New Zealand Film
1912–1996

Helen Martin

Sam Edwards

Auckland
OXFORD UNIVERSITY PRESS
Oxford   New York   Melbourne

OXFORD UNIVERSITY PRESS NEW ZEALAND

Oxford New York
Athens Auckland Bangkok Bombay
Calcutta Cape Town Dar es Salaam Delhi
Florence Hong Kong Istanbul Karachi
Kuala Lumpur Madras Madrid Melbourne
Mexico City Nairobi Paris Port Moresby
Singapore Tapei Tokyo Toronto
and associated companies in
Berlin Ibadan

OXFORD is a trade mark of Oxford University Press

© Helen Martin and Sam Edwards 1997
First published 1997

All rights reserved. No part of this publication may be
reproduced, stored in a retrieval system, or transmitted,
in any form or by any means, without the prior
permission in writing of Oxford University Press.
Within New Zealand, exceptions are allowed in respect
of any fair dealing for the purpose of research or private
study, or criticism or review, as permitted under the
Copyright Act 1994, or in the case of reprographic
reproduction in accordance with the terms of the
licences issued by the Copyright Licensing Limited.
Enquiries concerning reproduction outside these
terms and in other countries should be sent to the
Rights Department, Oxford University Press,
at the address below.

ISBN 019 558336 1

Edited by Jill Brown
Cover design by Steve Randles
Typeset by Scriptorium Desktop Publishing Pty Ltd
Printed by Impact Printing
Published by Oxford University Press,
540 Great South Road, Greenlane, PO Box 11–149,
Auckland, New Zealand

Contents

Preface		1
The Book's Methodology		2
A Chronology of New Zealand Cinema		7
List of Feature Films		16
List of International Films Associated with New Zealand		19

Year	Title	Page
1913	Loved by a Maori Chieftess	20
	Hinemoa	21
	How Chief Te Ponga Won His Bride	22
1914	Hinemoa	23
1916	The Test	24
	A Maori Maid's Love	25
	The Mutiny Of The Bounty	26
1921	Beyond	27
	The Betrayer	28
1922	The Birth Of New Zealand	29
	My Lady of the Cave	30
	Ten Thousand Miles In The Southern Cross	31
1923	The Romance of Sleepy Hollow	32
1924	Venus of the South Seas	33
1925	Rewi's Last Stand	34
	The Adventures of Algy	35
	Glorious New Zealand	36
1927	Carbine's Heritage	37
	The Romance of Hine-Moa	38
	Under The Southern Cross	39
	The Te Kooti Trail	40
1928	The Bush Cinderella	41
1929	Under The Southern Cross	42
1930	The Romance Of Maoriland	43
1934	Romantic New Zealand	44
1935	Down On The Farm	45
	Hei Tiki	46

Contents

1936	Phar Lap's Son	47
	The Wagon and the Star	48
	On The Friendly Road	49
1940	Rewi's Last Stand	50
1950	British Empire Games 1950	51
1952	Broken Barrier	52
1954	The Seekers	53
1964	Runaway	54
1966	Don't Let It Get You	55
1972	To Love A Maori	56
1973	Rangi's Catch	57
1974	Games '74: Official Film of the Xth Commonwealth Games, Christchurch, New Zealand, 1974	58
1975	Test Pictures: Eleven Vignettes from a Relationship	59
1976	The God Boy	60
1977	Wild Man	61
	Landfall	62
	Off the Edge	63
	Sleeping Dogs	64
	Solo	66
1978	Angel Mine	67
	Skin Deep	68
1979	Middle Age Spread	69
	Sons for the Return Home	70
1980	Lincoln County Incident	71
	Squeeze	72
	Nutcase	73
	Nambassa Festival	74
	Beyond Reasonable Doubt	75
	Goodbye Pork Pie	76
1981	Wildcat	77
	Smash Palace	78
	Pictures	79
	Race for the Yankee Zephyr	80
1982	The Scarecrow	81
	Battletruck	82
	Carry Me Back	83
	Bad Blood	84
	Hang On a Minute Mate!	85
	Prisoners	86
1983	Utu	87
	Dead Kids	89
	War Years	90
	Patu!	91
	Strata	93
	It's Lizzie To Those Close	94
	Savage Islands	95
1984	Trespasses	96
	Constance	97
	The Silent One	98

Contents

1984	Wild Horses	99
	Merry Christmas Mr Lawrence	100
	Death Warmed Up	101
	Second Time Lucky	102
	Came a Hot Friday	103
	Trial Run	104
	Other Halves	105
	Vigil	106
	Heart of the Stag	108
	Iris	109
	Mesmerized	110
1985	Should I Be Good?	111
	The Lost Tribe	112
	The Quiet Earth	113
	Kingpin	114
	Sylvia	115
	Leave All Fair	116
	Shaker Run	117
	Mr Wrong	118
	The Neglected Miracle	119
	Restless	120
1986	Pallet on the Floor	121
	Bridge to Nowhere	122
	Dangerous Orphans	123
	Arriving Tuesday	124
	Queen City Rocker	125
	Footrot Flats: The Dog's Tail Tale	126
	Mark II	127
1987	Ngati	128
	The Lie of the Land	130
	Starlight Hotel	131
	The Leading Edge	132
	Among the Cinders	133
	Bad Taste	134
1988	Illustrious Energy	135
	The Navigator: A Medieval Odyssey	137
	Mauri	138
	Never Say Die	139
	Send a Gorilla	140
	Chill Factor	141
	The Grasscutter	142
1989	Zilch!	143
1990	Mana Waka	144
	Flying Fox in a Freedom Tree	145
	Meet the Feebles	146
	User Friendly	147
	An Angel At My Table	148
	Ruby and Rata	149
	The Returning	150
	The Shrimp on the Barbie	151

CONTENTS

1991	A SOLDIER'S TALE	*152*
	REBELS IN RETROSPECT: THE POLITICAL MEMOIRS OF SOME MEMBERS OF CHRISTCHURCH AND WELLINGTON PYM	*153*
	TE RUA	*154*
	OLD SCORES	*155*
	THE END OF THE GOLDEN WEATHER	*156*
	CHUNUK BAIR	*158*
	GRAMPIRE	*159*
	UNDERCOVER	*160*
1992	BRAINDEAD	*161*
	CRUSH	*163*
	THE FOOTSTEP MAN	*164*
	ALEX	*165*
1993	ABSENT WITHOUT LEAVE	*166*
	DESPERATE REMEDIES	*167*
	BREAD AND ROSES	*169*
	THE PIANO	*171*
	JACK BE NIMBLE	*173*
	SECRETS	*174*
1994	ONCE WERE WARRIORS	*175*
	HEAVENLY CREATURES	*177*
	THE LAST TATTOO	*178*
	HERCULES AND THE LOST KINGDOM	*179*
	COPS AND ROBBERS	*180*
1995	WAR STORIES: OUR MOTHERS NEVER TOLD US	*181*
	LOADED	*182*
	BONJOUR TIMOTHY	*183*
	CINEMA OF UNEASE: A PERSONAL JOURNEY BY SAM NEILL	*184*
	WHO'S COUNTING? MARILYN WARING ON SEX, LIES AND GLOBAL ECONOMICS	*185*
1996	THE OFFERING	*186*
	CHICKEN	*187*
	FLIGHT OF THE ALBATROSS	*188*
	BROKEN ENGLISH	*189*
	THE FRIGHTENERS	*190*
	THE WHOLE OF THE MOON	*192*
	SOMEONE ELSE'S COUNTRY	*193*
	HERCULES: THE LEGENDARY JOURNEYS	*194*

INTERNATIONAL FILMS ASSOCIATED WITH NEW ZEALAND	*196*
APPENDIX: NEW ZEALAND FILM COMMISSION ACT 1978	*200*
BIBLIOGRAPHY	*201*
ACKNOWLEDGMENTS	*204*
INDEX	*205*

PREFACE

Beginning with the first footage shot by A.H.Whitehouse in 1898, New Zealand film consists of a great number of newsreels, promotional material, short dramas and documentaries, and feature length dramas and documentaries. Of these some have had theatrical release, some have been released theatrically and on video, and some on video only. A smaller number were made to be screened on broadcast television. Some feature length films have failed to secure a release of any kind.

New Zealand Film 1912–1996 is a reference book which aims to chronicle all New Zealand's feature films with the exception of 'adult movies', such as **On Tour in New Zealand** (1994).

Each entry records the major production information and technical and cast credits of the individual films. These are compiled by the entry's writer. They are followed by a brief synopsis and critical comment based on the writer's reading of the film. Further information on the film's history and critical and popular reception is included where pertinent.

The Bibliography lists books, magazines, journals and study guides which provide information on New Zealand film. Source books used in screenplays are included, as are novels and 'the making of' books published after a film's production. Films and radio programs on New Zealand film are also listed.

The Acknowledgments appear on p. 204. We would like to record here, however, our gratitude to Lindsay Shelton, Marketing Manager of the New Zealand Film Commission, whose knowledge of New Zealand films and whose support of the book have been invaluable. Thanks also to Diane Pivac of the New Zealand Film Archive for her excellent work in providing resources for the book, and to the National Film and Television Archive (U.K.) for their continuing collegial support.

New Zealand Film 1912–1996 had its genesis in research begun independently by Sam Edwards and Helen Martin in the early 1980s. The stills, tapes and documentation in Sam Edwards' extensive collection, which now make up a major resource for continuing research in New Zealand film, have made completion of this book possible. Much valuable information was also obtained through the authors' discussions and correspondence with the film-makers themselves. Helen Martin wrote the majority of the entries post-1976, while Sam Edwards researched the more sparingly documented period prior to New Zealand film's renaissance. He also sourced most of the stills.

The Book's Methodology

To aid readers in the use of this book, here is a description of the methodology used in the selection of entries and the reproduction of credits.

Defining the feature film

As the New Zealand film industry has evolved, definitions of what constitutes a feature film have shifted. When George Melies released his fictional narrative **Loved by a Maori Chieftess** in 1913, the trade journal *The Moving Picture World* described it as a two-reel feature, even though it was only 2000 feet.[1] Only 500 feet longer, George Tarr's 1914 version of the Hinemoa legend has been traditionally recognised as New Zealand's first feature. These films, and others like them, have been included in this book even though they may not reach the standard archival definition of a feature as being of 4000 feet because they are important in setting the context in which the feature film industry has developed. Thus the definition we have taken to give the best general guidance for features made prior to 1977, when the Interim New Zealand Film Commission was established, is that of the Library of Congress, 'films which consist of 4000 or more feet of 35 mm film or 1600 or more feet of 16 mm film, i.e. with a running time of 40 minutes or more.'[2] The FIAF Documentation Commission also uses the 4000 foot length to differentiate between short films and features by defining a short film as 'any film of four reels or less (approximately 4000 feet or 1200 metres in 35 mm').[3]

While guided by the world archivist standard of defining features as being of more than 60 minutes in length, for films made after 1976 we have deviated from the standard's definition of features as 'dramas' and have included feature-length documentaries. Also in the interests of inclusiveness a broader scope is achieved by including telefeatures and video features along with theatrically released films. The term 'telefeature' is used here to describe films made for television.

New Zealand film

As with all cultural products any New Zealand film is a hybrid of influences, with overseas input including such diverse contributions as the make-up brought to New Zealand by Lee Hill and used in **The Wagon and the Star** in the mid 1930s; the influence of overseas training institutions such as the Australian Film, Television and Radio School (formerly the Australian Film and Television

School); the presence of 'imported' actors (Warren Oates, Eleanor David, Jodie Foster) and production personnel (Michael Anderson, Ferdinand Fairfax); and the models provided by imported genres, as can be seen in such films as **Bad Taste**, **Wild Horses** and **Goodbye Pork Pie**.

In defining what constitutes a 'New Zealand film' we have been guided by the description in the *Film Commission Act* (1978) which established the New Zealand Film Commission. Under the Act 'significant New Zealand content' is defined with regard to subject; nationalities and places of residence of creators, production teams and casts, financiers and copyright holders; money sources; ownership and whereabouts of equipment and technical facilities (see Appendix).

Many films do not fit all of these categories but we have included them because of their significant New Zealand association. Examples include **The Devil's Pit** and **The Piano**, which were financed from overseas but set and shot in New Zealand; **A Soldier's Tale** and **Leave All Fair**, which were shot overseas but financed and produced from New Zealand; and **Merry Christmas Mr Lawrence**, which, although not a New Zealand story, had input from New Zealand money and personnel and was partly shot in New Zealand.

Where a film is of hybrid nationality this is indicated in the entry. Films with a minimal, but nevertheless interesting, connection to New Zealand are listed on pp. 196–9. Such films include, for example, the John Wayne classic **The Sands of Iwo Jima**, which was filmed partly in New Zealand.

Availability of films

Although we have seen many of the films in this book at theatrical screenings, we have viewed them again on video. Many early films, however, have been lost or destroyed. George Tarr's **Hinemoa** and **The Romance of Sleepy Hollow**, for example, have been completely lost to nitrate degradation. Of necessity then, assumptions have been made about the significance or the place of limited items of information and there is still much to be uncovered. We hope that as an outcome of this publication readers will provide information from their family histories that will fill the gaps.

The only recent film not available in any form is **Prisoners** (1982), which has never been released.

Availability of stills

The New Zealand Film Commission, the New Zealand Film Archive and individual copyright holders have been generous in granting permission for the use of stills. Where no stills are available entries are illustrated with images with some connection to the film.

Dating

Of the several dating methods available we have chosen to list films chronologically according to the month and year in which a film's censorship certification was registered in New Zealand. These dates have been obtained from the Film Censor's Register held at the National Archive, the Office of Film and Literature Classification (formerly the Office of the Chief Censor of Films) or, from 1976 onwards, from the New Zealand Gazette.

Where a film has no New Zealand censorship record, we have used the broader classification of the year of the first public screening of the film in completed form. Where this information is unknown, we have used the date of the completion of a film's production. This date, the date of a film's copyright, is given in each entry's production information after the production company listing. If a film's release has been delayed the years of censorship classification and copyright may differ considerably. We have noted the few cases where a film does not record its copyright year.

THE CREDITS

A set of credits, with an explanation of entries, is reproduced below.

1 9 8 4
THE SILENT ONE

Gibson Film Productions in association with the New Zealand Film Commission and South Pacific Merchant Finance Ltd. © 1984. *Budget*: approx. $1.9 million. *Locations*: Aitutaki, One Foot Island. *Distributor*: Gibson Group. *Rating*: G June, 1984. 35 mm. Dolby Stereo. Colour. 97.5 mins. (amended to 92 mins, September, 1987). 　　*Director*: Yvonne Mackay. *Producer*: Dave Gibson. *Executive producer*: David Compton. *Screenplay*: Ian Mune. *Source*: Joy Cowley, *The Silent One*. *Director of photography*: Ian Paul. *Underwater photographers*: Ron Taylor, Valerie Taylor. *Editor*: Jamie Selkirk. *Production designer*: Tony Rabbit. *Wardrobe supervisor*: Joan Grimmond. *Turtle wrangler*: Allan Watters. *Music*: Jenny McLeod. *Conductor*: William Southgate. *Players*: The Wellington Regional	Orchestra. *Vocals*: Kathy Blennerhassett, The Bach Choir. *Sound*: Ken Saville, John Gilbert, Ron Purvis, Les McKenzie, Malcolm Cromie, Jamie Selkirk, Tony Johnson. *Cast* Telo Malese (Jonasi), George Henare (Paui Te Po), Pat Evison (Luisa), Anzac Wallace (Tasiri), Rongo Tupatea Kahu (Taruga), Jo Pahu (Etika), Reg Ruka (Bulai), Anthony Gilbert (Aesake), Bernard Kearns (Redbeard), Teina Tetoa (Timi), Rangi Staski (Tomasi), Roy Staski (Matiu), Prince Tui Teka (Postmaster), Teraki Tokorangi, Turi Tama (Baby Jonasi), Panapa Tekopua, Tiki Pare, Tuatonga Tekopua, Rurutaura Tauta, Taeta Tekopua (Diggers), Mama (Turtle).

The pre-1977 films

Over the years production, crew and cast credits have become more detailed and specific. Information provided in the credits of early films is often incomplete or does not conform to style. For that reason the credits for the early films often deviate from the example.

The title

The title given is that which appears on the film print. Subtitles are indicated by the use of a colon, as in **The Navigator: A Medieval Odyssey**. Where a film has an alternative title this is indicated after the name of the production company. Many film titles are written in graphics that indicate something of the nature of the film. The title **Sleeping Dogs**, for example, appears above a gun. In the main such graphics have not been reproduced here.

Production information

The production company is recorded as it is named at the beginning of the film.

Financial assistance, such as that from the New Zealand Film Commission, is recorded when it is acknowledged in the film's credits. The wording is taken from the film (for example, 'with the assistance of'; 'in association with'; 'Script Development assistance from').

Budgets, which have been provided by the New Zealand Film Commission, by producers or directors or by publicity information, range from precise to approximate. Not all budgets were obtainable. In some cases producers can not accurately calculate them (as when two films share a float), in others they will not release the information for commercial reasons.

While a film may have many locations (**The Quiet Earth** had 92) only major locations are given.

Running times are those recorded on the censorship classification. We also indicate amendments to running times and censorship ratings.

Co-productions/overseas finance

The term 'co-production' is often loosely used to describe a film where finance has been provided by sources in two or more countries. Unless the term appears on a film's credits we have used it only where it applies to productions which have official approval in terms of New Zealand participation with another country under our official co-production agreement, under the 1985 Amendment to the *Film Commission Act*, with the New Zealand government or its agency (see Appendix). In cases where finance is provided by more than one country the term 'financed from' appears immediately after the copyright year.

Crew credits

Crew credits follow a standard format, with some additions where appropriate.

Camera operators are recorded if they appear on a film's credits as separate from the director of photography. Differences in the recording of key design department people are the result of the fact that some films credit a production designer while others credit an art director only, some credit a costume designer while others credit a wardrobe supervisor only.

Credits are included to indicate where a film has a special character. Thus **The Silent One**'s credits for the underwater photographers and the turtle wrangler are recorded; the foley artists are recorded in **The Footstep Man**; and the puppet-makers and puppeteers are named in **Meet the Feebles**.

In recognition of the contribution music makes to a film soundtrack credits are given for composers, conductors, arrangers, vocalists and players. Sound departments' credits are given without a specific designation on the nature of the contribution (designer, recordist, editor, dialogue editor, mixer).

Cast credits

Space limitations mean that not all cast can be listed, but we have attempted to list as many actors' names as possible within the designated space. This results in variations in the number of character names given. Where casts are large character names of the major roles only are given. Where casts are very large actors in minor roles are not included. Where casts are small even the most minor roles are noted. Thus for Gaylene Preston's film **Bread And Roses** there is room to record only 50 of the 173 actors, whereas for her film **Ruby and Rata**, which has a cast of 31, even Luna's role as 'barking dog' is recorded.

Character names are given as they appear in the credits.

Awards

Major awards won by a film appear at the end of the entry, with the date and nature of the award given for all films, except in the case of **The Piano**, where for reasons of space the information has been summarised.

Spelling

All credit lists have been rigorously checked to make sure spellings are reproduced as they are on the film's credits, even when they are incorrect. In the case of video copies with barely legible credits some guessing is involved. To name just a few of the many inconsistencies: Kevin Chisnall appears as Kevin Chiznell in the credits of **Chill Factor**; Finola Dwyer is listed as Phenola Dwyer in the credits of **Hang On a Minute Mate!**; Sarah Peirse can appear as Sarah Peirce, Elizabeth McRae as Liz McRea and Barry Harbert as Barry Harbet. Sometimes the form of a name will differ from film to film, as in the cases of Tama (Tom) Poata, Harley Cokliss (Cokeliss), Nathaniel (Nat) Lees and Michael (Mike) Firth.

In general, character names are more accurately recorded on the credits, but where inaccuracies occur, as in **Utu**'s listing of Colonel Elliot as Colonel Elloit, they are reproduced as listed.

Omissions

It has been our intention to include all New Zealand and New Zealand-related feature-length films. Information on any inadvertent omissions will be included in future editions of this book.

Helen Martin
Sam Edwards

---

[1] *The Moving Picture World*, vol. 15, no. 11, 15 March, p. 1171.
[2] *Moving Image Materials: Genre Terms*. 1988. Cataloguing Distribution Service. Library of Congress, Washington, p. 48.
[3] Harriet W. Harrison. 1991. *The FIAF Cataloguing Rules for Film Archives*. K.G. Saur, Munchen, New York.

A Chronology of New Zealand Cinema

This chronology provides a context for the evolution of New Zealand feature cinema. It lists some of the key films which have been made or screened in New Zealand; legislation or events which affected films in New Zealand; changes in technologies which affected both the making and screening of films; significant people; and the dates of important events. Entries are selected according to their influence on the development of cinema in New Zealand, but they are indicative, rather than exhaustive in scope. The chronology is illustrated more by fiction film than documentary, and feature film rather than short, simply because feature films are the focus of this book.

The early entries demonstrate how New Zealanders were introduced to the conventions and practices of emerging photographic technologies. The most significant of these was the patenting of Fox Talbot's Calotype negative to positive process in 1841, which allowed for the first time multiple reproductions of the same photographic image, an advance in visual information technology akin to the invention of Gutenberg's printing press. For the first time, mass audiences were able to see copies of the same image—what is more, copies which were indistinguishable from the original from which they came. In addition, they were replications of what people believed they saw in the 'real' world, limited only by the frame and the position of the camera.

The effect of the multiplication of images, and their apparent authenticity, was to suggest common truths about the world in which we live, truths which are founded on our common experience of the same image. Photographs of early New Zealand, whether the ethnographic representations of the Burtons or the architectural recordings of Willie Melhuish, provide a perspective which viewers accept as the 'real' New Zealand, a perspective which is confirmed by others who see the same images. The strongly authenticising images of nineteenth century photographers, taken often from the attitude considered most sellable by commercial image-makers, had a great deal of influence in constructing views of ourselves which were held then, and which are still held today.

Learning to 'see', to accept the visual conventions, was the intellectual, social and emotional equivalent of the industrial revolution. The nineteenth century became the century of the visual image, laying the foundation for the image-saturated, screen-addicted culture of the twentieth.

1456 (Germany) Gutenberg's presses print multiple copies of the same text for the first time.
1558 (Italy) Giovanni Battista Della Porta describes the Camera Obscura.
1769 6 October, James Cook sights New Zealand and his artists record the first representational images of the country.
1827 Augustus Earle arrives in New Zealand and spends eight months in the Bay of Islands and the Hokianga, painting representations of Maori in a variety of natural situations.
1834 (United Kingdom) The Zoetrope, a revolving drum giving the illusion of movement, is patented by William Horner.

A CHRONOLOGY OF NEW ZEALAND CINEMA

1839 (France) Louis Daguerre is probably the first inventor to provide a practical medium on which a photographic image can be successfully and permanently recorded.

1840 6 February, the date accepted as that of the first formal signings of Te Tiriti O Waitangi/ the Treaty of Waitangi.

1841 Fox Talbot patents the Calotype, a photographic process permitting unlimited image replications to be made from one original.

1844 George French Angas (1822–86) arrives in New Zealand and paints a series of landscapes and portraits of Maori chiefs, producing an important, if Eurocentric, record of Maori life in the 1840s.

1850 The first recorded photographic image of Maori is taken in Boston. The magic lantern, projecting a variety of images, becomes a popular means of entertainment.

1852 The first surviving photographic image of Maori taken in New Zealand, a daguerrotype portraying Caroline and Sarah Barrett, daughters of Rawinia Wakaiwa of Ngati Te Whiti and whaler entrepreneur Dicky Barrett.

1858 Introduction in New Zealand of the first customs regulations intended to prevent the importation of obscene or indecent material.

1863 Publication of the first edition of the *New Zealand Herald* in Auckland on Friday 13 November.

1864 31 March–2 April, General Cameron and Rewi Maniapoto clash at Orakao where Rewi is reputed to have spoken the now legendary lines:

'Ka whawhai tonu matou, Ake! Ake! Ake!'

('We shall fight on for ever and ever.')

The battle provided the narrative base for Rudall Hayward's feature **Rewi's Last Stand** (1925) and its remake in 1940.

1865 The *New Zealand Herald* of 17 June advertises 'A Splendid Series of Dissolving Views On a Large Scale … Illuminated by the Oxyhydrogen or Lime Light.'

1868 William Meluish, then in Dunedin, gives what is probably the first illuminated lantern lecture in Australasia. Walter and Alfred Burton set up their photographic business in Dunedin.

1871 Elizabeth Pulman takes over her husband's photographic business in Shortland Street, Auckland. Specialising in scenic photographs and portraiture, she becomes the first female professional photographer in New Zealand.

1880 The *New York Graphic* prints the first half-tone photographs. Prior to this the most representational illustrations came from line drawings based on photographs.

1889 Augustin Le Prince takes the first moving pictures on Leeds Bridge in Britain, with his single lens camera.

George Eastman invents perforated celluloid film, enabling Edison and others to take a major step in developing motion picture machines.

1892 The first act of the New Zealand parliament designed solely for the purpose of censorship, the *Offensive Publications Act*, outlawing 'any picture or printed or written matter which is of an indecent, immoral, or obscene nature', is passed.

In Nelson, William Tyree begins giving evening limelight slide exhibitions which he makes public by projecting images from his studio.

1894 After a visit to the World Columbian Exposition in Chicago A.H.Whitehouse goes on a tour of New Zealand exhibiting the Edison Phonograph.

1895 A.H.Whitehouse becomes the first person in New Zealand to exhibit motion pictures. He uses Edison's Kinetoscope. The first New Zealand advertisement for a motion picture appears in the *New Zealand Herald* of 29 November. The Lumières make their first public screening of projected motion pictures on 28 December in Paris.

1896 13 October, the first projected moving pictures are exhibited by 'Professors Hausman and Gow' in the Opera House, Auckland, using Edison's Kinematograph.

14 October, the *New Zealand Herald* carries New Zealand's first film review.

8

Alfred Hill's cantata 'Hinemoa' premieres in Wellington and is the first significant New Zealand musical work to mix Maori and European musical traditions.

1897 A.H. Whitehouse takes his Kinematograph, the first in New Zealand to use electric light, and his Edison Phonograph to the Tauranga A.&P. Show where he 'was in trouble for some time, there being some difficulty with the electric light.'

1898 A.H. Whitehouse films the opening of the Auckland Exhibition on 1 December and race day at Ellerslie in Auckland on 26 December, and becomes the first person recorded as shooting film in New Zealand. When, at Bartlett's Studio on Christmas Eve, he shows the film of the Governor and his wife arriving at the exhibition, he also becomes the first person to give a public screening of a New Zealand film.

1901 In the first recorded use by officialdom of the new medium the Salvation Army's Limelight Department films the visit of the Duke and Duchess of York to this country at the request of the New Zealand Government.

Film-maker James McDonald joins the New Zealand Tourist Department where he tours extensively with historian James Cowan.

Robert James Kerridge, who will become the dominant figure in film exhibition in New Zealand, is born at Christchurch.

1902 The Biorama Company of the Salvation Army begins the first of two film-making tours of New Zealand.

1905 The Biorama Company pioneers the 'develop it on the road' approach to film, where a film-maker takes shots of local people and scenes, develops them virtually overnight and screens them the following day. Such local interest movies developed eventually into the community comedies of Rudall Hayward and Lee Hill.

Henry Hayward, touring England with T.J. West's Baby Cinematograph and the Brescians, decides to come to New Zealand.

1906 The Edison spectacular **America At Work** screens in Auckland. It is 10 000 feet long and requires two projectors and two operators.

1907 The first Australian feature, **The Story Of The Kelly Gang**, screens in New Zealand.

1908 His Majesty's Theatre, Wellington, becomes the first building in New Zealand to be converted for film screenings on a permanent basis.

Henry Hayward and his brother Rudall, father of Charles Rudall, purchase the Royal Albert Hall in Auckland for use as a picture theatre.

1909 Britain introduces the *Cinematographic Act 1909*, designed primarily to establish adequate fire regulations. It is quickly adopted by local authorities to control both screening practices and content.

1910 The *Indecent Publications Act* (NZ), which remains in place unchanged until 1954, is passed into law.

Wellington's King's Theatre becomes the first purpose-built cinema in New Zealand.

1911 The first suburban cinemas appear. The Queens, a 500-seat Auckland cinema, opens on 25 November and is the first in New Zealand to run continuous shows, starting at 11.00 a.m. and running to 11.00 p.m.

The first colour films (not handpainted) are shown at two cinemas in Auckland, by Fullers at the Kings and by Haywards at the Globe. They require two projectors that overlap, one with a green light and the other with a red, and have to be run at twice the normal speed.

1912 James McDonald joins the Dominion Museum as Art Assistant and over the next decade also acts as assistant film censor.

The first fan magazines appear in the United States.

Gaston Melies, brother of pioneer film-maker Georges Melies, arrives in New Zealand. He shoots five scenic films and three narratives, **Hinemoa, How Chief Te Ponga Won His Bride**, and the short feature, **Loved by a Maori Chieftess**.

1913 Haywards and Fuller join forces in the distribution company NZ Picture Supplies.

1914 George Tarr makes the short feature **Hinemoa**.

1916 The *Cinematographic Film Censorship Act* (NZ) is passed, making it illegal to show any film which has not been approved by the state appointed censor, Mr W. Joliffe. As first chief censor he is charged with not passing any film depicting 'any matter that is against public order and decency, or the exhibition of which for any other reason is, in the opinion of the censor, undesirable in the public interest.'

1919 James McDonald begins a series of ethnographic photography expeditions in the Wanganui Valley, the East Coast and Rotorua. During these tours he produces four films which are the most extensive record of traditional Maori life of the period.

1920 Australian director Beaumont Smith is in New Zealand making **The Betrayer in Rotorua**, on which Rudall Hayward is a production assistant. Hayward also begins working for Harrington Reynolds in Howick as assistant director on **The Birth Of New Zealand**.

Len Lye begins developing his concept of 'art of motion' which led ultimately to his internationally recognised kinetic sculpture.

John O'Shea is born in New Plymouth on 20 June.

1921 Rudall Hayward makes his first film, **The Bloke From Freeman's Bay**. His uncle Henry thought the film so bad that he offered Rudall £150 to burn it.

On 3 September, the *New Zealand Herald* begins publication of a serial written by Waihi headmaster and friend of the Hayward family, Mr H.T. Gibson. Called 'My Lady Of The Cave', it becomes the first novel to be made into a film in New Zealand when Rudall Hayward films it in 1922.

1922 Edwin Coubray begins his career as assistant cameraman on **The Birth Of New Zealand**.

1923 Rudall Hayward marries his laboratory assistant Hilda Moran, who does much of the developing as well as the editing of such major features as **The Te Kooti Trail**.

The film censor bans the first New Zealand feature, **The Romance of Sleepy Hollow**, until some 900 feet are removed.

1925 Rudall Hayward, working for the production company Maori War Films, the same company which produced the first version of **Rewi's Last Stand**, records the arrival of the American fleet in New Zealand.

1927 Mr W. H. Tanner becomes chief censor.

The *New Zealand Herald* begins serialising 'The Te Kooti Trail' by Frank H. Bodle. During this year Hayward shoots **A Takapuna Scandal**, the first of the films which are to become the community comedies.

1928 Brothers Michael and Joe Moodabe form Amalgamated Theatres Ltd, which, despite the Depression, managed a circuit of 32 theatres by 1932, second only to that of Robert Kerridge.

Around this time Rudall Hayward begins work on the construction of a camera for sound recordings. Edwin Coubray documents his meeting with the Maori spiritual leader Rua Kenana in **Journey into Rua's Stronghold**.

Jim Manley works as second unit camera operator on Alexander Markey's film **Taranga**, later to be called **The Devil's Pit**.

1929 Edwin Coubray conducts New Zealand's first sound tests for NZ Radio Films Ltd.

Rudall and Hilda Hayward shoot and screen another seven community comedies.

The 3500-seat Civic Theatre is opened in Auckland on 20 December at a cost of £205 000, screening the talkie **Three Live Ghosts**.

1930 During the first full year of talkies 102 films, or 3.9% of the 2626 films examined by the censor, are banned, including Lewis Milestone's **All Quiet On The Western Front**. It is later released on appeal.

Ted Coubray makes the first New Zealand talkie, the first edition of **Coubray Tone News**.

Fuller Haywards is hit by the Depression and goes bankrupt. Henry and Phil Hayward form their own smaller company, Auckland Cinemas Ltd.

Alexander Markey begins production on **Hei Tiki** at Waihi, Lake Taupo.

1931 Alfred Hill is commissioned to write the music score for Markey's **Hei Tiki**. After disagreements Markey discharges Hill, who later accuses Markey of plagiarising his score.

Rudall Hayward records the results of the Napier earthquake for Australia Cinesound for whom he was New Zealand representative for a number of years.

1932 In the US, the Academy of Motion Picture Arts and Sciences recognises the 'Academy' ratio of 1.33:1 or 4:3 as the standard screen size ratio, naming and confirming the screen size most frequently used since the turn of the century.

1934 Parliament sets up a Committee to Enquire into the Cinema Industry, one result of which was to amend the *Cinematographic Films Act* to allow the Minister of Internal Affairs to appeal the censor's rulings. More liberally, the amendments also allowed for a new classification, RFS, which restricted some films to Film Society screenings only.

1935 Uncle Scrim—Colin Scrimgeour, soon to be a central figure in Rudall Hayward's film **On The Friendly Road**—has his broadcasts on social issues, seen as pro-Labour, jammed by post office workers on the orders of the government.

Len Lye has a successful release in Britain of his short direct film **A Colour Box**.

1937 Jim Manley, with the support of Te Puea Herangi, begins a three-year project recording the construction of three *waka taua* or great canoes.

By installing cameras at check points around the Ellerslie course in Auckland Rudall Hayward brings a new dimension to racetrack photography in New Zealand.

1938 Jim Manley forms Eppics Ltd to produce New Zealand films, especially those which have a Maori and historical focus.

Mr W.A. Von Keisenberg becomes chief censor.

1939 Alfred Hill composes the music for Hayward's **Rewi's Last Stand**.

1940 Gordon Mirams and others lobby the Labour government to establish a national film production unit to encourage New Zealand film-makers to extend their output, both in tourist films and in documentary.

1941 Len Lye is hired to make documentary films in Britain in support of the war effort, and does freelance shooting for the weekly cinema news review, **The March Of Time**.

Stanhope Andrews is appointed to lead the newly established National Film Unit. Rudall Hayward becomes an NFU photographer.

1942 The National Film Library is established by Walter Harris to make films available to schools as teaching support material.

1944 Len Lye moves from Britain to the US to become full-time director of **The March Of Time**.

1945 Gordon Mirams publishes the first critical and descriptive commentary on New Zealand filmgoing characteristics in his book, *Speaking Candidly*.

Robert Kerridge's Kerridge Odeon chain, with 133 cinemas, becomes the biggest exhibition circuit in Australasia.

1946 Rudall Hayward leaves for the UK where he is employed by the BBC as a news cameraman. Before he leaves he marries Ramai Te Miha, and they form a newsteam with Ramai as sound operator.

1947 Roger Mirams and Alun Falconer freelance as Fox Movietone reps in Australasia.

Rudall Hayward in the UK makes **The Goodwin Sands** for Warner Brothers and a documentary **The World Is Turning (Towards the Coloured People)** for Twentieth Century Fox.

1948 After a period working at the National Film Unit, Roger Mirams as cameraman and Alan Falconer as director set up the Pacific Film Unit.

New Zealand actor and film-maker Bathie Stuart, star of **The Adventures of Algy**, presents her first film lecture in the US.

1949 Gordon Mirams becomes chief film censor.

Largely as a result of the pressure from the new censor, the *Cinematographic Films Act* is amended to require the censor to use a series of recommendatory certificates, the R certificates, channelling films to audience groups rather than banning or cutting.

Rudall Hayward goes to Australia where he works in early Australian television, employed by the company C.G. Scrimgeour's Associated TV Programmes.

1950 John O'Shea and Roger Mirams form Pacific Film Productions Ltd.

1952 Pacific Films shoots the first New Zealand feature since before World War II, **Broken Barrier**.

Rudall Hayward returns to New Zealand from Australia and begins making documentaries, notably **Opo The Amazing Dolphin from Opononi** and **MacKenzie and His Dog.**

1954 Pacific Films begins **Pacific Magazine**, a monthly magazine format newsreel which continues until 1957.

Pauline Parker and Juliet Hulme are tried for murder after they admit battering Parker's mother to death with a brick, an event recaptured in Peter Jackson's award-winning film **Heavenly Creatures.**

1955 **The Wild One** is banned in New Zealand for a second time, and **Rebel Without a Cause** is released on appeal.

1957 Rudall and Ramai Hayward visit China at the invitation of the Chinese government and make a series of documentaries, including **Ramai Hayward's Children of China** and **Inside Red China.**

1959 Gordon Mirams is appointed to the permanent staff of UNESCO in Paris in the mass media division. One of his primary projects is the introduction of screen education to schools and colleges.

Doug McIntosh becomes chief censor, a post he holds until 1977.

1960 Regular television programs, first broadcast in the Auckland area, are transmitted throughout New Zealand by June, and cinema attendances and numbers of cinemas begin to drop.

John O'Shea and the Moodabe family of Amalgamated Theatres set up Pacific Television, but after Twentieth Century Fox buys into Amalgamated the company reverts to Pacific with a major emphasis on television commercials.

1961 A revised *Cinematographic Films Act* consolidates regulations, but makes little change.

The *Broadcasting Corporation Act* is introduced to cover broadcasting of both radio and television. All imported programs until 1968 are vetted by the film censor.

1964 After releasing **Runaway**, John O'Shea reports that a government bureaucrat had told him that 'never again would it [Pacific Films] make another feature film, because "films should be happy."'

1966 Pacific Films produces New Zealand's first popular musical **Don't Let It Get You.** Kiri Te Kanawa has a minor role.

1967 **Ulysses** is released for segregated audiences only. Censor McIntosh is concerned that some dialogue would cause embarrassment in mixed company.

1968 The New Zealand Broadcasting Authority is established to act as a standards watchdog for television screenings.

1969 Pacific Films employs 22 permanent staff and derives around 77% of its income from television commercials.

1970 **Rewi's Last Stand** in its British quota format, renamed **The Last Stand**, becomes the first New Zealand feature film to be broadcast on NZBC TV.

Patricia Bartlett forms the Society for the Promotion of Community Standards, a conservative lobby group aiming to tighten censorship laws.

The Acme Sausage Company of Bruno Lawrence and Geoff Murphy produces the short fiction film **Tankbusters.**

Pacific Films begins work on the series **Tangata Whenua.**

New Zealand's first television colour transmissions are made during the second week of February.

The Drama Studies department at Victoria University offers the first university film course, Film Analysis, for third-year undergraduates.

1972 The first Wellington Film Festival is held under the founding directorship of Lindsay Shelton. A program of 17 features is presented.

Stanley Kubrick's film **Clockwork Orange** is released by the censor with an R20 Certificate, but the attempt by Film Societies to screen **I Am Curious—Yellow** fails when the film is banned.

Alternative Cinema, a journal containing reviews and commentary on the developing film culture in New Zealand, begins publication in December.

1974 Rudall Hayward dies in Dunedin from pneumonia contracted during a promotional tour for **To Love A Maori**.

1975 In the English Department of Auckland University, Roger Horrocks offers the first graduate Film Studies paper.

1976 The *Cinematographic Films Act 1976* is intended by Internal Affairs Minister Alan Highet to liberalise film censorship by making the film censor responsible for determining whether or not a film was 'likely to be injurious to the public good'. As a result, **I Am Curious—Yellow** is passed for exhibition to Film Society audiences.

1977 With lawyer Bill Sheat in the chair, the first meeting of the Interim Film Commission in November is called 'to advise the Government on legislation, to establish a permanent commission, and to establish policy guidelines for developing a sound motion picture industry.' Don Blakeney is appointed first chief executive.

Now internationally recognised as an artist of world stature, Len Lye returns to New Zealand to oversee the installation of his sculptures in the Govett Brewster Gallery in New Plymouth where they will form the basis of the collection of the Len Lye Foundation.

Bernie Tunnicliffe becomes chief censor.

1978 In November the New Zealand Film Commission is established by act of parliament 'to encourage and … assist in the making, promotion, distribution, and exhibition of films … enabling the world to see New Zealanders as they see themselves.' It produces a small house journal titled *Rough Cut*.

Ian Cross as Chairman of the Broadcasting Corporation of New Zealand offers 'grants of between $5000 and $50 000 to independent film and television producers for television programs which reflect and develop New Zealand's identity and culture.'

John O'Shea is awarded an honorary D. Litt. by Victoria University of Wellington.

1979 *New Zealand Film*, journal of the New Zealand Film Commission, publishes its first issue in March under the editorship of Lindsay Shelton.

Vincent Ward makes **A State of Siege**.

Sir Robert Kerridge dies.

1980 Lawyers and tax accountants find loopholes in the New Zealand tax laws which allow film production to become a means of obtaining tax relief. This contributes to a burgeoning of feature film production, from two features in 1980 to five in 1981, six in 1982 and 1983 and 14 in 1984 when the loopholes are closed. The New Zealand Film Commission takes New Zealand films to the Cannes Film Festival for the first time. **Goodbye Pork Pie** and **Sons for the Return Home** become the first two features to screen in the market at Cannes.

On 15 May Len Lye dies in New York. He is recognised in New Zealand by the establishment of the Len Lye Foundation.

Sixty-seven per cent of New Zealand households now have colour television.

1981 The New Zealand Film Archive is established as a charitable trust with Jonathan Dennis as its founding director.

          Middle Age Spread becomes the first New Zealand feature telecast by the BBC.
          Pacific Films produces **Pictures**, its first feature since 1966.

1982 **The Scarecrow**, directed by Sam Pillsbury, becomes the first New Zealand feature selected for the Director's Fortnight at Cannes.

1983 Jim Booth becomes the second executive director of the New Zealand Film Commission, remaining in office until 1988, during which time 27 features are produced and the Short Film Fund is established.

        The Manley film footage is received and preserved by the New Zealand Film Archive.

        In December founding editor Sue May launches an industry magazine, *On Film*, intending to 'provide news, views, and background stories on the New Zealand motion picture industry.'

        Patu! is the first feature length film directed by a woman in New Zealand, Merata Mita.

        Expatriate Australian Roger Donaldson becomes the first New Zealand film director to move to California. Geoff Murphy's **Utu** is an official selection out of competition at Cannes.

1984 The gradual closure of tax loopholes by the Government causes a decline in production which results in only four features being produced in 1986.

        Vincent Ward's film **Vigil** becomes the first New Zealand feature selected to be in competition at the Cannes Film Festival.

1985 Founding chair Bill Sheat leaves the New Zealand Film Commission and is succeeded by lawyer David Gascoigne.

        A special screening of the preserved Manley film footage is arranged for Te Arikinui, Dame Te Atairangikaahu and elders at Turangawaewae.

1986 *Illusions*, a film, television, arts and theatre journal, containing commentaries and reviews and focusing primarily on New Zealand-produced entertainment, begins publication in Wellington under the editorship of Reid Perkins and film-maker associate editor, Russell Campbell.

1987 The *Video Recordings Act* establishes the Video Recordings Authority to censor pre-recorded video tapes.

        John O'Shea is presented with the Rudall Hayward Memorial Award by the Guild of Film and Television Arts (GOFTA) for 'exceptional contributions to the industry.'

        Barry Barclay's feature **Ngati**, the first dramatic feature written and directed by Maori, is selected for Critics' Week at Cannes.

1988 Jim Booth leaves the New Zealand Film Commission to become an independent producer. Judith McCann becomes the Commission's third executive director.

        Mauri is the first fiction feature to be directed by a Maori woman, Merata Mita.

        In the US, home video outranks the theatre box office as the primary dollar earner for filmed entertainment.

1990 Ninety-six per cent of New Zealand households now own a colour television set, and some 35% have more than one. Remote control units have increased from a few percentage points in 1980 to 60%, and video recorders in households have increased in the decade from virtually nil to 68%.

        Merata Mita incorporates the Manley films into her 85-minute documentary **Mana Waka**, which becomes the official film for the IV Commonwealth Arts Festival in Auckland.

        John O'Shea is awarded the OBE for services to film.

        The National Association of Media Educators is established in Auckland.

        Jane Campion's **An Angel At My Table** is the first all-female collaboration across roles of writer/director/producer, and is the first New Zealand feature to compete at the Venice Film Festival where it wins seven awards.

1991 Jane Wrightson becomes Chief Film Censor

1992 John O'Shea is presented with the New Zealand Film Commission's first Lifetime Achievement Award by Minister for the Arts, Doug Graham.

Alison McLean's **Crush** is the third New Zealand feature selected for competition at Cannes.

1993 The Peter Wells/Stewart Main film **Desperate Remedies** is selected for *Un Certain Regard* at Cannes.

Anna Paquin wins the Best Supporting Actress at the Academy Awards, the first New Zealand actor to win an Oscar, and Jane Campion takes another New Zealand first with the Best Original Screenplay for a feature film, **The Piano**.

Banker Phil Pryke succeeds David Gascoigne as only the third chairman in the 16-year history of the New Zealand Film Commission.

In November, the Moving Image Centre in Auckland publishes the first issue of *the big picture*, edited by Keith Hill.

1994 The three acts dealing with censorship in New Zealand, the *Indecent Publications Act 1963*, the *Films Act 1983* and the *Video Recordings Act 1987*, are combined. One office, the Office of Film and Literature Classification, is established under the new *Films, Videos, and Publications Classifications Act*. Australian Kathryn Paterson is appointed chief censor of Film and Literature Classification.

Ex New Zealand Film Commission CEO Jim Booth dies on 4 January aged 48, at the Mary Potter Hospice in Wellington, just before the completion of **Heavenly Creatures**, which he produced.

Once Were Warriors, directed by Lee Tamahori, is the first feature to gross more than $6 million at the New Zealand box office.

Australian Richard Stewart is appointed as the New Zealand Film Commission's fourth chief executive.

1995 In January Ken Mair, a descendant of Gilbert Mair who defeated Te Kooti in 1870, enters the news studio of Television New Zealand/TV One, holding up the 6.00 p.m. news broadcast as a protest against government handling of Treaty of Waitangi issues and TV One's summer dropping of Maori language news.

Bruno Lawrence, the best known of New Zealand's screen actors, dies.

The Film and Electronic Media Industry Training Organisation, FaEMITO, is established.

The television screening of the Peter Jackson/Costa Botes mockumentary *Forgotten Silver* arouses interest in 'film-maker' Colin McKenzie and some ire from people who object to being 'tricked'.

1996 New Zealand celebrates its Centenary of Cinema.

NZ Post produces a special edition of four Centenary of Cinema stamps.

The short film *Planet Man* wins Best Short Film at the Cannes Film Festival's Critics' Week.

The annual Asia-Pacific Film Festival is held in Auckland.

The Moving Image Centre and Auckland University's Film and Television Centre hold a Documentary Film Conference.

Waikato University holds a New Zealand Film Conference.

SE

List of Feature Films

The films in this list are ordered according to the dating system outlined in the section entitled The Book's Methodology.

1913	Loved by a Maori Chieftess
	Hinemoa
	How Chief Te Ponga Won His Bride
1914	Hinemoa
1916	The Test
	A Maori Maid's Love
	The Mutiny Of The Bounty
1921	Beyond
	The Betrayer
1922	The Birth Of New Zealand
	My Lady of the Cave
	Ten Thousand Miles In The Southern Cross
1923	The Romance of Sleepy Hollow
1924	Venus of the South Seas
1925	Rewi's Last Stand
	The Adventures of Algy
	Glorious New Zealand
1927	Carbine's Heritage
	The Romance of Hine-Moa
	Under The Southern Cross
	The Te Kooti Trail
1928	The Bush Cinderella
1929	Under The Southern Cross
1930	The Romance Of Maoriland
1934	Romantic New Zealand
1935	Down On The Farm
	Hei Tiki
1936	Phar Lap's Son
	The Wagon and the Star
	On The Friendly Road
1940	Rewi's Last Stand
1950	British Empire Games 1950
1952	Broken Barrier
1954	The Seekers
1964	Runaway
1966	Don't Let It Get You
1972	To Love A Maori
1973	Rangi's Catch
1974	Games '74: Official Film of the Xth Commonwealth Games, Christchurch, New Zealand, 1974
1975	Test Pictures: Eleven Vignettes From a Relationship
1976	The God Boy
1977	Wild Man
	Landfall
	Off the Edge
	Sleeping Dogs
	Solo
1978	Angel Mine
	Skin Deep
1979	Middle Age Spread
	Sons for the Return Home
1980	Lincoln County Incident
	Squeeze
	Nutcase
	Nambassa Festival
	Beyond Reasonable Doubt
	Goodbye Pork Pie
1981	Wildcat
	Smash Palace

LIST OF FEATURE FILMS

	PICTURES		AMONG THE CINDERS
	RACE FOR THE YANKEE ZEPHYR		BAD TASTE
1982	THE SCARECROW	1988	ILLUSTRIOUS ENERGY
	BATTLETRUCK		THE NAVIGATOR: A MEDIEVAL ODYSSEY
	CARRY ME BACK		MAURI
	BAD BLOOD		NEVER SAY DIE
	HANG ON A MINUTE MATE!		SEND A GORILLA
	PRISONERS		CHILL FACTOR
1983	UTU		THE GRASSCUTTER
	DEAD KIDS	1989	ZILCH!
	WAR YEARS	1990	MANA WAKA
	PATU!		FLYING FOX IN A FREEDOM TREE
	STRATA		MEET THE FEEBLES
	IT'S LIZZIE TO THOSE CLOSE		USER FRIENDLY
	SAVAGE ISLANDS		AN ANGEL AT MY TABLE
1984	TRESPASSES		RUBY AND RATA
	CONSTANCE		THE RETURNING
	THE SILENT ONE		THE SHRIMP ON THE BARBIE
	WILD HORSES	1991	A SOLDIER'S TALE
	MERRY CHRISTMAS MR LAWRENCE		REBELS IN RETROSPECT: THE POLITICAL
	DEATH WARMED UP		MEMOIRS OF SOME MEMBERS OF
	SECOND TIME LUCKY		CHRISTCHURCH AND WELLINGTON PYM
	CAME A HOT FRIDAY		TE RUA
	TRIAL RUN		OLD SCORES
	OTHER HALVES		THE END OF THE GOLDEN WEATHER
	VIGIL		CHUNUK BAIR
	HEART OF THE STAG		GRAMPIRE
	IRIS		UNDERCOVER
	MESMERIZED	1992	BRAINDEAD
1985	SHOULD I BE GOOD?		CRUSH
	THE LOST TRIBE		THE FOOTSTEP MAN
	THE QUIET EARTH		ALEX
	KINGPIN	1993	ABSENT WITHOUT LEAVE
	SYLVIA		DESPERATE REMEDIES
	LEAVE ALL FAIR		BREAD AND ROSES
	SHAKER RUN		THE PIANO
	MR WRONG		JACK BE NIMBLE
	THE NEGLECTED MIRACLE		SECRETS
	RESTLESS	1994	ONCE WERE WARRIORS
1986	PALLET ON THE FLOOR		HEAVENLY CREATURES
	BRIDGE TO NOWHERE		THE LAST TATTOO
	DANGEROUS ORPHANS		HERCULES AND THE LOST KINGDOM
	ARRIVING TUESDAY		COPS AND ROBBERS
	QUEEN CITY ROCKER	1995	WAR STORIES: OUR MOTHERS NEVER
	FOOTROT FLATS: THE DOG'S TAIL TALE		TOLD US
	MARK II		LOADED
1987	NGATI		BONJOUR TIMOTHY
	THE LIE OF THE LAND		CINEMA OF UNEASE: A PERSONAL JOURNEY
	STARLIGHT HOTEL		BY SAM NEILL
	THE LEADING EDGE		

LIST OF FEATURE FILMS

Who's Counting? Marilyn Waring on
sex, lies and global economics

1996   The offering
Chicken
Flight of the Albatross

Broken English
the Frighteners
The Whole of the Moon
Someone Else's Country
Hercules: The Legendary Journeys

List of International Films Associated with New Zealand

1947 GREEN DOLPHIN STREET
1949 THE SANDS OF IWO JIMA
1957 UNTIL THEY SAIL
1958 CINERAMA SOUTH SEAS ADVENTURE
THE DECKS RAN RED
1961 SPINSTER
1962 IN SEARCH OF THE CASTAWAYS
1964 QUICK BEFORE IT MELTS
1969 YOUNG GUY ON MOUNT COOK
1982 NEXT OF KIN
BROTHERS
1984 THE BOUNTY
1986 ACES GO PLACES IV
1988 MIDNIGHT RUN
THE RESCUE
WILLOW
1989 WILDFIRE
1991 DEATH IN BRUNSWICK
1993 ADRIFT
MAP OF THE HUMAN HEART
1994 RAPA-NUI

1913

LOVED BY A MAORI CHIEFTESS

[No known footage of this film remains.] Melies Films. *Location:* Rotorua. *Distributor:* USA Melies, although Melies was negotiating with Hayward's Picture Enterprise Ltd for the New Zealand release.[1] 35 mm. Black and white. Silent. 2000 ft (two reels).

Director and producer: Gaston Melies. *Screenplay:* Edmund Mitchell, from an original story by Mitchell. *Photographer:* George Scott. *Assistant Director:* attributed to Pastor Bennett (described by Melies as 'a half-blood Maori Minister who has a great influence on his fellow creatures.' He is probably the same Rev. F. Bennett who led the Maori Choir Party which provided the cast for George Tarr's version of *Hinemoa* in 1916.). The crew included Mr Bracken, Mrs Mildred Bracken, Sam Weil, Ehfe, Stanley and Miss Tracey.

Cast

Actor credits are unavailable, but leading characters were Wena, a Maori princess (probably Maata Horomona of Ohinemutu), Chief Te Rangi-Ka-Haruru of Ngatairuu, Chief Te Heuheu of Ngati Kahungunu, Chadwick (an English trapper) and a sorceress.[2]

Wena, a Maori woman of high rank, is told by a sorceress that 'she will marry a white man, tall and handsome, with eyes as blue as the sky and a fair beard.' As she plays with the poi, the young chief Te Heuheu arrives to court her. At the same time Chadwick, hunting in the bush, is taken prisoner and is brought to the pa to be burned at the stake to provide 'white man's meat'. Wena, recognising Chadwick as the man of the prophecy, helps him escape. The two swear eternal love, and Wena promises to elope with him that night. Chadwick guides her among the geysers to his hut on the lake, where they are eventually discovered by chief Te Heuheu. When Chadwick is threatened with death if Wena remains with him, she consents to return to the tribe and her father the chief, where she pines for her lost love. Five days later her father finds her close to death, her illness caused by the long separation from her husband. Her plight causes her father to relent, and Chadwick is made a chief of the tribe, whereupon Wena recovers and the tribe celebrates with a great feast.

The synopsis suggests a dramatic linking of the emerging melodramatic style of American cinema and the dynamic stories available in exotic cultures. Reviewed in *The Moving Picture World* by W. Stephen Bush, the film is described as 'of exceptional value as a scenic and educational subject ... With but one exception all of the characters in this play are Maoris and they all show that singular mimic gift which seems to be a heritage of all primitive peoples and always forms a welcome contrast to the more artful ways of our own white brothers ... *Loved by a Maori Chieftess* will be admired by all.'

Like the other films by Melies, **Loved by a Maori Chieftess** is now presumed lost, but its making is a significant event in New Zealand film history. Two reels, or 2000 feet in length, and made at a time when the feature film was still in its infancy, it is long enough for the publicity to describe it as the 'Unusual Two-Reel Feature'. Like features today, the distribution package included one, three, and six sheet posters. The narrative form appears well-developed, with parallel story lines necessitating cross-cutting, and the stock characters of melodrama are made novel by settings, events and relationships which have a specifically New Zealand flavour. Marketed as a 'New Zealand Production' it is described as 'enacted by genuine natives of that country' as a major draw card for the American release market. There is, however, no apparent record of its screening in New Zealand, and the chances of that are slim as Melies sent his exposed footage back to the United States for post-production treatment.

Melies shot the film with the crew that he had brought with him from Tahiti, as he did with **Hinemoa** and **How Chief Te Ponga Won His Bride**. The crew caused him considerable problems, and in a letter to his son Paul, written on 26 September 1912, he writes, 'Stop sending money to Messrs Bracken and Sam Weil the 15th October. I've dismissed them—and they're leaving this morning at 9.00—Bracken, his wife (Mildred), Sam Weil, Ehfe, Stanley, and Miss Tracey. Johnny, ill and left in hospital at Wellington with syphilis caught in Tahiti ... Bracken is more and more unbearable, and he's very coarse with Mitchel (a scriptwriter). He works when it pleases him, and Bracken, Stanley, and Sam have decided that taking one shot a week is sufficient work ... Ehfe is a big bully and Tracey was useless ...'* SE

Director Gaston Melies. Courtesy of the National Film and Television Archive, London.

---

[1] **Loved by a Maori Chieftess** was first reviewed in *The Moving Picture World* by W. Stephen Bush on 8 March 1913 (vol. 15, pp. 1001 and 1018), the same date given by the American Film Index, while in the Calendar of Licensed Releases from MPW an 'Advance Release' was scheduled for Friday 14 March. This appears to have been the first public screening. In the Catalogue of Copyright entries for the Library of Congress, Melies registered the film as two reels on 17 February 1913, cat. no. LP 391 under the company title G. Melies Inc.

[2] Melies had his own travelling cast of actors which included Johnny the Cowboy, Ray Gallagher and Melies's second wife, Hortense. Few of them were used in the three Rotorua based fiction films, however, where the cast was predominantly Maori.

Reference

*Quote from Melies' letter from the collection held in the New Zealand Film Archive.

1913

HINEMOA

[No known footage of this film remains.] Melies Films. *Location:* Rotorua. *Distributor:* USA Melies, although Melies was negotiating with Hayward's Picture Enterprise Ltd for the New Zealand release. *Registered:* March 27 1913.[1] 35 mm. Black and white. Silent. 1000 ft (one reel).

Director and producer: Gaston Melies. *Screenplay:* Edmund Mitchell, from the traditional Maori legend. *Photographer:* George Scott. *Assistant director:* attributed to Pastor Bennett (described by Melies as 'a half-blood Maori Minister who has a great influence on his fellow creatures.' He is probably the same Rev. F. Bennett who led the Maori Choir Party which provided the cast for George Tarr's version of **Hinemoa** in 1916.). The crew included Mr Bracken, Mrs Mildred Bracken, Sam Weil, Ehfe, Stanley and Miss Tracey.

Cast

The Moving Picture World notes that 'In taking motion pictures of this story, native actors played all the parts ... The native "leading lady" Maata, played the part of Hinemoa.' The only named cast member, she was Maata (Martha) Horomona of Ohinemutu, who Melies had retained as his leading lady during his stay in New Zealand. Melies also makes reference to 'the Maori chief Kenoi' who accompanied Maata on a visit to the Melies company.

Hinemoa is a Maori woman of high rank and exceptional beauty living in pre-European times on the shores of Lake Rotorua, opposite the island of Mokoia. Mokoia is the home of a tribal group led by the chief Whakaue, who has three legitimate sons, and one illegitimate son, Tutanekai.

Hated by his half-brothers, but cared for by the old chief, Tutanekai also happens to have the love of Hinemoa, much to the anger both of his brothers and Hinemoa's family. To resolve a growing dispute over who was an acceptable husband for Hinemoa, a race is held. It is won against the odds by Tutanekai, but after Hinemoa's parents refuse to keep their side of the bargain, Tutanekai is exiled from Mokoia.

Every evening at dusk, however, Tutanekai serenades Hinemoa on his flute, and eventually she can bear the separation no longer. One night, guided by the flute, she swims the three miles to the island. Exhausted and chilled after the swim, she hides in a natural warm bath until Tutanekai's servant comes for water. Hinemoa breaks the servant's water container each time he appears, until eventually Tutanekai himself appears. Then she shows herself, and they go immediately to his hut, because under Maori law, for a woman to be found by a man and taken into his sleeping hut means that she has to become his wife.

The legend of Hinemoa, traditionally a key narrative for the Arawa people, captured the colonial imagination, not only because it was a separated lovers' narrative in the vein of great classics such as *Romeo and Juliet*, but also because it provided some wonderful opportunities for the expression of romantic idealism in the Victorian tradition. In contrast to such idealistic possibilities, however, the figure of Hinemoa also provided artists and photographers (including the composer Alfred Hill) with an eroticised subject which satisfied and legitimated a Victorian interest in sexual display. Hill, who was later to provide the musical score for Alexander Markey's film **Hei Tiki**, wrote a cantata for the dramatic events to a libretto written by Arthur Adams who based his story on Governor Sir George Grey's version of the Arawa legend. Hill's *Hinemoa* had first been performed on 18 November 1896, but it was to be another 15 years before the first film version of the legend—a one reeler still much in the George Grey vein, but informed by local Arawa—was shot by Melies in October 1912.

The Moving Picture World noted that 'there is nothing theatrical about the film at all ... [it has] a quality something like the stories in Homer. A Maori girl loves a warrior and finds a way to win him despite her father. It is beautiful and delightful and we can find nothing but good to say about it.' Melies himself said of the film, 'I don't know if people will like 'Hinemoa', which is the most attractive and best-known Maori legend, but for myself I find very well done all the section where Hinemoa goes into the water, crosses the lake (two hours of swimming), lands exhausted, and regains her strength in the bath of natural hot water. All these shots were taken in the very sites where the story took place.' SE

---

[1] The American Film Index gives 17 March as the registration date, which is also the date of the issue of the trade paper *The Moving Picture World* where a synopsis is provided.

Hinemoa played by Maata Hurihanganui, Gustav Pauli's film **The Romance of Hinemoa** *(1927). Courtesy of the National Film and Television Archive, London.*

1913
HOW CHIEF TE PONGA WON HIS BRIDE

[No known footage of this film remains.] Melies Films. *Location:* Rotorua. *Distributor:* USA Melies, although Melies was negotiating with Hayward's Picture Enterprise Ltd for a New Zealand release.[1] 35 mm. Black and white. Silent. 1000 ft (one reel).

Director and producer: Gaston Melies. *Screenplay:* Edmund Mitchell, from a traditional tribal story. *Photographer:* George Scott. *Assistant Director:* attributed to Pastor Bennett. The crew included Mr Bracken, Mrs Mildred Bracken, Sam Weil, Ehfe, Stanley, and Miss Tracey.

Cast

Melies had brought his own troupe of actors, including Johnny the Cowboy, Ray Gallagher, and Melies's second wife, Hortense. None of them were used in this film, however, where the cast was entirely drawn from local Maori. No details of cast membership survive, but it is likely that the same actors who worked with Melies on his other two narratives would have continued here, especially as Melies was photographed 'in the midst of his Maori crew in the Pah (fortified village) of Whakarewarewa N.Z.' This would have been the same location where Melies found it necessary 'to redo a scene in a Maori Village with a lot of people in it … '

A state of war exists between two Maori tribes, the Ngati Awhitu and the Waikatu. Word reaches the young chief Te Ponga, of Ngati Awhitu, of the extraordinary beauty of Puhuhu, daughter of the elderly paramount chief of the Waikatu. In order to meet Puhuhu, Te Ponga flies a flag of truce, and appears ready to discuss peace.

The old Waikatu chief welcomes Te Ponga with traditional ceremony at a great hui, or meeting, and during the evening feasting Puhuhu dances for him. Chief Te Ponga falls instantly in love with her and she with him. After the ceremony, one of Te Ponga's young warriors manages to arrange a clandestine meeting of the two lovers, who plan to elope the following day. After Puhuhu returns secretly to her sleeping hut, Te Ponga and his warriors creep to the water's edge and remove all the paddles from the waka, or canoes, of the Waikatu and place them in their own waka.

When Te Ponga takes his leave of the Waikatu the next morning, he is ceremonially accompanied by the tribe's young women, including Puhuhu. Watching from a distance, the Waikatu men see the women returning and notice that Puhuhu is not with them. Realising that she has left with Te Ponga, the old chief orders his warriors to pursue the couple, but foiled by the loss of their paddles, they are left enraged on the shore, powerlessly chanting imprecations, while Te Ponga and his new bride paddle swiftly away to safety.

This, the third and last of Melies's New Zealand stories, underlines the universal film-making practice of creating fiction by taking greater or lesser liberties with material which has a degree of historical foundation. Waikatu is probably a simple alternative spelling of Waikato, or else a plain mistake, and the story itself probably recounts an actual conflict between Waikato tribes and tribes from the Bay of Plenty. It also has some remarkably interesting similarities to the plot line of the film **Hei Tiki**, directed by Alexander Markey during the 1930s. Markey's film is also based on the Romeo and Juliet notion of lovers from two opposing clans or tribal groups, clandestine meetings, the subterfuge or trick which enables the lovers to escape and the final escape by canoe across a lake.

How Chief Te Ponga Won His Bride also underlines the filmic potential of the dramatic landscapes and indigenous stories which exist in the turbulent volcanic areas of New Zealand. These continue to be used as recently as Alison McLean's 1992 award winning feature, **Crush**.

The Moving Picture World comments 'Another of this company's folk-lore stories played by Maori people in New Zealand. It is a simple love story, giving insight into the lives of these primitive folk and so is instructive and valuable. The great value of such offerings will be most apparent to those who know most. The average spectator looks upon them as something new and different; we have never had anything like them before and they seem to be taking very well. The photography is clear in most of the scenes; in some it is poor.'[1] SE

---

[1] *The Moving Picture World* lists the release date as 24 April 1913, although the American Film Index lists it as 19 April.

Vera James, a New Zealand actress who worked extensively in Australia, in the Maori costume made popular by films such as this. Courtesy of the National Film and Sound Archive, Canberra

1914

HINEMOA

[No known footage of this film remains.] Hinemoa Films (?).[1] *Location:* Rotorua. *Opened:* Lyric Theatre, Auckland, 17 August 1914. 35 mm. Black and white. Silent. 2500 ft.

Director and producer: George Tarr. *Screenplay:* George Tarr, based on the Maori legend. *Photographer:* Charles Newham.

Cast

Hera Tawhai, a.k.a. Sarah Rogers (Hinemoa), Rua Tawhai (Tutanekai), Miro Omahau (Tiki), Taimai Omahau (Ngararanui), with members of the Rev. F. Bennett's Maori Choir Party.

Tarr's telling of the legend of Hinemoa and Tutanekai appears to be based on the George Gray version. In this narrative Rangiuru, who already has three children by her husband Whakaue, elopes with Tuwharetoa of the Ngati Tuwharetoa, and as a result of the affair, gives birth to Tutanekai. Later she is reconciled to Whakaue and returns home to the island of Mokoia in Lake Rotorua, bringing Tutanekai with her. This sequence serves as a prologue to the main action of the film which begins when Tutanekai's friend Tiki brings him news of the beautiful puhi, Hinemoa, who lives on the mainland. Tutanekai meets Hinemoa and they fall in love, but Tutanekai's older brother, Ngararanui, becomes extremely jealous and Tutanekai is forbidden to see Hinemoa. Tutanekai, however, has arranged with Hinemoa that she should come to him when she hears the sound of the putorino, the flute. Eventually the call comes, and at night Hinemoa, supported by hollow gourds, manages to swim across the lake to the island where, exhausted and cold, she takes refuge in a hot pool called Wai-Kimihia, which is just below Tutanekai's village. Tutanekai's servant comes to the lake to get water. Hinemoa tricks him into giving her the calabash in which the water is carried, and breaks it. She does this several times, and eventually Tutanekai comes to find out what is happening. The lovers are united, and the sun sets over Lake Rotorua with, as Tarr writes, 'Happiness of All.'

In an interview recorded when he was 81, Tarr said that he had wanted to make a picture about Maori customs for screening in England. The declaration of World War I by Britain on 4 August 1914 meant that finance was not available, and Tarr decided to make a 'smaller' fiction film based on the legend of Hinemoa and Tutanekai. By preparing a careful shooting sequence to avoid editing time, he was able to shoot the film and complete preparation of the screening print in eight days. He said, 'as a matter of fact, I've been on the stage all my life, you see, and I've been in drama and musical comedy and everything, and I made it per the script. And I did it as much as possible with the scenes following each other … As a matter of fact, our cuttings were nil, practically.' But he had his problems. Hera Tawhai had dived into a hot pool which was too hot and had been scalded, so Tarr found a cousin who closely resembled the star, especially in profile, and finished the film in 'semidarkness and profiled her.'

Hinemoa was one of the first of New Zealand's feature films, and a day bill advertising the screening includes an insert which claims it as 'the first photo-play produced in New Zealand by entirely local enterprise … It is the first picture on record which has been acted entirely by Natives—every part being taken by the members of the Rev. F. Bennett's famous Maori Choir Party.'

Gaston Melies might take issue with that claim, as the 'Rev. F. Bennett' is probably the same person who rendered assistance to Melies when he made a shorter version of the legend two years earlier and many of the cast could well have been well-rehearsed through that earlier experience. Sadly the nitrate stock on which it was made has long since disintegrated, and the film is lost. All that remains are stills, daybills and an interview with Tarr. SE

Hera Tawhai-Rogers (Hinemoa). Courtesy of the Stills Collection, New Zealand Film Archive.

---

[1] The film was funded with a £50 advance from a Mr Anderson, president of the Auckland Chamber of Commerce, and shares were taken by Anderson, George Tarr and others. A handbill advertising the film notes that it was 'Kinematographed by Chas. Newham (Hinemoa Films)', which is the likely company name.

1916

THE TEST

[No known footage of this film remains.]
Release date: 1916. (Probably) 35 mm. Black and white. Silent.
Director: Rawdon Blandford.

There are tales that are told in the darkness
and tales that are told in the light,
And some are fit for the morning star
and some for the secret night,
But the tale Jim told is the tale to tell when
the camp fire's wan and grey,
And the dawn breaks into the house of night
with the blood red hammers of day.*

The obviously very filmable romantic melodrama, *The Ballad of Stuttering Jim*, of which the quoted extract is the second stanza, forms the basis of the story of **The Test**. The film probably concentrated on the eternal triangle which drives the story and used the New Zealand landscape as the setting for the tragedy. Jim is a close neighbour of another farmer who has a marriageable daughter. He courts her and wins her hand. An Englishman, probably a ne'er-do-well younger son, arrives at the neighbour's farm, and the daughter falls in love with him. She remains faithful to her betrothal vows, but one day returning home from a picnic, the two rivals and the daughter become lost in dense bush. They begin to starve while they wait for rescue, until eventually the Englishman follows Jim away from their bivouac to find that he had stored food which he alone is eating. The Englishman returns to the camp, collapses in the young woman's arms and, breathing his last, tells her of Jim's infamous behaviour. The young woman then tells Jim of her love for the Englishman before she too dies, and Jim is left to carry the burden of guilt for the rest of his life. Book-ended by the convention of beginning and ending around a campfire, it is wonderfully dramatic material for both camera and actor.

Very little is actually known about the film. Its producer/director, Rawdon Blandford, probably also starred in the photoplay. He worked extensively in film, particularly as an actor playing secondary leads, and during the 1920s was associated with the distribution firm of J.C. Williamson. He is reported to have acted in **A Maori Maid's Love**, directed by Raymond Longford in 1915, Franklyn Barrett's **The Breaking Of The Drought** (1920), F. Stuart Whyte's **Painted Daughters** (1925), Longford's **The Bush Whackers** (1925), and his melodrama, **Peter Vernon's Silence** (1926). Because he would have been in New Zealand for **A Maori Maid's Love** at the time **The Test** was made, it is interesting to surmise that Raymond Longford and Lottie Lyell may have known about the film credited to Blandford, and that others of the company brought over or employed by Longford may also have worked with Blandford on **The Test**.

This film is irretrievably lost. SE

Reference
* William Satchell. 1900. *Patriotic and Other Poems*, p. 34.

Director Rawdon Blandford. *Courtesy of the National Film and Sound Archive, Canberra.*

1916

A MAORI MAID'S LOVE

Lottie Lyell in the lead role. Courtesy of the National Film and Sound Archive, Canberra.

[No known footage of this film remains.] Vita Film Corporation and The Zealandia Photo Play Producing Co. *Country of origin:* Australia. *Location:* Rotorua. *Australian distributor:* The Eureka Exchange (N.Z. distributor unknown). *Opened:* probably 3 November 1915 (N.Z.). 35 mm. Black and white. Silent. 5000 ft (five reels).

Director: Raymond Longford. *Producers:* Raymond Longford and Lottie Lyell who worked together on Longford's films. Here Lyell was co-scriptwriter and director as well as taking the leading female role.

Cast

Lottie Lyell, Raymond Longford, Kenneth Carlisle, Rawdon Blandford.

Set in New Zealand during the period of early colonisation, the story builds on the attempts of a surveyor named Graham to avoid his wife by spending much of his time in the field. During the course of one of his surveys, he meets a Maori woman who becomes pregnant by him. She gives birth to a daughter who is placed in the care of a character known as Maori Jack. After a number of years the daughter grows up and falls in love with a jackeroo. Graham is killed by Maori Jack, but his daughter lives happily ever after.

With its five reel length exceeding the 4000 foot standard recognised by archivists, and Longford's growing capacity for innovation and narrative control, **A Maori Maid's Love** can claim to be the first full length New Zealand feature. Longford made the film when he was forced out of Australia during a dispute over distribution rights and studio ownership. He expected to be able to release his film in New Zealand, but found that the distribution combine which had closed ranks on him in Australia had also allied with the Hayward-Fuller organisation in New Zealand. Consequently after the first private screening, he was unable to release the film in this country.*

The original title, **The Surveyor's Daughter**, appears to be more in keeping with the plot, but was probably changed for marketing purposes when Longford returned to Australia with the film. In New Zealand a letter from J.N. Rolfe, whose father was invited to attend the first screening, notes, 'It appears that the film was made with the latter title (The Surveyor's Daughter) and later changed to A Maori Maid's Love. I cannot recall my father ever referring to the film as being anything but "The Surveyor's Daughter." '

Apart from authenticating that first screening, and providing the alternative title, the invitation also refers to the production company as The Zealandia Photo Play Producing Co. SE

Reference
* John Tulloch. 1981. *Legends on the Screen*, p. 155.

1916

THE MUTINY OF THE BOUNTY

[No known footage of this film remains.] Crick and Jones. *Country of origin:* Australia. *Location:* Rotorua. *Distributor:* Hughes (New Zealand). *Registered:* 15 September 1916. 35 mm. Black and white. Silent. 5000 ft.

Director and producer: Raymond Longford. *Screen-play:* Raymond Longford, assisted by Lottie Lyell, based on the history of Captain Bligh and the *Bounty* mutiny taken from Bligh's journals and ship's records. *Photographers:* Franklyn Barrett, A. Segerberg, Charles Newham.

Cast

George Cross (Captain Bligh), V. Power (Fletcher Christian), D.L. Dalziell (Sir Joseph Banks), Reginald Collins (Midshipman Heywood), Ernesto Crosetto (Midshipman Hallett), Harry Beaumont (Mr Samuels), Meta Taupopoki (Otoo), Mere Amohia (Mere).

Based on Bligh's own log book and other records of the voyage, the story appears to have dealt with the recognised elements of the Bligh story—a ship's captain who was a stickler for the letter of the regulations under which he commanded, and the tension and conflict with the crew which ensues when those regulations are strictly applied. Bligh's actions eventually result in a mutiny led by Fletcher Christian. Christian, as Bligh's own records observe, casts the captain adrift in a whaler and then takes the *Bounty* to Pitcairn Island where the mutineers settle.

Precisely how Longford and Lyell treated the *Bounty* mutiny is not known, although Pike and Cooper in their text *Australian Film 1900–1970* refer to their use of Bligh's log and other primary sources. These were to provide a picture of Bligh and the crew which was somewhat different from the Hollywood picture of Bligh the monster, an attitude epitomised in the opening screen comment from the 1935 version which refers to the mutiny as 'mutiny against the abuse of harsh eighteenth century sea law.'* The consequent image of Charles Laughton's Bligh was bereft of the balance which this 1916 version appears to provide.

Much of the film was shot around Rotorua, the same general location as Longford and Lyell's previous film, **A Maori Maid's Love**, and its New Zealand connection was furthered by Longford's use of Maori actors in the Tahitian scenes. There have been at least five versions of the Bounty story beginning with the Longford one in 1916. There was an Australian production by Charles Chauvel in 1933 starring the young Errol Flynn and called **In the Wake of the Bounty**; the 1935 version with Laughton as Bligh; one in 1962 directed by Lewis Milestone and starring Marlon Brando, also called **The Mutiny on the Bounty**; and finally New Zealand director Roger Donaldson's film of 1984, simply called **The Bounty**. Interestingly, in the latest version Maori actors again appear, the most notable being Wi Kuki Kaa as King Tynah. Like the Longford/Lyell version, Donaldson's Bligh and Christian were much more rounded characters, both of whom combined positive characteristics with more violent and negative ones. Clearly, however, the 1916 film had no problems with ethnic accuracy. Longford used both Maori actors and Rotorua locations to stand in for the Tahitian episodes. SE

Reference
* **Mutiny on the Bounty.** 1935. Director: Frank Lloyd.

Sailors from the **Bounty** *taking leave of their island sweethearts, played by Maori women from Rotorua. Courtesy of the National Film and Sound Archive, Canberra.*

1921

BEYOND

[No known footage of this film remains.] Famous Players–Lasky. *Country of origin:* U.S. *Distributor:* Paramount. 35 mm. Black and white. Silent. 5248 ft (five reels).

Director: William Desmond Taylor. *Producer:* Jesse L. Lasky. *Screenplay:* Julia Crawford Ivers. *Source:* Henry Arthur Jones, *The Lifted Veil*.

Cast

Ethel Clayton (Avis Langley), Charles Meredith (Geoffrey Southerne), Earl Schenck (Alec Langley), Fontaine La Rue (Mrs Langley), Winifred Kingston (Viva Newmarch), Lillian Rich (Bessie Ackroyd), Charles French (Samuel Ackroyd), Spottiswoode Aitken (Rufus Southerne), Herbert Fortier (Dr Newmarch).

Avis Langley is entrusted by her dying mother with the care of her wayward and profligate twin brother, Alec Langley. Avis is about to be married to her fiancé Geoffrey Southerne when she learns that brother Alec has gone missing. He had been working in New Zealand for Samuel Ackroyd and had become engaged to Ackroyd's daughter Bessie, but had taken to the drink and disappeared. Her mother's ghost appears and reminds Avis of her promise to look after her brother.

Honouring her promise, Avis goes to New Zealand, finds Alec, persuades him to dry out and marry Bessie, then leaves for England by steamer. During a storm the ship is wrecked. Avis manages to survive, but is washed up on a small island where she spends almost a year waiting to return to England. Her fiancé Geoffrey, believing her dead, marries Viva Newmarch, whom he does not love. On her return Avis conceals her presence from Geoffrey and is consoled during the waiting period by her mother, until the accidental death of Viva makes it possible for her to be reunited with Geoffrey.

Beyond seems only peripherally associated with New Zealand, but it represents the first example of a feature utilising exotic New Zealand as a setting while actually being shot in the U.S. It is typical also of the melodramatic romances which appeared on screens around the world and which influenced film-makers far beyond Hollywood's environs, despite their rapid production time and rather unremarkable production values. Furthermore it was typical of what audiences would see, as within the next five or six years the American studios would supply between two-thirds and three-quarters of all the films registered by the New Zealand censor's office. Trade reviewer Edward Weitzel describes Ethel Clayton as an actress of 'deep emotional power', but notes also, 'The material for the story is generally interesting, but the big dramatic points seem to miss fire and the death of the second wife is a trick of the dramatist's to bring about a happy ending. Through the fault of either the director or the actors … there is a feeling of perfunctoriness about most of the complications.'* SE

Reference
* Edward Weitzel. *The Moving Picture World*, 17 September 1921, p. 319.

Charles French (Samuel Ackroyd), Ethel Clayton (Avis Langley) and Earl Schenck (Alec Langley). *Courtesy of the National Film and Television Archive, London.*

1921

THE BETRAYER

[No known footage of this film remains.] Beaumont Smith Productions. A.k.a. Our Bit o' the World. A.k.a. The Maid of Maoriland. *Country of origin:* Australia. *N.Z. location:* Rotorua. *Distributor:* Beaumont Smith. 35 mm. Black and white. Silent. 5500 ft.

Director and producer: Beaumont Smith. *Screenplay:* Beaumont Smith. *Photography:* Lacey Percival.

Cast

Stella Southern (Iwa), Cyril Mackay (Stephen Manners), John Cosgrove (John Barris), Marie D'Alton (Mrs Manners), Mita, Chief of the Arawa (Hauraki), Bernice Vere (Eleanor Barris), with Maggie/Bella Papakura, Guide Susan, Herbert Lee, Raymond Hatton, Dunstan Webb.

Following a similar theme to Raymond Longford's **A Maori Maid's Love**, **The Betrayer** sets up a relationship between a pakeha, Stephen Manners, and a high-ranking Maori woman. When she dies in childbirth, her daughter is named Iwa and raised by her grandfather Hauraki, a rangatira. After a break of 20 years Manners returns to New Zealand where he is attacked by Hauraki, who appears to want to kill him for his past actions. However, the old chief suggests that a more fitting course of action would be for Stephen Manners to take Iwa back to Australia and by introducing her to Australian society, atone, at least in part, for his neglect of his daughter and his desertion of her mother. Iwa knows nothing of Manners's relationship with her mother.

Travelling with Manners is the dissolute John Barris, who is told by the old chief in a deathbed confession that Iwa is really the daughter of a missionary, not Manners. Barris keeps the information to himself, and in turn makes unwelcome approaches to Iwa. Rescued by Manners, Iwa tells him she is in love with him. He confesses that he is her father, and Iwa returns to Rotorua where she is again harassed by the importuning Barris. Told by Barris's wife of the truth, that Iwa is not his daughter, Manners realises his love for the young woman, returns to New Zealand, rescues her again from Barris and the pair live happily ever after.

Beaumont Smith had a fruitful association with New Zealand. His second and hugely successful Claude Dampier comedy, **The Adventures of Algy**, was mostly shot in New Zealand, and his distribution company was responsible for releasing films like **Venus of the South Seas** in Australia. **The Betrayer** was another melodrama driven by false information, miscegenation, and tangled relationships. Characters were eminently recognisable as villain and vamp, hero and unprotected heroine, and their actions included stock situations from deathbed confessions to dramatic, nick-of-time rescues. Where this film becomes significant in the annals of New Zealand film, however, is in its more positive treatment of a miscegenated relationship. Certainly the wages of interracial fertilisation is death for the mother; and typically too, the white male is the survivor while the dusky maiden of nineteenth century fantasy is the victim. However, Beaumont Smith gives the interracial relationship a different twist when he allows the couple not only to come together, but also to suggest that in the end Iwa and Stephen Manners survive and enjoy a regular and fruitful marriage for the rest of their lives.

Locating his film in Rotorua as well as in Australia, as so many other film-makers had done and were to do, suggests that there is a history to be written about the place of Rotorua in the early days of cinema production. New Zealand directors like George Tarr, as well as international film-makers such as Smith himself, Raymond Longford, and Gaston Melies, found in the dramatic geomorphology of craters, steam vents, geysers, boiling mud and the lakes a magnificent setting for the melodramas they were making. The Maori village of Ohinemutu, and the welcoming and supportive attitude of the Arawa, the Maori tribal group which populated the area, provided characters and sets which lent those early movies not only a unique and exotic appeal, but some superb actors as well. SE

Stella Southern (Iwa) and Cyril Mackay (Stephen Manners). *Courtesy of the National Film and Sound Archive, Canberra*

1922

THE BIRTH OF NEW ZEALAND

Tiki Films. *Rating:* U, 1922. 35 mm. Black and white. Silent. 8000 ft. 132 mins. *Remaining footage:* 154 ft. New Zealand Cinema Enterprises Ltd Palmerston North (Managing directors: Mr Fred Jackson and Mr H.E. (Kosy) Bennett).

Director: Harrington Reynolds. *Camera:* Frank Stewart. *Assistant camera and stills:* Edwin Coubray. *Scenic artist* (production designer): B.G. Lindvall. *Assistant director:* Wally Tate.

Cast

Stella Southern (Dorothy), **Norman French** (Tom Campbell), **Harrington Reynolds** (Con O'Hara), **George Kingsland** (Septimus), **Maisie Carte** (Mrs Campbell).

Only fragments of this film remain—a few minutes from an original 8000 feet—but posters and comments recorded from those who were responsible for the production, especially second cameraman Edwin Coubray, indicate that it was constructed episodically. A surviving poster lists the following headings:

- The Landing of Captain Cook
- Annexation of New Zealand by Governor Hobson
- Ancient Maori Wars Fought Once Again on the Screen
- Burning and Sacking of Kororareka
- Signing of the Historic Treaty of Waitangi
- Gabriel's Gully Gold Rush
- Queen Street Auckland 1842

In addition, remnants of film which have been restored by the New Zealand Film Archive include a French naval contingent arriving at Akaroa in the South Island only to find that HMS *Britomart* had already established a British presence. This sequence is followed by the cryptic intertitle, 'And so, but for the small indiscretion of a French Officer, how different things might have been.' The remaining film also shows part of a bush ranging sequence which appears to have been used in a later film called **The Romance Of Maoriland** (see below), and a love story involving a young officer, who according to surviving stills, eventually marries.

The Birth Of New Zealand was praised widely for its educational value and morally uplifting qualities. It intended to tell the story of New Zealand from 'The landing of Captain Cook to the Present Day', and was constructed to be of epic proportions, influenced, no doubt, by the success of D.W. Griffith's 1915 epic, **Birth of a Nation**. But in the end it did not return an adequate profit, and was sold to Edward Brown, who recycled portions of it in his **Romance Of Maoriland**.

It was, however, an important collaboration among film-makers, several of whom were to have a major influence on the development of film in New Zealand. Reynolds and Tate brought Australian film-making experience with them to New Zealand, Edwin Coubray eventually became a key figure in the development of movie sound in New Zealand, and there is evidence in the remaining stills that Rudall Hayward, arguably the father of New Zealand film, participated in the crewing. Stella Southern (real name Billie Winks), fresh from her leading role in **The Betrayer**, had remained in New Zealand and **The Birth Of New Zealand** was her next starring role. SE

The lost scene of the Treaty of Waitangi. Courtesy of the Stills Collection, New Zealand Film Archive.

1922

MY LADY OF THE CAVE

Bay Of Plenty Films. *Budget:* £1000, from a 20 person syndicate contributing £50 each. *Locations:* Mayor Island and Waihi. *Rating:* G, February 1922. 35 mm. Black and white. Silent. 5000 ft. 83 mins. Only portions of the original remain.

Director and producer: Rudall Hayward. *Screenplay:* Rudall Hayward from an original story by H.T. Gibson published as a serial in the *New Zealand Herald* during 1921. *Cameraman:* Frank Stewart using a 1912 35 mm 'Pathe' handcranked camera. *Assistant cameraman and assistant director:* Arthur 'Darkie' Bestic. *Costume designer for Miss West:* George Courts Ltd. of Auckland.

Cast

Gordon Campbell, real name Bob Ramsay (The Mill Clerk), Hazel West, real name Hazel Bodley, later Hazel de Montalk ('My Lady', Beryl Trite). The actors' names are unknown for Rau, the faithful Maori of the cave and Dick Trite, the mill clerk's friend and uncle of Beryl.

The story is told in a combination of real time events and flashbacks. It opens with the Mill Clerk going sailing on a scow and being lost overboard. He reaches the shore of a small island, exhausted. Awakened by a dog licking his face he follows the animal to a sheltered area under a cliff where he discovers his Lady of the Cave, a nubile young woman dressed rather like a Roman goddess, who speaks a form of language only she and her faithful guard Rau can understand. This opening sequence allows the following chronology to be unravelled.

A group of Maori have attacked the homestead of a family named Trite who have unwittingly broken a tapu. Their small daughter, Beryl, is rescued and hidden by a Maori family friend named Rau. The family is killed and Rau is tortured, mutilated and has his tongue torn out by the attacking Maori. Nonetheless, he manages to escape with Beryl to an island where he hides her successfully until the Mill Clerk finds her. After some problems with an antagonistic group on the island, our hero takes his find back to the mainland where she is progressively reintroduced to civilisation and prepared for the time when she will become the Mill Clerk's wife.

The Mill Clerk's problems on the island are developed by some clever narrative interaction with a sub-plot involving a gang of moonshiners. It not only adds action and excitement, but also provides the reason for the eventual death of the faithful Rau. On his deathbed he provides the material for the final dénouement as he hands over a small box which, when eventually opened back on the mainland, is seen to contain a description of the original Maori attack and identifies Beryl as belonging to the Trite family.

The narrative form is a sophisticated interplay of time sequences which ultimately provide the necessary elements of 'My Lady's' life, rescue, and rehabilitation by 'My Man Who Found Me'. Shot largely on Mayor Island, it is the first feature by the 22 year-old Rudall Hayward, whose uncle Henry was a major distributor of film in New Zealand, and whose family had been involved with the entertainment industry and the arts for many generations. Here Hayward provides a superb example of sympathetic colonialism, but one which demonstrates some important myths. 'My Lady' is the canvas upon which the hero writes, and as he does so he constructs the perfect wife for a successful pioneer—the essence of purity, willingly subject to every desire of 'Her Man Who Found Her', and completely untouched by hand or mind so that she has to be taught how to be, and thus becomes the template for pioneer womanhood. Hayward's fantasy, however, shows the beginnings of the respect in which he held Maori, and is a fascinating picture of attitudes and beliefs held by some privileged New Zealanders in the 1920s. It is solid early support for the talent Rudall Hayward showed as a visual storyteller dealing with early days in the colonial life of New Zealand.
SE

Hazel de Montalk, formerly Hazel West, as My Lady of the Cave, Beryl Trite. *Permission from The Hayward Historical Film Trust and Stills Collection, New Zealand Film Archive.*

1922
TEN THOUSAND MILES IN THE SOUTHERN CROSS

Documentary feature
Director: George Tarr.

In 1922 George Tarr toured the South Pacific in the vessel *Southern Cross*, documenting both indigenous cultures and the environments in which they developed. Thought to be entirely lost, in 1995 approximately 16 minutes of the film were found in Australia and returned to the New Zealand Film Archive. The footage is silent, and there are no subtitles or notes identifying precise locations or individuals, although further research, including screenings of the material in the Solomon Islands where some of the film was shot, will help fill some of the gaps. The images appear to be of missionaries and indigenous peoples from the Solomon Islands and from four or more locations in the Melanesian triangle. The visual emphases are on environments: architecture and the location of houses and other buildings; people: their physical appearance and costume; rituals: particularly dance and re-enactments of the hunt; subsistence activities such as fishing; and the presence of European missionaries. There are a number of references to the Christian church in the early footage, including a lengthy ecclesiastical procession with a bishop in full canonicals, indicating the presence of a major Melanesian mission.

Tarr's documentary approach is primarily not to comment, but simply to record images. Some of these are obviously enacted for the camera, including a bizarre shot of a small child smoking a cigarette as tears begin to run down his cheeks, an image which derives specifically from the exploitive traditions of nineteenth century photographers of indigenous peoples. The various ritual dances are also clearly enacted for the camera, allowing time for Tarr to shift his point of view and begin filming again. Some shots are posed, especially those of figures displaying physique or decoration, and these make up the bulk of the mid shots in the film. Some sequences include the few pans which explore the landscape, allowing the viewer to take in the coral walls and foundations of buildings in the third location, or the arrangement of buildings in villages along the shoreline. There are occasional records of events, a fisherman casting and pulling in his net, the landing of supplies brought in by boat from an off-shore vessel, and the ecclesiastical procession.

The style of the surviving footage, however, suggests that Tarr made little attempt to utilise the potential of the camera for locating the viewer within the environment which he was placing on record. Approximately three-quarters of the shots are wide shots, and less than 10% are close-ups which provide intimate detail. This gives a distanced and generalised sense of the area, acceptable in setting locations, but needing the balance of the closer view for the viewer to be able to have a sense of involvement. There is little camera movement, and while this is to be expected of much of the camera operation of the time, it means that the point of the viewer is essentially static. The interestingly innovative use of a boat to provide the equivalent of a seagoing tracking shot on two or three occasions is a welcome diversion.

Essentially, though, Tarr's beautiful black and white images speak for themselves. Apart from the presence of the child smoker, there is little of the Eurocentric rhetoric or exploitation associated with many early photographic records of South Pacific cultures, and Tarr's images leave the viewer with a satisfying sense both of freshness and enlightenment. SE

The poster from the film. Courtesy of the Stills Collection, New Zealand Film Archive.

THE ROMANCE OF SLEEPY HOLLOW

[No known footage of this film remains.] Maoriland Pictures. *Rating:* G, submitted November 1923, but returned for excisions to be made, and a new registration was issued on 20 December 1923. *Distributor:* Makepeace. 35 mm. Black and white. Silent. 5700 ft (November 1923). 4800 ft (December 1923).

Director and producer: Henry J. Makepeace.

Cast

Francis X. Bouzaid of Onehunga, June Phillips of Dominion Road, with Miss Lola Montesse of Mount Eden, Miss Angela Olivera of Devonport, Miss Olive Tayne of Ponsonby, Miss Peggy Carr of Parnell.

Nothing of the original film remains. The only indication of its content comes from a poster announcing that it would open at the Grand in Auckland on Friday 22 August 1924, which would appear to be almost a year after registration by the censor. There it is described as 'A Bright Sparkling Comedy-Drama … The first to be produced in New Zealand', a similar claim to many of New Zealand's early features.

This is one of a number of early New Zealand films made on nitrate stock which appear to be irretrievably lost. Whereas there are fragments of most other early titles, there is no trace of any surviving portion of **The Romance of Sleepy Hollow**. That makes all the more tantalising the mystery surrounding the censor's initial rejection of the film in November 1923. Following extensive cuts—some 900 feet or around 15 minutes of screen time—it was finally released for exhibition. The local casting suggests that **The Romance of Sleepy Hollow** could have been a melodrama of the kind which utitlised local interest, an approach later to be developed in one reel community comedies such as **Tillie of Thames**. However, as with many lost films where there is no evidence of supporting documentation by way of screenplay or press coverage, critical commentary can be no more than surmise. SE

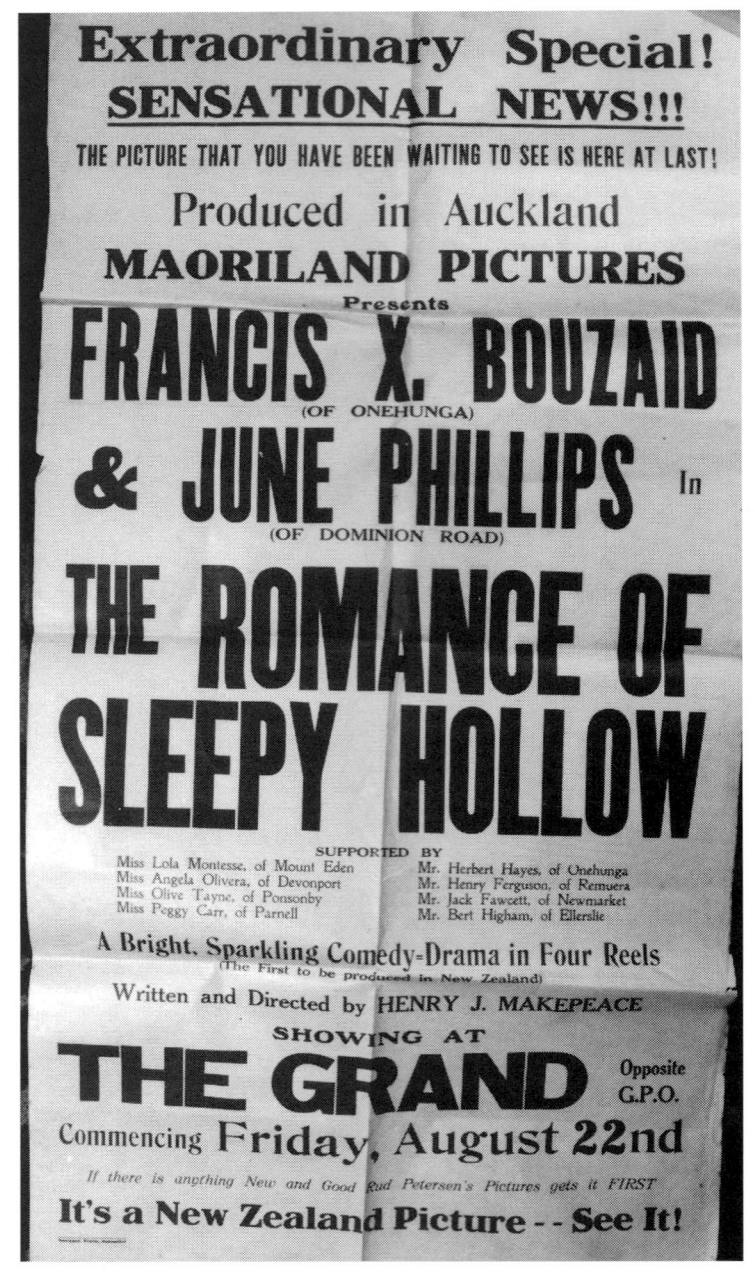

The only surviving visual material from the film. Courtesy of the Stills Collection, New Zealand Film Archive.

1924

VENUS OF THE SOUTH SEAS

Lee Bradford Corporation and New Zealand Dominion Productions Ltd. A.k.a. Venus of the Southern Seas. *Location:* Nelson. *Distributor:* New Zealand Picture Supplies. *Rating:* U, April 1924. 35 mm. Black and white. Silent. 7000 ft (five reels).

Director: James R. Sullivan. *Assistant cameraman:* Bert Bridgeman. *Processor:* Charlie Barton.

Cast

Annette Kellerman (Shona Royal), Roland Purdu (John Royal), Norman French (Captain John Drake), Robert Ramsey (Robert Quayne Jnr).

Shona Royal, the daughter of a South Sea island pearl trader, believes that her father is being systematically robbed of pearls by the divers who fish for him. An expert swimmer, she goes down among the divers and is supplied with proof of her suspicions when she catches one of them in the act. The thieves sell their pearls to John Drake, the captain and owner of the supply ship the *Southern Cross* when it makes one of its regular calls to the island. Drake, not satisfied with what the crooked divers bring in, wants to marry Shona and thus gain possession of the pearl fishing grounds. Shona, however, will have none of him. One night when a pleasure yacht anchors off-shore, she swims out to see what is on board. She is discovered by Robert Quayne, son of the owner, then dives overboard and swims back to shore pursued by Quayne. They fall in love, but Quayne is forced to leave by his father and, left on her own, she tells and performs an aquatic fairy story for a group of local children. Quayne eventually returns to the island as a deckhand on Drake' supply ship, and after a series of adventures, during which Shona's father dies, Drake attempts to murder Quayne, and Shona saves the day with her quick wit and remarkable swimming abilities. Finally they sail off into the proverbial sunset.

Venus of the South Seas is a wonderful example of the way New Zealand took to the fledgling film industry. The citizens of Nelson, where the film was shot, were entertained and absorbed as the original town reservoir was turned into a studio set for Annette Kellerman to perform her stunts. Locals drove the steam engine which provided the power for both pool heating and light, waves were generated on the surface by a handcranked windmill, the local taxi driver had the daily bonus of transporting the camera crew to and from the reservoir and local boats were used for the seagoing scenes.

But the film was as much a vehicle for star Annette Kellerman as it was glamour for the people or a potential profit-maker for its New Zealand investors. Kellerman was one of the success stories of her time. Born in Marrickville, Sydney, she was a talented swimmer and before she became a professional performer, she held a wide variety of swimming records. Her ability as an underwater swimmer gave her a number of roles in which she performed underwater in specially constructed glass tanks, just as she did in the fantasy princess sequence in **Venus of the South Seas**. Film roles and publicity stunts took her from being the first Australian to star in Hollywood productions to playing the first nude scene to an arrest for having the audacity to wear a one-piece bathing suit to a continuing concern for women who could benefit from increased physical fitness. Her roles were invariably melodramas such as the fantasy **A Daughter of the Gods**, released in the U.S. in 1916, where she played a mysterious beauty named Anitia who invariably escaped trouble by diving into the sea, but the film is still given an original twist by her remarkable aquatic abilities. Looking back on it some 70 years after its release, the viewer is left more with a memory of a remarkable performer bound by the conventions of the silent screen, and some fascinating and remarkably effective attempts at underwater effects, than with any great sense of originality in the narrative. SE

Annette Kellerman (Shona Royal). *Courtesy of the Stills Collection, New Zealand Film Archive.*

1925

REWI'S LAST STAND

[Only portions of the film remain.] Maori War Films Ltd (Directors: Henry Hayward, L.A. Eady, W.W. Wright and Phil Hayward). *Location:* Rotorua. *Distributor:* New Zealand Picture Supplies. *Rating:* G, 24 July 1925. 35 mm. Black and white. Silent. 8000 ft.

Director and producer: Rudall Hayward. *Scenario:* Rudall Hayward. *Source:* James Cowan FRGS, *The New Zealand Wars,* vol I and *The Old Frontier. Director of photography:* Frank Stewart with special scenes by Edwin (Ted) Coubray, J. Makepeace. *Continuous printer:* Edwin (Ted) Coubray. *Editing:* Rudall and Hilda Hayward. *Settings:* Edward Armitage, Jack Goessi, Cecil Todd. Furnishings and antiques supplied by Andrews & Clark, G. and W. Alexander. *Composer:* Marcella Doreen, accompanying Maori melody 'Mere'.

Cast

Frank Nemo (Dr Wake), Nola Casselli (Cecily Wake), M. Millington (Miss Jessica Wake), Eric Yates (Colonel Grey), Edmund Finney (Kenneth Gordon), Fred Mills ('Colonel Dobby'), Cadia Taine (Mrs Wake), Wightman McCombe (Sir George Grey), Chief Abe (Rewi Maniapoto), Chief Mita (Hitiri Paerata), H.J. Bentley (The Hon. Mr–a cabinet minister), Mr Alexis (Von Tempsky), Chas Archer (General Cameron), W. Surrell (Lieutenant-Colonel McDonnell), Miss Tina (Takiri), with unidentified Maori cast as Rangi (a small Maori boy), Mako (a fighting chief of the Maniapoto), Te Waro (a tohunga or priest).

During 1863 the New Zealand Wars had become serious enough to take the full attention of the governor, Sir George Grey. In the Waikato area a corps of forest rangers, under the command of Gustavus Von Tempsky and attached to the 40th Regiment, became renowned for its ability as a successful fighting unit. Newly arrived from England and working as a clerk, the young Kenneth Gordon is attracted by the regiment's reputation and joins up as a recruit, an action which forces him to part from his new acquaintance, the beautiful Cecily Wake. Out in the field, Ken Gordon leaves camp in order to find von Tempsky and his lieutenant (then sergeant), McDonnell, who have gone on a scouting expedition, but he becomes lost in the bush and is posted by his unit as a deserter. In the course of his wanderings, Gordon rescues a young Maori woman, a rangtira named Takiri, from drowning. Shortly afterwards the pair are captured by a taua, a war party of Maori, and Gordon is kept prisoner. He plans to escape and return to his unit with substantial information, but on finding that Takiri's young brother, Rangi, has disappeared, he goes with her to find him. Their search leads them to the Orakei pa, the fortified post the Maori have been building at Kihikihi, near Te Awamutu, where the presence of a pakeha (a white man) so enrages the paramount chief, Rewi Manipoto, that he is tied up and thrown into a rua, or dugout pit.

The British attack the pa and the battle rages for three days, after which the Maori abandon the fortification, and Ken Gordon, with Takiri, attempts to rejoin the British. Takiri, however, is shot, and dies in Gordon's arms. He eventually rejoins his unit, the charges of desertion are dropped, and he is reunited with Cecily.

Less than 30 minutes of **Rewi's Last Stand** remains. That footage, however, gives some indication of the vitality and dramatic intensity of this major historical reconstruction. It is based firmly on James Cowan's highly Eurocentric but factually well-researched description of the events leading up to the siege by the British of Orakei Pa during the New Zealand Wars of the 1860s. Director Rudall Hayward's balanced portrayal of Maori and their British attackers is unusual and rare in the cinema of New Zealand, as is his portrayal of the battlefield from the point of view of both parties in the combat.

His direction, together with Frank Stewart's photography, is economical and sound, with solid narrative control, an intelligent and creative presentation of image and classical assemble editing. On an important technical note, this was the film in which Edwin Coubray built a continuous printer which could do lap dissolves. Coubray notes, 'I think I accomplished some of the first lap dissolves in New Zealand.'

The narrative is held together by the simple device of a young colonial male, fresh from the mother country, England, becoming embroiled in the conflict between the indigenous people, the Maori, and the colonists, who were largely British. He undergoes the rites of passage required of a male, and in a singularly New Zealand turn of the narrative, forms a relationship with a young Maori woman of chiefly rank which gives him a view of Maori quite different from that of most of his fellow colonials.

In the program notes from its screening at the Strand Theatre in Auckland, Henry Hayward, father of the director, says, 'We believe that every unit of our great Empire should provide its quota in helping to make British pictures for British people, and that is solely why this little New Zealand producing company has made "Rewi's Last Stand."'

Rewi's Last Stand was remade in the late 1930s by Rudall Hayward as a sound feature. In its U.K. release, which is now the only extant print, it is titled **The Last Stand**. SE

MONDAY, 2nd NOVEMBER, 1925.

A Special Attraction.
Matinee at 3 p.m.
Evening at 8 p.m.

The Management is Proud to Announce New Zealand's First Super Feature:

REWI'S LAST STAND
REWI'S LAST STAND
REWI'S LAST STAND
 REWI'S LAST STAND
 REWI'S LAST STAND
 REWI'S LAST STAND

An Historically True Tale of Love and War Time Adventures in the New Zealand Bush, including the Exact, Amazing, and Graphic Description of the

BATTLE OF ORAKAU
BATTLE OF ORAKAU

From a Prominent Schoolmaster: "I feel it my duty as a Schoolmaster to tender my appreciation of the efforts of the local film company in their production of 'Rewis Last Stand.' I wish I could take all my pupils to see it.— (Signed) H. T. GIBSON."

"Rewi's Last Stand" is the greatest Education Entertainment ever offered. Book Your Seats for the Night Showing.

PRICES.—Matinee 1/6; Children 6d.
Evening, 2/- and 1/6; Reserves 2/-; Children 9d.

This advertisement appeared in the Te Awamutu Courier *of Tuesday 27 October 1925, the town adjacent to the historical location of the events in the film. Courtesy of the Te Awamutu* Courier.

1925

THE ADVENTURES OF ALGY

Bathie Stuart (Kiwi McGill). Courtesy of the National Film and Sound Archive, Canberra.

Beaumont Smith Films. A.k.a. Beaumont Smith's Productions. *Countries of origin:* New Zealand, Australia. *Distributor:* Beaumont Smith Films. *Rating:* G, September 1925. 35 mm. Black and white. Silent. 8000 ft (N.Z.), 6500 ft (Australia).[1]

Director and producer: Beaumont Smith. *Screenplay:* Beaumont Smith. *Director of photography:* Lacey Percival, Frank Stewart, Syd Taylor, Charles Barton, Edwin (Ted) Coubray.

Cast

Claude Dampier (Algernon Allison), Bathie Stuart (Kiwi McGill), Billie Carlyle (Mollie Moore), George Chalmers (John McGill), Eric Harrison (Murray Watson), Lester Brown (Stage Manager), with Eric Yates, Hilda Attenborough, Verna Blain, Beaumont Smith.

Algy Allison and his cousin Murray Watson have been left an estate in New Zealand by their uncle Geoff. The terms of the will pit the cousins against each other in a test of intelligence and resourcefulness, qualities much needed in the new colony. The first man to arrive in New Zealand will have first choice of the farms their uncle has left them. Delayed by considerable comic foul play by his devious and unprincipled cousin, Algy eventually arrives in New Zealand to find that cousin Murray has taken possession of the best farm. Algy's farm is reputed to bear oil, but his attention is distracted as he falls besottedly in love with Murray's farm manager's daughter, Kiwi McGill. Her father falls on hard times, and Kiwi, who has developed a repertoire of Maori dances, takes off to Sydney where she performs on stage to earn money to help her father. Murray, who has acquired an interest in the theatre where she performs, decides that Kiwi would be a great catch, but when she refuses to marry him, he has her fired and she returns to New Zealand with her new friend Mollie. In the best possible tradition, Algy, a confirmed crossword addict, sees the solution to his problems in a crossword clue, his farm strikes oil, Kiwi agrees to marry him, and even Murray turns out to see the error of his ways, helped by the goodness of Kiwi's friend Mollie.

As he did in **The Betrayer**, Beaumont Smith calls on New Zealand for colour and settings, although **The Adventures of Algy** is markedly different in tone from the sympathetic treatment of race and culture which characterised the earlier film. Here the star, New Zealand actress Bathie Stuart, is dressed in tourist Maori costume, and she performs a series of dances which are derived from, but are really a pastiche of, those of New Zealand's indigenous people. Beaumont also makes use of Maori as comic figures, confirming the nineteenth century stereotype of Maori as clown. While this did not appear to run counter to the prevailing attitudes of New Zealand in the 1920s, today it provokes questions about the evolution of cultural values and the roots of national identity.

Contemporary reviews of **Algy** also underline prevailing interest and approval. The *Christchurch Star* of 14 December 1925 notes, 'The Liberty Quality Orchestra … approaches the acme of perfection in providing music which is suitable … Waiata Poi (Hill) and Waiata Maori are numbers eminently suited for the Maori scenes … ' The *Evening Post* of 21 November 1925 in Wellington comments, 'From start to finish, the film is novel and amusing … the leading feminine role is Bathie Stuart, a New Zealand actress and a credit to her country … There is a strong supporting cast and the entire production is excellent in every respect.' SE

---

[1] The restored footage lodged with the N.Z. Censor on 17 February 1984 has a running time of only 70½ minutes.

1925

GLORIOUS NEW ZEALAND

The New Zealand Government Publicity Office. Directed and produced under the supervision of Arthur H. Messenger. A New Zealand Publicity Film. Documentary feature. *Registered*: September 1925. 35 mm. Black and white. Silent. 12 000 ft. (Note that it is the practice in government publications not to list authorship or individual credits.)

Glorious New Zealand is a New Zealand Government publicity film. As such, it has a clear agenda, which is to attract both tourists and new settlers. Consequently, it provides a fascinating insight into prevailing attitudes and popular myths about New Zealand as a geographical location and as an emerging society. The tone is clearly set in the opening frames which show Maori in a waka (canoe), looking towards a rising sun as if to welcome the new age. They are followed by the figure of a man carrying what appears to be a briefcase as he walks along a beach with the sails of the ship which brought him clearly evident in the background.

The images which remain in the ten minutes of surviving film provide a series of views of lakes, fjords, and rivers, as the intertitles emphasise, in a landscape where 'Snow clad mountains rear their noble heads o'er verdant valleys.' Brief references to Auckland 'Queen City of the North' and images of tram and pedestrian traffic shift the viewer to Northland's vineyards and citrus growing before moving to Lake Wanaka and Queenstown for the remainder of the footage. The film ends on a cutesy image of a child playing with a washboard and wiping suds off her nose.

Despite the small number of surviving images, however, **Glorious New Zealand** confirms the myths of empty landscapes ripe for the plough which were perpetuated in the nineteenth century by companies attracting settlers to New Zealand from Europe. People scarcely exist in this 'panorama of scenic gems', and when they do, they are predominantly male, and invariably pakeha.

The tourist New Zealand of **Glorious New Zealand**, 'this little nation within the Empire—and outpost, as it is, on the Rim of the World' clearly harks back to its British ancestry for a definition of progress and development, 'representing but eighty-five years of toil and enterprise', which is 'a glowing tribute to those hardy pioneers who laid the foundations of our prosperity.' In doing so, it also reinforces the strongly patriarchal, Eurocentric views held by the dominant groups in New Zealand society and politics in the mid 1920s. This is quite consistent with a government production designed to encourage immigration.

What the film lacks, however, is a sense of cinema. The camera acts to capture a series of 'views' in the tradition of the nineteenth century travelling magic lantern entrepreneurs, except that these views move. There is no sense of continuity, shots are predominantly wide shots, and there is no attempt to make use of the potential of the camera to explore time and space and make new connections and links among the images it records. The introduction of 'the second horse to climb the 5747 foot Ben Lomond above Queenstown' and the cute wee girl clearly rubbing suds on her nose at the instigation of an off-camera director are standard devices of the market rather than the documentarist, and so viewers need to judge this film on its attitudinal and social subtexts rather than treating it as an accurate visual portrayal of New Zealand of the mid 1920s.
SE

The title frame. *Courtesy of the Stills Collection, New Zealand Film Archive.*

CARBINE'S HERITAGE

Ted Preston (Tim Hogan). Courtesy of the Coubray Collection, New Zealand Film Archive.

[No known footage of this film remains.] Moa Films Ltd (Coubray noted that it was a New Zealand Radio Films production). *Location:* Auckland. *Registered:* March 1927. (A red X in the censor's register indicates that cuts were made.) 35 mm. Black and white. Silent. 8000 ft.

Director and producer: Edwin (Ted) Coubray. *Screenplay:* Edwin (Ted) Coubray. *Director of photography:* Edwin (Ted) Coubray. *Casting:* Capt Clewes. *Intertitles:* Edwin (Ted) Coubray. *Sound:* Edwin (Ted) Coubray. Sound equipment made by Kelvin Guff. *Poster design and publicity:* Mr MacDonald.

Cast

Queenie Grahame (Alice Wylie), Stuart Douglas (Harold Wylie), Ted Preston (Tim Hogan), Tom Patten (Pat O'Connor), Captain Martin, stage name Captain Lionel Clewes (Angus Macdonald), Con Ingsby (Mr King), John Haddock (Arthur Mack), C.M. Alain (Harrison Wylie), Maurice Field (Claude Montague), Cook Brothers (the Two Crooks), Margaret Roft (Mrs King), Frances Pardy (Mrs Wylie), Mlle Lola D'Ormonde (Molly King).

In an edited interview, Ted Coubray gave the following summary:

'The script … was more or less everybody's. Captain Clewes came along with a rough idea of a young fellow finding a horse when he was returning from a horse show in Hamilton. He knew that a lovely colt like that would be advertised for, so he looked after it, looking in the papers and so forth, but after a year no one had advertised for it, and he had discovered that this young horse had great capabilities, galloping well and even jumping. He entered it at a show, jumping, and that's where the young lady and the father come along and discover that it is their missing colt. A bit of trouble occurs, but they come to arrangements. The young fellow thinks that it's got great possibilities, and they explain it's a descendant of the famous Carbine. They enter the horse in a race, and near the training stages for the race it's stolen by the villain. Oh, and there were two elderly ladies, dressed in dark, and long skirts, and one was blaming the other for putting them off the horse they wanted the bet to lie on. There was a lot of side play like that.'

The Coubray style, witty, casual, but both perceptive and hugely knowledgeable, comes through in this extract and provides an interesting insight into the probable tone of his film. For it was his film. Despite the input of people like Lionel Clewes, **Carbine's Heritage** was the result both of Coubray's artistry and his ability to make the camera work for him.

Usually known as Ted, Edwin Coubray is one of New Zealand's most innovative film-makers. Not only did he have a prolific output, but he also built much of his own equipment, including that used for New Zealand's first sound test as he readied himself to present New Zealand's first newsreel under the title **Coubraytone News** in 1929.

The climactic sequence ending **Carbine's Heritage** was filmed at an actual running of the Auckland Cup at the Christmas meeting in 1926. The horse which starred, Maori Boy, while not the actual cup winner, did have some success on the track on other occasions. The first public screenings of the film, on 6 April 1927, were in the Hippodrome and Empress, Auckland, two theatres which were part of what became Amalgamated Theatres Ltd, formed by the Moodabe brothers, Michael and Joe, in 1928. This company became one of the most influential and longest lasting cinema companies in New Zealand cinema history.

Supportive critics included one enthusiastic reviewer who commented, 'The shots of the running of the Auckland Cup are perhaps the finest pieces of photographs yet produced in the Dominion.' The *New Zealand Herald* critic was less effusive, 'Mr Coubray is to be congratulated on a good piece of work and it is to be hoped that, the initial difficulties over, the company will extend itself to further efforts.' Coubray went on to work on other features, and to develop new sound technologies both for his own company, New Zealand Radio Films and for other producers such as Alexander Markey, and to make a series of industrial documentaries. SE

1927

THE ROMANCE OF HINE-MOA

Akuhato (Tutanekai) and Maata Hurihanganui (Hine-moa). *Courtesy of the National Film and Television Archive.*

[No known footage of this film remains.] The Gaumont Co. Ltd., *Country of origin:* U.K. *Location:* Rotorua. *Distributor:* Ginger. *Rating:* G, April 1927 (U.K. release December 1926). 35 mm. Black and white. Silent. 5500 ft (six reels).

Director and producer: Gustav Pauli. *Director of photography:* Gustav Pauli.

Cast
Maata Hurihanganui (Hine-Moa), Akuhato (Tutanekai), Tingarue, Chief of Omaho Village (Umukarai, Chief of Arawa tribe), Tane Herewini (Whakane, Chief of Ngati Tribe), Tai Amohau (Tai), Paora Tamati, (the Fat Warrior).

The trade journal *Bioscope* said, 'IN BRIEF: Charming love story illustrating an old Maori legend, acted entirely by Maoris in beautiful and interesting native surroundings. A simple and dramatic theme which by the realism of the acting and the unique quality of the settings makes a production of unusual and novel interest. Suitability: Will please any audience.'

The *Bioscope* story varies the well known legend by sending Tutanekai to seek new territory for his people. He pays a friendly visit to Umukari, chief of the Arawa tribe, and there falls in love with the chief's beautiful daughter, Hine-Moa. His advances are favourably received by the young woman's father and the young chief is regaled with feasting and dances, but he rouses the jealousy of Tai, a warrior of the Arawa, who also seeks the hand of Hine-Moa. Tai forms a plot by which Tutanekai appears to be guilty of having violated Umukari's hospitality by stealing the chief's food, which is tapu and for which the punishment is death. Out of respect for his father, Tutanekai's life is spared, but he is condemned to pass through the Valley of Fire, which leads him through the crater of an active volcano.

Hine-Moa is left to mourn for her lover until, on receiving a message from Tutanekai, she sends him word that she will join him at the next full moon. Tai hears of this, and when Hine-Moa tries to make her escape she finds all the canoes closely guarded. Nothing daunted, Hine-Moa plunges into the lake, and arrives safely at the island of her lover.

The traditional release date for **The Romance of Hine-Moa** is 1927, but in fact it was screened in Britain in 1926. New Zealand's Prime Minister of the time, the Right Honourable Gordon Coates attended the screening at the Gaumont company's trade show 'at the New Gallery Kinema on Thursday, December 16th, at 11.15 a.m … (to see) … an authentic picturisation of the most widely known Maori legend … (starring) … Maata Hurihanganui, who had just returned from a tour of Australia with a company of Maori dancers … '

Pauli seems to have shifted the emphasis in this version of the Hine-Moa narrative from her legendary lake crossing to the problems experienced by Tutanekai in the period leading up to his lover's famous swim. He develops his own version of the story by sending Tutanekai through a volcanic valley, 'The Valley of Fire', to face the 'Ordeal of the Four Elements', so that the presence of Hine-Moa in the narrative becomes more of a catalyst than the primary plot line. In so doing Pauli becomes an early member of that large group of film-makers from outside New Zealand who have used the dramatic settings to provide spectacle in stories which, despite their superficial exotic appeal, actually run along well-established European and American tracks. The settings, summed up in the descriptive material for Hine-Moa, are 'sinister and fire swept volcanic areas, with their hot springs, geysers, choking vapours of sulphur, and gushing wells of boiling mud, which are New Zealand's eerie heritage.' That heritage is one of a number of indicators of New Zealandness in films made prior to the sudden eruption of a new cinema ushered in by **Sleeping Dogs** and the New Zealand Film Commission in the late 1970s. SE

1927

UNDER THE SOUTHERN CROSS

[No known footage of this film remains.] The Gaumont Company Ltd. (?) *Country of origin:* U.K. *Distributor:* Ginger. *Registered:* April 1927. 35 mm. Black and white. Silent. 5000 ft. *Director:* Gustav Pauli.

Cast

Charles Aubrey Ashford (David Byrne), Moataa Doughty (Garrick Carlisle), Tui Fryer (Hazel Carlisle), A. Judde (Alex Dermott), Mrs Judde (Mrs Dermott), Barton Ginger (Robert Fenton), Jean Leckie (Jean).

A young man emigrates from England having been wrongly accused of a crime. In New Zealand he takes a job on a farm where he quickly adapts to the life and falls in love with Hazel, joint owner of a nearby sheep station. The station manager also fancies Hazel, who rejects his advances. It transpires that the manager, in fact, was the person who had committed the crime back in England, and after he is arrested, the young couple are happily united.

The New Zealand Film Archive holds an undated scenario entitled **Under The Southern Cross** which notes that the film was 'Released throughout New Zealand and Australia by Cinema Art Films Ltd, Wellington', and describes the film as 'A glimpse of station life—played by an amateur cast of New Zealanders.' The cast list above comes from that document, as does the suggested synopsis. The fact that the film was submitted to the censor by the distribution company Ginger is perhaps at odds with the reference to Cinema Art Films Ltd, and there is actually nothing specific to connect this scenario with the film directed by Gustav Pauli other than the title, and the fact that there is no record of registration by the censor of another film of that name.

The scenario, which appears to consist of an intertitle list, also contains two footage references which add to a total of only 1827 feet, although the scenario is clearly incomplete, and the foot length may refer to only section or reel length. Nevertheless, the story is typical of the pioneer plot, where the hero is forced to leave 'Home' as a result of a false accusation (Rudall Hayward uses it in **The Te Kooti Trail** in the same year), comes to New Zealand and meets his true love but cannot marry her because of the accusation of crime. Supported by his friends in the new country, however, he is eventually cleared and goes on to marry and become a successful new settler. It is possible that Pauli did, in fact, utilise that storyline, and the inclusion of two players with Maori names would tie in with the other film he made in 1926–1927 which was the last silent version of the legend of Hine-Moa.

A letter written in 1974 from Mr M. Michell to Mr George Hayes of the National Film Library further compounds the difficulties of accurate identification when he says, 'In 1929, a film was released in Britain under the title of *Under The Southern Cross*. In her history of the British film, Rachel Low suggests that this film was a reworking of the material from **The Romance of Hine-Moa** ... Also in 1929, a film entitled **Under The Southern Cross** was released in the U.S.A. as a silent. This version of **Under The Southern Cross** would seem to have no connection with the one in your collection, save that perhaps Pauli worked on them both ...'

The U.S. release more probably refers to a title directed by Lew Collins, and was certainly not the same film as the British version. The circumstantial evidence which informs this commentary on Pauli's film is an excellent illustration of the difficulties encountered in providing accurate records of New Zealand's cinematic past, especially when neither documentation nor film exists in any more than tantalisingly brief glimpses. SE

Akuhato as Tutanekai in The Romance of Hine-Moa, *made by Pauli in the same year as* Under The Southern Cross. *Courtesy of the National Film and Television Archive.*

1927

THE TE KOOTI TRAIL

Whakatane Films Ltd. *Distributor:* Hayward. *Rating:* G, November 1927. 35 mm. Black and white. Silent. 7100 ft.[1]

Director and producer: Rudall Hayward. *Screenplay:* Rudall Hayward, Frank Bodle. *Source:* James Cowan FRGS, *The New Zealand Wars*, vol II. (The story, written by Frank Bodle, appeared during September and October 1927 in the *Otago Witness*, the *Auckland Weekly*, and the *New Zealand Herald* prior to the release of the film.) *Director of photography:* Rudall Hayward (1st camera), Oswald Caldwell (2nd camera). *Editor:* Hilda Hayward. *Processing:* Hilda Hayward. *Interiors:* Tornquist Studios, Auckland. *General assistants:* Oswald Caldwell, R.L. Lees 'and the citizens of Progressive Whakatane'.

Cast

Jasper Calder (Rev. J. Winslow), Billie Andreasson (Alice Winslow), Arthur Lord (Eric Mantell), Eric Yandell (Geoffrey Mantell), Edward Armitage (Sir Richard Mantell), Te Pairi Oterangi (Te Kooti Arikirangi TeTuruki), Captain H. Redmond (Jean Guerrin, a.k.a. Hoani Te Wiwi, from John the Frenchman by Maori), Mary Kingi, later Mrs M. Davies (Erihapeti or Peti, from Elizabeth, originally Riki Rangi, daughter of Manuera Kuku of Ngati Warahoe), Tina Hunt (Monika or Nika), A.P. (Patrick or Patiti) Warbrick (Taranahi), Joe Tennant (Barney O'Halloran), James (Jim) Warner (Jules Vialou), Thomas McDermott (Lieutenant, later Captain, Gilbert Mair), Arapeti Tuati, from Albert Stewart (Te Rangatahi), Tipene, from Steven, Hotene (Eru Peka Te Makarini from Baker McLean). George Tarr and Johnny Keepa are also named as participating in the production.

The narrative begins with a prologue in which a young British officer is accused of stealing money which has been planted in his room by his unscrupulous brother. The young officer is then sent 'to the colonies or to the devil' and becomes a member of the Corps of Guides in New Zealand, led by Lieutenant Gilbert Mair. In the main narrative which follows, the Maori leader Te Kooti launches a crippling attack on a flour mill near Whakatane as he pursues his war against the invading settlers. He kills all its occupants except for two sisters. One of the sisters captured by Te Kooti is ruthlessly executed for refusing to reveal the whereabouts of hidden ammunition despite an attempt by Gilbert Mair to prevent the tragedy. Te Kooti evades capture and continues his forays against the pakeha and Mair spends another year attempting to defeat Te Kooti before finally succeeding in an attack near Rotorua.

Although Hayward had used historical events to focus **Rewi's Last Stand**, and **The Birth Of New Zealand** presented early events in New Zealand's history, in **The Te Kooti Trail** Rudall Hayward was to construct New Zealand's first significant docudrama. He clearly knew what constituted a good story, however, and developed and shot it with considerable skill, although much of the credit must also go to his first wife Hilda, who was instrumental in editing, and therefore constructing, the subtleties of the narrative. Some of the sequences are clearly derivative of Hollywood westerns and melodramas, and the relationship between Maori and military is reminiscent of the Indian versus cavalry action adventures which were the stock-in-trade of studios like Warners. Hayward photographed Te Kooti's lieutenant Peka Makarini using cinematic codes of lighting and make-up which made clear that here was a significant villain, although he also humanised the same character by giving him a pet dog of which he was extremely fond.

In his way he respected and recognised the place Maori occupied in the history of New Zealand, and in his films dealing with Maori, and especially those which reconstructed historical events, he was at pains to acknowledge the significance of both Maori and pakeha as much as he recognised their differences. Hayward had taken his story from Cowan's Eurocentric classic history, although he added a prologue which took lines from Kipling and Kiplingesque sentiments deriving from the story of the Lost Legion, a mythical tale about a Roman legion which went out to subdue the Scots and was never heard of again. He also added lines of intertitle dialogue and intertitle comments which made it very clear that the presence of the British was seen as completely beneficial to nineteenth century New Zealand. It should be remembered, then, that this is in the first instance cinema, and only secondarily an historical record, despite Hayward's determination to shoot on the actual sites of the original events. The result is a well-told, somewhat jingoistic apology for colonial imperialism, unexceptionable at the time the sentiments were uttered, but ready for reappraisal 70 years later. SE

Te Pairi Oterangi (Te Kooti Arikirangi Te Turuki) and Tipene (Steven) Hotene (Eru Peka Te Makarini, from Baker McLean). *Courtesy of the Hayward Historical Trust.*

---

[1] Later descriptions of this film show a running time of 90 mins, which probably refers to a shortened version which Hayward deposited with the National Film Library.

THE BUSH CINDERELLA

Rudall Hayward. *Distributor:* Ginger/Hayward. *Rating:* G, August 1928. 35 mm. Black and white. Silent. 6000 ft.

Director and producer: Rudall Hayward. *Screenplay:* Rudall Hayward. *Director of photography:* Rudall Hayward. *Editor:* Hilda Hayward. *Production assistant:* Hilda Hayward. *General assistant:* Lee M. Hill. *Art titles:* A. D.-Crafts. *Properties and locations:* Thomas McDermott.

Cast

The Prologue: Dale Austen (Margaret Cameron), Walter Gray (Andrew Cameron), Tony Firth (Sergeant Bennett). *The Story:* Dale Austen (Mary Cameron), Ernest Yandall (Michael Murgatroyd), Thomas McDermott (Sam Codlin), May Bain/Mrs Mary Dreaver M.P. (Mrs Codlin), Cecil Scott (Lieutenant Neil Harrison R.N.), Al Mack (Sammy), Frank Willoughby (Dr Stanway), W. Scott (Lawyer), Jack de Rose (Crook).

The Prologue describes how Margaret, orphaned niece of crusty and conservative Andrew Cameron, became pregnant after she and Sergeant Bennett made love when they learned he was to be posted to action in the Boer War. When he was killed while delivering despatches, Margaret had to carry the pregnancy alone. Thrown out by her uncle, she is taken in by a backblocks farmer and his wife, but contracts pneumonia and dies after giving birth to a daughter. The only evidence of her link with her uncle is a pair of booties and an address to be used 'if the child is ever in need'.

The narrative then goes on to describe how Mary grows up with the Codlin family, is courted by the farm hand Sammy, but falls in love with a naval officer who is on leave. When the old uncle's grasping secretary, Michael Murgatroyd, realises that there may be a legitimate heir, he hires the Crook and the crooked Doctor to ensure that Cameron dies before Mary Cameron appears. Cameron dies, but leaves a will which allows Mary to inherit provided that she reaches his lawyer by a specified date and time. Murgatroyd kidnaps Mary, but she is rescued by her naval officer. They reach the lawyer's office in the nick of time, and the story ends with scenes of their marriage.

The Bush Cinderella is something of a departure from Hayward's other features where he places a strong focus on Maori–pakeha relations. It is a simple romantic melodrama in a style typical of the Hollywood formula equivalents of the period, although without the same degree of technical or cinematic sophistication. Despite its lack of narrative originality, however, there is a sense in which this film picks up the pioneering theme of Hayward's earlier **My Lady of the Cave**, and translates the relationship to a period where New Zealand is showing a degree of colonial stability. Maori are completely absent as Hayward investigates a new set of conditions, and uses his female lead to show the audience poverty and wealth in the new dominion.

Links with Empire are sympathetically stated through the presence of the pipe-smoking, trout-fishing, naval officer who is both complete potential husband—and therefore acceptable new generation New Zealander—and archetypal representation of the civilised world, defined as the British Empire. There are also interestingly disparaging comments about the Irish, who were the least accepted of the early European immigrants in New Zealand, and an equally revealing picture of the huge burden placed on women of both childbirth and child rearing.

The Bush Cinderella was described by one reviewer as showing 'the film industry in the Dominion, which is practically centred on the efforts of one man, (Hayward) gradually emerging from its infancy ... far and away his finest production to date ... (although) Mr Hayward would not pretend that his film is up to the standard of an American special ... " The comments place the film firmly in that corpus of early New Zealand movies which were low budget, limited release and amateur cast productions, and were the training ground for the successes which were to emerge three or four decades later. SE

Title page of the song dedicated to the star Dale Austen by composer Daniel S. Sharp. Courtesy of Alexander Turnbull Library

UNDER THE SOUTHERN CROSS

Witarina Mitchell (Miro) and Patiti Warbrick (Patiti).

[Only fragments of out-takes remain.] Universal. A.k.a. The Devil's Pit. A.k.a. Taranga. *Location*: White Island. 35 mm. Black and white. Silent (1929), sound (1930). 5579 ft U.S. silent release, 5606 then 6279 ft U.K. release, 6642 ft U.S. sound release.[1]

Director: Lew Collins. *Producer*: Carl Laemmle. *Screenplay*: Lew Collins. *Director of photography*: Wilfred Cline, Howard Smith. *Editor*: Hugh Hoffmann. *Musical arrangement (sound version)*: Bathie Stuart. *Titles*: Walter Anthony.

Cast

Patiti Warbrick (Patiti), Witarina Mitchell (Miro), Hoana Keeha (Rangi), Ani Warbrick (Anu), Apirihana Wiari (Te Kahu), Te Paiaha (Paiaka), Paora Tomati (Tamanui, the Fat Carver), Ewa Tapiri (Wura, the Carver's Wife).

The *Bioscope* synopsis of the film, which introduced it to the trade, suggests that the story ran along the following lines. In pre-European New Zealand/Aotearoa, there were two Maori tribes, one of which was known as the Waitai, which were continually hostile to each other. When the beautiful Miro, daughter of the paramount chief of the other tribe, reaches marriageable age it is remembered that her father believed that a political marriage, in which Miro would marry a Waitai chief, would bring a lasting peace between the two tribes. The idea is not welcomed by Rangi, a sullen and vicious young warrior. In order that the best possible husband be chosen, however, a traditional contest is held, and the victor will take Miro as his bride. An invitation is sent to the Waitai to participate in 'The Challenge of the Spear', which will be fought on neutral ground. When Miro visits the Waitai camp to deliver the invitation, Patiti, a chieftain's son, sees her and they fall in love. By resorting to trickery, Rangi wins the contest, and a tapu is placed on Miro, effectively isolating her from any contact with Patiti. But Patiti rows across the lake and the lovers meet nightly in a cave, until the suspicious Rangi finds them. A deadly struggle on the edge of a volcano takes place, and Patiti throws his rival in. War is resumed, but love brings about a compromise, and Miro and Patiti marry.

Unlike the repeated use of Rotorua and its extensive thermal areas in many other films, Collins shifted his location to the dramatic and somewhat dangerous active volcano on White Island, just off the east coast of the Bay of Plenty. This provided the backdrop to some of the final fight scenes left in the existing out-takes.

Under The Southern Cross is another excellent example of the difficulties involved in providing accurate reference material for early cinema. The film began life when Universal, under Carl Laemmle, agreed to back a somewhat eccentric film-maker named Alexander Markey and sent him to New Zealand to make a feature which Markey originally called **Taranga**. Unfortunately he neither kept to a schedule nor completed any effective footage, and the result was that Lew Collins, who had been Markey's Assistant Director, took over the production, and the picture was finally completed as **Under The Southern Cross**. It first appeared in Britain with this title at the Polytechnic Theatre in London on Easter Monday in April 1929. In the U.S.A., still with the same name, it was registered on 24 November 1929, but almost immediately reflected the introduction of sound by being given a soundtrack and re-titled **The Devil's Pit**. New Zealander Bathie Stuart (who had played the part of Kiwi in Smith's **The Adventures of Algy**) arranged the score, and the length increased for registration to 6642 ft. Stuart also wrote an introduction to the film, although this was apparently never used. SE

---

[1] This film was registered as **The Devil's Pit, a.k.a. Under the Southern Cross**, with a length of 6140 ft in September 1929 with a 500 ft prologue registered in August 1929.

THE ROMANCE OF MAORILAND

Edward T. Brown. August 1930, but never released. 35 mm. Black and white. Sound/silent. 11 300 ft. *Remaining footage: approx. 30 mins.*

Director and producer: Edward T. Brown. *Compilation/script:* E.T. Brown. *Photography:* Edwin Coubray. *Sound:* Coubraytone. *Titles:* H.T.G.

Cast
(Includes) Patch Mason, Tom Campbell.

The Romance Of Maoriland was set up to be New Zealand's first feature length talking picture. The intention of its makers was made clear in the opening intertitles, words on screen which were still important despite the intention to use sound. It was to remind viewers of the 'romantic foundation upon which our far-flung Empire is built. No lands embody more of the romance of real life than do the isles of New Zealand. To portray this romance, and to yield a glimpse into the development of our Dominion are the main objects of this film. Kia Ora!' The intertitles go further, to assure the viewer that the film retells only what 'is perfectly true, without deviation from Historical Fact.'

Edwin Coubray's sound system, Coubraytone, recorded the first New Zealand produced talkies in September 1927, newsreel footage under the title **Coubraytone News**. Coubraytone was to provide the soundtrack to **The Romance Of Maoriland**. An entry in the *Auckland Sun* of 7 October 1929 headlines 'New Zealand operators taking first talkies on Mount Mangere'. The occasion was the shooting of part of the additional footage which was to be used by producer/director Edward Brown to link and supplement the footage from **The Birth Of New Zealand** which he had purchased for **The Romance Of Maoriland** project. The completed film was never released, despite obtaining registration from the Chief Censor on 14 August 1930, but it is included here as a title which explains in part the fate of **The Birth Of New Zealand**, and which provides further information on the film career of Edwin Coubray.

The film, which included some scenic footage, was primarily constructed as a series of docudramas, chapters in New Zealand's history which would capture the ambience of different periods from reconstruction of what the film-makers believed to be pre-European culture, to a re-enactment of the signing of the Treaty of Waitangi, to New Zealand's first western, designed to give a feeling for the period of the major goldrushes in the South Island by setting a robbery and kidnapping in the gold rich Gabriel's Gully in Otago. That saga begins with a hold-up of a Cobb & Co. coach which incorporates a stock set of western cliches—masked hold-up agents on horses pointing sixguns and rifles, the driver with hands held high, jewellery ripped from women—and the kidnapping of a boy passenger whose film mother appears to be Australian actress Stella Southern who had a major role in **The Birth Of New Zealand**. Following the return of the coach a posse is organised and sets out after the outlaws, and in an interestingly tragic twist, the heroic rescuer, the kidnapped boy's Uncle Con, is shot and dies. While the style of this restored nine minute segment is that of the Hollywood western, it nevertheless underlines the standard values of pioneering New Zealand, strong resolute men, pure women, inevitable defeat for criminal action, a final reward of a cottage and children, and a landscape curiously devoid of Maori after the arrival of pakeha colonists. SE

Anzac Wallace as Te Wheke in Utu (1983), *a more graphic recreation of early New Zealand. Courtesy of the New Zealand film Commision.*

Romantic New Zealand

The title frame. Courtesy of the Stills Collection, New Zealand Film Archive.

Filmcraft Studios. A Filmcraft Sound Production produced with the co-operation of the New Zealand Government and Trucolour Film Limited. *Locations:* General throughout New Zealand. *Registered:* April 1934. 35 mm. Colour (Trucolour Process) and black and white. 6100 ft.

Director and producer: Filmcraft Studios. *Camera:* Bert Bridgman, Cyril Morton, Charles Barton. (Note that it is the practice in government publications not to note authorship or individual credits.)

Designed as a successor to **Glorious New Zealand** (1925), this extended travelogue includes the use of the then new colour process Trucolour in two selected sections of the film, one dealing with views from the West Coast of the South Island and finishing with a stunning lake sunset, and the other covering a sequence in which Guide Rangi describes aspects of Maori life in Rotorua. The black and white material, which makes up the bulk of the film, takes viewers on a guided tour of New Zealand's major cities and tourist spots, with a strong emphasis on the Southern Alps and the fjords and adjacent landscapes. It also includes re-enactments of early road construction, clearing of virgin bush, surveying, and settlement, provides images of the tuatara, a native lizard, and deals in some detail with New Zealand birdlife from kea to kiwi.

The male voice-over narration provides a viewing context for the film in which New Zealand is portrayed as 'A world in a nutshell' and 'a fully established outpost of the great British Empire', although it is less prone to the nationalistic enthusiasm which characterised its official predecessor, **Glorious New Zealand**. At the same time, the social attitudes and early 1930s sense of social history which prevailed in government circles of the time saw no trace of colonial paternalism in statements such as 'axe and saw blazed the trail of civilisation', or New Zealand moving 'from savagery to civilisation in less than a century.' Neither was there any sense of misrepresentation in showing the contemporary New Zealand landscape virtually devoid of Maori.

This is cinematically more interesting than its predecessor, with intelligent editing giving the narrative a sense of structure and continuity. It demonstrates an ability to locate audiences firmly in the filmed environment.

Of specific interest in this feature length travelogue are the two sections in colour. The first, around two and a half minutes long, provides some memorable images of the wild 1930s landscape of New Zealand's South Island's West Coast, ending with the sun setting in the western sea. The second, lasting around six minutes, provides a vehicle for Rangitiaria Ratema, universally known as Guide Rangi, to conduct a cinematic tour of Whakarewarewa and Rotorua, showing Maori using thermal waters for cooking and washing, and providing a record of ritual dances, poi and haka.

Trucolour was a two-colour process being developed simultaneously in a number of different areas around the globe—France, the United States and New Zealand, where the New Zealand version of the name added the 'u' to the word color. The New Zealand inventors took their highly developed process on a promotional trip to the U.S., and in showing it to a developer there, inadvertently enabled him to release the blocks which impeded his own progress toward a colour system. The New Zealand process was never patented, and as a consequence a potential world first was taken by the United States.

Notably, too, **Romantic New Zealand** became the first feature length New Zealand sound film to be recorded with the censor's office when it was given registration on 27 April 1934. SE

DOWN ON THE FARM

Hamner Nine Syndicate. *Location:* Woodside, near Outram, Otago. *Opened:* Empire De Luxe Theatre, Dunedin, 2 May 1935. *Registered:* April 1935. 35 mm. Black and white. 6300 ft.

Director: Stewart Pitt. *Associate producers:* Lee Hill, Stewart Pitt. *Director of photography:* Lee Hill. *Sound:* Jack Welsh. *Composer and lyricist:* David S. Sharp, 'Down on the Farm'.

Cast

George Claridge (Donald), Daphne Murdoch, Florence Hastie (Cookie), Ra Hould (Rupert Hickmott), Mabel Larkins (Fat Woman), Andy Fraser (Conductor), Stuart Dick ('Orace 'Opkins), Sydney Lock (Sir Henry Hicks), Erana Newbold (Petrie, 'A Yeoman'), with three unidentified characters, Peggy a parlour maid, Arnold, Swaggy.

It is not possible to provide a full synopsis as little of the film remains and there is no supporting script. There is surviving footage which suggests a plot containing standard melodramatic elements regarding wealthy landowners and their families, including their children's romantic associations. There are also suggestions of a running sub-plot in which staff at the house provide a comic thread. This involves landowner family and staff attending a wrestling match, and reference to a lost Art Union ticket. A note at the New Zealand Film Archive adds these comments: 'Sir Henry Hicks, a gentleman dairy farmer, has a rival for agricultural honours in Petrie, a yeoman. Both have families, and in the process of time, their children form friendships which ripen into love, thereby consolidating New Zealand domestic and industrial life … ' *

The first New Zealand made sound fiction film is arguably Lew Collins's **The Devil's Pit** (1929), to which was added a soundtrack consisting of music and dialogue. The fact that the additions were made in the U.S.A., however, makes Collins's claim to have made the first New Zealand talkie somewhat problematic. Alexander Markey began work with Ted Coubray on the sound for **Hei Tiki** as far back as 1930 when the N.Z. *Freelance* reported that Coubray was using his sound camera on the set of **Hei Tiki**. That film, however, was not released in the U.S. until 1935, and did not return to New Zealand for distribution until 1939. The next fictional story with sound was Rudall Hayward's **Hamilton Talks**, a formulaic comedy melodrama using amateur local actors and a stock plot which included Hamilton's version of the Keystone Kops. Hayward, with Jack Baxendale, had developed his own sound camera for that movie, as had both Edwin Coubray and Jack Welsh, although the latter two had been initially concerned with the making of sound newsreels. Then in 1935, all three were engaged on sound features, Hayward on **On The Friendly Road**, Coubray on **Hei Tiki**, and Jack Welsh on **Down On The Farm**.

The footage of **Down On The Farm** which survives is disconnected and mostly unrelated, but it provides a glimpse of the two levels on which the story was told, and the conventions of acting and character which were beginning to shape New Zealand made films. The serious leads clearly had their role models set firmly back in upper middle-class England, emulating both dress and manners of the world the colonists had left behind, a world which represented both civilisation and high culture. As in other New Zealand films of the period, however, the amateur actors simply lacked the sophistication to do more than provide an unintentional parody of the characters they were taking so seriously. The farm staff, on the other hand, showed the beginnings of the irreverent and egalitarian humour which has since become a hallmark of New Zealand's films. But New Zealand was not to fare well. A line of dialogue from the film, supplied by Jim Tannoch who remembers its screening in Dunedin, 'I don't think they like our butter back home' did not augur well for the dairy trade. Neither was the lack of sophistication which brought the following comment from the trade journal, *The Kinematograph Weekly*, the best of omens for future film production in this country: 'The picture is ambitious … but its august aim is deflected by a feeble story, indifferent treatment, inferior acting, and indistinct photography. The film is poor entertainment and worse propaganda.'
* SE

Jack Welsh with the sound cinema. *Courtesy of the Stills Collection, New Zealand Film Archive.*

Reference
* New Zealand Film Archive files.

1935

HEI TIKI

The recreation of combat in pre-European New Zealand: an attack on Manui's pa.
Courtesy of the Stills Collection, New Zealand Film Archive.

Markey Films, A First Division Picture (President Harry J. Thomas). A.k.a. Primitive Passions. A.k.a. Hei Tiki: A Saga Of The Maoris. *Location:* Waihi in southern Lake Taupo. *Registered:* June 1939 (1935 [U.S.] 1936 [U.K.]). 35 mm. Black and white. 7300 ft.

Director and producer: Alexander Markey. *Associate Producer:* Zoe Varney. *Screenplay:* Alexander Markey. *Director of photography:* Howard Bridgman. *Camera assistant:* Henry Hopecross. *Crew cook:* Margaret Goulding. *Native melodies:* Alexander Markey. *English lyrics:* Billy Hill. *Symphonic score:* Oscar Potoker, recorded by RCA Photophone System. (Note that Markey also employed, but then discharged and did not credit, Edwin Coubray for initial camera and sound, and Alfred Hill for original music.)

Cast

Nowara Kereti (Mara), Ben Biddle (Manui), with uncredited characters Te Rangi, Tere, Tonga, Inu. *Extras:* Jimmy Eru, John Murray, Nepia Nikorima.

On the fictional Isle of Ghosts in a lake in central New Zealand, Mara, the daughter of a chief, has been set aside to become the wife of the tribal war god. Her future life would see her cut off from any physical contact with others, but finding a secret tunnel she slips out at night to enjoy at least a measure of freedom. She is observed by Manui, a young chief from an enemy tribe who is on a spying expedition, and they fall in love. They concoct a plan to help her escape. Manui sets up a complicated ruse which enables him to appear to Mara's people as the war god to whom Mara has been dedicated. When Mara is led out to him they seem to disappear, but in fact make their way to Manui's canoe. The ruse is discovered, and Mara's warriors pursue the couple across the lake and attack the fortified village belonging to Manui's people. A fierce battle follows, but Mara persuades the opposing forces to stop fighting and instead have the benefit of a peaceful alliance through their marriage across the two tribes.

The making of **Hei Tiki** is itself far more dramatic than anything offered by the movie. Markey, apparently somewhat eccentric from the descriptions of people who worked with him, was helped to make the film with £10 000 of capital from New Zealand investors, a great many taonga or cherished tribal artefacts from Maori who participated in the film, and a great deal of unpaid labour from the many Maori extras who appeared. During the filming, Markey fired his original sound cameraman, Ted Coubray, but commandeered Coubray's camera, and shortly afterwards sold it to Coubray's rivals in the race for New Zealand sound-on-film leadership. They were the Welsh brothers, one of whom, Jack, worked on New Zealand's first full sound feature, **Down On The Farm**. Markey employed composer Alfred Hill to write original music for the film, then fired him after an argument, but retained his material. When shooting was finished, Markey left for the U.S.A. with the film footage, many of the artefacts he had borrowed from Maori, a great many unpaid bills and his partner Zoe Varney.

Hei Tiki was originally designed as a silent feature, but on his return to the U.S. Markey added both music and voice-over narration, the latter to overcome problems of synchronisation. The result was less than gripping, although it was released widely in the U.S. and Britain. The *New York Times* wrote, 'For all the conviction it carries, the picture might as well have been filmed on Staten Island or in Hollywood', and *Variety* of 5 February 1935 said, 'There is not sufficient entertainment value in a primitive romance to propel unusual enthusiasm commercially. Picture will need support.' Some of that support came from the notoriety it received when scenes of nudity were cut in state after state in its U.S. release, but in the end **Hei Tiki** remains interesting because of its history and place in the corpus of New Zealand cinema, rather than for any great quality as a film in its own right. SE

1936

PHAR LAP'S SON

[No known footage of this film remains.] South Seas Films Ltd. A.k.a. Phar Lap's Son? *Budget:* An undated film history file in the N.Z. Film Archive notes that the cost of Phar Lap's Son was £15 045, 19/-. *Location:* Dunedin. *Registered:* March 1936 (N.Z.) and early 1938 (U.K.). 35 mm. Black and white. The U.K. release in 1938 showed 5623 ft, 63 mins.

Director and screenplay: Dr A. L. Lewis. *Technical advisers:* Jack Welsh, Lee Hill.

Cast
Harry V. Smith, Peggy/Peggie Collie.

The *Monthly Film Bulletin* of 31 March 1938 provides a brief synopsis which shows that one of the progeny of the famous antipodean racehorse Phar Lap is owned by a colonel who has got himself into debt. When he is visited by a touring theatrical company led by an American entrepreneur, the colonel invites the company to his estate. The company arrives dressed as hikers, and are entertained by the colonel's stable hands. The son of Phar Lap wins a race at a New Zealand track meet, and the resultant winnings enable the colonel both to wipe out his debt and be accepted by the leading lady from the troupe of visiting players, whom he marries.

Despite the paucity of information about the film, it is known to be one of an interesting trilogy made in the Dunedin area during 1935–1936 at the beginning of New Zealand's sound production era. The three films, **Down On The Farm**, **Phar Lap's Son** and **The Wagon and the Star**, made use of the experience of Lee Hill. Ronald Sinclair, who used the stage name Ra Hould in **Down On The Farm**, said in a later interview, 'It was Lee Hill that all of us relied on for guiding us in the production. He came to New Zealand from Hollywood, with a Hollywood background to put to use. Such background was considered vital, and Hill was highly revered by all of us because of the experience he brought with him.'[1]

All three films used local actors, drawn mainly from the ranks of local repertory and operatic society groups, and all three relied on the use of sound equipment built in New Zealand. They all used songs and dances as part of their repertoire of attractions, with **Down On The Farm** and **The Wagon and the Star** having songs written especially for them; and it is likely that **Phar Lap's Son** had the same. It is interesting to speculate whether it was the influence of the local operatic society singers in the cast which encouraged the introduction of musical interjections, or whether the Hollywood musical was already making its presence felt in New Zealand's deep south. The presence of Jack Welsh in particular indicated that this pioneer of purpose-built film sound systems was able to use these films as virtual test beds for the development of his equipment. The tests did not help **Phar Lap's Son**, however, where the sound was apparently of poor quality. Hill on the other hand, brought not only camera and acting experience, but also arrived in New Zealand with a range of make-up designed for black and white filmmaking. He took his expertise to a large number of films, and also directed several short formula fictions in the community comedy style used by Rudall Hayward in the early 1930s. The film was not particularly well-received when it eventually arrived in Britain, *The Monthly Film Bulletin* describing it as, 'The photography is very inferior, and it is often impossible to hear what is said. The actors stand in the picture, and recite their parts strictly in turn. The story develops desperately slowly and is padded with trite remarks and almost unbelievably amateurish songs and dances.'[2] SE

Technical adviser Jack Welsh. *Courtesy of the Stills Collection, New Zealand Film Archive.*

References
[1] Letter to Mr Peter Sakey dated 14 April 1991 at the New Zealand Film Archive.
[2] *The Monthly Film Bulletin*, vol 5, no. 51, 31 March 1938.

THE WAGON AND THE STAR

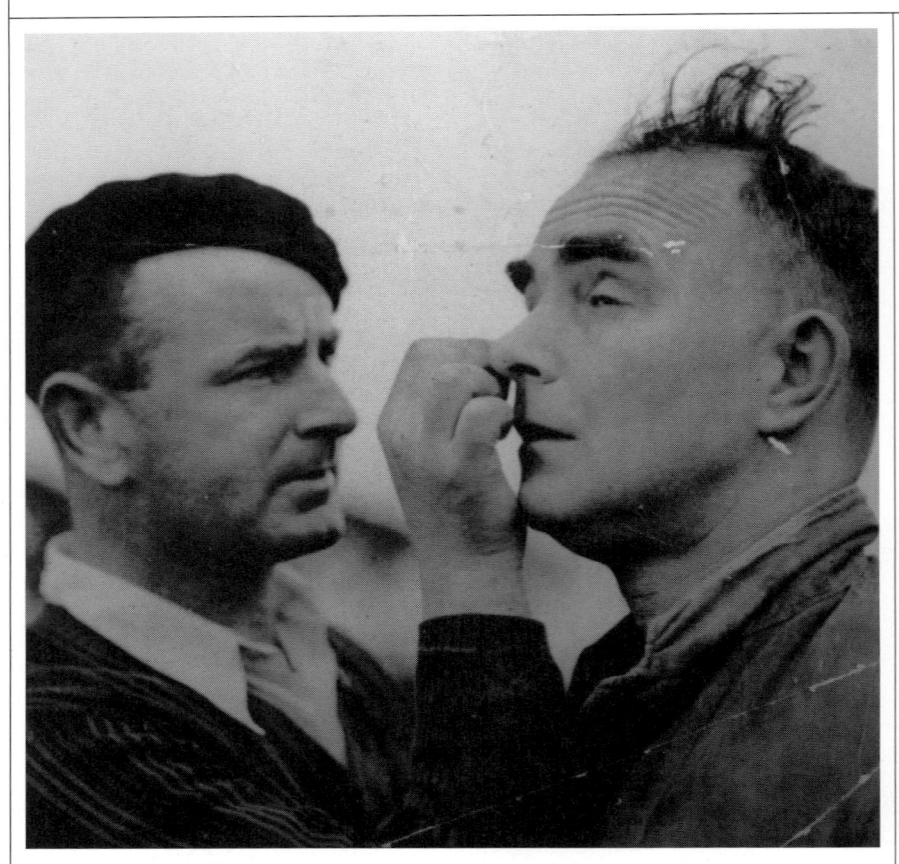

Lee Hill applying make-up to William (Bill) Buchanan (Andrew Henderson). Courtesy of leading lady Faye Jennings née Hinchey (Mary Tyson).

[Only one reel and some out-take footage of this film remains.] Southland Films Ltd. (*Note:* Southland Films Ltd was incorporated on 18 July 1935 with a nominal capital of £15 000.) A.k.a. The Waggon and the Star. *Opened:* The Regent Theatre, Invercargill, 16 July 1936. *Distributor:* Southland Films Ltd. 35 mm. Black and white.

Director and producer: J.J.W. Pollard. *Screenplay:* J.J. W. Pollard. *Script clerk:* Betty Rutherford. *Director of photography:* Lee Hill. *Sound:* Jack Welsh (sound engineer). *Music:* Howard Moody. *Lyrics:* Shaun O'Sullivan. *Make-up:* E. Stewart. *Casting:* Lee Hill. *Film processing supervisor:* Jack Walsh.

Cast

John Peake (John Hawthron), Faye Hinchey (Mary Tyson), William (Bill) Buchanan (Andrew Henderson), T.R. Vanity[1] (Hubert Throstle), A. Frank Grenfell (Peter Tyson), Mrs A.C. MacEwen (Aunt Harriet), Miss Moira O'Neill (Anne). Other named but uncredited characters include Mr Nicholas, the storekeeper and Wilson, one of the road gang.

The original story by Pollard is actually a traditional colonial narrative. John Hawthron has recently come to New Zealand from 'Home', but has been unable so far to make the expected fortune in the new country of opportunity. He goes to work on a road building gang and makes friends with another expatriate, a Scot named Andy Henderson, who lives by his own uniquely optimistic brand of homespun philosophy. Hawthron meets Mary Tyson, the daughter of a local landowner and the star of the title to which he hitches his personal wagon. He is inspired to go into business on his own account. His attempts to build his business and court Mary Tyson are thwarted by the presence of a lawyer villain, Hubert Throstle, but he succeeds in the end, marries his Mary, and proceeds to become the owner of a business which controls the transport and accommodation facilities of the lower South Island. A comic sub-plot is added which stems from the frustrating romance between Hawthron's friend Andy Henderson and Mary Tyson's maid Anne.

The plot synopsis has been pieced together from some fragments of film found, literally, under a house in Berhampore, Wellington, 50 years after it was made, and the John Hawthron dialogue script, which omits any footage where John Peake as Hawthron was not present, and the Mary Tyson script, supplied by the actress Faye Jennings (Hinchey). The available material suggests that the narrative is a typical 1930s rites of passage romantic melodrama, complete with lawyer villain and two-tiered society. It was, however, virtually the last of the New Zealand productions which gave credence to hierarchical social structures as desirable transplants to the new country, and later films are characterised by rejection of superior status arising from class difference.

While the setting is clearly New Zealand, the leading roles keep looking back to the U.K. for verification and example, even though New Zealand in the 1930s was beginning seriously to examine its relations with Mother England in the arts, if not in politics.

Only the road gang cutting bus and car routes through the mountains and bush, and a sequence which covers an agricultural show, bring some original New Zealand characters to the screen. The presence of the road gang, however, is a clear signpost to the pioneering themes of later New Zealand titles where engagement with the testing physical environment of the new country was the passage to manhood and acceptability, underlining the continuing preoccupation with masculinity which still defines New Zealand society.

The Wagon and the Star is also characteristic of the homegrown product which was to bedevil New Zealand film for many years. Southland Film Ltd made only one film. It was written by the editor of the local newspaper, *The Southland Times*. For many of the amateur cast, drawn mainly from the local operatic society, it was to be their only film experience. It was recorded using the handbuilt camera that Alexander Markey had confiscated from Edwin Coubray on the set of **Hei Tiki** and which Jack Walsh was still developing. The lack of experience for both cast and crew shows, and the non-recognition of that lack was to be a feature of much first-tier feature production in New Zealand for the next four decades. SE

---

[1] T.R. Vanity was the pseudonym of Mr Tom Pryde, a practising lawyer who was bound by professional ethics to avoid identification, public display or advertisement.

1936

ON THE FRIENDLY ROAD

New Zealand Film Guild. *Budget* (initial estimate) £800. *Location*: Auckland. *Rating*: G, August 1936.[1] 35 mm. Black and white. 7592 ft. 84 mins.

Director and producer: N.Z. Film Guild/Leonard P. Leary. *Screenplay*: George Altier/L. P. Leary, *Source*: A letter from Leonard Leary confirms that the idea for the film came from Rudall Hayward. *Director of photography*: Rudall Hayward. *Second camera*: Jack McCarthy. *Editor*: NZ Film Guild/Rudall Hayward. *Sound*: Jack Baxendale. *Assistant sound engineer*: Gerhard Diedrichs, *Music score*: Sam Raymond. Theme song, 'On The Friendly Road', sung by Robert G. Simmers.

Cast

Rev. C.G. Scrimgeour (Uncle Scrim), Stanley Knight (Old Bill, the swaggy), John Mackie (Mac McDermitt), Jean Hamilton (Mary McDermitt), Neville Goodwin (Harry McDermitt), James Martin (Alec 'Stinker' McDermitt), James Swan (Stevenson), Gladys Swan (Mrs Stevenson), Phillipa Hayward (Stephenson's daughter), Arnold Goodwin (Mike, an escaped convict), Harold Metcalfe (Sniffy, an escaped convict), Alan Leonard (policeman), Wharepaia (Hori), Kahu (Chieftainess), with Taffy the terrier and John Bell, Roland Medland, Ian Moir, Ethel Rae, Fred McCallum. *Garden party extras*: Ray Thompson, Alison Firth, Denise Didsbury, Leslie Waller, Althea Parker, Kathleen Milne, Doreen Saunders, Beryl Mowbray, Bettina Edwards.

The original poster from the film. Courtesy of the Stills Collection, New Zealand Film Archive.

McDermitt, accused of theft and wrongfully imprisoned because he would not turn informer, returns to his farm after serving his time. To make ends meet, he goes to work for Stevenson, the magistrate who had originally convicted him. Former fellow convicts turn up at the farm, and blackmail McDermitt into not reporting them to the police. The convicts steal a valuable gold chain from Stevenson, a gift to him from local Maori after he had returned a greenstone treasure found on the farm by one of McDermitt's boys. Old Bill, the swaggy, and McDermitt himself are accused, but son Harry hears the robbers plotting and adapting the advice given him by radio personality Uncle Scrim, foils the thieves who confess all. The stolen goods are returned and McDermitt's name is fully cleared

Uncle Scrim, the Rev. Colin Scrimgeour, was a key figure in the social and political history of New Zealand. He had joined the church mainly out of a concern for those below the poverty line, and employed radio as a way of communicating awareness of the situations people faced. His radio sessions under the byline 'The Friendly Road' included a section where he responded to letters from listeners, and this was the catalyst which drove **On The Friendly Road**. Unlike any other New Zealand feature before it, this was feelgood movie-making. It was didactic, allowing the advice from Uncle Scrim to be seen to be working, and employed a mawkish combination of suffering and sacrifice to give the film general appeal. And it appeared to work. A review in the *Auckland Star* of 29 August 1936 noted, 'The audience was ready to appreciate the higher qualities of the film and frequently showed its appreciation.'

Despite the experience of the 36 year-old Rudall Hayward, who had already made four features and a score of short comedies, and whose daughter Phillipa appears as Stevenson's daughter, the film had a bland reception when it was offered outside New Zealand. The *Auckland Star* referred to its weakness in dialogue, and 'an occasional hiatus in the action which technical difficulties have created', and the best *The Monthly Film Bulletin* of March 1938 could come up with was that it had 'a pleasant tone.'

A re-examination of the film from a contemporary standpoint shows a series of remarkably one-dimensional characters which are more portrayals of value characteristics than of characters. There are some notable scenes in which the lead Maori is stereotypically pictured as simple and comic, and the sense of complexity which accompanies any kind of serious social comment is entirely lacking. The technical difficulties exist not only in the camera (which tends to be static and uninteresting) and in the sound (which is not unexpected as Baxendale was still working on the sound camera systems), but also in the acting and dialogue. Acting is often risible, turning intended drama into melodrama, and the accompanying dialogue is stilted and unconvincing. It is one of our features which, unlike good wine, has not improved with age. SE

---

[1] The British release data incorrectly attributes the direction to Nicholas Colasanto, and names the production company Renshaw.

REWI'S LAST STAND

Frontier Films Ltd. Produced with the assistance and co-operation of the Te Awamutu Historical Society. A.k.a. The Last Stand: An Episode Of The New Zealand Wars. *Location*: Te Awamutu. *Distributor*: Hayward. *Opened*: Auckland April 1940. 35 mm. Black and white. 5750 ft. 64 mins.[1] (British quota cut, 1949.)

Director and producer: Rudall Hayward. *Screenplay*: Rudall Hayward. *Source*: James Cowan FRGS, *History of the New Zealand Wars*, vol. I and *The Old Frontier*. *Photography*: Rudall Hayward, Edwin Coubray, Jack McCarthy. *Stills*: Mr Williams. *Editor*: Rudall Hayward. *Sound*: Jack Baxendale. *Sound engineer's assistant*: Ron Purdy. *Narration*: Kenneth Melvin. *Original musical score*: Alfred Hill. *Publicity*: R.M. Iver. *Electrician for firings*: Les W. Spence. *Cast extras*: J. Rust.

Cast

Leo Pilcher (Robert Beaumont), Ramai Te Miha (Ariana), Henare Toka (part role) (Tama Te Heu Heu), Stanley Knight (Corporal Ben Horton), John Gordon (Brigadier General Carey), A.J.C. Fisher (Sir George Grey), Peter Hutt (A.D.C. to Grey), Colonel J.D. Swan (General Cameron), Bernard Britain (Captain Jackson), Rud Peterson (the only member of the cast who also appeared in the 1925 silent version), (Pat Madigan, a forest ranger), with local cast Raureti Te Huia (Rewi Maniapoto), Mr C.S. Wood (Rev. John Morgan), Phoebe Clarke (Mrs Morgan) Rongo Paerata (part role) (Tama Te Heu Heu), H.A. Swarbrick (Ensign Mair), James Oliphant (Lieutenant Hurst), Tawhiurangi Huihuia (Ahumai), Tom Moisely (Jim Taylor, the wagonner).

The story is centred on a major battle between Maori and military forces which took place during the 1860s. Around that event is woven the fictional narrative of a young settler, Robert Beaumont, meeting and falling in love with a young Maori woman, Ariana. Her father has been a sea captain who has left her mother, but who has now joined the British forces engaged with the Maori in the Waikato. When the mission at which Ariana lives is in danger of attack, she is smuggled out, but walking with Beaumont in the bush, she is discovered and recaptured by her people. Beaumont joins von Tempsky's Forest Rangers and goes off on a scouting expedition in an attempt to find Ariana. He does, but Ariana has promised to stay with her people, and they part. Following the major battle at Orakaupa, Ariana attempts to escape, but is shot, and apparently dies in Beaumont's arms.

Hayward's attempt to remake his 1925 version of this story in sound began with a letter to the Te Awamutu Historical Society on 10 Feb 1936 where he writes, 'It has been suggested to me that the historical sections of the film should be reissued with the addition of sound effects and a descriptive comment so that the coming generations might have a visual impression of the heroism of the Maoris in this action.' The consequence was that local citizens formed a company, Frontier Films Ltd, to support Hayward and to break into the apparently lucrative industry, and the Historic Society gave their support in casting and costume. The film, however, had a chequered career. By 1943, the company reported difficulty in selling it in the U.S., and earnings for the year were a mere £78 13/- 4d. The print promised by Hayward in his original letter had never eventuated, and he had taken what appeared to be the only negatives to Great Britain where it was recut as a British Quota title and reissued in shorter form, the version which is the only remaining footage of what was originally a much longer film.

The sound version lost much of the toughness and tightly woven drama of the original. The romantic melodrama which was intended to provide a human face for the conflict failed to convince, as Hayward did not seem able to decide whether he wanted a film which was identifiably New Zealand in style, or the soft focus sentimentality and overstated images which characterised low budget Hollywood material. A comment in *Te Iwi* records a Maori view, '(Hayward) made an attempt at historical accuracy—but distorted the significance of the facts to suit obvious preconceived ideas about what should have been in the minds of the protagonists ... but couldn't have been. Orakau was a bloody, almost genocidal confrontation by Maori and European with no quarter given.'* SE

Special Feltex Award presented to Rudall Hayward for the first television screening of a New Zealand film.

[1] In keeping with the intention of Rudall Hayward to allow his films to be used for educational purposes, a new 16 mm print was lodged with the National Film Library, and a new censor's certificate showing a running time of 63 mins, was issued on 23 April 1980.

Reference
* *Te Iwi*, February 1990, p. 19.

Stanley Knight (Corporal Ben Horton) and Leo Pilcher (Robert Beaumont). *Courtesy of the Hayward Historical Film Trust.*

BRITISH EMPIRE GAMES 1950

New Zealand National Film Unit for the New Zealand Organising Committee for the 1950 British Empire Games. *Location*: Auckland. *Distributor*: Eagle-Lion Distributors (N.Z.) Ltd. *Rating*: G, February 1950. 35 mm. Black and white. 9500 ft. 106 mins. (*Note*: It is the practice in government publications in New Zealand not to list authorship or individual credits.)

Director and producer: NZ National Film Unit

The context for **British Empire Games 1950** reflects the status of the New Zealand National Film Unit of the time as a government body, conveying an officially generated position on its subject. Thus, the film is seen not only as an official record of the games, but as a window on the host country, New Zealand. It is this role that locates the film geographically and culturally at its beginning with the touristy reference to New Zealand's Southern Alps and central Otago landscapes, and a voice-over comment, 'Blue skies and open air call us (New Zealanders) to sport, and we like sport.' Viewers are then taken on a short tour towards the north, through a variety of rural areas to the geothermal activity and Maori cultural focus which is Rotorua in the North Island, and on to Auckland where the Games were held. Over the accumulated images of international transport bringing athletes to the Games and being welcomed by a Maori cultural group as they come down the gangplank of their ship or plane is reiterated Auckland's and New Zealand's desirability as a location.

The nationalistic and, by today's standards, market driven emphasis continues through a sober and ritualistic opening to the Games, reflecting the esteem in which establishment New Zealand held the traditions and cultural influences which characterised the foundations of its own development and which were the common currency of the British Empire. The formality is underlined through the almost exclusive use of long shot in the opening ceremony, a technique which emphasises formality and ritual by distancing the viewer. Through the entire sequence of athlete entry, oath-taking, flag ceremonies and even the release of flocks of pigeons, there is a sense of respectful observation rather than individual involvement.

Stylistically, **British Empire Games 1950** is closer to newsreel than feature. The selected black and white images offer a record of events and winners, with unvarying medal ceremonies doing little to relieve the rather unimaginative cinematic landscape. There are moments of escape, however. During the marathon, for example, when heavy rain makes conditions frustratingly difficult for athletes, officials, and spectators alike, the ubiquitous New Zealand dog comes into shot and continues with the runners for a brief time. Use of a telephoto lens in the javelin event adds a sense of drama when the javelin appears constantly to fall dangerously close to the feet of the officials with the tape measure. And the so-carefully constructed music score surges up the scale when cyclists head uphill and accompanies them down the other side, and offers dramatic emphasis at each moment of visual drama. The viewer cannot, however, escape the continuing sense of nationalistic promotion, even in the jokes where, after a false start in the men's 100 yards, the narrator comments, 'As usual, Australia beats the gun.'

British Empire Games 1950 is an important record of New Zealand's past, but in the end its lack of narrative structure means that it is in fact no more than a feature length compilation of newsreel reports. SE

The poster from the film. Courtesy of the Stills Collection, New Zealand Film Archive.

1952

BROKEN BARRIER

Pacific Films Ltd. © 1951. *Location*: Mahia Peninsula. *Opened*: The Regent Theatre, Wellington, 10 July 1952. 35 mm. Black and white. 6350 ft. 69 mins.

Directors and producers: Roger Mirams, John O'Shea. *Screenplay*: John O'Shea. *Director of photography*: Roger Mirams. *Photographer's assistant*: Bill Hopper. *Sound*: Ian Houston. *Sound assistant*: Ron Skelley. *Recorded*: The National Film Unit Studios, Wellington. *Music*: Sydney John Kay. *Waiata*: Nuhaka Maori Choir. *Dialogue*: William Moloney. *Maori adviser*: Bill Parkin.

Cast

Kay Ngarimu (Rawi), Terence Bayler (Tom Sullivan), Mira Hape (Kiri), Bill Merito (Johnny), George Ormond (Alec), Lily Te Nahu (Maata), Dorothy Tansley (Mrs Sullivan), F.W. French (Mr Sullivan), Ata Ananu (Mirama), Carol Chapman (Faye Sullivan), Andrew Ormond (Peter), Lloyd Morgan (the Doctor), Bill Parker (the Maori Doctor), Pegs Davies (the Landlady), Vima Prue (Girl in the street, Anne Munz (Girl in the powder room), Guy Smith (Narrator).

Tom, a young and somewhat cynical freelance journalist, is looking for stories about New Zealand life which might be sold to overseas magazines. He appears to be looking for work, and a Maori family he meets hospitably offer him a job on their farm. Their daughter Rawi, who is home on holiday from her nursing job in a city hospital, looks after Sullivan, and they quickly fall in love. Tom does not tell her that his intention is to write a story about her family and Maori life in general. Her parents are not happy about the relationship, and when they invite Sullivan to a hui, or gathering, he realises how much the cultures differ. The tensions of his relationship with Rawi break out in an angry exchange and they part. He leaves and finds a job as a timber worker, making friends with Johnny Ngaie, who helps him appreciate some of the differences. In a forest fire, Johnny loses his life while saving Tom's, and realising his mistakes, Tom returns to Rawi and they prepare for marriage.

This, the first serious attempt at full feature film production in New Zealand since World War II, was a training ground for the newly revived industry and a site for an examination of cultural difference and interracial intolerance. Under the auspices of Pacific Films Ltd, many New Zealand filmmakers were able to gain practical experience, and while production values are limited, and the values stated somewhat heavy-handedly, **Broken Barrier** is nevertheless a crucial film in the post-war movement towards the establishment of a fully fledged industry. Like so many New Zealand financed features before it, it was a shoe-string production. O'Shea, commenting on the making of the film, said, 'We had little money between us, but we had two mute 35 mm 200 ft load Arriflex cameras, one on loan from Movietone News and the other picked up from an allegedly dead German in the Western desert ... a rickety dolly and some lights cobbled together from scrap metal ... we stuck to the storyline as best we, with all the weight of our inexperience, could.'*

In an apparent attempt to authenticate the bi-cultural position taken by the film, much of the footage has a strong documentary style. On an expedition to gather kai moana (sea food) the camera follows the processes and the reactions of the gatherers as if its concern was to inform and educate rather than to excite the emotions of and entertain the audience. In its endeavour to remain solidly supportive of both cultures it tends to overstate the obvious, and the consequence is a film that takes itself rather seriously. This feeling is exacerbated by the financial straits which caused the film-makers to opt for voice-over narration rather than synchronised sound, a style which tends to distance the viewer from involvement with the characters and their relationships.

Despite these limitations, and the clear understanding of the immensity of what the young cinematographer had taken on—he described it as '*Folie des grandeurs*'—writer-director O'Shea produced the most professional of New Zealand's features since **Rewi's Last Stand** (1925). SE

Reference
* Note held by the New Zealand Film Archive.

Bill Merito (Johnny). Courtesy of the Pacific Films Collection, New Zealand Film Archive.

1954

THE SEEKERS

Group Film Productions, Fanfare Films. A.k.a. Land of Fury. *Country of origin*: U.K. *Location*: Whakatane. *Rating*: G (Parts of this film may be unsuitable for young children), June 1954. 35 mm (also released in 16 mm). *Colour*: Eastmancolour. 8100 ft. 89 mins.

Director: Ken Annakin. *Producer*: George H. Brown. *Executive producer*: Earl St John. *Production managers*: George Maynard, Frank Sherwin Green. *Assistant directors*: Robert Asher, Peter Manley. *Screenplay*: William Fairchild. *Director of photography*: Geoffrey Unsworth. *Editor*: John D. Guthridge. *Production designer/Art director*: Maurice Carter. *Costume design*: Julie Harris. *Make-up*: George Blackler. *Special effects*: Bill Warrington, Filippo Guidobaldi. *Music*: William Alwyn. *Choreography*: David Paltenghi. *Sound*: Peter Messenger, Gordon K. McCallum. *Technical adviser*: Maharaia Winiata.

Cast

Jack Hawkins (Philip Wayne), Glynis Johns (Marion Southey), Noel Purcell (Paddy Clarke), Inia Te Wiata (Hongi Tepe), Kenneth Williams (Peter Wishart), Laya Raki (Moana), Patrick Warbrick (Awarua), Anthony Erstich (Rangiruru), Francis de Wolf (Captain Bryce), Norman Mitchell (Grayson), Maharaia Winiata (Hongi Tepe's father), Thomas Heathcote (Mackay), Edward Baker (Toroa).

The narrative consists of two periods in New Zealand separated by a brief visit to England, and follows the fortunes of Philip Wayne as he settles in the new country. Wayne, exploring on the coastline, enters a sacred burial cave. He is forced to race against Rangiruru, a noted warrior who will try to kill him. When Wayne wins, Hongi Tepe takes him under his cloak and gives him land to settle on, but at a feast at night where the chief's wife Moana dances, Wayne is insulted by Awarua, a tohunga or priest.

Wayne returns to England, but is arrested for unwittingly smuggling contraband goods. After paying his fine he leaves for New Zealand with his new wife Marion where he builds a house and settles on the land Hongi Tepe had given him. Marion, who is pregnant, introduces Hongi Tepe to Christianity, while Hongi Tepe's wife, Moana, seduces a not unwilling Wayne, but is observed by her husband. When one of the settlers shoots a Maori, Wayne has to intercede with Hongi Tepe. He is successful, but the settlement is attacked by a rival tribe, and despite a counterattack by Hongi Tepe, all the settlers, except the new baby, are killed.

The Seekers, the first colour feature to be made in this country, saw the post-war return to New Zealand of overseas funding and a professional crew and cast. Working in the small coastal town of Whakatane, which Rudall Hayward had used as a base when making The Te Kooti Trail, director Ken Annakin employed a combination of local talent and European experience to construct a mixture of colonial commentary and sensational entertainment.

The images which characterise The Seekers emerge from Eurocentric fantasies about cannibal islands, evil witch doctors, and dusky maidens. Maurice Carter's set designs and Julie Harris's costumes confirm the records of visual history for the settlers and thoroughly distort the evidence from Maori history. That in itself simply confirms the capacity of film-makers to produce a good story without the need for historical accuracy. In fact, this film could have been set on any unidentified island without damage to the fabric of the story, even though in his foreword in the souvenir program, J. Arthur Rank says, 'The spirit which inspired the growth of the great Dominions, which transformed vast wildernesses into rich territories, demands stories as bold as those pioneers who left their native lands more than a century ago to found new nations across the seas. I am confident that New Zealand will be proud of *The Seekers*, a film which tells so vividly that splendid first chapter in her history. It is a story written with the blood of the first settlers and the fine Maori people.'

It was at least the third film after The Te Kooti Trail and The Devil's Pit in which Patrick Warbrick, who played Awarua the tohunga, had appeared, making him one of New Zealand's most experienced actors in film. The Maori actors as a whole, however, demonstrated both power and authority in their roles, and it was their presence, rather than issues of script or camera, which validate this film's place in New Zealand film history. SE

Jack Hawkins (Philip Wayne) and Noel Purcell (Paddy Clarke) are confronted by Patrick Warbrick as the tohunga Awarua. Courtesy of the Rank Organisation Plc.

1964

RUNAWAY

Pacific Films Ltd. A.k.a. Runaway Killer. © 1964. *Locations*: Northland, Auckland, Westland. *Distributor*: N.Z. Film Services. *Rating*: A, September 1964. 35 mm (also released in 16 mm). Black and white. 9810 ft. 102 mins. Recut as Runaway Killers, 80 mins.

Director and producer: John O'Shea. *Screenplay*: John Graham, John O'Shea. *Director of photography*: Anthony Williams. *First assistant camera*: Michael Seresin. *Second assistant camera*: Patrick O'Shea. *Production advisor*: Margaret Thompson. *Production manager*: Bob Ash. *Editor*: John O'Shea. *Sets*: Tom Rowell, Selwyn Muru. *Technical advisor*: Ian Houston. *Make-up and hair*: Jenny MacDonald. *Dresses*: Bess Keam, David Start (courtesy Fibremakers N.Z. Ltd.). *Continuity*: Helen Smith, Judy Larkin. *Cutter*: Susan Pritchard. *Music*: Robin MacOnie. *Conductor*: Patrick Flynn. *Title song*: Rim D. Paul and the Quin Tikis. *Sound*: Lindsay Anderson, Ron Skelley, John McCormick.

Cast

Colin Broadley (David Manning), Nadja Regin (Laura Kossovich), Deidre McCarron (Diana), Kiri Te Kanawa (Isobel Wharewera), Selwyn Muru (Joe Wharewera), Barry Crump (Clarrie), Gil Cornwall (Tom Morton), Sam Stevens (Tana), Tanya Binning (Dorothy), Doraine Green (Sandra), Clyde Scott (Athol), Rim D. Paul (Simon Rangi), Alma Woods (Mrs Milligan), William Johnstone (Alex Manning), Murray Smith (Driscoll), Mary Amoore (Helen Manning), John Atha (Bellamy), Kauri Toi (Mrs Wharewera), Ray Columbus (Bandleader), with Pat Tuxford, Harry Lavinton, Tom Rowell, Harold Kissin, Russell Woods, Jean Suhas, Clarence Hall, Dene Lyon, Ken Flood, Richard Sie.

A high-living, high-flying accountant, David Manning, who regularly spends more than he makes, gets heavily into debt and has to leave his job. He goes on the road where he is given a ride by the wealthy Laura who sees him as a potential lover. Laura shows a jealous streak when her passenger becomes friendly with a young Maori woman, and after a fight Manning takes Laura's car and begins a journey back to the mountains of his childhood. It is a journey which is fraught with problems, and these are compounded by a police pursuit. As he crosses between the islands on the ferry, he meets Diana who offers him both friendship and company on his trek through the bush to the mountains. The police close in and the pair head up into the snow. Diana is left behind after she falls, and Manning continues his hazardous journey up the glacier making for the pass across the mountains.

Runaway is archetypal New Zealand cinema. Its elements, Man Alone, Man on the Run, Man against Man and Landscape, Man Against the Odds, its sea, bush, and mountain settings and the full range of iconographic images, make it quintessential Kiwi myth. Ironically, the catalyst which began the flight in the stolen car was a character played by a budding actress, a young Maori woman named Kiri Te Kanawa, who is now one of the best-known New Zealanders of all time. At the other end of the cultural spectrum, another character is played by the prototypical Kiwi joker himself, Barry Crump.

There is a sense in which the film defines its position in the slowly reviving industry as exploratory and tentative by trying out a range of possibilities from settings to ideas and attitudes. The result is a strong feeling that the story has been as consciously constructed as the images which convey it, and that awareness makes the suspension of disbelief rather more difficult than one would want. At the same time, it is a film which had to be made if the industry were to expand into something more than the well-meaning country cousin cinema which had been so representative of the 1930s.

Cut from its original 102 minutes to 80 for its British release, it tended to become a series of disconnected episodes rather than a portrayal of character disintegration. *The Monthly Film Bulletin* of June 1965 commented, 'The strange, downbeat story, rendered perhaps a little more disjointed and apparently unmotivated by the loss of over twenty minutes from the original running time, and misleadingly retitled to attract an audience unlikely to enjoy it, impresses only by the unsentimental and evocative way in which it uses its immensely varied settings ... ' In hindsight, what **Runaway** really offered was an indication that film-making in New Zealand was inexperienced rather than inept, that there were creative talents with great potential, that while the influence of Hollywood's melodramatic realist narratives was clear, they could be adapted in new and original ways. However, **Runaway** was also the first of many New Zealand productions which threw a dark shadow over their characters, which displayed an almost Hardy-esque world view in which the fates were greater than the individual, and in which the man alone protagonist was destined for death rather than glory. SE

Colin Broadley (David Manning) and Deidre McCarron (Diana) meet Barry Crump (Clarrie). Courtesy of the Pacific Films Collection, New Zealand Film Archive.

1966

DON'T LET IT GET YOU

Pacific Films Ltd. *Budget*: £40 000. *Locations*: Sydney, Rotorua. *Distributor*: N.Z. Film Services. *Rating*: G, August 1966. 35 mm. Black and white. 7200 ft. 80 mins.

Director and producer: John O'Shea. *Associate producer*: D. Russell Rankin. *Screenplay*: Joseph Musaphia. *Director of photography*: Anthony Williams. *Camera assistants*: Michael Seresin, Patrick O'Shea. *Editor*: John O'Shea. *Continuity*: Susan Pritchard. *Graphics and set design*: Patrick Hanley. *Make-up and hair*: Jenny McDonald. *Key grip*: Patrick O'Shea. *Grips*: John Wool, Bernard Reid. *Musical director*: Patrick Flynn. *Editing of musical numbers*: Anthony Williams. *Sound*: Les McKenzie, courtesy of Supreme Sound, Sydney. *Recording*: Les McKenzie, Brian McElwain, John McCormick.

Cast

Howard Morrison (as himself), Carmen Duncan (Judith Beech), Gary Wallace (as himself), Harry Lavington (William Broadhead), Tanya Binning (Australia's Queen of the Surf), Alma Woods (Mrs Beech), Eric Wood (Service station attendant), Ernie Leonard, Normie Rae (Special guest stars), Kiri Te Kanawa (guest artist), with Rim D. Paul, Herma Keil, Lew Pryme, Eliza Keil, Gwynn Owen, Garry Merito, Eddie Lowe, Paul Walden, the Quin Tiki Show Band.

A young Australian seeing New Zealand as a land of musical opportunity sells his drums to buy an air ticket across the Tasman, but ends up in this country with only his drumsticks for support. He is good, and he knows he can succeed with a top band given the opportunity, but he has difficulty finding a job as a musician despite the promise he feels the country offers. On the way over in the plane he meets Howard Morrison who is promoting a music festival in Rotorua, but even Morrison's support cannot get him a job. He keeps looking, and finds a constant irritant in a second-rate percussionist named William Broadhead, but eventually wins both fame and his girl.

This, O'Shea's third film for Pacific Films, takes him from the didactic pressures of **Broken Barrier** through the dark thriller pursuit themes of **Runaway** to the musical. The plot is minimal, and is a barely disguised excuse to showcase a range of New Zealand groups from the mid-sixties. There is no intention to hide what the film is doing. Most of the characters, Howard Morrison, Lew Prime, Kiri Te Kanawa, play themselves, and only the plot bearing characters need fictional roles.

Setting the film in the context of a musical festival also provides a traditional motivation for the musical numbers, and these turn up as soon as a car goes on the road or a group gets together. There are short set pieces interspersed with the music. Some, like the pig hunt provide comic relief. Most provide an opportunity for real life drummer Gary Wallace to display his potential with the sticks, and his drumless rhythms become a continuing motif. But it is the music which gives the film its focus, and each number receives the creative visual treatment which was beginnning to characterise the television located musical video genre.

Don't Let It Get You was well received and the press made much of the way it pulled crowds across the Tasman. Even allowing for a degree of patriotic license, it was a film that worked. Headlines such as 'Australia praises N.Z. film', 'N.Z. film a hit', 'Bright effort', 'Film provides boost for N.Z.' and 'Don't Let It Get You Does' underlined both audience and critical support for a film which 'stunned Australian reviewers, who agreed that New Zealand's first big production movie was a polished, exciting embarrassment to their own film industry.'* SE

Reference
* *Sunday Times*, 9 October 1966.

Howard Morrison and Gary Wallace as themselves. *Courtesy of the Pacific Films Collection, New Zealand Film Archive.*

TO LOVE A MAORI

Rudall and Ramai Hayward Film Productions. *Location*: Auckland. *Distributor*: Rudall and Ramai Hayward Film Productions. *Rating*: S (Suitable for family audiences), December 1972. 16 mm. Colour. 3850 ft. 104 mins.

Directors and producers: Rudall and Ramai Hayward. *Screenplay*: Rudall and Ramai Hayward and Diane Francis. *Source*: Case studies by Diane Francis. Camera: Alton Francis assisted by Randall Francis, Rowan Francis, Abel Francis. *Editors*: Rudall Hayward, Alton Francis. *Music*: Ray Gunter. *Singers*: Maria Finnigan, Marene Edward. *Choreography*: Matangi Kingi. *Choir*: Putaki Choir. *Sound*: Alton Francis.

Cast

Val Irwin (Tama), Marie Searell (Penny), Desmond Lock (Mr Davis), Sybil Lock, a.k.a. Sybil Westland (Mrs Davis), Pam Ferris (Deirdre), Robin Peel Walker (Fancy), Toby Curtis (Mr Muru), Olive Pompallier (Mrs Muru), Rau Hotere (Riki), Connie Rota (Tina), Matangi Kingi (Matangi), Peter Sharp (Butch), Vincent Sharp (Mr Lukers), Tom Newnham (Mr Thompson), Tama's Aunty (Ramai Hayward), Hinerangi Deller (Hinerangi), Harold Kissin (Lawyer), Tony Blackett,(Burglar), Tairongo Amoamo (Burglar), Courteney Bradley (Mechanic), Phil Shone (Barber), Helen Hart (Maori girl), Peter Benson (Gardener).

Tama, a bright and capable school leaver from a rural settlement, decides to leave home and head for the city, Auckland, where he will qualify as a mechanic by attending the technical institute for trade training. He is accompanied by Riki, who has had difficulty at school and is not felt to be ready for city life. The boys stay with relatives in the city and while Tama does well and falls in love with a pakeha girl, Penny, Riki is attracted by the flash clothes and the decadent lifestyle of Fancy. The story of Tama's success is dramatically enlivened by the gradual change in Penny's parents' opposition to their friendship, while Riki increasingly flirts with crime until he realises the error of his ways and joins the army.

This is the last of Rudall Hayward's seven feature films, his first colour feature, and the first colour feature made by a New Zealander in New Zealand. Hayward died after contracting pneumonia in 1974 during a gruelling promotional tour for the film. Hayward's first four films, made in the silent days of the 1920s, showed him at his strongest, and that contribution to New Zealand cinema is his real legacy.

Val Irwin (Tama) and Marie Searell (Penny). Courtesy of the Hayward Historical Film Trust.

They were tough, incisive, dramatically powerful for their time, and the small operating budgets allowed Hayward to demonstrate his enormous resourcefulness. His first wife, Hilda, a photographer in her own right, appeared to have assisted him extensively and professionally in those productions, although her name does not appear in credit lists. Following a period of solid documentary-making and newsreel production in a number of countries, but particularly Great Britain, Australia, Albania and China, he put his efforts into the production of non-fiction. In this he was driven in part by an altruistic belief in the importance of film as an educational medium, and in part by the co-operation and support of his second wife Ramai Hayward, formerly Ramai te Miha.

To Love A Maori shows every evidence of that altruism. It is intended as a dramatic documentation of the problems and successes of young Maori coming into the city from their rural communities, a situation which concerned New Zealanders, particularly during the 1950s and 1960s. That intention is all too obviously clear, and a theme that could have been of real interest turns up a decade too late. Even then, it could have been resurrected had the production values been commercially viable. Unfortunately, shooting on 16 mm did not produce a cinema verité graininess in keeping with the documentary intention. Instead, it reinforces the already apparent problems with editing in both sound and visuals, underlines a tendency to uncontrolled camera and a difficulty in handling the aesthetics of colour. It is accompanied by dialogue which is difficult for the comparatively inexperienced actors to handle. Together, these qualities make the suspension of disbelief in this, the last film of Hayward's rich career, much more difficult than in his earlier titles. SE

1973

Rangi's Catch

Michael Forlong Productions for the Children's Film Foundation. *Country of origin*: U.K. Telefeature. *Location*: Marlborough Sounds. *Rating*: G, June 1973. 35 mm. Colour. 8460 ft, 72 mins (theatrical release). 11 520 ft, 128 mins for the original eight episode television series.

Director and producer: Michael Forlong. *Production manager*: Hugh Harlow. *Screenplay*: Michael Forlong. *Director of photography*: William Jordan. *Editor*: Reginald Beck. *Music*: David Palmer. *Sound*: William Howell. *Sound rerecordists*: Phil Sanderson, Tony Anscombe, Harry Fairbairn.

Cast

Andrew Kerr (Johnny Murray), Temuera Morrison, (Rangi), Kate Forlong (Jane Murray), Vernon Hill (Hemi), Ian Mune (Jake), Michael Woolf (Bill), Don Selwyn (Mr Rukuhia), Hannah Morrison (Mrs Rukuhia), Peter Vere-Jones (Mr Murray), Christine Elsdon (Mrs Murray).

Four children live on a remote sheep farm in the northern part of the South Island. They swim and play in idyllic rural surroundings until, on a day when their parents have made one of their regular trips to town for supplies, they hear a radio broadcast warning of the escape of two convicts. The children have been aware that several things have gone mysteriously missing, and assume, correctly, that the convicts are in their vicinity.

Finding that their house has been burgled while they were swimming, the children go in search of the crooks to find them escaping by boat. The children give chase in the farm launch, but the men turn the tables and set the children adrift in a dinghy. They manage to land and find the convicts boarding the Cook Strait Ferry for Wellington. The children smuggle themselves aboard but are found and handed over to the police where a friendly policeman rings their parents. As they wait, they see the convicts again and, managing to hide in the boot of their car, go with them to where they have hidden a cache of stolen money in a cave. Further chases follow until the children eventually manage to catch the crooks at a Maori concert party performance in Rotorua, receive a reward for the capture and return to their idyllic rural existence again.

Made initially as an eight episode series for children's television by the Children's Film Foundation of Great Britain, **Rangi's Catch** was recut for theatrical release. In the process the narrative was simplified and edited to about two-thirds of its television length. The result was oddly gratifying. Well-lit, with bright Eastmancolor stock making the beautiful New Zealand countryside an appropriate setting for endless childhood memories, the story bowls along at great pace. It provides an interesting addition to the corpus of films which take much of their interest from an extended pursuit through a dramatic countryside. The landscape is used with understanding and affection by New Zealand-born Michael Forlong, and presented with the singular qualities normally associated with full characters—interest, unpredictablity, depth and variety.

The characters themselves are the stuff of well-told stories everywhere where the play's the thing, rather than confusing character complexity. Ian Mune's superb convict persona is not only immediately accessible, but also enlivened by touches such as the memorable spectacles supplied him by props which balance perfectly on the fine line between comic excitement and unintentional self-parody.

At the same time, the inability of the convict characters to handle the rural environment in which the children are so much at home again reinforces the very New Zealand belief in the myth of urban incapacitation. A very young Temuera Morrison, the complete antithesis of the muscular arrogance of his Jake Heke character in **Once Were Warriors**, is a superb Rangi, making the links which united the children with those of normal childhood, and providing a convincing affirmation of the most positive of friendships between Maori and pakeha.

The final theatrical release cut seemed to get a little less disciplined toward the end so that the pace slowed somewhat, and the story became a series of picaresque episodes rather than a more coherent and interconnected whole; but as an entertaining piece of televisual New Zealand mythology, it works. SE

The young Temuera Morrison with friends. Courtesy of the Children's Film and Television Foundation Ltd and the Stills Collection, New Zealand Film Archive.

GAMES '74: OFFICIAL FILM OF THE XTH BRITISH COMMONWEALTH GAMES, CHRISTCHURCH, NEW ZEALAND, 1974

New Zealand National Film Unit. *Rating*: U, 1974. 35 mm. Colour. 106 mins.

Directors: John King, Sam Pillsbury, Paul Maunder, Arthur Everard. *Producers*: David H. Fowler, Lance J. Connolly, *Associate Producer*: Derek Wright. *Camera unit*: Murray M. Greed, Lynton Diggle, Bruce Dunn, Stephen Gibb, John Hoyle, Dale Pomroy, Paul Thompson, Brian E. Cross, David Dry, Kell Fowler, Sam Gray, Don L. Oakley, Barry Thomas, Bayley Watson. *Editors*: Paul Maunder, Beth Butler, Stanley Harper. *Technical unit*: Mac Ashley, Kerry Coe, Bob Curtice, Ron Hiddleston. *Location assistants*: Stanley Harper, Denis Harvey, Sam Neill. *New Zealand Broadcasting Corporation liaison*: Ash Lewis. *Processing*: New Zealand National Film Unit Laboratory. *Music*: Malcolm Smith. *Musical director*: Garth Young. *Sound unit*: Val Federoff, Don Reynolds, Brian Shennan, John Lowe, Kit Rollings, Geoff Shepherd. *Sound editor/mixer*: Don Reynolds.

Games '74 is a production of the New Zealand National Film Unit, and as such could be expected to reflect the official line and become a vehicle for the promotion of New Zealand both at home and overseas. In one sense it does just that, but rather than offering the traditional introductory settings of sparkling mountains and pristine valleys, the film-makers go directly to the heart of the Games, the stadium in Christchurch in the South Island, and the military planning and precision which set the opening ceremony and the Games in motion. From that opening footage, introduced by an untypically taciturn narrator, the stylistic character of the film is located in viewer involvement.

The spectator's-eye camera is busy and a variety of shots both inform and entertain. The continuing involvement with competitors and crowd through seemingly unscripted, but in fact carefully edited, close-ups and medium shots humanises an otherwise endless procession of events followed by winners collecting medals. That humanising process has the effect of avoiding camera comment and letting events speak for themselves. The consequence is a surprisingly (for the time) gender-balanced and apolitical narrative which underlines the humanity of the competitors as much as it shows the drama of success and failure. At the same time, in conventions which are well-established in screen coverage of sports events in New Zealand, there is a clear ordering of priorities. Track events are prime targets, closely followed by field. Sprints are covered in their entirety, while long distance events are intercut with inserts from interviews to other events. The male weightlifters provide elephantine drama, and the marathon provides a useful device for taking viewers out of the stadium. Women's events receive scant coverage, even though this film bears all the hallmarks of professional and exploratory cinema.

Dick Taylor winning the 10 000 metre race at the 1974 Commonwealth Games in Christchurch. Frame enlargement courtesy of the New Zealand Film Archive.

Despite that qualification, the film is a cinematically appealing record rather than a simple recording of events. Gradual movement of camera from a wideshot on the track, to individual competitors, to a close-up of a finger squeezing the trigger of the starter's gun and a freeze frame finish in the 100 yards, for example, involves and informs. There is beauty in selected images from the diving in which the divers are captured in slow motion as the camera follows their balletic descent into the pool below. There is a sense of comedy as a series of high jumpers, using similar techniques to cross the bar are edited in collapsed sequence, reminding viewers of salmon exploding up a waterfall.

The liveliness and originality of so much of the film is no coincidence. The crew is composed of many of the film-makers who would be prominent in New Zealand film-making in the next couple of decades. Sam Pillsbury, Paul Maunder, Arthur Everard, David Fowler, and many others in the full crew—even a newcomer listed as a location assistant, Sam Neill—are part of a growing cadre of successful New Zealand screen professionals. SE

1975

TEST PICTURES: ELEVEN VIGNETTES FROM A RELATIONSHIP

Hinge Film Productions. Produced with assistance from the Queen Elizabeth II Arts Council of New Zealand. *Rating*: R18, May 1975. 16 mm. Black and white. 965 m. 87 mins.

Director: Geoffrey Steven. *Producers*: Geoff Chapple, Erik Braithwaite. *Production supervisor*: Peter King. *Screenplay*: Denis Taylor. *Director of photography*: Geoffrey Steven. *Camera assistant*: Philip Chapman. *Editor*: Geoffrey Steven. *Sound*: Philip Dadson. *Sound assistant*: Carin Svensson.

Cast

Denis Taylor (Man—Nick), Lee Feltham (Woman—Lindy), Francis Halpin (Master of ceremonies), Moira Turner (Pianist), Geoff Barlow (Roadworker), Dora Warren (Roadworker's mother), Barbara Saipe (Young girl), Mark Elmore (Young boy), Mike Fitzgerald (Storekeeper).

The film is loosely structured around the relationship between a man and a woman, Nick and Lindy, as they move out into a small enclosed community in the country and an alternative lifestyle. In the course of a series of 11 episodes which pick up the ordinariness of everyday living, as well as the memorable moments and plot points of life, their relationship is seen to break down under the limitations of a lack of communication and a consequent loss of feeling for each other.

Geoff Steven's film was regarded as the harbinger of a new age, both when it was released to festival audiences and when it received an audience on the Film Society circuit. In the early 1970s Steven led a small group of film-makers, which included Philip Dadson, in the formation of a film-makers' co-operative, Alternative Cinema. Unlike in Australia, which was beginning to receive significant funding for its fledgling film industry, New Zealand film-makers had to work on the proverbial shoestring. The co-operative, using 16 mm formats and with no significant financial support other than the occasional grant from the Queen Elizabeth II Arts Council and the Auckland City Council, was the catalyst for the development of film-making which led in due course to the establishment of a climate which produced the first commercial film of the new age, **Sleeping Dogs**, and to the setting up of the New Zealand Film Commission.

Test Pictures took on a significance beyond its public reception, as its production period in 1973 provided a training ground and a collaborative meeting place for many of the film-makers who were to become influential in the upcoming period of rapid growth which would be obvious five years later. It was shot on location at the Hinge Estate, with crew and cast working without wages. In what was to become a hallmark of New Zealand productions, a creative problem-solving approach allowed the film to be completed on a budget of $14 000, $7000 of which came from the Arts Council.

On release it achieved some notoriety, as it had been given an R18 rating by the censor as a result of content which included nudity and marijuana use. This was widely publicised by the Society for the Protection of Community Standards. However, **Test Pictures** was no commercial exploiter of the sensational. It was exploratory and experimental, and in his concentration on images rather than narrative Steven made life difficult for critics and audiences alike. Even as an example of experimental cinema, it was not particularly successful, and occasionally feels cumbersome and self-conscious. At the same time, the impetus it gave film-makers as a result of its co-operative base in Alternative Cinema, and the opportunity it provided for exploring the medium, was to have a significant catalytic effect. SE

The original poster from the film. Courtesy of Geoff Steven and the Stills Collection, New Zealand Film Archive.

THE GOD BOY

1976

Television One. © 1976. Telefeature. *Locations*: Featherston, Whakatane, Martinborough. No censorship rating (in-house production). 16 mm. Colour. 88 mins.

Director and producer: Murray Reece. *Screenplay*: Ian Mune. *Source*: Ian Cross, *The God Boy*. *Director of photography*: Allen Guilford. *Camera operator*: Alun Bollinger. *Editor*: Simon Reece. *Production design*: Ron Highfield. *Wardrobe supervisor*: Julia Feehan. *Music*: John Charles. *Conductor*: William Southgate. *Players*: Members of the New Zealand Symphony Orchestra. *Sound*: Russell Hay, Dick Reade.

Cast

Jamie Higgins (Jimmy Sullivan), Maria Craig (Mrs Sullivan), Graeme Tetley (Mr Sullivan), Sandra Reid (Molly Sullivan), Ivan Beavis (Bloody Jack), Judie Douglass (Sister Angela), Harold Kissin (Mr Waters), Colleen McColl (Mrs Waters), Damien Wilkins (Hector), Idris Minke (Legs), Brendon Mune (Joseph), Graham Peters (Sniffy), Mark Scott-Smith (Joe Waters), Steven Daniells (Steven), Bernard Kearns (Father Gilligan), Yvonne Lawley (Sister Theresa), Dorothy McKegg (Sister Francis), with Alma Black (Abortionist), Marius Verlijsdort (Fisherman), Charles Krinkel (Policeman), Gael Anderson (Policewoman), Bill Juliff (Greengrocer), Allona Priestley (Lady), Roy Pearce (Man).

Colleen McColl (Mrs Waters), Harold Kissin (Mr Waters), Mark Scott-Smith (Joe Waters) and Jamie Higgins (Jimmy Sullivan). Courtesy of Murray Reece.

Eleven year-old Jimmy Sullivan, growing up Catholic in the small, working-class seaside town of Raggleton after World War II, is deeply troubled. His parents war continuously in what Mr Sullivan calls 'the heavyweight championship of the world' and although Jimmy attempts to tell others of his increasing anxiety he is unable to reveal the full truth. Boiling point is reached when Mr Sullivan, to curry favour with Jimmy and provoke his wife, buys Jimmy a bike the family cannot afford. Jimmy watches his parents fight and, believing God has turned against him, goes on a stone-throwing rampage in the village. That night his mother kills his father, but when arrested lies to Jimmy, telling him he is being sent to a convent because she and Mr Sullivan have to 'go away for a while'. In the convent Jimmy fantasises to his sister Molly that their parents are happy together, and defiantly tells a nun he can look after himself.

The God Boy is a skilful adaptation of Ian Cross's novel, a rite of passage psychodrama where the surface calm of private and public lives in small town 1950s New Zealand masks repression, abuse, violence and dishonesty. Raggleton seems the setting for an idyllic childhood and for a time young Jimmy thinks God is on his side, that he is a 'God boy'. In that society sex roles are sharply delineated and Jimmy's violent father, a war trauma victim, makes his wife the scapegoat of his disappointments. As well as being used as his father's stalking horse at home, Jimmy is trapped in the violence of a punitive convent education. An imaginative boy, he comes to see Catholicism's iconography and its strictures on love, sin and penance as inextricably linked to his sense of guilt. In his fantasies he comes to see himself as a Christ-like victim, railing against God ('If I went after God I could beat him too unless he killed me') and anaesthetising himself against pain with rituals of his own. Young Jamie Higgins gives a fine portrayal of inarticulate suffering as Jimmy chooses to live in denial of how things really are, to 'care about nothink.'

Screenwriter Ian Mune maintains the spirit of the novel while simplifying its complex structure. The main body of the narrative is framed as a flashback and shot in an 'objective' style. Jimmy's experiences are described from his point of view, as if with the benefit of hindsight. His emotional responses are signalled in the way images are framed, in the often discordant soundtrack and in slow motion and montage. Jimmy's interpretation of God's complicity is verified by high angle shots giving a God's-eye-view of the action.

The God Boy, the first feature made for New Zealand television, was made when, the NZBC having been replaced by Television One, Television Two (later known as South Pacific Television) and Radio New Zealand (1975), television drama production was reorganised and flowered as senior executives became program—rather than administration—oriented. The telefeature screened in 1976 to mark Television One's first birthday and on 20 June 1985 to mark New Zealand's first 25 years of television.
HM

1976 Feltex Award: Best Actress, Judy Douglass.

WILD MAN

1977

Endeavour (Endeavour T.V. Productions Ltd) and the Acme Sausage Company, Blerta. *Location*: Foxton. *Distributor*: Endeavour T.V. Productions Ltd. *Rating*: G, May 1977 (The first application for registration was for Wild Man From Borneo on 19 April, the second on 19 May was for a 16 mm print with the name by which the film is now known, and a third application on 20 May was for the 35 mm release print. MGM released a film called The Wild Man Of Borneo directed by Robert Sinclair in 1940.) 16 mm and 35 mm. Colour. 73 mins.

Director: Geoff Murphy. *Producers*: Bruno Lawrence, Roy Murphy. *Executive producer*: John Barnett. *Screenplay*: Bruno Lawrence, Geoffrey Murphy, Martyn Sanderson, Ian Watkin. *Director of photography*: Allun Bollinger.

Cast

Bruno Lawrence (Wild Man), Ian Watkin (the Colonel), Tony Barry (Dombey Morgan), Martyn Sanderson (Snake), Bill Stalker (Willie Masters), Patrick Bleakley (Village Idiot), Val Murphy (Bar Room Singer).

In a narrative which demonstrates that honour among thieves is as mythical as political altruism, two travelling confidence tricksters, the Colonel and the Wild Man, play the gold fields of the South Island during the latter part of the nineteenth century. The Wild Man is brought into each town dressed in a leopard skin and travelling chained in a cage, scattering chickens and small children before him as he rants and postures, establishing his reputation as a ferocious battler who never loses a fight. The Colonel challenges the best fighter in each town to put up a no-holds barred contest with the Wild Man, and happily collects the bets the townspeople place on their own champion, knowing that the Wild Man indeed never loses.

On the final leg of a successful tour, they come to a town where the going will be hard. The townspeople rightly suspect a con and attempt to lynch the Colonel when he returns to the local bar to collect his winnings. However he is too sly to be caught that way and ends up shouting the bar. In the drunken revelry which follows, he slips away with Morgan and the money, leaving the locals to vent their spleen on the Wild Man who has been deserted, left still chained in his cage outside the pub.

The con man-as-comedy theme, later picked up in films like **Came A Hot Friday**,

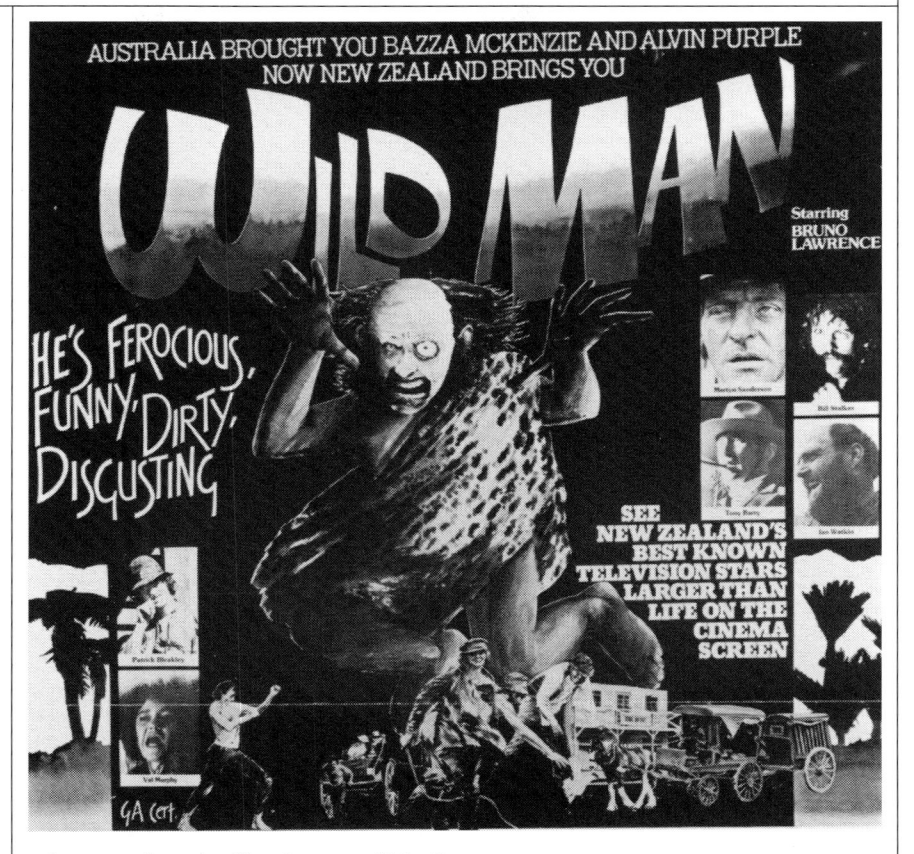

The poster from the film. Courtesy of John Barnett.

is dear to the New Zealand psyche. It embodies a combination of admiration of native cunning and an ability to live by one's wits, as well as a willingness to laugh at those who are caught out by their own inability to spot the con.

The Wild Man's antics emerged from ideas developed in the small Hawkes Bay settlement of Waimarama where Murphy, Lawrence and others of the cast and crew lived, and demonstrate the anarchic and individual attitudes which were to characterise the work of film-makers from the Waimarama community, especially those of Murphy and Lawrence. The posturer pricked, authority as a kind of divinely inspired comedy, tall poppies felled, self-importance as a constant source of laughter, set in or against a backdrop of the dramatic New Zealand landscape, have provided essential material for post-war film-makers from Murphy to Peter Jackson.

Wild Man is essentially exploratory, a template for later productions rather than a milestone feature, and there is a clear lack of the technical sophistication which was to characterise Murphy's later films. At the same time, there is a raw energy evident in Ian Watkin's Colonel, a frenetic insanity in Bruno Lawrence's Wild Man and a hissing extravagance in Martyn Sanderson's Snake, which make this film more than simply an historical curiosity.

Maintaining the sense of illogical and irreverent comedy, the 73 minute **Wild Man** was released with a vehicle for actor John Clarke's iconic New Zealand character, Fred Dagg. **Dagg Day Afternoon**, with a 37 minute running time, had the character Fred Dagg with his seven brothers, all named Trev, attempting to find the dreaded bionic ram, which had mysteriously gone missing. Like **Wild Man**, produced by the Acme Sausage Company, **Dagg Day Afternoon** was written by John Clarke and Geoffrey Murphy, directed by Murphy and produced by John Barnett. The cast included John Clarke (Fred Dagg), Derek Payne (Army Officer), Mike Wilson (Station Attendant), Peter McDonald (Shop Assistant), Robert Burst (Elder Trev). SE

LANDFALL

New Zealand National Film Unit for the Broadcasting Corporation of New Zealand. *Rating*: RFF, May 1977. (The film was actually shot in 1975, but problems with finance meant that it was not finally released until 1977.) 16 mm. Colour (Eastmancolour). 3100 ft. 86 mins. (The censor's certification shows 82 mins and specifies no cuts, but the synoptic material released with the film for festival viewing specifies 86 mins.)

Director: Paul Maunder. *Producer*: David H. Fowler. *Assistant director*: Stanley Harper. *Screenplay*: Paul Maunder. *Director of photography*: Lynton Diggle. *Camera operator*: Bayly Watson. *Camera assistant*: Barry Thomas. *Editors*: Paul Maunder, Maxine Schurr. *Production designer*: Martin Townsend. *Make-up*: Christine Reynolds. *Sound*: Geoff Shepherd. *Sound assistant*: Malcolm Moore.

Cast

Denise Maunder (Sandra), John Anderson (John), Sam Neill (Eric), Gael Anderson (Elizabeth), Rowena Zinsli (Girl), Russell Duncan (Tramp), Michael Haigh (Policeman), Pat Evison (Visitor), Jonathan Dennis (Reporter), Olwen Taylor (Addict).

Gael Anderson, Jonathan Dennis (later founding director of the New Zealand Film Archive) and Denise Maunder during the filming of Landfall *near Foxton.* Courtesy of Jonathan Dennis and the Stills Collection, New Zealand Film Archive.

Two women and two men move into an old rambling house in Foxton to set up a communal life style. Eric, lapsed Catholic and Vietnam veteran, and Elizabeth, a woman in search of herself, are single. The other male, John, is married to the childless Sandra. The four adopt their version of the alternative lifestyle of the late 1960s—gardening, building and attempting to reject the conventions of the society they have left. Because each of them brings tensions from the past, and each appears to be using the communal life as much to exorcise those tensions as to lead a revolutionary new existence, relationships fragment and the group begins to disintegrate. During a farewell party, Elizabeth shoots a policeman who has come to investigate claims of drug use. They turn themselves into a group of self-styled revolutionaries, but unable to resist the residue of the past or the pressures of the present world outside their gates, the group appears to collapse and its members are arrested—or perhaps they stay together to continue to develop a more harmonious and peaceful lifestyle together.

Paul Maunder is one of a group of filmmakers from the 1970s in New Zealand who were concerned with exploring the alternative possibilities of film, rather than pursuing the more mainstream developments which were taking place under the direction of filmmakers like Roger Donaldson and Ian Mune. Maunder's films displayed both a strong social conscience and a willingness to use the medium to direct public attention to new ways of seeing his world. His footage was intended to do more than merely entertain with the sanitised worldviews which characterised much contemporary New Zealand documentary production.

In **Landfall**, Maunder rejects many of the principles of cause and effect of the classic Hollywood narrative and instead adopts an approach which reconstructs time and space to present an internal reality. Characters are motivated by their past and by their own perceptions rather than by the actions of others. Much of the motivation, therefore, is not easily accessible. Elizabeth's shooting of the policeman, for example, is not so much pivotal to the plot as to an essentialist statement about the difference between the reality of a chaotic world and the fantasy of a world where people believe falsely in a kind of cosmic logic.

Both **Landfall** and Geoff Steven's **Test Pictures**, however, made essential additions to the melting pot of the cinematic 1970s in New Zealand. The nascent industry was to be given direction not merely from eventual commercial viability, although that was to be a major influence, but from a peculiarly New Zealand willingness to experiment, to ask questions of the establishment, to construct narratives outside traditional frameworks and to use what appeared to work best rather than what custom or convention dictated. Pragmatism, rather than prescription, underlay the decisions of the new directors. Such a climate allowed for the development of the new vision of Vincent Ward and Peter Jackson, as well as the erratically entertaining action comedies of Geoff Murphy and Roger Donaldson.

As a film, **Landfall** tries too hard to extend its narrative boundaries and has a rather self-conscious art school feel about its very clear intentions. From the standpoint of the late 1990s, it focuses on topics in ways which had already been dramatically exhausted. Viewing the nearly 90 minutes now gives the impression that the film serves as a vehicle for Maunder's own ideologies, but that there are often occasions when the viewer is left in the dark as to what, precisely, these are. SE

1977

OFF THE EDGE

Air New Zealand and Everard Films present a Pentacle Films Production. Copyright date not recorded. Documentary. *Budget*: $300 000. *Location*: Mount Cook National Park. *Distributor*: Kerridge Odeon Film Distributors. *Rating*: GY, May 1977. 16 mm. Colour. 77 mins.

Director and producer: Mike Firth. *Associate producers*: Michael Economou, Jeff Campbell. *Screenplay*: Molly Gregory. *Director of photography*: Mike Firth. *Camera operators*: Mike Firth, Geoff Cocks, Geoff Steven, Tony Lilleby. *Editor*: Michael Economou. *Alpine guides*: Gavin Wills, Harry Keys. *Helicopter pilots*: Bill Black, Mel Cain. *Music*: Richard Clements. *Additional music*: Exit, Richard Degray, Tom Hollyer, Greg Charland. 'Higher Trails' composed and sung by John Hanlon. *Sound*: Geoff Cocks.

Cast
Jeff Campbell, Blair Trenholme. *Narration voices*: Ron Hajek, Ron Roy.

After a voice-over discussion about the remoteness of New Zealand, and some map shots establishing where it is, skiers Jeff Campbell and Blair Trenholm arrive at Mount Cook National Park to ski and hang-glide. Making their way to Pioneer Hut, which at 8000 feet is bolted to a narrow mountain ridge, they travel first on horseback and then on foot. For their skiing adventures they travel in a wide arc, to altitudes of over 10 000 feet, always looking for new challenges. A blizzard has them confined to their hut for a week. Highlights include a venture into previously unexplored ice caves in Tasman Glacier and a swim and a joint in hot mineral springs at the base of a mountain. Occasional glimpses of other life—birds and goats—are a reminder of the inhospitability of the terrain. The accompanying voice-over describes the feelings of freedom that can be gained through having faith in yourself, overcoming your fear and going beyond your limits. In the hang-gliding sequences, particularly unnerving when they lose wind flying over the Tasman Glacier, the narration points out there is 'no place as unforgiving as the air.'

Distinguished as the first New Zealand feature film to receive an Academy Award nomination, **Off the Edge** had its genesis in the meeting of New Zealander Michael Firth, American Jeff Campbell and Canadian Blair Trenholm when skiing in France during the 1970–1971 winter. Two years later, at Firth's invitation to take part in a film, Campbell and Trenhom travelled to New Zealand to ski and hang-glide in the Southern Alps. The terrain was treacherous and the high altitudes remote. Difficulties included high winds (sometimes over 200 miles-an-hour) and juggling the logistics of filming on skis and hang-gliders and from a helicopter. While Campbell and Trenholm stayed in the ski hut, the camera crew flew up each day then skied to the site of the shoot. Because of the dangerous conditions, the ice caves sequence was shot in about 25 minutes.

The exploits of Campbell and Trenholm are extraordinary—especially given that they ski the entire film wearing jeans—and are matched by the brilliant capturing of the sounds and images of those exploits on film as the camera takes the viewer onto skis and up into the air.

On its release reviewers described the film with such epithets as 'beautiful … awesome … stunning … thrilling … a triumph'.
HM

1977 Academy Award Nomination: Best Documentary Feature.
Festival of the Americas: Gold Medal.

Off the edge and up in the air in New Zealand's Southern Alps. *Courtesy of the New Zealand Film Commission.*

1977

SLEEPING DOGS

Aardvark Films Ltd, in association with Broadbank Corporation Ltd, The New Zealand Development Finance Corporation of New Zealand, Television One and with the assistance of the Queen Elizabeth II Arts Council. © 1977. *Budget*: $450 000. *Locations*: Coromandel, Auckland, Waikato, Huia. *Distributor*: Aardvark Films. *Rating*: GA, August 1977. 35 mm. Colour. 107 mins.

Director and producer: Roger Donaldson. *Screenplay*: Ian Mune, Arthur Baysting. *Source*: C.K. Stead, *Smith's Dream*. *Director of photography*: Michael Seresin. *Camera operator*: Paul Leach. *Sykhawk sequence photographer*: Roger Donaldson. *Editor*: Ian John. *Art directors*: Roger Donaldson, Ian Mune. *Wardrobe supervisors*: Rosan McLeod, Lesley Mclennan. *Special effects director*: Geoff Murphy. *Stunt co-ordinator*: Jerry Popov. *Music*: Murray Grindlay, David Calder, Mathew Brown. *Sound*: Craig McLeod, Peter Fenton.

Cast

Sam Neill (Smith), Nevan Rowe (Gloria), Ian Mune (Bullen), Ian Watkin (Dudley), Clyde Scott (Jesperson), Donna Akersten (Mary), Bill Johnson (Cousins), Warren Oates (Colonel Willoughby), Don Selwyn (Taupiri), Davina Whitehouse (Elsie), Snuffles (Dog), with Melissa Donaldson, Dougal Stevenson, Bernard Kearns, Raf Irving, Cass Donaldson, Tommy Tinirau, Roger Oakley, Dorothy McKegg, Tony Groser, Bernard Moody, Laurie Dee, Ron Cameron, Rod Collison, Ken Smith, Richard Moss, Norman Fawsey, Peter Bols, Chris Parkinson, Bill Juliffe, Pat Hoff, Tom Binns, Les Hunt, Shirley Duke.

Smith leaves his family in the city after his wife, Gloria, takes up with his best friend, Bullen. Intercut with Smith setting himself up on an idyllic rural retreat, Maori-owned Gut Island, striking city workers combat government forces. Increasingly repressive government tactics result in martial law being declared, the establishment of an anti-terrorist force, the Specials, and the calling in of American advisers. Smith is steadfastly apolitical, but guerrillas set him up as a scapegoat and a force of Specials arrests him after finding a cache of arms on his island. Jesperson, the vicious head of the secret police, offers to lift Smith's death sentence if he confesses to 'revolutionary activities' on television. Escaping from captivity Smith takes refuge as the caretaker of a country motel. There, at the urging of Bullen, who is now a revolutionary guerrilla, he is the catalyst for the death of an entire American army detachment. On the run, he spends a night with his wife, also now a revolutionary. He escapes in a sheep truck with Bullen and, after learning of Gloria's death at the hands of the Specials, the two men take off into the bush. United in their shared goal of escape they are hunted and gunned down by army helicopters.

Sleeping Dogs, set in an imagined totalitarian future, depicts a marriage, a friendship and a society in collapse. Economic pressures from overseas enable opportunists at home to seize power while loss of civil liberties and oppressive government tactics make revolutionaries of people who, like Bullen, were former supporters of the status quo. As a kind of Everyman Smith's position is more ambivalent, adding complexity to the moral questions posed. Unable to maintain his stoic 'man alone' status he is drawn finally to act as a revolutionary through sexual jealousy (his lover Mary has sex with an American commander), but refuses to commit himself to the political cause, having also seen guerrillas commit atrocities. For ordinary bloke Smith personal politics are much more immediate and real. Central to his inarticulated anguish over his marriage break-up is not Gloria's infidelity, but Bullen's betrayal of their friendship. His final defiance of the armed forces is a personal gesture, fuelled by renewal of the friendship, and his emotional victory in death is that he has beaten Jesperson by avoiding capture.

Manipulation by the media, Asian guerrilla conflicts and questioning of the nature of political power provided the reference points by which C.K. Stead charted his novel **Smith's Dream** (1971). The book foresaw some of the confrontations in police, army and protester action that occurred in the 1981 Springbok Tour. In **Sleeping Dogs** those conditions are the spur to a fast-paced political thriller/action/buddy movie. Street riots, chases, napalm, rocket attack, Skyhawk aerobatics, phallic guns and fickle women provide the framework for Smith's emotional journey, involving some mistaken identity and much coincidence, where marriage and society remain in tatters, but mateship is joyously reaffirmed.

Country and western-style music gives a sentimental edge to relationship issues and provides a 'broken heart' theme song ending with 'Turn your back on it all, let sleeping dogs lie' while the music in the action sequences uses action/thriller codes. Effective special effects, tight editing (the opening sequence is excellent) and convincing performances mark a step forward in film-making confidence in New Zealand and, although some overseas reviewers found fault with things like character motivation and the over-the-top ending (still the longest individual death scene in a New Zealand film), local audiences, hungry to see their own stories on screen, received the film with enthusiasm. With the bonus drawcard of name American actor Warren Oates, **Sleeping Dogs** launched the careers of several film-makers and actors, most notably Sam Neill and Roger Donaldson.

When **Sleeping Dogs** was released in the United States *Variety* magazine praised it for its 'sharp directorial flair ... taut performances ... and a handsome technical gloss in all departments.' It is recognised as the film that marked the beginning of contemporary New Zealand cinema. Its success was followed by the announcement of the establishment of an Interim Film Commission.
HM

Ian Mune (Bullen) and Sam Neill (Smith). Courtesy of the New Zealand Film Commission.

1977

SOLO

David Hannay-Tony Williams Productions Pty Ltd, Sydney and Wellington, with the assistance of The Seven Television Network, Australia, The New Zealand Queen Elizabeth II Arts Council and the Solo Investment Fund. © 1977. Financed from New Zealand and Australia. *Budget*: $250 000. *Locations*: Waimarama, Tokoroa, Mamaku, Rotorua, Martinborough, Wellington, Southern Alps. *Distributor*: Amalgamated Theatres. *Rating*: GY, December 1977. 35 mm (shot on 16 mm). Colour. 97 mins.

Director: Tony Williams. *Producers*: David Hannay, Tony Williams. *Executive producers*: Bill Sheat, John Sturzaker. *Associate producer*: Tony Troke. *Screenplay*: Tony Williams, Martyn Sanderson. *Director of photography*: John Blick. *Aerial photography director*: Steve Locker-Lampson. *Editor*: Tony Williams. *Art director*: Paul Carvell. *Wardrobe supervisor*: Christine Reynolds. *Music*: Dave Fraser, Robbie Laven, Marion Arts. *Vocals*: Marion Arts, Al Bowlley. *Sound*: Robert Allen, Dell King, Phil Judd.

Cast

Martyn Sanderson (Jules Catweazle), Lisa Peers (Judy Ballantyne), Vincent Gil (Paul Robinson), Perry Armstrong (Billy Robinson), Davina Whitehouse (Rohana Beaulieu), Maxwell Fernie (Crispin Beaulieu), Frances Edmund (Schoolteacher), Uncle Roy (Man on bike), Jock Spence (Radio operator), Gillian Hope (Woman on train), Veronica Lawrence (Sue), Val Murphy (Anita).

On the road in New Zealand after recently separating from her partner, Judy, a young Australian woman, meets fortyish aerial fire patrol pilot Paul when he extinguishes a fire she has lit near a pine forest. Later, seeing Judy hitchhiking in town, Paul and his teenage son Billy offer her a bed for the night. They detour in a light plane to make some deliveries to Jules, also known as Catweazle, an eccentric who sits in a fire-watching tower playing with gadgets and developing theories about UFOs. Next day, on the maiden flight of Paul's Tiger Moth bi-plane, an oil leak forces the trio to land on an isolated beach and they are looked after by two elderly, eccentric farmers. Jealous of the attention Judy and Paul are paying each other, Billy takes off on a solo flight and crashes the plane but is unhurt. Judy and Paul exchange proclamations of love and spend the night together. When they return to Paul's home Judy, afraid of commitment, announces she is leaving. Ignoring Paul's admonitions to stay she visits Catweazle, telling him she will write to Paul. She hitches a ride with a couple of hippies and, on the road again, sheds some tears over the man she has left behind.

Billed as 'a love story of our time', **Solo** draws on ideas about freedom, commitment, risk-taking and environmental protection popularised by the counterculture movement in the 1960s and 1970s, framing them in the 'flying solo' metaphor. Catweazle's self-imposed isolation in a tower is explained in terms of his philosophy ('Most people need less than they think'), Billy is singular in his eccentric personality, Judy runs from the tedium of long-term relationships and Paul, having spent years as a solo father, has made a virtue of anaesthetising himself against feeling. Working against the stereotypes of the day—Judy isn't focused on marriage, lateral-minded Billy is the anti-thesis of the macho adolescent in spite of his obsession with sex, Paul cries when he lets his guard down and the farmers are quite bizarre—the characterisation is refreshingly different. The musical score supports the narrative without being obtrusive. Credibility is sacrificed in telescoping events into a couple of days and in the obvious lack of chemistry between the actors. Although there is a sense of time-filling in the copious flight footage, sequences over the North Island forest at Tokoroa cut together with Southern Alps footage provide a spectacular maiden flight.

Solo was partly financed by Australian money and was regarded as the first New Zealand co-production. Australians appeared in the roles of Judy and Paul. It was the first feature for many of the crew and, like **Sleeping Dogs** which was shot at the same time, served as a training ground for many film-makers. Director/co-writer/co-producer/editor Tony Williams described the film as 'rushed in the writing and shooting'*. On its release New Zealand-based critic Catherine de la Roche described **Solo** as 'our best film ever.' HM

1978 Asian Film Festival: Merlion Award for Most Outstanding Music.

Reference
* **Cowboys of Culture**, Director: Geoff Steven.

Lisa Peers (Judy Ballantyne). Courtesy of the New Zealand Film Commission.

1978

ANGEL MINE

I.L.A. Productions with assistance from the NZ Interim Film Commission and the Queen Elizabeth II Arts Council. Copyright date not recorded. *Budget*: $13 000. 35 mm blow-up: $26 000. *Location*: Auckland. *Distributor*: ILA Productions. *Rating*: R18 (Contains punk cult material), October 1978. 35 mm (shot on 16 mm). Colour. 67 mins.

Director: David Blyth. *Producers*: David Blyth, Warren Sellers. *Associate producers*: Larry Parr, Jennifer Jakich. *Screenplay*: David Blyth. *Director of photography*: John Earnshaw. *Camera operator*: John Earnshaw. *Editor*: Philip Howe. (No production designer credited). *Wardrobe supervisor*: Elizabeth Mitchell. *Music*: Mark Nicholas. *Players*: Auckland Youth Orchestra, Peter Kerin, Suburban Reptiles, Charisma. *Sound*: Mike Westgate, Brian Shennan.

Cast

Derek Ward, Jennifer Redford, Myra de Groot, Mike Wilson.

A man in an old-fashioned sailor suit emerges from the sea and dresses a naked woman sitting on a toilet in the sand. Looking to camera the man offers a bottle of pills while a voice-over, advertisement style, tells how the drug Angel Mine alleviates marital problems. In their Pakuranga subdivision Lockwood home the couple bicker as they dress for a party while their leather-clad alter egos (both couples played by Derek Ward and Jennifer Redford), cruising the sterile, treeless streets, plan to murder the first couple they come across whose fridge is empty. The rest of the narrative alternates 'real' and fantasised episodic sequences in which the suburban couple act out a number of roles while their alter egos close in on their prey. The suburban couple are eventually killed following discovery of their empty fridge.

Inspired by the surrealistic images of Louis Buñuel (in **Un Chien Andalou**, for example), David Blyth made his film while still a university student at a time when the 'little boxes' of suburbia were often in the satirical firing line. **Angel Mine** satirises the lifestyle of middle-class suburban New Zealand in the 1970s as barren and alienating. The couple, seduced into a materialistic, consumer-led lifestyle, are so absorbed in media images that real communication is stifled and they communicate only through soap opera and talkback radio. They search for 'real' images of themselves in media-fed escapist fantasies, playing with societal taboos involving nudity, sado-masochism, sex, abortion, religion, death and violence. Borrowed from a current commercial, Captain Hotshot, for example, enjoys anal sex with Mr Suburbia. The doppelgangers are the manifestation of their repressed physical, sensual selves but they, too, are media inventions.

Angel Mine, described by Blyth as 'more a visual essay, more a Buñuellian journey', contains some interesting, bizarre images (the Grim Reaper relaxing with a beer after mowing a desert-like suburban lawn, fellation of a doorknob, a slow-motion ballet danced around a revolving clothesline) and ideas (the empty fridge as a symbol of meaningless suburban lives) which had not hitherto been broached in New Zealand film. Awkward dialogue and roughly synched dubbing make the performances seem stilted. The inventive soundtrack provides useful narrative links, with music played by the Auckland Youth Orchestra, Charisma, Suburban Reptiles and Peter Kerin. Described on its release as a 'black comedy', the film today looks dated but retains its satirical edge.

Angel Mine was an important departure from realism in New Zealand cinema. A sexually explicit, experimental psychodrama, it was described by the director as marking 'the coming of age of New Zealand erotic cinema.' Media reports described it as 'controversial', 'shocking' and a 'sex-in-the-suburbs satire', while the community standards group led by Patricia Bartlett expressed horror that taxpayers' money was being 'squandered' on such a project. The censor's certificate, devised especially to describe **Angel Mine**, bears no relation to the film's actual contents. HM

Alter ego fantasy figures played by Derek Ward and Jennifer Redford. Courtesy of the New Zealand Film Commission.

1978

SKIN DEEP

Phase Three Film Productions Ltd, with assistance from the New Zealand Interim Film Commission. Script Development Grant: The Queen Elizabeth II Arts Council. © 1978. *Budget*: $180 000. *Location*: Raetihi. *Distributor*: Amalgamated Theatres. *Rating*: R16, November 1978. 35 mm. Colour. 110 mins.

Director: Geoff Steven. *Producer*: John Maynard. *Screenplay*: Piers Davies, Roger Horrocks, Geoff Steven, from an original idea by Geoff Steven. *Dialogue*: Robert J. Williams. *Director of photography*: Leon Narbey. *Camera operator*: Paul Leach. *Editor*: Simon Sedgley. *Art director*: Ron Highfield. *Wardrobe supervisor*: Lesley Vanderwalt. *Original music*: Neil Hannan, Jan Preston. *Lyrics*: Deryn Cooper, Arthur Baysting. *Vocals*: Beaver and the Country Flyers, Bunny Walters. *Sound*: Graham Morris, Don Reynolds, Brian Shennan.

Cast

Ken Blackburn (Bob Warner), Deryn Cooper (Sandra Ray), Alan Jervis (Vic Shaw), Grant Tilly (Phil Barrett), Bill Johnson (Mike Campbell), Arthur Wright (Les Simpson), Kevin J. Wilson (Policeman), Glenis Levestam (Alice Barrett), Heather Lindsay (Rita Warner), Bob Harvey (Stephen Douglas), Jim Macfarlane (Boxing manager), Wendy Macfarlane (Motel manageress), Mike Bajko (Young man), Christine Lloyd (Waitress), Peter Rowell (Youth), Rene Hall (Public relations girl), Bob Harvey (Stephen Douglas), with Don Sutherland, Alan Graham, Graham Sutherland, Darcy Newson, Trevor Reynolds, Garrick Workman, Robert Williams, Maurice Oliver, Errol Vincent and with Monty Betham, Alesana Sua, the Wanganui Axeman's Association, Rev. Bob Peck, the Ohakune Brass Band and D.J. Rocky O'Toole as themselves.

In rural Carlton the barometer, Big Red, indicates the progress of the Progressive Association's fundraising campaign, established to attract tourists and industry. Bob, President of the Association, encourages gym owner Vic to import a city masseuse to pep up the town's image. Sandra wants a quiet life but soon finds the Carlton men in general, and Bob in particular, on the prowl to press her into parlour-style service. The wives retrench and prepare for battle. At a celebration dance Sandra's boogie with Phil adds significantly to his muddled passions and her unpopularity. Then all hell breaks loose when the cop finds Bob naked and Sandra topless at the gym parlour. In despair Phil destroys the massage room. Bob and committee absolve themselves from blame with Sandra as their scapegoat. As she drives out of town Bob and his cronies stand in the road with the advertising manager planning the promotional film they hope will put Carlton on the map.

Skin Deep deftly satirises small town hypocrisy, conformity and capacity for exploitation using the Western device of the outsider as a catalyst showing up the community's values. The townsfolk want to ape city life, from private sexual practices to the public arena of the National Government's Think Big projects. Although many foibles are scrutinised, the inarticulate longing and rage stirred by the male libido figure most. The narrative is acutely observed, economically scripted and rich in familiar, documentary detail. Revealed are the tedium beneath the bleak facade of good citizenship and gung-ho communal bliss ('We know how to make our own fun here'), where men and boys follow obsessive athletic pursuits and 'girls' make the tea. Skin Deep is bleak and laced with irony. Bob, for example, looks rapaciously for extra-marital excitement while his wife, scantily-clad as she enjoys painting the phallic barometer (Bob calls his penis 'Big Red' when propositioning Sandra), is a much more willing sexual partner than the world-weary woman from the city.

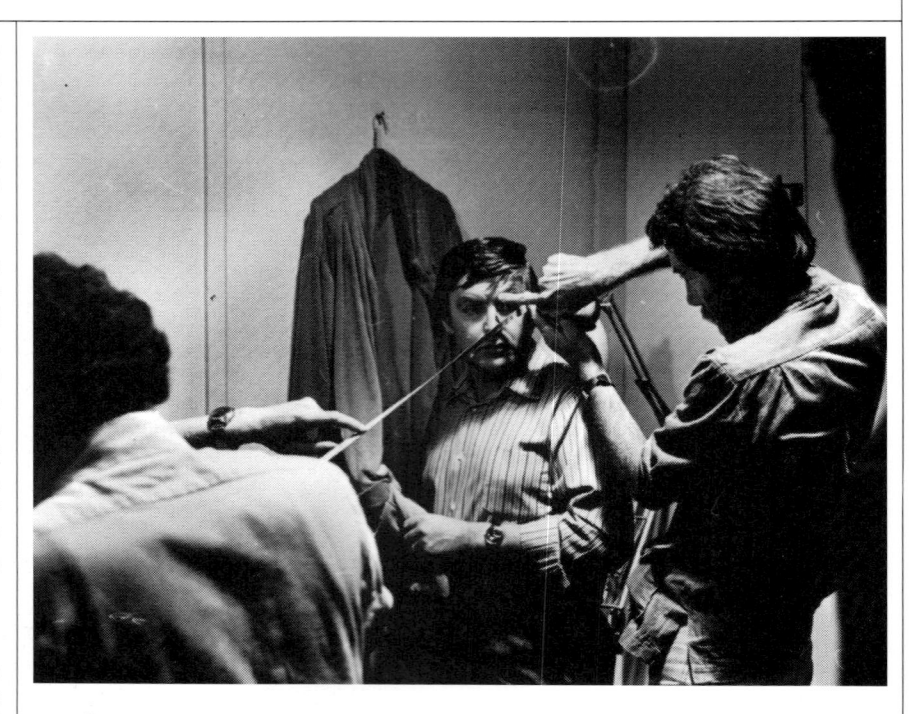

Geoff Steven directing Grant Tilly (Phil Barrett). Courtesy of Geoff Steven and the Stills Collection, New Zealand Film Archive.

The opening has Monty Betham shadow boxing in front of the gym window that at the end is smashed by Phil. Rich in images of illusion and mirror-gazing, the film underlines self-deception, hypocrisy and exploitation. The only character to see through the facade is streetwise Sandra. Although she too is exposed for her romanticised, city-dweller's view of small town New Zealand, she at least displays some wisdom in her assertion that massage 'goes deeper than skin—it should get into your mind as well as your body.'

Geoff Steven developed his idea from a three-screen video presentation on Raetihi, **Aspects of a Small Town**, made for the Auckland City Art Gallery in 1976. **Skin Deep** was the Interim Film Commission's first feature project. Many involved in the production were new to feature-making (John Maynard says in *Cowboys of Culture* 'We were making it up as we went along.') but the end result is of a quality that belies their inexperience. *Variety* (4 October 1978) said, 'As a work of art it is New Zealand's long-awaited breakthrough film.' HM

1980 Asian Film Festival: Mitra Award for Best Depiction of a Small Town.

MIDDLE AGE SPREAD

Endeavour Entertainment and the New Zealand Film Commission in association with South Pacific Merchant Finance Ltd. © 1979. *Budget:* $120 000. *Locations:* Auckland, Avondale College. *Distributor:* Endeavour Productions. *Rating:* R13, June 1979. 16 mm. Colour. 97.5 mins.

Director: John Reid. *Producer:* John Barnett. *Screenplay:* Keith Aberdein. *Source:* Roger Hall, *Middle Age Spread*. *Lighting cameraman:* Alun Bollinger. *Camera operator:* Paul Leach. *Editor:* Michael Horton. *Production designer:* Gaylene Preston. *Wardrobe supervisor:* Pat Murphy, Liz Jowsey. *Music:* Stephen McCurdy. *Sound:* Craig McLeod, Don Reynolds, Brian Shennan.

Cast

Grant Tilly (Colin), Dorothy McKegg (Elizabeth), Peter Sumner (Reg), Bridget Armstrong (Isobel), Donna Akersten (Judy), Bevan Wilson (Robert), Kerry McGregor (Jane), John Linaker (Roddy), Sophie Perkins (Caroline), David Mahon (Stephen), Ian Watkin (Wrightson), John Atha (Macintosh), Yvonne Lawley (Miss Reidy), Bernard Moody (Mailman), Wiki Oman (Diana), Peter McCauley (Man in pub), staff and pupils of Avondale College, Auckland.

Colin, who has been promoted to Principal of his city high school, and his wife Elizabeth give a dinner party. Guests are Judy and Robert, who have recently reconciled after a separation, and neighbours Isobel and Reg. As the evening wears on present-day dramas, aired in increasingly hostile conversation, are interwoven with those of the past, shown in flashback. Colin's jogging, ostensibly undertaken to combat his increasing girth, is revealed as a cover for his love affair with guest Judy, a relief teacher at his school. Reg, a teachers' college lecturer who beds his students, reveals a massive ego that makes nonsense of his left-wing political pronouncements. Colin and Elizabeth learn their daughter is pregnant to Reg and Isobel's son. In the resulting furore Reg tells Robert of Judy and Colin's affair and the party breaks up in acrimony. Beaten in his efforts to break out of the straitjacket of middle age, Colin heaps his coffee with cream and sugar and suggests to his stunned wife they do the dishes.

Reflecting New Zealand's 1970s white, suburban middle-class, the film adaptation of *Middle Age Spread* is provocative, accurate, sad and funny. Made at a time when the dinner party, with its creaking conversations and predictable menus, had become

Grant Tilly (Colin) and Donna Akersten (Judy). Courtesy of the New Zealand Film Commission.

a funnel for middle-class social ritual, the film skewers the post-1960s pretensions of its trapped, ageing, self-deceiving characters. Colin's attempt to run away from the tedium of his life, summed up in the jogging metaphor, is as bleakly futile as Reg's sexual diversions and cynical political posturing, Elizabeth's immersion in domestic trivia, Isobel's endless cottage industry and Robert's clinging to old-fashioned 'virtues'. Only Judy retains anything of the free-spiritedness of youth, but duty sends her back to Robert and the prospect of a life without passion. For the teenagers whose passion has borne fruit, their parents' examples offer little in the way of hope. There is something to like in all the characters in their very credible human frailty. In particular Colin's sharp sense of irony enables him to salvage dignity from his mortification.

Keith Aberdein's adaptation, with advice from dramatist Roger Hall, is based on Hall's dialogue and characters (minor characters are added in the film). The opening out of settings, the addition of action to replace explanatory dialogue and an economical shooting style ensure the production is cinematic. The significant events have occurred before the dinner party begins, thus the narrative's movement is in revelation. There is pleasure in watching the revelations unfold and in being party to the consequences, although some of the flashbacks are unclearly signposted. The wit sparkles, with the script adding new jokes while retaining Roger Hall's excellent ear for caustic dialogue and capacity for the brilliant one-liner. Although the specifics of the film have dated, the underlying assumptions about middle age and the middle class retain some force.

Middle Age Spread was the first New Zealand feature telecast by the BBC. The film struck a chord with audiences in New Zealand and abroad. Hungarian film director Istvan Szabo was reported as asking John Reid, 'How can you know Hungarian life so well?' HM

1979

SONS FOR THE RETURN HOME

Pacific Films in association with The New Zealand Film Commission. *Postproduction assistance*: New Zealand National Film Unit. © 1979. *Budget*: approx. $420 000. *Locations*: London, Western Samoa, Wellington, Taupo. *Distributor*: New Zealand Film Commission. *Rating*: R16, October 1979. 35 mm. Colour. 117 mins.

Director: Paul Maunder. *Executive producer*: Don Blakeney. *Screenplay*: Paul Maunder. *Source*: Albert Wendt, *Sons For the Return Home*. *Director of photography*: Alun Bollinger. *Editor*: Christine Lancaster. *Art director*: Vincent Ward. *Costume designer*: Christine Hansen. *Music*: Malcolm Smith. *Sound*: Don Reynolds, Brian Shennan.

Cast
Uelese Petaia (Sione), Fiona Lindsay (Sarah), Moira Walker (Sione's mother), Lani Tupu (Sione's father), Amalamo Tanielu (Malie), Anne Flannery (Sarah's mother), Alan Jervis (Sarah's father), Malama Masina (Receptionist), Sean Duffy (Sarah's first love), Tony Groser (Headmaster), Peleti Lima (Sione aged 15), with Eric Kemys, Des Kelly, George Mxlanga, Richard Newman, Mark Prain, Don Selwyn, Fou Simpson, Wendell Sisnett, Bill Smith, Lesley Stevens, Debbie Tait, the people of Matautu Falealili village, Western Samoa, the staff and students of Wellington College, members of the Wesley Samoan Fellowship, Wellington Te Rangiita Marae, Taupo.

In the opening scene Sarah, a young palagi (European) New Zealander, hears people discuss racism in a London pub. In the penultimate scene she leaves the pub to join a group of protesters in Trafalgar Square. The rest of the story is told in flashbacks in three time frames. One shows scenes from Western Samoan Sione's childhood and his family's move to New Zealand when he is four. A second time frame details his relationship with Sarah, whom he meets while studying at Victoria University. The third shows Sione's return to Western Samoa with his parents after graduation. After spending the night with a local woman, Sione realises he must return to New Zealand even though Sarah has terminated her pregnancy and their relationship and has gone to England. Returning to his parents' new, palagi-style home, Sione disowns his mother when he learns she advised Sarah to have an abortion. He tears up the poems he has written for Sarah as he flies back to New Zealand.

This adaptation of Albert Wendt's novel (the first published novel by a Samoan), while toning down the novel's sexual explicitness, captures the mood of its times. The first New Zealand feature film about the effects on Pacific Islanders of their immigration, its depiction of personal and institutionalised racism is damning. As demonstrated through Sione's experiences, immigrants face racial prejudice, cultural dislocation, rootlessness, alienation and exile. Institutionalised racism is seen in the dramatisation of one of the Muldoon Government's infamous Dawn Raids, indiscriminately undertaken by police allegedly looking for overstayers (immigrants whose visas had expired). In their ignorance palagi New Zealanders are unable to distinguish between Pacific Islanders and indigenous Maori, while sexual jealousy plays a large part in the viciousness of the racism of young males. To survive, Sione remains aloof, initially resisting Sarah's overtures of friendship.

Back home in Western Samoa pressure from palagi culture is weakening traditional customs and provides no haven for the returning immigrant. The fallout from family dysfunction, caused in Sione's case by his mother's overweaning ambition and lack of insight (she thought her sons would be happy to return to their cultural roots after growing up in an alien land) and in Sarah's by her wealthy parents' failed and bitter marriage and her father's alcoholism, contributes to the final failure of Sione and Sarah to cement their relationship. In the fragments of information given about the couple's grandfathers there is also a sense that this failure is a legacy from the past. Left begging is the question why Sione's brother readily adapts, firstly to immigration and later to the return to Western Samoa, as he is thinly drawn.

The three time frames, which include flashbacks within flashbacks, cause some confusion in the narrative and there is a tendency to romanticise with soft focus and mood music. Nevertheless **Sons for the Return Home** is a compelling story with a wealth of social and historical information conveyed with an eye for documentary detail. **Sons for the Return Home** and **Goodbye Pork Pie** were the first New Zealand films to screen in the market at Cannes. HM

Uelese Petaia (Sione) and Fiona Lindsay (Sarah). *Courtesy of the New Zealand Film Commission.*

1980 Karlovy Vary Film Festival, Czechoslovakia: Best Actor, Uelese Petaia.

1980

LINCOLN COUNTY INCIDENT

Lincoln Films with financial assistance from the National Film Unit and Queen Elizabeth II Arts Council of New Zealand. Copyright date not recorded. *Budget*: Approx. $14 000. *Locations*: Provincial Council Chambers, Lincoln Studios, Castle Hill Station, Canterbury, Lincoln High School, Otahuna Estate. *Distributor*: T. Brittenden. *Rating*: G, May 1980. 16 mm. Colour. 47 mins.

Director and technical producer: Tony Brittenden. *Production assistant*: Rosemary Barnett. *Screenplay*: Tony Brittenden. *Director of photography*: Bob Brittenden. *Camera operator*: Bob Brittenden. *Editor*: Tony Brittenden. *Costume designer*: Rosemary Barnett. *Clapper loader/clawhammer guitar player*: Fluff the Wonder Cat. *Special effects*: David Foulkes. *Composer/conductor*: Dorothy Buchanan. *Sound*: Bob Brittenden.

Cast

Steven Trail (Narrator), Shane Simms (Samson Peabody-Jones), Cornelia Schaap (Bar girl), David Wright (Bartender), Stephen Meyer (Miner), Grant McPhie (Bandit leader), with Robin Alfeld, David Clark, Kathryn Stewart, Fluff the Wonder Cat, Hermione Kluk, Pablo Rickard, Stuart Foster, Ross Mills, Peter Townsend, Peter Lagan, Neil Grant, Lorraine Dawkins, Helen Burkes, Kathryn Guthrie, Belinda Harvey, Karen Nicholas, Robyn Terras, Janet Tweedie, Murray Alfeld, David Strange, Gregory Tucker, Bruce Jowsey, Geoff Mills, Brian Saxelby, Linda Bryant, Julie Foster, Sandra Holmes, Paula Kortegast, Theresa Kortegast, Patricia Neale, Frances Pluck, Jane Sheppard, Susan Sheppard, Joanne Tucker, Richard Taylor, Wendy Wason, Bruce Gledhill, Edmund Lee, Roy Strange, Ian Roberts, William B. Fraser, Peter Curtis, Ralph Douglass, Barry Gamble, Mark Holmes, Roger McLenaghan, Barry Moir, Roger Parr, Richard Strange, Stephen Ward, Brian Williams, Trevor Williams.

Edmund (Ted) Lee as a tall cowboy. Courtesy of Tony Brittenden. Photograph by David Scott.

New Mexico, Spring 1881. In search of adventure, velvet-suited itinerant Samson Peabody-Jones (aged 13) finds a map to a gold mine on the body of a prospector killed by Indians. Arriving in town he is threatened by heavies but faces them down. Next morning he sets out to find the mine and is followed by the hotel's bartender, who, spying on him, has seen the map. Outlaws waylay the bartender while Peabody-Jones meets the ghost of a friendly old miner who gives him gold and a package to be opened if he is ever in fear for his life. In town the outlaws take P-J's gold and map, threatening to kill him on their return at 6 o'clock if they find nothing at the mine. Opening the parcel while his guards sleep P-J and his pet hen find *The Yellow Pages* and a telephone. Phoning 'Dial-a-Cowboy' he enlists the assistance of Royce Rogers, the Lone Rangerette, Tonto, a posse of Indians and the Seventh Cavalry (Women's Division). After a long and bloody shoot-out P-J and the hen walk into a glorious sunset with the bar girl.

This spoof, Sergio Leone-style Western was planned in 1974 as a $350 10-minute piece to accompany the rock opera that Lincoln High School art teacher, Tony Brittenden, was planning as a school production. As the script grew the rock opera evaporated and over 100 staff, students and parents set to work on the mammoth task of making the film. The principal was cast as a whisky-swilling gambler. The woodwork department turned the school hall into a saloon, the clothing department made costumes and the composer-in-schools, Dorothy Buchanan, wrote a Morricone-style score for 60 musicians, many of them students. The film was shot in four months and Tony Brittenden took leave to finish and distribute it. Postproduction, aided by funding from the National Film Unit and the QEII Arts Council, and with a large input from the director's brother Bob, took some five years. (Some of the students in the cast had married by the time they saw the finished film.)

Issued with a warning that some people may be disturbed by the film's use of inoffensive language, **Lincoln County Incident** is a pastiche of allusions and clichés parodying Western conventions. The narrative begins as drama and ends as farce. Played as a dumb show and with all sound done post-sync, the film is enlivened by over 1000 sound effects. Synched dialogue is avoided by use of a voice-over narrator. Witty and ingenious, the film makes good use of montage, the stunts and performances are impressive and the production design, helped by the authenticity of the Castle Hill Station locations, is excellent. The film is dedicated to wonderful star performer Shane Simms, who died tragically in a car accident before postproduction was completed.

In 1980 **Lincoln County Incident** had a good run in New Zealand theatres and screened in Cannes at the MIP-TV market, where sales to France, Denmark and Sweden were a forerunner of continuing overseas interest. Enthusiastic reviews include the *Time Out Film Guide*'s description of it as 'an extremely polished comedy Western … full of charm.' HM

1980

SQUEEZE

Trilogic Film Productions with script development assistance from the Queen Elizabeth II Arts Council. © 1980. *Budget*: approx. $100 000. *Location*: Auckland. *Distributor*: Richard Turner. *Rating*: R18, May 1980. 16 mm. Colour. 79 mins.

Director and producer: Richard Turner. *Screenplay*: Richard Turner. *Director of photography*: Ian Paul. *Wardrobe*: Barker's Menswear, Man to Man Fashion, Pussy Footing, Jeanmakers, Sabra, Cue Fashions. *Editor*: Jamie Selkirk. *Music*: Andy Hagan, Morton Young. *Bands*: Toy Love, The Features, Street Player, Marching Girls. *Sound*: Cinema Sound.

Cast

Robert Shannon (Grant), Paul Eady (Paul), Donna Akersten (Joy), Peter Heperi (Riki), David Herkt (John), Faye Flegg (Kate), Eileen Swann (Linda), Arthur Wright (David), Lyn Robson (David's Wife), Sandy Gauntlett (Jeremy), Ian Westbury (Simon), Murray Gauntlett (Maureen), Martyn Sanderson (Paul's father), Dinah Russell (Paul's mother), Don Farr (Boss), Geoff Rivers, Keith Dent (Grant's pub mates), Yvette and Giselle (Girls at bus stop), Roger Monk (Young men in club), Jonathon Tidbull (Young man in hamburger bar), Andrew Short (Young man outside club), Sandra Jones (His girl), Bruce Weston (Jack the client), Jackie Dunn and Maggie Maxwell (Wives), Penn Hsieng (Japanese sailor), David Souter and David Arundel (Policemen), the Proud Scum (Three toughs).

While his parents hope he has a girlfriend, lonely post-office worker Paul wanders around Auckland city's night streets, ending up in a gay bar recently sensationalised in the press. He goes on to a gay nightclub with stranger Grant, a suited executive, and a group of gay men including lovers John, a university student, and Riki, a prostitute. Paul stays the night with Grant and has sex for the first time. A love affair develops and Paul, tired of his parents' homophobia, leaves home. Grant won't let Paul move in and Paul discovers he is engaged to Joy. Grant introduces Paul to Joy as his cousin. Paul flirts with the idea of becoming a prostitute, but instead begins a relationship with John. Grant is arrested in a public toilet frequented by gay men, but is not charged. Grant and Joy meet Paul by chance in a gay bar. Grant defends Paul against a bully and tells Joy that Paul was his lover. After thanking Grant, Paul leaves with John. Grant is left drinking alone in the bar. As the sun rises Paul and John pause in a park for a see-saw.

The script grew from actors workshopping personal experiences and the episodic plot, often more documentary than drama, veers towards didacticism. In long, slow scenes Paul and friends mooch the streets, drifting from club to pub. The red-lit bars are the night time home for the gays and a place of voyeuristic thrills for the straights. The lesbian/gay scene is both bitchy (there are several 'queen' stereotypes) and warm, but the heart-to-heart conversations sound like text book lessons on 'being gay in a repressive society'. Uneven performances (lines are often delivered as though read), the thinness of some of the characterisation (particularly the straight characters) and the looseness of the narrative structure (some scenes are fillers) give something of a home-movie look, but the main characters are convincing. Paul, at first vulnerable and fragile, rejects the exploitative Grant and finds strength in his committed, open relationship with John while Grant, in the increasingly painful dilemma of leading a double life, has to face the truth.

Richard Turner hoped in making the film to break 'the conspiracy of silence' about homosexuality. The Society for the Protection of Community Standards led by Patricia Bartlett campaigned against the film and although the New Zealand Film Commission denied Richard Turner finance on the grounds that **Squeeze** did not have marketing appeal, the film's press kit maintained money was denied because of the film's content.

Bold for its time, **Squeeze** is an important landmark in New Zealand's film history as its first gay-themed feature. The *Los Angeles Times* described it as 'perhaps the first feature anywhere to deal seriously with bisexuality'.* On the film's release the New Zealand Gay Rights movement criticised it for not being radical enough. Some of the songs on the soundtrack were released as singles. HM

Reference
* *The New Zealand Listener*, 1 August 1981.

The first New Zealand film poster to advertise a gay relationship. Courtesy of the New Zealand Film Commission.

1980

NUTCASE

Ardvaark Endeavour Productions in association with South Pacific Merchant Finance Ltd and the New Zealand Film Commission. *Location:* Auckland. *Distributor:* Family Fare Productions. *Rating:* G, May 1980. 35 mm, Colour. 49 mins.

Director: Roger Donaldson. *Producer:* John Barnett. *Production manager:* Warren Sellers. *Assistant director:* Michael Firth. *Screenplay:* Keith Aberdein, Ian Mune. *Director of photography:* Graeme Cowley. *Editor:* Mike Horton. *Art director:* Kai Hawkins. *Continuity:* Jackie Sullivan. *Wardrobe:* Melvine Clark. *Props:* Louise Doyle. *Grip:* Stuart Dryburgh. *Gaffer:* Alun Bollinger. *Make-up:* Lesley Vanderwalt. *Special effects:* Geoff Murphy. *Music:* Shade Smith. *FX music:* Schtung. *Sound:* Graham Morris.

Cast

Melissa Donaldson (Nikki), Peter Shand (Jamie), Aaron Donaldson (Crunch), Jon Gadsby (Chief Inspector Cobblestone), Nevan Rowe (Evil Eva), Ian Watkin (Godzilla), Michael Wilson (McLooney), Ian Mune (U-boat Commodore), Clyde Scott (Murphy), Jim Coates (Gribble).

The city of Auckland is being held to ransom by a gang of sinister agents who have planted a nuclear device in the core of Rangitoto, one of the city's volcanoes which, when fired, will reactivate the dormant volcanoes upon which the city is built. The gang is led by Evil Eva who, with her thuggish off-siders Godzilla and McLooney, has set the ransom at five million dollars, and who has put the police team out of action with Happy Chappy powder, a drug which causes laughing and dancing preventing them from following up the crime. At the same time a group of children use discarded electrical components to build an antigravity device in their hut hideout. When the device works, the children take it to an old house where coincidentally the gang are hiding out, and, frightened by a ferocious mask, drop the device and run off. Eva, Godzilla and McLooney find it and accidentally set it off, ending up stuck to the ceiling. They then manage to lose the firing mechanism for the nuclear device in a rubbish collection and go off after it, followed by the children who have returned to collect their invention. The gang in turn see the children on TV, and lay ambush and capture them. They tie up the children, then radio the captain of a U-boat, 'U2', waiting off-shore, and Evil Eva repeats her threat to blow up the city if the ransom is not paid. The children, however, manage to escape in the nick of time, and the chase continues to Takapuna Beach, where the U-boat is waiting. Driven off by reinforcements in the form of hundreds of other kids, one of Eva's henchmen falls on the firing mechanism for the nuclear device. Rangitoto begins to erupt, but the antigravity machine reverses the movement, Auckland is saved and the children are heroes.

Made as a vehicle for children's television and holiday theatrical release, **Nutcase** was the children's equivalent of **Wildman**. Zany, slapstick comedy, a real sense of the ridiculous and exploiting the well-established convention of lunatic police doing the dramatic driving, it is included here as it helps to identify the cadre of film-makers who were to be responsible for the development of mainstream New Zealand cinema. Despite the development throughout the previous few years, there was still only a small group of relatively experienced working film-makers. Balancing the need for funds, the need to produce viable and cost-effective film, and the need to provide experience for greater numbers of employees in the budding screen industry in productions like **Nutcase**, members of this group (including Barnett, Firth, Bollinger, Murphy, Dryburgh, Aberdein and Mune, and comics like Gadsby and Watkin) were at the centre of most major developments.

Nutcase is not a world beater. It has difficulties with dialogue and character which are not significantly reduced by the combination of volume and slapstick gags. A lack of experience shows in script and acting, and a sometimes distracting tendency to lead the audience too obviously into the gags. At the same time, there is strong evidence of the anarchic comic philosophies which were to drive some of the films of Geoff Murphy, and a sense of the ridiculous shared by most New Zealanders who were soon to enjoy New Zealand's most successful movie of the start of the new wave, Murphy's **Goodbye Pork Pie**. SE

Nevan Rowe (Evil Eva) and Ian Watkin (Godzilla). Courtesy of the New Zealand Film Commission.

Nambassa Festival

The Nambassa Trust with Dale Films with the assistance of the New Zealand Film Commission. A.k.a. Nambassa. Copyright date not recorded. Documentary. *Budget*: approx. $46 000. *Location*: Golden Valley, Waihi. Distributor: Nambassa Trust. *Rating*: GY, June 1980. 16 mm. Colour. 105.5 mins.

Directors: Philip Howe and Dale Farnsworth. *Producer*: Dale Farnsworth. *Photography*: John Earnshaw, Kevin Hayward, Chris Strewe, Alan Locke, Andy Roelants, Andy McAlpine. *Editor*: Philip Howe. *Stage lighting*: Jay McCoy. *Studio mix downs*: Dave Hurley. *Final film mix*: Video Lab. *Sound*: Graham Morris, Mike Westgate, David Tossman, Doug Jane.

Held on an 84 ha farm in Golden Valley, Waihi, in January 1979, the second Nambassa rock and alternative lifestyle three-day festival was organised by Nambassa Trust as part of their fundraising activities to further their alternative community. It was envisaged by principal organiser Peter Terry as providing a model of 'the co-operative village of a spiritual new age direction, nonsectarian, with education of ourselves and our wider community as our ultimate goal'.* The Nambassa Trust approached film-maker Dale Farnsworth to film the festival and a large crew was assembled to cover it, capturing the atmosphere, the music and the range of workshops and demonstrations on offer.

Following **Woodstock**, the 1970 Academy Award-winning documentary of the festival in August 1969 in the U.S., **Nambassa Festival** opens with vistas of empty farmland, quickly moving on to the invasion of the 50 000 spectators (25 000 were expected) negotiating narrow country roads, creating a traffic jam that turned the 16 km drive from Waihi to the site into a five hour ordeal. On site a young man, à la Woodstock, informs the crowd, 'There's a lot happening you know. It's so big. It's so big', and warns of a drug bust. People of all ages get into the spirit of the festival—listening to the music (more than 30 bands and individuals performed) and watching mime, dance and puppet theatre. Highlights include Split Enz, in harlequin attire, singing 'You and me we can do whatever we please' and Limbs Dance's lithe performance, shot in part from below, through a glass floor.

An early morning gathering at the Festival. *Courtesy of Dale Farnsworth.*

Whereas the music is central to **Woodstock** and is used often to back up sequences not showing the performers, in **Nambassa Festival** the montage of off-stage happenings, incidental and planned, uses the sounds captured with the images. This gives the film an interesting cinema verité feel as enthusiasts expound the virtues of saving whales, powering tractors with wood-burners, acupuncture, Hare Krishna, Christianity … At times image and sound are ironically counterpointed, as in the sequence where a woman preaches religion while nearby kids swing on tent ropes, absorbed in their own thoughts. Background colouring-in includes ample footage of preparing, cooking and eating food and toilet and showering sequences that attest as much to the ingenuity of the festival organisers (showers come via tin cans) as to the corporeal needs of the campers.

Five three-person crews battled fatigue and high winds that threw up camera-threatening dust to shoot some 20 hours of film. The first cut was 140 minutes in length. Lack of availability of the released 105.5 minute version, which includes interviews by Hamish Keith, meant that for this entry the 50 minute version cut for television was viewed. Performers include Golden Harvest, Schtung, Steve Tulloch, Cockroach, Acorns Puppets, Swami Satchidananda, Chapman and White, John Hore, Serendipity, Dragon Dance, Plague, Neville Purvis, Limbs Dance, Split Enz. The Australian Little River Band was the only group to refuse filming permission. HM

Reference
* The *New Zealand Herald*, 7 April 1979, section 2, p. 7.

1980

BEYOND REASONABLE DOUBT

Endeavour Productions with Fay, Richwhite and Co., Brierley Investments Ltd and Bob Jones in association with the New Zealand Film Commission. © 1980. *Budget*: $360 000. *Locations*: Auckland, Pukekawa. *Distributor*: Endeavour Productions. *Rating*: GA, August 1980. 35 mm. Colour. 129 mins. (Reviewed September, 1980. 127 mins).

Director: John Laing. *Producer*: John Barnett. *Screenplay*: David Yallop. *Source*: David Yallop, *Beyond Reasonable Doubt?* *Director of photography*: Alun Bollinger. *Camera operator*: Paul Leach. *Editor*: Michael Horton. *Art director*: Kai Hawkins. *Wardrobe supervisors*: Julie d'Lacey, Sian Jones. *Music*: Dave Fraser. *Vocals*: Eddie Low, The Chapta. *Sound*: Don Reynolds, Brian Shennan.

Cast

David Hemmings (Inspector Bruce Hutton), John Hargreaves (Arthur Allan Thomas), Tony Barry (Detective John Hughes), Martyn Sanderson (Len Demler), Grant Tilly (David Morris), Diana Rowan (Vivien Thomas), Ian Watkin (Kevin Ryan), Terence Cooper (Paul Temm), Bruno Lawrence (Pat Vesey), with Marshall Napier, John Bach, Bruce Allpress, Peter Hayden, Mark Hadlow, Dawn Blair, Harold Kissin, Laurie Dee, Desmond Locke, Allan Nixon, Tristan Amos, Michael Kent, Brian Saipe, Timothy Lee, Mike Gill, Ken Harris, Noel Appleby, Fred James, Norm Keesing, Arthur Wright, John Bullock, Marie Bullock, Paula Keenan, Helen Smith, Fiona Bunce, Susan Burberry, Pat Gott, Robert Shannon, Kate Harcourt, Heather Lindsay, Michael Booth, John Givins, John Batstone, Karl Bradley, Patrick Smythe, Alba, Philip Laing, Ian Harrop, Bill Johnston, Gil Cornwall, Bernard Moodie, Gray Syms, Lex Calder, Clyde Scott, Jack Bongard, Hazel Cole and 15 members of the Thomas family.

On 22 June 1970 Harvey and Jeanette Crewe were reported missing from their bloodstained Pukekawa farmhouse. After three months' intensive search their bodies were found in the Waikato River. **Beyond Reasonable Doubt** dramatises what followed as, with little to go on, police suspicion focused first on Jeanette's father, Len Demler, because of his apparent motive and apparent lack of concern for his missing daughter. The investigation shifts focus when police inspector Bruce Hutton, rounding up the district's 22 rifles, finds two which could have been the murder weapon. Ignoring evidence pointing to one local rifle owner with a reputation for violence, Hutton homes in on ingenuous farmer Arthur Thomas. Thomas's arrest, conviction and subsequent re-trial provide the rest of the narrative. In the final scene Thomas, after nine years in jail and with his marriage over, returns home on 17 December 1979 after being pardoned by Prime Minister Robert Muldoon.

In his investigative book David Yallop calls Thomas's prosecution 'a game where evidence was put in and taken out to serve one purpose: that Thomas was convicted' and the investigation 'one of the most crass, banal, amateur investigations ever undertaken in the country's history.' His screenplay follows the book with a carefully constructed view of justice wilfully miscarried. Leading the investigation Inspector Bruce Hutton displays corruption in police practice. Under his leadership lies are told, evidence is falsified and suppressed, witnesses are intimidated, the justice system is abused and cronyism is rife. The film notes that, at the conclusion of the re-trial, which was significant as the first in British Commonwealth legal history, Hutton was awarded a Certificate of Merit and promoted to Chief Inspector.

David Yallop's book set in motion the events leading to Thomas's eventual pardon. As the film's narrative unfolds drama and docudrama overlap, as when members of Thomas's family appear as themselves and in voice-over explanations. The narrative provides a careful selection of information from Yallop's painstaking investigation, telescoping complex details while providing enough to illuminate the Kafkaesque web being spun around Thomas. The restrained visual style of documentary realism makes for compelling viewing and the musical score, with songs from Eddie Low and The Chapta, is aptly spare and moody. There is the occasional lapse into 'telling' rather than 'showing', as in a prison visit scene. The landscape and people of rural New Zealand are well depicted, but at times the identity of characters in the large cast is not clear. In particular, the role of the group working to have Thomas freed is underplayed. Ends are tied up hurriedly because Thomas's pardon and release, which came fortuitously at the end of 1979, took place when **Beyond Reasonable Doubt** was in postproduction.

Benefiting from the immense public interest in the case, **Beyond Reasonable Doubt** was New Zealand's most successful commercial film until the release of **Goodbye Pork Pie**. Some overseas reviewers criticised it for lack of clarity and found the documentary style unsuited to the drama. HM

1982 Cognac Film Festival of Thrillers: Grand Prix.

John Hargeaves, centre (Arthur Allan Thomas). *Courtesy of the New Zealand Film Commission.*

GOODBYE PORK PIE

A.M.A. with the assistance of the New Zealand Film Commission, New Zealand United Corporation Ltd, New Zealand Railways, New Zealand Motor Corporation. © 1980. *Budget*: $350 000. *Locations*: New Zealand (Kaitaia to Invercargill). *Distributor*: Pork Pie Productions. *Rating*: R13, October 1980. (Amended GA Contains Coarse Material, January 1985). 35 mm. Colour. 106 mins.

Director: Geoff Murphy. *Producers*: Geoff Murphy, Nigel Hutchinson. *Screenplay*: Geoff Murphy, Ian Mune. *Director of photography*: Alun Bollinger. *Camera operator*: Graeme Cowley. *Editor*: Michael Horton. *Art directors*: Kai Hawkins, Robin Outterside. *Wardrobe supervisor*: Robin Murphy. *Special effects*: Andy Grant. *Stunt driver*: Peter Zivkovic. *Music*: John Charles. *Additional music*: Street Talk. *Musical direction*: Dave Fraser. *Sound*: Don Reynolds, Jay Berryman, Annie Collins.

Cast

Tony Barry (John), Shirley Gruar (Sue), Kelly Johnson (Gerry), Claire Oberman (Shirl), Bruno Lawrence (Mulvaney), Stephen Tozer (Traffic cop), John Bach (Snout), Frances Edmond (Annette), with Geoff Murphy, Don Selwyn, Clyde Scott, Ian Watkin, Marshall Napier, Jackie Lowitt, Shirley Dunn, Paki Cherrington, Christine Lloyd, Maggie Maxwell, John Ferdinand, Phil Gordon, Adele Chapman, Bill Juliff, Liz Simpson, Alan Wilks, Paul Watson, Timothy Lee, Michael Woolf, Andrew Dungan, Frank Prythetch, Doug Aston, Charles Barlow, Len Bernard, Mike Booth, Norris Bruce, Bill Carson, Norman Fairley, Norman Fletcher, John Galvin, Des Kelly, Max Kennard, Melissa Lawrence, Chris Lines, Linus Murphy, Mathew Nieuwlands, Danny O'Connel, Paul Paino, David Pottinger, Keith Richardson, Roy Sanders, Gene Saunders, Ged Sharp, Peter Sledmere, Kevin Simpson, The Wizard, Brian Ward, Jim Woodfine.

In Kaitaia unemployed 19-year-old Gerry Austin finds a wallet and using its driver's licence as ID hires a yellow Mini Minor. An impulsive joyride takes him to Auckland where he is saved from a traffic cop's questioning by John, a man on his way to Invercargill to renew his relationship with estranged partner, Sue. At a loose end, Gerry decides to drive John to Invercargill. They pick up hitchhiker Shirl and after a misunderstanding over payment for petrol they are running from the law. An all-out chase, involving New Zealand's traffic department and, by Invercargill, its army, sees the protagonists arrested at different points along the way and the Mini reduced to a shell. Adventures in transit include encounters with off-beat, shady characters. Meanwhile Gerry and Shirl strike up a relationship of sorts and John acknowledges the depth of his feelings for Sue.

A comic, buddy/road movie, **Goodbye Pork Pie** uses irreverent humour to gain sympathy for the inarticulate Kiwi blokes while the women function as irritating plot devices. As the men become folk heroes their surface devil-may-care is undercut with hints of the bleaker side to anarchic freedom. But although neither get away with their rebellion, benefits accrue. Gerry, self-proclaimed leader of the 'Blondini Gang' and seen initially as callow, arrogant and misogynistic, gains depth as, in the course of the chase, he learns about commitment and loyalty. His assumption of a series of names signifies a search for identity that is fulfilled by commitment to the quest. John, in running from society's expectations of male achievement, also learns about commitment.

In celebrating 1960s counterculture hedonism the film playfully exploits audience disdain for authority and support for the underdog while avoiding the violence common to the chase genre. The many stunts are well-executed and the music enhances the up-beat tone. **Goodbye Pork Pie** is stylistically accomplished, with inventive camera work and editing. Dramatic tension is weakened by the loosely episodic nature of the quest and the dim lighting in some interior scenes obscures detail. Most working on **Goodbye Pork Pie** were learning the craft of film-making on the job. Several of the production roles were taken by director Geoff Murphy's family and friends, who became known as 'The Murphia', and some production crew, including Murphy, also had small roles.

Despite charges of anarchy, lawlessness, tastelessness, drug-taking and 'explicit' sex scenes (it wasn't until later that commentators wrote of the film's sexism), the film was a huge box office success at home, with one Auckland audience of 1900 giving it a standing ovation. It was the first New Zealand film to recover its costs from the domestic market alone. **Goodbye Pork Pie** and **Sons for the Return Home** were the first New Zealand features to screen in the market at Cannes. **Goodbye Pork Pie** altered New Zealanders' reluctance to watch locally made movies and, in proving that a local film could pay its way in the home market, was a breakthrough film for the industry. With its success, cinema was well and truly established as a vital part of New Zealand's popular culture. HM

John Bach (Snout). Courtesy of the New Zealand Film Commission.

WILDCAT

1981

Vanguard Films for the Combined Council of Delegates, New Zealand Timberworkers' Union. Made with the assistance of the Queen Elizabeth II Arts Council. *Budget*: $15 000. *Rating*: GA, May 1981. 16 mm. Colour. 70 mins.

Directed, produced, written and filmed: Rod Prosser, Russell Campbell, Alister Barry. *Additional photography*: Alun Bollinger. *Music*: Stefan Tyler-Wright. *Composer*: Bo Diddley, 'Timber'. *Additional sound*: Lee Tamahori. *Library footage*: Television New Zealand.

In the period following World War II New Zealand, as many other countries, became a site for industrial tension as a new balance of power was fought out among governments, employers and workers. On occasion a fourth element was added where unions, or groups within unions, ended up in opposing camps. The timberworkers' action of late 1977 was one such situation, where a group within the New Zealand Timber Workers' Union formed the Combined Council of Delegates to protest the leadership of the Timber Workers' Union. The consequent strikes and stopworks were later described by leader Willie Wilson, when defining 'wildcat' in a meeting where the customary meaning of 'illegal strike' was unacceptable, as 'the expression of the rank and file workers'. **Wildcat** documents the development of the timber workers' struggle from August 1977 to the beginning of 1978 when the dispute went to the industrial court. Structurally the film extends that time by depending extensively on interviews conducted after the court action, but the focus is very clearly on the period of the wildcat strikes and the timber workers who participated.

Stylistically and in its selected point of view, **Wildcat** is a trailblazer for the later documentary **Patu!** While the subject matter is quite different, the same sense of having to provide an alternative history to that of the establishment presses and screens is clear. The narrative unfolds with the camera behind the lines of the Combined Council of Delegates. That was the location where the then Minister of Forests, the Hon. Venn Young, said 'avowed communists pitting unionist against unionist' could be found. Similarly, the press described the situation with headlines like 'Small Timber Towns Enveloped In Fear Of Communist Rebels'. The consequence of that camera position, however, is a different story, told from the point of view of the timber workers themselves, and that perspective is both searing and effective in restating the balance of argument.

Russell Campbell, one of the three film-makers in the collective which constructed the film, noted that because of a tight budget—the Combined Council of Delegates had raffled a car to raise money for the film, and a grant was obtained from the QEII Arts Council—scripting was exceedingly tight. Interviews were carefully planned, the archival footage from Television New Zealand tightly edited and the only unscripted footage came from a shot of union leader Ray Hamilton pushing over the camera operator, an event which was fortuitously and dramatically captured by a second camera. Additional footage came from leading cameraman Alun Bollinger who, acting as a still photographer's assistant, concealed a 16 mm camera in a shoulder bag and recorded footage on site despite the hostility of management.

What is significant about **Wildcat** is not just its ability to offer a convincing alternative view, but the fact that it was made by experienced film-makers who were concerned that the discourse of the film itself should match the material they were covering. The result is a documentary feature which is dramatically gripping, visually entertaining and which provides a significantly cinematic gloss on a major event in the history of class struggle in New Zealand. SE

A forestry worker preparing a log for removal. Courtesy of Russell Campbell and Vanguard Films.

1981

SMASH PALACE

Aardvark Films Ltd in association with the New Zealand Film Commission. © 1981. *Budget*: $1.2 million. *Locations*: Horopito, Ohakune, National Park. *Distributor*: Aardvark Films Ltd. *Rating*: R16, September 1981. 35 mm. Colour. 108 mins.

Director and producer: Roger Donaldson. *Associate producer*: Larry Parr. *Screenplay*: Roger Donaldson. *Director of photography*: Graeme Cowley. *Camera operator*: Paul Leach. *Editor*: Michael Horton. *Art director*: Reston Griffiths. *Wardrobe supervisor*: Annabel Blackett. *Music*: Sharon O'Neill. *Sound*: Michael Westgate, Brian Shennan, Don Reynolds, Patrick Monaghan, Derek Morton.

Cast

Bruno Lawrence (Al Shaw), Anna Jemison (Jacqui Shaw), Greer Robson (Georgie Shaw), Keith Aberdein (Ray Foley), Desmond Kelly (Tiny), Sean Duffy (Frank), Lyn Robson (Linda), Margaret Umbers (Rose), Roy Sturch (Car crash driver), Jazz the dog (Buick), with Bryan Johnston, Terence Donovan, Dick Rollo, Ian Barber, Ray Littlewood, Doug McKenzie, Don Lee, Mike Beytagh, Brian Chase, Ross Davies, Colin Fredricksen, Thomas King, Chris Pasco, Evan Sommerville, Frank Taylor, Mike Wiggins.

Bruno Lawrence (Al Shaw). Courtesy of the New Zealand Film Commission.

In his wrecking yard, Smash Palace, Al Shaw works on his racing car, refusing to discuss sale of the yard with his unhappy French wife Jacqui. She begins a relationship with Al's best friend Ray, a local cop. After an argument Al rapes Jacqui and she leaves with their daughter, Georgie. The relationship deteriorates further when Jacqui takes a non-molestation order out against Al and when he is brutally beaten by a cop seeking revenge for a past incident. Al kidnaps Georgie, faking a fatal accident. They go bush, but return to town when she becomes ill. Cornered in the hubcap room at Smash Palace, Al hands over Georgie in return for Ray. Al forces Ray to drive onto a railway line in the Model A Ford he has restored for him. Al enjoys his 'victory' as an approaching train passes behind them on another track. Jacqui and Georgie wait at the car graveyard.

Having met Al as a successful grand-prix driver, Jacqui saw his inheritance of Smash Palace as their ticket to the world. To emotionally inarticulate Al, Smash Palace is the world. Horopito's roads offer him the thrill of fast driving, but for Jacqui they lead nowhere. Constant visual references to crashed and rusting cars represent the Shaws' disintegrating relationship and the 'Palace' reference ironically contrasts Al's idea of a palace with Jacqui's, whose European and feminine sensibilities baffle him. As in **Sleeping Dogs** and **Goodbye Pork Pie** the phallic connotations of the gun are not wasted, and even a pool game underscores male rivalry for 'ownership' of a woman. Al sees no need to make his relationship work as to him marriage is a lottery. Georgie, the pawn in the tug-of-love, watches all this with increasing panic. Sympathy is initially built for the victims of Al's male ego, but in scenes where he is beaten by a policeman and where lust persuades Jacqui to neglect her duties as a mother, sympathy is elicited for him as the wronged party.

Al's spiralling obsession is charted in some great cinematic moments produced by an imaginative script and excellent performances, especially those of laconic Bruno Lawrence and ten-year-old Greer Robson. The observational style effectively sketches in local detail. Long racing sequences provide a visceral visual correlative to Al's increasingly tense emotional journey and unexpected moments of humour lighten the tone. Sharon O'Neill's lyrics provide a bluesy edge while the spare score underlines the characters' desolation.

Smash Palace was successful at home and abroad, although not without detractors criticising it for misogyny. In the U.S. critics compared it favourably to **Kramer vs Kramer**. In *The New Yorker* Pauline Kael described it as 'amazingly accomplished' and *The New York Times* chose it as one of the year's ten best films. It won an international reputation for its director, Australian Roger Donaldson, who, soon after its completion, moved to Los Angeles but rejected American offers of a re-make as 'bloody silly'. Nude shots of Bruno Lawrence and the rape scene were cut for the film's first New Zealand television screening and not restored when it re-screened as tribute to the late actor in 1995.
HM

1982 Manila Film Festival: Best Actor, Bruno Lawrence.

1981

PICTURES

Pacific Films in association with the New Zealand National Film Unit, the New Zealand Film Commission and Broadbank Corporation Ltd. © 1981. *Overseas festival screenings*: 1981. *New Zealand release*: 1983. *Budget*: $460 000. *Locations*: Dunedin, Alexandra, Queenstown, Oamaru, Wanganui. *Distributor*: Pacific Film Productions Ltd. *Rating*: G, October 1981. 35 mm. Colour. 87 mins.

Director: Michael Black. *Producer*: John O'Shea. *Screenplay*: Robert Lord and John O'Shea, from an idea by Michael Black. *Director of photography*: Rory O'Shea. *Camera operator*: Michael Hardcastle. *Editor*: John Kiley. *Art director*: Russell Collins. *Costume designer*: Gwen Kaiser. *Special effects*: Kevin Chisnall. *Music*: Jan Preston. *Players*: Jan Preston, The Auckland String Quartet. *Sound*: Graham Morris, Geoff Shepherd, Brian Shennan.

Cast

Kevin J. Wilson (Alfred Burton), Peter Vere-Jones (Walter Burton), Helen Moulder (Lydia Burton), Elizabeth Coulter (Helen Burton), Terence Bayler (John Rochfort), Matiu Mareikura (Ngatai), Ken Blackburn (James Gilchrist), John Callen (Casey), Frank Edwards (Payton), Peter Hayden (Algy), the Maori People of Ati Hau-Nui-Apapa-Rangi Whanganui (Villagers), with Ron Lynn, Suzanne Furner, Louise Petherbridge, Murray Hutchinsin (Photographer), Winiata Tapa (Ploughman), Peter Wiari (Whiti), Billy Te Hore (Wiremu), Michael Bennett (Police sergeant), Honey Thompson (Girl in bush), Maria Toho (Girl at whare), George Williamson (Old soldier), Charles Mareikura, Robert Te Huia, John Tuka, Alf Te Koari, Lala Tururangi (Canoeists).

As the New Zealand Land Wars end government troops fight to destroy Maori resistance. Maori sabotage the efforts of surveyors preparing for a railway through the North Island. Dunedin photographer Walter Burton, commissioned to travel with railways surveyors to record their work, is refused permission by the Colonial Office to display his revealing photographs, including wretched Maori prisoners in chains just before execution, judged to show the colony in a bad light. Walter is joined by his brother Alfred, also a photographer, but cannot settle to the studio portraits that would earn him a living and a good reputation. He takes to drink. After photographing scenic wonders Alfred travels to Wanganui with railways supervisor Rochfort, an alcoholic womaniser contemptuous of the indigenous people. On their return to Dunedin Maori guide Ngatai is jailed as a troublemaker. Alfred is feted for his picturesque photographs of Maori and for saving the life of Rochfort, imprisoned by a Maori tribe after trying to seduce one of their women. Walter defiantly displays his photographs and, after paid thugs destroy his plates, commits suicide. Alfred becomes an elocution teacher. A postscript notes the Burton brothers' glass plates are decomposing in Wellington's National Museum.

This story of the founding fathers of photography in New Zealand is a fictionalised biography fabricating the circumstances of its story (the photographs in the film are fictions) to illuminate attempts by the Colonial Office to increase the settler population while dispossessing and slaughtering the indigenous people. Powerless to show the truth in his photographs, Walter escapes in drink then death. Alfred initially supports the system and his scenic photographs are appropriated by colonists to extol the virtues of New Zealand's landscape. A dream where pakeha and Maori roles are reversed brings home settler savagery, but Alfred changes profession rather than protest. Ngatai, acting as a guide to both brothers, provides a Maori perspective. He is happy to take the settlers' money while waging his own guerrilla war, but with the loss of his land life loses meaning.

Five years were spent collecting the period props, which included the Burton brothers' actual cameras and more than 500 costumes. In shooting style, musical score and production design **Pictures** recreates Victorian formality and rigidity (some critics have described the film as ponderous and stilted), while exposing its violent consequences. The idea that things are not what they seem is constantly underlined by the constructions of still photography and of the film itself. Alfred's hinted relationship with Walter's wife Helen is a structural weakness. Having encouraged audience speculation about how the relationship will develop, concluding on-screen information reveals that Alfred lived to a ripe old age while giving no news of Helen.

New Zealand reviewers were generally positive, hailing it as the first local film to make a coherent social statement, and the London *Daily Telegraph* nominated it one of the year's ten best. Sandra Coney's alternative view in *Broadsheet* (August 1983) called **Pictures** a 'breathtaking act of artistic dishonesty' that 'distorted history to pakeha advantage' by creating a 'fiction of the good pakeha who cared about the Maoris ... while giving it the validity of truth by overlaying it on real events.' HM

1981 Moscow Film Festival: Press Award for Humanism.
1982 Asian Film Festival: Best Music, Best Editing.

Peter Vere-Jones (Walter Burton) in potential difficulty. Courtesy of the New Zealand Film Commission.

RACE FOR THE YANKEE ZEPHYR

1981

The poster from the film. Courtesy of John Barnett.

Endeavour Productions Ltd and F.G.H. Film Consortium Pty Ltd. Financed from New Zealand and Australia. A.k.a. *Treasure of the Yankee Zephyr*. Copyright date not recorded. *Budget*: $6 million. *Location*: Queenstown. *Distributor*: International Film Distributors. *Rating*: GY (Contains coarse language), November 1981. 35 mm. Cinemascope. Colour. 111 mins.

Director: David Hemmings. *Producers*: Antony I. Ginnane, John Barnett, David Hemmings. *Executive producers*: John Daly, Michael Fay, William Fayman. *Associate producer*: Brian W. Cook. *Screenplay*: Everett de Roche. *Director of photography*: Vincent Monton. *Camera operator*: Freddie Cooper. *Editor*: John Laing. *Production designer*: Bernard Hides. *Costume designer*: Aphrodite Kondos. *Special effects*: Kevin Chisnall. *Stunts*: Dennis Hunt, Glen Boswell, Fiona McConchie. *Helicopter co-ordinator*: Don Spary. *Composer/conductor*: Brian May, Dave Fraser. *Sound*: Graham Morris, Don Reynolds, Derek Morton, Brian Shennan.

Cast
Ken Wahl (Barney), Lesley Ann Warren (Sally), Donald Pleasence (Gibbie), George Peppard (Brown), Bruno Lawrence (Barker), Grant Tilly (Collector), Harry Rutherford-Jones (Harry), Robert Bruce (Barman), with Tony Sparks, Clark Walkington, Frank Taurua, Steve Nicolle, Dick Jones, Dennis Hunt (Henchmen).

Helicopter deer hunters Barney (young, handsome, American), and Gibbie (old, unfit, alcoholic) are flying over the Southern Alps when Gibbie falls into a remote lake. There he discovers the wreck of a DC3, the Yankee Zephyr, that went down during World War II while carrying $50,000,000 worth of gold bullion for operational aid in the Pacific. In town Gibbie sells the medals he has taken from the plane and borrows money from his daughter Sally so he and Barney can salvage the wreck. Businessman-thug Brown and his henchmen snatch the medal dealer and follow Barney, Sally and Gibbie into the mountains. In the ensuing chase Gibbie is captured, then dramatically rescued. The chase continues by jetboat, with Barney delighted that Sally is happy to use skills she learned as Auckland's 1976 Jetboat Champion. On finding the plane laden with gold bars the threesome cut it free. The squabbling henchmen sink with the plane and Gibbie finds a box of gold bars on shore. Brown emerges from the lake calling for help.

Made with U. S. cinema audiences in mind, the film has a cartoon spirit and a blithe disregard for logic (a $50,000,000 haul lying untouched for 40 years?). Clichés of the action/chase genre abound. Shared danger loosens up the prim, repressed Sally (she shrieks a lot) and brings a small measure of emotional depth to heroic action man, Barney. To repeated strains of 'Beautiful Beautiful Brown Eyes' romance flourishes in this fertile ground and on-screen information at the end confirms happy endings — Sally and Barney marry and set up a Helijet tours business; Gibbie, meanwhile, uses his share of the loot to buy The Donkey Club in Port Said. Not mentioned is whether Gibbie's liver holds out long enough for him to enjoy his new-found wealth. The bad guys, accompanied by military-style music, ham it up as goons with guns who can't hit a single target. Humour is slapstick and everyone talks in speech bubbles. Most unsuccessful of the caricatures is Pleasence's Gibbie, whose alcoholism and wheezing cackle are unfunny. A British actor, Pleasence tries for the New Zealand accent with little success.

The shoot involved a large second unit (also directed by David Hemmings) and, in the spirit of the genre, most of the film's ingenuity and energy occur in the numerous stunts, chases and explosions. The helicopter sequences are particularly well-shot. The most successful 'character' is the landscape and the beauties of Queenstown and Fiordland are exploited to the full. In this respect **Race for the Yankee Zephyr** helped establish New Zealand's reputation as an excellent film-making location.

At the time the film was made co-productions such as this were regarded by some as likely to contribute to the destruction of the New Zealand film industry. Others believed the employment of local crews on such co-productions would help build a more substantial infrastructure for the industry. HM

1982. First International Knokkeheist Film Festival, Belgium: Best Actor, Donald Pleasence.

THE SCARECROW

1982

Oasis Films Ltd and the New Zealand National Film Unit in conjunction with the New Zealand Film Commission. A.k.a. *Klynham Summer*. © 1981. *Budget*: $650 000. *Location*: Thames. *Distributor*: Kerridge Odeon. *Rating*: GA (Contains coarse language), February 1982. 35 mm. Colour. 87.5 mins.

Director: Sam Pillsbury. *Producer*: Rob Whitehouse. *Associate producer*: Sam Pillsbury. *Executive producers*: Douglas Eckhoff (National Film Unit), Ross Jennings (Television New Zealand). *Screenplay*: Michael Heath, Sam Pillsbury. *Source*: Ronald Hugh Morrieson, *The Scarecrow*. *Director of photography*: James Bartle. *Editor*: Ian John. *Production designer*: Neil Angwin. *Costume designer*: Glenys Hitchins. *Music*: Andrew Hagen, Morton Wilson, Phil Broadhurst. *Sound*: Don Reynolds, Brian Shennan, Jamie Selkirk, David Keane.

Cast

Jonathan Smith (Ned), Tracy Mann (Prudence Poindexter), Daniel McLaren (Les), John Carradine (Salter), Bruce Allpress (Uncle Athol), Philip Holder (Constable Len Ramsbottom), Stephen Taylor (Poindexter), Des Kelly (Pa), Anne Flannery (Ma), Denise O'Connell (Angela Potroz), Jonathan Hardy (Charlie Dabney), Martyn Sanderson (Ned's adult voice), Greer Robson (Lynette), Roy Billing (Mr Potroz), Sarah Smuts-Kennedy (Daphne Moran), Yvonne Lawley (Miss [sic] Fitzherbert), Doug Hastings (Channing Fitzherbert), Simon Phillips (Chote Fitzherbert), Elizabeth McRae (Usherette), Ted Coyle (Alf Yerby), Elizabeth Moody (Mabel Collinson), Mark Hadlow (Sam Finn), Greg Naughton (Victor Lynch), Paul Owen-Lowe (Jim Coleman), with Margaret Blay, Duncan Smith, Bill Walker, John Kempt, Norm Forsey, Anna Marbrook, Sarah Nathan.

Small town N. Z., 1950s. In rapid montage a woman's murder is intercut with a theft as Ned and friend Les steal hens from school bully, Victor Lynch. The Lynch gang want revenge, and, like Les, lust after Ned's sister, Pru. Also lusting after Pru are Len Ramsbottom (the local cop), Chote Fitzherbert (the son of wealthy eccentrics), Charles Dabney (the undertaker) and Hubert Salter, an old itinerant magician revealed through Ned's narration as the necrophiliac killer whose handiwork was displayed in the opening scene. While Ned, Les, Pru and her friend Angela avoid the Lynch gang, Salter murders the music teacher and her simple-minded admirer. After killing and raping Angela he disappears, resurfacing as Pru's kidnapper. In a scuffle with Pru's brother Herbert Salter dies and his body is dumped. Len and Ned rescue Pru from the undertaker's. They are kissed by two girls.

The Scarecrow details the rite of passage of pre-pubescent Les and Ned and sexually aware Pru, showing up adults as criminally irresponsible. Outsider Salter epitomises sexual deviance, but his appetites merely magnify the corruption and degeneracy of other Klynham males. Although Pru and Les recognise the evil that others embrace, Ned and Les are also potentially corrupt. The adult women might be expected to offer protection and guidance, but eccentric Mrs Fitzherbert is a conspirator in her husband's attempt to rape Pru while Ma Poindexter is too buried in domesticity to notice.

The film is less bleak than Ronald Hugh Morrieson's novel set in the 1930s — there is more laughter and colour in the Heath/Pillsbury Poindexter house and the family is less grindingly poor. The visibility of sex and masturbation are toned down while the gothic atmosphere of excess and black humour are maintained. While the camera depicts Pru as a luscious sex object as much for the benefit of the audience as her pursuers, the deviance and degeneracy of the Klynham men is conveyed through distancing caricature. This ambiguity of tone generates readings that both book and film are misogynistic, despite the rationale that events are seen as filtered through Ned's mind with the wisdom of hindsight. The 'thriller' element is not in wondering 'whodunit' but in watching a consummate cosmopolitan 'sexo' draw Klynham's citizens into his ghastly web. Salter's mesmeric sexual appeal to Pru when he holds his knife against her saying, 'Behold, my child, its length. See how its razor-sharp edge would sink into your lush virginal body …' is faithfully recreated and although Salter gets his just desserts we are perhaps meant to derive a shudder of perverse pleasure from his deviance.

The narrative is at times confusing and disjointed. Consummate Hollywood character actor John Carradine, who received $20 000 of the film's budget, is well-supported by the large cast, although the Lynch gang look too old for their roles. The atmospheric musical score and cinematography are excellent (50% of the film was shot at night) and the depiction of 1950s small town New Zealand, puritanical on the surface and depraved to its depths, is realised in carefully designed detail.

The Scarecrow was the first New Zealand feature selected for the Director's Fortnight at the Cannes Film Festival. HM

1982 Cannes Film Festival: Official Selection, Director's Fortnight.
Mystfest, Italy: Best Ensemble Acting.

Jonathan Smith (Ned Poindexter). Courtesy of the New Zealand Film Commission.

1982

BATTLETRUCK

Battletruck Films Ltd. © 1981. *Budget*: $1.5 million. *Locations*: Alexandra, Central Otago. *Distributor*: International Film Distributors. *Rating*: GA, March 1982. 35 mm. Colour. 92 mins.

Director: Harley Cokliss. *Producers*: Lloyd Phillips, Rob Whitehouse. *Screenplay*: Irving Austin, Harley Cokliss, John Beech, from a story by Michael Abrams. *Director of photography*: Chris Menges. *Camera operator*: Mike Hardcastle. *Editor*: Michael Horton. *Production designer*: Gary Hansen. *Wardrobe supervisor*: Christine West. *Vehicle designer*: Kai Hawkins. *Special effects supervisor*: Jonnie Burke. *Stunts arranger*: Buddy Joe Hooker. *Motorcycle stunts*: Brian McGuinness. *Stunt driver*: Ewan Baxter. *Battletruck driver*: Brian McGuiness. *Composer/conductor*: Kevin Peek. *Music co-ordinator*: Dave Fraser. *Players*: Dave Fraser, Martin Winch, Bruce Lynch, Frank Gibson Jnr, New Zealand Symphony Orchestra. *Sound*: Grahame Morris, Don Reynolds, Brian Shennan, David Ginnane, Jamie Selkirk.

Cast

Michael Beck (Hunter), Annie McEnroe (Corlie), James Wainwright (Straker), Bruno Lawrence (Willie), John Bach (Bone), Randolph Powell (Judd), John Ratzenberger (Rusty), Diana Rowan (Charlene), Kelly Johnson (Alvin), Ross Jolly (Shotgun), Mark Hadlow (Orrin), John Banas (Reuben), Marshall Napier (Driver), Peter Rowell (Feathers), Timothy Lee (Hacker), Oona Menges (Zoe).

Set in the future in an indeterminate place, Battletruck sets up a post-oil wars scenario where the iron fist and lawlessness rule. In a plot borrowed from any number of post-holocaust films, a gang of ex-army thugs, led by ruthless outlaw army commander, Colonel Straker, ride the plains in their rhino-like battletruck in search of precious oil. Meanwhile the more peaceable holocaust survivors in Clearwater Commune avoid the food riots and martial law of the cities by organising themselves democratically and scratching out a living from the land. Straker and his gang have stumbled on an oil supply and pitched camp when Straker's daughter Corlie, refusing her father's order to kill a prisoner, makes a run for it. Rescued by loner Hunter, an ex-commando running his motorbike on gas produced from chicken faeces, Corlie is taken in by the commune. Straker raids the commune in the battletruck, but Corlie escapes and is again rescued, then bedded, by Hunter. In the ensuing chase and shoot-out Hunter and his helpers eventually vanquish the raiders and the battletruck is destroyed. He says his goodbyes and rides into the sunset.

Battletruck was described by its New Zealand producers during pre-production as 'a thinking man's action movie'. It does play perfunctorily with matters emotional and philosophical. Straker gets sentimental about immortality. There are hints Corlie is running from incest and when she asks plaintively, 'Why do men have to fight?' Hunter tells her, 'It's always about who gets more.' Philosophy aside, **Battletruck** is an all-out chase film, with lots of violence, fast action and stroppy vehicles. Evil Straker, thoroughly cartoon as he shoots from the hip, is in the end no match for noble Hunter's cunning. The vehicles are ingenious and the rest of the production design has a futuristic ambience. The Central Otago Plains are magnificent: brown, dusty and almost lunar in their barrenness.

Battletruck was financed by New Zealand investors. The production company had a pre-sale to Roger Corman, who had all U. S. rights. Corman was adamant about the casting, insisting on pre-approved U.S. actors, including the lead roles (Michael Beck and James Wainwright) as the film was to be made with U.S. cinema audiences in mind. **Battletruck**'s production exacerbated worries among the local film-making community that New Zealand was in danger of becoming a Hollywood satellite with overseas interests exploiting our cheap actor and crew rates and great locations. HM

Hunter's improvised dune buggy sends one of Straker's men flying. Courtesy of R. H. Whitehouse.

1982 International Festival of Fantasy and Horror Films: Best Actress, Annie McEnroe.

1982

CARRY ME BACK

Grant Tilly (Arthur Donovan) from a reverse angle as he loads his father into the car. Courtesy of the New Zealand Film Commission.

A Kiwi Films production in association with the New Zealand Film Commission. © 1982. *Budget*: $600 000. *Locations*: Wellington, Picton, Marlborough. *Distributor*: Kiwi Film Productions Ltd. *Rating*: GA (Contains coarse language), July 1982. 35 mm. Colour. 101.5 mins.

Director: John Reid. *Producer*: Graeme Cowley. *Associate producer*: Peter Barker. *Executive producer*: Gary Hannam. *Screenplay*: Derek Morton, Keith Aberdein, John Reid, from an original idea by Joy Cowley. *Director of photography*: Graeme Cowley. *Camera operator*: Paul Leach. *Editors*: Simon Reece, Michael Horton. *Art director*: Jim Barr. *Wardrobe supervisor*: Robin Murphy. *Music*: Tim Bridgewater, James Hall. *Sound*: Don Reynolds, Brian Shennan, Ross Chambers.

Cast

Grant Tilly (Arthur Donovan), Kelly Johnson (Jimmy Donovan), Dorothy McKegg (Aunty Bird), Derek Hardwick (TK Donovan), Joanne Mildenhall (Girl), Alex Trousdell (George), Frank Edwards (Brian MacAlister), Michael Haig (Craig), John Anderson (Geoff), Brian Sergeant (Andy), John Bach (Winton), Fiona Samuel (Housemaid), Peter Tait (Stanley/the body), Paul Murphy and Peter Barker (the body), with Ian Dredge, Len Assheton-Harbord, Alex Aitchison, Tolis Papazoglou, Angelique Meyer, Yvonne Kennedy, Lorena Carmell, Ian Watkin, Katy Platt, Kate Harcourt, Bruno Lawrence, Murray Reece, John Batstone, Tony Hiles, Gilbert Goldie, Joe Musaphia, Ross Logan, Paul Wallace, Grant Edgar, John Ensor, John Anderson, Ross Low, Peter Bayley, Marshall Napier, John Reid, Bill Juliff, Eric Gardener, David McKenzie, Willie Newman. Terence Burtenshaw, Phyl Rhodes, Lol Harrison, Audrey Cooper, Theresa Deacon, Robert Thomson, Chris Cooper, Sarah Randle, Richard Barron, Mollie Newton, David Mercies, Hugh Duncan.

Brothers Jimmy and Arthur are furious when their cantankerous old father TK, who hasn't been off their Marlborough family farm for years, decides to accompany them to Wellington to watch the home team play a Ranfurly Shield rugby game. After a rough, boozy inter-island ferry crossing with some mates, they are all delighted with a home team win. TK, wandering home from the celebration in a sauna parlour, meets a waitress who goes to his motel for a chat. Jimmy and Arthur wake with hangovers to find TK has died in his sleep. A quick look at the will TK fortuitously carries with him reveals that the Rugby Union will inherit the farm unless he is buried there. Complicating this, TK can't be buried legally on the farm unless he dies there. Jimmy and Arthur set about smuggling the body back to the farm in a truck belonging to a wily relative, Aunty Bird. With TK concealed in a wardrobe, their efforts are thwarted in a comedy of errors including theft of the truck, a second body in a wardrobe, a ferry strike, a fierce storm, encounters with the law and with the drunken mates. Back on the farm, mission accomplished, Jimmy asks the Wellington waitress, who they have picked up along the way, if she would like to stay and Aunty Bird decides to stay too.

Carry Me Back is a shaggy dog story with graveyard and scatological humour, sheep-shagging jokes, slapstick and kiwi-joker ribaldry. Sex roles are clearly delineated from the opening on-screen message fixing the period as 'when blokes were blokes and sheilas were their mums.' Lest we feel sympathy for TK as his malodorous body is ignominiously carted down country, he is a grumpy patriarch who belittles his sons by calling them 'sheilas'. The country jokers on the bash in the big smoke are very recognisable but, in keeping with the good-natured tone, their drunken hoonery is affectionately played. Women have some leverage in Aunty Bird, a magnificent caricature of the emasculating middle-aged woman, and in the wonderfully bored indifference of the strip joint masseuse who sees the revellers for the silly little boys they are. The nameless Wellington waitress, sweet as she seems, fares less well, along for the ride to take part in Jimmy's fantasy rather than as an individual character.

Local features are well exploited and the cinematography excellent. Told in a manner reminiscent of the Ealing comedies, the story, enlivened by a sub-plot involving an escaped prisoner, romps along at a cracking pace. The numerous mix-ups, most involving the body in the wardrobe and many including some tricky driving, are cleverly choreographed. While raucous comedy provides the main raison d'être the musical score, played by the Evening Post Onslow Brass Band, persistently introduces a rueful tone, suggesting a serious side to Jimmy and Arthur's task. This is borne out in the final shots of the picturesque and verdant farm laid out as a jewel worthy of the quest. HM

1982

BAD BLOOD

Southern Pictures Ltd with the assistance of the New Zealand Film Commission. Financed from the U.K. © 1982. *Budget*: £900 000. *Locations*: Kowhitirangi, Hokitika. *Distributor*: Kerridge Odeon. *Rating*: GA, August 1982. 35 mm. Colour. 115.5 mins.

Director: Mike Newell. *Producer*: Andrew Brown. *Executive producers*: Mark Shivas, Al Burgess. *Screenplay*: Andrew Brown. *Source*: Howard Willis, Manhunt — The Story of Stanley Graham. *Director of photography*: Gary Hansen. *Art director*: Ron Highfield. *Costume designer*: Joan Grimmond. *Firearms specialist*: Robin Cagney. *Composer/conductor*: Richard Hartley. *Sound*: Bob Allen, Ron Davis, Doug Turner, Bryan Tilling.

Cast

Jack Thompson (Stanley Graham), Carol Burns (Dorothy Graham), Dennis Lill (Ted Best), Elizabeth Watson (Pat Graham), Michael Teen (John Graham), Donna Akersten (Doreen Bond), Martyn Sanderson (Les North), Marshall Napier (Trev Bond), Cliff Wood (Henry Growcott), David Copeland (George Lindsay), Ken Blackburn (Tommo Robson), John Bach (Bert Cropp), John Banas (Macko Hager), John Black (Greg Hutchison), Karl Bradley (Maxi Coulson), Greg Naughton (Anker Madsen), Alan Jervis (Ralph Frederic), Grant Edgar (Colin Howatt), Caroline Claver (Bessie Best), Pat Evison (Dulcie Lindsay), Dulcie Smart (Evelyn Gibson), Miranda Harcourt (Ivy Smith), Dorothy McKegg (Mrs Webster), with Julie Gray, Dennis Smith, Ray Tinsley, Berwyn Smith, Bob Kluts, Tony Pattison, Bruce Allpress, Ian Watkin, Michael Haig, Phillip Holder, Kelly Johnson, Arthur Wright, Mervyn Glue, Desmond Kelly, Tony Wahren, Brian Aitken, George Carter, Peter Vere-Jones, Paul Breeze, Paul Baty, Geoffrey Snell.

Koiterangi, 1941. Dot Graham and her husband Stan are at odds with their small farming community. Tensions escalate and Stan refuses to hand in his .303 rifle to policeman Ted Best for the war effort. Dot's view that 'everyone's hounding us' is confirmed for her by other incidents like the rejection of their milk. When Stan surrenders the gun Dot buys another. Best arrives to confiscate it and Stan chases him off. When Best returns with reinforcements Stan shoots him and two other policemen. He then shoots a school inspector and takes off into the bush. Locals, police, home guard and soldiers join in the hunt. They finally find and shoot Stan and he dies later in hospital. While the locals hold a dance some of the men, in an act of exorcism, torch the Graham house. Next morning Dot surveys the smoking ruin, then turns on her heel and strides off down the road.

Bad Blood is based on the true story of a massive 12-day manhunt on the West Coast of the South Island. Stan Graham was born in Koiterangi (later renamed Kowhitirangi), but his Christchurch wife Dot was said to always feel an outsider. The film offers as cause for the bloodbath bad luck in hard times and community ostracism leading to the Grahams fuelling each others' paranoia. Dot is played as the more crazed of the pair, fanning inarticulate Stan's disappointment over the loss of his beloved guns 'like a draft to a fire.' Tension springs from the Grahams' unpredictability, from the role reversal when, in hunting Stan, the community become paranoid in turn, and from the sympathy that shifts in his favour as he is hunted. In excellent performances from the lead actors (both Australian), Stan becomes a kind of national hero in his courageous man-alone defiance of the law while Dot remains unbowed and proud in the midst of the horror they have wrought.

In powerful images, shot where the tragedy took place, the beauty and calm of sky and landscape are antithetical to the chaos about to explode. Insistent and telling motifs are tracking shots through bars and glass underlining the Grahams' entrapment and alienation. Constant West Coast rain adds to the sense of hopelessness and the shooting scenes are brutal and messy. Local colour is provided in cameo scenes, like a kids' footy practice, and fleshed out in painstaking production design (original photographs were used to replicate the setting and locals were brought in for advice). The narrative, enhanced by a first-class musical score, never misses a beat.

New Zealand-born Andrew Brown learned of the story through a documentary by Howard Willis, who later wrote the book on which the screenplay is based. The film was produced by Southern Pictures, the then film-arm of the British company, Southern Television, to fill a tax loophole. Director Mike Newell is British. Aside from a few technicians the film unit was from New Zealand. **Bad Blood**, which first screened on British television, received rave reviews in Britain and later in New Zealand. HM

Carol Burns (Dorothy Graham). Courtesy of the New Zealand Film Commission.

1982

HANG ON A MINUTE MATE!

Hang on a Minute Mate Film Partnership with the assistance of the Broadcasting Corporation of New Zealand. © 1982. Telefeature. No censorship rating (in-house production). *Location*: South Island. 16 mm. Colour. 71 mins.

Director and producer: Alan Lindsay. *Executive producer*: John Mathewson. *Screenplay*: Alan Lindsay, based on stories by Barry Crump. *Script editors*: Barry Crump, Grahame McClean, Coral Davison. *Lighting cameraman*: Peter Read. *Editor*: Jamie Selkirk. *Wardrobe supervisor*: Trixie Woodhill. *Music*: Bernie Allen, Tony Baker. *Sound*: Phenola Dwyer, Russell Hay, Graham Morris, Diane Twiss.

Cast

Alan Jervis (Sam Cash), Kelly Johnson (Jack Lilburn), Alex Trousdale (Tom Bine), Arthur Chapman (T. Burke), Patric Carey (Larry), Lawrence Ford (Ponto), Gwyneth Hughes (Sahra), Sara Jones (Mrs Cash), Tony Warren (Traffic officer), James Moynahan (Policeman), Linda Speirs (Girl at the door), Harold McNaughton (Teetotaller), John Goodliffe (Roller protector), Irene Macdonald (Mrs Wagner), Ross McPherson (Barman), Mathew Watkins (Boy), Mervyn Glue (Barman 2), John Milligan (Warder), Charles Drace (Tourist), David Telford (Big man), Patrick Smyth (Narrator).

1958. Sam Cash covers to the police for a young stranger, Jack Lilburn, caught siphoning petrol outside his house. Returning the favour, Jack agrees to drive Sam down country in his Model A Ford. Sam sneaks out without telling his wife. Jack and Sam get into trouble, drink and get out of trouble, thanks to Sam's incessant talking. On Sam's initiative they part company and Sam goes on alone, getting into trouble and drinking and talking himself out of trouble. At Hokonui pub, run by his old friend Tom, business booms when Sam shoots holes in the pub and invents a legend around them. When he hears Tom asking his wife to come back he sneaks away. After stealing a road roller Sam goes to jail where he refuses a visit from Jack. Released, he returns to his wife, ignoring her shrieked demands to tell her where he's been for the past two years and demanding his tucker.

This is an aimless road movie about an aimless Kiwi joker. Intensely misogynistic and devoid of irony, Sam Cash lives by his philosophy about women, 'I'd rather go to bed with a wet dog and cook me own tucker.' His idea of a good time is to live by his wits, tell shaggy dog yarns over a beer (he's

Alan Jervis (Sam Cash). Courtesy of Di Wilks.

fascinated by the sound of his own voice) and move on. Sam's version of mateship is superficial and Jack, like the other characters, is merely an audience for Sam, although he's so besotted with his new mate that, when Sam announces his intention to shoot through, the scene plays like the break-up of a sexual relationship.

Presenting Sam as a resourceful wag who can turn his hand to anything and from whom there is much for a young bloke to learn, **Hang On a Minute Mate!** (Sam's catchphrase) is one of the yarns that has made Barry Crump a household name and sold numerous books worldwide. Cash is one of a gallery of Crump characters perpetuating the Kiwi joker mythology set in motion by John Mulgan's *Man Alone*. Some of the film's stories are adaptations, with large chunks of dialogue lifted, unchanged, from the eponymous episodic novel. The roller theft and the Hokonui Hank episodes are from Crump's follow-up book on Sam Cash, *There and Back*.

Although interesting as a period piece (in pubs beer is squirted from a hose into 5oz glasses) the film is clumsy in shooting style and, with the exception of the Hokonui Hank sequence, barely cinematic. The camera moves little, zooms where it should cut, and is reluctant to provide information via the close up. The tinkly piano score adds a little energy, but not much. Also weakening the film are amateurish acting, a wordy script, out of synch dubbing and a deathly pace. It screened on New Zealand television on 28 September 1984. HM

1982

PRISONERS

Lemon Crest Pty Ltd and Endeavour Film Management Ltd for release by Twentieth Century Fox Film Corporation. Shot in 1982. No theatrical, video or television release. *Budget*: $US4 288 719. *Locations*: Brookby, South Auckland. 35 mm. Panavision. Colour. Running time unknown.

Director: Peter Werner. *Producers*: Antony I. Ginnane, John Barnett. *Executive producers*: David Hemmings, Keith Barish, Craig Baumgarten. *Associate producer*: Brian Cook. *Screenplay*: Meredith Baer, Hilary Henkin, from a story by Meredith Baer. *Director of photography*: James Glennon. *Camera operator*: David Burr. *Editor*: Adrian Carr. *Production designer*: Bernard Hides. *Wardrobe designer*: Aphrodite Kondos. *Composer/conductor*: Peter Sullivan. *Sound*: Gary Wilkins.

Cast

Tatum O'Neal (Christie), Colin Friels (Nick), Shirley Knight (Virginia), David Hemmings (Wilkens), Bruno Lawrence (Peeky), Ralph Cotterill (Holmby), John Bach (Bodell), Ira Seidenstein (Shadow), Michael Hurst (Sciano), Reg Ruka (Monkey), Rob Jayne (Maslow), Norman Fairley (Lewitt), Peter Rowley (Hapstood), Karl Bradley (Steel), Richard Moss (Dunham), Tim Lee (Watts), Heather Bolton (Elizabeth), Peter Nicholl (Warren), Norman Fletcher (Minister of Justice), Hone Kaa (Prison chaplain), Greg Newbold (Weasel), with Frank Allison (Tiny), Onno Boelee (Squeeze), Lance Cash, Dennis Boyd, Steve Kopae, Karam Hau, Joe Hohepa, Paul Callin, Wayne Cardell, Ralph Lawson (Prison group), Simone Curtis, Alison Wall (Elizabeth's friends).

An overseas prison expert, Superintendent Wilkens, comes to New Zealand from the United States to implement rehabilitation programs at Pukemahoe prison. One group of prisoners is assigned to his farm, a place Wilkens's 17-year-old daughter Christie sees as a prison because of her role as the go-between in her parents' unhappy relationship. The inmates and local prison officers see Wilkens as weak. Opposition from the man passed over for the Superintendent's job, Holmby, is especially bitter. Christie, not allowed to leave, withdraws into herself. When convicted murderer Nick comes to work on the farm he and Christie begin a tumultuous affair which sends shock waves through the community.

Prisoners was shot in South Auckland. A New Zealand production, Twentieth Century Fox acquired worldwide distribution rights in perpetuity. The film has not been released theatrically, on video or on television anywhere in the world. One rumour has it that a relative of one of the actors bought the film to prevent its release.

The film has not been viewed for this entry. The notes have been taken from Endeavour Productions' press kit, with further information provided by producer Antony I. Ginnane. HM

Tatum O'Neal (Christie Wilkins) and Colin Friels (Nick Skinner). Courtesy of Antony I. Ginnane.

1983

UTU

Utu Productions Ltd in association with the New Zealand Film Commission. © 1983. *Budget*: approx. $3 000 000. *Locations*: The Hawke's Bay District, Napier, Hastings, Te Pohue. *Distributor*: Utu Productions Ltd. *Rating*: GA, January 1983. 35 mm. Colour. Mono sound version, 124 mins. Re-cut Dolby Stereo version, 103.5 mins.

Director and producer: Geoff Murphy. *Executive producers*: Don Blakeney, Kerry Robins. *Screenplay*: Geoff Murphy, Keith Aberdein. *Director of photography*: Graeme Cowley. *Camera operator*: Paul Leach. *Editor*: Michael Horton. *Production designer*: Ron Highfield. *Costume designer*: Michael Kane. *Special effects make-up*: Bob McCarron S.M.A. *Special effects*: Kevin Chisnall. *Cultural advisor*: Joe Malcolm. *Armourer*: John Osborne. *Stunt co-ordinator*: Peter Rowell. *Music*: John Charles. *Conductor*: William Southgate. *Players*: New Zealand Symphony Orchestra, Joe Malcolm (Maori flute). *Waiatas*: Jane and Paul Mareikura, Rangi Dewes. *Sound*: Graham Morris, Ross Chambers, David Keene, Don Reynolds, Brian Shennan, Malcolm Cromie, John Van Der Reyden.

Cast

Anzac Wallace (Te Wheke), Bruno Lawrence (Williamson), Wi Kuki Kaa (Wiremu), Kelly Johnson (Lieutenant Scott), Tim Elliot (Colonel Elloit [sic]), Merata Mita (Matu), Tania Bristowe (Kura), Martyn Sanderson (Vicar), John Bach (Belcher), Ilona Rodgers (Emily), Faenza Reuben (Henare), members of the Te Whetu Ote Rawhiti Maori Club (Te Wheke's people), people of Waipatu Marae (Church crowd), people of Te Haroto Marae (Villagers and Waiata mourners), Hawke's Bay Black Powder Club (Militia), with Geoff Murphy, Tom Poata, Jeff Kennedy, Cook Te Huia, Wayne Allen, Dick Puanaki, Sean Duffy, Ian Watkin, Joe Malcolm, Ian Stewart, Ronnie Smith, Connie Gilbert, George Waaka, Stephen Tozer, Rawiri, Desmoine Swan, 'Tiny', Betty MacKay, Awatea Mita, Puni Rangiaho, Robin Ruakere, Tim Shadbolt, Al Ford, Bill Juliff, Manuel Echevarria, Paul Hewitt, Hingawaru Grant, Peter Rowell.

New Zealand, 1870. When troops sack his village, Maori militia scout Te Wheke deserts the British-led colonial army, has his face tattooed in full moko and vows revenge (utu). After beheading a fanatical minister he attacks a farm, reading *Macbeth* while his men loot the house. When his wife is killed Williamson, the owner, vows revenge. Lieutenant Scott and army scout Wiremu plan to wage guerrilla warfare against Te Wheke, against the better judgement of the corrupt British colonel, Elliot. Scott falls for Kura, a young Maori woman spying for Te Wheke. In the ensuing stalking and shoot-outs Te Wheke and Williamson become increasingly fanatical. The showdown comes when, camped at a one-horse town, the army is attacked by Te Wheke's followers using an ambushed supply wagon as a Trojan horse and creeping up on the soldiers disguised as bushes. Te Wheke murders Kura, blaming her for the army's advance warning. He is caught, summarily tried in a drumhead court martial and sentenced to death by Scott. Williamson, Scott and Kura's Aunty Matu all offer to carry out the execution. Saying they are unfit because they all seek utu, Wiremu reveals that Te Wheke is his brother and carries out the execution himself, shooting Te Wheke in the head.

With the New Zealand Land Wars as the spur to action **Utu** is a fiction rich in cul-

Anzac Wallace (Te Wheke).

87

tural detail. Because of Maori sensitivity to tribal matters the film is deliberately vague about locations and tribes. Te Wheke (The Octopus) is fashioned after such Maori leaders as Te Kooti Rikirangi, Wiremu Tamihana and Te Rauparaha. The court martial was based on James Cowan's short story about the death of Wi Heretaunga, *A Bush Court Martial*. Political points, broadly made, are that in the history of colonial expansion differences between cultures are irreconcilable and that violence is futile.

In representing different allegiances the characters are also drawn in broad, sometimes absurd, strokes: Colonel Elliot, the sadistic usurper, works on the premise of racial superiority; Wiremu the pragmatic intellectual, sides with the colonists and provides hints of twentieth century racial tensions; Williamson, the wise fool, goes mad in his search for utu; Te Wheke seeks revenge for the wrongs done to his race but loses his reason and turns on his own people. Te Wheke and Williamson raise questions about the responsibilities of those whose loved ones have been senselessly slaughtered, but the film's inconsistency of tone wastes their potential to become tragic heroes.

Set 30 years after the signing of the Treaty of Waitangi, **Utu** (working titles **Shoot the Bastard** and **Shoot 'em Up**) is an action/chase entertainment adapting codes from the Hollywood western to the local scene. The laconic humour is a recognisable Geoff Murphy feature, down to the sexual plea from Kura 'Didn't you say your gun could fire seven times without stopping?' Because **Utu** is loosely episodic there are dead spots but there is great energy and flair in the action scenes. (A steadicam was a novelty brought in for shooting in rugged landscapes.)

Lushly shot, exuberantly choreographed and richly scored, **Utu** was made on a budget large for the time and its scale is epic (a large second unit was employed). Many in the large cast were local Maori used as extras. Much care was taken to achieve period authenticity in the production design — each day, for example, it took up to four hours to apply Wallace's especially designed moko. **Utu** was the first New Zealand feature to use the full New Zealand Symphony Orchestra.

At home **Utu** received mixed reviews, some quite negative about its macho 'puha western' aspect. But the public responded well and it became for a time the country's second highest grossing film (after **Goodbye Pork Pie**). For marketing reasons and on the instigation of Don Blakeney it was re-cut by Ian John for its overseas release and 15 minutes were cut from the film to focus it more on Te Wheke's point of view. The bush court martial scene was recut into a series of flashbacks culminating in Te Wheke's execution and the mono sound was remixed into Dolby stereo. It was warmly received overseas, with a rave review in *The New Yorker* from Pauline Kael, who described Murphy as a director with an eye for 'a deracinated kind of hip lyricism' U.S. audiences saw **Utu** as providing them with historical information about Maori culture while in France *Fantastique* hailed it as 'a spectacular adventure film.' HM

1983 Cannes Film Festival: Official Selection, Out of Competition.

Tim Elliot (Colonel Elliot). *Courtesy of the New Zealand Film Commission.*

1983

DEAD KIDS

Hemdale and Fay Richwhite present a South Street Films Production. Endeavour Productions Ltd and Bannon Glen Pty Ltd. A.k.a. Strange Behaviour. A.k.a. Shadowlands. © 1982. Financed from New Zealand and Australia. *Locations*: Remuera, Epsom, One Tree Hill, Avondale College (Auckland). *Distributor*: Kerridge Odeon. *Rating*: R16, April 1983. 35 mm. Panavision. Colour. 103mins.

Director: Michael Laughlin. *Producers*: Antony I. Ginnane, John Barnett. *Executive producers*: John Daly, David Hemmings, William Fayman. *Associate producer*: Bill Condon. *Screenplay*: Bill Condon, Michael Laughlin. *Director of photography*: Louis Horvath. *Camera operator*: Ronald Vidor. *Editor*: Petra. *Production designer*: Susanna Moore. *Costume designer*: Bruce Finlayson. *Special make-up*: Craig Reardon. *Music*: Tangerine Dream. *Sound*: Paul Clarke, Steve Edwards, Peter Fenton.

Cast

Michael Murphy (John Brady), Dan Shor (Pete Brady), Louise Fletcher (Barbara), Fiona Lewis (Professor Gwen Parkinson), Arthur Dignam (Dr Le Sange/Nagel), Dey Young (Caroline), Marc McClure (Oliver), Elizabeth Cheshire (Lucy), Charles Lane (Donovan), Beryl Te Wiata (Mrs Haskell), Jim Boelson (Waldo), with Billy Al Bengston, Nicole Anderson, Bill Condon, B. Courtenay Leigh, William Hayward, Jack Haines, Cindy Arnold, Howard Crothall, Richard Moore, Andrew Glover, John Clarke, Susan Van Ravenswaay, Joe Harner, Mary Ruth Harner, Susanna Moore, Summer Ramer, Bob Houston, Lulu Sylbert, Neil McLachlan, Scott Brady, Jessica Kenny, Alma Woods, Maurice Keene, Brenda Casey, Bob Gentil, Greg Dower, Jane Dower, Simon Nesbitt, Rod Collison, Terry Donovan, Maryke Mann, Stephen Jackson, Wally Parks, Campbell Hegan, Le Roy Sisnett, Peter Walker, Kerry Brown, Melodie Batchelor, Kathryn Collins, Ngila Dickson, Louise Franklin, Mark Hadlow, Michael Hammond, Marcus Le Grice, Peta Rutter, Adair Wheeler, Janet Wells.

In the quiet mid-western college town of Galesburg, Illinois (Remuera), students are stabbed to death and mutilated, apparently indiscriminately and by different killers. Local cop John Brady realises all the victims are sons of men who supported him in his campaign to have the college's psychology department behavioural modification program shut down. The instigator, Dr Le Sange, thought by John to have had an evil influence on his late wife when she worked at the lab, is now officially dead, but lives on in videotaped lectures and in the work of Professor Parkinson and her assistant, Nagel. To earn a proferred $200, Brady's son Pete joins the program that, unknown to him, has produced the killers. He is firstly given a pill to improve his brainpower and then injected in the eyeball with a giant syringe. Programmed to kill his father, Pete staggers around feeling ill. Meanwhile John and friend Barbara have investigated Le Sange's grave and found it empty. Confronting the disguised Le Sange in the lab (he has been masquerading as Nagel) John is surprised when Pete arrives. On Le Sange's order to kill his father Pete stabs Le Sange to death. John marries Barbara.

Attempting a B-Grade campus/horror splatter with a sideline in satirising American junk culture, **Dead Kids** has a poorly constructed script, weak acting and clumsy cinematography. Attempts at irony are lost in the welter of plot twists, both in the present and in explanations of past events. In the video version viewed for this entry bad editing exacerbates the script problems. Because the Panavision format has not been scanned for video, actors disappear on the edges of the frame, a murderous 'fat woman' looks of average build and slim actors look emaciated.

On its release some saw **Dead Kids** as an example of cultural colonialism with overseas interests appropriating New Zealand locations for commercial gain (most of the film was shot in Remuera). One of the producers and some production crew were New Zealanders. A few locals were hired as extras and Beryl Te Wiata has a speaking role. HM

The video slick from a later release. Courtesy of Antony I. Ginnane.

WAR YEARS

Sir Apirana Ngata farewells members of the Maori Battalion. Courtesy of the New Zealand Television Archive.

New Zealand National Film Unit. © 1983. Documentary. *Locations*: New Zealand, overseas territories. *Distributor*: New Zealand National Film Unit. *Rating*: G, May 1983. Compiled on 35 mm. Black and white. 103 mins.

Director: Pat McGuire. *Producer*: Hugh MacDonald. *Executive producer*: Frederick Cockram. *Devised and directed*: Pat McGuire. *Editor*: Chris Lancaster. *Rostrum camera*: Nikki Dennis. *Film archivist/restoration*: Clive Sowry. *Laboratory technicians*: Ron Cameron, Les Bloomfield. *Additional maps and graphics*: Larry Nelson, Owen Mapp. *Sound*: Kit Rollings, Brian Shennan, David Newton.

National Film Unit Footage 1941–1945. *Producer*: Stanhope Andrews. *Cameramen overseas*: Ron McIntyre, Mervyn Elias, Stan Wemyss (Italy); Roger Mirams (Middle East); Stan Wemyss, Bert Bridgman, Frank Dyer, Harold Paton (Pacific). *Camera, sound, editing, scriptwriting, graphics*: Robert Allen, Charlie Barton, Bill Bailey, Syd Brookes, Michael Forlong, Free Grant, James Harris, Rudall Hayward, Oxley Hughan, Bert Male, Cyril Morton, John Pike, Russell Reid, Geoffrey Scott, Arnold Townsend, Claude Wickstead. *Commentators*: Cyril Bradwell, Martin Cock, Doug Campbell, Doug Edwards, Doug Elliot, Ernest Le Grove, Michael Miles, Bob Pollard, Rex Walden, Peter Whitechurch, Miss Jackson, Mrs Whatley.

The opening sequence backgrounds the lead-up to World War II, including a clip from New Zealand Prime Minister Michael Savage's 'where Britain goes, we go' speech. The 1941 establishment of the National Film Unit in New Zealand is described as a means of promoting the war effort, and its **Weekly Review** as a pioneer of documentary film-making in this country. A compilation of footage, taken from **Weekly Reviews**, which screened in local cinemas from 1941 to 1945, loosely follows the enlistment of soldiers through to their service in Egypt and the Western Desert, Greece, Crete, El Alamein, Italy and the Pacific and their return home after Japan's surrender. The Women's Auxiliary Army Corps is shown serving in the Middle East and the Maori Battalion is given coverage. While battle campaign details are deliberately vague, footage shows the necessity for the overseas campaigns, the evil of the enemy and the resourcefulness and resilience with which New Zealand soldiers tackle their work and leisure.

On the home front American troops stop off for R & R and to guard the country against Japanese invasion, the Home Guard practise with jam-tin bombs and molotov cocktails and talented inventors find ways of alleviating hard times. Women throw themselves into 'the war effort'. Some make up food parcels and hospital supplies, others take happily to what was formerly regarded as men's work, driving taxis and trucks, farming and delivering milk and mail. **The Weekly Reviews** exhort the populace to make sacrifices and live frugally. Bob Hope asks that people buy war bonds. A returned soldier comments, 'I want to say how darned glad I am to be back in little old Enzed. After being right around the world I'm quite sure that it is God's Own Country.'

World leaders are represented and information on war developments is provided by the **Weekly Reviews** and by the maps and graphics added by the makers of **War Years**, but the focus is on ordinary people and on the sense of community generated as they worked towards a common cause. In clear sharp images, and with a fondness for the drama of the low angle shot and stirring, upbeat music, the **Weekly Reviews** served as home-front propaganda aimed at boosting morale and at persuading people to make the sacrifices necessary for 'the war effort'. War is not glorified, but shown as the appalling manifestation of the machinations of 'foreign' evil. The rhetorical voice-over style is declamatory and loud, insistent with such moral assertions as, 'evil has a stranglehold on decency' and 'there is no goose-stepping here, just the swinging stride of free men'. New Zealand is portrayed as paradise and its people as heroes.

War Years is a fascinating record of documentary film-making at a crucial time in the country's history. The film, which screened theatrically, followed Pat McGuire's 50 minute television film, **Dreams in Black and White**, a documentary on the immediate post-war period in New Zealand. HM

PATU!

Awatea Films with the assistance of the New Zealand Film Commission and the Queen Elizabeth II Arts Council of New Zealand. © 1983. Documentary. *Locations*: Gisborne, Whakatane, Christchurch, Wellington, Hamilton, Auckland, Palmerston North, London. *Distributor*: Merata Mita. *Rating*: GY, July 1983. 16 mm. Colour. 112.5 mins.

Director & producer: Merata Mita. *Co-ordinators*: Gaylene Preston, Gerd Pohlmann, Martyn Sanderson. *Photography*: Barry Harbet. *Additional photography*: W. Attewell, C. Barrett, A. Barry, J. Bartle, A. Bollinger, P. Carvell, R. Donaldson, M. Fingel, E. Frizzell, C. Ghent, A. Guilford, R. Long, L. Narbey, R. Prosser, M. Single. *Editor*: Annie Collins. *Original theme music*: Diatribe, Tia Kingi. *Additional music*: Syd Melbourne, Haruru Mai. *Sound*: G. Pohlmann, B. Allen, H. Bollinger, R. Brittenden, R. Campbell, T. Johnson, O. Goodman, D. Keene, G. Phillips, D. Newton, B. Thomas, T. Woollams. S. Upston, B. Shennan.

Over a still of black South African activist Steve Biko, who died in police custody, Merata Mita's voice explains that on 12 September 1980, the anniversary of Biko's death, the New Zealand Rugby Football Union invited white South Africa's Springbok team to New Zealand. Coalitions of anti-tour groups marshal New Zealand's resistance. On 22 July the first Springbok rugby match is held in Gisborne and the first blows are struck as protesters attempt to enter the grounds. At the Hamilton game 1000 protesters occupy the field and on cancellation of the game the crowd erupts in violence. In Wellington's Molesworth Street police batons injure marchers. In Palmerston North army-erected barbed wire barricades create a city under siege. Motorbike helmets and body padding become required protester protection and frontliners carry wooden shields. Behind a motel the Red Squad practise their moves. In Auckland jumbo bins barricade Eden Park. The final game, a test match, is held on the anniversary in 1981 of Biko's death. Called the Day of Rage by protesters, the protest is huge, violent and climactic, as protesters take to police with fence palings, and as police fight back unrestrained. At the film's end on-screen notes inform, during the tour over 2000 were arrested and many were jailed, some people were maimed for life, the tour cost nearly $8 million and a rugby tour is due to take place in 1985.

Television reporters and police photographers filmed the 1981 Springbok Tour protests for their own purposes, but it is the work of the many independent film-makers, shown in *Patu!*, that tells the protesters' stories. Described by *New Zealand Listener* reviewer Peter Wells as 'the hottest documentary ever made in New Zealand' and by the 1983 London Film Festival Director Ken Wlaschin as 'a major documentary of our time' *Patu!* is film-making at its best, a powerful historical record and a great feat of direction and editing. ('Patu' is a Maori word meaning 'to strike, chastise, subdue, or kill', a patu is also a hand-weapon not unlike a police baton.)

Eschewing political analysis, the film uses visceral, impressionistic montage, but although having the look of cinema verité it is artfully constructed. Woven into the montage of sounds and images is evidence of changes in consciousness as the tour progresses. From the beginning, Maori and Polynesian protesters draw parallels between oppression in racist South Africa and racism at home, but white, middle-class protesters have a naive idealism to lose.

The film captures the theatricality and lighter moments of the anti-tour struggle. Telling details are well chosen — protesters and rugby supporters fight over a cross on the park at Hamilton, an elderly Polynesian woman watches, mesmerised, from her window as police and protesters battle in the streets below, plainclothed police hover uneasily on the edges of a crowd — and this creates the texture.

The soundtrack is evocative, combining news reports, the noise of violent confrontation and music which comments on, and at times mocks, the visuals. Varied arrangements of 'God Defend New Zealand' reflect the patriotism and solidarity claimed by both sides and, when distorted, make ironic comment on the depths to which state forces have sunk — a heavy metal version, for example, accompanies the army putting barbed wire in place. Stirring Sibelius played over the flour bombing of Eden Park adds a light touch. Not mentioned is the incident in which protesters put glass on the field at Gisborne.

Filming was dangerous and difficult. At times crews were beaten along with marchers. Police push cameras and camera crews aside. Protesters scream at camera operators to get out of the way, or to get involved. Through lack of footage *Patu!* records the aftermath of the Hamilton cancellation in stills. Merata Mita reported police harassment as the film was shot, and footage was sent out of the country to thwart confiscation.

Funded by a QEII Arts Council grant of $13 000 and an $18 000 loan from the New Zealand Film Commission, *Patu!* was made with scrounged film stock and voluntary labour (although people were eventually paid). Footage not used in the film was given to the Film Archive. While much footage was shot by Barry Harbert, important contributions came from several other professional film-makers and from amateurs. *Patu!* was the first New Zealand feature-length film directed by a woman. Postproduction took two years and the film was distributed in New Zealand through independent cinemas. It has screened to positive reviews in festivals at home and overseas. HM

1983 Amiens Festival of Films Against Racism (Mouvement Contre Le Racisme et Pour L'Amitié Entre Les Peuples): MRAP Prize. Leipzig Festival: International Students' Prize.

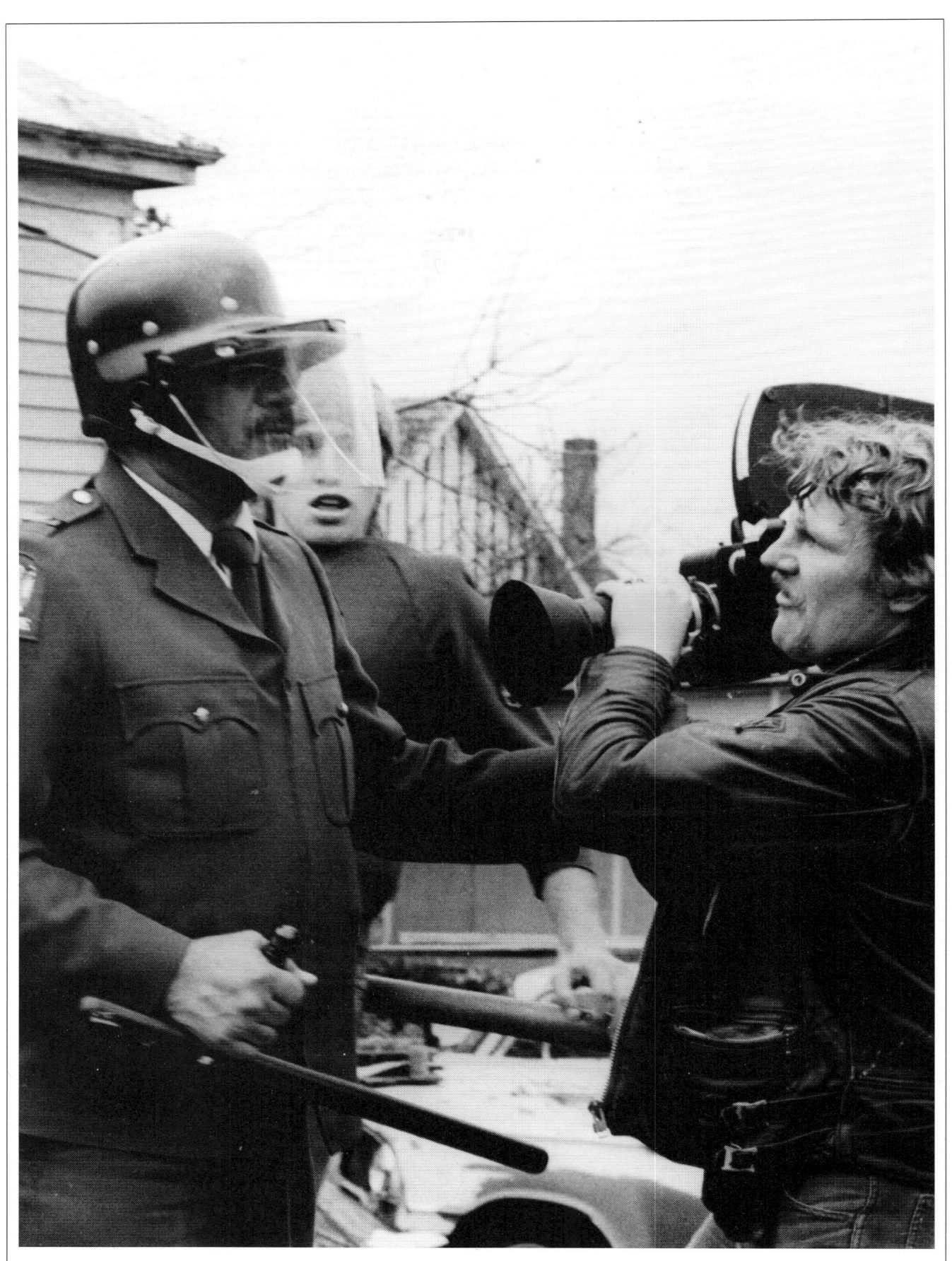

***Cameraman Barry Harbert and two of the riot squad in* Patu.** *Photograph by Kapil Arn.*

1983

STRATA

Phase Three Films Ltd. © 1982. *Locations*: Tongariro National Park, Desert Road, White Island. *Distributor*: Phase Three Films Ltd. *Rating*: GA, September 1983. 35 mm. Colour. 109.5 mins.

Director: Geoff Stevens. *Producer*: John Maynard. *Executive producer*: Gary Hannam. *Associate producers*: Piers Davies, Gary Hannam. *Screenplay*: Ester Krumbachova, Geoff Steven, Michael Havas. *Director of photography*: Leon Narbey. *Camera operator*: Alan Locke. *Editor*: David Coulson. *Art director*: Dean Cato. *Wardrobe supervisor*: Elizabeth Mitchell. *Music*: Mike Nock. *Sound*: Graham Morris, Alf West, Prue Birch, Don Reynolds, Brian Shennan.

Cast

Nigel Davenport (Victor), John Banas (Steve), Judy Morris (Margaret), Tom Brennan (Eric), Roy Billing (Keith), Peter Nicoll (Tony), Mary Regan (Gaylene), Ctibor Turba (Thomas), Patrick Smyth (Quarantine Director), Norman Forsey (Dr Hunter), Phillip Holder (Orderly), Phillip Gordon (Helicopter Pilot), Anne Walls (Receptionist), John Watson (Doctor).

Journalist Margaret and photographer Steve observe eminent vulcanologist Victor working on a volcanic plateau. Meanwhile, four passengers from an international flight, interned after a cholera outbreak, escape and set out for the nearest town. Eventually the group — Eric, an American businessman in his sixties, Keith, an ill-tempered thirty-something drifter, and honeymooners Gaylene and Tony — realise they are lost. They are joined by Thomas, a fellow passenger who speaks little English. Group tensions increase, with much carping from Gaylene who, while making sexual advances to fellow traveller Keith, berates him for his laziness. Eric reveals himself to Thomas as an arms dealer while Thomas tells of his work as a revolutionary trained to kill and of his assignment to assassinate Eric. The group split up, Eric dies of a heart attack and Thomas walks on alone. Victor tricks Margaret and Steve into staying longer on the plateau and at a lake they meet Thomas, then Gaylene, Tony and Keith. In front of Margaret Thomas kills Steve when he refuses to stop photographing him. When Margaret later launches *Surface Readings*, her biography of Victor, he watches through a window but refuses to go in and join her.

Looking like an arid planet, the inhospitable landscape is the perfect symbolic setting for this allegorical film, with the eeriness of the North Island central plateau made even more alien by footage of smouldering White Island, shot at no small cost to the nerves of the crew. Initially titled **Figures Beyond Glass**, **Strata** is a 'journey' film posing questions about the nature of reality, freedom, relationships and happiness and about the struggle for survival. Plot details slowly unfold as the lost travellers are reduced to their basic instincts by the limitations of the environment, while to Margaret and Steve the environment is merely a setting for studying a human subject. Frequent references to glass indicate self-examination and distanced observation of others, but ironically **Strata**'s characters are too self-centred to learn much. Only Victor is habitually introspective, and his self-imposed isolation shows up the hollowness of his pronouncements on the meaning of life.

Co-writer Ester Krumbachova, prominent in Czechoslovakian cinema in the 1960s, approached Geoff Steven after seeing **Skin Deep** and with Michael Havas they worked on an original idea by Steven. Although billed as a psychological thriller, **Strata** lacks narrative tension and the climax packs no punch. The characters represent ideas and are never credible as people. There is no indication why the newly-weds are so fractious and no apparent motivation for Gaylene's sexual encounter with Keith. Nor does the narrative make believable that three of the party abandon their companions without water. The revolutionary and the arms dealer work up some spark in their encounters but, again, motivation appears limp.

Strata is a slow-paced, art house, European-style film favouring continuous shots over montage. Despite its narrative drawbacks it is visually striking and evocatively scored. As an experiment in style it was important in the development of New Zealand film. HM

Judy Morris (Margaret). Courtesy of the New Zealand Film Commission.

1983
IT'S LIZZIE TO THOSE CLOSE

Filmcraft with the assistance of Television New Zealand, the New Zealand Film Commission and the National Film Unit. A.k.a. Lizzie. A.k.a. A Woman of Good Character (television drama title). © 1982. *Location*: Wakatipu. *Distributor*: South Pacific All Media Distributors Ltd. *Rating*: R16, October 1983. 16 mm. Colour. 74 mins (telefeature version), 50 mins (television drama version).

Director: David Blyth. *Producer*: Grahame McLean. *Screenplay*: Elizabeth Gowans. *Director of photography*: John Earnshaw. *Editor*: Jamie Selkirk. *Production designer*: Grahame McLean. *Costume designer*: Glenys Hitchens. *Composer*: Mark Nicholas. *Musical co-ordinator*: Morton Wilson. *Sound*: Hammond Peek, Brian Shennan.

Cast

Sarah Peirse (Lizzie), Jeremy Stephens (Reginald Bowen Jnr), Derek Hardwick (Reginald Bowen Snr), Bruno Lawrence (Younger son), Ian Watkin (Stock buyer), Martyn Sanderson (Reverend). (No character names are listed in the credits.)

In the mid-1800s a young English servant woman travels to New Zealand to take up a position as a servant. Her expectations of making a new life for herself 'like nothing we've never seen' are shattered when she is taken by horse and dray to a remote, dirty, run-down Canterbury sheep farm. When she arrives the farmer immediately shoots her dog. With no means of escape she stays on to keep house for the taciturn farmer, his simple-minded brother and his silent old father. The farmer tells her he and his father have not spoken for 12 years. With plans to sell off the footrot-blighted sheep and move into town with the servant woman as his wife, the farmer makes her the gift of a dog and proposes marriage. He later rapes her. She learns the farmer has posted marriage banns in town and that he and his father are both named Reginald Bowen. Reginald Snr speaks for the first time in protest at his son's selling the sheep. Reginald Jnr leaves with the sheep money and a parson persuades Reginald Snr and the woman to marry. That night the woman goes berserk in the barn. Her husband takes her inside and sorrowfully confides in her that his wife never knew he loved her. The woman tells him her name is Lizzie and reveals she was raped by Reginald Jnr. The old man hangs himself and Lizzie, pregnant, inherits the farm.

The script, written by an English woman, Elizabeth Gowans, who had lived in Canterbury for some time, was brought from England by David Blyth after a stay there studying film-making. Ostensibly a folk tale, the story attempts to fit pioneer New Zealanders into an archetypal framework (strong, resourceful woman, inarticulate rural hicks), but offers little insight into the people or the times. As an attempt at painting a picture of pioneering New Zealand, it is visually cute and the narrative lacks motivation.

Shot initially as a 50 minute television drama **A Woman of Good Character** was stretched to 74 minutes and re-named **It's Lizzie To Those Close** on the initiative of producer Grahame McLean, who shot extra footage for the longer version. The added-on 20 minutes, which consist mainly of extra shots of paddocks and sheep accompanied by Lizzie ruminating in voice-over, do little to advance character or motivation. The film was shot on Grahame Maclean's own small holding, an original miner's title in the mountains above Moke creek. It marks an early gig in the careers of several up-and-coming actors and film-makers and includes a lovely performance from Bruno Lawrence.

In 1985 the Phillips Whitehouse production company made a television mini-series, **Heart of the High Country**, using the story as its raw material. Lizzie's name was changed to Ceci. The series was scripted by Elizabeth Gowans, directed by Sam Pillsbury and shot by James Bartle. Sarah Peirse was casting director. HM

1982 New Zealand Feltex Award: Best Actress, Sarah Peirse.

Sarah Peirse (Lizzie). Courtesy of the New Zealand Film Commission.

1983

SAVAGE ISLANDS

Phillips-Whitehouse Productions. A.k.a. Nate and Hayes. © 1983. *Budget*: Approx. $13 million. *Locations*: Bay of Islands, Rotorua, Fiji. *Distributor*: Kerridge Odeon Film distributors. *Rating*: GA, November 1983. 35 mm. Colour. Dolby Stereo. 101 mins.

Director: Ferdinand Fairfax. *Producers*: Lloyd Phillips, Rob Whitehouse. *Screenplay*: John Hughes, David Odell, based on a story by Lloyd Phillips. *Director of photography*: Tony Imi. *Editor*: John Shirley. *Production designer*: Maurice Cain. *Costume designer*: Norma Moriceau. *Special make-up effects*: Bob McCarron S.M.A. *Special effects*: Peter Dawson, Kevin Chisnall. *Stunt co-ordinator*: Peter Diamond. *Armourer*: Robin Cagney. *Maritime consultant*: Cliff Hawkins. *Maori liaison*: Wally Hori. *Music*: Trevor Jones. *Players*: The London Symphony Orchestra. *Conductor*: Marcus Dods. *Sound*: John Ireland, K. McCallum, Terry Poulton.

Cast

Tommy Lee Jones (Captain Bully Hayes), Michael O'Keefe (Nathaniel Williamson), Max Phipps (Ben Pease), Jenny Seagrove (Sophie), Grant Tilly (Count Von Rittenberg), Bill Johnson (Rev. Williamson), Kate Harcourt (Mrs Williamson), Peter Rowley (Louis Beck), David Letch (Ratbag), Bruce Allpress (Mr Blake), Prince Tui Teka (King of Panape), Pudji Waseso (Fong), Reg Ruka (Moaka), Roy Billing (Auctioneer), Peter Vere-Jones (Gunboat captain), Mark Hadlow (Gun operator), Philip Gordon (Timmy), Tom Vanderlaan (Count's Lieutenant), with Norman Farley, Warwick Simmons, Paul Farrell, Frank Taurua, Norman Keesing, Robert Bruce, Timothy Lee, Peter Bell, Peter Diamond, John Rush, Grant Price, Karl Bradley.

Buccaneer Bully Hayes is captured by Ben Pease, whose testicles he has shot off in a previous altercation. Awaiting execution Hayes recounts an adventure, shown in flashback, beginning when he delivers missionary Nathaniel and his fiancée Sophie to a Pacific Island to convert the locals. When Pease torches the island Sophie is captured, along with islanders snatched to be sold into slavery ('blackbirding'). Following Pease to 'Samoa' (the Bay of Islands), Hayes and Nate (now buddies in spite of Hayes' declared love for Sophie) kill and maim several Pease men, but can't rescue Sophie. They follow Pease and Count Von Rittenberg to Penape (Rotorua) where Pease intends to bribe the evil king to sign a treaty. Bully et al kill the king and rescue Sophie. After a swordfight sea battle the Count's ship blows up and Pease escapes. Back in the present, Hayes prepares to hang when Nate, disguised as a padre, and Sophie, disguised as a nun, rescue him. Hayes hangs Ben Pease before they escape into the sunset.

Set in the mid-nineteenth century near the end of the pirate era, **Savage Islands** is an action/ buddy fantasy attempting to reprise the spirit of 1930s Saturday matinée serials in the manner of **Raiders of the Lost Ark** (1981). The borrowings of writers John Hughes (**National Lampoon's Vacation**) and David Odell (**Dark Crystal**) include Amazon women, ninja, a King Kong/Fay Wray encounter and Errol Flynn-style swashbuckling. In one Tarzan-ish episode an assailant cries 'Aaaahyeeeaaaah Pakeha!' But in using the characters of myth, the film-makers neglect a modern sensibility. Sophie loosens her stays a little but she, like the others, is cartoon. Most hideous are the Maori and Pacific Island characters who, in their representation as savage, cunning heathens, are limited to dialogue like 'Ooga booga'. The buccaneers say more and cackle a lot.

The swordfights and sailing boats are classy and the settings gorgeous. There is some character development. Nate learns not to be a sissy. Sophie learns she wants Nate now he's not a sissy. As a historical character Bully Hayes was generally described as a blackguard with scant regard for others. Biographer Frank Clune maintains that, while Hayes was often described as 'a rogue, villain, cheat, swindler, barrator, buccaneer, bilker, bigamist, freebooter, polygamist, seducer, murderer, pirate, slave-trader, robber, rapist, hooligan and bully', and while he was capable of these crimes, he was 'never convicted in any civil court of law for any serious criminal offence'.* Clune also maintains Pease and Hayes were partners, not enemies. In **Savage Islands** Hayes is the number one hero, demonstrating his morality in a new career running guns to anti-colonialists.

Savage Islands was financed by New Zealand investors taking advantage of tax loopholes. It was onsold to Paramount Pictures, who released it worldwide. It was directed by an Englishman, produced by New Zealanders and cast in Los Angeles, Australia, the United Kingdom and New Zealand. Postproduction was done in London. Music is played by the London Symphony Orchestra. HM

Tommy Lee Jones (Captain Bully Hayes). *Courtesy of R. H. Whitehouse.*

Reference
* F Clune. 1970. *Captain Bully Hayes: black-birder and bigamist*.

TRESPASSES

Finlayson-Hill Productions Ltd in association with Broadbank Investments Ltd. © 1983. *Locations*: Bethells Beach, Puhoi. *Distributor*: Kerridge Odeon Film Distributors. *Rating*: R13, January 1984. 35 mm. Colour. 101 mins.

Director: Peter Sharp. *Producers*: Tom Finlayson, Dean Hill. *Associate producer*: Logan Brewer. *Screenplay*: Maurice Gee, Tom Finlayson. *Director of photography*: Leon Narbey. *Camera operator*: Barry Harbert. *Production designer*: Lindsay Waugh. *Costume designer*: Glenys Hitchens. *Editor*: David Coulson. *Music*: Bernie Allen. *Music supervisor*: Tony Baker. *Players*: New Zealand Symphony Orchestra. *Sound*: Graham Morris, Alfred West, Pru Burch, Brian Shennan, David Newton.

Cast

Patrick McGoohan (Fred Wells), Emma Piper (Katie Wells), Andy Anderson (Albie Stone), Terence Cooper (Doug Mortimer), Frank Whitten (Stan Gubbins), Sean Duffy (Dave Gilchrist), Don Selwyn (Bob Storey), Vivienne Laube (Sandra Foster), Paula Keenan (Billie MacIntyre), Kate Harcourt (Mrs Mac), Peter Rowley (Andy MacIntyre), Richard Moss (Colin Dobbs), Christopher White (Philip Brewer), Reg Ruka (Barman), Alistair Douglas (Fingerprint specialist), Robert Gould (Pathologist), William Kircher (Constable), Karl Bradley (Detective Buckley), with Maggie Eyre, Michael Baxter-Lax, Christine Bartlett, Timothy Lee, Geoffrey Snell, Philippa Dann (Commune dwellers).

Living in a small coastal town with her restrictive father, Fred, who has a fundamental, calvinistic faith and an iron devotion to his dead wife, 25 year-old Katie Wells sees possibilities for another lifestyle in her relationship with Albie, a man from nearby Still River Commune. Against Fred's warnings Katie moves to the commune, but finds it impossible to 'open' herself. After Fred goes to the commune demanding his daughter's return, guru leader Stan rapes Katie to 'initiate' her. Katie flees and finds work on a farm up north but returns when she finds she is pregnant to Stan. With her father in a state of personal neglect and more fanatical then ever, she coaxes him into quasi 'normality' by convincing him she is back to stay. Hearing of Katie's pregnancy Albie attacks Stan. Later that day Katie confronts Stan, forcing him to see he has no power over her. Fred, unseen by the viewer but seen by Katie, bursts in and murders Stan. Action shifts to the police investigation into Stan's death and Katie's disappearance. Policeman Mortimer quickly deduces what has happened. Fred prepares to ritualistically kill the unrepentant Katie, whom he has imprisoned in his private clifftop church, but she escapes. When the police arrive Katie helps Fred, by now almost catatonic, into the police car, then walks free on the beach.

Made when there was much public curiosity about the goings-on in communes espousing free love, **Trespasses** is a psychological drama about the emotional journey of a woman dominated by fanatical, possessive men. The film is as hostile to the commune's hedonistic philosophy as it is to Fred's soulless religion, using Stan's jealous partner to show the free love philosophy as hurtful and destructive. While Stan merely seeks pleasure, Fred at least has a discernible, if twisted, motive, rationalising the death of his wife in childbirth in terms of a divine plan and believing she will continue to share the house with him and Katie as long as their daughter stays and as long as they adhere to God's stern dictates. The MacIntyre family on the Northland farm show Katie there is a sane middle way, although Billie MacIntyre warns against the folly of seeing rural life as idyllic.

Bethells Beach on the wild west coast provides an excellent primeval backdrop. The commune scenes are overplayed, at times with a look of amateur dramatics and the script allows Frank Whitten no room to convince of Stan's charisma. The increasingly fraught father/daughter relationship gives the narrative a thriller edge, with Katie's disappearance turning up the temperature.

The film was developed when producer Tom Finlayson bought the rights to the characters of the television cop show, **Mortimer's Patch**, and asked series writer Maurice Gee to write them into a feature. Terence Cooper, Sean Duffy and Don Selwyn appear in the film as their **Mortimer's Patch** characters. On Patrick McGoohan's insistence the story grew away from its origins, making the police search superfluous, and Finlayson and Gee, for whom this was his first screenplay for theatrical release, both believe the film fell between the police drama and the psychological thriller. HM

Patrick McGoohan (Fred Wells) and Emma Piper (Katie Wells). Courtesy of Thomas Finlayson.

1984

CONSTANCE

Donogh Rees (Constance Elsworthy). Courtesy of the New Zealand Film Commission.

Mirage Films Ltd with the assistance of the New Zealand Film Commission. © 1983. *Locations*: Auckland, Thames. *Distributor*: Mirage Films Ltd. *Rating*: GA, February 1984. 35 mm, Colour. 104 mins.

Director: Bruce Morrison. *Producer*: Larry Parr. *Screenplay*: Jonathan Hardy, Bruce Morrison, from a story by Bruce Morrison. *Director of photography*: Kevin Hayward. *Camera operator*: Paul Leach. *Editor*: Philip Howe. *Production designer*: Richard Jeziorny. *Costume designer*: Judith Crozier. *Make-up artist*: Anne Pospischil. D*onogh Rees's make-up*: Abby. *Hair designer*: Shayne Redford. *Composer*: John Charles, with Dave Fraser. *Music producer*: Dave Fraser. *Vocals*: Edith Piaf, Marlene Dietrich, Kay Star, Bing Crosby. *Sound* : Mike Westgate, Finola Dwyer, David Newton, Brian Shennan.

Cast

Donogh Rees (Constance), Hester Joyce (Noeline), Dana Purkis (young Constance), Martin Vaughan (Alexander Elsworthy), Judie Douglass (Sylvia Elsworthy), Lee Grant (Mrs Barr), Graham Harvey (Errol Barr), Donald McDonald (John Munroe), with Miranda Pritchard, Roman Watkins, Beryl Te Wiata, Elric Hooper, Lenore Truscott, Stephen Taylor, Mark Hadlow, Paul Owen-Lowe, Don Kjestrup, Shane Briant, Yvonne Lawley, Jonathan Hardy, Joan Foster, Dai Evans, Noel Appleby, Marc Wignall, Gay Dean, Susan Trainer, Barbara Doherty, Susan Paterson, Joanne Power, Kathryn Lawrence, Kit Surring, Elizabeth Hill, Jules Regal, Lois Haynes, Ellen Phillips, Mrs Fitzwilliams, Mrs Scott, Phillip Peacocke, Phillip Rikihana, Frank Mitchell, Bill Le Marquand, Paul Grinder, Kate Hood, Jack Cormack, Harold Frazer, Rod Collinson, William Kircher, Gay Dean.

Auckland, 1948. Beautiful Constance Elsworthy watches entranced as femme fatale Rita Hayworth vamps it up in Gilda (1946), while alternating shots show Constance as a child pirouetting in her mother's coat, to her father's pleasure and her mother's disgust. Reprimanded when her students act out a scene from Gilda, Constance leaves teaching and becomes secretary of the Leprosy Society, a job arranged for her by an admirer's mother, leading socialite Mrs Barr. Ostracised by the Barrs for mismanaging the Leprosy Fund, Constance shows them up for fools at their garden party, catching the eye of Simon Malyon, an expatriate New Zealander and one of Hollywood's leading still photographers. Her initial excitement at being photographed by Malyon turns to terror and self-loathing when he brutally rapes her. In despair she accepts a marriage proposal, then rejects it in horror at the thought of becoming a Thames housewife. The deaths of her parents leave Constance alone. After rejecting her father's friend John, she invites the patrons of a working-class pub home to party at her large Mission Bay home.

The mess young Constance makes of painting her face prefigures a lifetime of bungled attempts to live glamorously and with passion. Stifled by the gentility and hypocrisy of provincial 1940s New Zealand and seduced by the Hollywood ideal, Constance creates her own dramas. The Oedipal theme provides some motivation for Constance's inability to be content with any man, yet ironically it is her men friends' attachments to their mothers she most resents. Hallucinatory dreams, often including her father, suggest Constance's fantasising may be caused more by psychosis than boredom. For all that Constance initially enjoys flouting convention and flaunting her sexuality, her more homely friend Noeline ends up having a much better time in the suburbs with her plumber.

Constance is a melodrama in the manner of the movies its heroine apes and is peppered with ironic humour. It is self-consciously stylish, although the dialogue is at times so stilted as to make its delivery difficult. The set pieces are beautifully choreographed and the production design painstaking and authentically detailed. Costumes, make-up and hair styles are superbly done. Images of entrapment and the song 'Bird in a Gilded Cage' provide symbolic reference to Constance's predicament and her three-sided mirror is used to suggest narcissism and a fractured personality. The melodramatic staging of the rape, the turning point for Constance when she is finally forced to separate fact from fantasy, provides a ghastly, fitting shattering of her illusions. The boldest and most melodramatic symbolic reference is the last shot of the film, a large, beautiful and unattainable moon. A period piece with an 1980s perspective, the film is both a parody of Hollywood and a dig at the pretensions of the rising middle-class.

Donogh Rees, in her first film role, is superb as the self-styled vamp, beautifully mimicking such Hollywood sirens as Greta Garbo, Marlene Dietrich and Rita Hayworth. Critics hailed her performance as 'magnificently realised', 'stunning', 'moving' and 'New Zealand's answer to Meryl Streep'. HM

1984 Taormina Festival, Italy: Bronze Charybdis Award.

THE SILENT ONE

1984

Gibson Film Productions in association with the New Zealand Film Commission and South Pacific Merchant Finance Ltd. © 1984. *Budget*: approx. $1.9 million. *Locations*: Aitutaki, One Foot Island (Rarotonga). *Distributor*: Gibson Group. *Rating*: G, June 1984. 35 mm. Dolby Stereo. Colour. 97.5 mins. (Amended to 92 mins, September 1987.)

Director: Yvonne Mackay. *Producer*: Dave Gibson. *Executive producer*: David Compton. *Screenplay*: Ian Mune. *Source*: Joy Cowley, *The Silent One*. *Director of photography*: Ian Paul. *Underwater photographers*: Ron Taylor, Valerie Taylor. *Editor*: Jamie Selkirk. *Production designer*: Tony Rabbit. *Wardrobe supervisor*: Joan Grimmond. *Turtle wrangler*: Allan Watters. *Music*: Jenny McLeod. *Conductor*: William Southgate. *Players*: The Wellington Regional Orchestra. *Vocals*: Kathy Blennerhassett, The Bach Choir. *Sound*: Ken Saville, John Gilbert, Ron Purvis, Les McKenzie, Ross Chambers, Malcolm Cromie, Jamie Selkirk, Tony Johnson.

Cast

Telo Malese (Jonasi), George Henare (Paui Te Po), Pat Evison (Luisa), Anzac Wallace (Tasiri), Rongo Tupatea Kahu (Taruga), Jo Pahu (Etika), Reg Ruka (Bulai), Mana Kuriraki (Kohi), Douglas Hosking (Manu), Mareta Tane (Hene), Mabel Wharekawa (Marama), Anthony Gilbert (Aesake), Bernard Kearns (Redbeard), Rangi Staski (Tomasi), Roy Staski (Matiu), Teina Tetoa (Timi), Prince Tui Teka (Postmaster), Mabel Wharekawa (Marama), with Teraki Tokorangi, Turi Tama (Baby Jonasi), Panapa Tekopua, Tiki Pare, Tuatonga Tekopua, Rurutaura Tauta, Taeta Tekopua (Diggers), Mama (Turtle).

Ron and Valerie Taylor (underwater photographers) with Telo Malese (Jonasi). Courtesy of the New Zealand Film Commission.

A baby washed up on a Pacific Island is raised by childless Luisa, who names him Jonasi. The villagers call him the Silent One and treat him as an outcast because he is deaf and mute. This rough treatment is exacerbated by Chief Taruga's kindness to him, as the Chief's position is threatened by tohunga Paui Te Po and the power-seeking Tasiri. When Jonasi befriends a white turtle, believed by the islanders to be evil, he is blamed for the island's drought. The turtle's call is irresistible and Jonasi disobeys orders to stay away from it. In a confrontation between Taruga and Paui Te Po the villagers are set to follow the tohunga when it begins to rain and the storm becomes a hurricane. Tasiri attacks Jonasi and is killed by a shark. Blaming the turtle, the villagers are turning on Jonasi when Taruga kills Paui Te Po. Jonasi is rescued by a friendly trader and the chief's son, Aesake. At sea Jonasi dives overboard and swims away with the turtle. Luisa mourns his loss until he visits her in turtle form. Two white turtles swim together out to sea.

The film allegorises the outsider theme, exploring oppositions of prejudice and acceptance, good and evil, pagan and Christian superstition and traditional and new ways. It is mythic and universal in implication, while not set on any specific island nor based on any specific Polynesian myth. Shades of *Macbeth* (Tasiri urged to vaulting ambition by a shaman) and of *Moby Dick* (the white sea creature feared as the embodiment of evil) add depth to the allegory. The perniciousness of shaman Paui Te Po's fear and ignorance is set against the pragmatism and open-mindedness of Chief Turaga. His son Aesake, who has been educated in New Zealand and who sees Jonasi's disability for what it is, offers hope for a more enlightened future. Jonasi's role is as the catalyst forcing the conflict into the open.

Ian Mune's accomplished adaptation of Joy Cowley's children's novel is the first New Zealand fictional feature directed by a woman to be submitted for a censorship certificate. (Melanie Read's **Trial Run** was submitted for censorship in September 1984.) Overall the film, with its eerie score using Cook Island orchestral and electronic music, is affecting and powerful. Viewer identity with the outsiders is secured in scenes containing segments shot from Jonasi's and the turtle's points of view. Jonasi 'hears' the call of the turtle and finds his voice when he thinks he is going to lose his friend. Although the plot is overloaded with incident, and at times the choreography of the crowd scenes is overly theatrical and some performances are overplayed, the boy and the turtle are a winning buddy pair. The cinematography is striking and lighting and use of colour are particularly effective. The many underwater scenes, which establish and sustain the boy/turtle relationship, are visual magic. The storm scene, enhanced by excellent special effects including use of a DC3 engine to generate wind, is a spectacular highlight. **The Silent One** is dedicated to 100 year-old Mama Turtle, who died shortly after the underwater scenes were filmed. HM

1984 New Zealand Music Awards: Best Film Soundtrack, Jenny McLeod.
Frankfurt Film Festival for Children and Young People: Best Children's Film.
Giffoni Festival of Films for Children and Young People, Italy: Silver Griffon and Special Award.
1985 Moscow Film Festival: Silver Medal, Children's Section.
Figuera de Foz Festival, Portugal: Best Children's Film.
1986 Chicago Children's Film Festival: Best Cinematographer.
First Paris Festival of Films for Children and Young People: Best Actor, Telo Malese; Special Jury Prize for Best Film.

1984

WILD HORSES

Endeavour Productions in association with the New Zealand Film Commission. Copyright date not recorded. *Budget:* $2 million. *Locations:* North Island Central Plateau. *Distributor:* Endeavour Productions Ltd. *Rating:* GY (Content may disturb), August 1984. 35 mm. Colour. 89.5 mins.

Director: Derek Morton. *Producer:* John Barnett. *Executive producer:* Gary Hannam. *Original screenplay:* Kevin O'Sullivan. *Director of photography:* Doug Milsome. *Camera operator:* Mike Hardcastle. *Editor:* Simon Reece. *Production designer:* Joe Bleakley. *Costume designer:* Julia Mansford. *Special effects:* Kevin Chisnall. *Stunt co-ordinator:* Robert Bruce. *Car stunt co-ordinators:* Geoff Murphy, Peter Zivkovic. *Master of horse:* Peter McKenzie. *Music:* Dave Fraser. *Vocals:* The Four Fours, The La De Das, The Avengers. *Sound:* Mike Westgate, Jamie Selkirk, Finola Dwyer, John Gilbert, Don Reynolds, Brian Shennan.

Cast

Keith Aberdein (Mitch), John Bach (Jack), Kevin J. Wilson (Harry), Sara (Robyn Gibbes), Tom Poata (Sam), Bruno Lawrence (Tyson), Marshall Napier (Andy), Martyn Sanderson (Jones), Michael Haigh (Benson), Kathy Rawlings (Mary), Matiu Mareikura (Kingi), Peter Tait (Joe), Richard Poore (Ranger), Derek Hardwick (Mill manager), Shirley Gruar (Barmaid), Helena Wilson (Anne).

Dan Mitchell moves to Tongariro National Park to make a living rounding up and selling wild horses. He is joined by brothers Jack and Harry Sullivan. Their bad luck turns when they team up with Sam and Sara, whose success comes from their conservationist approach. Deer hunters working for a 'venison recovery' firm declare war on Mitch and team, maintaining the horses disturb the deer and make shooting impossible. The National Parks Authority Ranger and the venison firm recovery manager hire a professional horse exterminator, Tyson, who encourages the deer hunters to join him in wiping out every last horse. As enmity builds Mitch develops a passion, which quickly turns to obsession, to catch one of the horses, a beautiful silver. First his wife, then the Sullivans, leave. Mitch and Sara pursue the silver, the last horse, and the deer hunters molest Sara. In a showdown Tyson and Mitch vie for the silver and Tyson dies in a bungled attempt to lasso it. Mitch sets it free, then sets his own mare free to ensure future generations of wild horses.

Wild Horses compresses events in New Zealand during the 1960s and 1970s into one year, 1970. Increasing numbers of wild horses roaming the Tongariro plateau at that time were regarded as a threat to the plateau's ecology and a hazard to motorists on the state highway, so the Government auth-orised a ranger to manage the park. Shooting of the horses was encouraged and people made their living catching and selling them. In the film Sara's mystical attachment to the horses is set against the pragmatism of the Park Ranger and the deer hunters and the cold indifference of the exterminator. Thematically a dichotomy is established between progress and old-fashioned values, with Mitch as the visionary seeing the silver horse representing the struggle of the individual to survive in a world increasingly driven by big business greed.

Shot in B-grade western style, **Wild Horses** makes excellent use of locations — sweeping, tussock-covered plains, crystalline rivers, glorious snow-capped mountains and a portentous horizon — but the genre clichés look comical and the stern messages are much too heavy for the disjointed narrative, which is full of holes, non sequiturs and unexplained incidents and relationships. Mitch's obsession, for example, develops in a few seconds' screen time. Attempts at humour fall flat and characterisation is minimal. Black-clad, black-horsed Tyson, borrowed from Sergio Leone, is, in fact, a mild-mannered man only doing his job. In conservation terms Mitch is actually on the wrong side, but sympathy for his plight is maintained through his passion for the beautiful silver horse and in the nastiness of his foe.

Director Derek Morton, who took no part in the postproduction, disassociated himself from **Wild Horses**, saying he 'couldn't make head or tail of what the story was. And I shot the bloody thing.' *HM

Onfilm, vol 3, no. 1, December 1985.

John Bach (Jack). *Courtesy of the New Zealand Film Commission.*

1984

MERRY CHRISTMAS MR LAWRENCE

Jeremy Thomas Productions in association with Cineventure Productions, Recorded Picture Company, Asahi National Broadcasting Company Ltd, Broadbank Investments Ltd, Oshima Productions. A.k.a. Happy Christmas Mr Lawrence. © 1982. Financed from New Zealand, Japan and the United Kingdom. *Locations*: Auckland, Rarotonga. *Distributor*: Kerridge Odeon. *Rating*: GA (Contains war violence. English and Japanese dialogue with subtitles), August 1984. 35 mm. Panavision. Dolby Stereo. Colour. 124.5 mins.

Director: Nagisa Oshima. *Producer*: Jeremy Thomas. *Executive producers*: Masato Hara, Eiko Oshima, Geoffrey Nethercott, Terry Glinwood. *Associate producers*: Joyce Herlihy, Larry Parr. *Screenplay*: Nagisa Oshima, with Paul Mayersberg. *Source*: Sir Laurens van der Post, *The Seed and the Sower* and 'A Bar of Soap' and 'The Sword and the Doll'. *Director of photography*: Toichiro Narushima. *Camera operator*: Hiroaki Sugimura. *Editor*: Tomoyo Oshima. *Production designer*: Jusho Toda. *Wardrobe supervisor*: Christine West. *Special effects*: Akira Houma. *Armourer*: Ralph Gardiner. *Music*: Ryuichi Sakamoto. *Brother's song*: Stephen McCurdy. *Sound*: Mike Westgate, Akira Honma, Tetsuya Ohashi.

Cast

David Bowie (Celliers), Tom Conti (Lawrence), Ryuichi Sakamoto (Yonoi), Takeshi (Hara), Jack Thompson (Hicksley), Johnny Okura (Kanemoto), Alistair Browning (De Jong), James Malcolm (Celliers's brother), Chris Broun (Celliers at 12 years), with Yuya Uchida, Ryunosuke Kaneda, Takashi Naito, Tamio Ishikura, Rokko Toura, Kan Mikami, Yuji Honma, Daisuke Iijima, Hideo Murota, Barry Dorking, Geoff Clendon, Grant Bridger, Ian Miller, Don Stevens, Richard Adams, Geoff Allen, Michael Baxter-Lax, Mark Berg, Marcus Campbell, Colin Francis, Richard Hensby, Richard Hoare, Martin Ibbertson, Rob Jayne, Richard Mills, Mark Penrose, Arthur Ranford, Steve Smith, Stephen Taylor, Richard Zimmerman, Yoichi Iijima, Satoshi Ito, Masaki Kusakabe, Kunihide Kuruma, Hiroshi Mikami, Akihiro Masuda, Tokuhisa Masuda, Takeshi Nagasawa, Takeshi Odashima, Masanori Okada, Shoetsu Sato, Rintaro Shibata, Masamichi Shibasaki, Kaname Shimura, Kenzo Shirahama, Hisao Takeda, Hidenobu Togo, Atsuo Yamashita, Heiwa Yoshihara, Takeshi Yu.

A Japanese prisoner of war camp, 1942. Sergeant Hara orders a guard, Kanemoto, caught having sex with prisoner De Jong, to commit harakiri. Camp commander Captain Yonoi intervenes. At a military trial Yonoi saves English Major Jack Celliers from execution. Colonel Lawrence, who speaks fluent Japanese, asks Hara for protection for De Jong. Kanemoto dies in a drawn-out harakiri/execution and De Jong suicides. When the British soldiers express disgust Yonoi orders their confinement without food or water. Celliers finds food for the men and flowers to mark De Jong's death. Yonoi, obsessed with Celliers, has manoeuvred to make him camp commander in place of the encumbent, Captain Hicksley. Celliers insults Yonoi by defiantly eating flowers in front of him and Yonoi has him beaten and jailed. Lawrence, accused of smuggling in a radio, is also jailed. Celliers tells Lawrence of the terrible guilt he feels about betraying his brother when they were schoolboys. Because Hara gets drunk on Christmas Eve Lawrence avoids execution. When Hicksley won't tell him about British arms capacity Yonoi orders the prisoners into the compound and prepares to execute him. Celliers comes between them, kissing Yonoi on both cheeks. Yonoi has Celliers buried up to his neck in sand. Before Celliers dies he fantasises reconciliation with his brother. Four years later Lawrence visits Hara on the eve of his execution for war crimes. They discuss right and wrong and Lawrence tells Hara that Yonoi, who has been executed, gave him a lock of Celliers' hair to place on a shrine in Japan.

With singing as its motif for freedom of expression, the film is explicit in depicting British public school cruelty as stemming from the same source as Japanese wartime cruelty. In the collision of East/West cultures different attitudes to freedom, sexuality and responsibility to the state are represented, but the implicit sexual nature of Yonoi's obsession with Celliers, and Celliers' obsessive need for redemption, make it more than a merely schematic line-up of positions. Cultural reconciliation is signalled in the final scene, with Hara and Lawrence concluding that nobody is right and that through Yonoi's recognition of his courage, Celliers has sown a seed in everyone.

Merry Christmas Mr Lawrence, much of which was shot in Auckland, is an ambitious film. It is Oshima's first film in English and some dialogue is hard to catch. There are lapses in the sound editing — one of Celliers' beatings occurs with no sound effects for some punches and in some scenes the sound is very flat — and occasional out-of-focus shots irritate. Excellent production design, an evocative score by prominent musician Ryuishi Sakamoto (who plays Yonoi) and convincing performances bring the story to life in spite of the theatricality of much of the choreography of scenes. The film was financed by New Zealand, British and Japanese money channelled through New Zealand's Broadbank. Its mixed reviews include the *Time Out Film Guide* calling it 'a fair old mess' and Leonard Maltin in *Movie and Video Guide* describing it as 'a strange, haunting drama'. HM

The crew has a break between takes. Courtesy of Jeremy Thomas and the Stills Collection, New Zealand Film Archive.

1983 Cannes Film Festival: Official Selection.

DEATH WARMED UP

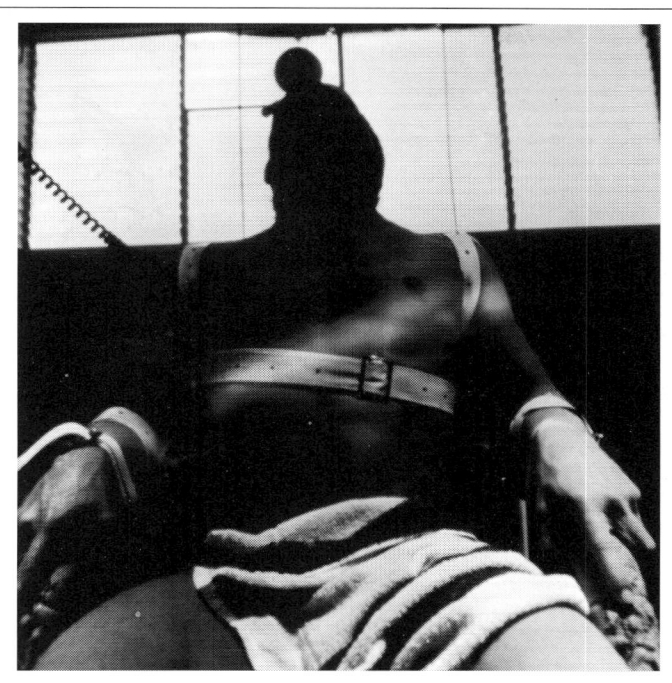

A waiting moment from David Blyth's fantasy. Courtesy of the New Zealand Film Commission.

Tucker Production Company Ltd in association with the New Zealand Film Commission. © 1984. *Budget*: $860 000. *Locations*: Auckland, Waiheke Island. *Distributor*: Endeavour Productions. *Rating*: R 16 (Violent content may disturb), August 1984. 35 mm (shot on 16 mm). Dolby Stereo. Colour. 84.5 mins.

Director: David Blyth. *Producer*: Murray Newey. *Screenplay*: Michael Heath, David Blyth. *Director of photography*: James Bartle. *Camera operator*: Alan Locke. *Editor*: David Huggett. *Production designer*: Michael Glock. *Costume designer*: Barbara Darragh. *Make-up effects*: Bryony Hurden, Rosalind McCorquodale. *Prosthetics*: Keith Pine. *Special effects supervisor*: Kevin Chisnall. *Stunt co-ordinator*: Robert Bruce. *Composer*: Mark Nicholas. *Music production manager*: Wayne Laird. *Vocals*: Suzanne, Annie Crummer, Peter Morgan. *Sound*: John McKay, Mike Westgate, David Huggett, Brian Shennan.

Cast

Michael Hurst (Michael Tucker), Margaret Umbers (Sandy), William Upjohn (Lucas), Norelle Scott (Jeannie), David Letch (Spider), Gary Day (Dr Archer Howell), David Weatherley (Prof. Tucker), Tina Grenville (Netty Tucker), Jonathan Hardy (Ranji Gandhi), Nat Lees (Jackson), Norm Fairley (Barman), Judy McIntosh (Nurse), Geoff Snell (Jannings), Bruno Lawrence (Tex Monroe), Ian Watkin (Bill), Karam Hau (Berry), Eva Radich (Sister Scott), Ken Harris (Janitor), Robert Bruce, Peter Bell, Ono, Dave Brown, Phillip Thorogood, Tim Lee, Alistair Douglas (Stunt men), Melissa Miles, Rebecca Saunders, Donna Oldnall, Julie Cooper, Michelle Yates, Dianne Guthrie, Rochelle Drumm, Angela Needham, Erina Larson, Victoria Bogle, Betty Wok (Nurses), David Parry (Milkboy), with Dave Clark, Rochelle Lawrence, Deborah McKinlay.

Dr Raymond Tucker and megalomaniacal genetic surgeon Dr Archer Howell win the Rothschild Award for Scientific Advancement. Howell, knowing his colleague intends to denounce his unethical experiments, programs Tucker's son Michael to shoot his parents. After seven years in a psychiatric institution Michael seeks revenge. On the ferry to Howell's island hospital, Trans Cranial Applications, Michael and friends Sandy, Lucas and Jeannie meet ghastly mutant Tex and fight off other hideous mutants Spider and Jannings, casualties of Howell's 'immortality' operations. As Howell drills into a brain and Tex's brains explode through his skull, Michael and friends explore a tunnel beneath the island. In a mad chase Jeannie is badly injured by Spider and Jannings, who is eventually impaled by Lucas. Spider evades Howell's execution order and frees a mob of murderous mutants who go on the rampage. Unable to defend themselves Lucas and Jeannie are killed. Michael drives off with Sandy but, deranged and raving, gets out of the car and, amidst the mayhem, is electrocuted by a collapsed pylon. Sandy runs away.

Targeted at a youth audience, **Death Warmed Up** celebrates B-movie splatter/horror. Technically the film is accomplished and uses the genre's conventions well, with atmospheric lighting, driving Dolby soundtrack, off-centre camera angles, clever choreography of action and shooting style, particularly in the chase scenes, convincingly gruesome special effects, a lively score and unconventional editing. The inventive production design, with its surreal use of colour, corrugated iron, high-tech clinical interiors and sci-fi props and costumes creates an effectively futuristic world of mechanistic menace. Some scenes were shot in Hellaby Meats' killing room.

Although the brain surgery is convincing enough to terrorise, the film lacks pace, a coherent plot and some character development to glue the episodes together. Dr Howell calls himself a new messiah and sets the film up for apocalypse with his 'we are the generation of the end', but does little more than drill brains and snarl. Spider, who becomes the focus of evil, is motiveless beyond the fact that he's had a personality-changing operation and, because Michael has no plan beyond some vague notion of revenge, he and his friends basically just lurch about, utter banal dialogue and fight whichever zombie happens by. The women are particularly irritating as they merely make up the numbers and make a lot of noise. Jeannie's death throes go on for so long it's a relief when she finally breathes her last. There's a Peter Sellers-style Indian spoof that's racist and unfunny (director David Blyth described the scene as a comment on the public mania for Gandhi and on the number of Indians running shops) and although the film attempts a high camp parody of the genre, its wit is wide of the mark.

Film Commission money was justified on the grounds that the production would help foster a commercial base for New Zealand films. **Death Warmed Up** was the first New Zealand film with a locally mixed Dolby stereo soundtrack and the first to be filmed entirely using a Steadicam. HM

1984 International Festival of Fantasy and Science Fiction Films, Paris: Grand Prix.

1984

SECOND TIME LUCKY

Jon Gadsby (the Angel Gabriel). Courtesy of Antony I. Ginnane.

Eadenrock Ltd. © 1984. *Locations*: Auckland, Thames, Twickenham Film Studios, England. *Distributor*: Kerridge Odeon Film Distributors. *Rating*: GY, September 1984. 35 mm. Panavision. Colour. 101 mins.

Director: Michael Anderson. *Producer*: Anthony I. Ginnane. *Associate producer*: Jon Turtle. *Co-producer*: Brian W. Cook. *Screenplay*: Ross Dimsey, Howard Grigsby, from a story by Alan Byrns, David Sigmund. *Additional screenplay*: Ron Challoner, Allan Byrns. *Director of photography*: John McLean. *Camera operator*: Michael Roberts. *Editor*: Tony Paterson. *Production designer*: David Copping. *Costume designer*: Bruce Finlayson. *Special effects*: Kevin Chisnall, Selwyn Anderson, Ralph Gardiner. *Composer/conductor*: Garry McDonald and Laurie Stone. *Players*: Roger Wilson, Rick Bryant's Band. *Sound*: Don Connolly, David Coulson, James Currie, Peter Smith.

Cast

Diane Franklin (Eve), Roger Wilson (Adam), Jon Gadsby (Gabriel), Robert Helpmann (The Devil), Robert Morley (God), John-Michael Howson (The Devil's assistant), Bill Ewens (Chuck), Eunice Ewens (Abby), Erna Larsen (Suzy), John Hudson (Jimmy), Gay Dean (Spinster), Brenda Kendall (Dykin), Onno Boelee (Ripperus), Melissa Miles (Sue), Paul Owen-Lowe (Roman guard), Derek Payne (Colonel Anderson), Norman Fairley (German officer), David Weatherley (British officer), Don Kjestrup ((Inn keeper), with Simon Forster, Karl Bradley, Darien Takle, Faye Flegg, Richard Poore, Donna Oldmall, David McKenzie, Grant Bridger, Alistair Browning, Peter Rowley, David Cameron, Graeme Moran, Terry Hayman, Teresa Woodham, Bob Parker.

The Devil bets God that Adam and Eve would fail on a second chance. Chosen by Angel Gabriel (Gaby) to undergo the test, nerdy American students Adam and Eve make chaste acquaintance at a frat party. After cops break it up Gaby whisks A and E off to the Garden of Eden (a 65 acre garden near Thames) where, for 20 minutes' film time, they nakedly and innocently cavort. The Devil persuades Eve to eat an apple. God, having lost the first round, transports them to Rome (Auckland War Memorial Museum), where Evia, Caesar's bride-to-be, attempts to seduce legionnaire Adameus. For offending Caesar he is thrown to a gladiator and dies. The pair turn up in World War I (downtown Auckland) where Eva is a French nurse spying for the Nazis. Soldier Adam resists her seduction attempt. As a gangster's moll in Prohibition America, Evie assures the doubting Lieutenant Adam that she can change, but it is not until they turn up as a rock star and a chick in the pay of evil rock producer Lew Seffer that Adam believes she really means it. In the showdown Eve is killed but, persuaded by Gaby, God gives them a second chance. Back at the frat party house, nerds Adam and Eve get together.

Ostensibly about Woman as Devil-inspired seducer, most attention is fixed on ways of taming the male member. In Eden Gaby warns Adam off sexual congress and hangs around to make sure Eve's seductions come to nothing. In wondering about their genitals, the innocents decide Adam has a banana and two berries, while Eve laments, 'It's not fair, I have nothing!' But, Adam reassures her, she has her 'lumps', thus drawing attention to the film's other fixation. Women's breasts appear in abundance, unlike the male penis which is much discussed but which remains hidden from view. This makes for some awkward shooting and editing in the Garden of Eden segment, as director and naked actor look for ways to coyly cover the banana and berries. There are no corresponding problems with Eve's lumps, however, as they are on constant show.

Screaming queen stereotypes and anti-gay sentiment abound and the Devil and his offsider are high camp. Ironically, with the exception of Eve and her two friends in the opening sequence, all the speaking parts are played by males. British actor Robert Morley is cute as God, but in his conversations with Gabriel the sequences are so badly shot and edited (they're obviously not in the same room) they look pasted together.

New Zealand investors financed the film through Broadbank Investments Ltd. British director Michael Anderson (**Around the World in Eighty Days**) was hailed in New Zealand at the time of the shoot as being the most experienced overseas director yet to work here. The film was cast in Los Angeles, Australia, New Zealand and England. New Zealand actors Jon Gadsby and Derek Payne were joined by about 25 other locals in speaking and non-speaking roles. In order to enhance the film's international appeal, Anderson chose actors whose New Zealand accents were not pronounced. HM

1984

CAME A HOT FRIDAY

Mirage Film Productions in association with the New Zealand Film Commission. © 1984. *Budget*: approx. $2.2 million. *Locations*: Wanganui, Waiuku, Whangaehu River. *Distributor*: Mirage Film Productions. *Rating*: GY, September 1984. 35 mm. Dolby Stereo. Colour. 102.5 mins.

Director: Ian Mune. *Producer:* Larry Parr. *Screenplay:* Dean Parker, Ian Mune. *Source:* Ronald Hugh Morrieson, *Came a Hot Friday*. *Director of photography:* Alun Bollinger. *Camera operator:* Paul Leach. *Editor:* Ken Zemke. *Production designer:* Ron Highfield. *Costume designer:* Barbara Darragh. *Musical director/composer:* Steven McCurdy. *Vocals:* Beaver, Prince Tui Teka. *Sound:* Hammond Peek, Greg Bell, Finola Dwyer, Brian Shennan, John Lipke.

Cast

Peter Bland (Wes Pennington), Phillip Gordon (Cyril Kidman), Michael Lawrence (Don Jackson), Billy T. James (Tainuia Kid), Marshall Napier (Sel Bishop), Don Selwyn (Cray), Marise Wipani (Esmerelda), Erna Larsen (Dinah), Phillip Holder (Dick), Tricia Phillips (Claire), Bruce Allpress (Don's Dad), Michael Morrissey (Morrie), Roy Billing (Darkie Benson), Hemi Rapata (Kohi), Bridget Armstrong (Aunt Agg), Stephen Tozer (Cop), Duncan Smith (Commercial traveller), Leslie Gregory (New Plymouth bookie), Alistair Douglas (Vicar), Peter Rowley (Bar man), Trudy Olson (Dance girl), Derek Hardwick (Capstan), Gaylene Wright (Balcony girl), Francis Cullenberg (Pop Simon), with Ian Watkin, Norm Keesing, Sean Duffy, Richard Stevenson.

New Zealand, 1949. City conman Wes and his sidekick Cyril are discovered running a horse-racing betting scam. Turning up on the Friday of Anzac weekend in Tainuia Junction, they dragoon local innocent, Don, into joining their con. Meanwhile gambling den proprietor Sel Bishop, in an insurance fraud, orders his lover Claire's brother, Morrie, to burn down the local billiard saloon and the old man living there dies. In a third storyline the Tainuia Kid, a Maori who thinks he's a Mexican bandito/Zorro cross, drives Sel to homicidal mania by letting down his tyres. After Don wins a thousand pounds off him in the pub, bookie Norm goes after the trio at Sel Bishops' Saturday night party. In an eventful night Don loses his virginity and Wes wins a thousand pounds, only to lose it when a cop breaks up the party. Wes, Cyril and the Tainuia Kid join forces against Norm and Sel. The climax sees Sel burned to death, Norm tipped into the river, Wes and Cyril parted then reunited and the Tainuia Kid throwing Wes's money to an imagined Taniwha. At the dénouement, Wes and Cyril pull up outside the town cenotaph where residents, gathered to remember the war dead, turn their backs on the troublesome pair. Watched wistfully by Don, Wes and Cyril speed towards Napier in search of their next scam.

Came a Hot Friday is a sprawling, rollicking tale in the spirit of the Ealing comedies. It is without the source novel's sexual perversion and sadistic violence and rejoices in its larger than life, parodic characters. Good-natured, nostalgic fun is made of small town 1940s New Zealand where Friday night's excitement is a pie and chips at the boozer. The cinematography is excellent and the plot rich in detail, with the minor characters' eccentricities adding to the fun. The pace, ably aided by tight editing and an upbeat 1940s musical score, never flags. Much of the humour's success results from the comic timing of the actors, who were encouraged to improvise. Crime itself is a joke because the crims are bunglers while the only vicious one, Sel, gets his just desserts. Ironically the con men, for all their sophistication, are the eventual losers, outclassed by the local 'fools' — Don gets Esmerelda and the Tainuia Kid gets a horse.

Slapstick, knockabout, running gags (shirtless Cyril shooting his cuffs, Wes jamming his finger), sight gags, irony and puns pepper the narrative which, while driven by crime, has mateship as its thematic glue. Wes and Cyril regard females as necessary for sport and pornographic pictures as a useful aid to masturbation, but their deepest felt emotions are those they feel for each other. Like antipodean Marx brothers, shrewd, grandiloquent Wes and naive, American-obsessed Cyril are a brilliant, unforgettable pair.

While British reviewers described the film as 'likeable' and 'amiable', Tom McWilliams's comment in *The Listener* (31 August 1985) that **Came a Hot Friday** was a 'fresh, funny, exuberant, childlike hoot of a film' exemplified the enthusiasm of local reviewers and audiences, who welcomed it as a 'Kiwi classic'.
HM

1986 Melbourne Film Festival: One of the Ten Best.
New Zealand Listener Film and Television Awards: Best Adaptation. Best Director. Best Editing. Best Film. Best Film Score. Best Male Performance, Peter Bland. Best Male Performance in a Supporting Role, Billy T. James.

Billy T. James (The Tainuia Kid). *Courtesy of the New Zealand Film Commission.*

1984

TRIAL RUN

Cinema and Television Productions in association with the New Zealand Film Commission. © 1984. *Budget*: less than $1 million. *Locations*: Auckland, Whangaparoa Peninsula. *Distributor*: Mirage Film Productions. *Rating*: GA, September 1984. 35 mm (shot on 16 mm). Colour. 90.5 mins.

Director: Melanie Read. *Producer*: Don Reynolds. *Associate producer*: Alane Hunter. *Screenplay*: Melanie Read, from an idea by Catarina De Nave and Melanie Read. *Director of photography*: Allen Guilford. *Penguin photographer*: Robert Brown. *Editor*: Finola Dwyer. *Production designer*: Judith Crozier. *Wardrobe supervisor*: Pat Murphy. *Music*: Jan Preston. *Sound*: Graham Morris, Brian Shennan, Annie Collins.

Cast

Annie Whittle (Rosemary Edmonds), Judith Gibson (Frances Hunt), Christopher Broun (James Edmonds), Philippa Mayne (Anna Edmonds), Stephen Tozer (Michael Edmonds), Martyn Sanderson (Alan West), Lee Grant (Mrs Jones), Frances Edmond (Police Constable Miller), Teresa Woodham (Publisher), Allison Roe (Allison), Karen Sims (Reporter), Maggie Eyre (Miss Walsh), Margaret Blay (Ghost), Roy (Smiley, the dog).

Rosemary is a former middle-distance runner who, in spite of opposition from her teenage children Anna and James, moves on assignment to a cottage on the coast to photograph rare, yellow-eyed penguins. She observes the birds daily and follows the training schedule devised on computer by James, which has her timing her 1500 m run to a public telephone box. Her family and her friend Frances visit often. Disturbed in her work by misogynistic neighbour Alan West and his aggressive dog Smiley and by inexplicable events like the destruction of her flower garden, Rosemary refuses to move back home, even when she survives a suspicious fire. Events climax when James stumbles in the door injured and she runs, followed by an unknown pursuer, to the telephone box to seek help. Driving to her aid, her family and Frances accidentally run over the pursuer who, under his disguise, is revealed to be James. In flashback James commits some of the acts by which he terrorised his mother into running her fastest time.

In line with Melanie Read's determination to make films 'that present a broader reality than that reflected in mainstream film and television' (*New Zealand Herald*, 22 September 1983) **Trial Run** is a psychological thriller of interest for its feminist intentions both in its production (75% of the crew were women) and in its subversion of the genre. Political points made are that the security of 'home' is not inviolate, that a thriller need not objectify its female victim via a voyeuristic shooting style and physical violence, that a female victim can fight back, that women can play roles, like that of police constable, traditionally reserved for men and that men do not have to play the lead. The question of identity is important for all the characters but especially for Rosemary, whose juggling of her roles is repeatedly reflected in photographic images as she looks back over her life and contemplates her budding independence. Rosemary's identification with Alan West's estranged wife, who inhabited the cottage before her death and whose ghost makes itself known to her, aims to deepen the thriller but is poorly integrated.

The slow build-up threads frightening events into a realistic framework. Smiley's campaign to kill the penguins and his owner's indifference to their fate runs nicely parallel to James's attacks on his mother. The ominous piano-and-percussion score and thriller conventions of lighting, shooting style, enigmatic characters and suggestive incidents build tension. Night scenes lose impact because the low blue lighting obscures detail and continuity is at times disjointed. Some incidents are left unexplained and the ending is disconcertingly abrupt.

Annie Whittle's training program was devised by runner Allison Roe, who appears briefly in the film. HM

Annie Whittle (Rosemary Edmonds). *Courtesy of the New Zealand Film Commission.*

OTHER HALVES

Orringham Ltd. © 1984. Financed from New Zealand and the United Kingdom. *Location*: Auckland City. *Distributor*: Finlayson-Hill Productions. *Rating*: R13 (Contains offensive language), October 1984. 35 mm. Colour. 106 mins.

Director: John Laing. *Producers*: Tom Finlayson, Dean Hill. *Associate producer*: Logan Brewer. *Executive producer*: Christopher J. Kirkham. *Screenplay*: Sue McCauley, from her novel *Other Halves*. *Director of photography*: Leon Narbey. *Camera operator*: Barry Harbert. *Editor*: Harley Oliver. *Production designer*: Robert Gillies. *Costume designer*: Judith Crozier. *Music*: Don McGlashan. *Lyrics*: Sue McCauley. *Vocals*: Jacqui Fitzgerald. *Sound*: Graham Morris, Prue Burch, Julian Ellingworth.

Cast

Lisa Harrow (Liz), Mark Pilisi (Tug), Paul Gittins (Ken), Clare Clifford (Aileen), Bruce Purchase (Irwin), Emma Piper (Audrey), Temuera Morrison (Tony), Fraser Stephen-Smith (Michael), Alison Routledge (Paula), Nathaniel Lees (Court clerk), David Weatherley (Judge), Stephen Tozer (Lawyer), Yvonne Lawley (Alice), John Bach (Jim), Grant Tilly (Dr Wray), Raymond Reid (Billy), Allan Sio (Max), Olaf Ulberg (Bones), Roy Billing (Harry Daniels), Judy McIntosh (Nurse), with Robert Gould, Alistair Topham, Paula Keenan, Derek Neville, Lottie Neville, Onno Boelee, Michael Baxter-Lax, Iva Seidenstein, Karam Hau, Karl Bradley, Kariba Mata'afa-Hanson, Aniva Mata'afa-Hanson, Joan Chalmers, Falala Valli, Maggie Maxwell, Lyndon Peoples, Nigel Carpinter, Rex Merrie, Norman Keasing, Peter Smith, Christopher Winn, Amy Colman, Stephen Barbarick, Susan Trainer, Don Kjestrup, Shirley Gruar, Gay Dean, Mathew Hunter.

Lisa Harrow (Liz Harvey) and Mark Pilisi (Thomas 'Tug' Morton). Courtesy of the New Zealand Film Commission.

Thirty-two year-old Liz, a well-educated, affluent, middle-class pakeha woman, becomes a voluntary patient in a psychiatric hospital after suburban neurosis and a dying marriage lead her to a suicide attempt. There she strikes up a tentative friendship with Tug Morton, a 16 year-old semi-literate Polynesian with a criminal record. Out of hospital Tug moves in with Liz, who is renting an anthropologist's designer loft, continuing his life of petty crime and drug-taking while she waits on tables. They become lovers, with Liz providing emotional security and Tug love without judgment. Tug is still drawn to the old life of hooning with his mates and promiscuous sex. Tensions are caused by his volatility, lack of self-esteem and emotional immaturity and after he beats Liz she stays away for some time. Eventually, facing her feelings for Tug, she returns to the loft and Tug accepts her offer for him to stay.

Based on Sue McCauley's award-winning autobiographical novel the film, subtitled 'a dangerous love story', eschews the novel's rural episodes in favour of an urban Auckland setting. Liz and Tug are outsiders from different sides of the track, divided by age barriers but drawn together in their mutual need. Shot when New Zealand was still touted as an egalitarian, non-racist society, **Other Halves** depicts insidious class and racial conflicts. Social services are either ineffective or obstructive and police are often brutal and racist. Issues of gender and sexuality are also explored, with none of the men, whatever their class, age and race, caring for monogamy.

Much of the success of this off-beat romance rests on the fine performances of the lead actors. Mark Pilisi was a 16 year-old Nuie Islander with a police record when he landed the role after being 'discovered' in a group of unemployed street kids in a community drama project. He is a natural, playing Tug with grace and assurance. As a counterpoint in acting technique Lisa Harrow, who is RADA trained, researched her role with a Reichian therapist. For visual interest the production design bypasses realism in favour of a more up-market, futuristic look in Liz's designer clothes (which become brighter and less blanket-like as she becomes more free), in the loft design and in Tug and his friends' jewellery and clothing. In lighting and design the film, with an international audience in mind, has a glamour that makes it less raw than the novel. The rumble with the skinheads was written in at the behest of Mark Pilisi and others in the cast who insisted on it for authenticity.

Other Halves was well received at home by audiences knowing the story was autobiographical. Some overseas reviewers were sceptical. David Robinson, for example, wrote in *The Times* (10 September 1986) that the film 'looks rather like the wish-dream of a middle-aged, middle-class woman, and severely strains credulity.' HM

1984

VIGIL

John Maynard Productions in association with the Film Investment Corporation of New Zealand and the New Zealand Film Commission. © 1984. *Budget*: a little under $2 million. *Locations*: Taranaki, the foot of Mount Messenger. *Distributor*: John Maynard Productions. *Rating*: GA, October 1984. 35 mm. Colour. 91 mins.

Director: Vincent Ward. *Producer*: John Maynard. *Executive producer*: Gary Hannam. *Associate producer*: Piers Davies. *Screenplay*: Vincent Ward, Graeme Tetley, assisted by Fiona Lindsay. *Director of photography*: Alun Bollinger. *Editor*: Simon Reece. *Production designer*: Kai Hawkins. *Costume designer*: Glenys Jackson. *Hawk trainer*: Rob Wheeldon. *Music*: Jack Body. *Sound*: Graham Morris, Ken Saville, Ross Chambers, Stewart Main, Dell King, Brian Shennan.

Cast

Bill Kerr (Birdie), Fiona Kay (Lisa Peers, 'Toss'), Gordon Shields (Justin Peers), Penelope Stewart (Elizabeth Peers), Frank Whitten (Ethan Ruir), with Arthur Sutton, Snow Turner, Bill Liddy, Maurice Trewern, Eric Griffin, Joseph Ritai, Emily Haupapa, Debbie Newton, Bob Morrison, Lloyd Grundy, Josie Herlihy, Sadie Marriner, Bill Brocklehurst, Rangitoheriri Teupokopakari.

A sheep farming family in a remote, windswept valley is shattered when the farmer, Justin, dies trying to rescue a trapped lamb. Justin's father-in-law Birdie hires poacher Ethan to help on the farm. Justin's wife Liz and daughter 12 year-old Toss resent Ethan's intrusion. Toss increasingly sees him as Lucifer, the angel with the sword, an enemy, like the hawks preying on the lambs, who must be expelled from the valley. While Birdie builds contraptions for the farm, Toss makes a shrine to her father. She lashes out at Ethan when her mother flirts with him, but later befriends him and, believing he can work magic, asks him to bring her father back. Enraged by Ethan's friendship with Toss, Liz, suspecting sexual impropriety, seeks him out in his hut. There they make love while Toss watches from a tree. Toss has nightmares of her father and Ethan duelling. Jealous of Liz and Ethan, Birdie and Toss shut themselves in Birdie's hut, where Toss, beginning her first menstruation, thinks she is dying. The farm is sold and Ethan leaves. When the family leave Birdie drives his hut away on the back of a tractor and Toss walks down the road away from the farm.

Observing the unities of time, character and place, **Vigil**'s simple narrative is the vehicle for a complex rite of passage story told largely from the point of view of an anxious, impressionable and highly imaginative child. In her growth towards puberty, Toss tries to make sense of her father's death and her mother's relationship with the enigmatic outsider through a mix of the imagery and rituals of Catholicism and her own animistic ideas. In exploiting the psychosexual impulses of mother and daughter, Ethan is a sinister figure, with his propensity for exposing the sexual in the everyday most tellingly shown in his repeated use of his finger as a phallic suggestion.

Nature is a mythical, archetypal force serving as a metaphor for the inner lives of the characters. The bleak harshness of the landscape and the elements and the relationships of the characters to each other and to the land are conveyed through expressionistic techniques; for example, where the arrangement of objects suggests dramatic tensions or where the visual image gives metaphoric force to human passion. Isolated, claustrophobic and embattled by indifferent Nature, the farm is an ideal correlative for the emotional states of its inhabitants. When the magic of childhood turns to nightmare, Toss has waking dreams that give visual shape to her emotional terrors. Motifs like the tractor, clothing, the hawks, the gun and Toss's stick acquire symbolic resonance and images of different ways of seeing (through smoke, mist, rain and distorting glass, for example) reveal the underlying theme, voiced by Birdie, that 'what you see depends on who you are.'

Vigil's production values are first class. Visually it is stunning, with the primary colours filtered out to give a luminous intensity to the grey/green images. The soundtrack is meticulously scored to build atmosphere. The actors, who endured a difficult shoot in very trying conditions, give convincing performances. Ward went to great lengths to get his film 'right', including driving and flying 30 000 kilometres around New Zealand looking for the right valley. When he found it, he had a road built and moved in all the buildings, animals and vegetation.

The film is open to many readings and on its release critics were divided. Some described it as pretentious, slow and unspontaneous. In *The Monthly Film Bulletin* (March 1985), for example, Robert Brown wrote, 'the persistent visual posturing and an irritating music-and-effects track evoke the grand themes of nature, family and survival, but without any notion of how they connect in reality with the mundane routines of sheep farming, rearing children and sharing living space.' Feminists criticised the way the love-making scene was shot from the male point of view. Other critics hailed **Vigil** as extraordinary and compelling, a poetic work of art and a sign of New Zealand film's coming of age. The *Los Angeles Times* (8 April 1986), for example, described it as 'a film of elemental beauty and growing tension' and Ward as 'the most gifted and original of New Zealand's filmmakers'. It established Vincent Ward's reputation as an exciting new talent. **Vigil** was the first New Zealand film selected to screen In Competition at Cannes where it received a standing ovation. HM

1984 Cannes Film Festival: In Competition.
Prades Film Festival: Most Popular Film.
1985 Imag Fic Festival, Spain: Best Film.
1986 New Zealand Listener Film and Television Awards: Best Cinematography. Best Original Screenplay. Best Production Design.

Fiona Kay (Lisa 'Toss' Peers). Courtesy of the New Zealand Film Commission.

HEART OF THE STAG

1984

Southern Light Pictures in association with the New Zealand Film Commission. © 1983. *Budget*: $1.2 million. *Location*: Chequers Sheep Station, King Country. *Distributor*: Southern Light Pictures. *Rating*: RP16 (Theme may disturb), October 1984. 35 mm. Colour. 94.5 mins.

Director: Michael Firth. *Producers*: Don Reynolds, Michael Firth. *Executive producers*: Rowan Chapman, Keith Gosling. *Screenplay*: Neil Illingworth, with additional writing by Bruno Lawrence, Michael Firth and Martyn Sanderson, from a story by Michael Firth. *Director of photography*: James Bartle. *Camera operator*: John Toon. *Editor*: Michael Horton. *Production designer*: Gary Hansen. *Wardrobe supervisor*: Mike Kane. *Technical farm adviser*: Gerald Chambers. *Stag co-ordinator*: John Wildman. *Composer*: Leonard Rosenman. *Players*: The New Zealand Symphony Orchestra. *Sound*: Hammond Peek, Brian Shennan, Dave Keen, David Newton, Ross Chambers.

Cast

Mary Regan (Cathy Jackson), Bruno Lawrence (Peter Daley), Terence Cooper (Robert Jackson), Anne Flannery (Mary Jackson), Michael Wilson (Jock Bestwick), Susanne Cowie (Young Cathy), John Bach, Tim Lee, Greg Naughton, Tania Bristowe (Shearing gang).

When his ute breaks down in remote King Country, Peter Daley seeks help from farmer Robert Jackson, who then hires him, but warns him off hunting 'his' stags. Farmhand Jock's cautioning, Jackson's daughter Cathy's timidity and her paralysed mother Mary's abortive attempt to speak warn Peter all is not well. He is sent to the tops to muster and, tentatively, he and Cathy become close during her illicit visits. Robert orders Peter to leave after mustering when the shepherd prevents him from shooting a stag. On Peter's last night Robert beats him in a stag roaring competition. Upset by the shearers' bullish behaviour, Cathy tells Peter about her father's incest. Persuaded to leave with Peter, she blocks her father's rape attempt. In a tense climax Robert, having killed his wife as she tries to intervene, stalks Cathy and Peter in the hills. Peter acts as a decoy, then calls a stag. Robert's gun jams and he is fatally impaled on the charging stag's horns. Peter hugs Cathy, but she steps back from his embrace.

Heart of the Stag is a tense, unsensationalised psychological drama. The actors workshopped the screenplay and Mary Regan researched her role with incest victims and support groups, with some of the resulting dialogue and information incorporated into the script. The performances are convincing and avoid caricature despite the archetypal roles. Too terrified to speak, Cathy slashes at garden plants and at her mirrored face. Mary Jackson fingers a gun she has not the strength to lift and Jock warns Daley off with the roundabout 'he doesn't like anybody to touch what's his.' Uncouth shearers reinforce Cathy's idea that all men are the same and widens the story's implications, while the hypocrisy of religion (the Jacksons are practising Catholics) is also implicated.

Growing intimacy between Peter and Cathy builds carefully and graphic father/daughter sex scenes bring home their vileness without prurience. By way of symbolism Cathy is like a startled deer while deerhunting represents male aggression, territoriality and sex drive. The link between Cathy and the stag as the victims of male power play is bald and the poetic justice of the stag's 'saving' Cathy contrived. Happily the ending more honestly suggests that, rather than quick-fix happy-ever-afters, for the incest survivor the road back to normality is not smooth.

Shot in rich browns and greens, **Heart of the Stag** is visually sumptuous and the mustering scenes gorgeous. Frequent use of shot/reverse shot, as when Robert and Peter each stand by a mounted stag's head and trade ideas about hunting, plays up the film's contrasts. The musical score is spare and effective in suggesting hidden horrors.

The film was received well, with the *Los Angeles Times* describing it as 'electrifyingly good' and *Newsday* seeing in Bruno Lawrence 'the tough tenderness of a young Brando.' HM

Bruno Lawrence (Peter Daley). *Courtesy of the New Zealand Film Commission.*

1984

IRIS

Endeavour Productions and Aotea Enterprises in association with TVNZ and Broadbank Investments Ltd. © 1984. Telefeature. *Locations*: Wellington, Paekakariki. No censorship rating (TVNZ in-house production,). Videotape. Colour. 90 mins.

Director: Tony Isaac. *Producers*: John Barnett, Tony Isaac. *Associate producer*: Murray Newey. *Screenplay*: Keith Aberdein. *Directors of photography*: James Bartle, Howard Anderson. *Camera operator*: Chris Reed. *Editor*: Michael Horton. *Production designer*: Josephine Ford. *Wardrobe supervisors*: Pam Wood, Chris Pickard, Mike Kane, Julia Mansford. *Research*: Jan Haynes. *Composer*: John Charles. *Music producer*: Dave Fraser. *Sound*: Graham Ridding, Geoff Shirkey.

Cast

Helen Morse (Iris/Sammie), Philip Holder (Dr Tothill/Kelly), John Bach (Mike), Donogh Rees (Simone/Kate), David Aston (Harry/Laurence), Liz McRea (Augusta Wilkinson), Roy Billing (John Wilkinson), Navit Harmor (Iris aged 10), Derek Challis (Derek Challis), Katy Platt (Maggie), with Jan Alexander, Michael Batley, Gerald Bryan, Peter Dennett, Leo Donnelly, Gilbert Goldie, Peter Hambleton, Chris Hampson, Kate Harcourt, Maria Heenan, Christopher Isaac, Roy Kellahan, Akira Kikuchi, Lew Martin, Alan Morris, Helen Moulder, Michael Noonan, Adam Ogilvy, Perry Piercy, John Reid, Patrick Smyth, Tandi Wright, Kay Melhuish.

Helen Morse (Iris/Sammie). Courtesy of the New Zealand Film Commission.

Born in Capetown in 1906, Iris Wilkinson emigrates to New Zealand as a child. Independent and imaginative, she finds in writing 'a mysterious sense of power'. As a journalist she graduates to parliamentary correspondent and falls for Harry, a fellow journalist, who rejects her to travel. She becomes lame after a fall from her horse. Pregnant, she travels to Australia where her son is stillborn and where she hears of Harry's death. Back home she takes the name of her dead son, Robin Hyde, as her pen name. After the birth of her second son Derek, despair leads her to a suicide attempt. Hospitalised, Iris continues writing and publishing. Her love for a resident doctor is unrequited and she leaves for England, going first to China, where she is brutally treated by invading Japanese. In England she continues writing, but, unable to live with despair, dies from an overdose of the sleeping pills to which she has become addicted. In a film-within-the-film film-makers struggle to produce a screenplay that truthfully captures Iris's life and art.

Television producer/director Tony Isaac originally planned to dramatise New Zealand writers' accounts of World War I. Although TVNZ rejected the idea, Isaac's fascination with Robin Hyde's writing led to the making of **Iris**. Through her son Derek Challis, Tony Isaac and Keith Aberdein had access to much of Iris Wilkinson's original writing in the form of manuscripts, journals and notes and they spoke with many of her contemporaries in their quest to find 'the woman behind the pseudonym Robin Hyde'.

The search occurs within the framework of a parallel contemporary drama. Suffering from writer's block, screenwriter Kelly struggles to do justice to his literary idol while actor Sammie tries to do justice to the writer in her performance. Kelly, sceptical about Sammie because of her reputation as a feminist, behaves obstructively in a way that parallels the obstacles Iris faced in the restrictive 1920s and 1930s. Chinese-box complexity occurs in the appearance of Iris's son Derek discussing his misgivings about the biopic with fictional characters Sammie and director Mike. Through their mutual regard for Iris, Kelly and Sammie develop a closeness that provides an upbeat ending, while the image of Iris remaining in front of the dressing room mirror as Sammie leaves is a reminder that for her there was to be no happy-ever-after.

Australian actor Helen Morse is excellent in both roles. Iris's poetry and prose, voiced-over throughout the narrative, give a clear sense of her talent. The contemporary story is at times contrived, particularly in the set-piece discussions, but Iris's troubled life, haunted by loss and the unsuccessful search for love, is dramatised without sensationalism. Iris's fascination with the pull for settlers between England as their cultural home and their adopted land, New Zealand, symbolised for her by the godwits' annual migration to Siberia, is a cornerstone of the film, as it is for her autobiographical novel *The Godwits Fly*. **Iris** screened on New Zealand television on 10 October 1984. HM

1984

MESMERIZED

The video slick from a later release of the film. Courtesy of Tony Ginnane.

Orinward Ltd and Manchester Productions for RKO Challenge. © 1984. A United Kingdom production financed from New Zealand. *Budget*: $5 654 930. *Locations*: Waimate Mission House, Bay of Islands, Auckland. No NZ theatrical release. *NZ video rating*: 16 (Sexual content may offend and/or offensive language). 35 mm. Panavision. Colour. 94 mins.

Director: Michael Laughlin. *Producer*: Antony I. Ginnane. *Executive producers*: Mark Seiler, Christopher J. Kirkham. *Associate producers*: Howard Grigsby, Richard Moore. *Co-producer*: Jodie Foster. *Screenplay*: Michael Laughlin, based on work by Jerzy Skolimowski. *Director of photography*: Louis Horvath. *Camera operator*: David Burr. *Editor*: Petra von Oelffen. *Production designer*: John Wingrove, Dan Hennah. *Costume designer*: Patricia Norris. *Composer/conductor*: Georges Delerue. *Sound*: Tim Lloyd, Mike Le Mare, Karola Storr, Trevor Pyke, Ian Turner, David Campling.

Cast

Jodie Foster (Victoria), John Lithgow (Oliver), Michael Murphy (Wilson), Dan Shor (George), Harry Andrews (Old Thompson), Beryl Te Wiata (Mrs Simmons), Reg Evans (Mr Simmons), with Sarah Peirse, Jonathan Hardy, Don Selwyn, Philip Holder, Derek Hardwick, George Spoors, Bob Gould, Jonathan Elsom, Norman Fairley, John Smith, Norman Fletcher, Ian Harrop, David Baxter, Tony Madigan, Curly del Monte, Ernie Stanley, Patrick Smith, David Cameron, John Wingrove, Sheila Summers, Jenni Matson, Carmen Heta, Kate Hood, Geoffrey Hill, Karl Bradley, Trevor Haysom, Rob Jayne.

New Zealand, 1880. A woman gives birth and her daughter, later named Victoria, is whisked away to be brought up in an orphanage. While Victoria is still a schoolgirl she inexplicably marries a much older merchant, Oliver, who comes back for her when she leaves school and takes her to his country home. Oliver peers at her through peepholes as she undresses. Unhappy, she attempts to leave with Oliver's younger and handsomer brother George, but in a struggle George seems to die. Victoria has a stillborn child. Things brighten when a visiting American reverend interests her in reading *Mesmer* and, in Oliver's presence, he hypnotises Victora. Inexplicably the reverend leaves town. Victoria finds a letter from George that Oliver has kept hidden. He becomes ill, and there are intimations that Victoria may be poisoning him. When he dies Victoria is tried and found innocent as there is no medical explanation for the death. She contacts George to say she wants to be alone and sails into the wide blue yonder.

At first **Victoria** says little, conveys her thoughts in voice-over, plays the piano and often wears black. A man sniffs her clothing. Unhappy in her arranged marriage she falls for someone not her husband, with violent results. Any temptations to see **Mesmerized** as a precursor to **The Piano**, however, are quickly dispelled. The video cover titillates with promises of erotic obsession, but the contents offer only a man peering through peepholes at his wife. The object of his gaze fancies his younger brother, but a fleeting few moments together, an unexplained pregnancy and a single letter are all that comes of that.

There is some toing-and-froing with a pair of scissors during the two mesmerising sequences, but it doesn't add up to much in the way of mystery. Attempts to reveal the plight of women in colonial times are sunk by a narrative that has no truck with cause and effect, tension or logic. The acting, including that of Jodie Foster, is uniformly wooden. Interesting touches include some lovely Saint Bernard dogs and an ending where, instead of staying within the codes of romantic melodrama, the Victorian woman chooses to live alone.

The film was shot mainly in the Bay of Islands and, although there were New Zealanders in the cast and crew, Actors' Equity was angered by the number of Americans in the cast and picketed the Auckland offices of Challenge Corporate Services, the film's backers, and threatened to disrupt the shoot. The film was distributed by RKO. It had a limited theatrical release but was not screened theatrically in New Zealand. It was released on video worldwide and has screened on television in many territories. HM

Should I Be Good?

Grahame J. McLean and Associates in association with Pan Asian Film Distributors Ltd, Hong Kong, with the assistance of Keith Hawke Films Ltd, Hong Kong, and Salon Films Thailand Co Ltd, Bangkok. © 1985. *Budget*: approx. $2.2 million. *Locations*: Wellington, Bangkok, Hong Kong. *Distributor*: Blondini Brothers Ltd. *Rating*: GA, February 1985. 35 mm (shot on 16 mm). Colour. 112.5 mins.

Director and producer: Grahame McLean. *Associate producer*: Narelle Barsby. *Screenplay*: Grahame McLean, based on original research by Lewis Pennington. *Director of photography*: Warrick Attewell. *Camera operator*: Richard Bluck. *Editor*: Jamie Selkirk. *Production designer*: John Roberts. *Wardrobe supervisor*: Catriona Caird. *Musical director*: Geoff Castle. *Composers*: Taj Mahal, Hammond Gamble, Geoff Castle, Julie Amiet, Mike Farrell, Stuart Pearce, Kim Fowley, Harry Lyon, Rob Winch, Billy Kristian. *Lyrics*: Harry Lyon, Beaver, Hammond Gamble, Rob Winch, Geoff Castle. *Sound*: Bob Clayton, John Gilbert, John Lipke.

Cast

Harry Lyon (Nat Goodman), Joanne Mildenhall (Vicki Strassbourg), Spring Rees (Anne-Marie Carre), Hammond Gamble (Ed Patterson), Beaver (Julie Patterson), Terence Cooper (Frank Lauber), Robin Dene (Robert Appleby), Simon O'Connor (Michael Elworthy), John Chico (Chico), Christine Higgs (Caroline Prendergast), Bruce Allpress (Neville Oswald), Alanna McLean (Pip), Renee Witting (Cees van der Groot), with Gilbert Goldie, Keith Richardson, Jason Saunders, Duncan Smith, Euan Upston, Christine Williams, Jean Budge, Katy Platt, Ann Pacey, Terry Mortensen, Trevor Morley, Stephen Taylor, Geoff Heath, Francie Chung, Lawrence Curry, Hamish McDonald, Loren Robb, Brent McDonald, Jean Palmer, Chris Ghent, Rob Schreiber, Joan Shute, Diana Johnston, Peter Morgan, Geoff Castle, Mike Farrell, Craig Walters, Bruce Kerr, Ross Burge, Betty Young, Mike Gregory, Kerry Dawson, Amy Bardsley, Kim Ackeus, Caroline Girdlestone, Catriona Caird, Dee Winterburn, Adrienne Frazer, Alan Elliot.

Would-be politician Frank Lauber pledges to destroy the evil of drug trafficking. Nat Goodman is released after doing time during the 'Mr Asia' drug busts and learns his former singing partner Anne-Marie is a prostitute with a heroin habit working for the underworld heavy van der Groot who owns the nightclub where Nat sings with Ed Patterson and his partner Julie. Television journalist Vicki has her interest in the Mr Asia affair re-awakened when a mutilated body is found in Wellington harbour. Looking for Anne-Marie Nat returns to the underworld where he meets Vicky and they team up to expose corruption. The Patterson's teenage daughter Pip, mistaken for Vicki, is shot dead. Bad guy Elworthy and van der Groot establish a 'casting agency' to launder money through Hong Kong. Vicki is threatened then fired and van der Groot is murdered. Anne-Marie is sent to Hong Kong to dry out. She meets Ed's band in Bangkok, resumes her singing career and frames Lauber by sending him heroin. In New Zealand police arrest Lauber.

Known as Mr Asia by international police New Zealander Martin Johnstone was about to be arrested on charges relating to his alleged leadership of a worldwide narcotics smuggling syndicate when he was murdered in Britain in 1980. The following year New Zealander Terence Clark, a.k.a. Alexander Sinclair, was jailed for the murder. Just before he was to reveal the powers behind the organisation he died in jail. Efforts to trace the continuing syndicate are dramatised in the film, which proposes 'the real Mr Asia' is a prominent businessman running the narcotics trade with a clique of respected lawyers and accountants.

When computer problems aborted producer/director Grahame Mclean's efforts to write a script he decided to shoot his film without one. During the shoot he dictated dialogue to be typed up while the camera crew set up. In the press kit taken with the film to Cannes McLean says, 'It was fun because we'd go on location and nobody would know what was happening except me.' Most of the actors were non-professionals and many were musicians. Singer Harry Lyon says 'I kept asking Grahame McLean … if he knew what he was doing … getting me for the part.'

There are things to like about this film. The musos and hangers-on look comfortable in their roles and the musical numbers are well done. Hammond Gamble and Beaver's raunchy rendition of 'Should I Be Good?' is a highlight. The Patterson family scenes with Ed, Julie, their teenage kids and mate Nat are very ordinary and credible and the nightclub and brothel scenes work. In particular Spring Rees performs well as Anne-Marie. Less credible are the comic-book big-time crooks. All the actors are hampered by lack of a coherent script and are obviously making it up as they go along. Gaping plot holes, non sequiturs and awkward filler scenes give the whole thing a stuck together look. There is no centre to the narrative and there are far too many characters. Just when the story seems to be going somewhere it lurches off in another direction.

The film screened for two weeks in Wellington but its season was cut short due to poor audience attendance. It also screened in Auckland when, in 1990, the director Grahame McLean showed it in a Travelling Road Show of films that also included **The Lie of the Land** and **Bad Taste**. HM

Harry Lyon (Nat Goodman) and Beaver (Julie Patterson) perform together as singers in **Should I Be Good?** *Courtesy of Grahame McLean.*

THE LOST TRIBE

Meridian Films and the Film Investment Corporation of New Zealand in association with the New Zealand Film Commission. © 1984. *Budget*: approx. $1.75 million. *Locations*: Wellington, Carey's Bay, Harrison's Cove, Milford Sound. *Distributor*: Amalgamated Theatres Ltd. *Rating*: R13, February 1985. 35 mm. Colour. 97 mins.

Director: John Laing. *Producers*: Gary Hannam, John Laing. *Screenplay*: John Laing. *Director of photography*: Thom Burstyn. *Camera operator*: Michael Hardcastle. *Editor*: Philip McDonald. *Art director*: Gerry Luhman. *Wardrobe supervisor*: Robin Laing. *Special effects*: Johnny Morris. *Composer*: Dave Fraser. *Sound*: Ken Saville, Philip McDonald, John Gilbert, Ross Chambers, Brian Shennan.

Cast

John Bach (Edward/Max Scarry), Darien Takle (Ruth Scarry), Emma Takle (Katy), Don Selwyn (Sergeant Swain), Terry Connolly (Inspector Ford), Ian Watkin (Mears), Martyn Sanderson (Bill Thorne), Keith Aberdein (Edward's double), Adele Chapman (Aileen Armstrong), Christopher Mills (Detective Sgt James), Joanne Simpson (Louisa), Alex Aitcheson (Ramsay), Bill Smith (Janitor), Nancy Renwick (Mrs Ball), Milne Cameron (Detective), Daryl Watt, Barry Lynch, Chris Cassin, Bert Cayless, Eric Coyle (Policemen), Sarah Ingram (Sandra Merrill), Michael Heath (Drunk).

In voice-over, young Katy Scarry explains that her father Max, an anthropologist, has gone missing while searching for the graves of a lost Maori tribe, the Hawea, which disappeared more than 100 years previously. In Wellington the body of prostitute Sandra Merrill is found and circumstantial evidence leads to the questioning of Max's identical twin brother, journalist Edward Scarry. Katy dreams she sees her father in 'a monster cave'. When Edward and Max's wife Ruth travel to Fiordland in search of Max, they are frustrated by the inaction of Sergeant Swain, who, believing Max has broken local tapu, refuses to mount a search. A prostitute identifies Edward as having been with Sandra the night she died. In voice-over Katy explains there is enmity between the twins because Edward and Ruth were formerly lovers. Edward and Ruth spend the night in Max's Fiordland island hut and as they make love Katy, staying at a hotel, 'sees' them in a mirror. Ruth, terrified by the 'presence' she feels in the cabin, returns to the hotel the next day. Edward stays at the hut and finds a burial ground Max has been excavating. In a confrontation between the brothers, Max murders Edward and places him, naked, in a burial cave. Dressed as his twin he returns to his family posing as Edward. In voice-over Katy explains her delight in having her father back and her mother's acceptance of the deception.

Billed as a psychological thriller, **The Lost Tribe** mixes madness (Max), murderous sibling rivalry (Max and Edward), supernatural prescience (Katy) and Maori mysticism (the tapu of the lost tribe). Character motivation is inadequately explained, with no plausible reason given for Max's murder of the prostitute, Mears' air of menace, Ruth's acceptance of Edward's sexual advances or her silence when her husband reappears disguised as his twin. A glaring implausibility occurs when the prostitute who identifies Edward in a police line-up fails to recognise him shortly afterwards on the grounds that she is drunk. Edward's lifetime domination by Max and Sergeant Swain's obstructiveness in the search for Max are explained in Katy's voice-over, the clumsy device providing much of the story's information and momentum. The premise that it may be possible to trace the occupation of the early Maori is an interesting story idea, but is all but swamped by the pakeha good/evil histrionics centred mostly on the Jekyll and Hyde conflicts of the Scarry twins.

The visuals are splendid. Excellent cinematography shows off the beauties of the Fiordland settings without reducing them to chocolate box banality. A prowling camera, superb film noir lighting and an effectively eerie soundtrack engender tension not provided by the narrative. The film was shot in 1982 but not released theatrically until 1985. HM

Don Selwyn (Sergeant Swain) and Emma Takle (Katy). Courtesy of the New Zealand Film Commission.

1983 Sitges Film Festival, Spain: Jury Prize.
Rencontres du Jeune Cinema, France: Jury Prize.
Orléans Film Festival, France: Special Jury Prize

1985

THE QUIET EARTH

Peter Smith (Api), Alison Routledge (Joanne) and Bruno Lawrence (Zac Hobson).
Courtesy of the New Zealand Film Commission.

Cinepro/Pillsbury Productions. © 1985. *Location*: Auckland. *Distributor*: Mirage Entertainments Ltd. *Rating*: GY, March 1985. 35 mm. Dolby Stereo. Colour. 91.5 mins.

Director: Geoff Murphy. *Producers*: Sam Pillsbury, Don Reynolds. *Screenplay*: Sam Pillsbury, Bill Baer, Bruno Lawrence. *Source*: Craig Harrison, *The Quiet Earth*. *Director of photography*: James Bartle. *Camera operator*: Paul Leach. *Editor*: David Huggett. *Production designer*: Josephine Ford. *Costume designer*: Mike Kane. *Special effects supervisor*: Ken Durey. *Composer*: John Charles. *Music producer*: Dave Fraser. *Sound*: Mike Westgate, Hammond Peek, Finola Dwyer, John McKay, Gethin Creagh, Martin Oswin.

Cast

Bruno Lawrence (Zac Hobson), Alison Routledge (Joanne), Peter Smith (Api), Anzac Wallace (Api's mate), Norman Fletcher (Perrin), Tom Hyde (Scientist).

Research scientist Zac wakes to find the city deserted and guesses that Operation Flashlight, the global top-secret energy project he has been collaborating on, has set off an 'Effect'—a distortion of the space/time fabric—and wiped out the population. All clocks are stopped at 6.12 a.m. As Zac kaleidoscopes through a tangle of emotions, he lives out several fantasies, shooting a Christ on the cross, commando-style, and announcing 'And now I am God.' He meets Joanne and they search for more people and make love. When they find Api the men become instant rivals. Swapping stories, the three conclude they were all at the point of death when the Effect occurred. Realising that continuing instability could cause a repeat of the first Effect they drive north, planning to blow up the satellite station linked to the power grid around the earth. Zac tricks the others into thinking he is returning to Auckland and in his absence they make love. Zac drives a truck loaded with dynamite into the laboratory and in the ensuing explosion is on the point of death when the Effect occurs again. Zac wakes on a beach, alone, facing an unknown planet.

With the film a sci-fi hybrid of the 'amoral scientist' and the 'last person on earth' stories, the plot McGuffin has American scientists concealing information about potentially devastating side effects of its system to fuel war planes. Colluding New Zealand scientists are culpable pawns and the source novel's question 'Who has the right to play God with the universe?' is reprised. Most successful is the first third where the 'last person on earth' scenario, while touched with humour, is effectively and chillingly wrought. Impetus is lost in the shift in focus and tone with the injection of male rivalry and its attendant adolescent macho posturing. As the men fight for sexual dominance, dialogue and performances become forced. Joanne overdoes the 'playing God' idea to the point where it seems possible that, last woman on earth or not, she might be outstaying her welcome. Racial tension arises through Api accusing Zac of seeking power through perpetuating the coloniser mentality.

The dramatic potential of apocalyptic depopulation is realised in James Bartle's excellent cinematography with judicious use of light, colour effects, movement, wide angle lenses and skew angles. The opening and closing scenes are visual highlights, while the rest of the imagery, particularly in the deserted city sequences, is effectively askew. Skilful use is made of models and surreal painted sets and the music, played by the New Zealand Symphony Orchestra, is powerful. Symbolism in names (Api and Zac suggest an A-Z range of possibilities) and in the timing of the Effect (the Book of Revelations 6:12) reinforce the archetypal dimension.

One apocryphal story has Bruno Lawrence burning an early version of the script.* The film, made under pressure because of the incipient lifting of tax concessions and with the added burden of 92 locations, was New Zealand's first sci-fi and the first where all the sound was done post-sync. Negative criticism included *The Monthly Film Bulletin* critic Philip Strick's view (April 1986) that the film is 'seriously adrift from sense and logic by its conclusion.' In general it was well-received, eliciting rave reviews such as that in the *Los Angeles Daily News* (18 October 1985) describing it as 'quite simply the best science-fiction film of the 80s.' Overseas reviewers were also keen to read the film as an expression of New Zealand's recently declared anti-nuclear stand, made in defiance of the superpowers. HM

1986 Madrid Film Festival: Best Director Award. International Fantasy Film Festival, Rome: Best Actor, Bruno Lawrence. Best Director. Tashkent Film Festival: Special Jury Prize For Peace.
1987 New Zealand Listener Gofta Awards: Best Film. Best Cinematography. Best Director. Best Editing. Best Male Performance: Bruno Lawrence. Best Male Performance in a Supporting Role, Peter Smith. Best Production Design. Best Screenplay Adaptation.

Reference
* *Onfilm*, vol. 3, no. 1, December 1985.

1985

KINGPIN

Morrow Productions and the Film Investment Corporation of New Zealand. *Script Development Assistance*: McKenzie Education Foundation, New Zealand Film Commission. © 1984. *Location*: Kohitere Boys Training Centre, Levin. *Distributor*: Hannam Productions Ltd. *Rating*: RP13 (Contains violence), March 1985. 35 mm (shot on 16 mm). Colour. 90 mins.

Director: Mike Walker. *Producers*: Gary Hannam, Mike Walker. *Screenplay*: Mike Walker, Mitchell Manuel. *Director of photography*: John Toon. *Editor*: Paul Sutorius. Art director not credited. *Wardrobe supervisor*: Margaret Austin. *Music*: Andrew Hagen, Morton Wilson (Schtung), Bruce Lynch, Mitchell Manuel, Fred King. *Sound*: Ken Saville, Ross Chambers, Brian Shennan, John Lipke.

Cast

Mitchell Manuel (Riki Nathan), Junior Amiga (Willie Hoto), Nicholas Rogers (Karl Stevens), Judith McIntosh (Alison Eastwood), Terence Cooper (Dave Adams), Peter McCauley (Paul Jefferies), Jim Moriarty (Mike Herewini), Wi Kuki Kaa (Mr Nathan), Ben Fox (Dog), with Kevin Wilson, Buddy Ruruku, Shane Campbell, Barnard Kahu, George Akavi, Niu Satele, Terence Griffiths, Peter Morgan, Jamie Rafferty, Eddi Lagilikoliko, Eddie Campbell, Marjorie Nees, Gilbert Goldie, Peter Rowell, Brenda Berry, Michael Dee, Teresa Campbell, Helen Johnson, Raewynne Jarmai Maria Falck, Rosemary Robertson, Brendon Molloy, Allison Busch, Richard Broughton, Shane Kendrick, Richard McFall, Regan Wood, Brent Ruruku, Chris Toto, Taku Ru, James Tohini, Tony Terita, Richard Hill, Sean Potter, Hayden Henry, Terry Williams, Aaron King, Tony Fifita, Dyon Whiti, Steven Lindop, Jimmy Arapoiti, Bruce Hilaire, Michael Hayes, Whiti Huiateroa, Carl Jensen, Steven Yopia, Michael Takapua, Ricky Heihei.

The mainly Maori and Polynesian inmates detained in a Child Welfare Training Centre are there for crimes ranging from burglary to assault. Propped up by sycophants, 15 year-old bully Karl sees the arrival of tough-looking newcomer Riki, also 15 and an accomplished burglar, as a chance to re-establish himself as the kingpin. Karl's image crumbles on a camping trip when he takes fright abseiling and is talked down by Willie, the smallest, youngest and most spirited inmate. Because those not in Karl's gang see Riki as a potential leader, Karl and his mates beat him up. Willie's attempts to

Junior Amiga (Willie). Courtesy of the New Zealand Film Commission.

contact his father, whom he hasn't seen for three years, come to nothing, his attempts at romance with teacher Alison turn sour, he is framed as a pantie thief and a budding friendship with Riki is thwarted when Karl causes an accident that hospitalises Riki. Defeated, Willie shelves his fear they might 'get catched' and escapes with two others. When their stolen car crashes Riki, believing Willie is dead, storms out of hospital and beats Karl with the rest of the inmates looking on. Locked up as punishment, Riki hears Willie's voice through the bars and discovers his new friend is alive.

Although named for the bully for whom violence is his only way of relating to others, **Kingpin** centres on Willie and Riki, both of whom are from homes destroyed by alcohol. The violence, fear and disappointment constantly at work in their lives is summed up acutely in the car flight/crash, a devastating reminder of the futility of running away. But the story builds to celebrate a friendship born of trust and intimacy. By keeping the action within the institution the story is very focused. It is simply told with a strong narrative drive, compelling in its capture of small, tender moments.

Extreme low angles and an ominous sound motif used for Karl's appearances underline the melodramatic image he has of himself and reinforce borrowings from the Western where the power of resident thugs is upset by a catalytic outsider. The film's raw energy is charged by the spirit of the kids: their music (scored by Schtung musicians Andrew Hagen and Morton Wilson); their talk; their humour; their sensuality and their graceful dance (highlighted by breakdance champion Niu Satele). The target audience is 12 to 20 and the purpose is to entertain but, while the film is anything but a didactic tract, the political message, that society's systems aren't working for the Centre's inmates, is inescapable.

Kingpin evolved from Mike Walker's employment of inmates of Levin's Kohitere Boys' Training Centre as assistants in the production of animated documentaries and television commercials. His first film venture with the boys was **Kingi's Story**, a television drama originally conceived as a training video for Social Welfare staff. Lead actor was inmate Mitchell Manuel, a New Zealand-born Rarotongan. The co-writer of **Kingpin**, which uses real-life stories in its script, Manuel was the only young person in the feature with any acting experience. Many of the actors were institution inmates. HM

1985 Moscow Film Festival: Special Prize for 'the clearest embodiment of the ideas of anti-imperialist solidarity, peace and friendship.'

1985

SYLVIA

Southern Light Pictures and Cinepro. Copyright date not recorded. *Budget*: $1.7 million. *Location*: Puhoi. *Distributor*: Proequity Entertainments Ltd. *Rating*: GA, June 1985. 35 mm. Colour. 100.5 mins.

Director: Michael Firth. *Producers*: Don Reynolds, Michael Firth. *Screenplay*: Michele Quill, F. Fairfax, Michael Firth. *Sources*: Sylvia Ashton-Warner, *Teacher* and *I Passed This Way*. *Director of photography*: Ian Paul. *Editor*: Michael Horton. *Production designer*: Gary Hansen. *Costume designer*: Anne McKay. *Research*: June McCartney. *Composer*: Leonard Rosenman. *Sound*: Graham Morris, M.J.F., Ronwen Proust.

Cast

Eleanor David (Sylvia), Nigel Terry (Aden), Tom Wilkinson (Keith), Mary Regan (Opal), Martyn Sanderson (Inspector Gulland), Terence Cooper (Inspector Bletcher), David Letch (Inspector Scragg), Sarah Peirce (Vivian Wallop), Joseph George (Seven), Eileen Glover (Lilac), Graham Glover (Ashton), Tessa Wells (Jasmine), Jonathan Porteous (Elliot), Cherie Nepia (Pearly), Robert Nepia (Ihaka), Erica Edwards-Brown (Olga), Paul King (Tiny), Frank Nathan (Wai), Awhina Soloman (Moana), Kristofer Hauraki (Hauwiti), Aaron Pako (Manu), Norma Taylor (Tweenie), Waione Te Paa (Caroline), Naomi Ruta (Rewi), Carol Henry (Kata), Andrew Glover (Jacob), with James Cross, Peter Thorpe, Roy Pearce, Ian Harrop, Te Whatanui Skipwith, Norman Forsey, Margaret Murray, Millie Bradfield, Brian Flegg, Arthur Wright, Ron McKitterick, Sheila Summers, Ngaire Horton, Deborah Cuzens, Ingrid Wahlberg, Mavis Tuoro, Nigel Harbrow, Joanna Paul, Debbie Dorday, Norman Fletcher.

Post-World War II. Sylvia, her husband Keith Henderson and their children move to rural Te Whenua to teach. Sylvia, recovering from a nervous breakdown, finds the Education Department's regimented teaching methods and resources unsuited to her mostly Maori pupils. The children's passive aggression brings her to near-relapse but her spirits lift when she stumbles on a teaching method tapping their need to use key words of fear, violence and sex and they begin to write their own stories and express themselves through dance, drawing and song. Sylvia befriends district nurse Opal and establishes a retreat where she can paint, draw, write and sculpt. School Inspector Aden approves of Sylvia's methods and takes her illustrated books to Wellington for publication. Mutually attracted, they kiss secretly at a picnic. Although the children are now reading, the Education Department refuses to grade Sylvia and refuses to publish her work. In Wellington to confront the Department Sylvia sees Aden with his wife and learns Keith has been posted to a city school. Her class is inherited by a strict, traditional teacher. On-screen information tells that Sylvia went on to write *Teacher* which was 'heralded throughout the world as a major advancement in the education of young children.'

Sylvia, an admiring portrait of a tenacious, multi-talented woman, is based on the period in Sylvia Ashton-Warner's life when she developed the teaching method that brought her international acclaim. Compressing nine years into a few months, and several locations into one community, the film is prefaced by an interview with Ashton-Warner, recorded 10 years previously. Most successful are the scenes with the school children, as through their growing excitement about Sylvia's methods the teacher's genius is revealed. Her sensitivity to and understanding of each child's individuality, spontaneity and creativity is the key to her success. Both she and her husband have a respect and empathy for the Maori culture lacking in the community.

Other story elements fare less well — the Education Department is caricatured, Sylvia's own children are barely seen, her attraction to Aden is unexplored and community violence, eventually to drive Opal away, is more discussed than seen. Dialogue explaining Sylvia's ideas occurs in stilted conversations sounding more read than felt. The pace is measured, with American composer Leonard Rosenman's piano score underlining the contemplative tone. The lovely autumn-toned cinematography gives a picturesque patina to the images.

The first film based on Sylvia Ashton-Warner's work was **Spinster** (U.S. title **Two Loves**), filmed in Hollywood in 1961 with Shirley MacLaine in the lead role. Ashton-Warner, who called that film, 'a minor movie but a major disgrace', supported Michael Firth's film, but died before production began. The decision to cast English actors (Eleanor David, Tom Wilkinson and Nigel Terry) caused controversy in New Zealand. Ashton-Warner's son Elliot Henderson was reported as saying of Eleanor David, 'I see my mother in her performance'. Reviewers were generally enthusiastic about **Sylvia** but Ron Mikalsen, writing in *Illusions 1* (Summer 1986), felt that it 'foregoes a ripe opportunity to articulate the past today.' HM

Nigel Terry (Aden) and Eleanor David (Sylvia Henderson). *Courtesy of the New Zealand Film Commission.*

1985 Andrew Sarris *of Village Voice* voted the film one of the year's ten best.
1986 *Sydney Film Festival*: Voted one of the ten best.
New Zealand Listener Film and Television Awards: Best Female Performance in a Supporting Role, Mary Regan.

LEAVE ALL FAIR

Jane Birkin (Katherine Mansfield/Marie Taylor). Courtesy of the New Zealand Film Commission.

Pacific Films in association with Goldeneye SARL (France) and SFA Ltd (Hong Kong) for Mansfield Films Ltd Co. with Challenge Corporate Services Ltd. © 1984. *Location*: Moulin d'Ande, St Pierre du Vauvray, France. *Distributor*: New Zealand Federation of Film Societies Inc. *Rating*: GA, June 1985. 35 mm. Colour. 90 mins.

Director: John Reid. *Producer*: John O'Shea. *Executive producer*: Dominique Antoine. *Associate producer*: Craig Walters. *Screenplay*: Stanley Harper, Maurice Pons, Jean Betts, John Reid, with selections from the works of Katherine Mansfield. *Director of photography*: Bernard Lutic. *Camera operator*: Allen Guilford. *Editor*: Ian John. *Art director*: Joe Bleakley. *Costume designer*: Rose Marie Melka. *Musical director*: Stephen McCurdy. *Players*: Brecon Carter, Rae Carter, Graeme Hemings, Bruce Greenfield, David Jenkins, Peter Scholes, Stanley Jackson. *Sound*: John Lipke, Robert Allan, Hammond Peek.

Cast

John Gielgud (John Middleton Murry), Jane Birkin (Marie Taylor, Katherine Mansfield), Feodor Atkine (André de Sarry), Simon Ward (young John), Louba Guertchikoff (Lisa), Maurice Chevit (Alain), Mireille Alcantara (Violetta), Leonard Pezzino (Alfredo), with Jean Betts, Michelle Bordier, Sylvie Bonnet, Jean Pierre-Briere, Gerard Heugues, Patrick de Hooghe, Jean-Francois de Travernier.

In 1956, 33 years after the death of his wife, New Zealand-born writer Katherine Mansfield, John Middleton Murry visits publisher André de Sarry in France to approve an edition of her collected letters and journals. At the home of de Sarry and his partner Marie, a New Zealander reminding him of Katherine (both roles played by Jane Birkin), Middleton Murry is haunted by his dying wife's instructions (conflated in the film into a single letter), 'I should like him to publish as little as possible ... He will understand that I desire to leave as few traces of my camping ground as possible' and 'All my manuscripts I leave entirely to you to do what you like with ... Please destroy all letters you do not wish to keep and all papers ... Have a clean sweep ... and leave all fair, will you?' As Middleton Murry struggles with his conscience, through flashbacks of Katherine ill and alone, Marie reads Katherine's work and, in Middleton Murry's papers, finds Katherine's letter. Concluding he exploited his wife, Marie confronts him and turns on André as another exploitative male. At the book launch Marie is disgusted by Middleton Murry's sanctimonious speech. An on-screen message notes Middleton Murry died the following year and Marie Taylor returned to New Zealand.

Talk and flashbacks advance the narrative which aims to bring the historical figure Middleton Murry and the fictional de Sarry to account, and to suggest a shift in Marie Taylor's consciousness through her understanding of Katherine's suffering. Although Middleton Murry's decision to publish almost all Mansfield's work over the years could have been determined more by the ambiguity of her 'destroy all you do not use' comment than by his own greed, **Leave All Fair** leaves no room for doubt, presenting Katherine Mansfield as an all-out victim. Through Marie's reading of the Mansfield stories, the film extends the idea of abuse to maintain that Middleton Murry ill-treated her while she lived.

Leave All Fair was developed in France by New Zealand director Stanley Harper and the New Zealand production company Pacific Films agreed to raise finance for the film, which had to be finished before the tax-break cut-off. John Reid was offered the project when Harper was fired two weeks before the shoot. Under his direction the 'ghost' element was introduced and the two-time-frame decision made. Beautifully shot in the European tradition, the film is slow and lyrical. The dialogue, much of it written on a day-to-day basis during the shoot, is at times 'wordy' and some conversations sound forced. Some time transitions are confusing and for Birkin's outbursts to be read as passion rather than histrionics one needs to be convinced of the truth of the film's basic premise.

Although hailed with such superlatives as 'arguably the best film to come out of New Zealand so far' (London Film Festival, 1985) and 'a new triumph for local achievement in cinema' (*Evening Post* 6 July 1985) other comments were less enthusiastic. Tom McWilliams, for example, wrote in the *New Zealand Listener* (1 February 1986), '*Leave All Fair*, by reducing Murry to a sexist exploiter for financial gain, simplifies the KM/Murry relationship into a cliché of our time ... ' HM

1985 Taormina Film Festival : Special Jury Citation Commendation, John Gielgud.
Orleans Film Festival: Best Actress, Jane Birkin.
1986 Karlovy Vary Film Festival, Czechoslovakia: Cidalic Prize.

SHAKER RUN

Mirage-Avicom Productions in association with Laurelwood Productions Inc. Financed from New Zealand and the U.S. ©1985. *Budget:* $5.3 million. *Locations:* Dunedin, Queenstown, Clyde, Blenheim, Wellington. *Distributor:* Mirage Films. *Rating:* GY (Contains violence), June 1985. 35 mm. Dolby Stereo. Colour. 91 mins.

Director: Bruce Morrison. *Producers:* Larry Parr, Igo Kantor. *Executive producer:* Henry Fownes. *Screenplay:* James Kouf Jnr, Henry Fownes, Bruce Morrison. *Director of photography:* Kevin Hayward. *Camera operator:* Alan Locke. *Editors:* Ken Zemke, Bob Richardson. *Production designer:* Ron Highfield. *Costume designer:* Barbara Darragh. *Special effects co-ordinator:* Kevin Chisnall. *Stunt co-ordinator:* Peter Bell. *Armourer:* Ralph Gardiner. *Music:* Stephen McCurdy. *Players:* Shona Laing, Simon Page, Leo Keane, Andrew Craig, David Berry. *Sound:* Malcolm Cromie, Ross Chambers, Tony Johnson, Brian Shennan, John Lipke, Tony Woollams.

Cast

Cliff Robertson (Judd Pierson), Leif Garrett (Casey Lee), Lisa Harrow (Dr Christine Ruben), Shane Briant (Paul Thoreau), Peter Rowell (Mr Carney), Peter Hayden (Michael Connoly), Ian Mune (Barry Gordon), Bruce Phillips (Dr Marshall), Fiona Samuels (Casey's girl), Deidre O'Connor (Judd's girl), Nat Lees (Squad Commander), Daniel Gillion (Driver), Geoffrey Heath (Car sales customer), Dave Smith (Car salesman), Barry Dorking (Storeman), Igo Kanitor (CIA man), John Bray (General).

American racing driver Judd Pierson and mechanic Casey are stunt driving their car, Shaker, in New Zealand when research scientist Dr Christine Ruben pays them to drive her on a four hour journey northwards from Dunedin. Unknown to Judd and Casey her cargo is a virus strain she and her colleagues have been using in experiments. Having mutated into a lethal strain it has killed three researchers. Dr Ruben is to hand it to the CIA to prevent it falling into the clutches of the New Zealand Security Service, led by the evil Thoreau, who want it for biological warfare. Judd drives at great speed and with much ingenuity weathering many explosions along the way from Dunedin to Picton, where they hide in a cargo ship. Escaping capture they race up the North Island, but are cornered by Thoreau and his goons. In fortuitous eleventh hour ingenuity Dr Ruben attaches Shaker by chains to a hovering CIA helicopter and, while she and her new friends fly to safety, their pursuers drive, lemming like, over a very high cliff. Amid much merriment Judd suggests to Casey they include the stunt in their act on their return to America.

Dr Ruben's desire to save the world, barely a plausible raison d'être for the chase, loses credibility when it becomes apparent she has not considered the consequences of handing over the virus to the CIA. To her credit she toughs out the chase with barely a squeal and at the end she can still laugh. Judd achieves redemption, of a sort, his great driving atoning for his causing Casey's father's death, while Casey, called on to drive when Judd is injured, overcomes his fear of speed. The CIA prove very callous indeed, just as Judd had said they would be, but not revealed is how Dr Ruben feels about having to hand them the virus post-rescue.

The film was shot chronologically, with the locations, and the roads and sea connecting them, a spectacular backdrop to the action. The credits end with the plea to viewers to 'Please Drive Home Safely.'

Shaker Run was made quickly in 1984 to beat the tax regulations cut-off date (but not released in New Zealand until 1986). The $5.3 million budget was massive by New Zealand standards of the day. Dialogue and characterisation receive little attention and attempts at humour fall flat, but the chase in two Pontiac Trans-American cars and the almost continuous stunt sequences, shot using multi-camera set-ups, are well executed. (Peter Bell's stunts included driving a blazing van over a four metre cliff and jumping a car from a ship onto a wharf 11 metres away). In *Onfilm* (volume 3, No. 2) director Bruce Morrison described the film's content as 'fantasy car violence' that is 'as unsexist and unviolent and unbloody as I could make it, while still making it unavoidable to watch.' In a *New Zealand Herald* interview he acknowledged that even though the film may be good of its kind, 'if I thought the rest of my career was going to consist entirely of *Shaker Run* films I would probably look for something else to do.' HM

The Dodge pick-up which was converted into a high speed camera chase truck. Courtesy of the New Zealand Film Commission.

1985

MR WRONG

Preston*Laing Productions Ltd in association with the New Zealand Film Commission and Barclays New Zealand Ltd. A.k.a. Dark of the Night. ©1984. *Budget:* $500 000. *Locations:* Wellington, Featherston, Paekakariki. *Distributor:* Preston*Laing Productions Ltd. *Rating:* GA, June 1985. 35 mm (shot on 16 mm). Colour. 89 mins.

Director: Gaylene Preston. *Producer:* Robin Laing. *Co-producer:* Gaylene Preston. *Associate producer:* Don Reynolds. *Screenplay:* Gaylene Preston, Geoff Murphy, Graeme Tetley. *Source:* Elizabeth Jane Howard, 'Mr Wrong'. *Director of photography:* Thom Burstyn. *Camera operator:* Alun Bollinger. *Editor:* Simon Reece. *Art director:* Mike Becroft. *Wardrobe standby:* Fiona Stewart. *Special effects/car wrangler:* Matthew Murphy. *Stunt drivers:* Peter Zivkovic, Mark Taylor. *Music:* Jonathan Crayford. *Lyrics/vocals:* Kelly Johnson. *Sound:* Ken Saville, Brian Shennan, Michael Hopkins, Tony Johnson, John Laing.

Cast

Heather Bolton (Meg), **David Letch** (Mr Wrong), Margaret Umbers (Samantha), Gary Stalker (Bruce), Suzanne Lee (Val), Danny Mulheron (Wayne), Michael Haigh (Mr Whitehorn), Kate Harcourt (Mrs Alexander), Phillip Gordon (Clive), Perry Piercy (Mary Carmichael), Jan Fisher (Edith), Lee Hatherley, Hampson and Hiles (radio voices), Meriol Buchanan (Woman with dog), Ross Jolly (Neighbour), Don Linke (Martin), John Bullock (Meg's father), Jonathan Crayford (Petrol pump attendant), Rebecca Gibney (Secretary), Lew Martin, Les Stone (Jag enthusiasts), Frank Slobbe (Tow truck driver), Ken Saville (Man in Jaguar), Phillip Mills (Man on bus), Matty (Cherry).

Driving her newly-bought Mark II Jaguar, Meg hears choking noises coming from the empty back seat and that night dreams of a ghostly looking woman. When she picks up a woman standing in the rain a man also appears in the car. Finding his insinuations threatening Meg asks him to leave and realises the woman she 'picked up' was from her dream. She finds an article about Mary Carmichael, a missing woman feared murdered. Her ownership papers reveal Mary Carmichael was the previous owner of her Jaguar and Meg guesses that, murdered in it by the hitchhiker, Mary haunts the car. Meg tries to sell the car but it refuses to unlock for men. Mr Wrong stalks her, a flatmate's boyfriend attempts to rape her and new friend Wayne Wright makes unthreatening overtures. Locked out of her flat Meg drives to Wayne's but finds the hitchhiker in the back seat. In response to his homicidal threats Meg attacks him with the car cigarette lighter and escapes. The car seals its doors and, with the killer inside, hurtles downhill and crashes in flames. The ghost of Mary Carmichael smiles at Meg and walks into the night.

In adapting Elizabeth Jane Howard's short story, the writers transferred the setting from England to New Zealand and updated the sexual politics. Mr Wrong subverts the thriller to look at sexual violence towards women and at the 'Cinderella syndrome' of rescue by a Mr Right. The initial con, where an oily car salesman sells tentative Meg 'a lady's car' he knows is haunted, contains the irony that, occupied by the ghost of a murdered woman, the Jag embodies something many women fear. Heather Bolton's spirited performance challenges the Hollywood idea that for viewer pleasure a heroine must be glamorous and creates a character inexperienced in the ways of the world, yet capable of using her terror as a spur to assertive self-defence. Meg's decision to tell no-one of her fears is unexplained, but drives the single narrative focus. By contrast other women believe they need a Mr Right although the end result of 'romance', as indicated by Meg's housebound friend Edith, is no alternative to independence. Although some of the men are well-meaning it is not for nothing that Wayne Wright and Mr Wrong send Meg identical roses. A visiting boyfriend scoffs at a televised self-defence program, affecting disbelief that such training is necessary, but the subtext is that such men do not want women unafraid.

The fairy-tale texture and comic touch ensure the film is no solemn feminist tract. The excitement of vicarious terror builds through well-crafted use of thriller conventions—prowling camera, noir lighting and production design, spooky soundtrack—and a carefully managed succession of red herrings reinforce the ideology. Unconventionally there is no violence or bloodletting until the explosive climax.

Mr Wrong was the first New Zealand film made by a female producer/director team. Reluctance on the part of the cinema chains to screen it led to Preston*Laing four-walling it themselves. It was well received overseas and locally, where audiences responded with noisy delight. HM

David Letch (Mr Wrong). *Courtesy of the New Zealand Film Commission.*

1986 New Zealand Film and Television Awards: Best Female Performance, Heather Bolton.
Creteil Women's Festival: Most Popular Film.

1985

THE NEGLECTED MIRACLE

The rich genetic diversity in third world countries is husbanded over the centuries by indigenous people. Courtesy of Pacific Films Collection, New Zealand Film Archive.

A Pacific Films Production for Mansfield Films Ltd and Co. with Challenge Corporation Services Ltd. Development Funding: UNESCO, United Nations Development Program, Threshold Foundation, Trocaire, International Coalition for Development Action, European Economic Commission, Television New Zealand, Australian Broadcasting Corporation. ©1985. Documentary. *Locations:* Netherlands, Australia, Belgium, France, Italy, Peru, Costa Rica, Nicaragua. No theatrical distribution. *Rating:* Exempted, July 1985. 16 mm. Colour. 120 mins.

Director: Barry Barclay. *Producers:* John O'Shea, Craig Walters. *Associate director:* Peter Hawes. *Director of photography:* Rory O'Shea. *Additional photography:* Michael Hardcastle, Allen Guilford, Molephe Pheto, Richard Bluck. *Editor:* Annie Collins. *Research/liaison:* Marta Haywood, Diana Pelaez. *Commentary:* Keri Kaa. *Stills:* Martyne van der Molen, Michael Hardcastle. *Music:* Jenny McLeod. *Sound:* Wouter Van Der Hoeven, Mike Piper, Ilse Acevedo, John Irwin, Guy Hiernaux, Steve Upston, Brian Shennan.

This superb documentary, shot over five years in several countries, raises questions about the stewardship of precious plant genetic resources. The film's journey, which shapes a journey of revelation for the viewer, is undertaken using what writer/director Barry Barclay calls 'the marae approach', that is, one in which all voices are heard and all speak as equals.* Speakers reveal how the rich genetic diversity in third world countries, husbanded over the centuries by indigenous people, is increasingly exploited by first world scientific plant breeders for first world profit. The consequences are partly scientific—the massive introduction of uniform seed varieties can quickly extinguish genetic variation and can favour bulk over nutritive value—but the consequences are also political and economic.

Points made include: in Australia, with flora pockets containing more plant varieties than in the entire United Kingdom, the government proposes to patent genetic resources; in Sweden flower bulbs are exported by companies only after they have been bred to a state of uniformity; French wheat growers search for new varieties to please the palates of first world customers; the Director General of a large European seed breeding company explains that third world countries, who have donated seed in the first place, have to buy it back when it has been improved through scientific breeding because 'value has been added through a lot of effort.'

By contrast Nicaraguans sing a moving hymn of praise and love to the goddess of maize and Moroccans visiting the Netherlands express in song and dance anxiety that their seeds have been taken into new countries where 'sometimes we hardly recognise them.' Their mission—'we come to ask which way our seeds will travel' because 'All seek riches but sometimes we do it at the cost of others'—is one shared by many countries. At a conference speakers call for sovereignty over their natural resources and ask why they should donate their seed to industrialised countries patenting it for their own interests. Positive programs, like one in Lima where the International Potato Centre has as its main task the breeding and supply of improved varieties to developing countries, provide a note of hope.

Using indigenous film crews where possible the film-makers interviewed 106 people and shot 56 hours of film. A 300 mm lens was used to enable the interviewee to forget the presence of the camera. There is some narration, but mostly the footage speaks for itself. Links are made by skilful editing, often in the form of cross-cutting between third and first world commentators, and the music of the indigenous people provides powerful accompaniment.

Barclay's interest in the topic was inspired by his reading of Canadian campaigner Pat Mooney's writing. **The Neglected Miracle** is compelling viewing, a metaphor, in Barclay's words, for 'the dignity of sovereignty.'* The film has encountered strong opposition from scientists and the release of **Seeds of Tomorrow**, a PBS documentary ostensibly similar to **The Neglected Miracle** but arguing that modern science has found solutions to the problems, effectively killed buyer interest in Barclay's film.

New Zealand footage was shot but has not been incorporated into the film. **The Neglected Miracle**, which David Bellamy called 'a documentary of epic proportions', has not had a theatrical release but has screened in a number of festivals worldwide and has sold on video through universities.
HM

References
* Barry Barclay. 'Amongst Landscapes' in J. Dennis & J. Bieringa (eds). 1992. *Film in Aotearoa New Zealand*, pp. 116-129.

1985

RESTLESS

Endeavour Productions and Wyndcross Ltd. A.k.a. Hot Target. *Locations:* Clevedon, Orakei, Parnell (Auckland). ©1985. Financed from New Zealand and the U.K. No theatrical or video release in New Zealand. *U.S. video rating:* R. *TVNZ rating:* AO.

Director: Denis Lewiston. *Producers:* John Barnett, Brian Cook. *Screenplay:* Denis Lewiston, from a story by Gerry O'Hara. *Director of photography:* Alec Mills. *Editor:* Michael Horton. *Production designer:* Jo Ford. *Costume designer:* Patrick Steel. *Composer/arranger:* Gil Melle. *Music director:* Dave Fraser. *Sound:* Gary Wilkins, John McKay, Gethin Creagh, Ross Chambers, Tony Johnson.

Cast

Simone Griffeth (Christine Webber), Steve Marachuk (Greg Sandford), Bryan Marshall (Clive Webber), Peter McCauley (Detective Inspector Nolan), Elizabeth Hawthorne (Suzanne Maxwell), Ray Henwood (Douglas Maxwell), John Watson (Ben), Renee Johansen (Sandy Webber), Elizabeth McRae (Mrs Harris), Viviene Laube (Nanny), with Frank Whitten, Karl Bradley, Arthur Wright, Terence Cooper, William Kircher, Ray Pearson, Derek Hardwick, Edward Newborn, Graeme Syms, Maggie Maxwell, Norman Fairley, Graeme Moran, Maggie Harper, Roxan Dautun, Judy McIntosh, Norman Fletcher, Ian Harrop, Glenn Scott.

Beautiful, rich, bored housewife Christine Webber, married to ruthless businessman Clive, meets an attractive drifter, Greg, while walking her dogs in the park. When Greg phones her to arrange a meeting Christine is frightened—Clive is very possessive—but intrigued. At Greg's apartment he and Christine instantly make love. Questioned, Greg reveals he is a criminal and the apartment is not his and, when Christine is out of the room, takes imprints off her keys. Suspicious of his wife, Clive has her tailed by his bodyguard, Ben. Breaking into the Webber house Greg steals half a million worth of jewels and is making love with Christine when they are disturbed by Clive. In the scuffle Greg kills Clive. The efforts of a suspicious cop to tie Christine to the murder come to little more than some desultory tailing and a futile racecourse chase. Back at the apartment Greg is surprised by the owner and in the scuffle the owner is killed and Greg stabbed. Christine drives him to his underworld mates and, in a sequence echoing Christine's dream in the opening scene, they surround the car menacingly. At Greg's supposed graveside the mates do not acknowledge Christine. Unknown to her, Greg watches her from behind a tree. Greg and Christine walk off in opposite directions.

Restless may be interesting for the amount of sweat produced during the lovemaking, the dogs are nice and the ending a surprise, but, in spite of its billing as a thriller, it's a film that never really happens. Hints of complications to come—in Clive's suspicion of his wife, in Ben's sinister aspect and in hinted-at business deals between ruthless partners—turn out to be no more than fillers to pad out an otherwise insubstantial plot.

The film provided work for local crews and actors. Although shot in Auckland it gives no hint of geography—the characters could be anywhere. Casting was in the U.S. (lead actors Simone Griffeth and Steve Marachuk), Australia and New Zealand. Most of the crew were hired in New Zealand. The film screened as **Hot Target** on New Zealand television on 17 March 1991. HM

Restless, *also known as* **Hot Target.** *The poster from the American release. Courtesy of John Barnett.*

PALLET ON THE FLOOR

Mirage Films Ltd. No copyright date recorded. *Locations:* Wanganui, Patea. *Distributor:* Mirage Films. *Rating:* RP13 (Some content may offend), January 1986. Made in 1983. 35 mm. Panavision. Colour. 88 mins.

Director: Lynton Butler. *Producer:* Larry Parr. *Screenplay:* Martyn Sanderson, Lynton Butler, Robert Rising *Source:* Ronald Hugh Morrieson, *Pallet on the Floor*. *Director of photography:* Kevin Hayward. *Camera operator:* Barry Harbert. *Editor:* Patrick Monaghan. *Production designer:* Lyn Bergquist. *Costume designer:* Christine West. *Musical director:* Bruno Lawrence. *Composer/arrangers:* Jonathon Crayford, Bruno Lawrence, Barry Johnstone. *Vocals:* Jo Tomlin, Beau Kaa. *Lyrics:* Sam Andrews, Bruno Lawrence. *Sound:* Hammond Peek, Simon Sedgley, Brian Shennan.

Cast

Peter McCauley (Sam Jamieson), Jillian O'Brien (Sue Jamieson), Bruce Spence (Basil Beaumont-Foster), Shirley Gruar (Miriam Breen), Alistair Douglas (Stan Breen), Tony Barry (Larkman), Jeremy Stephens (Spud McGhee), Michael Wilson (Shorty Larsen), Terence Cooper (Brendon O'Keefe), John Bach (Jack Voot), Marshall Napier (Joe Voot), Curly Del Monte (Mason Voot), Peter Rowley (Henderson), Ian Watkin (Amos), Sonny Waru (Mohi Te Kiri), Bruno Lawrence (Ronald Hugh Morrison), with Colin Kelly, Clair Ryan, Ngaire Mako, Norman Forsey, Karen Hammond, Ruth Clotworthy, Charmaine Gilbert, Bill Derby, Nigel Morris, Wayne Pettet, John Ward, Robin Farmer, Sam Haapu Jnr, Gerard Hipango, Margaret McGovern, Suzy Clyde, Suzanne Clarke, Suzanne Timms, Peter Calkin, David Le Compte, Sandra Dunlop, Mary Louise Pelizer, Andrea Kake, Erima Henare, Jim Day, Bill Brannigan, John Rist, Jonathon Crayford, Campbell McPherson, Dion Relose, Roslyn Refoy-Butler, Mack Abraham, Lesley Gregory, Stephen Piper, Robert Rising, Hori Broughton, Tina Penny, Carmel Marino.

Small town New Zealand, 1966. Freezing plant worker Sam Jamieson is told fiancée Sue has angered Miriam Breen, wife of local businessman Stan. At Sam and Sue's wedding her ex-lover Jack Voot makes a move on her and Sam's mate O'Keefe dies of a seizure. Later Miriam, who wants Sam, tells him the baby Sue is expecting was fathered by O'Keefe. When Sam confronts Sue she leaves but returns next morning. Jack Voot attempts to rape Sue and the house is wrecked. Sam and his mates return from the pub and Basil Beaumont-Foster (a.k.a. the Remittance Man) delivers Jack a death blow, watched by Miriam, which they pass off as an accident. Stan and Miriam blackmail Sam into agreeing to hand over his land. Jack's brother Joe comes looking for revenge and Basil accidentally kills him. The men's jobs at the freezing works are terminated. Basil agrees to drive Sam, Miriam and Stan to a lawyer to arrange transfer of the land title. On the way he drops Sue off at her family marae where she and Sam are to live. He persuades Sam to stay behind then drives over a cliff, killing himself, Miriam and Stan.

Martyn Sanderson's screenplay of **Pallet on the Floor** was a follow-up to the Sanderson-written documentary on Ronald Hugh Morrieson, **One of Those Blighters**. *Pallet* was Morrieson's last novel and the third to be dramatised on film. Butler and Robert Rising rewrote Sanderson's screenplay to focus on Basil, with Butler hoping Peter O'Toole would play the lead. Morrieson's trademark preoccupations are maintained—sex, death, mateship, voyeurism, violence, booze and mayhem in bleak small town New Zealand—along with his irreverent black humour.

Bruno Lawrence, whose jazz score is excellent, has a tiny cameo as Morrieson (the bass player at the wedding). Like **The Scarecrow**'s funeral parlour, the abattoir with its dodgy goings-on (workers watch through a peephole as lambs are slaughtered, meat theft is rife) is a major symbol of community corruption. Although billed as a comedy the film is corny rather than funny, the evil characters are comic book and the narrative too thick with incident for clarity. By shifting the focus to the British Remittance Man the impact of Sam's journey from inarticulate to more knowing Kiwi joker is diluted.

In depicting 1960s racism and class divisions the Voots quarry Maori land and speak of the Maori with contempt while worker Sam and his mates work on assembly lines with no job security. (Ironically the film was shot in Patea, the site of a closed-down abattoir.) Sam's initial refusal to go back to the pa where he and his Maori wife Sue grew up is motivated partly by male pride (he wants to support her) and partly by racism (he doesn't want to go 'back to the mat'.) He agrees only when Basil, a member of the British aristocracy who has fallen on hard times, rails against the injustices of the rat race, urging him to retreat to 'the pallet on the floor'. But life on the marae as a preferable lifestyle option is given little substance as, apart from the wedding, there are no marae scenes.

The film was made in 1983 but not released until 1986. HM

Bruce Spence (Basil Beaumont-Foster) and Peter McCauley (Sam). *Courtesy of the New Zealand Film Commission.*

BRIDGE TO NOWHERE

Mirage Films Ltd with the assistance of the New Zealand Film Commission. ©1985. *Location:* Raetihi. *Distributor:* Mirage Films Ltd. *Rating:* RP16 (Content may disturb), April 1986. Amended to R13 (Content may disturb), May 1986. 35 mm. Dolby Stereo. Colour. 87.5 mins.

Director: Ian Mune. *Producer:* Larry Parr. *Executive producer:* Henry Fownes. *Associate producer:* William Grieve. *Screenplay:* Bill Baer, Ian Mune, from a story by Larry Parr. *Director of photography:* Kevin Hayward. *Editor:* Finola Dwyer. *Art director:* Mike Becroft. *Costume designer:* Sue Gandy. *Stunt co-ordinator:* Peter Bell. *Composer:* Stephen McCurdy. *Music performance:* Annie Crummer, Low Profile, Ardijah, Car Crash Set, Peking Man, Marginal Era, Obscure Desire. *Sound:* Hammond Peek, Brian Shennan, John McKay, David Rawlinson, John McWilliam, Mike Westgate.

Cast

Matthew Hunter (Carl), Margaret Umbers (Tanya), Shelly Luxford (Julie), Stephen Judd (Gray), Phillip Gordon (Leon), Bruno Lawrence (Mac), Alison Routledge (Lise), Shirley Gruar (Julie's mother), Peter McCauley (Tanya's father), Norman Fairly (Gray's father), Fay Flegg (Tania's mother).

Matthew Hunter (Carl), Phillip Gordon (Leon), Margaret Umbers (Tanya), Stephen Judd (Gray) and Shelly Luxford (Julie). Courtesy of Larry Parr.

Five city teenagers go bush in search of adventure and meet Mac, a surly, black-garbed stockman and his flirtatious young companion, Lise, who tells them their destination, 'the bridge to nowhere', is a two-day walk away. With much horsing around and to loud pop music the youngsters set up camp and settle in for the night. Leon is wild Tanya won't have sex with him and Gray makes a tentative lunge at Julie. Next morning Leon lures Tanya's brother Carl to a bush, where Gray drops his trousers and farts loudly in Carl's face by way of a warning to him to keep out of their way. During more horsing around and farting, Mac's steers charge Leon, who shoots at them with the family shotgun. Mac appears and, enraged, hits Leon with the gun. Leon drags Tanya into the bushes and when she declares her love for him goes berserk, tries to rape her, then runs away. Finding the hut Mac shares with Lise, Leon is spying on Lise when she shoots him dead. The others go looking for him and find him hanging in a tree. Stalked and shot at by Mac, they kill Mac's dog then go to his house, where Tanya attacks Lise. Mac refuses to let Lise leave with the others and rages at her for writing in her 'secrets' book. Back in the bush Gray shoots Lise. Mac shoots his dogs and burns down the hut with the dead Lise inside. After more stalking Mac shoots Gray and Carl stabs Mac.

Bridge to Nowhere, targeted at 16 to 22 year-olds, aims to be a kind of NewZealand teenage **Deliverance**. Unfortunately, after a promising beginning it quickly deteriorates into a mindless scream and run affair in which sound and fury substitute for motivation and logical action. As the catalyst, Leon lurches inexplicably from playful to psychotic within seconds and the Mac/Lise relationship is unexplained. Mac may be holding Lise against her will, but because we are never privy to her 'secret writing' we have no way of knowing what she is thinking. The actors were given their heads to improvise (*Onfilm* quotes Ian Mune as saying, 'The actors are able to just follow their instincts, and its up to the techos … to capture that.')*. The resulting performances are overblown, amateurish and unconvincing.

Narrative aside, the cinematography makes good use of the magnificent location on and around a public works concrete bridge in an uninhabited ravine in mountain country north-west of Raetihi. (The bridge was built in the 1930s to service roading needs for World War I servicemen given land to clear for farms and the land has all now reverted back to bush. The bridge literally goes nowhere, with the only access to it by helicopter or by a tramping path from the Wanganui river.)* HM

1987 Media Women's Outrageous Media Award (MOMMA): The Cars, Guns, Horses and Maybe a Girl Oddfellow Award, shared with **Queen City Rocker** and **Dangerous Orphans**.

Reference
* *Onfilm*, volume 2, no. 3, April 1985.

1986

DANGEROUS ORPHANS

Jennifer Ward-Lealand (Teresa Costello). Courtesy of the New Zealand Film Commission.

Cinepro in association with the New Zealand Film Commission. ©1986. *Budget:* approx. $1.2 million. *Locations:* Wellington. 2nd Unit: Geneva, New York. *Distributor:* Mirage Film Distributors. *Rating:* RP13, August 1986. 35 mm. Colour/Black and white. 93 mins.

Director: John Laing. *Producer:* Don Reynolds. *Associate producer:* Robin Laing. *Executive producer:* Campbell Stevenson. *Screenplay:* Kevin Smith. *Director of photography:* Warrick Attewell. *Editor:* Michael Horton. *Costume designer:* Barbara Darragh. *Special effects:* Action Associates. *Stunts:* Tim Lee. *Armourer:* Jim Barber. *Music:* Jonathan Crayford. *Composer:* John Gibson. *Lyrics:* Kevin Smith, David Mahon. *Conductor:* Dave Fraser. *Players:* New Zealand Symphony Orchestra. *Sound:* Ralph Davies, Mike Westgate, Tony Johnson, Brian Shennan, Jamie Selkirk.

Cast
Peter Stevens (O'Malley), Jennifer Ward-Lealand (Teresa Costello), Ross Girven (Rossi), Michael Hurst (Moir), Peter Bland (Jacobs), Ian Mune (Hanna), Grant Tilly (Beck), Zac Wallace (Scanlan), Ann Pacey (Moony), with Peter Vere-Jones, Michael Haigh, Des Kelly, Michaela Banas, Tim Lee, Toby Laing, Alexis Banas, Eion Cox, Miles Tilly, Kevin Wilson, Marshall Napier, Paul Maunder, Patrick Smyth, Gerry Luhman, Richard von Sturmer, Simon O'Connor, Ruth Hampson, Lynette Williams, Roy Wesney, David Gascoigne, Tony Hiles, Nigel Hewat, Joanne Mildenhall, Stephanie Ash, Michael Horton, Geraldine York, Donna Akersten, Stephen Judd, Stephen Gledhill, Vivienne Plumb, John Bach, Mike Knudson, Eddie Campbell, Helen Moulder, Gerard Bryan, Ruth Thompson.

Friends O'Malley, Moir and Rossi execute a scam where O'Malley kills an American drug courier and steals his ID, with which Moir travels to Geneva, withdraws $US 5 million and deposits it in a Panama bank. O'Malley falls for Teresa, a singer in Rossi's nightclub. Heroin bosses Hanna and Jacobs discuss merger but fail to agree. Jacobs traces O'Malley's gun to arms dealer Moony, a middle-aged woman and his man, Scanlan, gets Moir's name from her, then kills her. O'Malley shoots Scanlan and Jacobs finds him in his fish tank. O'Malley plans to continue the vendetta against Hanna and Jacobs by stealing Hanna's safe and tying the crime to Jacobs. A flashback confirms the trio are out to avenge the death of O'Malley's father, a small-time crook killed by Jacobs and Hanna. O'Malley learns that Hanna fathered Teresa's child, Anna (Anna Hanna?), and has custody of her. The trio intercept a heroin drop, Teresa plants heroin on Hanna and he is shot in a raid by cops. In a raid on Hanna's safe Moir shoots Short, Hanna's henchman, and Rossi is shot trying to escape with a bag of money. The others rescue Teresa, shoot the American drug connection, tip Rossi's body over a cliff in Hanna's burning car and depart, O'Malley with Teresa and Anna, Moir alone.

Dangerous Orphans is a fast-moving urban action/thriller yarn with larger than life anti-heroes and villains. Described by producer Don Reynolds as 'unashamedly Boys' Own' the film looks stylish in spite of the low budget. Aimed at 13 to 26 year-olds it's a silly, far-fetched boys 'n' guns imitation of the American gangster movie and its occasional tongue in cheek has a particularly New Zealand flavour.

Excesses of theatricality are enjoyed in the characterisations. The cartoon bad guys have bizarre idiosyncrasies. Good guy O'Malley admits his TV role as a private eye is corny but likes the fame. On stage he revels in his bad/mad guy Shakespearian roles and joshes the others in the 'brother' triangle into a 'sword-fight' with French bread.

A noir style is used to good effect with Wellington's old buildings providing a suitably sleazy ambience. Action scene choreography is slick and well executed and the classical music and jazz score adds pace and mood. Much of the dialogue is awkward and over-written, too much of the complicated plot is revealed in obviously explanatory conversations and, because the flashbacks explaining the vendetta are placed well into the narrative, the start is an overloaded blur. The film's as corny as O'Malley's private eye stories and the point, that lust for revenge can escalate to damage the avengers, is all but buried in the skullduggery.

Dangerous Orphans was sold at the Cannes Film Festival for distribution in Europe in one of the largest single sales of a New Zealand film to that time. HM

1987 Media Women's Outrageous Media Awards (MOMMA): The Cars, Guns, Horses and Maybe a Girl Oddfellow Award, shared with **Queen City Rocker** and **Bridge to Nowhere**.

ARRIVING TUESDAY

1986

Cinepro in association with **Walker Films Ltd** and the **New Zealand Film Commission**. ©1986. *Budget:* $250 000. *Locations:* Auckland, Waiuku, Dargaville, Hokianga, Ninety Mile Beach. *Distributor:* Mirage Film Distributors. *Rating:* GA, September 1986. 35 mm. Colour. 88 mins.

Director: Richard Riddiford. *Producers:* Don Reynolds, Chris Hampson. *Executive producer:* Campbell Stevenson. *Associate producer:* Hammond Peek. *Screenplay:* Richard Riddiford, David Copeland. *Additional script:* Rawiri Paratene, Bruce Phillips. *Director of photography:* Murray Milne. *Editor:* John McWilliam. *Production designer:* Roger Guise. *Sculptures:* Graham Snowden. *Wardrobe:* Lyndsay Meager, Graham Snowden. *Music:* Scott Calhoun. *Players:* Henare Mahanga, Aotearoa, The Chills. *Sound:* David Madigan, Brian Shennan, Chris Burt.

Cast

Judy McIntosh (Monica), Peter Hayden (Nick), Rawiri Paratene (Riki), Heather Bolton (Jenny), Sarah Peirse (Carol), Lee Grant (Hotel manageress), Frank Whitten (Farmer), Te Paki Cherrington (George), Jon Smyth (Opossum man), Wayne Gilgren (Boatman), Dody Potter (Taxi driver), Jessie (Puss), members of Te Rito Performance Group.

Monica returns from Europe and goes back to Nick, a junk sculptor living in rural Waiuku. Nick is still stuck in his ways and Monica feels restless. She chivvies him into going up north, but while Nick settles happily on their beach campsite she soon wants to be off. At a Dargaville pub they meet troubadour poet Riki, a Ngapuhi who has left Auckland to return to his Northland roots, and his dog Puss. On the way to Hokianga Riki officiates at a mock marriage ceremony but Nick sulks, suspecting Monica of flirting with Riki. On the road they meet some Maori on a hikoi (a spiritual march), wheeling a large stone up north to erect as a monument to honour their ancestor, Waikura. Monica enjoys a night on a marae with their new friends but Nick sulks. In the Waipoua Forest Monica and Riki visit the ancient kauri Tane Mahuta while Nick sulks. With Monica back in the car Nick drives off, leaving Riki's gear in the road and with Puss in the back seat. After another fight Monica walks on alone. Puss escapes into a field and is shot by a farmer. In a temper Nick returns to Waiuku and Monica goes on, carrying the dead dog in a sack, looking for Riki. She finds him on a marae during a ceremony welcoming the hikoi and, realising his world is alien to her, returns to Waiuku. Nick spurns her, then follows her to the airport to return her saxophone. They kiss.

Arriving Tuesday is a quiet, modest drama about relationship shifts and, on a wider scale, national identity. The pakeha couple's bickering journey contrasts with the harmony and warmth with which the Maori group make their way northwards. Riki's certainty that the marae is the most comfortable place in the world and anger at pakeha exploitation of the kauri forests reveal a certainty Monica envies but feels unable to share.

The film is well paced, with warmth and wit cut through by moments of bitter anger, and the love and hikoi story lines are skilfully interwoven. Monica is blamed, by both Nick and Riki, for not knowing what she wants, but her 'new personality' (she fancies her overseas experience has made her more sophisticated) is a lot more attractive than Nick's sour obduracy. With no indication of what Monica 'does', besides travel and live with Nick, that identifies her as an individual, the viewer is left to wonder whether, having made her choice to go back to Nick, his junk sculptures and his view that 'you can't ingratiate yourself into another culture', Monica will have regrets. After all, at the end of the film he is exactly as he was at the beginning: emotionally withdrawn, jealous of her contact with other people and absolutely set in his ways.

The soundtrack provides moody atmosphere and the locations, many making their first appearance in a feature film, are beautifully shot. HM

1987 New Zealand Listener Gofta Award: Best Performance, Judy McIntosh. Best Supporting Actress, Heather Bolton.

Peter Hayden (Nick) and Judy McIntosh (Monica). Courtesy of the New Zealand Film Commission.

1986

QUEEN CITY ROCKER

Mirage Films with the assistance of the New Zealand Film Commission. A.k.a. Tearaway. ©1986. *Location:* Auckland City. *Distributor:* Mirage Film Distributors. *Rating:* RP16 (Violence and language may offend), October 1986. 35 mm. Colour. 89.5 mins.

Director: Bruce Morrison. *Producer:* Larry Parr. *Associate producer:* Finola Dwyer. *Executive producer:* Henry Fownes. *Screenplay:* Bill Baer, from an original idea by Richard Lymposs. *Director of photography:* Kevin Hayward. *Camera operator:* John Mahaffie. *Editor:* Michael Hacking. *Production designer:* Mike Becroft. *Wardrobe supervisor:* Sue Gandy. *Music director:* Dave McArtney. *Vocals:* Ardijah, Graham Brazier, Dave McArtney, Harry Lyon, Lisle Kinney, Ricky Ball, Simon Alexander, Fetus Productions, Kim Willoughby, Alan Jansson, Cheek ta Cheek, TAS, Tex Pistol, Shona Laing, Chrome Safari, No Tag, Wentworth, Brewster and Co. *Composers:* Dave McArtney, Ross Pearce, Ryan Monga, The Dickheads, Shona Laing and Bruce Lynch, Jed Town, Alan Jansson, Graham Brazier, Simon Alexander, No Tag, Irving Mills and Nat King Cole. *Sound:* George Lyle, Mike Hopkins, Mike Westgate, Gethin Creagh, John McWilliam, Graham Morris, Hammond Peek, Tim Field.

Cast

Matthew Hunter (Ska), Mark Pilisi (Andrew), Kim Willoughby (Stacy), Rebecca Saunders (Fran), Peter Bland (Jay Ryder), Riccardo Bribiesca (Sniper), Pevise Vaifale (Flak), George Henare (Buyer), Roy Billing (Stacy's father), Liddy Holloway (Stacy's mother), Greer Robson (Ska's sister), Simon Cornelius (Ska's brother), Michael Morrissey (Manager), Rob Jane (Ryder's driver), Norman Fletcher (Ska's father), Te Paki Cherrington (Andrew's father), Tasi Hunuki (Andrew's mother), S. Sapolu (Andrew's grandmother), Joe Tuaimau, Velesala Tuaimau, Sialasau Tuaimau, Charles (Andrew's brothers).

Matthew Hunter (Ska) deals with Peter Bland (Jay Ryder). Courtesy of the New Zealand Film Commission.

Rubbish collectors Ska, Andrew and Sniper, stealing gear on the job, are disgusted by the low price offered by the fence for underworld boss, Jay Ryder and Ska throws in his job. In the streets Ska and his mainly pakeha gang fight with a rival, mainly Polynesian, gang led by Flak. Escaping from the police Ska rescues Stacy, a stranger, from a gang rape. In town he sees his sister Fran, a prostitute who works for Ryder, with a client. He confronts Ryder, who gives him tickets to a rock concert he is promoting, then throws him out. After a futile talk with his alcoholic father, Ska resolves to rescue Fran and he, Andrew and Sniper trash Ryder's brothel with baseball bats. Fran and Andrew rekindle their relationship and Ska gets together with Stacy. Ryder's men beat up Ska and Andrew and Andrew dies in hospital. Ska persuades Flak to add his gang's weight to his plan to get back at Ryder by destroying his rock concert. The gangs stop the concert and Ska throws Ryder, then his suitcase of money, to the angry crowd. Fran takes their younger brother and sister to live with their grandmother. Ska and Stacy drive through the city, joking they have no money.

The original script was written by street kid Richard Lymposs. Described by its director as 'for people who want their video clips longer and with a few more words', the film targets its teen audience with music, comic book urban street violence and organised crime where the have-nots (the young) outmanoeuvre the haves (the middle aged) with the baseball bat as the preferred weapon. Ryder's underworld gang are caricatures of evil, while Stacy's rich parents, driven by greed for booze, possessions and status, are yuppie caricatures.

All the young people, whether in punk or rocker dress, are lost souls, although lack of adult responsibility is not always to blame for adolescent waywardness. Andrew lives with his large supportive Polynesian family in a state housing area and although they are poor his downfall is brought about not by family negligence but by his answering the call of the queen city's streets. Ska and sister Fran, on the other hand, 'parent' their kid brother and sister because their father decamped after their mother's death.

In becoming a prostitute Fran has given in to defeat, believing Ryder is invincible and things are unchangeable. Ska, the inarticulate hero, is bruised but not beaten as the film traces the four days in his life when, acting on his disgust with adult corruption, he brings Ryder and his criminal empire to their knees. Hunter's performance is very low key, although the missionary zeal with which he rescues his sister injects some vigour and not a little sentimentality into the performance. Stacy likes Ska, she says, because he is not afraid.

Locally, the song 'Give Me Your Number' made it to number 16 in the national charts. HM

1987 Media Women's Outrageous Media Awards (MOMMA): The Cars, Guns, Horses and Maybe a Girl Oddfellow Award, shared with **Dangerous Orphans** and **Bridge to Nowhere**.

1986

FOOTROT FLATS: THE DOG'S TAIL TALE

Dog, cut off from aid, is in trouble. Courtesy of John Barnett.

Magpie Productions Ltd in association with Independent Newspapers Ltd. ©1986. *Budget:* approx. $5 million (includes NZ and Australia distribution costs, production of the film, the soundtrack and albums, three books and two promo films). *Distributor:* Endeavour Entertainment Ltd. *Rating:* GY (Parental guidance recommended. Contains coarse language), November 1986. 35 mm. Dolby Stereo. Colour. 71.5 mins.

Director: Murray Ball. *Producers:* John Barnett, Pat Cox, Murray Ball. *Screenplay:* Murray Ball, Tom Scott, based on characters created by Murray Ball. *Animation director:* Robbert Smit. *Camera operators:* Jenny Ochse, Bob Evans, Kate Robinson. *Backgrounds:* Richard Zaloudek. *Special effects animation:* Henry Neville. *Composer:* Dave Dobbyn. *Music performers:* Herbs, Dave Dobbyn, Bruce Lynch, Ardijah. *Editors:* Michael Horton, Denis Jones. *Sound:* Soundworks Studio, Auckland, Associated Sounds in association with National Film Unit and Mandrill Studios, Graham Morris, Ken Saville, John McKay, Chris Burt, Ross Chambers. *Voice production*: Chris Hampson.

Voices

John Clarke (Wal), Peter Rowley (Dog), Rawiri Paratene (Rangi), Fiona Samuel (Cheeky Hobson, Pongo), Peter Hayden (Cooch, Irish Murphy), Dorothy McKegg (Aunt Dolly), Billy T. James (Pawai), Brian Sargent (Spit Murphy), Marshall Napier (Hunk Murphy), Michael Haigh (Rugby commentator).

Dog finds life on Wal Footrot's 400 acres of swamp/farm is not easy, but it's not dull either. Trying to prevent Wal from using up valuable energy before the rugby game in which he hopes to be selected as an All Black, Dog falls from favour, spoiling Wal's Friday night date with girlfriend Cheeky. Local villains, the Murphys, steal neighbour Cooch's prize stag. In the mayhem that follows in Saturday's flood, dog Jess and cat Horse battle the Murphys' dogs, the Hellhounds, a swarm of evil-minded rats led by king rat Vernon the Vermin, the riled Murphys and the even more ferocious swamp crocopigs. Rangi lures Wal away from the rugby game and with Cooch they find Dog, Jess and Horse on a raft floating out to sea. Jess is thrown onto the beach and the others are feared dead until they are spied surfing magnificently in to shore. Jess and Dog proudly trot ahead of a large litter of puppies looking just like them.

When the film was made Murray Ball's much-loved fictional Ureweras-inspired farming district, Raupo (population 406), celebrated in his cartoon strip 'Footrot Flats', was appearing in 120 newspapers in Australia and New Zealand and in translation in several other countries. The film reprises Ball's affectionate satire of the archetypal community, focusing on grubby, laconic farmer Wal and his smart best mate Dog, and adding some new characters for menace — Vernon the Vermin, the ghastly crocopigs and Spit and Hunk Murphy.

Appealing principally to an adult audience the narrative wallows in things earthy and visceral—mud, sexual innuendo, the elimination of body waste—and sets up Herculean good/evil battles where the honest country underdog briefly triumphs. Problems in pace and timing arise because the plot is basically episodic and some of the dialogue sounds forced. This is compensated for by the anarchic tone, which is kept rolling by visual and verbal humour and noisy slapstick. The animation of colour, light, movement and form is beautiful and the characters (animal and human) and the landscape are alive and real without a hint of Disney. The music is a highlight.

Footrot Flats: The Dog's Tail Tale, which took six years to plan and 15 months to make, comprises over 100 000 individually drawn and painted animation frames. The animation was done in Sydney, where armies of layout artists, animators, animation checkers, inbetweeners, line testers, colour stylists, xerox checkers, painters, paint checkers and renderers brought Ball's characters and settings to life in an exercise requiring replication of the originals down to the last hair. (Ball checked virtually every image for absolute accuracy.) The film was directed from New Zealand where Tom Scott collaborated with Murray Ball to develop the screenplay. Investor INL was the first New Zealand newspaper group to publish the cartoon strip. Fay Richwhite was also involved in the financing.

New Zealand's first, and to date only, animated feature film **Footrot Flats: The Dog's Tail Tale** was a huge success, grossing over $2 million at the local box office.
HM

1986 New Zealand Music Awards: Film Soundtrack of the Year, Dave Dobbyn.
Song of the Year: 'Slice of Heaven', Dave Dobbyn. Producer and Top Male Vocalist of the Year: Dave Dobbyn.
1987 International Animation Celebration, Los Angeles: First Prize.
New Zealand Listener Gofta Awards: Best Sound Design. Best Film Score. Best Original Screenplay.

1986

MARK II

Avalon, Television New Zealand. ©1986. Telefeature. *Locations:* North Island. No censorship rating (in-house production). Videotape. Colour. 72 mins.

Director: John Anderson. *Producer:* Dan McKirdy. *Screenplay:* Mitchell Manuel, Mike Walker. *Director of photography:* Peter Hudson. *Camera operator:* Renaud Maire. *Editor:* Paul Sutorius. *Production designer:* Richard Martin. *Wardrobe supervisor:* Joan Pearce. *Driving stunts:* Peter Zivkovic, Mark Taylor. *Music:* Rob Winch. *Vocals:* Annie Crummer. *Sound:* Gavin Wilsher.

Cast

Nicholas Rogers (Eddie), Mitchell Manuel (Kingi), Junior Amiga (Matthew), Joanna Briant (Judy), Jeff Boyd (Chris), Jim Moriarty (Rangi), Riwia Brown (Mary), Do Kahu (Uncle), Maria Rogers (Eddie's mother), Tama Poata (Eddie's father), Ellen Te Moni (Auntie Nell), Marise Wipani (Tina), Kevin Tako (Sniffbag), Kate Harcourt (Pump attendant), Bernard Kearns (Judge), Aileen Davidson (Shopkeeper), Ray Carroll (Farmer), Peter Gardiner, Greg La Hood, Peter Gray (Drug heavies), with Gwynn Amiga, Eddie Campbell, Sue Day, Jon Brazier, Stanley Churn, David Douglas, Robert Fifita, Dan Heke, Jim Hollis, Mac Kahu, Mary Lochore, Keith Hambleton, Arthur Henare, Vicky Hunwick, Steve Lillyston, Neville Pascoe, Donna McLeod, Alex Ranken, Joan Reid, Peter Sledmere, Ross Wilson, Sarah Major, Amilla Ranken, Jascinda Richmond, Colin Welsh.

Young Polynesian Eddie sets off down country in his restored Mark II Zephyr with his cousin Matthew and their friend Kingi. Unknown to Eddie and Matthew, Kingi is followed by dealers in pursuit of the drugs Kingi has, in fact, flushed down a toilet. The Turangi chapter of the Mongrel Mob help them fix a flat tyre. A farm visit to Eddie's relatives ends when a neighbour, incensed that Kingi has spent the night with his daughter Tina, chases them off. In a river swim Kingi rescues Eddie from drowning. Next morning Kingi breaks into a farmhouse in search of food and, pursued by a farmer, steals a tractor to escape. Eddie picks him up and, arguing, they drive to a town. Eddie rescues a young woman, Judy, from a beating, and Kingi and Matthew are pursued by the drug dealers. Joined by Eddie they beat the dealers in a fist fight. Eddie and Matthew are welcomed by their cousin Rangi's family. In another altercation with the dealers Kingi steals their van, is caught by police and charged with possession of hard drugs. Eddie spends a night with Judy. Provoked to fight her ex-boyfriend he is arrested and charged with assault. Judy's father hires a lawyer and Eddie is freed. He rages against the unfairness of his arrest, but is persuaded by Rangi to channel his anger into going back to Auckland to support Kingi.

Targeted at a young audience writer/adviser Mike Walker called **Mark II** 'a Polynesian **Goodbye Pork Pie**', although it was conceived well before that breakthrough film. The journey is essentially aimless and the narrative episodic, but there are strong connecting threads in the feelings shared by the young men and their extended families. The warmth with which their relatives receive them underlines the idea of community and the importance of their culture.

Kingi is the most troubled of the trio. He sees traditional ways as 'superstition', refusing to wash his hands after visiting a Maori burial ground, and lacks a sense of cultural belonging. In suggesting a way out the film balances the need for individual responsibility with the recognition that, whatever their circumstances, the Polynesian characters have to battle institutionalised racism.

The film is well scored and shot and the performances excellent, with Junior Amiga's solitary breakdance a highlight. John Anderson shared the directing decisions with writer Mike Walker and the three lead actors. Mike Walker wrote the original screenplay in the 1970s but shelved it, through lack of funding, and worked instead on **Kingi's Story**, a 50 minute television drama about the pressures facing young Polynesians in New Zealand. The script evolved from the experiences of inmates of the Kohitere Boys' Training Centre who Walker met through their work on his commercials productions. Walker and inmate/actor Mitchell Manuel followed **Kingi's Story** with **Kingpin** (1985), then collaborated on a revised version of the original Mark II screenplay when cancellation of the television series Roche II had TVNZ looking for work for its crew.

The first telefeature produced by TVNZ, Mark II is important in its dramatisation of the lives of young Polynesians in New Zealand. It screened on New Zealand television on 5 November 1986 and 11 July 1987. HM

1987 New Zealand Listener Film and Television Awards: Best Male Performance in a Television Drama, Mitchell Manuel. Best Television Drama.

Nicholas Rogers (Eddie). *Courtesy of the New Zealand Film Commission.*

1987

NGATI

Pacific Films in association with the New Zealand Film Commission. ©1987. *Budget:* approx. $1 million. *Locations:* North Island East Coast, Waipiro Bay, Iritekura Marae. *Distributor:* Pacific Films. *Rating:* GY (Contains coarse language. Some Maori dialogue/English subtitles), April 1987. 35 mm. Colour. 91.5 mins.

Director: Barry Barclay. *Producer:* John O'Shea. *Associate producers:* Craig Walters, Tama Poata. *Screenplay:* Tama Poata. *Director of photography:* Rory O'Shea. *Camera operator:* Kevin Riley. *Editor:* Dell King. *Art director:* Matthew Murphy. *Costume designer:* Sue Gandy. *Music producer:* Bob Smith. *Arrangements:* Dalvanius. *Vocals:* Te Roopu Ngati, Kara Pewhairangi. *Players:* Clarence Smith, Bob Smith, Rob Winch, Tony Noorts, Dave Parsons. *Sound:* Robert Allen, Annie Collins, Brian Shennan.

Cast

Michael Tibble (Tione), Oliver Jones (Ropata), Wi Kuki Kaa (Iwi), Kiri McCorkindale (Sue), Judy McIntosh (Jenny Bennett), Norman Fletcher (Dr Paul Bennett), Alice Fraser (Sam Bennett), Ross Girven (Greg Shaw), Iranui Haig (Nanny Huia), Ngawai Harrison (Hine), Connie Pewhairangi (Sally), Luckie Renata (Dike), Tuta Ngarimu Tamati (Uncle Eru), Sol Pewhairangi Jnr (Bus driver), Johnny Coleman (Drover), Barry Allen (Headmaster), Erica Hovell, Priscilla Hovell (Tione's sisters), Paki Cherrington (Mac), with Joe Davis, James Beaumont, Ken Blackburn, Edward Karauria, Timothy Bartlett, Paul Sonne, Buster Hanley, Mere Matahiki, Manare Tatare, Ken Pickett-Harrison, Tawai Moana, Red McClutchie, Kura Wharehinga, Whataaiwi Hapairangi Sadler.

1948. In the tiny (fictional) East Coast settlement of Kapua people gather around the bedside of a dying child, Ropata, and pray with tohunga Uncle Eru. Some Maori farmers, seduced by the offer of higher payments, are sending their stock to an out-of-town abattoir, precipitating the imminent closure of the freezing works. Curiosity is aroused by the arrival of Australian Greg Shaw whose father, a former Kapua doctor, has sent him to his birthplace as a graduation present. Schoolteacher Jenny introduces Greg to the community. Her doctor father, formerly in practice with Greg's father, explains Greg's heritage to him—he had not known his late mother was a local Maori. Ropata dies and at his tangi his friend Tione begins to comes to terms with the death, growing closer to Ropata's father Iwi and to Greg, who needs coaching in taha Maori. Iwi, offered management of a sheep station, prevents closure of the local works by proposing a solution, suggested by his daughter Sally, that will employ people and enable the community to buy the works. Sally decides not to return to the city. Immersed in community life Greg loses his racist assumptions and this, along with his growing affection for Jenny, influences his decision to return to Kapua as a practising doctor.

Ngati was the first New Zealand feature made principally by Maori and the world's first feature by an indigenous culture living within a white majority culture. Its story is of community survival in the face of tragedy and change. Through its three interwoven storylines, told in docudrama style, the film emphasises the immutability and timelessness of Maori spiritual values, where individuals gain their sense of identity from knowledge of and respect for their ancestry and ethnicity and where the community is valued above material possessions. Ropata's illness, spoken of as Maori sickness (mate Maori) and described as leukemia some way into the film, is a symbol of a community dysfunctional because conflict over how to deal with the threat to their livelihood is tearing it apart.

The clash of traditional and new ways, exacerbated by post-war urban drift, is voiced in conflicts over whether Ropata's family should use the tohunga's methods or modern medicine. The women and elders have great strength, but there are no heroes. Everybody counts, and the healing of the community is not effected until everyone listens and co-operates. Greg's journey from ignorance to empathy takes the viewer vicariously on the same journey while Tione's passionate refusal to obey his elders and abandon his dying friend shows traditional values adapted to fit changing times. Cross-cutting between parallel scenes works well in showing how all actions impact on the whole community and in this way the traditional oral and diffuse Maori storytelling style is reflected in the structure.

The script evolved from a one-hour screenplay by Tama Poata about the return of the Maori Battalion after World War II. With some events based on Ngati Porou writer Poata's East Coast childhood, the film, developed from his lifetime interest in Maori political issues, with its message about Maori autonomy relevant to all tribes even though it was shot on Ngati Porou land. Eschewing the Hollywood film model Poata and director Barry Barclay intended **Ngati** to be a political film in form, content, production and distribution, an attempt to say what it's like being Maori. Many of the young Maori who crewed on the film were part of a collective, Te Awa Marama, recruited from a training course. Most of the cast were non-actors, with the result that some of the performances look amateur. Barclay describes the necessity of having pakeha characters in a Maori film to attract audiences as 'the Costner factor'.* The pakeha bosses, portrayed as commercially driven and with no sense of humanity, are played as stereotypes.

Production design is simple and effectively conveys the period atmosphere, although the occasional documentary detail (such as the shoeing of the horse) seems misplaced. Form and content reveal the texture of community life in a leisurely and thoughtful manner. Long shots give time for images to be absorbed, with the observational shooting style enhanced by use of a long lens in place of a dolly. The sense of mysticism created by beautiful images and by events is enhanced by a haunting, other-worldly score drawing on traditional Maori music. Notwithstanding the seriousness of the themes, humour provides light relief. HM

1987 Cannes Film Festival: Critics Week.
Taormina Film Festival, Italy: Gold Charybdis Award, Best Film.
New Zealand Music Awards: Best Soundtrack, Dalvanius.

Reference
* B. Cairns & H. Martin. 1994. *Shadows on the Wall, a study of seven New Zealand feature films*, p. 116.

Michael Tibble (Tione) and Tuta Ngarimu Tamati (Uncle Eru). Courtesy of the New Zealand Film Commission.

The Lie of the Land

Creative Arts for South Pacific Broadcasting Corporation Ltd and Co. ©1984. *Locations:* Wellington, Waikanae. *Rating:* G, May 1987. No New Zealand theatrical release. *Censorship applicant:* Grahame J. McLean Associates. 35 mm (shot on 16 mm). Colour. 93.5 mins.

Director: Grahame J. McLean. *Producers:* Grahame J. McLean, Narelle Barsby. *Screenplay:* Grahame J. McLean, based on the screenplay *Small Farms* by Kevin Smith. *Director of photography:* Warrick Attewell. *Editor:* Jamie Selkirk. *Art department:* Rob Pearson, Caroline Girdlestone, Mark Robins, Johnny Morris, Yvonne Davidson. *Wardrobe supervisors:* Norman Forsey, Fiona Stewart. *Music:* Dale Gold. *Sound:* Malcolm Cromie, David Newton.

Cast

Marshall Napier (Huddy), Roberta Wallach (Alwyn), Dean Moriarty (Henry), Jim Moriarty (George Thompson/George's brother), Jonathan Hardy (Doctor Max Steiner), Terence Cooper (Clifford), Eileen Dean (Davina Whitehouse), Meriol Buchanan (Alice Perrin), Tom Poata (Bill Te Hau), Ann Pacey (Jenna Steiner), John Bach (Gorrie), Norman Forsey (Allard), Sonny Waru (Koro Mita), Witarina Harris (Kuia Thompson).

1920s rural New Zealand. Ex-army Major Martin Hudson, returned after World War I service, finds work on the farm of widow Alwyn, introducing himself as Huddy. Working with Alwyn's son Henry, he is attacked by neighbour Jack Clifford, a brute who wants Alwyn's land to augment his water supply. Huddy becomes ill as a result of wet weather exacerbating damage done to his lungs in trench warfare. While recuperating he is troubled by flashbacks to the War, reliving a court martial where he defended a Maori corporal refusing to fight, saying the land they were fighting for was not theirs. Before he was sentenced the man committed suicide. Alwyn visits the local marae and it is revealed her husband, said to have been killed in the War, was part-Maori and the grandson of a pakeha who gained much Maori land. Because of this kaumatua Koromita has put a curse on the family and the land. The doctor tells Huddy that although he has diagnosed George, the brother of Alwyn's husband, as schizophrenic, the Maori believe he has been cursed with mate Maori (Maori sickness). Aware that Huddy and Alwyn are becoming close Clifford and his gang of thugs try to scare him off the farm. Huddy ties a yellow ribbon in a tree by way of atonement for the horrors of the War. Spurned by Alwyn George goes berserk and kidnaps Henry. In the confrontations that follow Henry is returned safely, George kills himself and Clifford is thrown off the farm. A close-up of a photo of Alwyn and her dead husband reveals him to be the Maori Huddy defended in the war. Koromita lifts the curse and Alwyn, having given the farm back to the Maori, leaves on a horse-drawn cart with her new lover Huddy and Henry.

A period drama with romance, a Maori curse on the land, a water rights dispute, two suicides, a mystery prowler and eventual redemption, **The Lie of the Land** features a winning performance from young Dean Moriarty in the role of Henry. Big problems with the script are that much of the 'mystery' is explained in dialogue or flashback and plot holes and non sequiturs make for confusion and bathos. The 'watcher', for example, whose incessant prowling activities are shown via point-of-view shots and shots seen as if through binoculars, is revealed to be George by the clumsy and perfunctory device of Henry pointing it out to George that he knows he's the one. Doctor Steiner makes a reasonable fist of explaining to Huddy how the pakeha are stealing Maori land and ruining their culture, but the message loses impact because land-grabbing Clifford is a caricature. By way of light relief the doctor's wife, Jenna, affecting the dress and manner of a 20s flapper, is a caricature of sexual predation.

Made on a low budget and shot back-to-back with **Should I Be Good? The Lie of the Land** was made for the international television and video markets. Although made in 1984 it was not submitted for a censorship certificate until 1987. In 1990 the director, Grahame McLean, screened it at his Auckland Travelling Show with **Should I Be Good?** and Peter Jackson's **Bad Taste**. It has not had a theatrical release. HM

Dean Moriarty (Henry) and Marshall Napier (Martin Hudson). *Courtesy of the New Zealand Film Commission.*

STARLIGHT HOTEL

1987

Greer Robson (Kate Marshall). *Courtesy of the New Zealand Film Commission.*

Mirage Films/Challenge Film Corporation in association with the New Zealand Film Commission. ©1987. *Budget:* $1.7 million. *Location:* South Island. *Distributor:* Mirage Film Distributors. *Rating:* GY, June 1987. 35 mm. Colour. 95.5 mins.

Director: Sam Pillsbury. *Producers:* Larry Parr, Finola Dwyer. *Screenplay:* Grant Hinden-Miller [sic] from his novella *The Dream Monger*. *Director of photography:* Warrick Attewell. *Editor:* Michael Horton. *Production designer:* Mike Becroft. *Costume designer:* Barbara Darragh. *Music:* Morton Wilson, Andrew Hagen. *Sound:* Mike Westgate, John McKay, Gethin Creagh, Michael Hopkins.

Cast

Peter Phelps (Patrick Dawson), Greer Robson (Kate), Marshall Napier (Detective Wallace), The Wizard (Swaggie), Alice Fraser (Aunt), Mervyn Glue (Skip), Gary McCormack (Constable Murphy), Patrick Smyth (Uncle), Shirley Kelly (Mrs Skip), Bruce Phillips (Kate's father), Donogh Rees (Helen), with Sam Pillsbury, Elric Hooper, John Watson, Teresa Bonney, Duncan Anderson, Russell Gibson, Ken Cook, Lex Matheson. Norman Forsey, Craig Stewart, Craig Halkett, Geoffrey Wearing, Sherril Cooper, Louise Petherbridge, Peter McCauley, Bill Walker, Timothy Lee, Michael Brown, Peter Dennet, Yvonne Martin, Deanne Bryant, Kath Te Maiharoa, Jack Browne, Doug Randall, Janice Gray, Connie Hassan, David Telford, Patrick Paynter, Glennis Woods, Peter Brunt, Judy Cleine, John Melor, Vanessa Young.

New Zealand in the 1930s is feeling the bite of the worldwide Depression. Widower Dave Marshall leaves his central South Island home to find work in Wellington. His 13 year-old daughter Kate, unhappy in the care of indifferent relatives and picked on at school, heeds the advice of a passing swaggie and runs away to find her father. On the road she meets World War I veteran Patrick, a young man with bitter war memories. On the run from the police after injuring, perhaps fatally, an unscrupulous furniture repossession agent, he intends stowing away to Australia. Pursued by a zealous detective, the pair make their way up the South Island, sleeping under the night sky (the starlight hotel) and surviving many close calls with the law. Although they squabble at first, as they travel their relationship deepens. When Patrick is offered a place on a ship from Oamaru he chooses to stay with Kate as far as Christchurch. When Patrick is shot at by police and falls into a river he is presumed drowned. The police put Kate on a boat to Wellington and she finds Patrick stowed away. They exchange keepsakes and vow to meet again. As Kate leaves with her father she looks back at the boat, knowing Patrick's escape will be successful.

Starlight Hotel is a simply told odd-couple road movie which makes use of the dramatic potential of the Depression era setting while spinning a good yarn, exploring the possibility a hardened, inarticulate man can learn about life and love from a child. In the public realm the thuggery of the profiteers feeding off other people's misfortune exemplifies selfishness, while the swaggie acts as a knowing mouthpiece for the oppressed poor. The story has an air of fairytale and at times coincidence and chance stretch credibility, particularly with the number and nature of the runaways' narrow escapes. Given that he fought in the War it is questionable that Patrick would be in his twenties during the Depression. In spite of the leisurely pace, dramatic tension is maintained, largely by the quality of the performances of Greer Robson and Peter Phelps, but also by their encounters with many colourful characters on the way.

There is a painterly quality to the light and the images of land and sky that at times looks surreal. The environment, vast and beautiful, is a perfect motif signalling freedom to the travelling pair. Action scenes are equally well realised, as in the riot by the unemployed in Oamaru which, although quite brief, provides a vivid instance of Depression politics.

The source novella is pitched at readers in the 11 to 13 age group and Hindin Miller has adapted his story for a wider audience. The casting, too, has changed the complexion of the source story where the characters are aged 9 and 40. With Patrick twenty-something and Kate 13, as their journey progresses so too does an undercurrent of sexual tension. In keeping with the film's 'family' target audience, this is, however, never more than hinted at, although a single kiss at the end of the film was believed to have dissuaded the Disney organisation from buying **Starlight Hotel**. HM

1989 New Zealand Listener Film and Television Awards: Best Female Performance, Greer Robson.

1987

THE LEADING EDGE

Southern Light Pictures Ltd with assistance of New Zealand Film Commission. ©1987. *Locations:* Mount Cook National Park, Tongariro National Park, Westland National Park, Queenstown. *Distributor:* Everard Film Distributors Ltd. *Rating:* GA (Contains some coarse language), August 1987. 35 mm. Dolby Stereo. Colour. 78.5 mins.

Director and producer: Michael Firth. *Executive producer:* Barrie Everard. *Associate producer:* Robin Judkins. *Screenplay:* Michael Firth, Grant Morris. *Directors of photography:* Stuart Dryburgh, Michael Firth. *Camera assistants:* Neil Cervin, Richard Scott, Paul Richards, Matt Lunjevich. *Editor:* Patrick Monaghan. *Art director:* Greg Taylor. *River stunts:* Peter Bell. *Stunt pilot:* Gavin Wills. *Music:* Mike Farrell, Tom Whitlock. *Sound:* Mike Westgate, Mike Hopkins, Chris Todd.

Cast

Mathurin Molgat, Bruce Grant, Christine Grant, Evan Bloomfield, Mark Whetu, Billy T. James, Melanie Forbes, Jeff Campbell, Zachary Templin, Matthew Templin, Budgie Jones, Geoff Hunt, Steven Brooks, Melanie White, Tony Marcinowski, Andy Bayne-Jardine, John Howard, David Williamson, Gordon Rayner, Nikolaus Frithof, Richard Gallagher, Rosamond Grant, John Grant.

Canadian skier Matt Molgat, working in Telluride, Colorado, as a ski-patroller, looks forward to holidaying in New Zealand and meeting his friend Campbell's 'cowboy mates'. From Auckland Matt hitchhikes down country, skiing at Ruapehu on the way. At a South Island ski field he meets Campbell's mate Bruce, who offers to drive him to Queenstown for the Iron Man competition. At Mount Cook skifield Bruce breaks a leg skiing in dodgy conditions. With Matt driving the landrover they pick up Bruce's mates. After some glacier skiing, they pick up two female hitchhikers. En route to Queenstown they run out of petrol. A crazy pilot (Billy T. James) flies them over the mountains. Jet boating and rubber rafting on the Shotover River and a mountain obstacle race precede the Iron Man, a gruelling race involving a mountain run, skiing and kayaking. All five in the group complete the race.

The Leading Edge, financed principally by merchant bankers Fay Richwhite, is a sequel to the Academy Award-nominated **Off the Edge** in that Mathurin Molgat decides to go to New Zealand to ski on the advice of co-worker and **Off the Edge** star, Jeff Campbell. Again, skiing is the focus.

The Leading Edge is of hybrid genre, a semi-dramatised documentary with champion skiers playing themselves. At the time of filming Mathurin Molgat was a world-class skier and had won several international ski competitions; Bruce Grant was an Olympic representative skier and New Zealand's leading downhill racer; Evan Bloomfield was a New Zealand junior ski champion; Christine Grant was twice national ski champion; Mark Whetu was an alpine heli-ski guide; and Melanie Forbes was a top-line skier.

Scripted dialogue and dramatised sequences attempt to put flesh on the bones of the action sequences. Beyond ascertaining that Kiwis are down-to-earth, fearless blokes who say 'no worries, mate' at any suggestion of danger, there is little opportunity for the skiers' individuality to emerge and the bits of business calculated to convey group solidarity are clumsy. Matt's voice-over and the dubbing in of dialogue not spoken at the time are awkward. In his role as a crazy pilot and entertainer Billy T. James does an unfunny version of his 'dumb Maori' act.

Forty hours of film were shot over 14 weeks with only 14 crew involved in the shoot. The film comes into its own in the stunning action sequences. Accompanied by 1980s rock music the river, glacier and mountain sequences are brilliantly performed and shot. Many of the tumbles are left in—Bruce's leg was broken in an avalanche and the accident required the re-writing of much of the script—and the film creates a vivid sense of the thrills, dangers and rewards of the sport. With action focused tightly on the skiers having fun and daring all, a television news item describing Prime Minister David Lange's advocacy for a nuclear-free New Zealand provides a glimpse of the outside world. HM

Mathurin Molgat takes to the air. *Courtesy of the New Zealand Film Commission.*

1987
AMONG THE CINDERS

Paul O'Shea (Nick Flinders), Rebecca Gibney (Sally) and Derek Hardwick (Hubert Flinders). Courtesy of the New Zealand Film Commission.

Pacific Films in association with Nordeutscher Rundfunk, Hamburg, the New Zealand Film Commission and Broadbank Investments Ltd. No copyright date recorded. Financed from New Zealand and Germany. *Budget:* $1 202 454. *Locations:* Takaka, Golden Bay. *Rating:* R13, November 1987. Made in 1983. No New Zealand theatrical release. *Censorship applicant:* Kerridge Odeon. 35 mm. Colour. 112 mins.

Director: Rolf Haedrich. *Producer:* John O'Shea. *Associate producer:* Craig Walters. *Screenplay:* Rolf Haedrich, John O'Shea. *Source:* Maurice Shadbolt, *Among the Cinders*. *Director of photography:* Rory O'Shea. *Editors:* Inge Behrens, John Kiley. *Art director:* Gerry Luhman. *Costume designer:* Ulla-Britt Soederlund. *Music:* Jan Preston. *Maori ceremonies and songs:* Te Awhina Marae, Motueka Maori Committee. *Sound:* Graham Morris, Maria Jonderko, Malcolm Cromie, John Van Der Ryden, Dave Ginnane, Gerd Wicklaus.

Cast
Paul O'Shea (Nick Flinders), Derek Hardwick (Hubert Flinders), Yvonne Lawley (Beth Flinders), Bridget Armstrong (Helga Flinders), Maurice Shadbolt (Frank Flinders), Amanda Jones (Glenys Appleby), Marcus Broughton (Derek Flinders), Ngaire Woods (Kate), Rebecca Gibney (Sally), Ricky Duff (Sam Waikai), Christopher Hansard (Michael), Harata Solomon (Mrs Waiki), Michael Haigh (Sergeant Crimmins), Peter Baldock (Clergyman), Cherie O'Shea (Nurse), Des Kelly (Fred), Tom Poata (Ahu), Peter Dennet (Constable), Sal Criscillo (Photographer), Sela Apera (Tera), Helena Ross (Glenys' mother), Tamata Paua Bailey (Maori orator), Lorna Langford (Postmistress), Florence Langford (Lady with letter), David Hamilton (Photographer's assistant), Ken Nicholas (Golfer), Lil and Puti Te Runa (Golfer's family), Cindy Turipa (Sam's sister), Shelley Simpson, Jill Ann Davis (models).

Helga Flinders worries that her teenage son Nick is lonely and not like other boys. Her husband, Frank, initiates a father-son talk, but Nick won't communicate. He enjoys the companionship of his Maori friends, the Waikais, before he and Sam Waikai go hunting. In the bush they come across the derelict house of a family whose sons murdered their sisters and parents. Sam refuses to break tapu by entering the house, but Nick goes exploring, treating the tapu as a joke. The following day they fall off a ledge. Sam is killed and Nick blames himself. In his hearing his brother blames Nick's depression on homosexuality. When his grandfather visits and invites him to stay Nick cheers up. Because his parents refuse permission he runs away. Still depressed, and having to deal with his grandparents' bickering and the sexual advances of a girl from his school, Nick is pleased when his grandfather suggests they go to the gumfields he worked in as a young man. They find the derelict old house where the young couple brought up six children. Nick meets a young woman, Sally, and loses his virginity. He and his grandfather go on the run when they hear the police are looking for them. With his grandfather sick and supplies dwindling, Nick goes to a store and the police catch up with him. He learns his grandfather had found his grandmother dead and, not wanting Nick to suffer further, immediately took him away. Nick realises he has grown up and will in future be able to cope with what life brings.

Raised by puritanical parents living cramped, joyless lives, Nick has to work through self-imposed guilt to redemption by learning self-reliance. Notions of cultural belonging are effectively explored in the contrast between Nick's German mother's sense of alienation and dislocation and the comfort of the Waikais. Grandfather offers a portrait of the archetypal pioneer, down-to-earth, practical and hard working. In comparison Nick's parents, Sally's lover and a fashion photographer, have little sense of what really matters. These ideas are expressed symbolically through a range of dwellings from the Flinders' bird's cramped cage to the tapu house to the photographer's architecturally designed home hunched incongruously on open farmland.

The initiative to film Maurice Shadbolt's acclaimed novel came from German film-maker Rolf Haedrich who began correspondence with Shadbolt which eventuated in his directing the adaptation. Whereas Shadbolt's boy proves himself by cutting down a tree Haedrich insisted on a sexual rite of passage to cater to German audiences. Problems with pace are exacerbated by awkward dialogue and the voice-over technique doesn't work dramatically, as characters pause awkwardly in tableau while the words are spoken. Errors of judgement in direction include unmatched eyelines in shot/reverse shot sequences and unnecessary slow zooms. Characterisations sanction irascible misogyny in the old man and the photographer and sexist imaging of the young women. Given that it takes Nick so long to become interested in girls the film's preoccupation with women's naked breasts is a puzzle.

The film was made in 1983 but was not submitted to the New Zealand censor until 1987. It has screened on New Zealand television but has not had a New Zealand theatrical release. It has, however, screened often on German television and has sold to overseas territories. HM

1984 Karlovy Vary Film Festival, Czechoslovakia: Special Jury Prize For Acting Diploma, Derek Hardwick.

BAD TASTE

WingNut Films in association with the New Zealand Film Commission. ©1987. *Budget:* approx. $250 000. *Locations:* Makara, Pukerua Bay, Gear Homestead, Porirua. *Distributor:* Endeavour Entertainment Ltd. *Rating:* R16 (Violent content may offend), December 1987. 35 mm. Colour. 91.5 mins.

Director and producer: Peter Jackson. *Special assistants to the producer:* Mum and Dad (Joan Jackson and Bill Jackson). *Consultant producer:* Tony Hiles. *Screenplay:* Peter Jackson, additional material by Tony Hiles, Ken Hammon. *Camera operator:* Peter Jackson. *Editors:* Peter Jackson, Jamie Selkirk. *Art director:* Caroline Girdlestone. *Make-up effects/special effects:* Peter Jackson, Cameron Chittock. *Film crew:* Ken Hammon, Pete O'Herne, Terry Potter, Mike Minett, Craig Smith, Dean Lawrie, Philip Lamey. *Music:* Michelle Scullion. *Songs:* The Remnants, Madlight. *Sound:* Ken Saville, Brent Burge, Kit Rollings, Jamie Selkirk.

Cast

Peter Jackson (Derek, Robert), Pete O'Herne (Barry/3rd class alien), Mike Minett (Frank/3rd class alien), Terry Potter (Ozzy/3rd class alien), Craig Smith (Giles/3rd class alien), Doug Wren (Crumb), Dean Lawrie (Alien leader, special effects), Peter Vere-Jones (Crumb's voice), Ken Hammon, Michael Gooch, Peter Gooch, Shane Yarrall, Laurie Yarrall, Dean Lawrie, Costa Botes, Bob Haliburton, Clive Haywood, John Nelson, Steven Smith, Matt Noonan, Ray Battersby, Mike Appleby, Peter Appleby, Robert Johnston, Philip Lamey, Mark Lamey, Grant Taylor, Dean Taylor, Dave Hamilton, Tony Hiles, Kerry Underhill, Garry Brown, Peter Henderson, Robin Griggs, Graham Butcher, Andrew McKay, John McTavish, Graham Nesbitt, John Logan Jnr, Cameron Chittock, Mike Kane, Scott Bradshaw, Giles Forrest, Carol Taylor, Kim Taylor, Jock Fyfe, John Ruby, Robin Watene, Mark Jackson, Janine Riely, Margaret Byford (third class aliens).

When extra-terrestrials decimate Kaihoro (population 75) Internal Affairs sends in the Boys, a.k.a. the Astro Investigation and Defence Service. Derek and Barry massacre several aliens before Derek plunges over a cliff. Charity worker Giles is marinated by aliens in preparation for their farewell feast. AIDS reinforcements Ozzy and Frank join Barry and Frank learns the extra-terrestrials, on an intergalactic mission to supply meat for their fast-food chain, have packaged Kaihoro's population in preparation to space-shipping them home. Storming the house, the Boys free Giles. Derek returns, having secured his loose brains into his skull with a belt, and attacks the aliens with a chainsaw. Ozzy bazookas the house and a sheep and the only surviving alien, the leader, phones home. Launching the house into orbit, he meets his maker when Derek powers through his skull with the chainsaw and emerges, born again, between his legs. Cackling with glee Derek anticipates revenge.

Bad Taste is made in the spirit of small boys playing shoot-em-up in the backyard. A do-it-yourself comedy splatter, its Monty Pythonesque humour has been dubbed 'splatstick'. Fun is made of the horror/splatter genre and of New Zealand culture, with many parodic allusions to other films. Much care was taken with make-up, costumes, animation, prosthetic body parts, models, special effects and props. The ingenious special effects are home-made from cheap materials. Kilos of raw meat and buckets of fake blood provide the gore and the green vomit scene is a highlight. Weapons are made of cardboard and foam rubber and Jackson made gun replicas out of aluminium tubing, wood and Fimo. Gun flashes were achieved by double-exposing the film. Clever choreography in the battle scenes generally keeps them from seeming repetitive and with approximately 2300 shots in the film the cutting rate is very fast. The musical score reinforces the over-the-top tone and smooths over rough patches.

Peter Jackson's 10 minute splatter, **Roast of the Day**, began shooting in October 1983 and evolved into **Bad Taste**. With Ken Hammon (who dies 23 times in the film) he made up the story as he went along. Shot only on Sundays, the film was not completed until October 1987. The four year shoot made for logistical problems: the script changed according to who was available; the lead actor left the cast after two years then returned; Jackson himself played two parts because he knew he could be relied on to turn up (he also had most of the production roles); actors played aliens and their assassins; and actor Pete O'Herne had not shaved on the first day of the shoot so had to maintain the stubbly look for four years.

Jackson began filming using his own money. Three years into the shoot the Film Commission provided finance, most of which was used in post-production, when assistance was given by professionals Tony Hiles and Jamie Selkirk.

Bad Taste posters were banned in the London Underground and Australian censorship authorities cut out a minute before letting it into the country. The *Evening Standard* (London, September 1989) offered **Bad Taste** as 'the best reason yet for not having to visit New Zealand.' Locally and overseas the film has attracted a large cult following. HM

1988 Cannes screening, standing ovation. International Festival of Fantasy and Science, Paris: Prix de Gore.
1989 Fanta Festival, Rome: Special Public Prize.
1992 Wellington Fringe Festival Accolades: Peter Jackson, achievement in creating a new genre in New Zealand film-making, comedy splatter.

Doug Wren (Crumb). *Courtesy of the New Zealand Film Commission.*

1988

ILLUSTRIOUS ENERGY

Mirage Entertainment Corporation Ltd in association with the New Zealand Film Commission. ©1988. *Budget:* $1.5 million. *Location:* Central Otago. *Distributor:* Mirage Entertainment Corporation Ltd. *Rating:* GY, March 1988. 35 mm. Colour. 102 mins.

Director: Leon Narby. *Producers:* Don Reynolds, Chris Hampson. *Screenplay:* Martin Edmond, Leon Narbey. *Director of photography:* Alan Locke. *Editor:* David Coulson. *Production designer:* Janelle Aston. *Costume designer:* Trixie Woodill. *Chinese calligraphy:* Shaun Bao. *Original music:* Jan Preston. *Percussion and voices:* Don McGlashan. *Sound:* Bob Allen, Graham Morris, Michael Hopkins, Gethin Creagh.

Cast

Shaun Bao (Chan), Harry Ip (Kim), Peter Chin (Wong), Geeling (Li), Desmond Kelly (Surveyor), Peter Hayden (Reverend Don), Heather Bolton (Mrs Wong), David Telford (Stan), John Billington (Chicken thief), Andrea Cunningham (Patsy), David Sheridan (Clown), Herbert Wong (Opium man), Tim Yee (Sammy), Peter Lee (Fan), Ingram Washington (Circus hand), Bill Wong (Merchant musician), Charles Lum (Gambling den owner), Tony Loo, Lee Mung (Musicians), Eddie Chin (Referee), Christopher Tso Fang King, Trevor Sai-Louie, Choie Yee Hing (Gamblers), Stephen Burton, Alan Clarke, Scott Grayland, Matthew Hughes (Acrobats, courtesy of Circus Oz).

1860s, Central Otago goldfields. Three Chinese exhume a friend's bones and prepare them for shipment to China. Chan and his old father-in-law Kim discuss their longing for China and Wong, who established the claim they're reworking, reminds them they owe him money. Wong returns to his orchard and Chan and Kim work the stream near their camp. Kim worries nearby surveyors will force them out. Striking gold at last (Chan has mined for 12 years, Kim for 27) Chan and Kim work tirelessly and recover a fortune, hiding it in their cabin. In town for supplies, Chan discusses religion with a Reverend and is almost robbed in an opium/gambling den. Visiting Wong to pay their debts, he talks about his Chinese wife and the child he has never seen. Returning home he meets a travelling circus and is beaten by racist Europeans. He spends the night with the circus magician, Li, an Australian-born Chinese woman. Although invited to stay he returns to Kim, on the way repelling men after his gold. He and Kim get drunk and Kim tells Chan he has shifted the gold to a new hiding place in the hills. The next day Kim dies and Chan, after a futile search, realises he will never find the gold. He packs his few possessions and leaves the claim.

Illustrious Energy dramatises the way of life of Chinese prospectors in the waning days of the 1860s gold rush. Its title is from the diary of a Presbyterian minister, Reverend Alexander Don, describing an old Chinese man, Illustrious Envoy (read initially by the film's writers as 'Energy'), who was arrested and admitted to Seacliff Mental Hospital. Martin Edmond and Leon Narbey began with him in mind although their Chan is much younger.

To Chan and Kim, desire to return to China wars with the promise of prosperity in New Zealand. In asking how a person transplants from one culture to another, the film poses alternatives. Wong forgets his Chinese family, marries a Scot and prospers. Many immigrant Chinese while away their time with prostitutes and opium. Old Kim clings to superstition, insisting the appearance of a comet and the collapse of his plum tree are portents of ill fortune. Ironically, in hiding the gold from the surveyors he calls 'land butchers' Kim causes the bad luck he has predicted. Chan, complex and pragmatic, has shaken off the beliefs inherited from his culture and insists on the materialist philosophy that the world is as he experiences it. In the opium den men amuse themselves betting on cricket fights. Chan's cricket, which he cages but cares for as a pet, is a symbol to him of his own entrapment. He enjoys its singing, but when he knows finally he will never return to China he sets the cricket free.

There are alternatives to the vicious, self-serving racism of the British settlers, seen in the Reverend's easy companionship and the jovial warmth of the circus folk. In a sense the closing of the door that would lead him back to China has given Chan the freedom to put down roots in his new land. It is left for the viewer to speculate on whether he chooses to join Li in the circus.

While the characters are individually drawn, their story suggests myth and archetype, inviting the film to be read as an allegory asking questions about history and the human condition. The dream-like rhythm is created by a measured pace and by the extraordinary beauty of the images. From the opening shot the landscape dominates, from gorgeous, intractable sky to the bare plains with their coarse, towering rock faces, dwarfing the birds flying by and the men digging in the hard earth. The narrative is rich in documentary detail conveyed through meticulous production design which used Reverend Don's photographs as source material for costume ideas. The score, with its Chinese instruments and music, acts as a strong aural bridge between Eastern and Western cultures.

Lack of clarity in the dialogue results from the broken English spoken by some of the Chinese actors. In *Illusions 11* Tony Chuah took **Illustrious Energy** to task for 'nostalgia for a Chinese ethnicity of the distant past', 'use of conceptions of Chineseness that verge on cliché' and 'framing of Chan as a romantic hero',* but in general response was very positive, with reviewers using such epithets as 'near faultless', 'finely crafted', 'uncompromising' and 'arresting'. HM

1988 Taormina Film Festival: Bronze Charybdis.
Hawai'i Film Festival: East-West Centre Award (Best Film).
London Film Festival: Official Selection.
New Zealand Listener Film and Television Awards: Best Director. Best Cinematographer. Best Design. Best Music. Best Editing. Best Soundtrack. Best Supporting Male Actor, Peter Hayden. Best Supporting Female Actor, Heather Bolton.

Reference
* Tony Chuah. 'Chan Is Missing'. *Illusions 11*, July 1989, p. 41.

Harry Ip (Kim) in Illustrious Energy. *Courtesy of the New Zealand Film Commission.*

Paul Livingstone (Martin), Chris Haywood (Arno), Hamish McFarlane (Griffin) and Bruce Lyons (Connor) in The Navigator: A Medieval Odyssey. *Courtesy of the New Zealand Film Commission.*

1988

THE NAVIGATOR: A MEDIEVAL ODYSSEY

Arenafilm and the Film Investment Corporation of New Zealand with the assistance of the Australian Film Commission and the New Zealand Film Commission. ©1988. A New Zealand/Australia co-production. *Budget:* $4.3 million. *Locations:* Auckland, Wellington, Mount Ruapehu, Waitomo, Lake Harris (Southern Alps). *Distributor:* Maynard Productions Ltd. *Rating:* GY, June 1988. 35 mm. Dolby Stereo. Black and white/Colour. 93 mins.

Director: Vincent Ward. *Producer:* John Maynard. *Co-producer/executive producer:* Gary Hannam. *Screenplay:* Vincent Ward, Kely Lyons, Geoff Chapple from an original idea by Vincent Ward. *Director of photography:* Geoffrey Simpson. *Camera operator:* Allen Guilford. *Editor:* John Scott. *Production designer:* Sally Campbell. *Costume designer:* Glenys Jackson. *Research:* Lynda Fairbairn, Alison Carter, Clare Shanks. *Special effects pyrotechnics:* Ken Durey. *Special effects supervisor:* Paul Nichola. *Steeple-jack:* Russell Baldwin. *Music:* Davood A. Tabrizi. *Vocals:* Mara Kiek, Martin Doherty. *Sound:* Dick Reade, Liz Goldfinch, Lee Smith, Peter Townend, Phil Judd.

Cast

Bruce Lyons (Connor), Chris Haywood (Arno), Hamish McFarlane (Griffin), Marshall Napier (Searle), Noel Appleby (Ulf), Paul Livingston (Martin), Sarah Peirse (Linnet), Mark Wheatley (Tog 1), Tony Herbert (Tog 2), Jessica Cardiff-Smith (Esme), Roy Wesney (Grandpa), Kathleen-Elizabeth Kelly (Grandma), Jay Saussey (Griffin's Girlfriend), Charles Walker (Old Chrissie), Desmond Kelly (Smithy), Bill Le Marquand (Tom), Jay Lavea Laga'aia (Jay), Norman Fairley (Submarine Captain), Alister Babbage (Grigor).

Cumbria, 1348. In a remote copper mining village the leader Connor returns from a journey to tell of a plague, the Black Death, sweeping the land, and of how the seeds of the Death are dropped by the full moon. The villagers agree to act on the dreams of Connor's nine year-old brother Griffin, whose prophetic vision is that they must go on pilgrimage to raise a spike (a Celtic cross) of Cumbrian copper on a cathedral spire on the other side of the earth before dawn to deflect the 'evil'. With Griffin as navigator a group of men tunnel through a mine shaft and as they work Griffin tells them of his dream where they emerge in a brightly lit twentieth century city. When they cross a busy motorway frightened Ulf is left behind. Connor finds the cathedral and rigs it with a ladder on the spire while Griffin, Martin and Searle find blacksmiths, whose foundry is about to be closed down, who agree to cast the spike. The race is on to raise the spike before dawn. Travelling by boat the group retaliate when they are almost overturned by a monsterish nuclear submarine. Racing to find Connor Griffin, who has dreamed one of the group dies, is confronted in a shopping arcade by a video wall showing a Grim Reaper AIDS commerical, a nuclear submarine report and a hawk preying on a rabbit. Raising the spike before dawn with the smiths' help Griffin, as in his dream, falls from the spire. Back in Cumbria Griffin finds he has the plague and learns Connor has been a carrier of the disease but is now clear of it. Griffin berates Connor for his deception, then tells him the story of his dream has been his salvation. Griffin's coffin is floated out to sea.

As narrative **The Navigator** crosses genres as a mystery/thriller piecing together Griffin's dreams (are his predictions accurate? who will die?); a heroic mythic quest where people try against the odds to change the course of their lives; a parable about twentieth century demons (nuclear capability, AIDS) using the conceit of showing the modern world though medieval eyes.

Across the centuries the mining Cumbrians and the New Zealand blacksmiths are bonded by trade and class and by their logic-defying act of faith and redemption in erecting the spike. Elemental substances—earth, air, fire and water—are important in both centuries but the ironies in twentieth century technology's secular use of them (water is the medium of travel for the nuclear-powered submarine, the American *Queenfish*), are lost on visionary Griffin, whose 'sight' fails him in his view of Auckland as 'God's celestial city of light'. His world view is infused with medieval ideas about 'good' and 'evil', and he sacrifices his life, while New Zealand itself is shown to follow a kind of modern equivalent in its determination to remain nuclear-free in the sceptical, spiritually desolate present. While the intent of the pilgrims is serious, humour leavens the narrative. Ulf, for example, is a kind of Laurel and Hardy comic character.

The surreality of dream provides poetic and incongruous images and a structure for the narrative. Motifs of falling, of the moon, the glove and religious icons knit the two time frames together while the Black Death is an overarching metaphor for the ills of an industrial, dehumanised society. The black and white chiaroscuro photography of the snow-covered Dark Ages sequences is visually stunning, contrasting starkly with the light and colour of the present day time frame, and many of the images, like a white horse in a rowboat at night, are startling in their beauty and strangeness.

The contemporary world is portrayed in medieval blues and oranges to remind the viewer that the film is a medieval vision of the twentieth century. Ward's brilliant images have been compared variously to those of Bergman, Tarkovsky, Bosch, Bruegel and Dürer. The soundtrack, making use of Scottish, Celtic and Gregorian music, provides period atmosphere and reinforces the emotions in the narrative.

Originally to be a New Zealand production, Australia was brought in as a co-producer to help overcome problems funding the film. Casting was done in New Zealand, Australia, England and America.

Some reviewers found the characters shallow, the plot lacking in momentum and the contrasting timeframes too schematic, but most described the film in such super-latives as 'compelling', 'breathtaking', 'astonishing', 'dazzling'. Vincent Ward was given a five-minute standing ovation at the film's Cannes screening. HM

1988 Cannes Film Festival: Official Selection in Competition.
Fanta Film Festival, Rome: Jury Prize, Best Film.
Cinema Fantastic, Sitges Film Festival, Spain: Best Film.
International Festival of Fantasy Films, Munich: Best Film.
Australian Film Institute Awards: Best Film, Best Director, Best Cinematography, Best Editing, Best Production Design, Best Costume Design.
1989 Oporto Film Festival, U.S.A.: Best Film.
New Zealand Film and Television Awards: Best Film. Best Male Performance, Hamish McFarlane. Best Female Performance in a Supporting Role, Sarah Peirse. Best Male Performance in a Supporting Role, Noel Appleby. Best Cinematography. Best Soundtrack. Best Director. Best Editing. Best Film Score. Best Original Screenplay. Best Production Design.

MAURI

Sonny Waru (Hemi), Eva Rickard (Kara) and Rangimarie Delamere (Awatea). Courtesy of the New Zealand Film Commission.

Awatea Films in association with the New Zealand Film Commission and Radio Hauraki. ©1988. *Budget:* A little under $2 million. *Location:* Te Kaha. *Distributor:* New Zealand Film Commission. *Rating:* GA (Some content may offend), July 1988. 35 mm. Colour. 101 mins.

Director and producer: Merata Mita. *Associate producer:* Geoff Murphy. *Screenplay:* Merata Mita. *Director of photography:* Graeme Cowley. *Camera operator:* Paul Leach. *Editor:* Nicholas Beauman. *Production designer:* Ralph Hotere. *Wardrobe supervisor:* Rangitinia Otene Wilson. *Special effects:* Richard Rautjoki. *Musical director:* Hirini Melbourne. *Original music and performance:* Amokura. *Vocals:* Te Rita Papesch. *Sound:* Ru Rakena, Gethin Creagh, Michael Hopkins, Ross Chambers, Phil Benge.

Cast

Eva Rickard (Kara), Anzac Wallace (Rewi Rapana), Susan D. Ramiri Paul (Ramiri), James Heyward (Steve), Rangimarie Delamere (Awatea), Willie Raana (Willie Rapana), Geoff Murphy (Mr Semmens), Don Selwyn (Old cop), Temuera Morrison (Young cop), Ana Hine Aro Kura Thrupp (Hinemoa), Anthony Angell (Tawa), Sonny Waru (Hemi), Michael Insley (Dave Roberts), Joanna E. Paiana Paul (Doctor), John Algar (Pakeha minister), Mando Waenga (Sergeant-at-arms), Bernard Rua (Herb), Mas Campbell, Hiria Lake (Chief hula girls), Te Whanau a Apanui (Elders and extras), Martyn Sanderson (Hospital doctor — not credited).

1950s. Kuia Kara tells granddaughter Awatea that when she dies her soul will go over the hill to Hawaiki. Kara's niece Ramiri pleads for Rewi's love, but although they make love he rejects her as a partner. Pakeha farmer Semmens rages at his son Steve for his attraction to Ramiri and poses as a scarecrow to keep Maori children off his land. Kara warns her nephew Willie, visiting from the city, to be careful who he trusts and he is later killed. Steve and Ramiri marry and old Semmens dies. At a marae meeting Rewi is recognised as a former jail inmate and runs away. Ramiri tells him he fathered her son and he explains he is in hiding because there is blood on his hands. Steve and Ramiri shelter Rewi. He visits dying Kara, knowing cops are watching the road. At her bedside Rewi tells Kara he is not Rewi Rapana but Paki, a jail escapee who has taken the dead Rewi's identity. Kara tells Paki to return to where Rewi died and ask for forgiveness. That night she dies. As Awatea farewells Kara's spirit soaring over the hill Paki asks Rewi for forgiveness and is arrested.

A powerful film about Maori identity and birthright, **Mauri** was the first full-length dramatic feature to be made by a Maori woman and the first entirely from a Maori perspective. In its remote North Island coastal settlement land and life force (mauri) are inextricably linked, visually in beautiful cinematography and dramatically in relationships to tribal land. Old Semmens' appropriation of Maori land represents the increasing threat of European encroachment, while Rewi's story is allegorical as notions of birthright and the erosion of Maori culture are reflected in the catalytic effect of his return. Urban drift is taking hold and Willie, leaving his turangawaewae, is also lost.

The women show a way forward and in Kara is the knowledge and wisdom essential for the preservation of mauri. In Ramiri's cross-cultural marriage her pakeha husband has an empathy for her race antidotal to his father's racism. The child Awatea, watching and learning, represents hope for the continuation of tribal wisdom. The challenge **Mauri** offers Maori is to assert a clear Maori identity. Although the enemy is in institutions and individuals, the most insidious threat is posed as the enemy within, epitomised in the treachery of Herb and the young local cop, both Maori who put personal ambition first.

Shot by a largely Maori film crew with many non-professional Maori actors **Mauri**'s expressions of passion at times seem too big for the screen. Some dialogue is overwritten, making difficult demands on the actors, particularly when shown in tight close-up. As pakeha caricatures the government minister and old Semmens are least credible. Although not an experienced actor Eva Rickard is compelling as Kara. The withholding of information prevents narrative clarity, but details of the lifestyle are eloquently drawn. The soundtrack builds an eerie atmosphere of other-worldliness. Composer Hirini Melbourne used traditional Maori instruments, the koauau (nose or mouth flute), the putorino (flute) and the putatara (conch), and all the songs are in Maori.
HM

1988

NEVER SAY DIE

Pastrami and Rye in association with the New Zealand Film Commission. ©1988. *Budget:* $3 million. *Locations:* Los Angeles, Auckland, Waiheke Island, West Coast of the South Island, Wellington, Central North Island. *Distributor:* Everard Films Ltd. *Rating:* GA (Language may offend), October 1988. 35 mm. Dolby Stereo. Colour. 105 mins.

Director: Geoff Murphy. *Producers:* Geoff Murphy, Barrie Everard. *Executive producer:* Barrie Everard. *Screenplay:* Geoff Murphy. *Director of photography:* Rory O'Shea. *Editor:* Scott Conrad. *Production designer:* Bill Gruar. *Costume designer:* Barbara Darragh. *Armourer:* Steve Ingram. *Stunt co-ordinators:* Peter Bell, Peter Zivkovic. *Stunt drivers:* Peter Bell, Peter Stewart, Peter Zivkovic, Mark Harris, Mark Taylor, Mark Maloney, Lance Johnson. *Music:* Sam Negri, Billy Kristian. *Composers:* Murray Grindlay, Billy Kristian, Geoff Murphy, Denys Mateparae, Svarama. *Vocals:* Nigel Lee, Susan Lynch, Jacqui Fitzgerald, Ray Woolf, The Vocal Minority, Bunny Walters, Martin Winch, Svarama. *Sound:* Mike Westgate, Dick Reade, Gethin Creagh, Sam Negri, Kit Rollings.

Cast

Lisa Eilbacher (Melissa Jones), Temuera Morrison (Alf Winters), Tony Barry (Evans), George Wendt (Mr Witten), Geoff Murphy (Jack), with Colin Clarke, Barrie Everard, Murray Newey, Alan Sorrell, Jason Greenwood, Judy Fyfe, Phil Gordon, Ian Richard Stewart, Peter Bell, Marcel Kroes, Russell Smith, John Clarke, Elizabeth McRae, Jill Ranger, Martyn Sanderson, Matt Palmer, Steve Ingram, Steven Hall, Kenneth Young, Svarama, Peter Tait, Paul Murphy, Stephanie Leibert, John Old, Basil Swenson, George Carter, Sean Duffy, Tom Poata, Ralph Williams, Gay Dean, Selina Forsythe, Martin Horsefall, Matt Palmer, Jay Laga'aia, Peter Rowley, Tony Monk, Doug Aston, Anthea Baker, Nikki Walker, Thad Lawrence, Linda Cotter, Stuart Day.

World-weary investigative journalist Alf Winters is shocked when the inner-city Auckland house he shares with American partner Melissa blows up. Seeking sanctuary on Waiheke Island they are shot at and Alf kills the assailant in self-defence. Hard-nosed Inspector Evans, an old enemy cop, refuses to believe their story. Now wanted on a murder charge they flee by car down country where further attempts are made on their lives. Piecing together a conversation Melissa heard in the U.S. they guess she and not Alf is the target. They guess a planeload of rugby players, the Mavericks, is to be blown up on its way to South Africa in an act designed to discredit the anti-apartheid protest movement. Holed up on the West Coast they are fired on from helicopters. With Evans now on their side they learn a head cop is feeding the criminals information on their whereabouts and the chase intensifies, culminating in a confrontation between the fugitives and a large New Zealand Police Force contingent. At Auckland Airport American lawyer Witten reveals that the plans Melissa heard discussed in his office involve intentions to appropriate the formula for a potentially lucrative new soft drink invented by her late father. Alf thwarts Witten's plan to murder Melissa. While the couple make love waiting for the police to arrive the plane carrying the Mavericks explodes.

The production faltered when Mirage Entertainment was unable to finance the film, but it was rescued by a deal put together by Barrie Everard and the New Zealand Film Commission. Geoff Murphy's view of the film, stated in the press kit, was that 'New Zealanders want to have a bit of a laugh and a bit of bloody excitement.' A comedy chase thriller about international business and political intrigue, **Never Say Die** exploits the New Zealand landscape's beauty, most notably in remote West Coast bush.

The film rejoices in energetic chases, explosions and death-defying stunts, including one with Peter Bell driving a car on two wheels across an old, narrow bridge. A James Bond running gag pays homage to the genre (the working title was **007**). Boosted by the lively soundtrack, a childlike effervescence in the direction makes for a bruising pace and much slapstick, black humour and tongue-in-cheek bathos, although the cause of the plane's explosion remains a puzzle.

John Clarke's cameo as a used car salesman (shot in Melbourne because Clarke hates flying) and Peter Tait's **High Noon** muck-up are comic highlights. Temuera Morrison's parodic take on his character adds to the fun. Murphy reprises **Goodbye Pork Pie**'s anti-establishment tone and the film endorses anti-apartheid sympathies. Phallic gun references and male gaze shots feature. While Melissa's assertiveness in lovemaking and behind the wheel marks some attempt to inject a little equality into a cartoonish boy-film, unlike rebel journalist Alf she has little identity as an independent character.

An international name was a requirement of the film's financing and the presence of American actors Eilbacher and Wendt puts Hollywood in the mix. HM

Lisa Eilbacher (Melissa Jones) and Temuera Morrison (Alf Winters). Courtesy of the New Zealand Film Commission.

1988

SEND A GORILLA

Energy Source International presents, in association with the New Zealand Film Commission and Television New Zealand, a Pinflicks Production. ©1988. *Location:* Wellington. *Distributor:* Energy Source International Group. *Rating:* GA, December 1988. 35 mm. Colour. 96 mins.

Director: Melanie Read. *Producer:* Dorothee Pinfold. *Executive producers:* Peter Sainsbury, Dorothee Pinfold. *Supervising producer:* Robin Laing. *Screenplay:* Melanie Read, based on an idea by Perry Piercy, developed by Carmel McGlone, Rosemary McLeod, Katherine McRae, Perry Piercy. *Director of photography:* Wayne Vinten. *Camera operator:* Renaud Maire. *Editor:* Paul Sutorius. *Production designer:* Kirsten Shouler. *Wardrobe supervisor:* Lyndsay Meager. *Music:* Peter Blake. *Gram composers:* Rob Winch, Melanie Read, Peter Blake, Fiona Samuel. *Vocals:* Robyn Lynch, Diedre Elliott. *Valentine song:* Jackie Clarke. *Players:* Wellington Regional Orchestra. *Opera conductor:* William Southgate. *Sound:* Brian Shennan, John McKay, Chris Burt.

Cast

Carmel McGlone (Clare), Katherine McRae (Joy), Perry Piercy (Vicki), John Callen (Chris Dean), Rusty (Hermione), with Larney Tupu, William Kircher, Jim Moriarty, Nathan Waldron, Rima Te Wiata, Daniel Benseman, Michael Haigh, Stephen Clements, Kim Buchanan, Stanley Findlay, Ann Pacey, Miranda Harcourt, Ian Watkin, Joy Watson, Liz Mullane, Joanna Briant, Alice Fraser, Gerald Bryan, Kate Harcourt, Onehau, Peter Dennett, Ralph Johnson, Helen Lagen, Michael Wilson, Steven Naismith, Richard Lawrence, Mark Wright, Wiki Oman, Jane Waddell, Dulcie Smart, Renita Chan, Peter McAllum, Ross Jolly, Danny Mulheron, Whillow Patterson, Turei Reidy, Katy Platt, Christianne Phillips, Marianne Govaerts, Iain Rae, Stephen Lovatt, Felicity Samuel, Brian Carbee, Lorae Parry, Jon Brazier, Teresa Healey, Duncan Smith, Tony Box, Vivienne Brown, Sandra Coory, Joanne Simpson, Louise Graham, Keiko Kirk, Andra Albulescu, Heather Benfield, Murray Keane, Keith Richardson, Stephen Gledhill.

St Valentine's Day, Wellington. The Send-a-Gorilla Singing Telegram Company, usually performing 10 telegrams a day, is booked to perform 50. Boss Janine has gone away, leaving instructions for the day on videotape. Vicki, who runs a sideline business selling chocolate-covered strawberries, is in no mood to sing as she has caught her boyfriend two-timing with her friend Lisa. Clare, who delivers telegrams in a gorilla suit, has to take time out to see a lawyer over custody of her son, Toby. Joy, training to sing opera, is dragooned into filling in for her sister who has laryngitis. In other parts of town vile DJ Chris Dean loses his dog Hermione coming home from her artificial insemination session and even viler property developer and landlord Sir Richard Olphert plans to knock down the building housing Send-a-Gorilla. In an incident-packed day telegrams are delivered and mis-delivered, friendly cops offer assistance, Joy sings her way to an audition with a London opera examiner, Clare's ex-husband gives up the custody fight, Clare collects a reward for finding Hermione, the Send-a-Gorilla singers wreck a men's club party, the Send-a-Gorilla building is destroyed and Vicki's money is recovered.

Billed as an off-beat comedy, **Send a Gorilla**'s narrative creaks under the weight of a welter of issues—solo parenthood, child custody, inner city development, animal rights, relationship fidelity—and a jumble of sub-plots. Feminist intent is indicated in characterisation and narrative. Played with great verve, most of the women are assertive, independent and lively. In homage to **Mr Wrong** Clare drives a white Jaguar, with the figure in the back seat this time not the ghost of a murdered woman but the dog of a misogynistic male whose name Chris Dean, said quickly, echoes that of the haunted car in the eponymous Stephen King story. As if to counter the notion that feminists have no sense of humour anti-male rhetoric is delivered in a combination of corny slapstick and music-hall performance style, most tellingly exemplified in a fight over a penis cake at the working men's club. The overriding tone of the film is not wit and wisdom but rage.

'Romantic love' is satirised with cynicism—most of the telegrams are motivated by revenge or the desire to publicly humiliate the recipient—and in all the relationship permutations that develop most of the men are stereotypical creeps. While disguise is a motif suggesting women are better able to realise their potential by masking who they really are, the point is driven home with a sledgehammer.

The idea came from Perry Piercy who, as a sometime singing telegram deliverer, contributed many story ideas. With some 1600 shots, over 50 speaking parts and over 60 locations the film creates a frenetic atmosphere. A sense of the bizarre is achieved using wide angle lenses and a large number of close-ups. Two opera-singing sequences and the cop duo routines are highlights. Bubblegum pinks, yellows and oranges and bouncy music add to the comic-strip feel.

Originally planned as a telefeature **Send a Gorilla** was the first theatrical feature film to receive financial backing from TVNZ. Many of the crew were TVNZ employees on leave. HM

Perry Piercy (Vicki), Katherine McRae (Joy), director Melanie Read and Carmel McGlone (Clare). Courtesy of the New Zealand Film Commission.

1989 Montreal Women's Film Festival: Second Most Popular Audience Choice.

CHILL FACTOR

1988

Frank Whitten (Frank) as he appeared in a very different role in Vigil *(1984). Courtesy of the New Zealand Film Commission.*

An Intercontinental Releasing Corporation presentation. Associated Entertainment Releasing (U.S.A.) and Deco Corporation (N.Z.) present a Chillco Production. ©1988. Financed from New Zealand and the U.S. *Budget:* approx. $1.5 million. *Locations:* Auckland, Los Angeles. Not released in New Zealand. 35 mm. Colour. 95 mins.

Director: David L. Stanton. *Producers:* David L. Stanton, Dale G. Bradley. *Executive producer:* Grant L. Bradley. *Screenplay:* Rex Piano, Dan Goldman. *Director of photography:* Michael Delahoussaye. *Editor:* Bryan Shaw. *Art directors:* John Hagen-Brenner, Jackie Rabinowitz, Dave Cook. *Wardrobe supervisor:* Karen Galardi, Jeanette Woolcombe. *Original music:* John Ross. *Special effects:* Eddie Surkin, Kevin Chiznel. *Stunt co-ordinators:* Scott Hass, Peter Bell. *Pyrotechnics:* Larry Roberts. *Sound:* Phil Burton, Brent Englund, Chris Burt, Peter Dufaur.

Cast

Laura McKenzie (Katherine Sanders), Paul Williams (Clifford White), Patrick MacNee (Carl Lawton), Carrie Snodgress (Amy Carlisle), Patrick Wayne (Jerry Rivers), Harvey Shain (Samuel Hofritz), Andrew Prine (Kioshe Jones), Frank Whitten (Frank Robertson), with Gary Crosby, Warren Stevens, John Ross, Carl Bland, Byron Delves, Ray Pearson, Robert Horwood, Debra Turnbow, David Wray, Holley Setlock, Te Paki Cherrington, Brenda Simmons, Helen McGowan, Ben Mukogawa, David Sheridan, Stephen Hall, Philip Gordon, Jeffrey Whitman, Liddy Loree, Godfrey Hall, Richard Lawton, James Hook, Sam Woo, Satoru Nakamura, Milton Quon, Yokiohi Aita, Joe Ozaki, Francine Swift, Gary Chan, Tom Krishna, Nat Lee, Karen Lawrence, Maggie Harper, Greg Morman, Russell Gowers, Tim Lee, David Griffiths, Vittorio, Norman Forsey, George Hayashida, James Ogawa, Pamela Johnston, David Grierson, Heidi Paine, Christina Veronica.

In New Zealand to shoot a travelogue, an American television crew, headed by reporter Katherine Sanders, is persuaded by disillusioned hit man Clifford White to help expose a crooked, CIA-linked dirty tricks corporation, Chillco. Specialising in covert international political destabilisation, Chillco is paving the way for Japanese conglomerate Tsunami to acquire economic global supremacy. Chased around New Zealand and then to California as they gather information for their exposé, the television crew, the disillusioned hit man and others who have joined in along the way are systematically murdered, many by sadist Sam Hofritz. In his hour of triumph Sam in turn is horribly killed by his boss, Kioshe Jones. An American-Japanese conceived during World War II, Jones masterminds the Tsunami operation, the leading lights of which shared duties in a Japanese prisoner of war camp during the War and now seek economic might. Unhappily for Jones he barely has time to celebrate the elimination of all opposition before he sees their videotaped evidence of his dirty dealings screening on U.S. television and commits harakiri.

Chill Factor is formula action/thriller fare with numerous chases interspersed with big chunks of banal explanatory dialogue. Characterisation is minimal and there is no subtext beyond the set-up that the Japanese, defeated fairly in World War II, still have world domination on their minds. Sam's 'persuasion' scenes are nasty—he enjoys pulling out fingernails and sticking sharp things in his potential informants—and there is a large body count. Where the film does veer is in its egalitarian clean sweep. By the end credits none of the main characters, goodies or baddies, are still breathing.

Seventy per cent of the film was shot in New Zealand and the shoot provided work for local crew and actors. It was released in 16 countries, not including New Zealand, and has shown on cable television in the U.S. The film was the subject of litigation between its U.S. and N.Z. producers.[1] HM

---

[1] Information from executive producer, Grant L. Bradley.

1988

THE GRASSCUTTER

Finlayson Brewer Productions with development assistance from the New Zealand Film Commission. ©1988. Financed from New Zealand and the U.K. Telefeature. *Locations:* Dunedin, Queenstown. *NZ video rating:* 13 (Content may offend, violence and/or offensive language). Hi-Fi Stereo. 16 mm. Colour. 110 mins.

Director: Ian Mune. *Producer:* Tom Finlayson. *Associate producer:* Logan Brewer. *Executive producer:* Ted Childs. *Screenplay:* Roy Mitchell. *Directors of photography:* Matt Bowkett, Michael O'Connor. *Editor:* Patrick Monaghan. *Production designer:* Robert Gillies. *Costume designer:* Barbara Darragh. *Special effects co-ordinator:* Kevin Chisnall. *Stunt co-ordinator:* Peter Bell. *Armourer:* Steve Ingram. *Aerials co-ordinator:* Dave Kershaw. *Action vehicle co-ordinator:* Richard Barker. *Music:* Don McGlashan, Wayne Laird. *Players:* Mike Farrell, Auckland Philharmonia. *Sound:* Graham Morris, Gethin Creagh.

Cast

Terence Cooper (Jack Macready), **Martin Maguire** (Billy), **Ian McElhinney** (Brian Deeds), **Judy McIntosh** (Hannah Carpenter), **Mitchell Manuel** (Patu Beale), **Frances Barber** (Claire Deeds), **Raymond Hawthorne** (Keen), **James Coyle** (Jim Wallace), **Marshall Napier** (Detective Inspector Cross), **Temuera Morrison** (Detective Sergeant Harris) **Jon Brazier** (Detective Sergeant McKay), with Peter Vere-Jones, Terence Porter, Jon Waite, Kerry Waenga, Ian Todd, Jocky Jensen, Andrew Colby, Stuart Fever, Alfie Speight, Don Andrews, Hamish McFarlane, Kent Belcher, Eddie Campbell, Dave Kershaw, Nic Farra, Tans Robin, Tim Bartlett, Rex Dovey, John Mann, Kristen Gillespie, William Johnson, Lewis Rowe, Des Gotobed, Ken Blackburn, Stephen Hall, Joel Tobeck, Terry Hayman, Ross McKellar, Wolfgang Khiene, Martin Phelan, Hilary Norris, Katie Cribb, Jack Dacey.

Belfast, July 1988. A young Irishman shoots a terrified young victim. Dunedin, August 1988. Irish landscape gardener Brian Deeds and his apprentice Patu pack up after work and drive to Brian's apartment discussing the Ireland/All Black rugby test to be played at Dunedin's Carisbrook the following day. Arriving at Dunedin Airport that night on the same flight as the Irish rugby team are three Irishmen from the first scene. One of them, Jack Macready, phones Deeds' ex-wife Claire in Queenstown to say her son Billy is dead. Claire arrives at Deeds' seaside crib, where he is spending the weekend with lover Hannah, and tells him the news. Flashbacks and explanatory dialogue show Deeds to be an ex-member of the Ulster Volunteer Force, a terrorist sent by the British to New Zealand with a new identity after grassing on 23 fellow terrorists eight years previously. Macready, leading a hit squad set to destroy Deed's family, blows up his apartment, injuring Deeds and killing Patu. On the run Deeds tells Hannah that one of the many violent acts that turned him off terrorism was Macready's rape of his own sister, Deeds' ex-wife Claire. Things heat up when Detective Inspector Cross and his underlings, the British Honorary Consul and lastly the Armed Offenders Squad, join the chase. Hijacking a small plane, Deeds and Hannah fly to Queenstown to save Claire and the kids. In the final shootout it transpires Billy is not dead, but on the revenge trail with Uncle Jack. Claire, Macready and his oily accomplice, Wallace, are killed at the top of the cable car building and Billy, wounded, runs off. In a confrontation with Deeds, Billy learns Jack Macready was both his uncle and his father. Thinking Billy is going to shoot, an Armed Offender shoots him dead.

The set-up is novel—this is the first New Zealand-set film to dramatise the Irish 'troubles'—but apart from the landscaper/informer double entendre there's not much new in this standard action thriller. As a deceptively slow-witted cop, Temuera Morrison has some nicely laconic lines and accomplished British actor Frances Barber is a passionate Claire. There's some interest in the local Detective Inspector's dawning realisation that the people he pursues mean business, but any probing into the deeper issues of the Irish struggle is eschewed in favour of car and plane chases showing off the wonderful Southern Alps and lake scenery. The technique of gradually leaking information about motivation is calculated to build tension, as is the withholding of the facts of Billy's incestuous parentage until the last sequence.

The Grasscutter was released in New Zealand on video, the sleeve of which asserts the film 'left over 12 million U.K. viewers stunned.' Also on the sleeve the *Sunday Times* calls it 'a tense, beautifully edited and intelligent thriller' and asserts 'It was entirely absorbing to watch the local (New Zealand) detective come to terms with the fact that the horrors of Northern Ireland were being visited on his community.' The film was cast in London, Belfast and New Zealand. HM

Ian McElhinney (Brian Deeds) and Judy McIntosh (Hannah Carpenter). Courtesy of the New Zealand Film Commission.

1989

ZILCH!

Lucy Sheehan (Anna). Courtesy of the New Zealand Film Commission.

Park Avenue Productions and Vardex Group in association with the New Zealand Film Commission. ©1989. *Budget:* $700 000. *Location:* Auckland. *Distributor:* New Zealand Film Commission. *Rating:* RP13, December 1989. 35 mm. Colour. 99.5 mins.

Director: Richard Riddiford. *Producers:* Richard Riddiford, Amanda Hocquard. *Screenplay:* Richard Riddiford, Jonathan Dowling. *Director of photography:* Murray Milne. *Underwater photography:* Sigmund Spath. *Editor:* Chris Todd. *Art department:* Duncan Graham, Kerry Hessell, Colleen Forde, Adrian Greshoff. *Wardrobe supervisors:* Catriona Caird, Sandra Peacock. *Music:* Chris Knox. *Vocals:* The Holidaymakers, Straitjacket Fits, Jim 'An' Joe. *Sound:* Peter Walker, John McKay, Chris Burt, Brent Burge.

Cast

Michael Mizrahi (Sam), Lucy Sheehan (Anna), John Watson (Curtis), Eddie Campbell (Tony), Peter Tait (Eric), Roy Billing (Gary Hyde), William Bullock (Harbour commissioner), Sylvia Rands (Melissa), Andy Anderson (Lawyer), Louise Graham (Amber), Peter Stevens (Todd), Frank Whitten (Engineer), Lee Grant (Cara), Brenda Kendall (Tolls supervisor), with Marie Adams, Stefan Segedin, Anna Cahill, Catriona Caird, Johnny Green, Brenda Kendall, Eva Radich, Jonathan Dowling, Sue Ferens, Paula Green, Michael Hight, Sarah Gerrad, Malcolm McNeill, Michael Lamb, Grant Chilcott, Michael Steeneveld, Martin Whitehead, Angela Corry, Martin Findlay, Phillipa Sinclair, Sheila McCabe, Mark Dobson, Herschell, Steve Yeoman, Kevin Le Hat.

Anna, dressed in black plastic, throws tomatoes at a large, naked man standing in a bath. Unknown to them they are videotaped from above. As the cameraman, Eric, leaves the building, sirens start up and his getaway driver takes off. Before he is caught by police he hides the videotape in a phone box, calls a telephone operator, Sam, and asks him to ring a number. Sam, who eavesdrops on and tapes toll calls, tells his socialist, conspiracy-theorist friend Curtis and the pair resolve to follow up the call. Their sleuthing involves them in a web of corruption and intrigue. They learn, through a series of bizarre and farcical coincidences, that development company Infacorp is using the tomato-in-the-bath videotape to blackmail the harbour commissioner to secure a contract for a second harbour crossing via a harbour tunnel, even though their engineer's study has revealed that the subsoil is unstable and the project is doomed to disaster. Sam uses family connections to infiltrate the company. Infacorp's engineer, who has arranged to meet Sam, is murdered, but not before he videotapes an exposé that brings about Infacorp's downfall just as it celebrates securing the harbour tunnel contract. Sam, escaping death after a harrowing chase on foot on Auckland harbour bridge, celebrates by having Anna throw tomatoes at him in the bath.

Set in the heady boom days before the Black Monday stock market crash in 1987, **Zilch!** is an action/thriller yarn teeming with energy and good ideas. The comic treatment of the kinky tomato sex-substitute is novel and the satire of yuppie greed and the scorch-and-burn, wild west mentality of Auckland's developers timely. The film looks good and handsomely shows off its city locations, which include Kelly Tarlton's Underwater World and the harbour and its environs. Chris Knox's crisp musical score provides inventive accompaniment. Glaswegian nasty Tony, rabid socialist Curtis and quirky emotional-cripple-turned-committed-activist Sam are fresh characters. Mobile-faced Michael Mizrahi, required to swim through sharks and dangle from the Auckland harbour bridge, has a gift for comic timing.

The problems are with the script. Actors struggle with mouthfuls of unconvincing dialogue, often in the form of tedious explanations and the jigsaw puzzle plot is overloaded and confusing. There are indications that, as part of Sam's character development, he is meant to learn how to behave in a relationship. But because the two women he is involved with have nowhere to go in their roles (Anna throws tomatoes, Melissa nags and whines), no development is possible.

Script problems were exacerbated by the way the film was made. Richard Riddiford started principal photography in January 1988 using Film Commission script development money. There were constant script revisions while the shoot was in progress and many scenes were improvised. Actors doubled as crew and crew doubled as actors. Continuity was a nightmare as the filming schedule was drawn-out over a year while money was sought from investors reluctant to commit money in the wake of the stock market crash. HM

MANA WAKA

One of the wakataua/war canoes built for the 1940 centennial celebrations of the signing of the Treaty of Waitangi. Frame enlargement courtesy of the New Zealand Film Archive.

Nga Kaitiaki o Te Puea Estate/The Te Puea Estate and the Turangawaewae Marae Trust with the assistance of the Nga Kawhina/New Zealand Lottery Grants Board, the New Zealand Film Commission Short Film Fund, Te Komihana o 1990/1990 Commission, Elders Resources/NZFP. Copyright unavailable. Documentary. *Distributor:* Trustees of Te Puea Estate. *Rating:* Exempt, February 1990. 35 mm. Black and white. 85 mins.

Director: Merata Mita. *Camera:* R.G.H. Manley (filmed 1937–1940). *Editor:* Annie Collins. *Kai korero/narrator:* Tukuroirangi Morgan. *Film preservation:* Nga Kaitaiki o nga Taonga Whitiahua/The New Zealand Film Commission, Nga Kaitiaki o Nga Taonga Whitiahua/The New Zealand Film Archive, NFU Laboratory, NFU Sound. *Finecut:* Nga Kaitiaki o Te Marae o Turangawaewae. *Sound:* Merata Mita, David Madigan, Chris Verberg, Mike Hedges, Annie Collins.

Mana Waka, working title **Canoe**, is a feature-length documentary made to launch New Zealand's 1990 centennial celebrations. The documentary has a fascinating history. Princess Te Puea Herangi of the Turangawaewae Marae, Ngauruawahia, was a great Maori leader committed to work that would uphold, and be used for the benefit of, the Maori people. During the late 1930s she conceived the idea of celebrating the 1940 centennial of the signing of Treaty of Waitangi by re-building the seven wakataua/war canoes of the Great Fleet. According to legend these canoes had journeyed from Hawaiki to Aotearoa some 25 generations previously. Princess Te Puea asked stills photographer R.G.H. (Jim) Manley, who had not previously made a film, to film the re-building, and he did so over a period of three years. Up north in the Puketi Forest, a great kauri tree was felled for the building of the Nga-toki-matawhaorua canoe which is now housed at Waitangi. Two totara trees from the Oruanui Forest provided the timber for the canoes that were carved and built at Turangawaewae. Lack of government support meant that Princess Te Puea had to raise money herself through such activities as staging concerts and in the end the financial costs and the time taken by the canoe-building meant that not all of the canoes were completed.

The footage shot by R.G.H. Manley was stored, unedited, on the Turangawaewae Marae, where it remained for some 40 years until the Manley Family Trust and Jonathan Dennis of the New Zealand Film Archive organised the restoring and preserving of the nitrate film stock, a process which took five years. They then asked Merata Mita to shape it into a feature film and thus bring Princess Te Puea's vision to fruition. (The Manley family later withdrew from the project in the belief that Mita's film was not as their father had wanted it).

In 1989 the work began on Turangawaewae Marae, through the manaakitanga of Te Arikinui Dame Te Atairangikaahu, the Maori Queen. As Merata Mita, with editor Annie Collins, worked on the film at the marae, she became aware that it was more about Te Puea's vision for her economic development and independence for her people than the physical act of canoe construction. As Mita and Collins worked they were joined by people keen to watch it taking shape. Among them was Jim Kukutai, an elder who was one of the canoe builders.

The evocative soundtrack and skilful direction and editing bring Manley's wonderful silent images to life, building them into a story which is a spellbinding celebration of the slow canoe building process and the vision it symbolises. First the huge trees are felled and shaped into rough shapes, then they are dragged from the forest by bullock teams and painstakingly carved and finished. Most canoe builders worked for no wages and the work was tough, the day beginning with a two mile walk into the forest and, after prayers, a 10 to 12-hour day. The wholehearted commitment of the workers, for whom the spiritual dimension of their task was uppermost, is keenly evident.

The wakataua and the film are sacred and the film, which was the official film for the Fourth Commonwealth Arts Festival, is regarded as a gift from the Maori Queen to the people of New Zealand. Ownership remains with the Turangawaewae Trust. HM

FLYING FOX IN A FREEDOM TREE

Grahame McLean Associates in association with the New Zealand Film Commission. ©1989. *Budget:* $900 000. *Locations:* Apia, Matautu Falealili, Tauese, Falealupo. *Distributor:* McLean/JMP. *Rating:* RP13, February 1990. 35 mm. Colour. 92 mins.

Director: Martyn Sanderson. *Producer:* Grahame McLean. *Screenplay:* Martyn Sanderson. *Source:* Albert Wendt, *Flying Fox in a Freedom Tree*, and the expanded version of the story in *Leaves of the Banyan Tree*. *Director of photography:* Allen Guilford. *Camera operator:* Barry Harbert. *Editor:* Ken Zemke. *Art director:* Nicholas Dryden. *Wardrobe supervisor:* Amanda Butler. *Composer:* Michelle Scullion, assisted by Albert Umaga. *Players:* Michelle Scullion, Daniel Usage, Albert Umaga, Lani Umaga, Peter Tuitama, Steve Jessops, T. Umaga. *Vocals:* Mara Finau, Martha Samasoni, Peter Tuitama, Michelle Scullion. *Sound:* Anthony Johnson, Kit Rollings, Chris Verburg, Mike Hedges.

Cast

Faifua Amiga Jnr (Pepe), Richard von Sturmer (Tagata), Fuialo Molimau (Toasa), Aloema Anae (Pepe's mother), Peseta Sinave Isara (Pepe's father), Afatia Aloese (Susana), Sapio To'Ala (Susana's father), Pativaine Ainuu (Susana's mother), with Tavita Leaumoana, Tuiletufuga Papali'i Enele Hunkin, Maryanne McCarthy, Mata'u Uefa, Pule Nua, Ti'a Sausi, Tapuana Afamasaga, Moira Walker, Ane Leota, Povalu Fa'Avalea, Cindy, Tapu Feilo, Peter Hugginson, Beachcomber Band, Beachcomber Dancers, Vilima'a Salu, Kelvin Le Geyt, Lipine Pula, Sapati Sio, Folo Lavasi'i, Gavin Bartley, Vainu'upo Malietoa, Ekumeni Tinetali, Samaga Su, Tui Samau, Apineru Tavita, Amosa Laulu, Misi Malu, Osa Te'o, Tini Talaina, Viliga Ma'atusi, Uelese Petaia, Felix Crawley, Michael McGrath, Ilasa tiava'asu'e McLean, Martyn Sanderson.

Pepe, dying of TB, writes his life story. Born on Sapepe, a small Western Samoan island, he is sent to school in Apia by his wealthy father Tauilopepe, and forced to learn Western ways. High chief Toasa convinces Pepe he is a high chief, descended from the Samoan god Pepesa, born to lead his people in traditional ways. Pepe grows increasingly angry with Tauilopepe, whose business dealings contribute to destruction of priceless bushlands. At high school Pepe is unjustly accused of rape and expelled. With his only friend, half-caste dwarf Tagata, he burns down a church and robs his father's store. In court he claims descendance from Samoan gods and is sentenced to four years' hard labour. Released, he attends Toasa's funeral and publicly berates his father. Tauilopepe beats him and he leaves home and sets up a business in the markets with Tagata. Fed by movie images of romantic love, including John O'Shea's **Runaway**, he fathers a son and marries. Tagata, in despair that he has no place within the culture, hangs himself and is buried by his grieving friend Pepe. In the hospital bed Pepe waits for death.

In this bitter story about the effects of colonisation on Western Samoa, Pepe and Tagata are caught between a past that has lost its meaning and a present that has lost its way. They express their agony in savage retribution against society and themselves. To Pepe his ruthless, capitalistic father embodies all that is destructive in the breakdown of fa'a Samoa. He rejects the religion introduced by colonising Western missionaries and traders which worships Jehovah, money and success. Pepe's raw rage and lamentation are no match for progress and he has no option but death. Tagata, nicknamed 'the flying fox' because, like his mythical counterpart, he is an outsider, is sustained for a time by his sardonic wit but alienation's corrosiveness defeats him. The most bitter words are his, 'The palagi and his world have turned us and people like your rich but unhappy father, and all the modern Samoans, into cartoons of themselves—funny, crying, ridiculous shadows of themselves.'

Lushly filmed and with a moody score, the film is an excellent adaptation of its source, the second part of Albert Wendt's novel, *Leaves of the Banyan Tree*. Metaphysical themes are enhanced by contrasts: the calm beauty of the setting against the characters' bleak prospects; the certainty of old ways against anxiety wrought by the palagi customs and values. Scenes where Pepe enters the realms of the supernatural in speaking with Toasa, shot in surreal style and with ancient myth acted out in tableau, are especially powerful. The lava fields to which Tagata turns to understand life's 'meaning' eloquently represent existential alienation.

Many in the crew and cast were recruited locally and it was their first experience working in film. Shot mainly in English, there is some awkwardness in dialogue and action. Faifua Amiga Jnr is outstanding in the lead role. Martyn Sanderson's first script of the story was produced as a radio play in Apia. In writing the screenplay he liaised with Albert Wendt on each draft.
HM

Faifua Amiga Junior (Pepe). *Courtesy of the New Zealand Film Commission.*

1989 Tokyo International Film Festival: Best Screenplay.
La Ville D'Amièns: Grand Prix, for making the greatest contribution to the understanding of a culture and the identity of a people.

MEET THE FEEBLES

WingNut Films. ©1989. *Budget:* $750 000. *Location:* Wellington. *Distributor:* Pacer Kerridge. *Rating:* R16 (Contains gross material), April 1990. 35 mm. Colour. 98 mins.

Director: Peter Jackson. *Producers:* Jim Booth, Peter Jackson. *Screenplay:* Frances Walsh, Stephen Sinclair, Danny Mulheron, Peter Jackson. *Director of photography:* Murray Milne. *Camera operator:* Peter Jackson. *Editor:* Jamie Selkirk. *Production designer:* Mike Kane. *Costume designer:* Glenis Foster. *Special effects/armourer:* Steve Ingram. *Model maker:* Richard Taylor. *Puppet designer:* Cameron Chittock. *Puppet engineer:* Steven Greenwood. *Supervising puppeteers:* Jonathon Acorn, Ramon Aguilar. *Puppeteers:* Eleanor Aitken, Sarah Glensor, Carl Buckley, Danny Mulheron, George Port, Ian Williamson, Justine Wright, Terri Anderton, Sean Ashton-Peach. *Puppet co-ordinator:* Tania Rodger. *Music:* Peter Dasent. *Composers:* Peter Dasent, Fane Flaws, Danny Mulheron. *Lyrics:* Arthur Baysting, Fane Flaws, Garth Frost, Danny Mulheron, Frances Walsh, Peter Dasent. *Vocals:* Fane Flaws, Mark Hadlow, Stuart Devenie. *Sound:* Jamie Selkirk, Eric de Beus, Grant Taylor, Chris Todd, Neil Maddever.

Spoken performances

Donna Akersten, Stuart Devenie, Mark Hadlow, Ross Jolly, Brian Sergent, Peter Vere-Jones, Mark Wright. Heidi performed by Danny Mulheron.

Cheerful puppet troupe The Feebles rehearses a live television variety hour. Offstage prima donna hippo Heidi, a torchsong singer, is told, 'I've heard better singing from a mongoose with throat cancer.' While the director, Sebastian the fox, agonises over rehearsal disasters like the Indian contortionist getting his nose stuck up his rectum, dramas abound in the grotty backstage. M.C. Harry the hare contracts a disfiguring illness the doctor calls 'the big one', and hides from the fly, a gutter press reporter wanting the dirt on him. Naive hedgehog Robert falls for poodle Lucille and is devastated to see her copulating with Trevor the rat. Walrus Bletch, the show's producer and Heidi's lover, makes abortive drug deals and S.M. pornographic movies between sneaking sex with cat Samantha. Junkie knife-thrower Wynyard, a frog with a Vietnam trauma, hassles for a fix and depressive elephant Sidney tries to evade the paternity suit threatened by hen Sandy. Despite good news (Harry doesn't have the big one) the live performance climaxes badly. Heidi, rejected by Bletch, goes on a machine gun rampage and most Feebles die. An on-screen message up-dates the survivors.

A bizarre creation by the special effects team at WingNut Films. Courtesy of the New Zealand Film Commission.

Dubbed a 'spluppet creature feature' **Meet the Feebles**, initially planned as a 24-minute television short, evolved from musings about what Miss Piggy would do with Kermit were she to have her wicked way with him. A Japanese pre-sale enabled Peter Jackson to develop the idea into a full-length feature.

The disclaimer that no puppets were killed or maimed during production is a lie according to Jackson, who was quoted on the Australian release saying, 'the way that we abused and treated them, I doubt whether they would want to work with us again.'[1] In anarchic spirit Jackson and crew make every effort to offend, using a puppet front to grossly represent and heartily celebrate every kind of bodily emission and secretion, wallowing in sick jokes, splatter and sexual perversion.

Muppet cuteness, politics, tabloid journalism, the entertainment industry and human nature itself are satirised and allusions to other films (**The Godfather**, **The Deer Hunter**) add to the fun. Bizarre images like the black stretch Morris Minor limo add a surreal edge. Metaphors come alive in images like the drug switch which literally 'pokes the borax' at drug dealers.

The most used visual motif is the phallus, brought to a graphic climax in Sebastian's stonily received song, 'Sodomy'.

Shot in a disused Wellington railway shed, the film, with almost every shot requiring a special effect, has excellent production values. The 'cast' included over 90 puppets (mostly rubber) so well conceived and manipulated (the puppeteers worked under a false floor) that, aided by ingenious camera work, much of it hand held, they take on a life of their own. At times coherence suffers in the busy plot. The excellent musical score, with many Feeble numbers, enlivens the colourful, hectic narrative.

Meet the Feebles won worldwide recognition as the first creature film made for an adult audience. On its release Peter Jackson warned, 'It's a nasty little piece of work, this one, and people should know that.'[2] The major investor, the New Zealand Film Commission, did not take a credit on the completed film. HM

1990 Film Fantastique Festival, Paris: Grand Prize.
 New Zealand Film Awards: Best Contribution to Design.
1991 Madrid Film Festival: Audience Prize for Most Popular Film.
Fanta Festival, Rome: Best Director. Best Special Effects. Best Female Performance, Heidi.

References
[1] *On The Street*, Sydney, 27 March 1989.
[2] *Sydney Morning Herald*, 8 March 1989.

USER FRIENDLY

1990

Film Konstruction in association with the New Zealand Film Commission. ©1990. *Budget:* $1.3 million. *Location:* Auckland. *Distributor:* John Maynard Productions. *Rating:* RP13, April 1990. 35 mm. Colour. 90 mins.

Director: Gregor Nicholas. *Producers:* Trevor Haysom, Frank Stark. *Screenplay:* Gregor Nicholas, Norelle Scott, Frank Stark from an original story by Gregor Nicholas. *Director of photography:* Donald Duncan. *Camera operator:* Barry Harbert. *Editor:* David Coulson. *Production designer:* Kirsten Shouler. *Costume designer:* Ngila Dickson. *Composer:* Mark Nicholas. *Musical director:* Mike Chunn. *Players:* Auckland Youth Orchestra. *Conductor:* Michael McLellan. *Sound:* Graham Morris, John McKay, Garth Maxwell, Gethin Creagh.

Cast

William Brandt (Billy), Alison Bruce (Augusta), Judith Gibson (Miranda), David Letch (Wayne), Joan Reid (Marjorie), Lewis Martin (Monty), June Bishop (Doris), Noel Appleby (Barry), Nell Weatherley (Beverley), Dorothy Hurt (Eunice), Belinda Weymouth (Laura), Biggles (Cyclops), Alan de Malmanche (Mr Digman), Victoria Watt (Young Miranda), Eddie Hegan (Frank), Ishebashi Takahide (Interpreter), Mark Clare (Gas station attendant), Jeff Gane (Telecom worker), Alistair Douglas (Gas station manager), Timothy Smith (Jonathan).

Billy, who shears sheep at tourist promotions while writing a thesis on Melanesian art, is visited by ex-girlfriend Augusta and her bull terrier Cyclops. Gus presses Billy into sex then takes him to retrieve her belongings from Miranda, a cosmetics tycoon who has in her possession a stolen magical dog-goddess from the Pacific island Tokabaru. Miranda intends to use the dog-goddess in the production of anti-aging potions. At Miranda's, Billy watches Miranda and her partner Wayne in sexual foreplay in which, in full space regalia and with high-tech equipment, they speak dialogue from the Apollo space missions and act out manoeuvres inspired by **2001: A Space Odyssey** with Wayne in the role of the shuttle pod. Gus steals the dog-goddess and they escape, having been seen by Marjorie and Monty, a pair of mad old doctors who run an old folk's rejuvenation clinic out of the Balmoral Bowling Club's gardening shed and who are in search of a new elixir-of-life. The three-way chase is on. Marj and Monty deputise Barry and Doris to retrieve the dog-goddess. Billy tries to return the dog-goddess but he and Gus are kidnapped and trussed up in the Bowling Club garden shed. Injected with green goo from the eyes of the dog-goddess, Billy and Gus throw off their bonds and fall on each other for hot sex. Marj, impressed, administers doses to herself and Monty with similar results. Miranda, on the warpath with a speargun, gobbles a dog-goddess eyeball and is transformed into a child. Cyclops grabs the dog-goddess, with which he has fallen in love, and escapes with Billy and Gus. On-screen messages tell of prison sentences for Marj and Monty, a maximum security childcare centre for Miranda and domestic bliss on Tokabaru for Billy, Gus and Cyclops.

Aiming at being a quirky action comedy, **User Friendly** (the dog-goddess reciprocates kindness) was initially conceived as a short film. As the McGuffin, the dog-goddess is a good starter for a madcap romp (the film's tag-line reads 'A little dog goes a long way'), but after the set-up there is nothing for anyone to do but chase or be chased. The film relies on slapstick and sight gags, neglecting narrative development.

A major weakness is that the 'sympathetic' characters, Billy and Gus, are virtually without motivation, while the others, although ostensibly motivated by greed, are too one-dimensional to sustain interest or generate suspense. Most of the humour falls flat, as in the attempts to send up the New Zealand tourist industry with fluffy, life-sized kiwi fruit and an aborted sheep shearing session. In its favour, **User Friendly** has a fresh attitude to sex, but the novelty of seeing old people coupling on screen is undermined because their sexuality is portrayed as grotesque and aberrant.

The film looks stylish and the production design is inventive, particularly in Miranda's lair where props include a tank of anemones brought in from the Poor Knights Islands and the bizarre sex-in-space gear. The lively music goes some way to papering over plot hiatuses. The dog-goddess statue was based on a carving in the Pacific and Oceanic room of the Auckland Museum. HM

Lewis Martin (Monty) and Joan Reid (Marjorie). Courtesy of the New Zealand Film Commission.

1990

AN ANGEL AT MY TABLE

Hibiscus Films in association with the New Zealand Film Commission, Television New Zealand Ltd, Australian Broadcasting Corporation and Channel 4. ©1990. Feature film/television series. *Budget:* $2.8 million. *Locations:* Auckland, Helensville, Kareotahi Beach, Cook Strait, Catalonia, Paris, London. *Distributor:* John Maynard Productions. *Rating:* GA (Some scenes may disturb), May 1990. 35 mm (shot on 16 mm). 159.5 mins. Colour. (1″ Videotape. 3 × 54 mins.)

Director: Jane Campion. *Producer:* Bridget Ikin. *Co-producer:* John Maynard. *Screenplay:* Laura Jones. *Sources:* Janet Frame, *To the Is-land* (1983), *An Angel At My Table* (1984), *The Envoy From Mirror City* (1985). *Director of photography:* Stuart Dryburgh. *Editor:* Veronika Haussler. *Production designer:* Grant Major. *Costume designer:* Glenys Jackson. *Research:* Hilary Quick, Cheryl Cameron, Peter Long. *Wigmaker:* Cheryl Newton. *Composer:* Don McGlashan. *Music research:* William Dart, John Hopkins, Janet McIvor. *Sound:* Graham Morris, John Dennison, Tony Vaccher, Graeme Myhre.

Cast

Kerry Fox (Janet), Alexia Keogh (Young Janet), Karen Fergusson (Teenage Janet), Iris Churn (Mum), K.J. Wilson (Dad), Melina Bernecker (Myrtle), Andrew Binns (Bruddie), Glynis Angell (Isabel), Sarah Smuts-Kennedy (June), Martyn Sanderson (Frank Sargeson), David Letch (Patrick), William Brandt (Bernard), with Jessie Mune, Francesca Collins, Mark Morrison, Katherine Murray-Cowper, Mark Thomson, Brenda Kendall, Paul Moffat, Blair Hutchinson, David McAuslan, Ailene Herring, Faye Flegg, Carla Hedgeman, Timothy Bartlett, Richard Mills, Sassy Acorn, Tony Creamer, Hamish McFarlane, Geoff Barlow, Samantha Townsley, Sarah Llewellyn, Christopher Lawrence, Edith Campion, Fiona Kay, Brian Flegg, Eileen Clark, Margaret Gordon, Caroline Somerville, Lilian Enting, Fiona Brown, Maureen Duffy, Karla Smith, Willa O'Neill, Fritha Stalker, Melanie Reid, Natasha Gray, Kelly Stewart, Susan McGregor, Erin Mills, Virginia Brocklehurst, Natalie Ellis, Eddie Hegan, Colin McColl, Erin Dorricott.

Based on the autobiographies of poet/novelist/short story writer Janet Frame, **An Angel At My Table** was shot as a three-part series for television but first released as a feature film. Episode One, set in Janet's Oamaru childhood, shows her growing consciousness of the power and pleasures of words. Shaping forces include poverty, her father's wild rages, her brother Bruddie's disabling epilepsy and her sister Myrtle's drowning. In adolescence Janet, uncomfortable with her body, retreats into isolation and the solitary pursuit of writing. She leaves home for Teachers College training and university study. In Episode Two Janet retreats further, realises that teaching terrifies her and makes a half-hearted suicide attempt. In a psychiatric institution she is diagnosed schizophrenic. Institutionalised for eight years, she endures over 200 electric shock treatments, avoiding a leucotomy only because a doctor intervenes when her book of short stories, *The Lagoon*, wins a prize. Tragedy strikes again when her sister Isabel drowns. Her life takes a positive turn when writer Frank Sargeson takes her in. Her first novel, *Owls Do Cry*, is accepted for publication and Sargeson helps Janet secure a travel grant. In Episode Three Janet mixes shyly with the 1950s avant-garde in London and Ibiza, Spain. A rapturous romance with an American poet in Spain results in pregnancy, desertion and self-induced miscarriage. Struggling to survive in London, Janet has a relapse. In a psychiatric hospital she learns she is not schizophrenic. Janet, whose reputation as a writer has grown in her absence, returns to New Zealand to write.

Janet Frame's life is richly evoked through superb production design, an evocative score, a generally coherent, episodic narrative and impeccable performances. Following its source the film explodes the 'mad genius' legend and eloquently demonstrates how Frame's writing was her lifeline and her life's passion. Her love affair with language as a way of experiencing other realities is realised both in impressionistic flashes and in longer narrative scenes that open out and develop the conflicts tormenting Janet: wanting to be part of things while wanting to be alone; the struggle to accommodate the increasing importance of language and writing while feeling alienated from others; the desire to extricate herself from her 'illness' while lacking in assertiveness.

The impressionistic narrative style means that at times coherence suffers, as when Janet's first book is published with no indication she was still writing. Details are particularly effective in conveying a sense of Janet's external and internal worlds—the one often harsh and frightening, the other rich in imagination, made magical by the power of words. In keeping with the television format and the relatively low budget the shooting style favours tight shots and uncomplicated set-ups to create intimacy. Sound and visual motifs connect the episodes and reinforce thematic ideas, as in the use of trains as harbingers of change. **An Angel at My Table** was the first New Zealand film to screen in competition at the Venice Film Festival. The film has sold to 48 countries. It brought wider international attention to Frame's writing and resulted in many reprints and translations of her autobiography. It screened on New Zealand television episodically between 7 July 1991 and 21 July 1991 and as a feature on 19 March 1994. HM

Alexia Keogh as the young Janet Frame surrounded by her family. Courtesy of the New Zealand Film Commission.

1990 Venice Film Festival: seven awards, including Special Jury Prize. Sydney Film Festival: Most Popular Film. Australian Film Critics' Circle: Best Foreign Film. Festival of Festivals: International Critics' Prize. Valladolid Film Festival, Spain: Best Actress. New Zealand Film and Television Awards: Cinematography. Screenplay. Performance in a Supporting Role, Martyn Sanderson. Female Performance, Kerry Fox. Director. Best Film.

1991 Berlin Film Festival: Otto Dibelius Film Prize, Most Popular Film. Union of Critics, Belgium: Best Film.

1990

RUBY AND RATA

Preston*Laing Productions in association with the New Zealand Film Commission. ©1990. *Budget:* approx. $2 million. *Locations:* Mount Albert, Auckland. *Distributor:* Trans Tas. *Rating:* GA, July 1990. 35mm. Dolby Stereo. Colour. 111 mins.

Director: Gaylene Preston. *Producers:* Robin Laing, Gaylene Preston. *Screenplay:* Graeme Tetley, Gaylene Preston from an original idea by Graeme Tetley. *Director of photography:* Leon Narbey. *Camera operator:* Allen Guilford. *Editor:* Paul Sutorius. *Production designer:* Robert Gillies. *Costume designer:* Ngila Dickson. *Cultural advisors:* Keri Kaa, Dulcie Bolton. *Musical director:* Jonathon Crayford. *Vocals:* Vanessa Rare. *Conductor:* Ken Young. *Players:* Members of the New Zealand Symphony Orchestra. *Sound:* Kit Rollings, Graham Morris, Phil Judd, Brian Shennan, John Neill, Mike Hedges.

Cast

Yvonne Lawley (Ruby), Vanessa Rare (Rata), Simon Barnett (Buckle), Lee Mete-Kingi (Willie), Dr Debes Bhattacharyya (Ramesh), Russell Smith (Social worker), Russell Gowers (Sike), Ngaire Horton (Mrs Stickle), Alma Woods (Mrs Shearer), Vicky Burrett (Mrs Spindle), Iain Rea (Traffic officer), Simon White, Dave Clark, Tony Gallagher, Peter van Bergen (the Apocalypse), Des Culling (Party goer), Heather Bolton (Nurse), Matt Palmer (New tenant), Pratima Soma (Ramesh's wife), Sam Ford (Magician), Trudi Green (Rabbit), Peter Sharp (Father Christmas), Gary McCormick (Manhattan Mac), Steve La Hood (Morgan Cohen), Dot Barrington (Welfare clerk), Glynis Paraha (Cleaning supervisor), Andrew Binns (Salesman), Jeff Cane, Stephen Hall (Repo men), John Paul (Schwakker's voice), Luna (Barking dog).

An Auckland suburb, 1980s. Pakeha Ruby, 83, cajoles nephew Buckle into renting out part of her house, hoping to remain independent. She insists he rent to a young Maori, Rata, thinking she is a wealthy, childless businesswoman, whereas in fact Rata is a benefit fraud with a young son, Willie, working as a cleaner. Rata auditions for the band the Apocalypse and Buckle, instead of evicting her as Ruby orders, spends the night with her and becomes the band's manager. Ruby and Rata declare war despite Willie and Rata saving Ruby's life after she becomes stranded in her bath. Ruby covers for Willie when he is caught stealing chocolate fish at the corner dairy, and blackmails him into becoming her helper. Ruby and Willie grow to love one another and when Rata realises Social Welfare is on to her and decides to move on, Willie goes into hiding. Ruby falls and is hospitalised. Buckle renews his efforts to move her to the Golden Age Retirement Home, but instead Ruby signs her house over to Willie. Out of hospital she and Willie watch gleefully as Rata greets a prospective tenant.

Dr Debes Bhattacharyya (Ramesh), Yvonne Lawley (Ruby). *Courtesy of the New Zealand Film Commission.*

Originally conceived as a television series, **Ruby and Rata** is a wish-fulfilment comedy drama satirising social systems while celebrating ordinary people's brave struggles to get by. With different values and ethnic backgrounds the women initially have little in common. The narrative highlights their differences while gradually shifting the ground as, through Willie's intervention, they pool resources to survive. Both belong to an underclass created by government restructuring to foster a deregulated economy. Both struggle for independence and dignity surrounded by corporate prejudice and indifference represented by Conspec Corporation big business and Social Welfare patronage. Their 'using' of others is strictly pragmatic.

Willie is an unwittingly dangerous little boy, in trouble as an arsonist, truant and thief, and to keep him from Social Welfare's clutches Rata, an urban Maori out of contact with her whanau, has to have an address. Ruby fears living out her days in the Golden Age Retirement home. The stereotypes—irresponsible Maori solo mother defrauding the government, mean-minded, friendless pakeha pensioner—are cleverly undermined as the characters are established. Buckle, the Social Welfare Officer and three retirement home women who comment, like a spiteful Greek chorus, on Ruby's every move, are less successful as characters, as the comedy in their roles is laboured.

Visual motifs suggest the everyday can be larger than life and magical. Ruby sees Willie as a 'little space man' and, in his imagination, Willie invests Ruby with witch-like powers. Drawn to fire and brightness, his view of Ruby is coloured by magical lighting effects in her house and jewellery. Ironically Willie in the end is the alchemist, transforming the lives of Ruby, Rata and himself. The chocolate fish motif highlights the playful tone and moments of poignancy (when Willie and Ruby dance, for example) give depth. Excellent production design creates a believable urban setting and, in keeping with the comic intention, the musical score is light and up-beat. In his first role Lee Mete-Kingi gives a superb performance as Willie. HM

1990 New Zealand Film and Television Awards: Best Editing. Best Soundtrack. Best Film Score. Best Male Performance, Lee Mete-Kingi.
1991 Sydney and Melbourne Film Festivals: Third Place, Popular Choice.
Giffoni Film Festival: Gold Medal.

1990

THE RETURNING

Matte Box Films Ltd in association with David Hannay Productions Pty Ltd for Echo Pictures Ltd and the New Zealand Film Commission. ©1990. *Budget:* a little under $2 million. *Locations:* Auckland, West Otago. *Distributor:* Endeavour Entertainment Ltd. *Rating:* GA, December 1990. 35 mm. Colour. 98.5 mins.

Director: John Day. *Producer:* Trishia Downie. *Executive producer:* David Hannay. *Screenplay:* John Day, Clinton Phillips from an original story by Simon Willisson. *Director of photography:* Kevin Hayward. *Camera operator:* Kevin Hayward. *Editor:* Simon Clothier. *Production designer:* Mike Becroft. *Costume designer:* Christine West. *Special effects:* Brian Harris, Katrina Griffith, Geoff Clenden. *Music:* Clive Cockburn. *Sound:* Kit Rollings, John Neill, Philippa Anderton, John Van Der Reyden, Michael Hedges, Michael Westgate.

Cast

Phillip Gordon (Alan Steadman), Alison Routledge (Jessica Scott), Max Cullen (Father Donohue), Jim Moriarty (George), John Ewart (Steadman Senior), Grant Tilly (Dr Pitts), Jenny Ryken (Charlotte Heatherington), Frank Whitten (Mr Spiggs), Judie Douglass (Miriam), with Tony Grosser, Zak Becroft, Gavan Hogg, Arthur Baysting, Trishia Downie, David Hannay, Daniel Wrightson, Jim Mcfarlane, David Blacklock, Linda Dearing, Rochelle May, Bruce McDowell, Jim Dynes, Shirley Grace, Mrs Kilpatrick, Mrs Thompson, Antony Day, Dick Cook, Chrystal McKee, Margot Lane, Hone Tuwhare, Graeme Dickison, Margret MacDonald and the people of Tapanui.

Alison Routledge (Jessica Scott). Courtesy of the New Zealand Film Commission.

After contemplating his future as executor of his recently deceased grandfather's trust fund, lawyer Alan Steadman tells his scheming lawyer father he intends to start up his own law practice and run the trust alone. Moving into a Victorian country mansion, he is disturbed by dreams of passionate sexual encounters with a young woman and by sounds of a baby crying. He learns Charlotte Heatherington, whose father built the mansion, committed suicide there in 1893 on hearing her lover had drowned on his way out from Scotland. While Alan's father and crooked business associates scheme to get control of the trust by having him committed as a paranoid schizophrenic (his mother is thus diagnosed and kept comatose by medication) he becomes obsessed with the idea his destiny is linked to Charlotte's, to the chagrin of his lawyer associate Jessica, who wants him for herself. Evidence that in a past life he was Charlotte's lover leads Alan to sign over care of the trust to local gardener George. With the help of Charlotte's ghost, Steadman Senior dies horribly. Alan, carrying Charlotte's lace wedding dress, walks naked into the river and drowns.

While the text of this psychological thriller tells a ghost story, the subtext is about personal and global abuse. The closing down of a pesticides factory by Alan's grandfather foreshadows horticulturalist George's concern that acid rain and deforestation are destroying the planet and it is apt that the Steadman millions should be left in the care of one who will spend the money on trees. George's dictum, 'you treat nature bad, she takes revenge' is borne out in the manner of Steadman Senior's death, as he is the instigator of abuse as a ruthless lawyer and as a husband and father. Charlotte, too, was abused by her father, and this forges the connection between her and Alan. His redemption begins when Charlotte heals his crippled hand and is completed when he joins her in death, while Maori George's belief in the spirituality of nature promises redemption for the planet.

The Returning grew from a dream told by Simon Willisson to director/writer John Day. With its slow build and judicious use of light it generates a mysterious, dreamlike atmosphere. The shooting style, which favours an open frame, gives the film a European feel and the imaging of the Otago countryside/Hitchcockian house settings adds much to its visual richness. The music is apt, but overused.

Some credibility is lost in the caricatures of evil presented by Steadman Senior and his offsider Mr Spiggs and by the stereotypically Machiavellian psychiatrist. The scene where Pitts shows Alan a videotape of Mrs Steadman discussing her son's childhood suicidal tendencies and imaginary friend is an awkward plot contrivance. Ironically the 'ghost' story, which raises questions about madness, love and reality, is much more credible and involving than the 'here and now' plot strand involving the machinations of Alan's father and business associates. HM

1986 Madrid Festival: Best Director.
International Fantasy, Rome: Best Director, Best Actor. Tashkent Festival: Special Jury Prize for Peace.

1990

THE SHRIMP ON THE BARBIE

Bruce Spence (Wayne) as he appeared in **Pallet On The Floor** *(1986). Courtesy of the New Zealand Film Commission.*

An R. Ben Efraim Production for Unity Pictures Corporation. A.k.a. The Boyfriend From Hell. A.k.a. Boyfriend From Hell. Financed from the U.S. © 1990. *Locations:* Auckland, Sydney. *NZ video rating:* PG. 35 mm. Colour. 86 mins.

Director: Alan Smithee. *Producer:* R. Ben Efraim. *Executive producer:* Jerry Offsay. *Screenplay:* Grant Morris, Ron House, Alan Shearman. *Directors of photography:* James Bartle (N.Z.), Andrew Lesnie (Aus). *Editor:* Fred Chulak A.C.E. *Production designer:* Ron Highfield. *Costume designer:* Sue Gandy. *Kangaroo wrangler:* Evanna Chesson. *Music:* Peter Kaye. *Sound:* Dick Reade, Phillip Keros, James Williams, Robert Harman, Allen Stone, Clancy Troutman.

Cast

Cheech Marin (Carlos), Emma Samms (Alex), Vernon Wells (Bruce), Carole Davis (Dominique), Terence Cooper (Sir Ian Hobart), June Bishop (Lady Irene), Bruce Spence (Wayne), Jeanette Cronin (Maggie), Bruce Allpress (Mr Ridley), Val Lamond (Mrs Ridley), Herbs (Mariachi band), Hattie St John (BBQ singer), Gary McCormick (Gary Williams), Frank Whitten (Blue), David Argue (Kevin), Claire Glenister (Anchorwoman), Jonothan Coleman (Postman), Suzanne Chamberlain (Maid), Richard Hanna (Nigel), Eric Liddy (Eddison the butler), Michael Morrissey (Airport ticket agent), Ken George (Collins), Doug Aston (Old man), Leticia Bridges, Wendy Petrie (Teenage girls), Daryl Maguire (Spa clerk), Dennis O'Keefe (Spa bellman), Brian Gidley (Spa bartender), Neill Gladwin, Stephen Kearney (Bar guys), Alan Farquar (Travel agent), Noel Appleby (Slim), Kim Buchanan (Eve), Tracey Allen (Rugby bikini girl), Joel Tobeck (Lance), Kurt de Koster, Mike Finlayson (Bar guys).

Lured to Sydney by Paul Hogan's 'pop a shrimp on the barbie' television commercial, Mexican-American Carlos is fired from his Kings Cross engagement as Elvo, the Pakistani Elvis, beaten up by a flatmate's jealous kangaroo and cast emotionally adrift by his Los Angeles fiancée's Dear John letter. Employed as a waiter in a mock-Mexican restaurant, Mañana, Carlos's luck changes when spoiled heiress Alex Hobart offers him $5000 to masquerade as her new, grossly uncouth fiancé in a bid to force her father, Australia's richest man, to consent to her marriage to ex-Wallaby captain Bruce. Listening behind doors Sir Ian discovers Carlos is no buffoon and hires a private detective to tail and photograph Bruce, who is meanwhile frolicking naked in a restaurant fish tank with Alex's best friend Dominique. Alex loses her selfishness and arrogance and falls for honest, lovable Carlos, who wants her for herself alone. Bruce and Dominique are sent packing. Carlos is welcomed warmly into the family and they party at the Mañana, which Carlos and Sir Ian now own as business partners.

The first section endeavours to mine comedian Cheech Marin's talent for mimickry with routines plundered from the Basil Fawlty/Manuel duo and there is much slapstick and caricature. With the change in Alex's persona from stuck-up bitch to vulnerable and lonely poor-little-rich-girl the tone switches to romantic comedy mode and poor-but-honest Carlos becomes the embodiment of everything good and true. Oedipal conflict rages between Alex and Daddy. As Cinderella, Carlos gets to marry the princess because she and Daddy have fallen for his simple, foreign integrity.

Some of it works. When Sir Ian recalls a passenger plane so Alex can have the man she wants, he looks wryly into the camera and explains, 'I'm very rich.' Australian racism is briefly satirised in the character of Alex's uncle (Bruce Allpress) and fiancé Bruce is a recognisable stereotype of the gross Aussie jock. Ex-Wallaby captain Bruce makes his living endorsing a well-known brand of Australian beer, with references to the product so prolific that at times **The Shrimp on the Barbie/The Boyfriend From Hell** looks like a long advertisement with brief story breaks.

Initially Los Angeles producer R. Ben Efraim intended shooting in Australia, but industrial problems concerning the hiring of American actors drove the production to New Zealand. The film was made to look as though it was shot in Australia, with the only Australian footage from there being the Sydney Harbour Bridge sequence. The screenplay was written by New Zealander Grant Morris, there were many New Zealanders in the crew and Herbs and Hattie St John perform. Director Michael Gottlieb and producer R. Ben Efraim went to court over the film. The directorial credit is given to Alan Smithee, the non-existent figure whose name is used as a fill-in in such cases. The film has not had a theatrical release in New Zealand but is available on video under the title **Boyfriend From Hell**. HM

1991

A SOLDIER'S TALE

Mirage Entertainment Corporation and Atlantic Entertainment Group. ©1988. *Budget:* approx. $5 million. *Locations:* Normandy, Bordeaux. *Distributor:* Hoyts Entertainment. *Rating:* GA (Some content may disturb), February 1991. 35 mm. Colour. 95.5 mins.

Director and producer: Larry Parr. *Line producers:* Dominique Antoine, Finola Dwyer. *Executive producer:* Don Reynolds. *Screenplay:* Grant Hindin Miller, Larry Parr. *Source:* M.K. Joseph, *A Soldier's Tale*. *Director of photography:* Alun Bollinger. *Editor:* Michael Horton. *Production designer:* Ivan Maussion. *Costume designer:* Renee Renard. *Music:* John Charles. *Conductor/music producer:* Dave Fraser. *Player:* Deirdre Irons. *Sound:* Mike Westgate, Gethin Creagh, John McKay, Ross Chambers, Ken Sparks, Mike Hopkins.

Cast

Gabriel Byrne (Saul Scourby), Marianne Basler (Belle), Judge Reinhold (American soldier), Paul Wyett (Charlie), Maurice Garrel (M. Pradier), Jaques Mathou (Wolf), Benoit Regent (Father Superior), Bernard Farcy (Andre), Roch Leibovici (The kid), Claude Mann (Winterhalter), Matthew Byam Shaw (Lieutenant Mortimer), David Duffy (Private Smith), Nicholas Tronc (Balthazar), Veronique Muller (Simone), Claudine Berg (Older woman), Philippe Le Mercier (Gustav), Eric Galiano (Karl), Father Herman (The old monk).

1944, Normandy, France. Having broken the defences of occupying Germans, Allied troops are working their way up north. British working-class sergeant Saul Scourby saves soldier Charlie's life by cutting a German soldier's throat. On reconnaissance Charlie and Saul meet Belle, a French woman who members of the French Resistance claim is a traitor who colluded with occupying German officers, causing the deaths of twelve Resistance men. Saul offers to stay in her cottage until his regiment moves on in three days' time. Although Belle treats him with contempt they become lovers. Saul tries to save her by asking a priest to give her sanctuary and by asking his regiment to intercede. In flashback we learn of her love affair with a German soldier during the Occupation and of her later friendship with a member of the Gestapo who, jealous of her former friendship with Frenchman, Balthazar, has him and his fellow Resistance workers executed. Saul rapes Belle after a shooting scare, then explains he did it out of fear. She eventually accepts this and over the next few hours they become close.

Marianne Basler (Belle). Courtesy of the New Zealand Film Commission.

When Saul's efforts to save Belle fail, rather than leave her to be tortured and killed by the Resistance men when his regiment moves on, he stabs her to death. As he leaves her cottage in the rain a lecherous American who has been awaiting his turn and the three Resistance men move into the cottage and discover Belle's body.

M.K. Joseph's novel is a simple tale posing complex moral questions about loyalty, betrayal and culpability in wartime. The film's Scourby is more articulate and less misogynistic than M.K. Joseph's and the narrative concentrates on Belle's story as a microcosm of the moral ambiguities of war. Because Belle's guilt is hearsay and because the story is told from her perspective the French Resistance and the soldier/priest's refusal to grant her a fair trial appear brutal. Saul's rape of Belle highlights the violence of foreign occupation and the powerlessness of its victims. The narrative balances the harshness of war with the tenderness of the emerging love affair. Saul, unused to expressing his feelings and through his upbringing a prude in sexual matters, learns about love in his few days with Belle.

Shot mainly in Normandy and Bordeaux, the cinematography contrasts the timeless beauty of the lush green landscapes with the ugliness of war as shown in the brief opening sequence, the behind-the-scenes machinations of the Gestapo and French treatment of Belle. The music is spare and effective. The source novel was written in New Zealand but is a European story. Some crew were from France although the film is a New Zealand production. The French locations made it a complex production task.

The film, made in 1988, was to have been a co-production, but the French pulled out. This, combined with the bankruptcy of a contracted U.S. distributor who failed to pay a big advance, helped send the Mirage Entertainment Corporation into receivership. **A Soldier's Tale** has not had a general release in New Zealand. It has, however, screened in festivals. It screened on New Zealand television on 24 November 1995. HM

1992 New Zealand Film Awards: Best Female Performance, Marianne Basler. Best Soundtrack.

1991

Rebels in Retrospect: The Political Memoirs of Some Members of Christchurch and Wellington PYM

A Vanguard Films production. Produced with the assistance of Valdini Video and the Creative Film and Video Fund of the Queen Elizabeth II Arts Council of New Zealand, the New Zealand Film Commission and Television New Zealand. ©1991. Video documentary. *Location:* Christchurch. *Distributor:* Vanguard Films. Video, 1991. 16 mm. Colour. 74 mins.

Director and producer: Russell Campbell. *Screenplay:* Russell Campbell. *Camera:* Martin Long. *Production manager and additional photography:* Alister Barry. *Editor:* Russell Campbell. *Sound:* Steve Upston. *Music:* composed and performed by Bill Lake, Nick Bollinger, Andre Delahunty, Stephen Jessup, Alan Norman, Geoff Rashbrooke, Tim Robinson. Recorded by John Donoghue, Pacific Sound Titles. *Editing consultant:* Reid Perkins. *Film library research/VTR operator:* Julie Webb-Pullmann. *Library film:* Television New Zealand. *Excerpts from 8 mm movies:* Tony Currie. *Historical photo-graphs:* Tony Webster, Pip Alley. *On-line editor:* Peter Metcalf. *Track-laying and mix:* Grant Taylor, Village Sound Recorders. Thanks to Jan Nauta, Bob Leonard, Murray Horton, Tony Currie, Ann Hardy, Paul Maunder 'and all the old PYMers who helped.'

Cast

Named participants: Christine Bird, Richard Bolstad, Tony Currie, Mike Donaldson, Murray Horton, Pam Hughes, Richard Hill, Chris Klaus, Lana Le Quesne, Dave Mitchell, Therese O'Connell, Tama Poata, Dave Welch, Chris Wheeler.

Rebels In Retrospect revisits the sites of 1960s and 1970s conflict in New Zealand, decades when the political and social patterns of this country were being jolted from the complacent comfort which had characterised life until then. New Zealanders were having to respond to and sometimes participate in events which were bringing about irreversible change, without the experience or skills to cope with such change. Learning took place in the crucible of radical reappraisal of traditional beliefs, and frequently within the environs of one pressure group or another. For one woman, 'The PYM was my university,' and that comment could be made by almost all the politically active movers of the period.

In the course of re-examination of traditional beliefs and value systems, a number of pressure groups emerged, the most radical and arguably the most influential of which came from the political left. One such group was the Progressive Youth Movement, an organisation which developed a reputation for membership and action which, for the period, was right at the cutting edge of extreme political activity. **Rebels In Retrospect** provides a contemporary perspective on the events which brought about the founding of the PYM, and follows both membership and political activism through the next 20 years. By then the members of the Progressive Youth Movement had become middle-aged, the forces which ignited the movement had largely been superseded, and the fire of radical youth had been replaced with the inescapable logic of maturity.

Campbell's film begins with a reunion of members of the Christchurch group who, through commentary, discussion and nostalgic recalling of their participation in events, proceed to give a perspective on the period which differs markedly from media reportage of the time. That perspective is unashamedly that of the PYM, and is a position for which Campbell sees no need to apologise. He believes that the media, especially television, provide a propaganda base for the Establishment, and that through films such as **Rebels in Retrospect**, and his earlier film **Wildcat**, 'We are perhaps counteracting that potential for Establishment propaganda.'*

When the film was submitted to Television New Zealand for screening, negotiations had reached the stage of contract preparation, but the in-house censor for TVNZ who reviews intending programs for objectivity as well as for offensiveness, rejected the film on the grounds that it was biased.

The film makes no pretence at middle-of-the-road neutralism. It is arranged in 19 parts with a prologue to set the scene and, in a style which is typical of Campbell's political documentaries, constantly sets image against speaker and image against image, so that the viewer is provided with a succession of possible readings which seek to subvert the Establishment position. Against Prime Minister Keith Holyoake's political justification of New Zealand's involvement in Vietnam, Campbell places the photojournalist image which shocked the world, a burned, naked child running from a napalm attack. It is Campbell's ability to use the very cinematic codes which can conceal truth, to reveal it, and to utilise the potential of the medium to convey a message which print cannot, which makes his documentaries unique in the corpus of nonfiction features detailing New Zealand's past. SE

Reference
* *The Press*, 5 June 1991, p. 17.

Members of the PYM protesting against the Vietnam War. Courtesy of Russell Campbell and Vanguard Films.

1991

TE RUA

Pacific Films in association with the New Zealand Film Commission, Berlin Senate and Film Commission, Avalon/NFU Studios. © 1991. *Budget*: $4 346 000. *Locations*: Berlin, Wellington, Cape Palliser, Wairarapa Coast. *Distributor*: Trans Tas. *Rating*: GA (English and Maori dialogue, English subtitles), July 1991. 35 mm. Colour. 99.5 mins.

Director: Barry Barclay. *Producer*: John O'Shea. *Executive producer*: Renee Gundelach (Berlin). *Associate producer*: Craig Walters. *Screenplay*: Barry Barclay. *Additional Writing*: Jochen Brunow. *Directors of photography*: Rory O'Shea (Berlin), Warrick Attewell (N.Z.). *Camera operator*: John Mahaffie. *Editors*: Simon Reece, Dell King. *Production designer*: Ron Highfield. *Costume designers*: Monika Jacobs, Tina Harris. *Post-production Maori advisor*: Tahu Asher. *Uritoto carvings*: designed by Riaka Hiakati, carved by Te Hue Rangi Taneatua. *Music*: Dalvanius. *Additional music*: Jay Dee, Stuart Pearce. *'Turuturu Mai Ra' haka*: performed by Pipiwharauroa. *Maori dialogue /haka*: Huirangi Waikerepuru. *Sound*: Christian Moldt, Ken Saville, Kit Rollings, Mike Hopkins, John Neill, Michael Hedges.

Cast

Wi Kuki Kaa (Rewi), Nissie Herewini (Nanny Matai), Tilly Reedy (Mere Marangai), Maria Fitzi (Hanna Lehmann), Donna Akersten (Fiona Gilbert), Walter Kreye (Dr Sattler), Jürgen Thormann (Dieter Goetz), Carolyn Del Rosario (Teza), Vanessa Rare (Helen Marangai), Günter Meisner (Professor Biederstedt), Matiu Mareikura (Taki Ruru), Peter Kaa (Peter Huaka), Stuart Devenie (Hamish MacMillan), Anton Rattinger (Günter Schewer), Dalvanius (Dr Waru), Maximilian Held (Rüdiger), Özay Fecht (Museum cleaner), with Emilio de Marchi, Amadeus Flossner, Brigit Anders, Conrado Del Rosario, Thomas Schendel, David McKenzie, Paki Cherrington, Anne Budd, Bill Aspinall, Roimata Baker, Paku Kapene, Jim Grant, Duncan Smith, Whetu E.F. Fala, Toby Mills, Hori Ahipene, Nadja Reichardt, Lisa Riecken, Columbina Burton, Christian Camerota, Bubacar Jammeh, Elmar Gutmann, Jurgen F. Schmid, Melzie-Louise Hamrick, Phillip Nixey, Peter Warren, Ann Chamberlain, James Beaumont, Jan Rea.

In fictional Uritoto a Maori explains how one hundred years previously an ancestor stole three precious carvings for a German, then lived as an outcast in a kumara storehouse (a rua) before shooting himself. Kuia Nanny is resolved the carvings will be returned from Berlin. Wealthy patent lawyer Rewi Marangai, an Uritoto man, works on an anti-hacking patent in Berlin. His nephew Peter Huaka, a performance poet on tour in the city, is detained after performing a ritual dance before the Uritoto carvings in a museum basement. Rewi is called in to calm him. Peter is approached by a political action group asking him to take part in a campaign publicising the need to return indigenous art to its homeland. With translator Hannah, Peter plans to use the group to get the carvings back. Rewi returns to Uritoto and makes contact with his estranged wife and family and Peter returns with three young Maoris committed to retrieving the carvings. Nanny orders Rewi to accompany them to Berlin and moves into the marae meeting house, vowing not to eat until the mission is accomplished. Peter's group is unable to take the carvings from the Berlin museum and instead steals three ancient busts, hiding with them in a basement. After a confrontation with Berlin police Peter is shot and wounded, the busts are returned and the group arrested. The museum director, at the urging of an African diplomat and the action group, signs a document to release the carvings. At Uritoto the tribe celebrate the return while mourning the jailing of Peter, Rewi and the others.

Te Rua is an angry, passionate film about a quest for spiritual guardianship, mana tuturu, and its implications about cultural sovereignty for tribes whose taonga have been appropriated for financial gain. Central to the concept of mana tuturu is the notion that to achieve spiritual ownership a tribe must be united, and that 'it is more important to own what is inside than to have possession of the outside.' To this end internationally successful Rewi, disconnected from his cultural roots, undergoes a personal journey of rediscovery.

As key images the kumara storehouse (a rua) and the art 'storehouse' (the museum) are inappropriate homes for the tribe's spiritual treasures. Film and video cameras appear often, both as media weapons and, when rolling without an operator, as modern recorders of old tales. The museum director's objection to returning the carvings, that the move would have worldwide implications, underlines the universal nature of a story where, even though some pakeha are sympathetic, clearly the struggle must be fought by the indigenous people themselves.

Te Rua germinated partly from an idea by the West Berlin state fund to invest in a film linking a Maori story with Berlin.* Disagreement over the final cut caused a rift in the long-time director/producer team of Barry Barclay and John O'Shea. Structurally the narrative is overloaded with incidents and characters. Rapid cross-cutting is used to keep all the stories alive, but often not enough detail is given, with the result that the point of many scenes is lost. Dramatically the ending is an anti-climax because we do not see the carvings being returned. The marae sequences are shot and choreographed in a stylised, theatrical manner contrasting well with the more conventional scenes. Most memorable is the film's raw emotional power.

Te Rua failed to find an audience during its New Zealand release and has not been screened in Germany. HM

1991 Wellington Fringe Festival Accolade: Maori Composition, Huirangi Waikerepuru.

Reference
* J. Dennis & J. Bieringa (eds). 1992. *Film in Aotearoa New Zealand*.

Maria Fitzi (Hanna) and Peter Kaa (Peter Huaka). Courtesy of the New Zealand Film Commission.

OLD SCORES

1991

Acid and his All Blacks pose for a team photo. Courtesy of South Pacific Pictures.

A South Pacific Pictures and HTV/CYMRU production in association with Park Avenue Advertising, The New Zealand Film Commission and Television New Zealand Ltd. © 1991. A New Zealand/Wales co-production. *Budget*: approx. $3 million. *Locations*: Cardiff Arms Park, Abercynon, Piha, Whangaparoa. *Distributor*: Endeavour Films. *Rating*: GA, September 1991. 35 mm (shot on 16 mm). Colour. 93 mins.

Director: Alan Clayton. *Producer*: Don Reynolds. *Associate producers*: Jo Johnson (N.Z.), Manny Wessels (Wales). *Screenplay*: Dean Parker, Greg McGee. *Director of photography*: Allen Guilford. *Camera operators*: Matthew Bowkett (N.Z.), James Daniels (Wales). *Editors*: Mike Horton, Jamie Selkirk (N.Z.). *Art directors*: Jennifer Ward (N.Z.), Paul Laugier (Wales). *Costume designers*: Christine West (N.Z.), Graham Meethod (Wales). *Rugby advisors*: Steve McDowell (N.Z.), John Welch (Wales). *Composer*: Wayne Warlow. *Sound*: Hammond Peek (N.Z.), Paul Gaydon (Wales).

Cast
John Bach (Ewen Murray), Tony Barry (Barry Brown), Roy Billing (Frank O'Riordan), Alison Bruce (Ngaire Morgan), Robert Bruce (Jock McBane), Terence Cooper (Eric Hogg), Windsor Davies (Evan Price), Dafydd Emyr (Owen Llewellyn), Howell Evans (Lloyd Thomas), John Francis (David Llewellyn), Peter Gwynne (Winston Macatamney), Glynn Houston (Aneurin Morgan), Stephanie Millar (Helen Chatfield), John Moreno (Referee), Beth Morris (Bronwen Llewellyn), Andrew Powell (Glyndwr), Robert Pugh (Bleddyn Morgan), Keith Quin, (Rugby commentary), Martyn Sanderson (Acid Aitken), Clayton Spence (Dai Morgan), Stephen Tozer (Jim Farquhar), Jack Walters (Clifford), Steve McDowell and Alan Trotter as themselves, Ian Kirkpatrick, Waka Nathan, Grahame Thorne, Alex Wyllie (All Blacks players), Phil Bennett, Gerald Davies, Mervyn Davies, Gareth Edwards, Tony Faulkner, Dennis Hughes, Barry John, Allan Martin, David Morris, Graham Price, Mike Roberts, J.J. Williams, Bobby Windsor (Welsh players).

A dying touch-judge confesses to engineering the 1966 Welsh rugby team's victory over the All Blacks by denying try-scorer Bleddyn Morgan stepped into touch. Welsh Rugby Union President Evan Price announces a re-match. Morgan, now settled in New Zealand, first refuses to return to Wales because, later scenes reveal, his relationship with Bronwen, his best friend David's fiancée, ended bitterly. The 1966 All Blacks who reluctantly re-assemble and begin training include a tubby, unfit Catholic priest (star halfback Frank O'Riordan), a drunk (captain Barry Brown), a vote-seeking politician married to Lady Macbeth (reserve Jim Farquhar) and a peace-loving Salvation Army officer (Ewen Murray, the 'monster of Cardiff'). Needling them along is corrosive 1966 coach Acid. Back in Wales Bleddyn, persuaded to play because 'Wales expects', learns he is the natural father of Bronwen's son, Owen, who is coaching the Welsh veterans. Jealous, David refuses to play the old winning combination with Bleddyn, but in the big match the Welsh, aided by David and Bleddyn's reconciliation, play a blinder. When O'Riordan finds his boot, a revitalised Brown replaces the hopeless Farquhar and Murray finds 'the monster within', the full-time score evens at 16-all, with Brown to take a conversion. Via Evan Price's dirty tricks the match ball has been replaced with Old Lucky, a winning Welsh ball. In flight Old Lucky splits, deflates and settles on the crossbar. Price announces a re-match.

With a disclaimer explaining the disputed try in the 1905 Wales/New Zealand game is a similarity only, this shaggy dog tale, shot as a telefeature for the United Kingdom and released theatrically in New Zealand, wonderfully satirises its two countries' national obsessions. The film takes no sides: as Acid would say, everyone cheats and sometimes you get found out. Said to caricature Fred Allen, the All Black coach known as 'The Needle', Acid embodies all that is nasty in the rugby ethic. Also satirised is the new style of rugby, hyped for maximum media profits.

The game's attractions are well caught in the stirring pre-match haka, the Welsh crowd's singing at hallowed Cardiff Arms Park and the mateship of the players and their coteries. The 'star-crossed lovers' sub-plot strengthens the structure by adding depth. Written by a former junior All Black (Greg McGee) and a sometime soccer player (Dean Parker) the dialogue is witty and shrewd. More grimly, the ephemerality of first class competition is all too evident in the condition of the greats a few years on, all of whom trained for their cameo film roles, some with painful consequences.

While actors reported feeling overawed 'playing rugby' with, and getting tips from, their heroes, the four former All Blacks and 13 Welsh rugby nationals, who have no lines, were said to be equally daunted to be working alongside professional actors. Ex-All Black Steve McDowell supervised training and fitness and helped choreograph the games. In this Welsh director Clayton was also advised by Cardiff's television sports director. For the first half of the big match the Welsh team was required to play a very taxing open running game while the 'All Blacks' had an easier time of it filming a more contained attack.

Old Scores was released in New Zealand just before the 1991 Rugby World Cup. HM

1991 Welsh Bafta: Best Drama.
1992 New Zealand Film Awards: Best Screenplay. Best Supporting Actor, John Bach, Roy Billing.

THE END OF THE GOLDEN WEATHER

1991

South Pacific Pictures in association with New Zealand On Air, Television New Zealand and the New Zealand Film Commission. © 1991. *Budget*: $3 million. *Locations*: Te Muri Beach (Mahurangi Peninsula), Takapuna Beach and Takapuna Grammar School (North Shore), Wenderholm. *Distributor*: Endeavour Films. *Rating*: GY, October 1991. 35 mm. Dolby Stereo. Colour. 104 mins.

Director: Ian Mune. *Producers*: Christina Milligan, Ian Mune. *Executive producer*: Don Reynolds. *Associate producer*: Dorthe Scheffmann. *Screenplay*: Ian Mune, Bruce Mason. *Source*: Bruce Mason, *The End of the Golden Weather: a voyage into a New Zealand childhood*. *Director of photography*: Alun Bollinger. *Camera operator*: John Mahaffie. *Editor*: Michael Horton. *Production designer*: Ron Highfield. *Costume designer*: Barbara Darragh. *Composer*: Stephen McCurdy. *Vocals*: Colleen Rae-Gerrard, David Chickering, Stanley Jackson, Christine Mori, Peter Scholes, Tony Benfell. *Sound*: Greg Bell, Dick Reade, John McKay, Phil Judd, Chris Burt, Ross Chambers.

Cast

Stephen Fulford (Geoff), Stephen Papps (Firpo), Paul Gittins (Dad), Gabrielle Hammond (Mum), David Taylor (Ted), Alexandra Marshall (Molly), Ray Henwood (Rev. Thirle), Alice Fraser (Mrs Atkinson), Bill Johnson (Mr Atkinson), Greg Johnson (Uncle Jim), Alison Bruce (Auntie Kass), Steve McDowell (Jesse Cabot), Alistair Douglas (Sergeant Robinson), Francie Gray (Miss Effie), Andrea Kelland (Miss Sybil), Andrew Binns (Joe Dyer), with Ross McKellar, Lucy Lawless, Kate Miles, Francis Bell, Tricia Phillips, Alistair Browning, David Telford, Christian Teutenberg, Shirley Duke, Robert Horwood, Georgina Monro, Tim Raby, Leila Ford, Melissa Copp, Henry Dewey, David Fitchew, Christine McLay, Nicholas Pegg, Blessing Ross, Dorothy Tomlinson, Lucy White, Peter Stevens, Angus Cooper, Geoff Ross, Bob Harvey, Robert Hammond, Steve Westlake, Paul Thompson, Fraser Harvey, Rupert Harvey.

New Zealand summer, 1935. Twelve year-old Geoff Crome, escaping from the chores at his beachside Te Parenga home, finds a dusty hut in the bush at the top of a long flight of steps and sees it as an ideal place to write his novel. On a later visit he finds his story burning on a fire and his hut occupied by a thin, wild-eyed man who calls himself Firpo. Despite vigorous opposition from his father and community disapproval Geoff's friendship with Firpo flourishes as trust is established. At home Geoff occupies himself and his brother Ted and sister Molly in preparing a play, in which he is to star as an old man transformed by love, to present to family and friends on Christmas day. The local young men, amused that Firpo fancies his prospects as an Olympic competitor and wanting to make fun of him, challenge him to a race on the beach. Geoff, enthused by Firpo's belief he will win, dedicates himself to helping him train. Watched by the community Firpo loses badly and is publicly humiliated. He goes berserk, wrecking the hut and accusing Geoff of laughing at him along with the others. He is taken away to an institution. Geoff apologises to his father for not listening to him and in a look Mr Crome acknowledges Geoff's strength and autonomy. Geoff steps out along the beach in the new school uniform that signals his passage from boyhood to adolescence.

In telling the story from Geoff's point of view the sound, cinematography, music, production design, narrative and characterisation sharply realise the magic and intensity of a middle-class 1930s New Zealand childhood. As the sensitive innocents, bruised and damaged by the intrusion of adult pettiness and tyranny, Firpo (based on a man from playwright Mason's childhood) and Geoff (based on Mason's childhood self) form a bond transcending their many differences. Geoff's rich fantasies and desire to write isolate him from others and in making the painful discovery that his frail and vulnerable friend is not the mythical Made Man of his dreams Geoff leaves the golden weather of his childhood behind. There is comedy in his heightened perceptions of a world where, to him, fantasy and reality merge. Particularly colourful are the Felliniesque characters who people his days when, with a little help from his imagination and a bit of faith, for Geoff miracles are possible. Firpo is the catalyst for Geoff's rite of passage and while he and Geoff are kindred souls his illness dictates that what he 'learns' from his treatment on losing the race is not, 'life is like that' but, 'Geoff is as bad as all the rest.'

Insight into social pressures of the times, as Geoff journeys to the beginnings of adult understanding and compromise, is clear in its delineation of sex-role expectations. Symbolism, particularly in the way the physicality of the beach, hut, houses and the elements are used to reflect Geoff's states of mind, is well integrated. The operatic, Germanic-style music, almost all electronic, powerfully underscores Geoff's emotional life. The narrative is shaped as the reminiscences of a man looking back on his boyhood which is seen not in naturalistic terms, but as a palette of dramatically heightened sensual experiences. But because the narrative is presented as a real-time story and the man is never present, some critics described the film on its release as overwrought and inflated. The performances, in particular that of Stephen Fulford as Geoff, are excellent.

Playwright Bruce Mason, who performed **The End of the Golden Weather** solo over 1000 times, based his stage play on the conservative, middle-class Takapuna of his childhood and described his story as being about 'the failure of romantic idealism'. Ian Mune approached Bruce Mason to film the story, and the script was completed 15 years after it was begun, some time after the death of Bruce Mason. Although Mason's play strongly featured the 1931–1933 Depression, Mune chose to leave it out and to focus on the Geoff and Firpo story. Scenes not in the original are added (for example, Geoff's dramatised fantasies) and others omitted (most notably the 1932 Queen Street riots) while keeping to the spirit of the original.

The film is dedicated to the memory of Bruce Mason. Celebrated by many in New Zealand as evocative and authentic, it drew large, enthusiastic audiences at home. HM

1991 Wellington Fringe Festival Accolade: Location Management, Sally Sherratt.

1992 Children's Film Festival Giffoni: Gold Medal. New Zealand Film Awards: Best Film. Best Director. Best Cinematography. Best Editing. Best Score. Best Male Performance, Stephen Papps. Best Costume Design. Best Production Design.

1993 Los Angeles Youth in Film Awards: Best Actor in a Non-American Film, Stephen Fulford. Best Director of a Foreign Family Film, Ian Mune.

David Taylor (Ted), Stephen Fulford (Geoff) and Alexandra Marshall (Molly). *Courtesy of the New Zealand Film Commission.*

1991

Chunuk Bair

Avalon/NFU Studios and Daybreak Pictures. © 1991. *Budget*: approx. $1 million. *Locations*: Wainuiomata, Wellington studio. *Distributor*: Hoyts. *Rating*: GA, October 1991. 35 mm. Dolby Stereo. Colour. 111 mins.

Director: Dale G. Bradley. *Producer*: L. Grant Bradley. *Executive producers*: David Arnell, L. Grant Bradley. *Screenplay*: Grant Hindin Miller. *Sources*: Maurice Shadbolt, *Once on Chunuk Bair* and Chris Pugsley, *Gallipoli, the New Zealand Story*. *Director of photography*: Warrick Attewell. *Editor*: Paul Sutorius. *Production designer*: Kevin Leonard-Jones. *Scenic artist*: Mike Travers. *Wardrobe supervisor*: Norman Forsey. *Historical advisor*: Chris Pugsley. *Special effects make-up*: Cliff Hughes. *Special effects*: Wayne Rugg, Major Ian Juno, Staff Sergeant Ian Evans. *Gun wrangler*: Stephen McManus. *Army co-ordinator*: Major Mark Wheeler. *Composer*: Stephen Bell-Booth. *Sound*: John Neill, Don Paulin, Michael Hedges.

Cast

Robert Powell (Frank), Kevin J. Wilson (Connolly), Jed Brophy (Fred), John Leigh (Porky), Murray Keane (Smiler), Danny Mulheron (Bassett), Richard Hanna (Harkness), Lewis Rowe (Johnston), Norman Forsey (Hamilton), Darryl Beattie (Scruffy), John Wraight (Mac), Peter Kaa (Otaki George), Stephen Ure (Holy), Tim Bray (Lofty), Donald Holder (Nobby), David Cole (Temperley), with James MacLaurin, Stephen Hollins, Andrew Laing, Jonathan Hendry, Keith Richardson, Neil Holt, Vlad Titov, Des Stephens, Kim Andrews, Geoff Dolan, Stewart Turner, Regiment Sergeant Major Des Ratima, Damian Peters, Chris Brougham, David Kettley, Tony Bertinshaw, Crispin Field, John Fitzgerald, Campbell Hey, Kerin Kelly, Tony Meinan, Nigel Peacock, Karl Urban.

Gallipoli, 1915. Volunteer New Zealand troops land on the Peninsula. After fighting the Turks at Quinn's Post, the Wellington regiment are exhausted and debilitated. The British, promising support, order them to launch an offensive against the Turks holding Chunuk Bair, the highest point on the peninsula, which is the gateway to the Dardanelles, regarded as the key to the campaign. Sergeant Major Frank South thinks the exercise is futile, but Colonel William Connolly sees it as a chance for New Zealand glory. The Wellingtons go it alone in charge after charge. On 8 August 1915 they take Chunuk Bair, holding it for a day. A British navy ship fires on the summit, killing Connolly. Of the 700 who began the campaign only 54 are left alive. Fresh New Zealand troops watch as Frank, having shot his mortally wounded brother, walks down the hill carrying a bent bayonet. On screen information says the Turks eventually repelled the British from Chunuk Bair and Connolly, never recognised as a hero, was the subject of controversy and blame.

Chunuk Bair follows historical records and the source stage play to claim for the campaign rite of passage for New Zealand from British colony to nationhood. Focus is on the conflicts between the British commanders, who are boozing caricatures of callousness and cowardice with no regard for the lives of the New Zealanders they command, and Connolly,[1] a career soldier who talks about 'the art of war' and dreams of New Zealand nationhood. These oppositions are muddied by South, a communist who has turned down a commission believing war is an imperialist conspiracy and whose mission is to look out for his kid brother. Common sense tells the soldiers death is inevitable, but they obediently and bravely charge into a battle, in part because they have been stirred to it by Connolly's exhortation, but also because, given the rules of war, they have no alternative. New Zealand's nationhood, interpreted as its independence from Britain, is shown to be built on her soldiers' sacrifice and on Britain's calumny.

While the film vividly depicts the futility of the Chunuk Bair campaign, in relegating the common soldiers to the background much of the source play's irony and black wit is lost, along with the bawdy jokes and raw language that give the play's characters authenticity and individuality. Porky, for example, has gone from being the play's sardonic, insightful Everyman to the film's occasional joker. Much of the shoot took place in a 20 m by 13 m studio and the sets and lighting give the action a theatrical look. More convincing are scenes shot on the Wainuiomata coast. The cast is small and the viewer must imagine the scale of the campaign from information supplied by dialogue and sound effects. The slow motion charges are effectively choreographed. HM

1991 Wellington Fringe Festival Accolade: First Assistant Director, Joe Nolan.

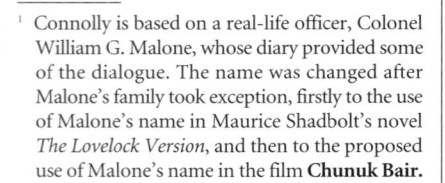

---

[1] Connolly is based on a real-life officer, Colonel William G. Malone, whose diary provided some of the dialogue. The name was changed after Malone's family took exception, firstly to the use of Malone's name in Maurice Shadbolt's novel *The Lovelock Version*, and then to the proposed use of Malone's name in the film **Chunuk Bair**.

Robert Powell (Sergeant Major Frank South) and Kevin J. Wilson (Colonel Connolly). Courtesy of the New Zealand Film Commission.

1991

GRAMPIRE

Noel Appleby (Ernie Noad) and Pat Evison (Leah). *Courtesy of the New Zealand Film Commission.*

Murray Newey and the Tucker Production Co. Ltd. in association with the New Zealand Film Commission. A.k.a. Moonrise. A.k.a. My Grandpa is a Vampire. © 1991. *Budget*: approx $2.3 million. *Locations*: Piha, Auckland. *Distributor*: Endeavour Films Ltd. *Rating*: GY, December 1991. 35 mm. Dolby Stereo. Colour. 94.5 mins.

Director: David Blyth. *Producer*: Murray Newey. *Associate producers*: Judith Trye, Brian Walden. *Screenplay*: Michael Heath from his radio play *Moonrise*. *Director of photography*: Kevin Hayward. *Camera operator*: Richard Bluck. *Editor*: David Huggett. *Production designer*: Kim Sinclair. *Costume designer*: Ngila Dickson. *Special effects*: Action Associates Ltd. *Special effects supervisor*: Kevin Chisnall. *Visual effects*: Digital Post Ltd, Zap Productions Ltd, Video Images Ltd, Optical and Graphic Ltd. *Stunt co-ordinators*: Peter Bell, Robert Bruce. *Music*: Jim Manzie, Pat Regan. *Additional music*: Matthew Brown. *Sound*: David Madigan, Gethin Creagh, John McKay.

Cast

Al Lewis (Cooger), Justin Gocke (Lonny), Milan Borich (Kanziora), Pat Evison (Leah), Noel Appleby (Ernie), David Weatherley (Sergeant Dicky Ticker), Sean Duffy (Derek), Sylvia Rands (Cheryl), Phoebe Falconer (Tammy), Chris McNair (Ben), Ian Watkin (Father Vincent), Beryl Te Wiata (District nurse), Alistair Douglas (Ghost train owner), Max Cryer (Compere), Rebekah Davies (Brigit), Louise Perry (Serena), Lyn Waldegrave (Polka-dot woman), Ann Morris (Betty Gutsell), Tina Grenville (Winona Ticker), Robert Bruce (Truck driver), Joel Tobeck (McDonald's cashier), Mark Sadgrove (Hamish McWhirter), Karl Burnett (Joe), Penelope Collins (Woman at carnival), Jim Scorrar (Cooger double).

Living with his middle-aged daughter Leah in a huge mansion by the sea, Vernon Cooger is a mischievous old man who, in spite of a weak heart, enjoys frightening people at a local funfair. His 12-year-old Californian grandson, Lonny, holidaying with his Kiwi relatives, is initially reluctant to go along with his friend Kanziora's theory that Grandpa Cooger is a vampire. When Grandpa dies of heart failure Lonny and Kenziora are left to mind the coffined body at the wake while Leah sneaks off for a rendezvous with repulsive lover Ernie. In response to the boys' keyboard playing Grandpa rises from the coffin and reveals himself to be an eighteenth century vampire. Kanziora hides him in the family shed. While he and the boys enjoy some night flying, Leah and Ernie plan to do him in by driving a stake through his heart. The chase climaxes at McDonald's where Leah regrets her unfilial behaviour and sends Ernie away. The local cop joins in the chase and Grampire turns in a dazzling performance at the funfair concert, literally bringing the house down. Leah and the boys take him home and in a ritualistic ceremony Grandpa goes to join his fellow undead. Saddened by his departure, the boys ponder the desirability of perpetual youth.

An affectionate, bloodless, Disney-esque romp bearing the message 'your imagination is more powerful than any movie', **Grampire** invites children to make up their own versions of popular stories while offering the viewer a reason for the liberties it takes with vampire myth conventions. Watered down as it is into a pantomime-style buddy movie, the vampire element offers an excuse for an old man and a couple of kids to do a little night flying, with the prospect of youthful joie-de-vivre as a healthy alternative to adult ennui. Grampire admits he's 'been a naughty boy' and, although Lonny and Kanziora do not want the adventure to end, they accept he has to join his own kind. In keeping with the need to woo a young audience all the adults except Grampire are bossy and self-centred.

With its inception as a radio play by Michael Heath, **Grampire** suffers in its screen version partly because the planned magic and special effects elements, intended to provide much of the film's interest, had to be modified because of lack of finance, although atmospheric lighting goes some way towards enhancing the other-worldly intent. The narrative is overloaded with explanatory dialogue, the plot lacks tension and the humour creaks.

Eighty-one-year-old Al Lewis, who grew his hair and fingernails for the role, gives a spirited performance. Although writer Michael Heath fought to retain New Zealand content, the attempt to increase the market by including American actors Lewis and Gocke gives the film a hybrid quality that dilutes local flavour, especially with the teenager's 'hip' act. HM

1991

Undercover

Gibson Group. Copyright date not recorded. Telefeature. *Location*: Wellington. *Video rating*: AO. Videotape. Colour. 90 mins.

Director: Yvonne Mackay. *Producer*: Dave Gibson. *Screenplay*: Arthur Baysting. *Director of photography*: Wayne Vinten. *Editor*: Mike Bennett. *Art director*: Matt Murphy. *Wardrobe supervisor*: Jodie Moller. *Music*: Sam Negri. *Vocal arranger*: Tony Backhouse. *Songs*: Baysting, Lake, Curtis, Ahipene, Tahu, Finau, Backhouse, Brendan Power, Luke Hurley, Sam Cooke, Circus Block Four, Back Door Blues Band, Beefhouse, Idles, Low Profile. *Sound*: Tony Johnson, Mike Hopkins, Simon Hughes.

Cast

William Brandt (Tony), Alistair Browning (Eddie), Jennifer Ludlam (Sandy), James Heyward (Robbo), Sylvia Rands (Nancy), Karen Holland (Treeza), Richard Mills (Preston), Cliff Curtis (Zip), with Hori Ahipene, Gerard Tahu, Mara Finau, Aaron Bold, Edward Campbell, Tina Regtien, John Wraight, Perry Piercy, Duncan Smith, Michelle Goulten, Kristen Gillespie, Harry Lavington, Peter McAllum, Graeme Tuckett, Lara Matheson, Wayne E. Lutton, Stelios Yiakmis, Christina Asher, Tony Loughran, Bill Humphries, Juliet Furness, Silvio Famularo, Tony Mosley, Richard Smith, Charles Hambling, Willie Clanachan, Ingrid Jensen, Yolanda Smythe, Keith Hambleton, David Cameron, Michaela Roony, Andrea Hobden, Dale Stephens, Judy Christian, Paul Nadas, Sandra McKay, Janet Fisher, Sima Urale, Murray Keane, Marc White, Sarah Major, Carol Clifton, Peter Kaa, Barry Wiki, Mike Woodley, Rachel Nash, Jed Brophy, Henry Vaeoso, Svon Mesarov, Du Kahu, Fred Twyford, Eteuati Ete, Gabe Giddens, Monique Van Resseghem.

Tony, a small town rookie cop, leaves his fiancée Nancy in Timaru to go undercover in Wellington. His assignment is to find the Mr Big in a heroin operation run by band manager Eddie and to learn how the drugs are shifted. In no time Tony is on good terms with Eddie's band, Zeroes, and lands himself a job in Eddie's club when barmaid Treeza, suffering from taking too many drugs, has to take a rest. Although Tony is beaten up by bikies early on his police superior, Robbo, reassures him his cover hasn't been blown. When Zeroes, jamming, are stuck for a line, and Tony offers one, he suddenly finds himself temporarily part of the band and Eddie's new mate. In scenes indicating that Tony likes his new lifestyle more than he should he helps Eddie's man Frog do a burglary then helps Eddie recover a heroin haul. Meanwhile he has moved in with ex-prostitute Sandy and her son Luke, who hopes to secure Tony as his stepfather. Learning that in his absence a mate has moved in with Nancy, Tony becomes involved with Sandy. Later he is told that Eddie is Luke's father. In Timaru on a gig Zeroes' lead singer Zip learns from Nancy that Tony is a narc. On hearing that Eddie beats Sandy up and goes looking for Tony. Treeza and Tony are taking Sandy to hospital when Treeza, wild that Tony is a narc, bails out of the van in the Wellington tunnel. At the hospital Sandy sends Tony away and he hears that Treeza has been run over and killed. Tony spikes Eddie's hamburger with LSD and the dealer falls in the sea and drowns. Through a telephone clue Tony traces Mr Big, who turns out to be a bigtime lawyer. Robbo's wife leaves him because he won't leave the drug squad and Tony resolves never to go undercover again. Sandy, Luke and Tony board a plane for Brisbane.

Undercover was inspired by the true-life story of Wayne Haussman, a Christchurch undercover cop convicted of drug trafficking after infiltrating a drug ring. Issues of police behaviour — how undercover cops lose their innocence and how cops on the beat lose crediblity when they treat people with disdain — are central to the narrative and of interest as a real social concern. Noir lighting, a handheld camera and a fluid shooting style create an atmosphere in keeping with the drug-trading genre and, unlike the unconvincing caricatures often appearing in this kind of television film, the characters are refreshingly ordinary and believable.

The chance to probe the psyches of the undercover cops and the robbers is missed. Tony and Eddie both gaze into mirrors as if searching for clues as to who they are and the shot superimposing their faces on different sides of a pane of glass baldly suggests good and evil easily merge, but that's as far as it goes. The narrative is standard fare, stretching suspension of disbelief with non sequiturs, coincidence and missed plot beats, most notably in Eddie's anti-climactic death and in the fact that the plot McGuffin, Mr Big, is never more than a name. There is an interesting variety of New Zealand music tracks, including the work of an a capella group formed especially for the film.

Undercover was produced as a pilot for a possible series but was not developed because TVNZ had made a commitment to the cop show **Shark in the Park**, also set in Wellington and because, in the words of TVNZ director of programming John McCready, 'there was nothing particularly indigenous about it.'* It screened on New Zealand television on 13 November 1991. HM

1993 New Zealand Film and Television Awards: Best Female Dramatic Performance in a Television Drama: Jennifer Ludlam. Best Television Drama.

Reference
* *New Zealand Herald*, 13 November 1991.

Jennifer Ludlam (Sandy) and Karen Holland (Treeza). Courtesy of the New Zealand Film Commission.

1992

BRAINDEAD

WingNut Films Ltd in association with the New Zealand Film Commission and Avalon/NFU Studios. A.k.a. Dead Alive. © 1992. *Locations*: Wellington, The Pinnacles. *Distributor*: John Maynard Productions. *Rating*: R16 (Content may offend), May 1992. 35 mm. Dolby Stereo. Colour. 105 mins. *U.S. release*: 89 mins.

Director: Peter Jackson. *Producer*: Jim Booth. *Associate producer*: Jamie Selkirk. *Screenplay*: Stephen Sinclair, Peter Jackson, Frances Walsh from an original idea by Stephen Sinclair. *Director of photography*: Murray Milne. *Camera operator*: Mark Olsen. *Editor*: Jamie Selkirk. *Production designer*: Kevin Leonard-Jones. *Costume designer*: Chris Elliott. *Make-up/wigs*: Debra East. *Creature and gore effects*: Richard Taylor. *Prosthetics design*: Bob McCarron. *Prosthetics/make-up supervisor*: Marjory Hamlin. *Special effects co-ordinator*: Steve Ingram. *Fight choreographer/stunts*: Damon DeBerry. *Stunt co-ordinator/stunts*: Peter Hassall. *Supervising puppeteer*: Ramon Aguilar. *Music*: performed and produced by Peter Dasent. *Composers*: Peter Dasent, Jane Lindsay, Fane Flaws, Stephen Hinderwell, Tony Backhouse, Arthur Wood, A. Amonau. *Vocals*: Kate Swadling, Tony Backhouse, the Maori Battalion. *Players*: Fane Flaws, John O'Connor, Jonathan Zwartz, Jim Lawrie. *Sound*: Mike Hedges, Sam Negri, Alex Paton, Tony Johnson, Beth Tredray.

Cast

Timothy Balme (Lionel), Diana Peñalver (Paquita), Elizabeth Moody (Mum), Ian Watkin (Uncle Les), Brenda Kendall (Nurse McTavish), Stuart Devenie (Father McGruder), Jed Brophy (Void), Elizabeth Brimilcombe (Zombie Mum), Stephen Papps (Zombie McGruder), Murray Keane (Scroat), with Glenis Levestam, Lewis Rowe, Elizabeth Mullane, Harry Sinclair, Davina Whitehouse, Silvio Fumularo, Brian Sergent, Tina Regtien, Bill Ralston, Tony Hopkins, Tony Hiles, Duncan Smith, Tich Rowney, Stephen Andrews, Nick Ward, Peter Jackson, Jim Booth, Kenny McFadden, Angelo Robinson, Johnny Chico, Fijian rugby club, James Grant, Michelle Turner, Sam Dallimore, Anna Cahill, Kate Jason-Smith, Frances Walsh, Norman Willerton, Robert Ericson, Morgan Rowe, Sean Hay, Vicki Walker, Chris Short, Jamie Selkirk, Brad Selkirk, Forrest J. Ackerman, Gim Bon, Sarah Davis, Anthony Donaldson, Jo Edgecombe, Mel Edgecombe, Melody French, Ken Hammon, Michael Helms, Mary O'Leary, Simon Perkins, Annie Prior, Vanessa Redmond, Chris Ryan, Tim Saywell, Paul Shannon, Belinda Todd.

Skull Island, Southwest Sumatra, 1957. Zoo official Stewart captures a rat-monkey and ignores warnings that evil spirits will get revenge. When the monkey attacks Stewart, his guides dismember him and ship the animal to Wellington Zoo. There timid Lionel, a man dominated by his emasculating, cleanliness-obsessed mother, meets Spanish Paquita. At the zoo Mum, spying on Lionel and Paquita, slips on a banana skin, lunges at the rat-monkey's cage and is bitten on the arm. That night Paquita and Lionel make love in Lionel's bedroom while, in hers, Mum's health deteriorates alarmingly. Entertaining 'society' next day, she begins to disintegrate. The party breaks up after Mr Matheson eats custard containing blood and pus from Mum's arm and Mum eats her own ear. Lionel, finding Mum devouring raw meat, promises to look after her. After eating Paquita's dog Mum dies, rising up again as a zombie. Lionel parks her in the cellar and persuades Nazi vet Heinrich to supply him with a tranquilliser, to be administered to Mum via nose injection. Matters escalate when Mum creates more zombies. Gross Uncle Les holds a party to celebrate blackmailing Lionel into handing over the house, but the zombies break out and in the ensuing blood fest Paquita and Lionel deal with the undead by liquefying them. Paquita feeds dismembered zombie parts into a blender. Lionel, aided by Paquita's grandmother's lucky talisman and having learned that his mother murdered his father, rampages with a motor mower. The last zombie to dispatch is Mum, even more grotesque than before. With the house alight in a purging fire Lionel and Paquita stroll away together.

Braindead is a brilliantly designed and executed comedy splatter, solemnly introduced by Queen Elizabeth, as is Jackson's **Bad Taste**. Parodic homage is paid to several films and great pleasure is shown in taking things, gross when they were conceived — the **Gremlins**' blender idea (the brand of Mum's blender is 'Gremlin'), the picnic in Monty Python's **Salad Days** — and winding them up. The key joke is that 1950s New Zealand — quiet, parochial, nice — is the setting for the mayhem. Wellington trams and a Kiwi Bacon van join other 1950s cultural icons, some turned to absurd use as Paquita fends off Uncle Les with a packet of Rinso, Uncle Les deals to a zombie with a garden gnome, and a blender and a lawnmower, symbols of domestic toil, are the implements for restoring 'normality'. On the soundtrack The Archers and Aunt Daisy provide ironic commentary. Middle-class taboos around table manners, sex and bodily emissions are defied again and again with gusto.

Oedipus drives the narrative as Mum, playing on Lionel's guilt (he has suppressed childhood knowledge of his father's murder), emasculates her son. To all appearances Mum Cosgrove is a pillar of respectable, upper middle-class society, but her zombie transformation manifests the murdering, sexually jealous, suffocating monster she really is. Lionel for a time becomes a 'parent' and, in caring for the zombies, grows up fast. His discovery of Mum's duplicity, through finding the family skeleton in the attic, encourages him to become a man. Images of birth abound, particularly in the visceral bloodbath sequences. Lionel 'gives birth' three times to a grotesque baby and in the final scene, when Mum, a massive creature all breasts, stomach and buttocks, sucks him back into her ghastly womb, Lionel births himself by hacking his way out with the lucky talisman. What Mum does for Motherhood gone awry, Uncle Les does for Manhood run amok. Believing himself to be a man with balls, and spending much time focused on his crotch, he can't understand why Paquita keeps kneeing him there. Paquita squeals a lot, but she's feisty and knows what she wants.

To bring its severed limbs, decapitated heads and decomposing bodies vividly to life, the large special effects unit used masses of maple syrup (for blood), pork fat, offal, latex, polyfoam and slime. Models make up many of the period street scenes. Humour comes in visual and verbal gags. The carnage at Uncle Les's party is the most absurd series of splatstick sequences, but, going on as long as it does, becomes repetitive. (This scene was shortened in the U.S. version.) Performances are excellent, with Peter Jackson's cameo as a crazed undertaker's assistant a highlight.

Although not without its detractors — *The Times* (13 March 1993) felt the director 'remains stuck with a schoolboy's coarse imagination' — **Braindead** received wide critical and popular acclaim (one reviewer called it 'a necrophiliac's wet dream'*). It was reported as one of the hottest films in the market at the 1992 Cannes Film Festival.

Braindead The Musical, co-written by Stephen Sinclair and Frances Walsh concurrently with the film script, was first staged in 1995. HM

1992 Wellington Fringe Festival: Creation of a New NZ Genre, Comedy Splatter, Peter Jackson. Rome Fantasy Film Festival, Rome: Best Actor, Best Special Effects.
International Cinema Fantastique Festival, Montreal: Grand Prix, Best Direction, Best Soundtrack.
1993 Avoriaz Film Festival: Grand Prize, Critics' Prize.
Oporto Fantastique: Best Film, Best Special Effects.
Sitges International Film Festival, Spain: Best Special Effects.
New Zealand Film and Television Awards: Best Film, Best Director, Best Male Performance, Tim Balme. Best Screenplay. Best Contribution to Design (Special Effects).

Reference
* *Film Threat* Issue 7, December 1992, p. 43.

***Diana Penalver (Paquita) and Timothy Balme (Lionel) in* Braindead.** *Courtesy of the New Zealand Film Commission.*

1992

CRUSH

Hibiscus Films in association with the New Zealand Film Commission, Avalon N.F.U. Studios and N.Z. On Air. © 1992. *Budget*: a little over $2 million. *Locations*: Rotorua, Auckland. *Distributor*: John Maynard Productions. *Rating*: RP13, June 1992. 35 mm. Dolby Stereo. Colour. 97.5 mins.

Director: Alison Maclean. *Producer*: Bridget Ikin. *Associate producer*: Trevor Haysom. *Screenplay*: Alison Maclean with Anne Kennedy. *Director of photography*: Dion Beebe. *Camera operator*: Ian Turtill. *Editor*: John Gilbert. *Production designer*: Meryl Cronin. *Costume designer*: Ngila Dickson. *Prosthetics*: Bob McCarron. *Composer*: Jean-Paul Sartre Experience. *Additional/orchestral music*: Antony Partos. *Players*: Russell Baillie, James Laing, Dave Mulcahy, Gary Sullivan, David Yetton, Greg Johnson, Guy Noble, Members of the Australian Opera and Ballet Orchestra. *Conductor*: Dobbs Franks. *Music consultant*: John Hopkins. *Sound*: Robert Allen, Greg Bell, Kit Rollings, Mike Hopkins, Ross Chambers, Michael Hedges, John Neill, John McKay.

Cast

Marcia Gay Harden (Lane), Donogh Rees (Christina), Caitlin Bossley (Angela), William Zappa (Colin), Pete Smith (Horse), Jon Brazier (Arthur), Geoffrey Southern (Patient), Shirley Wilson (Intensive care nurse), Denise Lyness, Jennifer Karehana (Physiotherapy nurses), David Stott (Stephen), Harata Solomon (Aunty Bet), Caroline De Lore (Colleen), Trish Howie (Stunt nurse), Phil McLachlan (Ward sister), Wayne McGoram (Nurse), Wayne Roberts (Physiotherapy patient), Alistair McConnell (Doctor), Terry Batchelor (Taxi driver), Martin Booker (Waiter).

Driving into Rotorua to interview has-been novelist Colin Iseman, critic/writer Christina is critically injured when the car, with her American friend Lane at the wheel, rolls on a bend. Leaving Christina crushed under the car, Lane appears at Colin's. His daughter Angela later visits Lane, who gives her a red velvet dress and invites her out that night. Lane repels two men and spends the night in Angela's bed. They visit Christina, who is hospitalised and in a coma, but seeing her badly injured they leave. Angela develops a crush on Lane, but Lane's sexual relationship with her father turns her infatuation to revulsion. Visiting brain-damaged Christina, Angela talks incessantly about Lane's treachery. Meanwhile Lane dismisses Colin's obsession with her. Colin, Lane and Angela stay at a lakeside bach and Christina appears on Angela's invitation. On a bush walk Angela and Colin leave the women together. Christina leaves her wheelchair and walks, encouraged by Lane who has asked for forgiveness. On a lookout, watched by Angela, Christina lurches towards Lane and pushes her over the railing, into the river many metres below.

Eating chicken, Christina asks Lane prophetically, 'Do you want my skin?' **Crush** is a psychological thriller about characters endeavouring, in the search for personal identity, to gain power over others. Unexpectedly the careless amorality of outsider Lane can't match Colin's lack of prescience, Angela's adolescent pique and Christina's fury. Ambiguity about sexuality is central and Angela's unformed sexual identity is open to influence. Rotorua, with its fragile earth crust, forms a visual metaphor for passions bubbling below the surface and for the less successful broader theme where Angela represents New Zealand's uncertain adolescence in the face of American sophistication and influence. The metaphor can also be taken to indicate that pressure is rupturing New Zealanders' puritanism. Images of New Zealanders asserting a unique identity on television (a Maori concert party, a pre-match haka) and in the efforts of the pakeha hospital therapist expounding the spirituality of Maoritanga are playfully undercut: Lane expertly swings the pois and Maori singer Horse focuses attention on the corporeal pleasures of sex, drugs and rock and roll.

Aided by a suggestive soundtrack (from New Zealand band JPS Experience) the tone, like Maclean's acclaimed short film **Kitchen Sink**, has a dark fairytale quality (Angela stuffing Lane's hair down a plughole reverses the catalytic opening sequence in **Kitchen Sink**) with Lane as the bad fairy undone. The women's red and black clothing indicates relationship links. Alienation is shown in many shots of characters alone and diminished in the frame and uncertainty about identity recurs in mirror shots.

There are credibility problems, especially with Lane's apparently motiveless abandonment of Christina. Melodrama as Christina begins to recover threatens to dominate and the narrative style of withholding information distances the viewer. Intense emotional entanglements are based on short acquaintance and the characters exist in a vacuum. Excellent performances from the actors ensure none of the characters are particularly likeable.

Alison Maclean's work on the script and the film's direction was aided by her participation in a Sundance Institute workshop. HM

Marcia Gay Harden (Lane). Courtesy of the New Zealand Film Commission.

1992 Cannes Film Festival: Official Selection in Competition.
1993 Wellington Fringe Festival Accolades: Superior Film Colour-Grading, Lynne Seaman.
New Zealand Film and Television Awards: Best Female Dramatic Performance, Caitlin Bossley. Best Female Supporting Performance, Donogh Rees. Best Soundtrack. Best Film Score.

1992
THE FOOTSTEP MAN

Steven Grives (Sam) and Jennifer Ward-Lealand (Mireille). Courtesy of the New Zealand Film Commission.

John Maynard Productions Ltd in association with the New Zealand Film Commission, Avalon N.F.U. and N.Z. On Air. © 1992. *Budget*: $2.5 million. *Locations*: Waipa River, Auckland. *Distributor*: John Maynard Productions. *Rating*: GA, June 1992. 35 mm. Dolby Stereo. Colour. 88.5 mins.

Director: Leon Narbey. *Producer*: John Maynard. *Associate producer*: Trevor Haysom. *Avalon/N.F.U. Studios production executive*: Sue Thompson. *Screenplay*: Leon Narbey, Martin Edmond. *Director of photography*: Allen Guilford. *Projection consultant*: Doug Harley. *Underwater camera:* Sigmund Spath. *Production designer*: Kai Hawkins. *Artists*: Ross Ritchie, Kate Lang. *Costume designer*: Barbara Darragh. *Editor*: David Coulson. *Composer*: Jan Preston. *Sound*: Kit Rollings, David Madigan, Robert Allen, Gethin Creagh, Don Paulin, Paul Sutorius, John Dennison, John McKay. *Foley recordist*: Helen Luttrell. *Sound supervisor/footstep recordist*: John Neill. *Footstep artist*: Carolyn Lambourn.

Cast
Steven Grives (Sam), Jennifer Ward-Lealand (Mireille), Michael Hurst (Henri de Toulouse-Lautrec/Barman), Sarah Smuts-Kennedy (Marcelle), Rosey Jones (Vida), Jorge Quevedo (Ricardo), Peter Dennett (Jake), John Ross (Cab driver), Harry Sinclair (Sescau), Geoff Snell (Maurice), Frances Edmond (Asst Madame), Glenis Levestam (Madame), Peta Rutter (Lucie), Johnny Bond (Doctor), John Parker (Policeman), Leanne Dore, Caroline Lowry, Genevieve McClean, Leah Seresin, Maggie Tarver, Dee Wernham, Sarah Wilson (Prostitutes), Grant McFarland (Terry), Mike Maher (Client), Jessica Maynard (Kirsty), Irene Malone (Nun), Camille Rosenfeldt (Sick woman), Andrew Couling (Soldier), Marque Kolack (Thin man), Kazuyuki Sugawara (Japanese guard), Norelle Scott (voice of Lyndi), Sean Condon (voice of Rory), Adrienne Scott-Kemp (voice of Kirsty).

Foley artist Sam works on a feature film about nineteenth century painter Henri Toulouse-Lautrec and his lover/model, prostitute Mireille. Writer/director Vida's script ends the film with Mireille finding she has syphilis, leaving Henri and her lover Marcelle and drowning herself in the Seine. Sam, recovering from a nervous breakdown and a suicide attempt after his wife left him, agonises over Mireille's fate, dreaming she makes love with him at night. He begins to see her as real. Vida's lover Lyndi asks her to change her film's ending, supporting Sam's plea to let Mireille live. Sam tells Vida about his attempted suicide and his decision to change his mind when he found in his daughter a reason to live. Vida tells Sam of her sister's suicide and her inability to come to terms with it. They make love on the beach. Vida recuts the film with an upbeat ending and Sam plans to visit his daughter in Dublin.

The film-within-the-film, using autobiographical details from Toulouse-Lautrec's life, enriches themes in the principal film. In Vida's original version the painter offers Mireille a kind of love but, in denying financial support, thwarts her plans for a better life. In this he is little better than the doctor who, examining prostitutes for syphilis, treats them like rotten meat. In parallel with Toulouse-Lautrec, Sam's obsession for his work has come before concern for his family. Through the intensity of his feeling for illusory screen character Mireille he learns about passion and commitment and is fired to persuade Vida, also vulnerable, to change her film's ending, thus beginning the healing process for both of them. **The Footstep Man** also highlights the transformative process by which art, in this case film-making and painting, is an 'illusion' made from life's raw materials. The notion of multiple identities deepens the illusion/reality theme.

Leon Narbey's fascination with Toulouse-Lautrec led him to recreate some of the paintings and their execution. Fascination with the work of footsteppers, or foley artists, who recreate sound effects for actions in a film, led to a film about the film-making process. With analogue sound recording on the way out and digital recording on the way in, Narbey's film is 'a homage to sprocket technology.'[*] Video technology is also shown as it is used in postproduction.

Excellent production design richly evokes the opulence of nineteenth century French brothels and salons, with Allen Guilford's lighting design based on the work of Degas. The bleakness of the street and hospital scenes is reflected in blue tones and Sam's blue studio echoes the drowning metaphor depicting his emotional state. The modern sequences are shot in realistic style while Sam's dreams are surrealistic.

Vida's producer was one of several characters written out when the script was reduced, for reasons of budget, by 20 minutes. This altered the original structure of **The Footstep Man**, leaving credibility gaps.
HM

1992 San Sebastian Film Festival, Spain: Official Selection.
1993 New Zealand Film and Television Awards: Best Cinematography. Best Editing.
Fantasporto International Film Festival: Official Selection. Wellington Fringe Festival: Superior Film Colour-Grading, Lynne Seaman.

Reference
[*] B. Cairns & H. Martin. 1994. *Shadows on the Wall: a study of seven New Zealand feature films*, p. 288.

1992

ALEX

Isambard Productions and Total Film in association with the New Zealand Film Commission, N.Z. On Air and Australian Film Finance Corporation Pty Ltd. © 1992. A New Zealand/Australia co-production. *Budget*: a little over $2 million. *Location*: Auckland. *Distributor*: Everard Films. *Rating*: G, December 1992. 35 mm. Colour. 94 mins.

Director: Megan Simpson. *Producers*: Tom Parkinson, Philip Gerlach. *Associate producer*: Alan Withrington. *Screenplay*: Ken Catran. *Source*: Tessa Duder, *Alex*. *Director of photography*: Donald Duncan. *Camera operator*: Neil Taylor. *Editor*: Tony Kavanagh. *Production designer*: Kim Sinclair. *Costume designer*: Sara Beale. *Swimming consultant*: Sandra Blewitt M.B.E. *Swimming coaches*: Jack Lyons, Dean Greenwood. *Original music*: Todd Hunter. *Additional music*: Johanna Pigott. *Sound*: David Madigan, Ashley Grenville, Helen Brown, Phil Heywood, Martin Oswin.

Cast

Lauren Jackson (Alex), Chris Haywood (Mr Jack), Josh Picker (Andy), Catherine Godbold (Maggie), Elizabeth Hawthorn (Mrs Benton), Bruce Phillips (Mr Archer), May Lloyd (Mrs Archer), Patrick Smith (Mr Benton), Grant Tilly (Cyril Upjohn), Rima Te Wiata (Female commentator), Mark Wright (Male commentator), Alison Bruce (Female journalist), Vicky Burrett (Gran), Kim Hanson (Julia), with Leon Woods, Gavin Endicott, Jaclyn Druitt, Christine Bartlett, Gilbert Goldie, Joy Watson, Susannah Devereux, John Summer, Nigel Harbrow, Teresa Woodham, David Stott, Tony Groser, John Mellor, Susan Story, Anne Hunter, Dana Purkis, Jan Saussey, Greg Johnson, Paul Benseman, Ketzal Stirling, Stuart Anderson, Eli Barkaway, Kirstie O'Sullivan, Alison Selman, Margot Hodgson, Kirsten Reade, Kathryn McKenzie, Stacey Bodger, Janine Service, Gaye Harman, Althea Tollemache, Michael Shirley, Kevin Goldsby, Jacqui Huitema, Natalie Hine, Kelly Wilson, Stephen Anderton.

Alex, a 15-year-old hoping to gain selection to swim the 110 yards freestyle in the 1960 Rome Olympics, meets a rival in new student Maggie Benton. Always busy, Alex takes piano and ballet lessons, plays hockey and has a part in the school musical. At Maggie's dance Alex hears girls ridiculing her height and build, but new boyfriend Andy assures her he likes tall girls. Playing hockey, a rival breaks Alex's leg with a well-aimed shot. Andy encourages her to will herself to recover but, back in the water, Alex is beaten by Maggie. After an argument with her coach Mr Jack, Alex decides to give up swimming. Saintly Andy persuades her to keep her faith in herself and they declare their love for each other. That night Mr Jack devises an exciting new training routine based on ballet techniques. Back home Alex learns Andy has been killed by a drunken driver. She gives up her other activities and returns to training. In spite of the machinations of Maggie Benton's mother and a spiteful swimming official Alex swims the Olympic selection race and, admitting to herself she has been unable to accept Andy's death, she swims a great race and wins.

Alex is a feelgood kidult movie designed to inspire the teenage girls in its target audience. It begins and ends with Alex telling the viewer in voice-over she has always known that in another life she was, or will be, a dolphin. But rather than taking the motivational lead from there, the rest of the film depicts a girl driven not by love of the water, but by ambition.

In the film's single focus the novel's depths and subtleties are lost. Conflicts arise in the shape of characters out to thwart Alex (sly Mrs Benton, nasty sports administrator Cyril Upjohn, a vicious hockey opponent and the partisan reporter), but all are paper tigers and can offer no real competition against Alex's superior talent and virtue. In support her grandmother offers platitudes like 'You're as good as them, dear.' Also problematic is that Alex, although played with natural grace by Lauren Jackson, is not particularly likeable. Some attempts are made to gain sympathy for her, but the focus is on her petulant, self-obsessed over-achieving and little time is taken to establish her as a whole person. Opportunities to develop her character as she relates to Maggie are lost — the only time she really warms up is when she beats Maggie and wins a place in the Olympic team. The role of Alex's friend Julia, intended to support the information that in the 1950s girls had to fight to break out of sex-role expectations, is unsubtle and overstated.

Alex looks like a telefeature (it was first released on Australian television), but the swimming scenes are well shot, with excellent underwater photography evoking the tension and excitement of match racing. Australian input includes that of the director, the editor, a co-producer (Philip Gerlach), several of the actors and postproduction. The film is dedicated to the memory of Alexander Clare Duder, 1968–1992. HM

1993 New Zealand Film and Television Awards: Best Male Performance in a Supporting Role, Josh Picker.

Lauren Jackson (Alex Archer). Courtesy of the New Zealand Film Commission.

1993

ABSENT WITHOUT LEAVE

Meridian Film Productions and the New Zealand Film Commission in association with Avalon/N.F.U. Studios and N.Z. On Air. © 1992. *Budget*: $2.3 million. *Locations*: Wellington, Wairarapa. *Distributor*: Everard Films Ltd. *Rating*: GY, February 1993. 35 mm. Colour. 106 mins. (Re-cut version 101 mins, March 1993.)

Director: John Laing. *Producer*: Robin Laing. *Screenplay*: James Edwards with Graeme Tetley. *Director of photography*: Allen Guilford. *Camera operator*: Richard Bluck. *Editor*: Paul Sutorius. *Production designer*: Rick Kofoed. *Costume designer*: Glenis Foster. *Military advisor*: Chris Pugsley. *Composers*: Don McGlashan, David Long, Mark Austin. *Vocals*: Don McGlashan, Janet Roddick. *Players*: David Long, David Donaldson, Don McGlashan, Neill Duncan, Paul Kentell, James Edwards. *Sound*: Ken Saville, Kit Rollings, Don Paulin, Gethin Creagh, Stephen Murphy, John Neill.

Cast

Craig McLachlan (Ed), Katrina Hobbs (Daisy), Tony Barry (Peter), Judie Douglass (Ella), Robyn Malcolm (Betty), David Copeland (Claude), Ken Blackburn (C.O.), Desmond Kelly (Daisy's father), Tony Noorts, Andre Lavelle, Frank Simkin, Bill Dick (Dance band), with Chloe Laing, Danny Mulheron, Tina Cleary, Joan Foster, Margaret Blay, Robert Bennett, Stephen Lovatt, Rebecca Hobbs, Chris Brougham, Jed Brophy, Murray Keane, Cameron Rhodes, Lewis Rowe, Francis Bell, Tony Burton, Matthew Sunderland, Michael Haigh, Stephen Hall, Kevin Woodill, Mark Hadlow, Grant Edgar, Patrick Smyth, David Copeland, Clinton Ulyatt, Lewis Martin, Barry Sivern, Keith Richardson, Brian Sergent, Tina Regtien, John Wraight, William Kircher, Peter Hambleton, Robert Roos, Tandi Wright, Tim Gordon, Don Langridge, Ross Jolly, David Yerex, Paul Shannon, Mark Spratt, Michael Haigh, David McKenzie, Stephen Gledhill, Helen Moulder, Robert Bennett, Turei Reedy.

1942. Sixteen-year-old Daisy falls pregnant and lover Ed marries her in what looks like an act of duty. Called up to the army, Ed is training in the Medical Corps near Wellington when Daisy miscarries. After six weeks in the army Ed learns from a sadistic corporal his unit is to be sent overseas with no final leave. Believing Daisy incapable of taking care of herself, Ed goes AWOL, planning to take her to Auckland to live with her father. With no money they begin hitchhiking up north. There are few cars on the road but they are eventually picked up by a farming couple, Ella and Peter Wilson. Offered work on the farm they stay happily for some time, leaving when the local cop warns Ed the army is looking for him. Daisy phones home and learns her father has died. Ed gives himself up and is sentenced to 60 days in prison. Daisy moves into a flat and Ed, jealous that American servicemen are in town, persuades the C.O. to let him have time alone with her. They make love. The C.O. demands payment in the form of Ed spying on the other prisoners. When Ed refuses his visiting rights are cancelled. Discharged from prison, he causes a scene in the tea shop where Daisy works when he sees an American flirting with her. Walking the streets he is told his unit had never been posted overseas. Back at Daisy's he finally finds words to express his frustration and loneliness and tells Daisy he loves her. Reconciled, she tells him she is pregnant.

The film, based on a true story that came to director John Laing's attention when he heard Jim Edwards recounting it on New Zealand radio, explores the implications of war as a young couple learn the hard way about trust, responsibility and love. The period's sex role divisions are evoked in behaviour and expectations and Daisy's resolution to defy convention and act independently is a focal point. The dominant symbol of the couple's journey from naiveté to wisdom is the road, while the musical motif of the first bar of 'Keep the Home Fires Burning' is an insistent reminder of Daisy's refusal to be a conventional wife and do as she's told.

Good casting and performances bring the story to life and the meticulous period production design is first class. There are problems with pace as initially the episodic narrative lacks tension and a sense of urgency is not created until Ed is imprisoned. HM

1993 Wellington Fringe Festival: Excellence in Props Buying and Set Dressing, Kirsty Clayton. Superior Film Colour-Grading, Lynne Seaman. New Zealand Film and Television Awards: Best Design.

Craig McLachlan (Ed) is reprimanded. Courtesy of the New Zealand Film Commission.

1993

DESPERATE REMEDIES

James Wallace Productions Ltd in association with the New Zealand Film Commission, N.Z. On Air and Avalon N.F.U. Studios. © 1993. *Budget*: $2 136 000. *Location*: Auckland. *Distributor*: Footprint Films. *Rating*: RP16, June 1993. 35 mm. Dolby Stereo. Colour. 94.5 mins.

Directors: Stewart Main and Peter Wells. *Producer*: James Wallace. *Associate producer*: Trishia Downie. *Screenplay*: Peter Wells, Stewart Main. *Director of photography*: Leon Narbey. *Camera operator*: John Day. *Editor*: David Coulson. *Production designer*: Michael Kane. *Costume designer*: Glenis Foster. *Make-up/hair*: Abby Collins, Dominie Till. *Special effects*: Jason Docherty. *Composer/music director*: Peter Scholes. *Concertmaster*: Brecon Carter. *Players*: Auckland Philharmonia Orchestra. *Sound*: Kit Rollings, Don Paulin, Graham Morris, John Neill, Michael Hedges, Mike Hopkins.

Cast

Jennifer Ward-Lealand (Dorothea Brook), Kevin Smith (Lawrence Hayes), Lisa Chappell (Anne Cooper), Cliff Curtis (Fraser), Michael Hurst (William Poyser), Kiri Mills (Rose), Bridget Armstrong (Mary Anne), Timothy Raby (Mr Weedle), Helen Steemson (Gnits), Geeling Ching (Su Lim), Irene Malone (Bar singer), Kate Bartlett, Johnny Bond, Ann Cockroft, Maya Dalziel, Alison du Fresne, Tony Gallagher, Richard Hanna, Bruce Hopkins, Ian Hughes, Murray Keane, Irene Malone, Andrew Kovacevich, Pete Mason, Buzz Moller, Mathew Sunderland, Peter Tait, Annaliese Patten-Williams (Chorus), Dorothy Piripi, Sam Williams, Gordon Hatfield, Michael Kem, Thomas Tina, Jack Chong, Amon Nikora, Dan Fantl, Lauren Morcom, Rua Acorn, Dominico Mosca, Sean Marshall, Jacki Sims, Amber Harris, Ella Mizrahi, Sam Smith, Rachael Main, Martyn Sanderson (Maori warriors and townspeople).

1860s. In a frontier Dickensian town called Hope in a far-flung colony of the Empire, beautiful Dorothea Brook, Draper of Distinction, offers money and land to sulkily handsome new immigrant Lawrence Hayes in return for an undisclosed favour. Lawrence, entranced by Dorothea and thinking she is offering herself, pursues the matter to learn Dorothea wishes him to marry her sister Rose and dispose of Rose's lover. Unknown to Lawrence, Rose is addicted to opium, sex-obsessed and pregnant to dastardly Fraser, a dandified blackguard who is blackmailing Dorothea. While the hoi polloi get on with their steamy debauchery at the seedy end of town, heavily-in-debt oily politician/profiteer William Poyser suggests he and Dorothea enter a business arrangement whereby he helps her sell serge for uniforms needed for an imminent war, at the same time proposing a marriage of convenience. Thinking it will provide them with a cover, Dorothea's lover Anne urges her to accept William's proposal. Dorothea offers Lawrence rubies to get Fraser on a boat bound for San Francisco but Lawrence, smitten with Dorothea and sure that desperate remedies are required, wants to dispose of Fraser by killing him. Fraser confronts Dorothea. Lawrence, hiding behind a curtain, learns the pair were formerly lovers and Fraser, who still lusts after Dorothea, is blackmailing her with his knowledge she was once pregnant to him. Fraser sails away. Rose marries Lawrence and goes north. Two years later Dorothea, by now married to William, learns Rose has died of typhoid. Fraser arrives to claim Dorothea and the rubies and is shot by Anne. In the scandal that follows, and as soldiers going to war are farewelled, Lawrence reappears looking for Dorothea and sees her in Anne's arms. Dorothea tells him her heart has made its choice.

Desperate Remedies is a superbly rich, no-holds-barred costume melodrama, operatic in style and farcical in narrative, with a setting entirely fictional apart from references to other dramas and to notions of how things were in the nineteenth century. (Dorothea Brook takes her name from George Eliot's *Middlemarch* and the film's title is taken from Thomas Hardy's first published novel.)

Because the complex web of relationships is revealed only gradually, the narrative sustains tension by drip-feeding information. Tackling the notion of love-as-commodity the story is a mystery, shot through with heart motifs to deliver the melodramatic message that although 'we are all strangers in this land of love' those who find happiness negotiate their way through subterfuge, deceit and sexual power-play by following their hearts. Not that everyone can win, as lovelorn Lawrence learns — Anne's victory over him in winning Dorothea's heart is the film's most triumphant, unexpected subversion. Sex-as-animal-act is also celebrated in images aligning sex and meat and in sex scenes featuring people copulating in various gender and positional combinations. In revealing the real passions beating away beneath the carefully structured surfaces, the appearance/reality theme is highlighted in images of disguise and in images of eyes and looking.

Shot entirely in an Auckland wharfside warehouse, **Desperate Remedies** evokes a richly wrought psychological landscape of societal entrapment from which the two women fight to break free. Their agitation is shown in the film's fast pace and in constant images of movement. Opulence in the production design includes dramatic use of light and shadow, gorgeous, increasingly bizarre costumes and vivid co-ordination of colour, texture and pattern. The camera finds strikingly odd angles and at times moves frantically as though taking part in the action. Tightly composed shots deny the wide view and focus on the significance of details in the frame, creating a sense of claustrophobia. The almost continuous music, the rich vein of humour and the performance style are straight from the conventions of melodrama. Much wit is contained in tongue-in-cheek, mock-Victorian dialogue ('there's a plague of Australians in town') and the exuberant performances.
HM

1993 Cannes Film Festival: Official Selection, Un Certain Regard.
Sitges International Film Festival: Best Actress, Jennifer Ward-Lealand. Kiev International Film Festival: Best Film, Best Design.
Wellington Fringe Festival: Superior Film Colour-Grading, Lynne Seaman.
1994 Torino Lesbian and Gay Film Festival: Audience Feature Film Prize.
New Zealand Film and Television Awards: Best Cinematography, Best Design. Best Costume Design. Best Male Performance in a Supporting Role, Cliff Curtis. Asia Pacific Film Festival: Best Directors. Best Art Direction.

Cliff Curtis (Fraser) and Kevin Smith (Lawrence Hayes) with Jennifer Ward-Lealand (Dorothea Brook) in **Desperate Remedies.** *Courtesy of the New Zealand Film Commission.*

1993

BREAD AND ROSES

Preston*Laing, in association with N.Z. On Air, Television New Zealand and the 1993 Suffrage Centennial Year Trust with the financial participation of the New Zealand Film Commission. © 1993. Television series/feature film. *Budget*: approx. $3 million. *Location*: Wellington. *Distributor*: Preston*Laing Productions. *Rating*: GY, July 1993. *Television rating*: AO. 16 mm. Colour. 195 mins and 4 × 52 mins.

Director: Gaylene Preston. *Producer*: Robin Laing. *Executive producer*: Dorothee Pinfold. *Associate producer*: Gaylene Preston. *Screenplay*: Graeme Tetley, Gaylene Preston. *Source*: Sonja Davies, *Bread and Roses: Sonja Davies, her story*. *Director of photography*: Allen Guilford. *Camera operators*: Alun Bollinger, Leon Narbey. *Editor*: Paul Sutorius. *Production designer*: Rick Kofoed. *Costume designer*: Chris Elliot. *Researcher*: Cheryl Cameron. *Music*: John Charles. *Vocals*: Lisa Schouw. *Players*: John Charles, Geoff Hughes, Nik Brown, Paul Dyne, Roger Sellars, Gary Stratton, Barry Saunders, Callie Blood. *Sound*: Tony Johnson, Gethin Creagh, Kit Rollings, Don Paulin, John Boswell.

Cast

Genevieve Picot (Sonja), Mick Rose (Charlie), Donna Akersten (Mrs Mackersey), Raymond Hawthorne (Mr Mackersey), Tina Regtien (Con), Erik Thomson (Red), Theresa Healey (Peggy), Frances Kewene (Maisie), Emily Perkins (Joan), Larissa Matheson (Dot), Joanna Briant (Barbara), William Walker (Wally), Katherine McRae (Syd), Janet Fisher (Ruth Page), Sarah Cathie (young Penny), Emma Hazlewood (12 year-old Penny), Mandy McMullin (Lyn), Joanne Mildenhall (Anne), William Kircher (Stan Whitehead), Kathryn Rawlings (Les Bennett), with Doug Aston, Bub Bridger, Judie Douglass, Meredith Parkin, Beryl Te Wiata, Annie Ruth, Alix Bushnell, Miranda Harcourt, Tina Cleary, Jonathan Hendry, Cameron Rhodes, Grant Ryan, John Laing, Matthew Chamberlain, Alan Skates, Richard Hanna, Tandi Wright, Barbara Laurenson, Ann Pacey, Emma Robinson, Merophie Carr, Susan Brady, Abbie Ralston, Kate Elliot, Emily Turner, Bronwyn Bradley, Perry Piercy, Ingrid Prosser, Lillian Enting.

Based on Sonja Davies's autobiography **Bread and Roses**, the film, made as a four-part television series and also screened theatrically in New Zealand and Australia, covers her early years up until the beginning of her political career proper with her election onto the Nelson Hospital Board in 1956. Born illegitimate in 1923, Sonja first lives with her grandparents then with her mother and stepfather. Unconvinced by her middle-class mother's view that 'the unemployed are lazy and don't want to work', Sonja's empathy is with the working-class. As a teenager she becomes involved in left wing politics. When her mother vets her sixteenth birthday party guest list to keep out the working-class, Sonja leaves home and makes a hasty and short-lived marriage. She goes nursing, continuing to develop political ideas through association with her conscientious objector friends. Her 'understanding' with Charlie Davies, a left-winger serving in the army corps as a non-combatant, ends when she becomes passionately involved with American soldier Red Brinsen. At the end of Episode One, Sonja confides in her friend Con she is pregnant. In Episode Two the focus shifts to Sonja's personal experiences of injustice. She is threatened with expulsion from the nursing profession when she inquires about establishing a nurses' union and her mother refuses support in her pregnancy. At first Red sends money, but the payments inexplicably cease. The tuberculosis Sonja contracted nursing becomes serious and, after finding a minder for her daughter Penny, she goes to hospital. For much of Episode Three Sonja is critically ill, but although news of Red's death further lowers her spirits she fights back. Released from hospital she retrieves Penny and marries Charlie Davies. Finally, thanks to a new drug, she is cured. Episode Four sees Sonja on her way as an active participant in political life. Her efforts to gain nomination for office within the Nelson Labour Party are opposed, largely by men who think she should be at home. She becomes the spokesperson for women trying by a campaign of civil disobedience to prevent the closure of the Nelson railway line and as a result is elected Deputy Chairman (sic) of the Nelson Hospital Board.

Sonja Davies takes her autobiography's title from James Oppenheim's poem celebrating a spontaneous walkout in Massachusetts in 1912 staged by 20 000 mill workers protesting cuts in working hours of women and minors. The women's banners declared 'We want bread and roses too'. Davies charts her growth from ingénue to shrewd politician and describes, without self-promotion, a life committed to peace issues and to improving living and working conditions, particularly those of women.

Rather than cover her whole career sketchily the Preston*Laing production, with Sonja in every scene, distils the formative events shaping the young woman's developing political consciousness. An opening shot of Sonja's great-grandmother reading her palm and predicting a lifetime of joy and sorrow points to the sense of destiny running through the narrative that is reinforced by repeated hand imagery. Growing up in a class conscious, sexist society, Sonja's personal experiences and observations of the experiences of others lead her to develop early a strong socialist and feminist sensibility as, with no role models to guide her and no sense of belonging, she learns to rely on her own resources. Along with many joyful, life-enhancing experiences Sonja suffers much sorrow and fear through separation, loneliness, loss, chronic illness and brushes with death.

As both evocation and documentation, **Bread and Roses** pays tribute to a remarkable New Zealand woman without sanctifying her. Her bluntness often looks like tactlessness, she is impatient with opposing views and, as her political career snowballs, her daughter Penny often waves for attention from the sideline. **Bread and Roses** is equally fascinating as a social history. The sexual politics of the times, along with issues of class and privilege, politics and power, are woven into the narrative with a lightness of touch avoiding didacticism. In realising the spirit of the times, the production design, music, cinematography and sound design work towards authenticity while preserving good storytelling as the primary concern.

In the demanding lead role, Australian Genevieve Picot is excellent. Her performance was described by Sonja Davies as 'wonderfully accurate'. **Bread and Roses**, made as a Suffrage Year tribute to the women of New Zealand, received enthusiastic reviews and popular acclaim, with more than one reviewer describing it as a masterpiece. The series screened on New Zealand television in four episodes between 3 October 1993 and 24 October 1993. HM

1993 Wellington Fringe Festival: Excellence in Props Buying and Set Dressing, Kirsty Clayton. Creative Flair and Strong People Skills in Casting and Management, Di Oliver. Superior Film Colour-Grading, Lynne Seaman.
1994 New Zealand Film and Television Awards: Best Female Performance in a Dramatic Role, (awarded in both the film and the television categories), Genevieve Picot. Best Male Performance in a Television Role, Mick Rose. Best Design (television drama).

Genevieve Picot (Sonja Davies) in Bread and Roses. *Courtesy of the New Zealand Film Commission.*

Harvey Keitel (Baines) in The Piano. *Courtesy of CIBY 2000 and Jan Chapman Productions.*

1993

THE PIANO

CIBY 2000 presents a Jan Chapman production with the assistance of the Australian Film Commission and the New South Wales Film and Television Office. © 1992. Produced by Australia, financed from France. *Budget*: $US7 million. *Locations*: Karekare, West Auckland, Matakana, Waitakere Ranges, Bay of Plenty, Mount Taranaki. *Distributor*: Everard Films Ltd. *Rating*: RP13 (Some scenes may disturb), July 1993. 35 mm. Dolby Stereo. Colour. 122 mins.

Director: Jane Campion. *Producer*: Jan Chapman. *Executive producer*: Alain Depardieu. *Associate producer*: Mark Turnbull. *Screenplay*: Jane Campion. *Director of photography*: Stuart Dryburgh. *Camera operator*: Alun Bollinger. *Editor*: Veronika Jenet. *Production designer*: Andrew McAlpine. *Costume designer*: Janet Patterson. *Researchers*: Colin Englert, Peter Long. *Maori dialogue and advisors*: Waihoroi Shortland, Selwyn Muru. *Special effects co-ordinators*: Ken Durey, Wayne Rugg. *Music*: Michael Nyman. *Players*: Munich Philharmonia, Holly Hunter (solo piano), John Harle, David Roach, Andrew Findon. *Maori performance and language advisor*: Temuera Morrison. *Sound*: Lee Smith, Tony Johnson, Peter Townend, Annabelle Sheehan, Gary O'Grady, Jeanine Chialvo, Gethin Creagh, Martin Oswin.

Cast

Holly Hunter (Ada), Harvey Keitel (Baines), Sam Neill (Stewart), Anna Paquin (Flora), Kerry Walker (Aunt Morag), Genevieve Lemon (Nessie), Tungia Baker (Hira), Ian Mune (Reverend), Flynn (dog), with Peter Dennett, Te Whatanui Skipwith, Pete Smith, Bruce Allpress, Cliff Curtis, Carla Rupuha, Mahina Tunui, Hori Ahipene, Gordon Hatfield, Mere Boynton, Kirsten Batley, Tania Burney, Annie Edwards, Harina Haare, Christina Harimate, Steve Kanuta, P.J. Karauria, Sonny Kirikiri, Alain Makiha, Greg Mayor, Neil Mika Gudsell, Guy Moana, Joseph Otimi, Glynis Paraha, Riki Pickering, Eru Potaka-Dewes, Liane Rangi Henry, Huihana Rewa, Tamati Rice, Paora Sharples, George Smallman, Kereama Teua, Poama Tuialii, Susan Tuialii, Kahumanu Waaka, Lawrence Wharerau, Eddie Campbell, Roger Goodburn, Stephen Hall, Greg Johnson, Wayne McGoram, Jon Brazier, Stephen Papps.

Nineteenth century New Zealand. Elective mute Ada travels from Scotland with her daughter Flora as a mail-order bride. They disembark on a wild beach and Ada's future husband Stewart refuses to transport her piano through the bush. Ada persuades a neighbour Baines to retrieve her piano. Against Ada's will Stewart gives the piano to Baines in exchange for land, and arranges for his wife to give Baines lessons. Baines bargains with Ada to give her piano back key by key in return for erotic favours. At a Christmas concert Maori believe a Bluebeard shadow play to be real violence and break it up. Baines persuades Ada to lie naked with him for 10 keys and Flora secretly watches. Catching Flora and some Maori children simulating sex with tree trunks Stewart forces her to scrub the trees. Baines, wanting an open relationship with Ada, gives her piano back. Ada visits Baines and, with Stewart spying on them, they make love. Stewart attempts to rape Ada then confines her to their cabin. Ada becomes withdrawn, but takes to fondling Stewart while refusing to let him touch her. Hearing Baines is leaving Stewart releases Ada, who sends Flora to Baines with a love note written on a piano key. Flora gives Stewart the key and, enraged, he chops off Ada's finger. About to rape Ada as she sleeps Stewart 'hears' her voice in his mind asking him to let Baines take her away. Ada, Flora and Baines leave by sea for Nelson. At Ada's bidding the piano is thrown overboard and she is dragged in after it. She saves herself by removing her shoe. In Nelson Baines makes her a metal finger, she teaches piano and learns to speak.

In contrast to emotionally inarticulate and sexually naive settlers like Stewart, the Maori have an open attitude to sexuality. Immigrant Baines, tattooed and fluent in Maori and embracing new world freedoms, is a means by which Ada can discover her sensuality and passion and learn to 'speak' both literally and sexually. Openness to sensory communication is the conduit to rich experience. The blind piano tuner has excellent hearing while Stewart, equipped with all his faculties but blind to Ada's needs, believes 'there is something to be said for silence'. Mute Ada is eloquent in communicating her thoughts through her mind and her emotions through facial expressions, sign language and piano playing.

A number of related motifs spin off the central significances of the piano: Flora is a mirror image of her mother, but with twentieth century sensibilities; clothing, and its handling and removal signals degrees of restrictiveness and freedom; Victorian codes of ownership, sacrifice, barter and appropriation apply equally to people, land and things; a pattern of phallic and castration imagery (piano keys, fingers, a stocking hole) makes sexual repression and exploration specific; the masking of true feelings is conveyed in images of dress, in lies and in images of obscured looking (through scarves, curtains, windows, keyholes and into small mirrors); lighting, space, the elements and the physicality of the environment are used expressionistically to convey emotions and relationships. Unexplained is how Baines was to read his love note, given that his illiteracy is clearly established. It is also unclear whether Ada deliberately puts her foot in the piano rope.

An epic, romantic melodrama tinged with Gothic, **The Piano** is visually stunning, brilliantly acted and technically superb. Multi-layered and richly textured, it causes intrigue with its openness to many readings and continues to be the subject of articles, reviews and critiques. (The post-film novel, *The Piano*, written by Jane Campion and Kate Pullinger, inexplicably draws back the veils and offers explanations for many of the film's mysteries, including the love note and the foot-in-the-rope.)

Although mostly described in terms like 'a total mastery of the art of cinema' (*Le Figaro*) there are detractors. Stanley Kauffman (*New Republic*), for example, called **The Piano** 'an overwrought, hollowly symbolic glob of glutinous nonsense.' Although the producers worked closely with Maori language, dialogue and performance advisers, Leonie Pihama spoke for some critics of the film when she described the imaging of the Maori as naive, simple-minded people who acted impulsively and spoke only in terms of sexual innuendo. HM

1993 Cannes Film Festival: Palme d'Or. Best Actress, Holly Hunter.
1994 Academy Awards: Best Original Screenplay. Best Supporting Actress, Anna Paquin. Academy Award Nomination: Best Cinematography.
Other Awards: Best Film (3), Best Director (4), Best Actress, Holly Hunter (7), Best Supporting Actress, Anna Paquin (3), Best Actor, Harvey Keitel (2), Best Screenplay (5), Best Cinematography (3), Best Music (3), Best Editing (1), Best Sound (1), Best Costume Design (2), Best Production Design (2).

Holly Hunter (Ada) and Anna Paquin (Flora) in The Piano. *Courtesy of CIBY 2000 and Jan Chapman Productions.*

1993
JACK BE NIMBLE

Essential Productions and the New Zealand Film Commission. © 1993. *Budget*: $1.6 million. *Location*: Auckland. *Distributor*: Rialto Cinemas. *Rating*: RP16, October 1993. 35 mm. Dolby Stereo. Colour. 97 mins.

Director: Garth Maxwell. *Producers*: Jonathan Dowling, Kelly Rogers. *Associate producer*: Judith Trye. *Executive producers*: Murray Newey, John Barnett. *Screenplay*: Garth Maxwell. *Additional screenplay*: Rex Pilgrim. *Director of photography*: Donald Duncan. *Camera operator*: Mark Olsen. *Production designer*: Grant Major. *Costume designer*: Ngila Dickson. *Make-up designer*: Viv Mepham. *Editor*: John Gilbert. *Music*: Chris Neal. *Prosthetics*: Marjorie Hamlin. *Special effects*: Kevin Chisnall. *Special effects models*: Chris Fitzpatrick. *Stunt co-ordinator*: Peter Bell. *Sound*: Dick Reade, Gethin Creagh, Paul Stent, Graeme Myhre.

Cast

Alexis Arquette (Jack), Sara Smuts-Kennedy (Dora), Bruno Lawrence (Teddy), Tony Barry (Clarrie), Elizabeth Hawthorne (Bernice), Brenda Simmons (Mrs Birch), Gilbert Goldie (Mr Birch), Tricia Phillips (Anne), Paul Minifie (Kevin), Sam Smith (Little Jack), Hannah Jessop (Little Dora), Nicholas Antwis (Jack aged 7), Olivia Jessop (Dora aged 8), Kristen Seth, with Amber Woolston, Tracey Brown, Wendy Adams, Nina Lopez, Beth Morrison, Ella Brasella, Joanna Morrison, Amy Morrison, Victoria Spence, Ricky Plester, Rohan Stace, Bridget Armstrong, Bridget Donovan, Caroline Lowry, Paula Jones (Tina), Rebekah Mercer, Shannon Grey, Tina Frantzen, Vicky Haughton, Helen Medlyn, Grant McFarland, Celia Nicholson, Chris Auchinvole, Peter Bell, Kaash, Eric Williams. *Psychic voices*: Raymond Hawthorne, Douglas George, Brenda Kendall, Peter Tait, Hester Joyce, Meryl Main, Michael Mizrahi, Johnny Caracciolo, Paula Sanchez, Kelly Rogers, Lucy Sheehan, Meremere Penfold.

Emotionally exhausted, Anne leaves home. Her daughter Dora is adopted by a kind, wealthy couple. Her son Jack's adoptive family, farmers Clarrie and Bernice and their four ghastly look-a-like daughters, treat him brutally. Pushed over the edge when drunken Clarrie beats him with barbed wire, Jack hypnotises his step-parents with a gadget he has made at school, leading them to horrible, self-induced deaths. Dora, who hears voices, is drawn to the home of psychic Teddy, who later drives her to find Jack. The siblings are delighted to meet again but there is instant rivalry for Dora's affections between the men.

Alexis Arquette (Jack) and Sarah Smuts-Kennedy (Dora). Courtesy of the New Zealand Film Commission.

Dora, who is pregnant to Teddy, and Jack go in search of their birth parents. Seeking revenge, the step-sisters kill Dora's stepmother. Dora and Jack find Anne. Jack, by now violent and psychotic, forces Anne to admit she hates them. When they find their father, Jack hynotises him and forces him to suicide. The sisters run their car off the road, kidnap Jack and kill him, sewing his eyes, mouth and ears shut and hanging him upside down from a tree. The sisters kill Teddy but Dora, using her psychic powers, repels them and they die horribly. Ensconced at Teddy's, Dora is visited by Anne. Dora's unborn baby communicates with her in Jack's voice, and she happily reassures Anne and the baby she will soon 'get him over the bridge'.

In setting up a situation of gross child abuse within a nuclear family, writer/director Garth Maxwell creates a revenge fantasy where violence is repaid in violence of equal horror and where redemption is achieved through regret and forgiveness. Eschewing realism, Gothic horror evokes family brutality. Initially a sweet little boy Jack, who with Dora inherited his mother's psychic powers, becomes psychotic through environmental damage. His alter ego Dora, suffering less, is merely psychic and through her redemption is achieved. The extent of the cruelty, suffering and revenge makes of the story a modern Grimm's fairytale stretching good and evil characters to archetypal limits, while the Molly Wuppy fairy story is integral to the resolution. The motifs — marigolds (redemption), light and dark (good and evil), wind-flapped blinds (psychic forces), cats (poetic justice), confining bars (entrapment) — tell of significance beyond surface events. Running through this is a strain of dark humour, seen in Jack's bizarre death machine and in the mad sisters-from-hell on the rampage in their battered farm truck.

Bruno Lawrence's role as psychic Teddy and Jack's sparing of the mad sisters are rather bald plot devices, the dialogue slips occasionally into banality and the mixing of genres makes for awkwardness in the narrative. Overall the film is striking and bizarre. American actor Alexis Arquette performs Jack with a passable Kiwi accent and he and the rest of the cast sustain a fittingly melodramatic performance style. Music, cinematography and production design match the melodrama with an eerie surreality.

Jack Be Nimble received mixed reviews, some judging the narrative disjointed and the tone inconsistent, some, including the *New York Times*, finding the film a bold, impressive debut and comparing Maxwell's work with David Lynch. With its literate script and first class production values **Jack Be Nimble** is an art house film inviting a cult following. HM

1994 Fantasporto Festival, Portugal: Best Screenplay. Best Actress, Sara Smuts-Kennedy.

1993

SECRETS

Beyond Films Ltd presents a Victorian International Pictures and Avalon N.F.U. Studios Production, made in collaboration with the Australian and New Zealand Film Commissions and with the participation of the Australian Film Finance Corporation Pty Ltd. Developed with the assistance of Film Victoria. © 1992. A New Zealand/Australia co-production. *Location*: Avalon Studios, Wellington. *Distributor*: Avalon TV Centre, Incorporating National Film Unit. *Rating*: GA, October 1993. 35 mm. Dolby Stereo. Colour/Black and white archival footage. 93 mins.

Director and producer: Michael Pattinson. *Executive producers*: David Arnell, Michael Caulfield, William Marshall. Avalon. *Screenplay*: Jan Sardi. *Director of photography*: David Connell. *Camera operator*: Ian Jones. *Editor*: Peter Carrodus. *Production designer*: Kevin Leonard-Jones. *Wardrobe supervisor*: Theresa Liand. *Archival footage research*: Sally Jackson. *Music*: The Beatles. *Arranger/producer*: Dave Dobbyn. *Sound*: Ken Saville, Roger Savage, Steve Burgess. Paul Sayers, Craig Carter M.P.S.E., Glenn Newnham.

Cast

Beth Champion (Emily), Malcolm Kennard (Danny), Dannii Minogue (Didi), Willa O'Neill (Vicki), Noah Taylor (Randolph), Steve Parr (D.J.), Joy Watson (Randolph's Mum), Joan Reid (Sister Anunzia) Peter Vere-Jones (Emily's Dad), Don Langridge (Cop), Lorae Parry (Reporter).

Willa O'Neill (Vicki) and Noah Taylor (Randolph). Courtesy of Michael Pattinson and Beyond Films Ltd.

1964. On their first trip to the Southern Hemisphere the Beatles have arrived in Melbourne and four besotted teenagers who are strangers to each other — farm girl Emily, hairdresser Vicki, schoolgirl Didi and schoolboy Randolph — join screaming crowds outside the hotel where the Fab Four are to stay. Also in the crowd, but there to jeer, is Danny, a greaser whose 'Elvis the King' leather jacket identifies his loyalties. In their efforts to see the Beatles the five make their way into the hotel, only to find themselves trapped in its vast plant room basement. As the day wears on their feelings about the Beatles act as the catalyst for their talk and by night each character's public persona has been peeled away to reveal the secret that their passion (or, in Danny's case, antipathy) for the Beatles is a panacea for deep fears: the consequences of unplanned pregnancy, abandonment in childhood, early marriage, inability to connect with the opposite sex and the demands of Catholicism. By morning they have paired off — Emily with Danny, Didi with Randolph and pregnant Vicki with Didi's doll — and group solidarity is firm as they face the television cameras and talk about the night's experiences before racing to the airport together to see off their idols.

Secrets is an ensemble teen movie in the manner of **I Wanna Hold Your Hand** (Robert Zemeckis, 1978), where teenagers struck by Beatlemania try to get close to their idols by crashing the Ed Sullivan show, on which they are to appear, and **The Breakfast Club** (John Hughes, 1985), where the enforced entrapment of a group of teenagers provides a space for them to talk about themselves and face things normally concealed. Repeated mirror shots reinforce that the most anxiety circles around questions of identity and 'normality'. Having seen themselves through their new friends' eyes the teenagers 'swap' names for their 'fifteen minutes of fame' in the television interview, thus recognising that each has learned from, and has taken on some of, the more positive aspects of the others.

Because the film is schematic with a point of discovery to be made from each confrontation and admission, the narrative flow is theatrical rather than cinematic and several scenes, like the one where they all decide at the same time they need to use the toilet, have a plodding 'set piece' choreography. The talented young cast give energetic performances but are confined by the two-dimensionality of their characters. The lighting and cinematography are excellent and archival footage of the Beatles' Melbourne visit is well integrated. The producer acquired the rights to four Beatles songs for the film and 'Do You Want to Know a Secret?' is used as the catalyst for the deepest revelations. Arrangements of other Beatles numbers were produced by New Zealand's Dave Dobbyn.

New Zealander Willa O'Neill was nominated for Best Performance by an Actress in a Supporting Role in the Australian Film Institute's Awards. Other New Zealand actors in the film include Lorae Parry, Steve Parr (a D.J. seen in the form of his mouth in close-up) and Peter Vere-Jones. The film was shot in New Zealand and postproduction took place in Australia.
HM

1994

ONCE WERE WARRIORS

Communicado in association with the New Zealand Film Commission, Avalon N.F.U. and N.Z. On Air. © 1994. *Budget*: approx. $1.4 million. *Location*: Auckland. *Distributor*: Footprint Films. *Rating*: R13 (Contains violence and offensive language), March 1994. 35 mm. Dolby Stereo. Colour. 104 mins.

Director: Lee Tamahori. *Producer*: Robin Scholes. *Film unit production executive*: Sue Thompson. *Screenplay*: Riwia Brown. *Source*: Alan Duff, *Once Were Warriors*. *Director of photography*: Stuart Dryburgh. *Editor*: Michael Horton. *Production designer*: Mike Kane. *Wardrobe supervisor*: Pauline Bowkett. *Carvings and tattoo designer*: Guy Moana. *Fight co-ordinator*: Robert Bruce. *Music*: Murray Grindlay, Murray McNabb, Herbs. *Maori music consultant*: Hirini Melbourne. *Guitar*: Tama Renata. *Sound*: Kit Rollings, Graham Morris, John Neill, Don Paulin, Ray Beentjes, John Van der Reyden, Michael Hedges, Emma Haughton, Annie Collins.

Cast

Rena Owen (Beth Heke), Temuera Morrison (Jake Heke), Mamaengaroa Kerr-Bell (Grace Heke), Julian Arahanga (Nig Heke), Taungaroa Emile (Boogie Heke), Rachael Morris Jnr (Polly Heke), Joseph Kairau (Huata Heke), Clifford Curtis (Bully), Pete Smith (Dooley), George Henare (Bennett), Mere Boynton (Mavis), Shannon Williams (Toot), Calvin Tuteao (Taka, gang leader), Ray Bishop (King hitter in pub), Ian Mune (Judge), Te Whatanui Skipworth (Te Tupaea), Rangi Motu (Matawai), with Robert Pollock, Jessica Wilcox, Stephen Hall, Wiki Oman, Israel Williams, Jonathon Wiremu, Richard Meihana, Edna Stirling, Ngawai Simpson, Spike Kem, Arona Rissetto, Fran Vivieaere, Brian Kairau, Charlie Tumahai, Tama Renata, Guy Moana, Riwia Brown, Mac Hona, Jason Kerapa, Eddie Tongalahi, Chris Mason, Percy Robinson, Robbie Ngauma, Sam Masters.

Contemporary New Zealand. An idyllic country scene is revealed to be printed on a billboard as the camera draws back to show a grimy, traffic-filled urban setting. Living by the motorway in a scruffy state house are the Heke's, a Maori family. The father Jake, known as 'Jake the muss' because of his reputation as an invincible fighter, has just lost his job and is content to drink away his dole money with his mates. While his wife Beth also drinks and parties she worries about their five children, particularly Nig, who undergoes violent initiation into a tough gang, and Boogie, who is up on a court charge. After a party at home Jake beats Beth so severely she is unable to attend court to support Boogie, and he is sent to a Social Welfare Institution. Thirteen year-old Grace persuades Beth to arrange a trip to visit Boogie but Jake, after initially supporting the idea, detours to the pub. That night Jake's friend Bully rapes Grace at her home and she later hangs herself in the garden. Jake refuses to attend the tangi on Beth's marae because he has never been accepted by her people. At the tangi Boogie performs the haka he has learnt in the Institution and Beth reconnects with her tribe. Beth invites Grace's homeless friend Toot to live with them. In Grace's book of writing Beth reads about the rape and confronts Bully in the pub. Jake beats him severely, stabbing him with a broken beer bottle. Beth leaves Jake at the pub, telling him she is going to look after her children and does not need him.

In adapting Alan Duff's controversial 1990 novel the producer, director and screenwriter felt that the story in which two of the Heke children die, Jake is implicated as his daughter's rapist and Beth is as negligent as her husband, was too bleak to form the basis for a successful feature film. Thus the focus was shifted from aggressive Jake, dispossessed of his culture and inarticulate in his rage, to his wife, Beth, who stays with Jake because, despite the violence and abuse, she still loves him. In changing her priorities Beth becomes the catalyst through whom change and hope for a better future can be effected when the cycle of violence is broken.

Despite the changes **Once Were Warriors** is a harrowing, brutal and passionate film which reflects the heritage of Britain's colonisation of Aotearoa. Jake, prompted by self-loathing and alcohol, can talk only with his fists, while the culturally dislocated gang to which his oldest son is attracted replaces the rituals of Maoritanga with those of macho self-aggrandisement. But young Boogie, whose home life is training him to emulate his father, learns another way when Social Welfare Officer Bennett shows him how pride in his culture can make him a new kind of warrior. Beth also finds her strength in regaining her heritage. Not explained is the explanation Jake gives for his venom — he tells his children he comes from a long line of slaves — an idea more the stuff of fiction than fact and one which some overseas reviewers took as an aspect of Maori history.

Excellent production values and all-round performances (Rena Owen was compared to Judy Davis and Anna Magnani) contributed to the extraordinary success of the film both at home and overseas. Negative reponses have included criticism of the uneasy stylistic mix which includes heightened realism (the fight scenes), some melodrama in the shooting style (the depiction of the gang) and on the soundtrack (underlining Jake's menace), nostalgic romanticism (the chocolate box marae) and the glamorous, futuristic design in the look of the young gang members. The atonal colouring and orange lighting, designed to show the city as it looks under sodium lighting, was criticised by some as inappropriately 'romantic' looking. In the narrative Bully's savage beating is a contrivance providing a kind of gratuitous retribution, but it does not shift focus from Jake as the main culprit.

In New Zealand **Once Were Warriors** became the first film to gross more than $6 million at the box office. Its ideas quickly entered the culture, with cases of domestic violence and 'home alone' children referred to in the press as 'Warriors families' and with many reports of the film changing people's lives. Depicting a lifestyle that is a reality for many people the film stirred discussion worldwide about societal problems of domestic violence, parental negligence, poverty, rape, gang violence and alcohol abuse.[1] HM

1994 New Zealand Film and Television Awards: Best Film. Best Director. Best Screenplay. Best Film Score. Best Soundtrack. Best Editing. Best Male Performance in a Dramatic Role, Temuera Morrison. Best Female Performance in a Supporting Role, Mamaengaroa Kerr-Bell. Best Juvenile Performance, Taungaroa Emile.
Durban Film Festival: Best Film.
Montreal Film Festival: Best Film. Best Actress, Rena Owen. Most Popular Film. Ecumenical Jury Award.
Venice Film Festival: Anica-Flash Best First Film.
Hawaii Film Festival: Special Jury Award.
Wellington Fringe Festival Accolade: For services beyond where any third assistant should ever go, Te Rangitawaea Reedy.
1995 Fantasporto Film Festival: Best Actress, Rena Owen.
Rotterdam Film Festival: Netherlands Best Film. Special Jury Award.
Santa Barbara Film Festival: Bruce Corwin Award for Artistic Excellence.
San Diego Film Festival: Best Actress, Rena Owen.
Asia-Pacific Film Festival: Best Supporting Actress, Mamaengaroa Kerr-Bell.

---

[1] Among the references is the 67 minute 'homemade' video, released to video rental outlets, **Once Were Warders** (1995), which explores, with amateurish film-making skills but with a refreshing determination to get beyond the soundbite, the reasons behind the protest of two remand prisoners who escaped and occupied a tower on the roof of Mount Eden prison in August 1994.

Rena Owen (Beth) and Temuera Morrison (Jake Heke) in Once Were Warriors. *Courtesy of the New Zealand Film Commission.*

Melanie Lynskey (Pauline Rieper), top and Kate Winslet (Juliet Hulme) in Heavenly Creatures.

1994
HEAVENLY CREATURES

WingNut Films co-produced with Fontana Film Productions GmbH in association with the New Zealand Film Commission. © 1994. *Location*: Christchurch. *Distributor*: Roadshow/Miramax/Buena Vista. *Rating*: GA, May 1994. 35 mm. Dolby Stereo. Colour. Panavision. 108 mins.

Director: Peter Jackson. *Producer*: Jim Booth. *Co-producer*: Peter Jackson. *Executive producer*: Hanno Huth. *Screenplay*: Frances Walsh, Peter Jackson. *Director of photography*: Alun Bollinger. *Editor*: Jamie Selkirk. *Production designer*: Grant Major. *Costume designer*: Ngila Dickson. *Prosthetic effects designer*: Richard Taylor. *Digital effects operator*: George Port. *Visual effects*: W.E.T.A. Ltd. *Scenic artist*: Ian McDonald. *Sculptors*: Maurice Quin, James Johnston, Rob Gordon, Bodhi Vincent. *Composer*: Peter Dasent. *Orchestration*: Bob Young. *Players*: Auckland Philharmonia Orchestra. *Conductor*: Peter Scholes. *Sound*: Hammond Peek, Michael Hopkins, Greg Bell, Michael Hedges, Michael Jones.

Cast

Melanie Lynskey (Pauline), Kate Winslet (Juliet), Diana Kent (Hilda), Sarah Peirse (Honora), Clive Merrison (Henry), Jed Brophy (John/Nicholas), Kirsti Ferry (Wendy), Peter Elliott (Bill Perry), Jean Guerin (Orson Welles), Geoffrey Heath (Reverend Norris), Ben Fransham (Charles), Simon O'Connor (Herbert), with Andrew Sanders, Ben Skjellerup, Jesse Griffin, Glen Drake, Chris Clarkson, Gilbert Goldie, Elizabeth Moody, Liz Mullane, Moreen Eason, Pearl Carpenter, Toni Jones, Nick Farra, Ray Henwood, John Nicoll, Darien Takle, Mike Maxwell, Raewyn Pelham, Glenys Lloyd-Smith, Lou Dobson, Wendy Watson, Jessica Bradley, Gina Parker, Stephen Reilly, Andrea Sanders, Alex Shirtcliffe-Scott, Barry Thomson, Michael Wilson, Nicky McCarthy, Peter Jackson.

1953. At Christchurch Girls' High School Pauline Rieper, a naive and moody loner, is enchanted by new girl Juliet Hulme's glamorous sophistication, extraordinary confidence and wild imagination. Their friendship flourishes with their common love of fantasy and ritual. They invent a non-Christian 'fourth world' of 'music, art and pure enjoyment', medieval Borovnia, and people it with plasticine characters. Mario Lanza is their idol and Orson Welles their bête noir. Pauline records their stories and plans in her diary. When Juliet is hospitalised with tuberculosis they write to each other as their fantasy characters, Charles (Pauline) and Deborah (Juliet). Pauline has sex with a boarder, but her heart is with Juliet. With her parents opposing the friendship Pauline becomes increasingly depressed and refuses to eat. Her antagonism towards her mother, Honora, is exacerbated by a doctor's conclusion the girl is homosexual. When Juliet's parents decide to separate, the girls are hysterical to learn Juliet is to be sent to South Africa. Allowed to spend a final three weeks together, intimations are that their relationship becomes sexual. Desperate that they stay together, Juliet falls in with Pauline's idea to 'moider Mother'. On 11 June 1954, they kill Honora in Victoria Park by bashing her repeatedly on the head with a brick. On-screen information explains that police used Pauline's diaries as evidence and that the girls served time in separate prisons before being released on the condition they never meet again.

A psychological study of obsessional friendship, **Heavenly Creatures** is an original, unsettling and chilling depiction of the infamous Parker-Hulme story (Pauline was charged under her mother's maiden name when it was discovered her parents had never married). The film opens with a 1950s Pictorial Parade, showing the city off as a genteel and orderly outpost of the British Empire that is abruptly interrupted by footage of two screaming, blood-covered teenage girls. Thus the first two sequences eloquently frame the central questions: by what path did two teenage girls at this point in New Zealand's history arrive at the ghastly act of mother murder? And how could this society's image of itself be so awry?

The film's triumph is that, using Pauline's own words from her diaries and an extraordinary collaborative film-making imagination, it provides credible insights without patronising the viewer with answers impossible to give. Both girls are outsiders and intensely passionate. Isolated through illness as children, they lack interest in their peers and are contemptuous of authority. Juliet, shaped by a British upbringing, the privileges of money and class and parental neglect, fascinates the other, more 'ordinary' girl. Oblivious to Pauline's social and financial inferiority, Juliet is delighted to find a friend willing to be caught up in the exhilaration of her wild ideas. It is in the dissolution of the boundary between fantasy and reality, and in the terrible fear of separation, that the seed of matricide is sown.

Meticulous attention is paid to historical detail, one example being that the Hulmes' actual house was used, enhanced by a computer-generated balcony added to it to show it as it was in the 1950s. Basing the script partly on interviews with people who knew the girls, the story is told with superb creative verve. Brilliant computer-generated visuals, the first to be used in a New Zealand feature film, take the viewer into the girls' fervid minds in startling and witty images, from unicorns and giant butterflies in a gorgeous manor garden to a castle peopled with life-sized 'plasticine' characters. 1950s Christchurch is in part evoked using the same technology and in the most startling scenes the 'real' and 'fantasy' worlds collide. The cinematic wizardry, which includes excellent widescreen cinematography, production design, editing, and musical score, is matched by a well-structured script full of wit and sympathy. Consummate performances are given by all the actors (casting was in England and New Zealand), but particularly by Sarah Peirse as the careworn, likeable moider victim and by the two young women, Kate Winslet and Melanie Lynskey, charged with bringing the passions and torments of Juliet and Pauline to life.

On the film's release the ethics of dramatising blighted lives were discussed as renewed interest in the case led to the whereabouts of both women being revealed. In a bizarre sequel Juliet Hulme, now the Scotland-based novelist Anne Perry, appeared on New Zealand television offering explanations for the murder. The film, a tribute to producer the late Jim Booth, marked a turning point for Peter Jackson, taking him beyond splatter into serious drama. Reviewers locally and overseas raved, 'a triumph', 'a remarkable achievement', 'a suspenseful, thrilling film'. HM

1994 Venice Film Festival: Silver Lion.
Toronto International Film Festival: Metro Media Award. Academy Award Nomination: Best Original Screenplay. U.S. Writers' Guild Nomination: Best Original Screenplay.
1995 Italy, Fantasia Film Festival: Best Film.
France, Fantastica Film Festival: Grand Prize.
New Zealand Film and Television Awards: Best Director. Best Screenplay. Best Editing. Best Actress, Melanie Lynskey. Best Supporting Actress, Sarah Peirse. Best Foreign Performer, Kate Winslet. Best Soundtrack. Best Film Score. Best Design. Best Contribution to Design.
Australian Film Critics' Circle: Best Foreign-language Film (shared with *Once were Warriors*).
1996 London Critics' Circle: Best British Actor of the Year (Kate Winslet). Empire Magazine: Best Actress (Kate Winslet).

1994
THE LAST TATTOO

Plumb Productions Ltd and Capella International Inc. © 1994. *Location*: Wellington. *Distributor*: Everard Films Ltd. *Rating*: RP13, July 1994. 35 mm. Colour. 113.5 mins.

Director: John Reid. *Producers*: Neville Carson, Bill Gavin. *Executive producers*: David Korda, Bridget Hedison. *Production manager*: Carole Pagonis. *Assistant directors*: Stuart Freeman, David Norris. *Screenplay*: Keith Aberdein, from a story by John Reid and Keith Aberdein. *Director of photography*: John Blick. *Camera Operator*: Richard Bluck. *Production Designer*: Ron Highfield. *Art Directors*: Joe Bleakley, Rob Outterside. *Editor*: John Scott. *Dialogue Editor*: Paul Sutorius. *Costume designer*: Barbara Darragh. *Chief make-up artist*: Viv Mepham. *Special effects*: Action Associates. *Music*: John Charles. *Sound recordist*: Tony Johnson.

Cast

Tony Goldwyn (Captain Mike Starwood), Kerry Fox (Kelly Towne), Robert Loggia (Colonel Conrad Dart), Rod Steiger (General Frank W. Zane), John Bach (Austen Leech), Timothy Balme (Jim Mitchell), Tony Barry (James Carroll), Peter Hambleton (Peter Davis), Elizabeth Hawthorne (Henrietta Simpson), Michelle Huirama (Grace Raukawa), Desmond Kelly (Monty McGurr), Martyn Sanderson (Ralph Simpson), Katie Wolfe (Rose Mitchell), Donna Akersten (Mrs Monahan), with Eddie Campbell, Matt Chamberlain, Danielle Cormack, Stella Reid, Peter Daube, Theresa Healey, William Kircher, Jacqui McPherson, Mark Rafferty, Michael Robinson, Mick Rose, Brett Tomkins, Stephen Tozer.

World War II. Thousands of U.S. marines are stationed at a huge barracks at Paekakariki, a small settlement on the coast just north of Wellington where a murder investigation resulting from the death of a marine sergeant is under way. Brothel keeper Austen Leech, who is responsible for the sergeant's death, uses his position as Hotel Worker's union boss both to exploit the 'girls' who are controlled by him and to avoid questions which could jeopardise the lucrative relationship he has with members of the marine corps. A parallel tale concerns a romantic relationship between the investigating officer, marine captain Mike Starwood, and a public health nurse, Kelly Towne, whose function it is to identify cases of VD and locate the source of the infection. When he comes too close to revealing the truth, Starwood is himself framed on a charge of murder, and is finally forced to ship out to the Pacific battle zone and leave Towne back in New Zealand.

The Last Tattoo which is a nicely ambiguous title, considering its military and literal implications, is set in 1943 when the presence of U.S. marines in New Zealand provided rest and recreation for the incoming servicemen but also led to tensions and difficulties. Reid's recreation of the period has a gritty authenticity and avoids the jingoism of films like **The Sands of Iwo Jima**, and the perpetuation of romantic myth. In doing so, he shows a Kiwi past superbly rendered and memorably recalled. In interview Reid said that he wanted a film which would paint the period both in the colours of the time and in tones which would make it accessible to viewers in the 1990s. Particular attention was paid to the way in which the film was lit, and the bold and luminous lighting plot is essential to the whole feel. Costume design also reflects the appearance and ambience of the period.

The Last Tattoo is a noir-ish suspense thriller with a strong narrative and a chewy and complex plot, highly entertaining for audiences in both New Zealand and the U.S., despite the comments it makes about corruption in America's military elite. There are some problems with pace, there are times when the script becomes a little overloaded, and the somewhat self-conscious style disconcerted some viewers as it received a less than enthusiastic critical response upon its New Zealand release. It is typical of the contemporary features which move towards the arthouse end of the audience spectrum. SE

1995 New Zealand Film and Television Awards: Best Cinematography, John Blick. Best Actor, John Bach. Best Supporting Actor, Peter Hambleton.

Katie Wolfe (Rose Mitchell). Courtesy of the New Zealand Film Commission.

1994

HERCULES AND THE LOST KINGDOM

Renaissance Pictures. © 1994. A United States production. Telefeature. *Location*: New Zealand. *Distributor*: Universal City Studios, USA. *Video rating*: PG (Contains violence). 35 mm (transferred to videotape). Colour. 86 mins.

Director: Harley Cokeliss. *Producer*: Eric Gruendemann. *Executive producers*: Sam Raimi, Robert Tapert, Christian Williams. *Associate producer*: Bernadette Joyce. *Co-producer*: David Eick. *Screenplay*: Christian Williams. *Director of photography*: James Bartle. *Camera operator*: Ian Turtill. *Editor*: Jon Koslowsky A.C.E. *Production designer*: Mick Strawn. *Costume designer*: Barbara Darragh. *Creature/make-up/digital effects*: Weta Ltd. *Special effects design*: Richard Taylor. *Special effects co-ordinator*: Tania Rodger. *Digital effects supervisor*: George Port. *Mechanical effects supervisor*: Wayne Rugg. *Project managers*: Jamie Selkirk, Peter Jackson. *Stunt co-ordinator*: Peter Bell. *Music*: Joseph Lo Duca, Ray Bunch (theme). *Sound*: Tony Johnson, Paul Urmson, Craig Berkey.

Cast

Kevin Sorbo (Hercules), Renée O'Connor (Deianeira), Anthony Quinn (Zeus), Eric Close (Telamon), Nathaniel Lees (Blue Priest), Robert Trebor (Waylin), Todd Rippon (Melus the Hood), Alex Beasley (Marathon messenger), Onno Boelee (Gargan the Giant), Elizabeth Hawthorne (Queen Omphale), with Chic Littlewood, Gilbert Goldie, John Sumner, George Boyle, Barry Hill, Te Whatanui Skipworth, Francis Bell, Peter Rowley, Brenda Kendall, Maggie Tarver, Lee-Jane Foreman, Darren Warren, Daniel Warren, Patrick Wilson, Jay Saussey, Stan Wolfgramm, Bevan Sweeney, Joshua McDonald, Nell Weatherly, Kenneth Prebble, Shane Blakey, Bruce Brown, Ryan Carey, Shane Dawson, Mark Harris, Annette Howell, Robert Lee, Aaron Lupton, Allan Poppleton, Paul Shapcott, Sam Williams, Barry Hill, Peter Bell.

Hercules rescues a town from a giant's evil clutches before setting off on a quest to find the lost Kingdom of Troy and rescue its usurped inhabitants. Along the way he rescues Deianeira, a young woman about to be sacrificed to bring rain, and together they look for the compass that will lead them to Troy. Opposition and adventure come in many forms, not the least being the vendetta waged by Hera, Hercules' stepmother, who is obsessed with the desire to destroy him. Deianeira's conviction that she is a king's daughter is confirmed when they reach Troy and with the help of Hercules and his father Zeus she avoids another sacrifice and they win back the city. Hercules rebuffs her attempts to establish a closer relationship but she is happy to rule Troy. Resisting the temptation to kill her stepson Hera whisks Hercules off to new adventures.

Kevin Sorbo (Hercules) astride Onno Boelee (Gargan the Giant). Courtesy of Pacific Renaissance Pictures Ltd.

Hercules and the Lost Kingdom is a playful pastiche on popular culture, borrowing from **Star Wars** and the Western as much as from Greek mythology. The god/hero is refreshingly secular, advising against sacrifice and obeisance to the gods because 'most of them are bums', and favouring self-motivation. When it comes to fighting the world's demons he does have an edge — he can sling a giant around his head like a rag doll — but he's never sanctimonious or smug.

The narrative line is straightforward with interest held by the tongue-in-cheek banality of the dialogue and the various creatures (human and otherwise) impeding Hercules's mission to save the world ('as long as there were people crying for help there was one man who would never rest'). Excellent special effects, many provided by Weta, bring the battle between good and evil to vivid life, as in the hair-raising sequence where Deianeira and Hercules fight their way out of the stomach of a murderous sea serpent. Also first class is the production design which matches the action with an appropriate comic book look.

Initially five 90 minute telefeatures were made, followed by 13, one-hour episodes, then another 24. **Hercules** currently screens on television in New Zealand and is in syndication on U.S. television as the top-rating one-hour action show. **Hercules and the Lost Kingdom** was the first New Zealand telefeature release from the New Zealand-based, American produced television production.

Although the writing and most of the directing is done by the American team, the production represents a creative breakthrough for New Zealand in that all heads of departments, some directors and line producer Chloe Smith are New Zealanders. The series is crewed by New Zealanders and has a largely New Zealand cast, including Michael Hurst as Hercules's sidekick Iolaus (although he is not in **The Lost Kingdom**). The spinoff series, **Xena, Warrior Princess**, has a New Zealander, Lucy Lawless, in the lead role. Most postproduction is in the U.S. but many of the digital effects are done in New Zealand by Weta. HM

COPS AND ROBBERS

Isambard Productions and Total Film and Television Australia in association with the New Zealand Film Commission and the Australian Film Finance Corporation Ltd with the assistance of the New South Wales Film and Television Office. © 1994. A New Zealand/Australia co-production. *Budget*: approx. $A2 million. *Location*: Sydney. No theatrical release. Super 16 mm. Colour. 85 mins.

Director: Murray Reece. *Producers*: Phil Gerlach, Tom Parkinson. *Associate producer*: Tammie Painting. *Screenplay*: Tim Bean. *Director of photography*: Steve Arnold. *Editor*: Simon Reece. *Production designer*: Tim Ferrier. *Wardrobe supervisor*: Jane Johnston. *Pig/ferret wrangler*: Grahame Ware. *Cocky wrangler*: Rhonda Hall. *Armourer/special effects*: John Bowering. *Composer*: Todd Hunter. *Additional music*: Johanna Pigott. *Sound*: Paul Brincat, Paul Stent, Dick Reade.

Cast

Grant Dodwell (John), Rima Te Wiata (Cop), Mark Wright (Kevin), Melissa Kounnas (Rita), Gosia Dobrowolska (Bitch), with Martin Vaughn, Lyn Collingwood, Norry Constantian, Harry Constantian, Anna Phillips, Julia Gardiner, Nick Stock, Shelly Smith, John Flower, Jean Bell, Cedric McLaughlin, Elspeth MacTavish, Jill Clayton, Cathren Mickalak, Keith Smith, Raymond Cole, Grant Page, Harry Dakanalis, Chim Shu, Mitchell Welfare, Wayne Kimber, Esther May Chee Cheah, Robyn Austin, Joan Miles.

In his Sydney warehouse John Barnesberg contemplates suicide because his cockatoo-exporting business is kaput and his ex-wife, the Bitch, is fleecing him. With their quarter million dollar insurance policy about to expire the Bitch sends her gormless, alcoholic lover Kevin to murder John. Kevin bungles the job and his arm is broken. A female cop arrives the next day to serve Kevin's writ for damages and John is still sitting around with a gun in his mouth. To distract him the cop does a striptease and, when John accepts her offer of sex, insists he go out in her car and buy a condom. She stays behind wearing only her underwear and tied to a chair. The bank next to the chemist shop is robbed. One of the victims, a nurse called Rita, leaps into the cop car and, believing John to be a cop, insists he chase the robbers.

Rima Te Wiata (the Cop) and Mark Wright (Kevin). Courtesy of the New Zealand Film Commission.

Rita and John confront the robbers in a shootout on the outskirts of Sydney. Meanwhile the Bitch orders Kevin back to murder John and he and the female cop get drunk. The film climaxes with the Bitch arriving at the warehouse to find three trussed-up robbers (two dead, one feigning death), John and Rita tied up, the female cop tied to a chair, a wino asking for a cut of the takings and Kevin negotiating for some of the bank haul. The Bitch is electrocuted, Kevin is arrested, the live robber escapes, the wino gets away with the bank haul and Rita accepts John's marriage proposal. In the last shot the Bitch's ferret, followed by her gloved hand, emerges from her grave.

Shot in 1992 and with postproduction completed in 1994, **Cops and Robbers** (working title **Kevin Rampenbacker and the Electric Kettle**) aims to be a black, off-the-wall, action-packed comedy drama. It inverts expectations (old women buy condoms, a wino drinks out of a wine glass) with a heavy hand and the pace drags. Problems with coverage dictate sequences are cut in a way that holds up action and dialogue. At the climax the Bitch inexplicably 'changes' outfits four times, including one change between her plugging in a kettle and falling to the floor. The soundtrack irritatingly insists on underlining the jokes.

Of the women only dumb little-girl Rita is named. All are caricatures of well-worn female stereotypes: beautiful, unattainable, ruthless bitch, semi-naked Catholic virgin with SM potential (the cop) and fat old shrewish frump (the boss robber). The male characters, all named, include the dumb fool (doubly played by robbers Larry and Curly), the alcoholic sleaze (Kevin) and dashing hero John.

New Zealand input includes actors Rima Te Wiata and Mark Wright affecting strong Australian accents, director Murray Reece, producer Tom Parkinson, editor Simon Reece and all postproduction. The film has screened in a New Hampshire film festival and has sold on video to Hungary. It has had no theatrical release. HM

1995

WAR STORIES: OUR MOTHERS NEVER TOLD US

Gaylene Preston Productions in association with The New Zealand Film Commission, N.Z. On Air, TV3 Network with the assistance of The Oral History Centre, Alexander Turnbull Library, National Archives of New Zealand, The Film Unit, Village Sound, Spectrum Communications Ltd, Kodak NZ Ltd, Protel NZ Ltd, Film Facilities, Ansett New Zealand. © 1995. *Budget*: $650 000. *Location*: Village Sound Studio. *Distributor*: Footprint Films. *Rating*: G, March 1995. 35 mm. Dolby Stereo. Colour/Black and white. 90 mins.

Director and producer: Gaylene Preston. *Executive producer*: Robin Laing. *Associate producer*: Jenny Bush. *Film Unit General Manager*: Sue Thompson. *Director of photography*: Alun Bollinger. *Editor*: Paul Sutorius. *Oral archive project manager*: Judith Fyfe. *Film archivist*: Clive Sowry. *Researchers*: Julie Adams, Julie Benjamin, Jenny Bush, Cathy Casey, Sarah Dalton, Michelle Erai, Susan Fowke, Brita McVeigh, Alison Parr, Queenie Rikihana Hyland, Jane Tolerton, Johanna Woods, Joan McCracken. *Composer/arranger*: Jonathan Besser. *Players*: Colin Hemmingson, Chris Selley, Nick van Dijk, George Packard, Noel Clayton, Ed Ware, Jonathan Besser, Gaylene Preston, Peter Barber, Yuru Gezentsvey, Matthew Ross. *Choral*: Ivan Patterson, Roger Wilson, Stephen Wells, Glen Schuitman, Ngati Poneke. *Young Maori Singers*: Captain Ward Whaitiri, Dovey Taiaroa, Mary Anne Shellock, William Nathan, Mere Tonia Nathan, Rawiri Shedlock, Michael John Priest, Keri Kaa. *Karanga*: Taukiri Thomason. *Sound*: Hugo Tichbourne, Beth Tredray, Don Paulin, Michael Hedges, Steve Murphy, John Neill, Paul Sutorius.

Interviewees: Pamela Quill, Flo Small, Tui Preston, Jean Andrews, Rita Graham, Neva Clarke McKenna, Mabel Waititi. *Interviewer*: Judith Fyfe.

Shot in mid-shot and close-up, seven elderly New Zealand women one-by-one discuss their World War II experiences. Pamela Quill was granted prime ministerial dispensation to follow her fiancé to England to marry. After he went missing in action, she and their infant daughter sailed home on the last free boat. Pamela didn't accept Paul's death until she visited his Belgian grave in 1963. Flo Small was abused by many when she married an American marine and when, after his death on active service, she had his child. Tui Preston, the director's mother, fell pregnant to and married an old friend, Ed. A passionate affair after Ed went missing in action ended when Ed came home and, as strangers, they struggled to rebuild their marriage. Of Ngati Raukawa/Te Atiawa tribal descent, Jean Andrews' family cared for American servicemen in Paekakariki. One tragic occasion she describes is a training session where 103 men drowned. Rita Graham and her husband Alan were abused because he was a Christian pacifist seeing out the war in detention as a conscientious objector. The death of their child brought further grief. Neva Clarke McKenna served overseas in Egypt and Italy and in one unforgettable incident fought off three rapists. Angered by the futility of war, she has never recovered from the deaths of two fiancés. Mabel Waititi, from the Ngatihere community, drove a school bus and ran the family trucking business while her husband fought with the Maori Battalion.

War Stories began as an idea during research for **Bread and Roses**. Unable initially to get funding for a film, Gaylene Preston, funded by the Lotteries Commission and the Suffrage Centennial Fund, organised interviewers to speak with 66 elderly women, all of whom had a unique story to tell. (The interviews are kept on audiotape in the Alexander Turnbull Library).

The stories of the seven gifted storytellers in the film are poignant, funny and riveting, describing the heroism in ordinary lives unheralded in official war histories. Brought up in a society still shaped by nineteenth century puritanism often the women tell of feelings and events previously hidden. (Gaylene Preston, for example, had not known her mother's 'war story' before the shoot.) They gain in stature as they vividly describe difficulties faced during the war and, in rebuilding their lives after the war, losses that could never be repaired.

Prompting from interviewer Judith Fyfe is minimal and non-intrusive. **Weekly Review** clips recall the tenor of the times when the propaganda of the National Film Unit was at a far remove from the reality of the people's lives. Accompanying stills from the women's pasts and a skilfully designed soundtrack, including background effects and tunes of the times, provide information and atmosphere.

The 30 hours of film shot was edited on an electronic editing machine, Lightworks. **War Stories**' production coincided with the fiftieth anniversary of the end of World War II. The film, which drew enthusiastic audiences, is dedicated to 'the children' and is in loving memory of Auntie Jean Andrews, who died shortly after the filming. HM

1995 New Zealand Film and Television Awards: Best Film.
Venice Film Festival: Official Selection.
Sydney Film Festival: Best Documentary. Best Film (Audience Poll).
Melbourne Film Festival: Best Documentary.

Tui Preston, Pamela Quill, Neva Clarke McKenna, Judith Fyfe (interviewer), Flo Small, Gaylene Preston (director), Mabel Waititi, Rita Graham. Courtesy of the New Zealand Film Commission.

Loaded

Catherine McCormack (Rose) and Thandie Newton (Zita). Courtesy of the New Zealand Film Commission.

British Screen and the New Zealand Film Commission in association with The British Film Institute, Channel Four and Geissendorfer Film, A Strawberry Vale and The Movie Partners production. © 1994. A New Zealand/United Kingdom co-production. *Budget*: $2.97 million. *Location*: just outside London, England. *Distributor*: Footprint Films. *Rating*: M, March 1995. 35 mm. Colour. 98 mins. (Original running time, 108 mins.)

Director: Anna Campion. *Producers*: Caroline Hewitt, David Hazlett (U.K.), John Maynard, Bridget Ikin (N.Z.). *Executive producer*: Ben Gibson. *Screenplay*: Anna Campion. *Director of photography*: Alan Almond. *Editor*: John Gilbert. *Production designer*: Alistair Kay. *Costume designer*: Stewart Meacham. *Special effects*: George Port, Weta Digital Effects. *Composer*: Simon Fisher Turner. *Sound*: Peter Lindsay, Gethin Creagh, Michael Hedges.

Cast

Oliver Milburn (Neil), Nick Patrick (Giles), Catherine McCormack (Rose), Thandie Newton (Zita), Matthew Eggleton (Lionel), Danny Cunningham (Lance), Biddy Hodson (Charlotte), Dearbhla Molloy (Ava), Caleb Lloyd (Young Neil), Joe Gecks (Dale).

Seven articulate and highly intelligent young school leavers spend the weekend at an English mansion outside London making an impossibly ambitious Celtic fantasy horror video. Tensions on the shoot, mostly in the form of fighting over the script, are shaped as a tight psychodrama revealing anxieties and emotional inadequacies. Neil wants to sleep with Rose, who is weighing up whether to lose her virginity. Giles is escaping anxious parents and Zita wants to escape poverty. Overachiever Charlotte desperately wants to have fun. Lance imagines the video will open doors for him and resents suggestions about how it should be shot. At first the mood is light. Tensions are explored and the film-making process is lampooned with cheerful black humour. The mood shifts as some begin arguing that intimate details from their lives are being fed into the script. In the evening they take LSD and play a 'truth' game, recording their fears and fantasies on video. Things climax later that night when Neil, whose visits to his therapist have revealed a mind tortured by guilt (as a child he failed to save his brother from drowning), runs over and kills Lionel, whom he resents as a competitor for Rose's affections. In a direct re-play of their horror video Neil's companions bury Lionel's body under leaves. Neil insists to Rose that he foresaw Lionel's and his brother's deaths and after an argument they make love. Next morning the group decide to return the body to the scene of the accident but they cannot find it. Neil rings the police.

Loaded features ordinary young Brits, all ambitious and untried and in some way troubled, and looks at how they unravel when pushed to extremes by circumstance. The film-making scenes suggesting the constructed nature of the stories people tell and video footage of the truth game and of Neil's visits to his therapist suggests 'truths' are also constructions. While they are 'free' in a way their parents never were, these are Thatcher's children and their questions about 'the meaning of life' are made bleak and angry because, in contemporary England, there seems to be no 'meaning' seems to be grasped.

An early scene hinting a secret room will later become important both symbolically and as a plot device is a frustrating dead end given that the film looks to exploring what is below the surface in youth culture, and plot twists are stretched rather too far. Impact is achieved by the skill of the young cast, the surprises in the script, the excellence of the edgy score and sharp cinematography.

Loaded is the first U.K./N.Z. co-production made in terms of a co-production agreement signed in April 1993. It was shot in the U.K. by expatriate Anna Campion, with many expatriate New Zealanders on the crew. Postproduction, financed by the New Zealand Film Commission, was in New Zealand. American distributor Miramax financed a re-cut of the original film which reduced its duration by 10 minutes. HM

BONJOUR TIMOTHY

Tucker Films and Cinar Productions Inc in association with New Zealand Film Commission with participation of FUND (Foundation to Underwrite New Drama for Pay Television). © 1995. A New Zealand/Canada co-production. *Locations*: Auckland, Avondale College, Westmere. *Distributor*: Tucker Developments. *Rating*: G, April 1995. 35 mm. Dolby Stereo. Colour. 97 mins.

Director: Wayne Tourell. *Producers*: Murray Newey, Micheline Charest. *Co-producers*: Judith Trye, Patricia Lavoie. *Supervising producer*: Madeleine Henrie. *Executive producers*: Antony I. Ginnane, Ronald A. Weinberg. *Screenplay*: David Preston based on a story by David Parry. *Director of photography*: Matt Bowkett. *Camera operator*: Mike Fuller. *Editor*: Jean-Marie Drot. *Production designer*: Brett Schwieters. *Costume designer*: Pauline Bowkett. *Composer*: Daniel Scott. *Sound*: Raymond Vermette, Dick Reade, Mario Rodrigue, Jean-Pierre Pinard.

Cast

Sabine Karsenti (Michelle), Dean O'Gorman (Timothy), Milan Borich (Nathan), Angela Bloomfield (Vikki), Richard Vette (Derek), Sylvia Rands (Mary), Syd Jackson (Roger), Mark Hadlow (Rugby Coach), Raewyn Blade (Miss Braithwaite), Stephen Papps (Mr Blisker), Nathaniel Lees (Mr Wiley), Wayne Wells (Thug Friend No. 1), Ryan McFadyen (Thug Friend No. 2), Jay Saussey (Melissa Anderson), Marise Wipani (Airport Clerk), Megan Nicol (Waitress).

Avondale College student Tim calls rich bully Derek a psycho and retribution comes when he is shut in a girl's locker. When Tim is discovered there by the girls the opportunistic Principal bribes him into hosting an international exchange student. Tim is shocked when his French-Canadian guest is a gorgeous girl, Michelle. Instantly smitten he tries, without success, to impress her. Michelle finds it hard to settle but is befriended by Vikki. Tim's friend Nathan pursues Vikki and Tim has a rival in Derek, who persuades Michelle to partner him at his party. Tim sees Michelle leave the party drunk and, following her to One Tree Hill, rescues her from Derek's abuse. Michelle is ill and Tim, putting her to bed, discovers a tattoo on her thigh. Nathan spreads the news. At the final assembly Derek and his mates lead the student body in a 'tattoo tattoo' chant. On a camping holiday with the family Michelle refuses to speak to Tim, but relents after a heart-to-heart with his mother, Mary. Michelle joins Tim, who is star-gazing, and they kiss. After tearfully seeing Michelle off at the airport, Tim resolves to become an exchange student and join her in Montreal.

Bonjour Timothy, with its middle-class suburban milieu, is a lively, comedic film about and for teenagers. With the original story written by David Parry when he was 20, it's a wish-fulfilment fantasy (the underdog gets the dream try and the girl) catering good-naturedly to adolescent preoccupation with, fear of and anxiety about sex.

The recurring motif is the gaze. Tim is initially set-up as a peeper, but from his meeting with Michelle he actually becomes one. The phallic implications of his telescope are thoroughly exploited and the comet does nicely as an orgasm motif, but Tim is not alone in his gazing. Almost every male in the film, including Tim's father, is hard at it, while the camera provides plenty of gaze shots for the audience. In one scene Michelle drools over the bums of the rugby players, but for the most part it is the male point of view that is privileged. For all that, this is an innocent film. Kissing is as far as anyone gets, the stimulants of choice are beer and wine and the strongest terms of abuse are 'jerk' and 'wanker'.

Much of the film was shot at Avondale College with its students as extras. The film is well cast and the performances polished and credible. To provide energy the camera moves a lot. Cultural and period references are made without fuss. Tim's father is a lovable beer-and-rugby blowhard and the teachers are comically flawed. The boys talk big — a girl is either a 'spunky babe' or a 'dog' — but their vulnerabilty shows in well judged action and dialogue, particularly in Nathan and Tim's exchanges. Appropriate to the 1990s Derek's bragging about his planned sexual conquest is rewarded by a smack on the face. The excellent soundtrack includes Canadian band Tragically Hip and New Zealand musicians The Headless Chickens, Dave Dobbyn and The Warratahs. HM

1995 Giffoni Film Festival, Italy: Gold Critic's Award.
Cinemagic Film Festival, Belfast: Best Film.
1996 19th Berlin Children's Film Festival: Special Jury Mention.

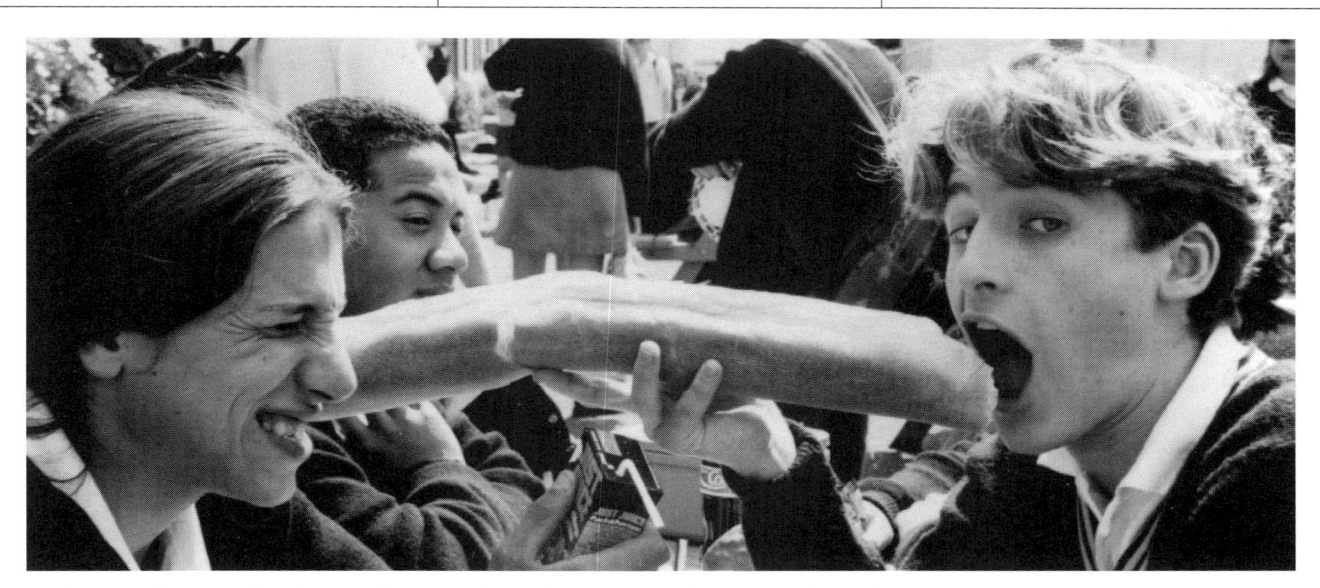

Milan Borich (Nathan) and Dean O'Gorman (Timothy). Courtesy of the New Zealand Film Commission.

Cinema of Unease: A Personal Journey by Sam Neill

BFI TV, the New Zealand Film Commission, N.Z. On Air, TV3 Network Services in association with Top Shelf Productions. A New Zealand/United Kingdom co-production. A.k.a. A Century of New Zealand Cinema (TVNZ title). © 1995. Documentary. *Budget*: $466 000. *Locations*: New Zealand, England. *Distributor*: Top Shelf Productions. *Rating*: Exempt, July 1995. 35 mm. Colour. 56 mins.

Directors: Sam Neill and Judy Rymer. *Producers*: Paula Jalfon, Grant Campbell. *Executive producers*: Vincent Burke, Colin MacCabe, Bob Last. *Director of photography*: Alun Bollinger. *Camera operator* (U.K.): Alistair Cameron. *Screenplay*: Sam Neill, Judy Rymer. *Editor*: Michael Horton. *Music*: Don McGlashan. *Performers*: The Mutton Birds. *Sound*: John McNicholas, Ross Chambers, Mike Hedges.

Cinema of Unease is the New Zealand contribution to the British Film Institute's Century of Cinema series in which 18 film-makers were invited to survey their national cinema. Whereas film-makers like Martin Scorsese (**A Personal Journey With Martin Scorsese Through American Movies**) and Stephen Frears (**Typically British: A Personal History of British Cinema**), both of whom have played full and influential roles in their countries' cinema histories, chose to present a comprehensive survey of their countries' films and to indicate how they shaped them as film-makers, New Zealand expatriate actor Sam Neill, with co-writer, documentary film-maker Judy Rymer, builds his journey around a single thesis, indicated in the title, that the country's film-making culture is dark and brooding and troubled and, as such, reflects a nation of the same ilk.

While the production values are first class, the film is fatally flawed, both in the pomposity and purple prose of Sam Neill's delivery and in the content. Firstly, in an autobiographical stroll down memory lane, Neill conveys embarrassment and distaste that the country of his birth provided him with such an unworldly, alienating and eventless childhood, where everyone longed for a return to a mythical England and where the country's most important statistic was its headcount of sheep. Film clips illuminate his memories — a clip from **The Scarecrow** illustrates that kids ate jaffas at the movies, a clip from **An Angel At My Table** evokes the spooky feelings Neill had about the local psychiatric hospital — and demonstrate that our films have reflected some significant moments in our history (**Patu!** for the Springbok Tour, **Weekly Reviews** for World War II).

Moving on to New Zealand's cinema history Neill briefly describes the significance of Rudall Hayward, John O'Shea and Pacific Films and the National Film Unit. The 1977 release of **Sleeping Dogs**, heralding the 'birth' of a national cinema, paved the way, in Neill's view, for a raft of archetypal, boy-film B-movies (**Goodbye Pork Pie**, **Smash Palace**) following in the wake of John Mulgan's seminal novel *Man Alone*, with the road as the central metaphor. Then cinema grows up, the boy-film is attacked and the introspective, psychologically probing A-feature is born: **Vigil**, **Desperate Remedies**, **Bread and Roses**, **The Navigator** and, putting New Zealanders 'centre frame' where we can 'see ourselves', **The Piano**.

A section on the distinctiveness of some New Zealand actors (Bruno Lawrence, Kerry Fox, Grant Tilly, Ian Watkin, John Bach, Martyn Sanderson) opens the possibilities out a little, but the problem with the 'New Zealand film history' aspect of **Cinema of Unease** is that clips are chosen to illustrate the 'dark and brooding and troubled' thesis. Thus, while some films are mentioned often (**Heavenly Creatures**, **Bad Blood**, **Braindead**, **The Piano**), there are many films, themes and genres not mentioned at all (the shaggy dog tale, the pot-boiler co-production, the film reflecting Pacific Island culture, the urban comedy, the feminist thriller, the Hollywood clone …).

The film was not favourably reviewed in New Zealand with many critics feeling a chance to celebrate the uniqueness of our film culture had been missed. It was, however, warmly praised by the *New York Times* and the *Los Angeles Times*. HM.

Sam Neill as himself. Courtesy of the New Zealand Film Commission.

1996 *TV Guide* Film and Television Awards. Best Documentary.

WHO'S COUNTING? MARILYN WARING ON SEX, LIES AND GLOBAL ECONOMICS

National Film Board of Canada, Studio B. Copyright 1995. Documentary. *Locations*: New Zealand, New York, Dubai, Philippines, Kenya, Montreal. *Distributor*: Media Services, NZ. Television rating: G. 1995. Dolby stereo. Colour. 35mm. 94 minutes.

Director: Terre Nash. *Producer*: Kent Martin. *Executive producers*: Colin Neale, Don Haig. *Associate producer/original film concept*: Pamela Adamson. *Source*: Marilyn Waring, *Counting for Nothing* (released in North America as *If Women Counted*). *Director of photography*: Susan Trow. *Dubai Airshow sequence*: Martin Duckworth. *Philippines sequence*: Anne Henderson. *Dubai interviewer*: Jooned Khan. *Radio interviewer*: David Gutnick. *Speaking of Nairobi excerpt*: Montreal New Film Group. *The War Series: Notes on Nuclear War excerpt*: National Film Board of Canada. *Research*: Sabine Pusch, Kent Martin, Terre Nash, Pamela Adamson, Lucie Winer. *Optical effects*: Susan Gourley. *Music*: Penny Lang, Penguin Café Orchestra, Brian Eno and Daniel Lanois, Jason Lang and Lance Neveu, J.S. Bach. *Vocalist*: Marilyn Waring. *Sound*: Diane Carriere, Jacqueline Newell, Danuta Klis, Jean-Pierre Joutel, Serge Boivin, Claude Hamel, Michel Chalut, Louis Hone, Chris Crilly.

Marilyn Waring, at the age of 22, became the youngest member of the 1975 New Zealand parliament. Three terms of office later, her refusal to vote in support of allowing nuclear-armed and -powered ships into New Zealand waters brought down the National Government. Freed from her role as a politician, and resolved to demystify economics, Waring set off on a process of discovery to test her theory that the world's national income accounting systems, set in place by John Maynard Keynes and Richard Stone, fail to measure or value the work engaged in by many on the planet and lead many people to a state of 'economics anxiety'. The fascinating documentary **Who's Counting?** pursues ideas expressed in Waring's book *Counting for Nothing*. The film's thematic glue is provided by an address she gave in Montreal to provide footage for the film, and it is given shape by a fifteen-part structure. Cut into the address is a wide range of footage: Waring's discoveries while in political power and later, when she travelled to New York to study the international rules of economics set down in the United Nations System of National Accounts; examples of the effects of this system on women and children in third and first world countries; interviews with Waring in Canada and on her farm in New Zealand; interviews with well-known identities like John Kenneth Galbraith, Gloria Steinem and the Hon. Katherine O'Regan, and with people without political power whose lives are profoundly affected by the global system of economics.

In the intelligent articulation of her thesis Marilyn Waring covers from a feminist perspective some of the territory Peter Watkins explores in his fifteen-hour film *The Journey*, which has screened constantly around the world since its release in 1987. Waring makes connections between the massive greed of arms race economics and world poverty and want. Like Watkins, she concludes that to save the planet from extinction each individual must act to bring about a shift to the view that in an 'economic' system there is more to be valued than the exchange of money and goods. In particular, Waring sees the measurement of time use and the development of qualitative environmental indicators as vital to an equitable system of wealth distribution and to a healthy planet. Her own answer to the challenge, in addition to widely publicising her ideas, has been to become a goat farmer, a lifestyle she sees as helping her restore the environment. In butting the camera operator Waring's handsome guard-goat Tofu has the last word.

The idea for the film came from associate producer Pamela Adamson, who was convinced of Waring's theories by her reading of *Counting for Nothing*. Independent film-maker Terre Nash (who made the academy award-winning Helen Caldicott film *If You Love This Planet*) worked with Waring to shape the film. Because all New Zealand agencies approached refused to become involved, the film was funded entirely by the National Film Board of Canada.

Who's Counting? has screened in festivals worldwide and on New Zealand's TV3 on 22 October 1995 and 21 January 1996. The videotaped version is being distributed in New Zealand, where the International Film Festival declined to screen the film when it was submitted for the 1995 event. HM

1996 Edinburgh Film Festival: Best Film.
 Colombus Film Festival, USA: Chris Award.
 Genie Award nomination, Canada.
 Bombay Film Festival: Film Award.

Marilyn Waring on her Wellsford farm. Courtesy of Marilyn Waring

1996

THE OFFERING

Quetzal Films. A Mexico/New Zealand/USA production. A.k.a. *Shadow of the Pepper Tree*. *Post-production consultants*: Tucker Films. (NZ). *Copyright*: 1995. *Location*: Mexico. *Distributor*: Blue Angel Films. *Rating*: M. January 1996. 35mm. Colour. Dolby stereo. 92 minutes.

Directors/producers/screenplay: Taggart Siegel, Francesca Fisher. *Director of photography*: Alex Phillips Jnr ASC. *Camera operator*: Guillermo Rosas. *Editors*: Dermot McNeillage (NZ), Sonya Polonsky (USA). *Production designers*: Genevieve Desgagnes, Daniel Sirdey, Rita Torlen. *Wardrobe supervisor*: Adolfo Ramirez. *Special effects*: Jose Lim. *Choreographer*: Gilbert Meunier. *Composers*: Wille Royal, Wolfgang Fink, Tribu. *Performers*: Willie & Lobo, Tribu. *Music producer*: Keith Ballantyne. *Sound*: Fernando Camara, Jorge Palomino, Dick Reade, Paul Stent, Gethin Creagh, Michael Hedges, John Neill.

Cast

Mayra Serbulo (Luna), Thom Vernom (Terence), Greg Sporleder (Willie), Zaide Sylvia Gutierrez (Luz), with Socorro Avelar, Javier Herrera, Malena Doria, Rodrigo Puebla, Adyari Chazaro, Claude Pru D'Homme, John Garvey, Maria Cespedes, Victoria Southern, Yolanda Orizaga, Lolo Navarro, Benjamen Gonzalez.

San Miguel de Allende, 1968. Luna, a young Mexican woman, informs the viewer in voiceover that, according to the calendar of her Aztec ancestors, she was born under a dark and dangerous sign. In spite of warnings she visits a witch, and her mother, a shaman healer, drags her away. Luna's mother refuses to teach her how to use her healing powers and demands that she leave. Living alone, Luna practises healing and meets a Spanish-speaking American beatnik, Terence, who lives with other beatniks and paints. Terence seduces her but refuses to marry her, preferring the company of his friends. Luna uses black magic to help a woman get rid of her husband's mistress. When she tells Terence she is pregnant he runs away and refuses to see her. She learns he has a Mexican fiancée, a dancer and, using black magic, kills the woman with a hex. In the next few years, Luna devotes her time to raising her son, Robio, until Terence, convinced that Luna is continuing to blight his life, kidnaps the boy. In an accident somehow contrived by Luna, Terence and Robio are killed. After a battle with dark forces Luna's good side triumphs, and she is welcomed back by her mother.

Freed from the constraints of a conventional cause and effect plot structure (Why won't Luna's mother tell her what she fears? Why does Terence decide after so many years that he wants his son?), **The Offering** tells a modern folk tale of obsession, revenge, witchcraft, and redemption. Images of evil (characterised by the snake as both Christian and pagan demon) and of the divided self (mirrors) dominate the film. In broad terms the mythic dimensions offer opportunities for some striking visual imagery and choreography and a haunting, beautifully executed musical score. Characters and events springing from a framework of realism provide ironic comment on the destructiveness of obsessive love as well as of outsiders' colonisation of other cultures. The case in point is the effects on Mexican culture of the pilgrimage made by droves of beatniks seeking freedom and enlightenment and sampling the cactus plant's hallucinatory properties, as enthusiastically advertised by Carlos Castaneda.

In 1992 the film, then titled *Eclipse* (a.k.a. *Wild Blue Moon*), was brought to New Zealand. After test screenings the film makers reshot some scenes in Mexico and had the film re-edited in New Zealand.

The Offering, shot in Spanish and subtitled in English, was made with money from New Zealand, the USA and Mexico. Fisher is a New Zealand-born film-maker who lives in Mexico, while her co-writer/director/producer Siegel is an American living in New Zealand. HM

Mayra Serbulo (Luna). Courtesy of Taggart Siegal.

1996

CHICKEN

Keirfilm Productions Ltd in association with the New Zealand Film Commission present a Senator Film International co-production. New Zealand/Germany. Copyright 1996. *Budget*: $2.7 million. *Location*: Wellington. *Distributor*: Essential Films. *Rating*: PG, April 1996. 35mm. Dolby Stereo. Colour. 90 minutes.

Director: Grant Lahood. *Executive producer*: Hanno Huth. *Producer*: John Keir. *Screenplay*: Grant Lahood. *Director of photography*: Allen Guilford. *Camera operator*: Simon Riera. *Editor*: John Gilbert. *Production designer*: John Girdlestone. *Costume designer*: Bev Hinchey. *Special effects coordinator*: Wayne Rugg. *Chicken trainers*: Hero Animals, James Delaney, Caroline Girdlestone. *Child wrangler*: Cushla Roughton. *Stunt coordinator*: Bruce Brown. *Score*: Michelle Scullion. *Song producer*: Ian Morris. *Sound*: Ken Saville, Michael Hopkins, Craig Tomlinson, Michael Hedges, John Boswell, Helen Luttrell.

Cast

Bryan Marshall (Dwight Serrento), Martyn Sanderson (Bryce Tilfer), Ellie Smith (Colette Milham), Cliff Curtis (Zeke), Jed Brophy (Will Tilfer), Claire Waldron (Vicky Serrento), Joan Dawe (Betty Junket), Sean Feehan (Otis Milham), with Adele Chapman, Desmond Kelly, Lucy Schmidt, Martin Csokas, Julia Truscott, Lewis Martin, Peter Hambleton, John Leigh, Bronwyn Bradley, John Wraight, Brian Sergent, Mick Rose, Phil Vaughan, Nick Ward, Tina Cleary, Dylan Tait, Alison Mau, Aimée Belton, Lillian Forrester, Lyndee-Jane Rutherford, Jacqui Pryor, Stuart Turner, Miki Magasiva, Alison Harper, Nancy Brunning, Justin Curry, Dominic Godfrey, Simon Alsford, Francesca Morton, Ray Columbus, Suzanne Lynch, Judy Hindman, Shane Hales, Bruce Warwick, John Harrison, Rick White, Meredyth Tamsyn, Peter Hall, Roger Watkins, Desna Sisarich.

Ageing, has-been 1960s pop singer Dwight Serrento, reduced to singing jingles promoting fast-food chicken for Lik'n'Chik, fakes his own death with the help of his agent Bryce in order to recapture the interest of his fans. For a while the ruse is successful. However, while in hiding with the help of his daughter Vicky, his longtime housekeeper Betty, Bryce, and Bryce's dim-witted son Will, Dwight is stalked by psychopathic eco-terrorist Zeke, who aims to save all poultry from the battery box by making an example of the rock star. Also after Dwight are police, who suspect a scam.

Bryan Marshall (Dwight Serrento). Courtesy of the New Zealand Film Commission.

In the mayhem that follows Dwight and his newly acquired bodyguard Colette forge a relationship, Colette's son Otis almost destroys, then saves, the day, Vicky finds her birth mother, Zeke murders loyal Betty, and Bryce, revealed to be a villainous traitor in collusion with Zeke, attempts to have Dwight's face disfigured by surgery. The happy ending sees Dwight transformed, minus the bad wig but with a black eyepatch to remind him of his lucky escape from the surgeon's knife, successful as a producer/songwriter, married to Colette and a confirmed vegetarian.

Chicken is an energetic romp, in the same vein as Lahood's acclaimed short films (**The Singing Trophy**, **Snail's Pace**, **Lemming Aid**), with the fickle nature of fame and the clash between the human and the animal worlds providing the spurs to the plot. Some of the gags work (Zeke bursts brilliantly into flames when annoyed, 1960s New Zealand Happen Inn pop stars, the Chicks among them, turn up as themselves at Dwight's 'funeral'). The excellent production design, the cinematography, with its skew and extreme angles, and the heat and explosion motifs give the visuals interest. Zeke's lair of 'rescued' hens is a highlight. Most successful is the film's neat juggling act, which has it lampooning animal rights activists while also asserting that activists have a lot to be heated up about.

But, in aiming at a **Raising Arizona** style of black comedy, **Chicken** is frantic where it should be deadpan. Although its characters and story are cartoon, the approach to the overloaded script is scattergun, and few of the characters manage to arouse much sympathy. In particular hyperactive Otis, whose allergy-induced destructive behaviour makes some comment on food industry practices but functions ultimately as a plot device, is an unfunny irritant. Dwight's mutation into a chicken inexplicably comes to a halt, Colette's posing as Vicky's birth mother has little payoff, and Betty's death seems thrown in to fill out the running time.

Although reviewers greeted the film with a plethora of poultry puns and a considerable amount of enthusiasm for the spirited tone, **Chicken** did poorly at the local box office. HM

1996

FLIGHT OF THE ALBATROSS

Taungaroa Emile (Mako) and Julia Brendler (Sarah). Courtesy of the New Zealand Film Commission.

Top Shelf Productions and Fritz Wagner Filmproduktion present in association with the New Zealand Film Commission, Zweites Deutsche Fernsehen, Avalon Studios, Filmboard Berlin Brandenberg and Portman Productions. New Zealand–Germany co-production. Copyright 1995. *Budget*: $4.4 million. *Locations*: Great Barrier Island, Berlin. *Distributor*: Footprint Films. Rating: G. April 1996. VHS. Dolby Stereo. Colour. 88 minutes.

Director: Werner Meyer. *Executive producers*: Rita Wagner, Susanne Wagner. *Producer*: Udo Heiland. *Screenplay*: Riwia Brown. *Source*: Deborah Savage, *Flight of the Albatross*. *Director of photography*: Martin Gressmann. *Editor*: Mike Horton. *Production designer*: Rick Kofoed. *Costume designer*: Kaumatua Rei Rakatau. *Ngati Wai liaison*: Whetu McGregor, Shona Rapira Davies. *Composer*: Jan Preston. *Performers*: New Zealand Symphony Orchestra. *Orchestration*: John Charles. *Flute*: Alexa Still. *Traditional Maori instruments*: Richard Nunns. *Sound*: Dave Madigan, Mike Hopkins, Ross Chambers, Craig Tomlinson, Michael Hedges, Helen Luttrell, John van der Reyden, John Neill.

Cast

Julia Brendler (Sarah), Taungaroa Emile (Mako), Suzanne von Borsody (Claudia), Diana Ngaromotu-Heka (Mari), Jack Thompson (Mike), Pete Smith (Huka), Peter Tait (Digby), Joan Reid (Margaret), Eva Rickard (Hatai), Peter Schmode (Walter), Gloria (Chubby) Park (Bartender), Ebony Kite-Bell (Atawhai), Phillip Barclay (Pilot), Grant Tilly (Narrator), Kate Harcourt, Jeff Thomas, Susan Wilson (Additional voice work).

As an albatross glides with grace over a perfect blue sea, an old Maori woman, Hatai, keens a karakia. Voice-over narration explains that the return of the bird heralds the arrival of one with the power to lift the curse on a desecrated sacred mountain burial ground, Pukeroimata. Teenage Maori Mako, released from prison, returns to his island home angry with and resentful of his pakeha stepfather. Refusing to take advice, he fishes in forbidden waters and is later hunted by a shark. Mako is watched over by the spirit of his dead Aunt Hatai, a tohunga. His relationship with Sarah, a flute-playing teenager who has come from Berlin to visit her distracted ornithologist mother Claudia, progresses from antagonism to friendship but is threatened when Claudia, seeing them kissing, resolves to send her daughter home. Pakeha Digby, struck dumb since he broke Pukeroimata's tapu, gives Sarah a gold comb belonging to her look-alike relative, Catherine, who was Digby's lover and who died on Pukeroimata. Sarah is told she must return the comb to the island. When bar owner Huka learns Sarah has rescued a trapped albatross he urges Mako to take the patu he has found belonging to Hatai and return it to the island. In a dramatic climax the comb and patu are reunited and the ancient curse lifted. Mako and Sarah escape as mine shafts collapse around them.

Flight of the Albatross revisits the spiritual territory of Maori cosmology in such films as **The Lost Tribe**, **Mauri**, **Mark 11**, **Ngati** and **Te Rua**. The curse is lifted through a double act of bravery crossing Maori and European cultures, and as a consequence family reconciliations and personal, cultural and spiritual redemption are effected. The film, the first feature to be shot on Great Barrier Island, has gorgeous cinematography taking maximum advantage of the island's natural beauty. Action is accompanied by an excellent soundtrack, particularly effective where it carries haunting suggestions of the supernatural. Targeted specifically at a teenage audience, the film focuses on dysfunctional families as a source of teenage anguish. The Maori mother, Mari, provides a loving role model that contrasts with the benign neglect of the Berliner Claudia, who has more time for her birds than for her daughter. Refusal to acknowledge traditional cultural values creates spiritual malaise in both Maori (Mako) and pakeha (Digby); it is cured only by a change in attitude and behaviour.

Many actors give spirited performances but, because some performances are wooden, and much of the dialogue is awkward, not all the characters convince. The plot is overloaded with twists and turns, and the symbolism weighs so heavily—shark, earring, albatross, patu, gold comb, bird incubations, flutes—that the narrative has the predictability of melodrama, and the 'message' (adults will let you down, take responsibility for yourself) is unsubtly delivered.

Flight of the Albatross had a short theatrical run locally. It is to screen overseas as a television miniseries. HM.

1996 TV Guide Film and Television Awards. Best Supporting Actor: Pete Smith.
1997 Berlin Film Festival: Best Film.

1996

BROKEN ENGLISH

Village Roadshow presents a Communicado Production in association with the New Zealand Film Commission and New Zealand On Air. Copyright 1996. *Location*: Auckland. *Distributor*: Roadshow Film Distributors. *Rating*: R16. Contains violence, offensive language and sex scenes. June 1996. Colour. 35mm. 95.28 minutes.

Director: Gregor Nicholas. *Producer*: Robin Scholes. *Executive producer*: Timothy White. *Screenplay*: Gregor Nicholas, Johanna Pigott, Jim Salter. *Additional dialogue*: Aleksandra Vujcic, Rade Serbedzija, Jing Zhao, Li Yang. *Director of photography*: John Toon. *Editor*: David Coulson. *Production designer*: Mike Kane. *Costume designer*: Glenis Foster. *Maori language/culture consultant*: Don Selwyn. *Croatian language/culture consultants*: Davorin Krnjal, Anna Jankovaic. *Chinese language/culture consultant*: Hou Dejian. *Music*: Murray Grindlay, Murray McNab, Nenad Romano. *Sound*: Tony Johnson, Graham Myhre, Steve Murphy, Michael Hedges, Don Paulin, Ray Beentjes, Kit Rollings, John Neill.

Cast

Rade Serbedzija (Ivan), Aleksandra Vujcic (Nina), Madeline McNamara (Mira), Marton Csokas (Darko), Elizabeth Mavric (Vanya), Michael Langley (Zura), Marena Tutugaro (Sashka), Mona Ross (Auntie Marja), Julian Arahanga (Eddie), Temuera Morrison (Manu), Jing Zhao (Clara), Li Yang (Wu), with Barbara Cartwright, Patrick Wilson, Greg Johnson, Stephen Hall, Stephen Ure, Vinko Bakich, Zejiko Bilcic, Rade Borkovic, Chris Ruka, Nui Tuakana, Teariki Vaerua, Shane Harris, Crystal Harris, Tepori Vaerua, Naomi Kino, Rocky Pepe, Romey Ruka, Chris Anderton, Dominic Blaazer, Dalmatian Club of Auckland, Taokotaianga Cultural Group.

A young woman in voice-over laments the destructive power of bombs while refugee buses flee a Croatian town after its fall to Serbia. In Auckland three years later the young woman, Nina and her sister Vanya, serve drinks as their father Ivan, who runs the family marijuana-growing business, hosts a gambling session. When Ivan finds Vanya having sex in a car, he and his son Darko wreck it with baseball bats. Nina resolves to escape her father's tyranny by marrying Wu, the Chinese boyfriend of her workmate Clara, to enable him to immigrate. With the payment she receives Nina buys a car. She moves in with her new boyfriend Eddie, a chef she meets at the restaurant where she works. Clara and Wu also move in, to provide cover for Wu's impending marriage to Nina. At a family party Wu, drunk, reveals Nina's plans to marry him, and Ivan beats him. Eddie, annoyed with Nina for exposing them all to Ivan's anger, takes off for the Bay of Islands. Ivan drags Nina back home and locks her in. Eddie rescues her, and they leave together. Later, they play with their child on a beach, and Nina laments her father's refusal to accept her relationship with Eddie.

A cross-cultural, *Romeo and Juliet*-influenced love story told in melodramatic style, **Broken English** is notable among New Zealand films for its representation of many ethnic backgrounds—Croatian (Nina's family), Pacific Island (their neighbours), Maori (Eddie and his brother Manu) and Chinese (Clara and Wu)—and its non-representation of the dominant European culture. While Maori Eddie expresses his pride in his cultural roots by way of passionate attachment to a pohutukawa tree, Chinese immigrants Clara and Wu, a political refugee, dream of producing 'a small Kiwi'. Clinging to old gender-linked behaviour, the male Croatian immigrants see themselves at the centre of 'normality' and, against a background of ethnic chaos in their homeland (seen most powerfully in a television broadcast), lord it over their women and their Polynesian neighbours. Although the immigrants might have escaped hard times in their homelands, the New Zealand urban setting where they make their lives is bleak and their prospects limited.

The target audience for **Broken English** is 16–25-year-olds, and the film relies on commercial-style film-making techniques. Part of the advertising campaign focused on the 'discovery' of beautiful young Aleksandra Vujcic in an Auckland bar during casting. While the heightened style (production design, soundtrack, editing and performance) casts the film as melodrama, several local reviewers were not convinced. They gave **Broken English** a negative reception, calling it contrived and mediocre, and criticising it for shallow characterisation using racial stereotypes, unsatisfying performances, and a minimal, predictable plot. Most praised the film's production values, but Philip Matthews[1] called the design 'an advertising agency's idea of lower socio-economic Auckland sprawl' that 'swims in art-directed poverty and stylised alienation'. The local box office, however, told a different story. **Broken English** became the third highest grossing film of the 1990s. Many overseas reviewers were positive about the film, praising it, for example, for being 'bold' and 'hard hitting'.[2] HM.

1996 Asia Pacific Film Festival: Best Editing.
TV Guide Film and Television Awards: Best Supporting Actress (Madeline McNamara). Best Foreign Performer: Rade Serbedzija. Best Editing. Best Design. Best Soundtrack.

References
1 *NZ Listener*, 21 September 1996
2 Jay Carr, *Boston Globe*.

Julian Arahanga (Eddie) and Aleksandra Vujcic (Nina). Courtesy of Communicado.

1996

THE FRIGHTENERS

Robert Zemeckis presents a WingNut Films Production. Universal Pictures. USA. Copyright 1996. *Budget*: $US29.66 million. *Locations*: Wellington, Lyttelton. *Distributor*: United International Pictures. *Rating*: M. Contains violence. August 1996. 35mm. Dolby Stereo. Colour. 110 minutes (amended to 106 minutes).

Director: Peter Jackson. *Executive producer*: Robert Zemeckis. *Producers*: Jamie Selkirk, Peter Jackson. *Co-producer*: Tim Sanders. *Associate producer*: Fran Walsh. *Screenplay*: Fran Walsh, Peter Jackson. *Directors of photography*: Alun Bollinger, John Blick. *Camera operators*: Richard Bluck, Allun Bollinger. *Editor*: Jamie Selkirk. *Production designer*: Grant Major. *Costume designer*: Barbara Darragh. *Effects make-up*: Rick Baker, Richard Taylor. *Visual effects*: WETA Ltd. *Digital effects producer*: Charlie McClellan. *Creature and miniature effects designer*: Richard Taylor. *Visual effects supervisor*: Wes Takahashi. *On set supervisor*: George Port. *Composer*: Danny Elfman. *Orchestrator*: Steve Bartek. *Conductor*: Artie Kane. *Music editor*: Ellen Segal. *Players*: the Muttonbirds, Sonic Youth. *Sound*: Randy Thom, Hammond Peek, Phil Benson, Mike Hopkins, Janet Roddick, Mark Herman, Cindy Bowles, Sam Negri, Brent Burge, Tim Prebble, Mike Jones, Craig Tomlinson, Ross Chambers, Helen Luttrell, Mike Hedges, Gethin Creagh, Chris Ward, John Neill, David Boulton, Charleen Richards, Chris Burt.

US Cast

Michael J. Fox (Frank Bannister), Trini Alvarado (Lucy), Peter Dobson (Ray), Jeffrey Combs (Milton), Dee Wallace Stone (Patricia), Chi McBride, John Astin, Jim Fyfe, Julianna McCarthy, Troy Evans, Jake Busey, R. Lee Ermey.

NZ Cast

Elizabeth Hawthorne, Jonathan Blick, Angela Bloomfield, Todd Rippon, John Sumner, Michael Robinson, Jim McLarty, Anthony Ray Parker, Paul Yates, Stuart Devenie, Desmond Kelly, Ken Blackburn, John Leigh, K. C. Kelly, Alan O'Leary, Lewis Martin, Danny Lineham, Melanie Linskey, Nicola Cliff, Genevieve Westcott, George Port, Liz Mullane, Billy Jackson.

In the small US town of Fairwater (Lyttelton), Frank Bannister, down on his luck, uses his paranormal abilities to eke out a living exorcising houses that have had the frighteners put on them by his three ghost friends. Frank is in trouble because the editor of the local paper is on to him. His problems are exacerbated when police think he is connected to a spate of deaths in the town. Frank sees that the perpetrator of the 'heart attacks' is none other than the Grim Reaper, who marks out his victims by carving a number into their foreheads. Joining forces with Lucy, a doctor whose bullying husband has been struck down by the ghoul, Frank and his ghost friends do battle with the Death figure. Meanwhile, Lucy ministers to Patricia, a woman living as a recluse since her release from jail, where she was incarcerated following her participation in psychopathic Johnny Bartlett's mass murder spree at the local hospital. Things turn nasty when Lucy and Frank learn that Bartlett is the Grim Reaper. The showdown, complicated by the ghastly stalkings of a mad FBI agent and by Frank's spasmodic transportation to the scene of the original mass murder, results in the friendly ghosts finding a comfortable place in heaven, the Grim Reaper and his sidekick vanquished, and the brave couple united.

The hybrid genre of this 'thrillomedy', described by Peter Jackson as '**Caspar** meets **Silence of the Lambs**',[1] allows room for slapstick, splatter, verbal gags, daredevil comic stunt driving and numerous film allusions to be combined with straight action. The frantic pace rushes the tightly packed narrative along. The over-the-top tone compensates for the sometimes perfunctory attention paid to plot logic and characters drawn in too-broad strokes. A good-natured romp, with Peter Jackson and his baby Billy making brief cameo appearances, the film is more amiable than frightening. Interest is sustained by details like the send-up of **Natural Born Killers**' psycho-sexual pair bond, the clever use of setting, and the excellent production design. In characteristic Jackson–Walsh style, Frank strikes a tongue-in-cheek blow for the sensitive new age man, while the monster-mother in **Braindead** resurfaces here as a reformed character. Special effects highlights include the antics of the film's numerous ghosts and the Grim Reaper's vicious hauntings.

The film employs an army of rotoscope artists, character animators, technical directors, digital compositors and the like. It was fully financed and released by Hollywood's Universal Pictures. Shot and post-produced in New Zealand, **The Frighteners** showcases some 500 complex, state-of-the-art special effects, created by WETA Ltd, that marked a watershed in computer graphics and raised the international profile of the country's film-making skills.

Although given a 1600-print release in the USA, **The Frighteners** was not the box-office blockbuster there it was expected to be. Reviews ranged from enthusiastic to damning. The *Washington Times* called the film 'a creative landmark', and the *New Zealand Listener*'s Philip Matthews described it as 'built so completely from its references that, if one brick came out, the whole structure would collapse'.[2] In New Zealand, however, the film did very well at the box office (locally it was the top grossing film in the 1995–96 summer holidays) and at the time of writing had more than ninety home pages on the Internet. It was recut, with 15 minutes added, for a special-edition laser disc as part of Universal's Signature Collection series. HM

1996 Capital City Accolades. Wellington Fringe Festival. Film Unit Management of Post-Production Schedule (Colin Tyler).
Sitges Festival of Fantasy Film. Spain. Special effects prize, model maker, Richard Taylor.

References
[1] Interview with Kim Hill. National Radio. 9 December 1996
[2] *New Zealand Listener*. 14 December 1996.

Jim Fyfe (Stuart), Michael J. Fox (Frank Bannister) and Chi McBride (Cyrus). Courtesy of Universal Studios.

The Whole of the Moon

Tucker Films Ltd and Cinar Productions Inc., in association with the New Zealand Film Commission and with the participation of TMN, Government of Quebec, Super Channel. A Canada–New Zealand co-production. *Copyright*: 1995. *Locations*: Auckland. *Rating*: PG. December 1996. *Distributor*: Columbia TriStar. 35mm. Colour. Dolby Stereo. 94 minutes.

Producers: Murray Newey, Micheline Charest. *Associate producer*: Brian Walden. *Co-producers*: Judith Trye, Patricia Lavoie. *Executive producers*: Ronald A. Wienberg, Antony I. Ginnane. *Supervising producer*: Madeleine Henrie. *Screenplay*: Richard Lymposs and Ian Mune, based on a story by Richard Lymposs. *Director of photography*: Warrick Attewell. *Camera operator*: Mark Olsen. *Editor*: Jean Beaudoin. *Production designer*: Brett Schwieters. *Costume designer*: Pauline Bowkett. *Visual special effects supervisor*: François Aubry. *Digital effects*: Topix. *Medical advisers*: Karen Olsen, Megan Brownhill, Jane Wilkinson. *Skating coordinators*: Carol Over, Bill Over, Chris Poipoi. *Music*: Daniel Scott. *Band*: Supergroove. *Sound*: Raymond Vermette, Graham Morris, Louis Collin, Katherine Fitzgerald.

Cast

Toby Fisher (Kirk Mead), **Nikki Si'ulepa** (Marty), Pascale Bussieres (Sarah), Paul Gittins (Alec Mead), Jane Thomas (Maureen Mead), Nicola Cliff (Tory Taylor), Elliot O'Donnell (Ronnie), Carl Bland (Mr Dixon), Greg Johnson (Mr Couper), with Ollie Rennie, Lee Metekingi, Sam Holland, Ezra Woods, Hannah Collins, William Sabin, Missy Erick, Suzie Taylor, McKay Tharp, Tinkeke Van Der Walle, Gina Binnie, Chloe Jordan, Judie Steele, Marion Holmes, Adam Middleton, Karen Routledge, Amber Cunliffe, Ashleigh Seagar, Scott Harman, Edwin Hussey, Ben Eastwood, Adam Biesharr, Robert Elliott, Kent Bowater, Kerryn Fowlie, Phoebe Falconer, Joe Folau, Misa Tupou, Anton Tobin, Alfred Aholelei, Joseph Naufahu.

Kirk Mead is a Palagi teenager living in an affluent New Zealand seaside suburb (Takapuna). He has a lot of friends, a new girlfriend, and a promising future as a champion roller-blader. Tested after a roller-blading accident, Kirk learns he has bone cancer in his leg. In a children's cancer ward he meets leukemia patient Marty, a homeless Samoan teenager, who angrily stages a roll-call each morning to highlight the fact that children among them are dying. With Kirk's family and friends unable to understand his emotional pain, he feels increasingly alone, particularly when his girlfriend finds him repulsive after chemotherapy leaves him bald and depressed. Marty uses harsh tactics to help Kirk confront his illness and regain the will to live. After her initial antagonism and his self-pity (his leg might have to be amputated), the pair become friends. When Marty's condition worsens she persuades Kirk to run away with her. On the run they realise they love each other. Marty collapses and is taken back to hospital, where she dies in Kirk's arms. Kirk takes the morning roll-call, and resolves to do whatever it takes to live.

Surprisingly, **The Whole of the Moon** tells an ultimately upbeat story. Excellent casting and performances, especially from leads Toby Fisher and Nikki Si'ulepa, carry off the many difficult emotional moments. Ineffectual adults on the periphery are unable to provide empathy as the teenagers cross barriers of race and socioeconomic backgrounds to form a bond in their fight against cancer. The story—boy meets girl from the other side of the tracks and learns much from her that his privilege could never teach him—is not new. However, its telling is refreshingly different and all the more powerful because, in spite of the co-production factor, it has a very New Zealand flavour. The moon symbolism is achieved without cliché, and Marty's insights about life and death are remarkably uncontrived. The authenticity of the script (Richard Lymposs is the former street kid who scripted *Queen City Rocker*; Ian Mune is a seasoned professional) was boosted by thorough research, in particular in the actors' meetings with young cancer patients.

Set-piece scenes, like those on the hospital rooftop and on the gulf island, lend an air of magic that balances the pace of action scenes like the roller-blade races and the dancing and fighting in a city nightclub. Strong, moody lighting and effective set design contribute to the polished look.

The film's first public screening was at a charity première in November 1996, with the proceeds going to the children's hospital, Starship, in Auckland. On its general release, in February 1997, **The Whole of the Moon** was very well received at the box office. Reviewers were generally enthusiastic, but Philip Matthews, while praising the film's power, criticised some of the production values and described the first part as looking like a ' "So you have cancer" instruction video for kids'.* HM

1996 Giffoni Film Festival: Best Picture. Best Actor (Toby Fisher). Best Actress (Nikki Si'ulepa).
TV Guide Film and Television Awards: Best Film. Best Cinematography. Best Screenplay. Best Actress (Nikki Si'ulepa). Best Contribution to Design (Make-up).
1997 Berlin Film Festival: Special mention.

NZ Listener, 15 February 1997.

Nikki Si'ulepa (Marty) and Toby Fisher (Kirk). Courtesy of the New Zealand Film Commission.

1996
SOMEONE ELSE'S COUNTRY

Community Media Trust, in association with Vanguard Films with the assistance of the Creative Film and Video Fund of the Arts Council of New Zealand. Copyright date not recorded. Documentary. *Budget*: less than $40,000. *Location*: New Zealand. *Distributor*: Starr Brothers. *Rating*: Exempt. December 1996. Videotape. Colour/Black and white. 98 minutes.

Director: Alister Barry. *Producer*: Community Media Trust, Vanguard Films. *Writer*: Alister Barry. *Script advice*: Russell Campbell. *Camera operators*: Shane Loader, Tony Sutorius. *Additional camera*: Peter Da Vanzo, Mark Derby, Jonathon Brough, Barry Thomas, Gerry Vasbenter. *Super 8 footage*: Andrea Bosshard. *Editor*: Shane Loader. *Additional editing*: Tony Sutorius. *On-line editing*: Dub Shop, TV3 Wellington. *Music*: Janet Roddick, David Donaldson. *Sound*: Tony Sutorius. *Additional sound*: Russell Campbell, Gerd Pohlman, George Rose, Peter Da Vanzo, Shane Loader, Steve Upston, Hamiora Williams, Andrea Bosshard. *Sound mix*: Tony Parkinson, Blue Bicycle Flicks. *Narrator*: Ian Johnstone. *Archival footage*: TVNZ, California Newsreel, ITN, BBC, NZ Film Archive, TV3, Deborah Schaeffer, Warren Sellers, PSA, Valhalla Prods, John Reid, Post Office Workers' Union, Vanguard Films, Chris Dillon, Patricio Guzman, Zee Films, Yeti Prods, Sparrow Film Unit. *Photographs*: NZ Listener, NZ Herald, Evening Post, Dominion, PSA Journal.

Marchers protesting unemployment. Courtesy of PSA Journal/Vanguard Films.

With an interest in documenting New Zealand's track record on democracy, Alister Barry began work on **Someone Else's Country** in 1993. Financed partly by an Arts Council grant of $26,000, the film took three and a half years to make. The aim was to document the politics of Rogernomics, initiated by the 1984 fourth Labour Government (when Treasury secured the willing ear of Finance Minister Roger Douglas) and continued by successive Labour and National governments, and to explain how the forces of the New Right overcame obstacles in the way of the 'reform' agenda. After extensive research Barry looked to archives to provide footage and interviewed many of those directly involved.

The film opens with a sequence demonstrating the coming to power in 1973 of a dictatorship in Chile that set about opening the country up to foreign capital, selling off state-owned enterprises, cutting welfare and education spending, privatising hospitals and facilitating takeover of natural resources by multinationals. A parallel is drawn between Chile and Aotearoa/New Zealand where, ten years later, a democratically elected government initiated a similar programme without a shot being fired. A wealth of archival footage, supported by interviews with critics and supporters of the New Right, builds to show the reforms driven by the dictates of Treasury economists, Reserve Bank officials, wealthy trans- and multinational executives, and the increasingly powerful Business Roundtable. Individuals who wielded enormous power in the reform process—Richard Prebble, Roger Douglas, Doug Myers, Ron Trotter, Peter Shirtcliff, Bob Jones, and Roger Kerr—feature prominently. While men generally dominate, women appear in more supportive roles—Labour Party president Margaret Wilson plays a strong part in persuading members to support the changes, and Anne Hercus, with Phil Goff, shouts down protesters outside parliament—until Ruth Richardson becomes Finance Minister in the National Government (Michael Laws calls this 'unleashing the dog').

Women are seen in greater numbers among the critics of the New Right—as the country's assets are sold off, as the welfare state is dismantled and laws are passed to cut wages and benefits, as working conditions are eroded. Politicians and working people alike explain why opposition was unsuccessful. Winston Peters describes the New Right tactic as 'hijack, ambush, speed ... move onto something else before they've got a chance to think'. Academics describe how, unheeded, they retreated to their universities when speaking out resulted in cuts in their research funding. Rare successes, like Auckland's managing to keep ownership of its assets in public hands and the overturn of the two-party system, are also highlighted.

While eschewing the commercial model of documentary film-making (Barry went for what he calls 'an old-fashioned style, unvarnished, no whizzy graphics—it just plods along telling the story'*), the abundant ironies are apparent in the film's skilful editing. New Zealand television's commercial channels refused to screen the documentary on the grounds that the television series *Revolution* covered the same ground. However, the film did screen on Max TV (a former music channel) on 29 September 1996, and many people around the country bought copies on videotape and attended festival and conference screenings. HM

---

*the big picture. Spring 1996, page 29.

1996

HERCULES: THE LEGENDARY JOURNEYS

Renaissance Pictures for Universal City Studios Inc. USA. Copyright 1994. Telefeature. *Location*: New Zealand. *Distributor*: CIC Video. *Rating*: M. Contains violence. Videotape. Colour. Approx. 87 minutes.

Executive producers: Sam Raimi, Robert Tapert, Christian Williams. *Producer*: Eric Gruendemann. *Associate producer*: Bernadette Joyce. *Co-producer*: David Eick. Created by Christian Williams. *Director of photography*: James Bartle. *Camera operator*: Ian Turtill. *Production designer*: Mick Strawn. *Costume designer*: Barbara Darragh. *Special make-up effects*: KNB EFX Group, Inc. *VCE Visual effects*: VCE/Peter Kuran. *Head scenic artist*: Paul Radford. *Mechanical effects supervisor*: Waynne Rugg. *Stunt coordinator*: Peter Bell. *Music*: Joseph Lo Duca. *Musical theme*: Ray Bunch. *Sound*: Tony Johnson, Craig Berkey, Stephen Buckland, John Ross, CAS, Patrick Giraudi, Tim Boggs.

Working to a tight formula, and in tongue-in-cheek style, each **Hercules** telefeature opens with a montage of clips from episodes in the television series and from the first telefeature, **Hercules and the Lost Kingdom**. With sorcery, romance, and battles with evil as their focus, and playing fast and loose with the myths from which they borrow (Hercules is exclusively heterosexual, the Amazon women retain their right breasts), the films feature a large cast of stunt players and an array of special effects. In recurring plot lines Zeus tries to get some quality time with his son, while the possibility that Hercules might not be immortal adds a frisson to threats to his life. Along with its sister series **Xena: The Warrior Princess**, the series spawned several other television adventure shows in the USA. In New Zealand the television series and the telefeatures have created much-needed work for many local film-makers and actors.

HERCULES AND THE AMAZON WOMEN

Released in New Zealand February 1996.
Director: Bill L. Norton. *Screenplay*: Jule Selbo, Andrew Dettmann, Daniel Truly. *Editor*: Steve Polivka. *Music editors*: Philip Tallman, Richard Bernstein. *Sound*: Paul Urmson, Craig Berkey, David Torres, Danielle Ghent.

Cast

Kevin Sorbo (Hercules), Anthony Quinn (Zeus), Roma Downey (Hippolyta), Michael Hurst (Iolaus), Lloyd Scott (Pithus), Lucy Lawless (Lysis), with Christopher Brougham, Tim Lee, Kim Michalis, Maggie Tarver, John Steemson, Helen Steemson, Rose McIver, Jennifer Ludlam, Nick Kemplen, Heidi Anderson, Jill Sayre, Murray Keane, Andrew Thurtell, Mick Rose, David Taylor, Nina Sosanya, Vicky Burrett, Margaret-Mary Hollins, Kristin Darragh, Tamara Waugh, Fiona Mogridge, Jacques Dupeyroux, Peter Malloch, Daniel James, Jeff Boyd, Simone Kessell.

Hercules strikes a blow for equity by persuading a village of men to respect and cherish their female partners, the Amazons. Hera fails yet again to vanquish Hercules, and Iolus prepares for matrimony.

HERCULES AND THE CIRCLE OF FIRE

Released in New Zealand March 1996.
Director: Doug Lefler. *Screenplay*: Barry Pullman, Andrew Dettman, Daniel Truly. *Editor*: Jon Koslowsky, ACE. *Creature, prosthetic, and digital effects*: WETA NZ Ltd. *Special effects designer*: Richard Taylor. *Project managers*: Jamie Selkirk, Peter Jackson. *Digital effects supervisor*: George Port. *Sound*: Joshua Schneider, Mathew Waters, David Grant.

Cast

Kevin Sorbo (Hercules), Anthony Quinn (Zeus), Tawny Kitaen (Deianeira), Kevin Atkinson (Cheiron), Stephanie Barrett (Phaedra), Mark Ferguson (Prometheus), with Christopher Brougham, Nell Weatherly, Simone Kessell, Alexander Gandar, Joseph Greer, Kerry Gallagher, Leonard twins, John Watson, Sharon Tyrell, Yvonne Lawley, Zo Hartley, Geoff Snell, Mark Newnham, Philip Gillis, Martyn Sanderson, Lisa Chappell, Kim Michalis, Letitia Bridges, Amy Morrison, Patrick Morrison, Joy Watson.

Hera's plan to destroy the world by extinguishing the eternal fire is thwarted just in time by Hercules and his new love, Deianeira (not the Deianeira from **Hercules and the Lost Kingdom**).

HERCULES IN THE UNDERWORLD

Released in New Zealand April 1996.
Director: Bill L. Norton. *Screenplay*: Andrew Dettmann, Daniel Truly. *Editor*: Steve Polivka. *Creature and prosthetic effects*: WETA. *Operations managers*: Jamie Selkirk, Peter Jackson. *Sound*: Craig Berkey, Joshua Schneider, Mathew Waters, David Grant.

Cast

Kevin Sorbo (Hercules), Anthony Quinn (Zeus), Tawny Kitaen (Deianeira), Marlee Shelton (Iola), Cliff Curtis (Nessus), Jorge Gonzales (Eryx the boxer), Timothy Balme (Lycastus), with Michael Hurst, Michael Mizrahi, Grant Bridger, John McKee, Pio Terei, Michael Wilson, Buzz Moller, Ross McIver, Paul McIver, Simon Lewthwaite, Jason Hunt, Simone Kessell, Greg Johnson, Yvonne Lawley, Rose Glucina, Andrew Kovacevich, Sydney Jackson, Vicky Burrett, Amber Jane Raab, Peter Morgan, Mario Gaoa, Hilary Cleary, Nic Fay, Nicky Mealings, Liseli Mutti, Phaedra, Vernon King, Sarah Litherland, Mark Ferguson, Stig Eldred, Gordon Hatfield, Stephen Hall, John Dybvig, Al Chalk.

Now married to the Deianeira of **Hercules and the Circle of Fire**, and the father of three children, Hercules ventures into the Underworld to save the world from extinction, in the process testing his own immortality.

HERCULES IN THE MAZE OF THE MINOTAUR

Released in New Zealand May 1996.
Director: Josh Becker. *Screenplay*: Andrew Dettmann, Daniel Truly. *Digital FX supervisor*: Kevin O'Neill. *Camera and prosthetic effects*: WETA. *SFX designer*: Richard Taylor. *Project managers*: Jamie Selkirk, Peter Jackson. *Sound*: Josh Schneider, Mathew Waters, David Grant, Louis Creveling, Jason Schmid.

Cast

Kevin Sorbo (Hercules), Anthony Quinn (Zeus), Tawny Kitaen (Deianeira), Michael Hurst (Iolus), Anthony Ray Perker (Minotaur), with Nic Fay, Andrew Turtill, Paul McIvor, Simon Lewthwaite, Rose McIvor, Katrina Hobbs, Warren Earl, Maya Dalziel, Sydney Jackson, Marise Wipani, Andrew Glover Snr, Terry Batchelor, Al Chalk, Lawrence Wharerau, John Mellor, Geoff Allen, Scott Freeman, Pio Terei.

Tired of tilling the soil, Hercules and Iolus do battle with the Minotaur, and Hercules learns that the evil creature is his brother. Seven lengthy fight sequences from earlier Hercules telefeatures pad out the running time in flashback. HM.

1996 TV Guide Film and Television Awards. Best Design. Hercules 11: Prince of Thieves.

Michael Hurst (Iolus) and Kevin Sorbo (Hercules). Courtesy of Pacific Renaissance Pictures Ltd.

International Films Associated with New Zealand

1947

Green Dolphin Street
VICTOR SAVILLE

M.G.M. *Country of origin*: U.S. 141 mins. *Producer*: Carey Wilson. *Screenplay*: Samson Raphaelson, based on Elizabeth Goudge's prizewinning novel in M.G.M.'s first annual contest. *Director of photography*: George Folsey. *Art directors*: Cedric Gibbons, Malcolm Brown. *Editor*: George White. *Music*: Bronislau Kaper. *Special effects*: Warren Newcombe, A. Arnold Gillespie.

Cast: Lana Turner (Marianne Patourel), Van Heflin (Timothy Haslam), Donna Reed (Marguerite Patourel), Richard Hart (William Ozanne), Hinemoa (Linda Christian).

William Ozanne emigrates to New Zealand, but misses his love, Marguerite. One drunken evening he writes to her and asks her to join him, but mistakenly addresses the letter to her sister Marianne. She arrives in New Zealand and becomes the object of rivalry between William and his partner Timothy Haslam before eventually happily returning to England with William. The New Zealand sequences in the film were shot in the Californian redwood forests, but producer Carey Wilson asked the New Zealand government for help, and Captain George Bennett was sent to the U.S. to supervise 'the Maori sequences' and to provide a degree of authenticity. Nevertheless, the film demonstrates the licence film-makers were prepared to take in the interests of the box office, and it is an interesting example of the way the rest of the world perceived colonial New Zealand.

1949

The Sands of Iwo Jima
ALLAN DWAN

Republic Pictures Corporation. *Country of origin*: U.S. 108 mins. *Producer*: Merian C. Cooper. *Screenplay*: Harry Brown. *Directors of photography*: R. Lanning, James Edwards Grant.

Cast: John Wayne (Sergeant Stryker), John Agar (Pfc Conway), Adele Mara (Allison Bromley), Forrest Tucker (Corporal Thomas).

This classic post WWII hero vehicle has veteran sergeant John Wayne befriending a rifle squad of recently recruited marines, training them in the arts of manhood and war, and leading them heroically until they raise the American flag in Hollywood's rendering of the famous photograph. During the early sections of the film, the R&R camp at Paekakariki in the lower half of the North Island was the setting for the meeting and bonding sequences prior to departing for battle. The same camp is the focus of the reminiscences of one of the women who contributed to Gaylene Preston's documentary **War Stories**.

1957

Until They Sail
ROBERT WISE

M.G.M. *Country of origin*: U.S. *Producer*: Charles Schnee. *Screenplay*: Robert Anderson. *Source*: James Michener, *Return to Paradise*. *Director of photography*: Joseph Ruttenberg.

Cast: Jean Simmons (Barbara Leslie Forbes), Joan Fontaine (Anne Leslie), Piper Laurie (Delia Leslie), and Sandra Dee (Evelyn Leslie).

The film tells the story of four sisters living in New Zealand during WWII when the American soldiers arrive. The consequent relationships that they develop with servicemen bring both tragedy and love. This adaptation of the Michener story is notable more for its Wellington and Christchurch settings against which a series of universal dramas is played out than for its accuracy in rendering the period. American servicemen in WWII New Zealand provide the focus for a number of New Zealand features. For an interesting and less glamourised update **The Last Tattoo** (1994) has more authenticity.

1958

Cinerama South Seas Adventure
A.K.A. South Seas Adventure
FRANCIS D. LYON & ORS

Stanley Warner Cinerama Corporation. *Country of origin*: U.S. *Producer*: Carl Dudley. *Screenplay*: Charles Kaufman, Joseph Ansen, Harold Medford. *Director of photography*: John F. Warren. *Narration*: Orson Welles.

Two young women travel the South Pacific and provide the link for a series of stopovers at major tourist points from Hawaii to New Zealand. This fifth Cinerama film, like the previous ones, was designed to exploit the possibilities of the Cinerama screen. Like the early 3D movies, the emphasis is on effect not character or story line, and as a result becomes both predictable and tedious. The New Zealand sequence combines tourist fishing, concert party Maori, and an ex-serviceman returning to his old WWII R&R hunting grounds, but is interesting for what constitutes the exploitist camera. Somewhat ironically, the views which are designed to sell New Zealand overseas are from the same stable as those freelance journalist Tom Sullivan eventually rejected in **Broken Barrier**.

1958

The Decks Ran Red
ANDREW L. STONE

Andrew and Virginia Stone, Loew's Incorporated. *Country of origin*: U.S. 84 mins *Producers*: Andrew and Virgina Stone. *Screenplay*: Andrew L. Stone. *Director of photography*: Meredith M. Nicholson. *Editor*: Virginia Stone.

Cast: James Mason (Captain Edwin B. Rumill), Dorothy Dandridge (Mahia), Broderick Crawford (Henry Scott), Stuart Whitman (Leroy Martin), Katherine Bard (Joan Rumill), David Cross (Mace) Joel Fluellen (Cook) Jack Krushen (First officer).

The story is a familiar one of attempted mutiny on the high seas. Ex-luxury liner first mate James Mason, now newly appointed captain on a rusty tramp steamer, picks up a new ship's cook in New Zealand. The cook is Maori and he is accompanied by his wife Mahia who is beautiful and seductive. Crew members Henry Scott and Leroy Martin unsuccessfully attempt to raise a mutiny in order to get rid of the ships' officers and claim salvage money on the ship and their consequent actions lead eventually to a running battle between loyal crew and captain, and the mutineering killers. Of interest is the fact that writer Stone chose not only to include a Maori character, even though she was played by African American actress Dorothy Dandridge, but to portray Mahia in almost identical fashion to nineteenth century erotic photographs of Maori women — available and sexual — and as the catalyst for tension among the men in the closed shipboard community.

1961

SPINSTER A.K.A. TWO LOVES A.K.A. I'LL SAVE MY LOVE
CHARLES WALTERS

Julian Blaustein Productions. M.G.M. *Country of origin*: U.S. 99 mins. *Producer*: Julian Blaustein. *Screenplay*: Ben Maddow from the novel by Sylvia Ashton-Warner. *Director of photography*: Joseph Ruttenberg. *Editor*: Frederick Steincamp. *Art directors*: George W. Davis, Urie McCleary. *Sound*: Franklin Milton. *Music*: Bronislau Kaper.

Cast: Shirley MacLaine (Anna), Laurence Harvey (Paul), Jack Hawkins (Abercrombie), Nobu McCarthy (Whareparita), Ronald Long (Headmaster Reardon), Juano Hernandez (Rauhuia), Edmund Vargas (Matawhero), Lisa Sitjar (Hinewaka).

Shot in Hawaii, this version of Sylvia Ashton Warner's book about life as a creative teacher in one of New Zealand's more remote rural schools has used much of the original material, but fails to develop the cultural ambience which was the essence of her writing and teaching. Maori advisor on the film was the Rev. Kingi Ihaka of Wellington, but despite his presence, the filmmakers were more interested in confirming their box office view of the world than representing what was a fascinating chapter in New Zealand's educational and social history. MacLaine's teacher begins her day with a cigarette, brandy and her piano, and this overstatement continues throughout the film. A different perspective was provided by Michael Firth in his film version of Ashton Warner's life, **Sylvia** (1985).

1962

IN SEARCH OF THE CASTAWAYS
ROBERT STEVENSON

Walt Disney Productions. *Country of origin*: U.K. 100 mins. *Producer*: Walt Disney. *Screenplay*: Lowell S. Hawley, from the novel by Jules Verne. *Director of photography*: Paul Beeson. *Editor*: Gordon Stone. *Art director*: Michael Stringer. *Sound*: Peter Thornton. *Music*: William Alwyn. *Special effects*: Peter Ellenshaw.

Cast: Maurice Chevalier (Jaques Paganel), Hayley Mills (Mary Grant), George Sanders (Thomas Ayrton), Wilfred Hyde White (Lord Glenarvan), Michael Anderson Jnr (John Glenarvan), Keith Hamshere (Robert Grant), Wilfred Brambell (Bill Gaye), Jack Gwillim (Captain Grant), Inia Te Wiata (Maori Chief).

Designed by Disney to make the most of a world tour of some of the earth's more dramatic geography, the film has three children and a somewhat overblown professor journey through South America and the Pacific in search of the children's seafaring father. On the search they encounter earthquakes, avalanches, waterspouts, lightning and volcanic eruptions, with a giant body snatching condor thrown in for good measure. The New Zealand segment allows the party to be captured by bloodthirsty Maoris from whom they escape by triggering an eruption in a nearby volcano. Te Wiata's presence makes the Maori contingent believable, albeit somewhat touristy in traditional piupiu rather than real fighting garb.

1964

QUICK BEFORE IT MELTS
DELBERT MANN

M.G.M. *Country of origin*: U.S. 97 mins. *Producers*: Douglas Laurence, Delbert Mann. *Screenplay*: Dale Wasserman. *Director of photography*: Russell Harlan.

Cast: George Maharis (Pete Santelli), Robert Morse (Oliver Cannon), Anjanette Corner (Tiare Marshall), Janine Gray (Diane).

A standard romantic comedy filtered through the lens of the military who are running an Antarctic base supplied by an operation codenamed Deep Freeze, the story has a journalist in search of a scoop passing through New Zealand on his way to Antarctica. Operation Deep Freeze was Christchurch based, and it is there that, predictably, the male leads respond to the attractions of New Zealand women. In **Quick Before It Melts** the two women, Diane Grenville-Wells, an English educated blonde, and Tiare Marshall, who is scripted as half Maori, are interesting reflections on what constitutes characters who are acceptable to M.G.M., but still identifiably from New Zealand.

1969

NYUJIRANDO NO WAKADAISHO A.K.A. YOUNG GUY ON MOUNT COOK
JUN FUKUDA

Toho. *Country of origin*: Japan. *Screenplay*: Yasuo Tanami. *Director of photography*: Shinsaku Uno.

The Mount Cook of the title is the setting which allows this tangled web of relationships to end in the traditional way. It is a story about a Japanese family and their romantic attachments seen largely through the eyes of the son, Yuichi, who himself falls in love with Setsuko, an employee of a trade group with business concerns in New Zealand industry.

1982

NEXT OF KIN
TONY WILLIAMS

A Film House/SIS production for Filmco Limited with financial assistance from the New Zealand Film Commission and the New South Wales Film Corporation. 35 mm. 89 mins. *Producer*: Robert Le Tet. *Co-producer*: Timothy White. *Screenplay*: Michael Heath, Tony Williams, *Director of photography*: Gary Hansen.

Cast: John Jarratt (Barney), Jackie Kerin (Linda), Charles McCallum (Lance), Gerda Nicolson (Connie), Alex Scott (Dr Barton).

Shot in Australia and premiered in the Cannes market in May of 1982, **Next of Kin** delivers a satisfying horror story motivated by the return of a young woman to the house in which she grew up. Her inheritance, however, is not the comfortable old family home she was expecting, but a nursing home inhabited by bizarre characters, both staff and inmates. Mysterious noises, murders and inexplicable events begin to make sense only after Linda discovers her mother's diaries and learns that her mother's psychotic sister is still alive and determined to take her revenge on those who have mistreated her.

The screenplay by New Zealanders Michael Heath, co-writer of Sam Pillsbury's film The Scarecrow (1982), and director Tony Williams was originally developed in New Zealand with assistance from the New Zealand Film Commission under the title Sticky Ends.

BROTHERS
TERRY BOURKE

Producer: Terry Bourke.
Cast: includes Moira Walker.

Parts of this film were shot in the rural district of Taihape in the central North Island.

1984

THE BOUNTY
ROGER DONALDSON

De Laurentis. *Country of origin*: U.S. 130 mins. *Producer*: Bernard Williams. *Screenplay*: Robert Bolt. *Source*: Richard Hough, Captain Bligh and Mr Christian. *Director of photography*: Arthur Ibbetson. *Editor*: Tony Lawson. *Production design*: John Graysmark. *Costume design*: John Bloomfield. *Music*: Vangelis. *Special effects*: John Stears.

Cast: Mel Gibson (Fletcher Christian), Anthony Hopkins (Lt William Bligh), Sir Laurence Olivier (Admiral Hood), Edward Fox (Captain Greetham), Daniel Day Lewis (Fryer), Wi Kuki Kaa (King Tynah), Jon Gadsby (Norton).

Shot partly in and around Gisborne, New Zealand, Roger Donaldson's **Bounty** shows how far he developed since his first feature, **Sleeping Dogs**, in 1977. It uses, rather than identifies, New Zealand locations and associations, just as the first Bounty movie, Raymond Longford's **The Mutiny Of The Bounty** did in 1916. This highflying film, originally scripted as two separate features but reconstructed under one title after the first idea failed to come to fruition, is carried more on the quality of its cast than its script or direction. Nevertheless it presents an interesting alternative view to the mythic villainy of Captain Bligh and his romanticised opponent, Fletcher Christian.

1986

ACES GO PLACES IV
A.K.A. MAD MISSION IV
RINGO LAM

Cinema City. *Countries of origin*: New Zealand /Hong Kong. 98 mins. *Producer*: Karl Maka.

Cast: Karl Maka, Sam Hui, Sally Yeh, Ronald Lacey.

This is a title which has had no release in New Zealand, but has a tenuous connection in that the plot derives from the New Zealand discovery of a rain-making compound, and the Aces, an investigatory group, come to New Zealand to find out more. **Aces Go Places IV** is one of very few New Zealand Hong Kong film connections.

AGAINST THE LAW
RINGO LAM

A.k.a. *The Y Project*. A quarter of this Hong Kong-produced, Cantonese-speaking action film was shot in Auckland and featured actor Cynthia Roderick. Post-production was in Auckland. Fifty per cent of the crew were from New Zealand and fifty per cent were from Hong Kong. New Zealander Kevin Chisnall produced the New Zealand section and was also responsible for the special action effects. The film boosted the career of Ringo Lam, who went on to become a very successful action director. **Against the Law** was not released theatrically in New Zealand, but a subtitled version is available on video.

1988

MIDNIGHT RUN
MARTIN BREST

Universal Pictures. City Lights Films. *Country of origin*: U.S. 122 mins. *Producer*: Martin Brest. (New Zealand crew are named in the following credits.) *Production supervisor* (N.Z.): Bill Borden. *Production manager* (N.Z.): Margaret Hilliard. *Location manager* (N.Z.): Trevor Haysom. *Screenplay*: George Gallo. *Director of photography*: Donald Thorin. *Editor*: Billy Weber, Chris Lebenzon, Michael Tronick. *Production design*: Angelo Graham. *Music*: Danny Elfman. *Special effects*: Roy Arbogast.

Cast: Robert De Niro (Jack Walsh), Charles Grodin (Jonathan the Duke Mardukas), Yaphet Kotto (Alonzo Mosely), John Ashton (Marvin Dorfler), Dennis Farina (Jimmy Serano), Joe Pantoliano (Eddie Moscone), Wendy Philips (Gail), Danielle DuClos (Denise).

The storyline sets up an apparently incompatible couple — a bounty hunter (De Niro) and his prize captive — to travel across country facing assorted dangers on the way as the bounty man attempts to bring in his bounty. Some of the shooting was done in New Zealand to take advantage of the qualities of light and the varieties of geographical location.

THE RESCUE
FERDINAND FAIRFAX

Walt Disney Pictures, Touchstone, Silver Screen Partners. *Country of origin*: U.S. 98 mins. *Producer*: Laura Ziskin. *Production manager* (N.Z.): Margaret Hilliard. *Location Manager* (N.Z.): Annie Dodman. *Screenplay*: Jim Thomas, John Thomas, Alvin Sergeant. *Director of photography*: Russell Boyd. *Editor*: David Holden, Tim O'Meara. *Production designer*: Maurice Cain. *Music*: Bruce Broughton. *Special effects*: Nick Allder. *Stunt co-ordinator* (N.Z.): Peter Bell. *Casting* (N.Z.): Diana Rowan. *Crowd casting* (N.Z.): Maria Saunders.

Cast: Kevin Dillon (J.J. Merrill), Christina Harnos (Adrian Philips), Marc Price (Max Rothman), Ned Vaugn (Shaun Howard), Ian Giatti (Bobby Howard), Charles Haid (Commander Howard).

Drawing on the tensions which exist between North and South Korea to provide opposing camps, director Fairfax uses the New Zealand landscape as the setting for a kidult exploitation film which had only limited release here, despite its New Zealand locations. It tells the improbable story of a group of teenagers who go on an expedition to rescue their fathers who have been captured by the North Koreans. What is significant is the willingness of overseas production companies to locate in New Zealand to utilise the cinematic potential of the landscape without specifically identifying locale.

WILLOW
RON HOWARD

Lucasfilm in association with Imagine Entertainment. *Country of origin*: U.S. 125 mins. *Producer*: George Lucas. *Screenplay*: Bob Dolman from a story by George Lucas. *Director of photography*: Adrian Biddle. *Editors*: Daniel Hanley, Michael Hill, Richard Hiscott. *Production designer*: Allan Cameron. *Music*: James Horner.

New Zealand crew: *Production co-ordinator*: Catherine Madigan. *Production manager*: Murray Newey. *Location manager*: John Bernard. *Assistant directors, 3rd Unit*: Deuel Droogan, Richard Barker. *Camera operators, 3rd unit*: John Mahaffie, Mike Fuller, Rick Allender. *Art director*: Kim Sinclair. *Special effects* (*N.Z. co-ordinator*): Kevin Chisnall. *Special effects technicians*: Steve Ingram, Clint Ingram. *Wardrobe*: Andres Fernandez, Julia Mansford, Barbara Darragh. *Make-up*: Trish Cohen, Robyn Austen. *Stunts*: Peter Bell, Michael Baxter-Lax, Tim Lee, Jo Lumsden, Karam Hau, Mark Harris, Barry Johnson, Martin Johnson, Shaughan Bruce, Ka Segerberg. *Horse co-ordinator*: Russell Olds. *Bird handler*: Sarah Purdy. *Opossum trainer*: Laurie Gaskill. *Dog handler*: Alan Symes.

Cast: Val Kilmer (Madmartigan), Joanne Whalley (Sorsha), Warwick Davis (Willow Ufgood), Jean Marsh (Queen Bavmorda).

A wonderful fantasy which invents its own myths and draws on classic fairy stories in which to place them, **Willow** covers the adventures of a little person who discovers a small child floating in a stream after an Herodian attempt by the evil queen Bavmorda to kill the nation's babies. He attempts to return her to her rightful family and heritage and in so doing, has great adventures and becomes a hero in his own right. Director Ron Howard chose to shoot much of the film in New Zealand's South Island, where the presence of the Southern Alps gives the perfect setting for such an elaborately constructed fantasy. The reputation New Zealand has for light quality, its limitless variety of landscapes, together with the reputation crew members have for innovative and rapid problem-solving on shoots has drawn increasing numbers of international film-makers to New Zealand in the past decade.

1989

WILDFIRE
A.K.A. ROGUE STALLION
HENRI SAFRAN

South Pacific Pictures. Grundy Television. *Producers*: Don Reynolds, Phil East. *Executive producer*: Roger Mirams. *Screenplay*: Ysabelle Dean, Rick Maier. *Director of photography*: Chris White.

Cast: includes Bruno Lawrence, Beaver.

1991

DEATH IN BRUNSWICK
JOHN RUANE

Meridian Films, Australia. 35 mm. 100 mins. *Producer*: Timothy White. *Screenplay*: John Ruane, Boyd Oxlade, from the novel by Boyd Oxlade. *Director of photography*: Ellery Ryan.

Cast: Zoe Carides (Sophie Papafagos), John Clarke (Dave), Yvonne Lawley (Mrs Fitzgerald), Sam Neill (Carl Fitzgerald).

The narrative of **Death In Brunswick** leaps frenetically from one unpredictable event to another, but on the way delivers some wonderful characters. The first is Carl, no longer in the first flush of youth, but unable or unwilling to make the adjustment to conservative maturity, while his dominating mother and friends try to help him get his life together, their way. His job as cook in a less than salubrious nightclub involves him in a killing which leads to a hilarious attempted exhumation in the company of gravedigger Dave, but also provokes a meeting with Sophie, with whom he falls unpredictably in love. The film has a strong New Zealand connection with three of the main characters being expatriate Kiwis. Sam Neill, John Clarke and Yvonne Lawley are typical examples of the strong connections between the Australian and New Zealand film industries.

1993

ADRIFT
CHRISTIAN GUGUET

Atlantis Films and South Pacific Pictures for CBS. Telemovie shot on location in New Zealand.

Cast: includes Kate Jackson.

MAP OF THE HUMAN HEART
VINCENT WARD

Polygram Filmed Entertainment, A Working Title Film, Australian Film Finance Corp. Australian Film Commission, New Zealand Film Commission. *Producers*: Tim Bevan, Vincent Ward. *Screenplay*: Louis Nowra, based on a story by Vincent Ward. *Director of photography*: Eduardo Serra.

Cast: Jason Scott Lee (Arvik), Robert Joamie (Young Arvik), Anne Parillaud (Albertine), Annie Gallipeau (Young Albertine), Patrick Bergin (Walter Russell).

Told in flashback by an old Inuit, Vincent Ward's Australia/Canada/France/U.K. joint production delivers the story of a young couple from different cultures who meet as children, reunite as lovers years later during WWII but find that the clash of their separate cultures with those of their European counterparts produces some impossible tensions. Ward's capacity for wonderful painterly images resurfaces here. While there appears to be more than a nod to the shareholding needs of the multiple backers, there is also a masterly directorial hand at work in the way the narrative is constructed and the images are arranged.

1994

RAPA-NUI
KEVIN REYNOLDS

Tig Productions, Majestic Films in association with R.C.S. *Country of origin*: U.S. *Producers*: Kevin Costner, Jim Wilson. *Screenplay*: Tim Rose Price, Kevin Reynolds. *Director of photography*: Stephen F. Windon. *Production designer*: George Liddle. *Costume designer*: John Bloomfield. *Editor*: Peter Boyle. *Music*: Stewart Copeland.

Cast: Jason Scott Lee (Noro), Esai Morales (Make), Sandrine Holt (Ramana), Anzac Wallace (Haoa), George Henare (Tupa), Eru Potaka-Dewes (Ariki Mau).

Rapa-Nui is set in the pre-European past of what is known as Easter Island in the South Pacific. The story uses the universal myth of opposing clans to create dramatic tensions with a young hero from each clan competing for the same female prize according to rules established in a fictitious myth created for the movie. Shot on location on the island, about the only authentic elements are the setting itself and the presence of some islanders as extras. The key male players are from Hawaii, Puerto Rico and New Zealand, and the female lead is a Canadian citizen and international model. With a strong Maori presence filling three major roles and providing a significant cultural link with the fictional past created for the film, however, there is in **Rapa-Nui** an interesting confluence of several exotic cultural streams.

SE

APPENDIX
New Zealand Film Commission Act 1978

Clause 18. Content of Films
(1) In carrying out its functions, the Commission shall not make financial assistance available to any person in respect of the making, promotion, distribution, or exhibition of a film unless it is satisfied that the film has or is to have a significant New Zealand content.
(2) For the purposes of determining whether or not a film has or is to have a significant New Zealand content, the Commission shall have regard to the following matters:
   (a) The subject of the film:
   (b) The locations at which the film was or is to be made:
   (c) The nationalities and places of residence of —
      (i) The authors, scriptwriters, composers, producers, directors, actors, technicians, editors, and other persons who took part or are to take part in the making of the film; and
      (ii) The persons who own or are to own the shares or capital of any company, partnership or joint venture that is concerned with the making of the film; and
      (iii) The persons who have or are to have the copyright in the film:
   (d) The sources from which the money that was used or is to be used to make the film was or is to be derived:
   (e) The ownership and whereabouts of the equipment and technical facilities that were or are to be used to make the film:
   (f) Any other matters that in the opinion of the Commission are relevant to the purposes of this Act.
((2A) A film shall be deemed to have a significant New Zealand content if it is made pursuant to an agreement or arrangement entered into in respect of the film between —
   (a) The Government of New Zealand or the Commission; and
   (b) The Government of another country or relevant authority of another country).
(3) In carrying out its functions, the Commission shall in relation to the content of any film have due regard to the observance of standards that are generally acceptable in the community.

Subs.(2A) was inserted by s.2 of the *New Zealand Film Commission Act 1985.*

BIBLIOGRAPHY

BOOKS

Allen & Unwin and the Department of Internal Affairs. 1990. *The Dictionary of New Zealand Biography, Volume One*. Wellington.

Barclay, B. 1990. *Our Own Image*. Longman Paul, Auckland.

Boyd-Bell, R. 1985. *New Zealand Television: the First 25 Years*. Reed Methuen, Auckland.

Bridget Williams Books and the Department of Internal Affairs. 1993. *The Dictionary of New Zealand Biography, Volume Two 1870–1900*. Wellington.

Broadley, C. & Jones, J. 1979. *Nambassa: A New Direction*. A.H. & A.W. Reed, New Zealand.

Blythe, M. 1994. *Naming the Other: Images of the Maori in New Zealand Film and Television*. The Scarecrow Press Inc., Metuchen, New Jersey and London.

Cairns, B. & Martin, H. 1994. *Shadows on the wall: a study of seven New Zealand feature films*. Longman Paul, Auckland.

Christoffel, P. 1989. *Censored: A Short History of Censorship in New Zealand*. Department of Internal Affairs, Wellington.

Clarke McKenna, N. *Angel in God's Office: My Wartime Diaries*. Tandem Press. 1996. Birkenhead, New Zealand.

Day, P. 1994. *The Radio Years: A History of Broadcasting in New Zealand*. Auckland University Press, Auckland.

Dennis, J. 1992. *Moving Images From Aotearoa/New Zealand*. Museum of Contemporary Art, Sydney.

Dennis, J. (ed.) & Sowry, C. (research). 1981. *The Tin Shed*. New Zealand Film Archive, Wellington.

Dennis, J. & Toffetti, S. (eds). 1989. *Te Ao Marama Il Mondo della luce il Cinema Della Nuova Zealanda*. Le Nouve Muse, Torino.

Dennis, J. & Bieringa, J. (eds). 1996 (2nd edn). *Film in Aotearoa New Zealand*. Victoria University Press, Wellington. (First edition 1992.)

Edwards, S.R. 1993. *Docudrama From the Twenties: Rudall Hayward, Whakatane, and the Te Kooti Trail*. Whakatane Historical Review, vol. 41, no. 2.

Hayward, B.W. & Hayward, S.P. 1979. *Cinemas of Auckland: 1896–1979*. Auckland Lodestar Press, Auckland.

Hayward, H.J. 1944. *Here's to Life: The Impressions, Confessions, and Garnered Thoughts of a Free-minded Showman*. Oswald Sealey Ltd, New Zealand.

Horrocks, R. 1985. *Meet the Filmmakers Catalogues Series*. Auckland City Art Gallery, Auckland.

Horrocks, R. 1991. *Composing Motion: Len Lye and Experimental Film-making*. National Art Gallery, Wellington.

Horrocks, R. & Curnow, W. (eds). 1984. *Figures of Motion: Len Lye/Selected Writings*. Auckland University Press, Auckland.

Horrocks, R. with Tremewan, P. 1989. *On Film 11*. Heinemann, Auckland.

Ingham, G. 1973. *Everyone's Gone to the Movies: the Sixty Cinemas of Auckland … and some others*. Cyclostyle, Auckland.

King, M. 1981. *New Zealanders at War*. Heinemann Reed, Auckland.

Lennox, B. 1985. *Film and fiction: studies of New Zealand fiction and film adaptations*. Longman Paul, Auckland.

Maddock, S. 1988. *A Pictorial History of New Zealand*. Heinemann Reed, Auckland.

Main, W. 1976. *Maori in Focus: A Selection of Photographs of the Maori From 1850–1914*. Millwood Press, Wellington.

Mirams, G. 1945. *Speaking Candidly*. Paul's Book Arcade, Hamilton.

New Zealand Film Commission and American Film Institute Festival Program. (Foreword by Roger Horrocks.) 1985. *New Zealand Cinema and Its Directors*.

Palmer, S. 1988. *A Who's Who of Australian and New Zealand Film Actors: The Sound Era*. The Scarecrow Press Inc., Metuchen, New Jersey and London.

Phelps, G. 1975. *Film Censorship*. Victor Gollancz Ltd, London.

Pike, A. & Cooper, R. 1980. *Australian Film 1900–1977: A Guide to Feature Film Production*. Oxford University Press, Melbourne.

Price, S. *New Zealand's First Talkies: Early Filmmaking in Otago and Southland 1896–1939*. Otago Heritage Books. Dunedin. 1996.

Reid, N. 1986. *A Decade of New Zealand Film: From Sleeping Dogs to Came a Hot Friday*. John McIndoe, Dunedin.

Reynolds, S. (ed.) 1995. *Australian Film 1978–1994*. Oxford University Press, Melbourne.

Rorke, J. 1984. *A.H. Whitehouse: An Early Film Pioneer*. Whakatane Historical Review, vol. 32, no. 1.

Sowry, C. 1984. *Film Making in New Zealand: a brief historical survey*. New Zealand Film Archive, Wellington.

Tulloch, J. 1981. *Legends on the screen: The Australian Cinema 1919–1929*. Currency Press and the Australian Film Institute, Sydney.

References to the Biorama Company are taken from a collection of *Warcry* entries in the form of a diary written by 'Rambler', probably a Captain Brodie, during the 1902 and 1905 tours. The material is held by the New Zealand Film Archive.

MAGAZINES AND JOURNALS

Writing on New Zealand film appears widely in specialist magazines such as *Sight and Sound* (U.K.), *Cinema Papers* (Australia), *Film Threat* (U.S.A.) and in other magazines and journals (*Sites*, *Pavement*, *Midwest*, *New Zealand Sociology*). This list gives New Zealand-based specialist references.

Alternative Cinema (published 1977–85).

the big picture, Moving Image Centre, High Street, Auckland.

Film Archive Newsletter, New Zealand Film Archive, Wellington.

Filmland, 1939.

Illusions, The Imaginary Partnership, Wellington.

New Zealand Film, New Zealand Film Commission Journal.

New Zealand Film Commission: Te Tumu Whakaata Taonga. *Annual Report*. 1996.

New Zealand Journal of Media Studies, Massey University, Palmerston North.

N.Z. Talkies and Theatre Magazine, 1920–39.

New Zealand Theatre and Motion Picture Magazine, 1930. (Ten issues.)

Onfilm, Napier Street, Freemans Bay, Auckland.

SCRIPT, National Association of Media Educators, Teachers' Centre, Herne Bay.

BIBLIOGRAPHY

Sklar, R. 'Rudall Hayward, N.Z. Film-Maker,' *Landfall*, no. 98, June 1971.

SOURCE PUBLICATIONS

Ashton-Warner, S. 1963. *Teacher*. Secker & Warburg, London.

Ashton-Warner, S. 1972. *Spinster*. Heinemann, London.

Ashton-Warner, S. 1980. *I Passed This Way*. A.H. & A.W. Reed, Wellington.

Bodle, F.H. 1927. 'The Te Kooti Trail.' Serialised in the *New Zealand Herald*, 24 September–14 October.

Clune, F. 1970. *Captain Bully Hayes: blackbirder and bigamist*. Angus & Robertson, Sydney.

Cowan, J. FRGS. 1922, 1923. *The New Zealand Wars: A History of the Maori Campaigns and the Pioneering Period*. Vols I and II. R.E. Owen and New Zealand Government Printer, Wellington.

Cowan, J. FRGS. 1922. *The Old Frontier: The Story of the Waipa Valley*. The Waipa Post Printing and Publishing Company Ltd, Te Awamutu.

Cowan, J. 1934. 'A Bush Court Martial', in *Tales of the Maori Bush*. A.H. & A.W. Reed, Wellington.

Cowley, J. 1984. *The Silent One*. Whitcoulls, Christchurch.

Cross, I. 1957. *The God Boy*. Whitcoulls, Christchurch.

Crump, B. 1961. *Hang on a Minute Mate!* Barry Crump Associates, Tauranga.

Crump, B. 1963. *There and Back*. A.H. & A.W. Reed, Auckland.

Davies, S. 1984. *Bread and Roses: Sonja Davies, Her Story*. David Bateman Ltd, Auckland.

Duder, T. 1987. *Alex*. Oxford University Press, Auckland.

Duff, A. 1990. *Once Were Warriors*. Tandem Press, Auckland.

Gibson, H.T. 1921–1922. 'My Lady of the Cave: A New Zealand Coast Tale', serialised in the *New Zealand Herald*, September 1921–February 1922.

Goudge, E. 1944. *Green Dolphin Country*. Hodder & Stoughton, London.

Hall, R. 1977. *Middle Age Spread*. Victoria University Press, Wellington.

Hindin Miller, G. 1985. *The Dream Monger*. Hodder & Stoughton, Auckland.

Howard, E.J. 1975. *Mr Wrong*, Jonathan Cape, London.

Hyde, R. 1938. *The Godwits Fly*. Hurst & Blackett, Great Britain.

Mansfield, K. 1974. *The Complete Stories of Katherine Mansfield*. Golden Press, in association with Whitcombe & Tombs, Auckland.

McCauley, S. 1982. *Other Halves*. Hodder & Stoughton, Auckland.

Morrieson, R.H. 1976. *Pallet on the Floor*. Dunmore Press, Palmerston North.

Morrieson, R.H. 1976. *The Scarecrow*. Heinemann Educational Books (N.Z.) Ltd, Auckland.

Morrieson, R.H. 1981. *Came a Hot Friday*. Penguin Books, Auckland.

Phillips, J., Boyack, N. & Malone, E.P. (eds). 1988. *The Great Adventure*. Allen & Unwin, Wellington.

Pugsley, C. 1984. *Gallipoli, The New Zealand Story*. Hodder & Stoughton, Auckland.

Satchell, W. 1900. 'The Ballad of Stuttering Jim' in *Patriotic and Other Poems*. The Brett Printing and Publishing Co. Ltd, Auckland.

Savage, D. 1990. *Flight of the Albatross*. Harper Collins. Auckland.

Shadbolt, M. 1982. *Once on Chunuk Bair*. Hodder & Stoughton, Auckland.

Shadbolt, M. 1988. *Voices of Gallipoli*. Hodder & Stoughton, Auckland.

Stead, C.K. 1971. *Smith's Dream*. Longman Paul, Auckland.

Van der Post, L. 1963. *The Seed and the Sower*. Hogarth Press, London.

Waring, M. 1988. *If Women Counted*. Auckland University Press, with Bridget Williams Books. Auckland.

Wendt, A. 1973. *Sons for the Return Home*. Longman Paul, Auckland.

Wendt, A. 1974. *Flying Fox in a Freedom Tree*. Longman Paul, Auckland.

Wendt, A. 1979. *Leaves of the Banyan Tree*. Longman Paul, Auckland.

Willis, H. 1979. *Manhunt — the story of Stanley Graham*. Whitcoulls, Christchurch.

Yallop, D. 1978. *Beyond Reasonable Doubt?* Hodder & Stoughton, Auckland.

POST-FILM PUBLICATIONS

Ball, M. 1986. *Footrot Flats, the Dog's Tail Tale: from the screenplay*. Inprint, Wellington.

Berry, J. 1989. *Footrot Flats in Focus: a 1990 perspective*. Gisborne Museum and Arts Centre, Gisborne.

Campion, J. & Pullinger, K. 1994. *The Piano: a novel*. Bloomsbury Publishing Ltd, London.

Duder, T. 1992. *The Making of Alex*. Ashton Scholastic, Auckland.

Fyfe, J. 1995. *War Stories Our Mothers Never Told Us*. Penguin Books, Auckland.

Heath, M. 1978. *Solo: from the screenplay*. Horwitz Publications, Australia.

Jones, L. 1990. *An Angel At My Table: the screenplay from the three-volume autobiography of Janet Frame*. Random Century, Auckland.

Piggott, J. 1996. *Broken English*. Hodder Moa Beckett. Communicado. Auckland.

Reed. A.W. 1939. *Rewi's Last Stand: from the film scenario by Rudall Hayward*. A.H. & A.W. Reed, Wellington.

Reynolds, K. & Rose Price, T. 1994. *Rapa-Nui: The Easter Island Legend on Film*. Newmarket Press, New York.

Stevens, L. 1986. *Footrot Flats: The Dog's Tail Tale: The Making of the Movie*. Magpie Productions Ltd, New Zealand.

Williams, R.J. 1979. *Skin Deep: the book of the film*. A.H. & A.W. Reed, Wellington.

Ward, V. 1990. *Edge of the Earth*. Heinemann Reed, Auckland.

STUDY GUIDES

'A Study of Utu' *Teaching Film and Television*. 1983. Margaret Hodson. Association of Film and Television Teachers. Kohia Teachers Centre.

Adventures in Maoriland: Alexander Markey and the making of Hei Tiki. 1994. Helen Martin. The Moving Image Centre. (Videotape and notes.)

Alex. 1991. Pat Quirke. Everard Films.

An Angel At My Table. 1990. Barbara Cairns. Hibiscus Films. New Zealand Film Education Trust.

Broken English. 1996. Rachel Stace, Helen Martin and Robin Scholes. Communicado.

Chunuk Bair. 1991. Includes videotape Chunuk Bair: the making of, the film trailer, the opening title sequence, audition tape (scene 153), rushes of scene 153, roughcut of scene 153, finished film version of scene 153. 1991. Study guide notes. Avalon Television Centre.

Ngati. 1990. Helen Martin. Learning Media. (Videotape and notes.)

Once Were Warriors. 1991. Robin Scholes, Helen Martin. Communicado.

Once Were Warriors. 1996. Peter Beale. Self-published. Palmerston North.

Ruby and Rata. 1990. Barbara Cairns. Association of Film and Television Teachers.

Runaway Revisited. 1995. John Reynolds. Learning Media. (Videotapes and notes.)

SCRIPT: the 1992 Collection. (Helen Martin & Anna Soutar eds.) National Association of Media Educators. Kohia Teachers Centre. Includes **The Navigator**. Ngaire Hoben.

Skin Deep. 1979. John Reynolds. Phase Three Films.

The End of the Golden Weather. 1991. Barbara Cairns. South Pacific Pictures.

The Scarecrow. 1982. Brian MacDonnell. Longman Paul, Auckland.

The Silent One. 1984. The Gibson Group.

The Whole of the Moon. 1996. Helen Martin. Tucker Films Ltd.

Vigil. 1985. Barbara Cairns and Margaret Henley. Hibiscus Films.

War Stories. 1995. Gaylene Preston. Australian Teachers of Media.

FILMOGRAPHY

In New Zealand there have been numerous television magazine items on aspects of New Zealand film on such programs as *Kaleidoscope*, *The Edge* and *Marae*. For reasons of accessibility they have not been included in this reference list.

The Internet

Adventures in Maoriland: Alexander Markey and the making of Hei Tiki. 1982. BCNZ/Phase Three. Producer: John Maynard. Director: Geoff Steven.

Cowboys of Culture. 1991. Vid-Com. Producer/director: Geoff Steven.

Cinema of Unease. 1995. BFI/NZFC/NZOA/TV3/Topshelf. Producers: Paula Jalfon, Grant Campbell. Directors: Sam Neill, Judy Rymer.

Chunuk Bair: the making of. 1991. Avalon Film Studios.

Bread and Roses: the making of. 1994. Nautilus Productions. Producer/director: Barbara Cairns.

Directions … Margaret Thomson. 1993. Tommy Productions. Producer/director: Julie Benjamin.

Doodlin' ... Len Lye. 1987. U.K. Director: Keith Griffiths.

Flip and Two Twisters: a documentary about the great film maker and kinetic sculptor Len Lye. 1995. Point of View Productions. Producers: Robin Laing and Shirley Horrocks. Director: Shirley Horrocks.

Good Taste Made Bad Taste. 1988. City Associates. Producer/director: Tony Hiles.

Jane Campion: The Grass is Greener. 1994. TVNZ. Documentary. Producer/director: Greg Stitt.

Making Utu. 1982. Scrubbs and Co. Producer/director: Gaylene Preston.

New Zealand Century of Cinema: Te Rautau O Te Whitiahua Ki Aoteaora. 1996. Trailer. In association with the New Zealand Film Commission. Director: Greg Page. Producers: Jan Bieringa, Jonathan Dennis.

New Zealand Century of Cinema: Te Rautau O Te Whitiahua Ki Aotearoa. 1996. Trailer. In association with the New Zealand Film Commission. Director: John O'Shea. Producers: Jan Bieringa, Jonathan Dennis.

Runaway Revisited. 1994. Learning Media. Producer/director: John Reynolds.

Seeing Red. 1995. James Wallace Productions Ltd. Producer: James Wallace. Director: Annie Goldson.

RADIO PROGRAMS

Voices on film: independent film-making in Aotearoa–New Zealand Film. 1. Radio with pictures — the start of it all. 2. The Persistence of realism — the documentary tradition. 3. The independent feature film industry. 4. Other stories to tell — Maori film-making. 5. Changing the language of film — experiment. 6. Against all odds — the possibilities and the potential. 7. The new generation — the major feature films of 1994 and 1995. Devised and presented by Jonathan Dennis. Produced for New Zealand public radio by Elizabeth Alley.

Acknowledgments

We wish to thank the New Zealand Film Commission for its support in the preparation of this book and in particular to recognise the contribution of Marketing Director, Lindsay Shelton. The New Zealand Film Archive made its staff and material resources freely available and we are particularly grateful to Diane Pivac for her contribution.

Other archives that were unstinting in their support and assistance were the National Archive, Wellington, the National Film and Television Archive, London, and the National Film and Sound Archive, Canberra.

Thanks to Russell Campbell, who brought to his reading of the manuscript a great knowledge of New Zealand film, to Keith Knewstubb, whose research assistance was invaluable, and to the Department of Film and Television at Waikato University.

In our research we called often on the goodwill of film-makers, writers, crews, actors, librarians and publicists. Many thanks to those who searched their files and their memories to provide us with information. The New Zealand film industry magazine *Onfilm* and the New Zealand Film Commission journal *New Zealand Film* have been much-used research resources.

Thanks to Balmoral Videon and Belmont Video Ezy for providing videotapes for the checking of credits.

Warm thanks to our families for their unstinting tolerance and support.

For permission to reproduce stills grateful acknowledgment is made to the following: the New Zealand Film Commission; the New Zealand Film Archive; the National Film and Sound Archive, Canberra; the National Film and Television Archive, London; the Hayward Historical Film Trust; the Te Awamutu *Courier*; Faye Jennings; the Rank Organisation Plc; the Children's Film and Television Foundation Ltd; Murray Reece; Geoff Steven; Jonathan Dennis; Tony Brittenden; Dale Farnsworth; Russell Campbell and Vanguard Films; Di Wilks; Antony I. Ginnane; New Zealand Television Archive; Jeremy Thomas; Thomas Finlayson; Larry Parr; John Barnett; CIBY Sales; Michael Pattinson and Beyond Films; Sue May; Kapil Arn; South Pacific Pictures; R. H. Whitehouse; Graham McLean; Pacific Films Collection, New Zealand Film Archive.

INDEX

A

Aardvark Films Ltd 78
Aberdein, Keith 69, 73, 78, 83, 99, 112, 178, 109
Abrams, Michael 82
Absent Without Leave 166
Acme Sausage Company, Blerta 61
Adventures of Algy, The 35
Ahipene, Hori 154, 160, 171
Air New Zealand 63
Akersten, Donna 64, 69, 72, 84, 123, 146 154, 169, 178
Alex 165
Allen, Bernie 85
Allpress, Bruce 75, 81, 84, 95, 103, 111, 151, 171
Almond, Alan 182
Altier, George 49
Alvarado, Trini 190
Alwyn, William 53
AMA 76
Amiet, Julie 111
Amiga, Junior 114, 127, 114, 127
Amohau, Tai 38
Amonau, A. 161
Among the Cinders 133
Anae, Aloema 145
Anderson, Andy 96 143
Anderson, Gael 60, 62
Anderson, Howard 109
Anderson, John 62, 83, 127
Anderson, Michael 102
Andreasson, Billie 40
Andrews, Harry 110
Andrews, Stanhope 90
Angel At My Table, An 148
Angel Mine 67
Angwin, Neil 81
Annakin, Ken 53
Anthony, Walter 42
Apanui, Te Whanau a 138

Appleby, Noel 75, 97, 137, 147, 151, 159
Arahanga, Julian 175, 189
Ardvaark Endeavour Productions 73
Arenafilm 137
Armitage, Edward 34, 40
Armstrong, Bridget 133, 103, 133, 167, 173
Armstrong, Perry 66
Arnold, Steve 180
Arquette, Alexis 173
Arriving Tuesday 124
Arts, Marion 66
Ash, Bob 54
Ashley, Mac 58
Ashton-Warner, Sylvia 115
Aston, Doug 76 139, 151, 169
Aston, Janelle 135
Atha, John 54, 69
Atkine, Feodor 116
Atkinson, Kevin 194
Atlantic Entertainment Group 152
Attewell, Warrick 111, 123, 130, 131, 154, 158, 192
Austen, Dale 41
Austin, Irving 82
Austin, Mark 166
Australian Film Commission 137, 171, 174
Avalon 127
Avalon N.F.U. Studios 158, 174, 175, 188
Awatea Films 91, 138

B

Bach, John 75, 76, 82, 83, 84, 86, 87, 99, 105, 108, 109, 112, 121, 123, 130, 155, 178
Backhouse, Tony 161
Bad Blood 84
Bad Taste 134
Baer, Bill 113, 122, 125
Baer, Meredith 86
Bain, May 41
Bair, Chunuk 158
Baker, Tony 85

Ball, Murray 126
Balme, Timothy 161, 161, 178, 194
Banas, John 82, 84, 93
Bannon Glen Pty Ltd 89
Bao, Shaun 135
Barclay, Barry 119, 128, 154
Barclay, Phillip 188
Barlow Geoff 59, 148
Barnett, John 69, 73, 75, 80, 86, 89, 99, 109, 120, 126
Barnett, Simon 149
Barr, Jim 83
Barrett, Franklyn 26
Bennett, H.E.(Kosy) 29
Broken Barrier 52
Barrett, Stephanie 194
Barry, Alister 153, 177, 193
Barry, Tony 61, 75, 76, 121, 139, 155, 165, 166 173, 178
Barsby, Narelle 130
Bartle, James 81, 101, 108, 109, 113, 151, 179, 194
Bartlett, Christine 96, 165
Bartlett, Timothy 128, 148
Barton, Charles 33, 35
Basler, Marianne 152
Batstone, John 75, 83
Battletruck 82
Battletruck Films Ltd 82
Baxendale, Jack 49, 50
Baxter-Lax, Michael 96, 100, 105
Bay Of Plenty Films 30
Bayler, Terence 52, 79
Baysting, Arthur 150, 160, 64
Bean, Tim 180
Beaudoin, Jean 192
Beauman, Nicholas 138
Beaumont Smith Films 35
Beaumont, Harry 26
Beaumont, James 128, 154
Beavis, Ivan 60
Beck, Michael 82

Index

Beck, Reginald 57
Becker, Josh 194
Becroft, Mike 125, 131, 150
Beebe, Dion 163
Beech, John 82
Behrens, Inge 133
Bell, Francis 156, 166, 179
Bell, Peter 95, 101, 139, 173, 179
Bennett, Mike 160
Bennett, Pastor 20
Bennett, Rev. F. 20,23
Bergquist, Lyn 121
Besser, Jonathan 181
Bestic, Arthur 'Darkie' 30
Betts, Jean 116
Beyond 27
Beyond Films Ltd 174
Beyond Reasonable Doubt 75
BFI TV 184
Bhattacharyya, Dr Debes 149
Biddle, Ben 46
Billing, Roy 81, 95, 93, 103, 105, 109, 125, 143, 155
Binning, Tanya 54, 55
Binns, Andrew 148, 149, 156
Bird, Christine 153
Birkin, Jane 116
Birth Of New Zealand, The 29
Bishop, June 147, 151
Black, Michael 79
Blackburn, Ken 68, 79, 84, 128, 142, 166
Blake, Peter 140
Bland, Carl 192
Bland, Peter 103, 123, 125
Blandford, Rawdon 24, 25
Blay, Margaret 81, 104, 166
Bleakley, Joe 99
Bleakley, Patrick 61
Blick, John 66, 178, 190
Bloomfield, Angela 183
Bloomfield, Evan 132
Blue Angel Films 186
Blyth, David 67, 105,159,
Bodle, Frank 40
Boelee, Onno 86, 102, 105, 179
Boelson, Jim 89
Bollinger, Allun 61, 70, 75, 76, 77, 103, 106, 152, 156, 177, 181, 184, 190
Bollinger, Nick 153
Bolstad, Richard 153
Bolton, Heather 86, 118, 124, 135, 149
Bond, Johnny 164, 167
Bonjour Timothy 183
Booth, Jim 146, 161, 177
Borich, Milan 159, 183
Bossley, Caitlin 163
Bouzaid, Francis X. 32
Bowie, David 100
Bowkett, Matt 142, 183

Boyd, Jeff 127
Boynton, Mere 171, 175
Bracken, Mildred 20, 21
Bradley, Dale G 141, 158
Bradley, Karl 75, 84, 86, 95, 96, 102, 105, 110, 120
Bradley, L. Grant 158
Braindead 161
Brandt, William 147, 148, 160
Brazier, Jon 127, 140, 142, 163, 171
Bread And Roses 169
Brendler, Julia 188
Brennan, Tom 93
Briant, Joanna 127, 140, 169
Briant, Shane 97, 117
Bridge to Nowhere 122
Bridgeman, Bert 33
Bridger, Grant 100, 102
Bridgewater, Tim 83
Bridgman, Howard 46
Bristowe, Tania 87, 108
British Film Institute 182
British Screen 182
Brittenden, Bob 71
Brittenden, Tony 71
Broadhurst, Phil 81
Broadley, Colin 54
Broken English 189
Brophy, Jed 158, 160, 161, 166, 177, 187
Brougham, Chris 158, 166
Broun, Christopher 100, 104
Brown, Andrew 84
Brown, Edward T 43
Brown, George H. 53
Brown, Mathew 64
Brown, Riwia 127, 175, 187
Browning, Alistair 100, 102, 156, 160
Bruce, Alison 147, 155, 156, 165
Bruce, Robert 80, 95, 101, 155, 159
Bryan, Gerald 109, 140
Buchanan, Dorothy 71
Buchanan, Kim 140, 151
Buchanan, Meriol 118, 130
Buchanan, William (Bill) 48
Bullock, John 75, 118
Burns, Carol 84
Burrett, Vicky 149, 165
Burstyn, Thom 112, 118
Bush Cinderella, The 41
Bussieres, Pascale 192
Butler, Lynton 121
Byrne, Gabriel 152
Byrns, Alan 102

C

Cahill, Anna 143, 161
Cain, Maurice 95
Caird, Catriona 111, 143

Calder, David 64
Calder, Jasper 40
Caldwell, Oswald 40
Callen, John 79, 140
Came a Hot Friday 103
Cameron, David 102, 110, 160
Campbell, Eddie 114, 123, 127, 142, 143, 171, 178
Campbell, Gordon 30
Campbell, Grant 184
Campbell, Jeff 63, 132
Campbell, Russell 77, 153
Campbell, Sally 137
Campbell, Tom 43
Campion, Anna 182
Campion, Jane 148, 171
Capella International Inc 178
Carbine's Heritage 37
Carey, Patric 85
Carlisle, Kenneth 25
Carlyle, Billie 35
Carradine, John 81
Carrodus, Peter 174
Carry Me Back 83
Carson, Neville 178
Carter, George 84, 139
Carter, Maurice 53
Carvell, Paul 66
Casselli, Nola 34
Castle, Geoff 111
Catran, Ken 94, 165
Chadwick 20
Challenge Film Corporation 131
Challis, Derek 109
Chalmers, George 35
Champion, Beth 174
Channel Four 182
Chapman, Adele 112
Chapman, Arthur 85
Chapman, Jan 171
Chappell, Lisa 167
Chapple, Geoff 59, 137
Charest, Micheline 183, 192
Charles, John 60, 76, 97, 109, 113
Cherrington, Te Paki 76, 124, 128, 125, 141, 154
Cheshire, Elizabeth 89
Chicken 187
Chico, John 111
Chief Te Heuheu of Ngati Kahungunu 20
Chief Te Rangi-Ka-Haruru of Ngatairuu 20
Chill Factor 141
Chillco Productions 141
Chin, Peter 135
Chulak, Fred A.C.E 151
Churn, Iris 148
CIBY 2000 171
Cinar Productions Inc 183, 192
Cinema and Television Productions 104

Cinema of Unease: A Personal Journey by Sam Neill 184
Cinepro 113, 123, 124
Cineventure Productions 100
Claridge, George 45
Clark, Dave 149
Clark, David 71
Clarke, John 89, 139
Clayton, Alan 155
Clayton, Ethel 27
Cleary, Tina 166 169
Clements, Richard 63
Clewes, Captain Lionel 37
Cliff, Nicola 192
Clifford, Clare 105
Cline, Wilfred 42
Close, Eric 179
Clothier, Simon 150
Cokeliss, Harley 82, 179
Collie, Peggy/Peggie 47
Collins, Annie 144, 91
Collins, Lew 42
Collins, Reginald 26
Collins, Russell 79
Collison, Rod 64, 89, 97
Combs, Jeffrey 190
Communicado 175, 189
Community Media Trust 193
Connell, David 174
Connolly, Terry 112
Conrad, Scott 139
Constance 97
Conti, Tom 100
Cook, Brian 120
Cooper, Deryn 68
Cooper, Terence 96, 108, 111, 114, 115, 120, 121, 130, 142, 151, 155, 175
Copeland, David 84, 166
Copping, David 102, 135, 147, 164, 167
Cops and Robbers 180
Cornwall, Gil 54, 75
Cotterill, Ralph 86
Coubray, Edwin (Ted) 29, 34, 35, 37, 43, 46 50
Coulson, David 96, 189
Coulter, Elizabeth 79
Cowan, James 34, 40, 50
Cowie, Susanne 108
Cowley, Graeme 78, 83, 87, 138, 173
Cowley, Joy 83, 98
Cox, Pat 126
Craig, Maria 60
Crawford Ivers, Julia 27
Crayford, Jonathan 118, 121
Creative Arts 130
Creative Film and Video Fund 193
Crick and Jones 26
Cronin, Meryl 163
Cross, George 26

Cross, Ian 60
Crozier, Judith 104
Crump, Barry 85
Crush 163
Csokas, Marton 189
Cullen, Max 150
Currie, Tony 153
Curtis, Cliff 160, 167, 171, 175, 187, 194

D

Dale Films 74
Dalziell, D.L. 26
Dampier, Claude 35
Dangerous Orphans 123
Dasent, Peter 146, 161, 177
Davenport, Nigel 93
David Hannay Productions Pty Ltd 150
David, Eleanor 115
Davies, Piers 68
Davies, Sonja 169
Davis, Carole 151
Dawe, Joan 187
Day, Gary 101
Day, John 150
Daybreak Pictures 158
De Groot, Myra 67
Dead Kids 89
Dean, Gay 97, 102, 105, 139
Death Warmed Up 101
de Roche, Everett 80
Dee, Laurie 64, 75
Del Monte, Curly 110, 121
Delahoussaye, Michael 141
Delahunty Andre, 153
Delamere, Rangimarie 138
Delerue, Georges 110
Dene, Robin 111
Dennet, Peter 131, 133, 109, 140, 164, 171
Desgagnes, Genevieve 186
Desperate Remedies 167
Dettmann, Andrew 194
Devenie, Stuart 146, 154, 161
Diggle, Lynton 62
Dignam, Arthur 89
Dimsey, Ross 102
Dobbyn, Dave 126, 174
Dobrowolska, Gosia 180
Dobson, Peter 190
Dods, Marcus 95
Dodwell, Grant 180
Donaldson, Aaron 73
Donaldson, Melissa 73
Donaldson, Mike 153
Donaldson, Roger 64, 73, 78
Donovan, Terence 78, 89
Don't Let It Get You 55
Doreen, Marcella 34

Doughty, Moataa 39
Douglas, Alistair 121, 96 101, 103, 121, 147, 156 159
Douglas, Judie 60, 97, 150, 165, 166, 169
Douglas, Stuart 37
Dowling, Jonathan 143, 173
Downey, Roma 194
Down On The Farm 45
Downie, Trishia 150
Dreaver, Mary MP 41
Dryburgh, Stuart 132, 148, 171, 175
Duder, Tessa 165
Duff, Alan 175
Duffy, Sean, 70, 78, 87, 96, 103, 139, 159
Duke, Shirley 64, 156
Duncan, Carmen 55
Duncan, Donald 147, 165, 173
Dunn, Shirley 76
Dwyer, Finola 104, 122, 131

E

Eadenrock Ltd 102
Eady, L.A. 34
Eady, Paul 72
Earnshaw, John 67, 74, 94
Echo Pictures Ltd 150
Economou, Michael 63
Edgar, Grant 83, 84, 166
Edmond, Frances 66, 76, 104, 164
Edmond, Martin 135, 164
Edwards, Frank 79, 83
Edwards, James 166
Efraim, R Ben 151
Eggleton, Matthew 182
Ehfe 20, 21
Eilbacher, Lisa 139
Elliot, Tim 87
Elmore, Mark 59
Emile, Taungaroa 175, 188
End of the Golden Weather, The 156
Endeavour (Endeavour T.V. Productions Ltd) 61
Endeavour Entertainment 69
Endeavour Film Management Ltd 86
Endeavour Productions 75, 80, 89, 99, 109, 120
Energy Source International 140
Enting, Lilian 148, 169
Essential Productions 173
Everard Films 63
Everard, Arthur 58
Everard, Barrie 139
Evison, Pat 62, 84, 98, 159
Ewart, John 150
Ewens, Bill 102
Ewens, Eunice 102
Eyre, Maggie 96, 104

Index

F

F.G.H. Film Consortium Pty Ltd 80
Faifua, Amiga Jnr. 145
Fairchild, William 53
Fairfax, F. 115
Fairfax, Ferdinand 95
Fairley, Norman 76, 86, 101, 122, 95, 102, 110, 120, 137
Famularo, Silvio 160, 161
Fanfare Films 53
Farnsworth, Dale 74
Farrell, Mike 111
Federoff, Val 58
Feehan, Sean 187
Feltham, Lee 59, 124, 143
Ferguson, Mark 194
Fergusson, Karen 148
Ferrier, Tim 180
Ferris, Pam 56
Filmboard Berlin Brandenberg 188
Film Investment Corporation of New Zealand, 106, 112, 114, 137
Film Konstruction 147
Filmcraft 94
Fink, Wolfgang 186
Finlayson Brewer Productions 142
Finlayson, Tom 96 105, 142
Finlayson-Hill Productions Ltd 96
Finney, Edmund 34
Firth, Michael 63, 108, 115, 132
Firth, Tony 41
Fisher, Francesca 186
Fisher, Simon Turner 182
Fisher, Janet 160, 169
Fisher, Toby 192
Fitzgerald, Mike 59
Fitzi, Maria 154
Flannery, Anne 108, 70, 81
Flaws, Fane 146 161
Flegg, Brian 115, 148
Flegg, Fay 72, 102, 122, 148
Fletcher, Louise 89
Fletcher, Norman 76, 86, 110, 113, 115, 120, 125, 128
Flight of the Albatross 188
Flying Fox in a Freedom Tree 145
Flynn, Patrick 54, 55
Fontana Film Productions GmbH 177
Footrot Flats: The Dog's Tail Tale 126
Footstep Man, The 164
Ford, Josephine 109, 113, 120
Forlong, Kate 57
Forlong, Michael 57
Forsey, Norman 81, 93, 115, 121, 130, 131, 141, 158
Foster, Joan 97, 166
Foster, Jodie 110
Fowler, David H 58, 62
Fowley, Kim 111
Fownes, Henry 117
Fox, Kerry 148, 178
Fox, Michael J. 190, 191
Frame, Janet 148
Francis, Alton 56
Francis, Diane 56
Franklin, Diane 102
Fraser, Alice 131, 128, 140, 156
Fraser, Dave 66, 75, 76 80, 97, 112, 152,
French, Norman 29, 33
Friels, Colin 86
Frighteners, The 190
Fritz Wagner Filmproduktion 188
Frontier Films Ltd 50
Fryer, Tui 39
Fuialo, Molimau 145
Fulford, Stephen 156
FUND (Foundation to Underwrite New Drama for Pay Television) 183
Fyfe, Jim 191

G

Gadsby, Jon 73, 102
Gallagher, Ray 22
Gallagher, Tony 149, 167
Gamble, Hammond 111
Games '74: Official Film of the Xth British Commonwealth Games, Christchurch, New Zealand, 1974 58
Garrel, Maurice 152
Garrett, Leif 117
Gaumont Company Ltd 38, 39
Gavin, Bill 178
Gaylene Preston Productions 181
Gee, Maurice 96
Geissendorder Film 182
Gerlach, Philip 165, 180
Gibbes, Robyn 99
Gibney, Rebecca 118, 133
Gibson Film Productions 98
Gibson Group 160
Gibson, Dave 98, 160
Gibson, H.T. 30
Gibson, John 123
Gibson, Judith 104, 147
Gibson, Russell 131, 141, 149
Gielgud, John 116
Gil, Vincent 66
Gilbert, Anthony 98
Gilbert, John 163, 173, 182, 187
Gillespie, Kristen 142, 160
Gillies, Robert 105, 142, 149
Ginnane, Antony I 80, 86 89, 102
Girdlestone, John 187
Girven, Ross 123, 128
Gittins, Paul 105, 156, 192
Gledhill, Stephen 123, 140, 166

Glennon, James 86
Glock, Michael 101
Glover, Andrew 89, 115
Glue, Mervyn 84, 85, 131
Gocke, Justin 159
God Boy, The 60
Godbold, Catherine 165
Goessi, Jack 34
Goldie, Gilbert 83, 109, 111, 114, 165, 173, 177, 179
Goldman, Dan 141
Goldwyn, Tony 178
Goodbye Pork Pie 76
Goodwin, Neville 49
Gonzales, Jorge 194
Gordon, John 50
Gordon, Philip 76, 93, 95, 103, 118, 122, 139, 141, 150
Gould, Robert 96, 105
Gowan, Elizabeth 94
Graham, John 54
Graham, Louise 140, 143
Grahame, Queenie 37
Grampire 159
Grant, Bruce 132
Grant, Christine 132
Grasscutter, The 142
Gray, Walter 41
Green, Frank Sherwin 53
Gregory, Mike 111
Grenfell, A. Frank 48
Grenville, Tina 101, 159
Gressmann, Martin 187
Griffeth, Simone 120
Griffin, Eric 106
Griffiths, Reston 78
Grigsby, Howard 102
Grindlay, Murray 64, 139, 189
Grives, Steven 164
Groser, Tony 64, 70, 150, 165
Group Film Productions 53
Gruar, Bill 139
Gruar, Shirley 76, 99, 105, 121, 122
Gruendemann, Eric 179, 194
Guertchikoff, Louba 116
Guidobaldi, Filippo 53
Guilford, Allen 60, 104, 145, 155, 164, 166, 169, 187
Guise, Roger 124
Gunter, Ray 56
Guthridge, John D. 53
Gutierrez, Zaide Sylvia 186

H

Hacking, Michael 125
Hadlow, Mark 75, 81, 82, 89, 95, 97, 146, 166, 183
Haedrich, Rolf 133

Hagen, Andrew 72, 81
Haig, Michael 62, 83, 84, 99, 118, 123, 133, 140, 166
Hajek, Ron 63
Hall, Roger 69
Hall, Stephen 141, 142, 149, 166 171, 175
Halpin, Francis 59
Hambleton, Keith 127, 160
Hambleton, Peter 109, 166 178
Hamilton, David 133
Hamilton, Jean 49
Hammon, Ken 134, 161
Hammond, Gabrielle 156
Hamner Nine Syndicate 45
Hampson, Chris 124, 135, 137, 165
Hang on a Minute Mate Film Partnership 85
Hang on a Minute Mate! 85
Hanlon, John 63
Hanna, Richard 151, 158, 167, 169
Hannam, Gary 112, 114
Hannan, Neil 68
Hannay, David 66, 150
Hansen, Gary 82, 84, 108, 115,
Hape, Mira 52
Harbert, Barry 91
Harbrow, Nigel 115, 165
Harcourt, Kate 75, 83, 95, 96 109, 118, 127, 140
Harcourt, Miranda 84, 140, 169
Harden, Marcia Gay 163
Hardwick, Derek 83, 94, 99, 103, 110, 120, 133,
Hardy, Jonathan 81, 97, 101, 110, 130
Hargreaves, John 75
Harlow, Hugh 57
Harmor, Navit 109
Harper, Maggie 120, 141
Harper, Stanley 116
Harris, Julie 53
Harrison, Craig 113
Harrison, Eric 35
Harrop, Ian 75, 110, 115, 120
Harrow, Lisa 105, 117
Hartley, Richard 84
Harvey, Bob 68, 156
Harvey, Graham 97
Hastie, Florence 45
Hatfield, Gordon 167, 171
Hau, Karam 86 101, 105
Haussler, Veronika 148
Havas, Michael 93, 114
Hawkins, Kai 73, 75, 76, 106, 164
Hawkins, Jack 53
Hawthorne, Elizabeth 120, 165, 173, 178, 179
Hawthorne, Raymond 169, 173
Hayden, Peter 75, 79, 117, 124, 135
Hayman, Terry 102, 142
Haysom, Trevor 110, 147
Hayward, Henry 34

Hayward, Hilda 34, 40, 41
Hayward, Kevin 74, 97, 117, 121, 122, 125, 150, 159
Hayward, Phil 34
Hayward, Ramai 56
Hayward, Rudall 30, 34, 40, 41, 49, 50
Hazlett, David 182
Healey, Theresa 169, 178
Heart of the Stag 108
Heath, Geoffrey 117, 177
Heath, Michael 69, 75, 76, 78, 81, 82, 83, 101, 112, 159, 175, 184
Heavenly Creatures 177
Hegan, Eddie 147, 148
Heiland, Udo 188
Helpmann, Robert 102
Hemmings, David 75, 80, 86
Henare, George 98, 125, 175
Henderson, Peter 134
Hendry, Jonathan 158, 169
Henkin, Hilary 86
Hennah, Dan 110
Henry, Arthur Jones 27
Hensby, Richard 100
Henwood, Ray 120, 156, 177
Heperi, Peter 72
Hercules and the Lost Kingdom 179
Hercules: The Legendary Journeys 194–5
Herewini, Nissie 154
Herewini, Tane 38
Herkt, David 72
Hewitt, Caroline 182
Heyward, James 138, 160
Hibiscus Films 148, 163
Hides, Bernard 80, 86
Higgins, Jamie 60
Higgs, Christine 111
Highfield, Ron 60, 68, 84, 87, 107, 117, 151, 154, 156 178
Hiles, Tony 83, 123, 134, 161
Hill, Alfred 46, 50
Hill, Billy 46
Hill, Dean 96, 105
Hill, Lee 41, 45, 47, 48
Hill, Richard 114, 153
Hill, Vernon 57
Hinchey, Faye 48
Hinden-Miller, Grant 131, 152, 158
Hinderwell, Stephen 161
Hinemoa 21, 23
Hinemoa Films 23
Horomona, Maata 21
Hinge Film Productions 59
Hobbs, Katrina 165, 166
Hocquard, Amanda 143
Hoffman, Hugh 42
Holder, Philip 81, 84, 93, 109, 103, 110
Hood, Kate 97, 110
Hooper, Elric 97, 131

Horrocks, Roger 68
Horton, Mike 73, 155, 188
Horton, Murray 153
Horton, Ngaire 115, 149
Horvath, Louis 89, 110
Horwood, Robert 141, 156
Hotere, Ralph 138
Hould, Ra 45
House, Ron 151
Houston, Ian 52
How Chief Te Ponga Won His Bride 22
Howard, Elizabeth Jane 118
Howe, Philip 67, 74, 97
Howell, William 57
Howson, John-Michael 102
Hudson, John 102
Hudson, Peter 127
Huggett, David 113, 159
Hughes 26
Hughes, John 95
Hunter, Holly 171
Hunter, Matthew 122, 125
Hunter, Todd 180
Hurihanganui, Maata 38
Hurst, Michael 86 101, 123, 164, 167, 194, 195
Hutchinson, Nigel 76

I

I.L.A. Productions 67
Ikin, Bridget 148, 163, 182
Illingworth, Neil 108
Illustrious Energy 135
Imi, Tony 95
Independent Newspapers Ltd 126
Ingsby, Con 37
Intercontinental Releasing Corporation 141
Ip, Harry 135
Iris 109
Irwin, Val 56
Isaac, Tony 109
Isambard Productions 165, 180
Isara, Peseta Sinave 145
It's Lizzie To Those Close 94

J

Jack Be Nimble 173
Jackson, Fred 29
Jackson, Lauren 165
Jackson, Peter 134, 146, 161, 190
Jalfon, Paula 184
James Wallace Productions Ltd 167
James, Billy T 103, 132
James, Kouf Jnr 117
Jayne, Rob, 86, 100, 110, 125
Jemison, Anna 78
Jenet, Veronika 171

209

Index

Jeremy Thomas Productions 100
Jervis, Alan 68, 70, 84, 85
Jessup, Stephen 153
Jeziorny, Richard 97
John Maynard Productions 106 164
John Paul Sartre Experience 163
John, Ian 64, 81, 116
Johnny the Cowboy 22
Johns, Glynis 53
Johnson, Bill 64, 68, 75, 95, 156
Johnson, Greg 156, 165, 171, 192
Johnson, Kelly 76, 82, 83, 84, 85, 87
Johnson, William 54, 142
Johnstone, Barry 121
Jolly, Ross 82, 118, 140, 146 166
Jones Oliver, 128
Jones, Denis 126
Jones, Laura 148
Jones, Rosey 164
Jones, Tommy Lee 95
Jordan, William 57
Joseph, M. K. 152
Joyce, Hester 97, 173
Judd, Stephen 122, 123
Juliff, Bill 60, 64, 76, 83, 87

K

Kaa, Peter 154, 158, 160
Kaa, Wi Kuki 87, 114, 128, 154
Kanawa, Kiri Te 54, 55
Kane, Artie 190
Kane, Michael 134, 167, 175, 189
Kaneda, Ryunosuke 100
Kantor, Igo 117
Karsenti, Sabine 183
Kavanagh, Tony 165
Kay, Alistair 182
Kay, Fiona 106, 148
Keane, Murray 140, 158, 160, 161, 166, 167
Kearns, Bernard 60, 64, 98, 127
Keeha, Hoana 42
Keenan, Paula 75, 96, 105
Keesing, Norman 75, 95, 103, 105
Keirfilm Productions 187
Keitel, Harvey 171
Keith Hawke Films Ltd Hong Kong 111
Kellerman, Annette 33
Kelly, Desmond 70, 76, 78, 81, 84, 123, 133, 166 178
Kem, Michael 167
Kendall, Brenda 102, 143, 148, 161, 173, 179
Kennard, Malcolm 174
Kennedy, Anne 163
Kent, Diana 177
Keogh, Alexia 148
Kereti Nowara 46
Kerr, Andrew 57

Kerr, Bill 106
Kerr-Bell, Mamaengaroa 175
Kiley, John 79, 133
King, John 58
King, Dell 128, 154
King, Peter 59
Kingpin 114
Kingsland, George 29
Kingston, Winifred 27
Kircher, William 96, 97, 120, 140, 166 169, 178
Kissin, Harold 54, 56 64,75
Kitaen, Tawny 194
Kite-Bell, Ebony 188
Kiwi Films 83
Kjestrup, Don 97, 102, 105
Knight, Shirley 49, 50, 86
Kofoed, Rick 166, 169, 188
Koslowsky, Joe 179, 194
Kounnas, Melissa 180
Kreye, Walter 154
Kristian, Billy 111, 139
Krumbachova, Ester 93

L

Laemmle, Carl 42
Lahood, Grant 187
Laing, John 75, 80, 105, 112, 123, 166, 169, 158
Laing, Robin 118, 149, 166, 169
Lake, Bill 153
Lancaster, Chris 90
Lancaster, Christine 70, 76
Landfall 62
Lane, Charles 89
Langley, Michael 189
Langridge, Don 166, 174
Larkins, Mabel 45
Larsen, Erna 102, 103
Lasky, Jesse L. 27
Last Tattoo, The 178
Laube, Vivienne 96
Laughlin, Michael 89, 110
Laurelwood Productions Inc 117
Laven, Robbie 66
Lavington, Harry 54, 55, 160
Lawless, Lucy 194
Lawley, Yvonne 60, 69, 81, 97, 105, 133, 149
Lawrence, Bruno 61, 75, 76 78, 80, 82, 83, 86, 87, 94, 99, 101, 108, 113, 121, 122, 173
Lawrence, Michael 103
Lawrie, Dean 134, 134
Leach, Paul 103
Leading Edge, The 132
Leary, L. P. 49
Leave All Fair 116
Lee Bradford Corporation 33
Lee, Nat 141

Lee, Suzanne 118
Lee, Timothy 75, 76, 82, 95, 86, 96, 101, 108, 123, 131, 141
Lees, Nathaniel 101, 105, 117, 179, 183
Lefler, Doug 194
Lemon Crest Pty Ltd 86
Leonard-Jones, Kevin 158, 161, 174
Lesnie, Andrew 151
Letch, David 95, 101, 115, 118, 147, 148
Levestam, Glenis 68, 161, 164,
Lewis, Al 159
Lewis, Dr A. L. 47
Lewis, Fiona 89
Lewiston, Denis 120
Liddy, Bill 106
Lie of the Land, The 130
Lill, Dennis 84
Lim, Jose 186
Lincoln County Incident 71
Lincoln Films 71
Lindsay, Alan 85
Lindsay, Fiona 70
Lindsay, Heather 68, 75
Lindsay, Jane 161
Lindvall, B.G. 29
Lithgow, John 110
Livingston, Paul 137
Loaded 185, 174
Loader, Shane 193
Lock, Desmond 56 75
Lock, Sybil 56
Locke, Alan 74, 135
Locker-Lampson, Steve 66
Lo Ducas, Joseph 194
Loggia, Robert 178
Long, David 166
Longford, Raymond 25, 26
Lord, Arthur 40
Lord, Robert 79
Lost Tribe, The 112
Lovatt, Stephen 140, 166
Loved By A Maori Chieftess 20
Lowry, Caroline 164, 173
Ludlam, Jennifer 160
Lutic, Bernard 116
Luxford, Shelly 122
Lyell, Lottie 25, 26
Lymposs, Richard 125, 192
Lynskey, Melanie 177
Lyon, Harry 111
Lyons, Bruce 137, 137
Lyons, Kely 137

M

MacDonald, Hugh 90
Macfarlane, Jim 68
Mackay, Yvonne 98, 160

Mackie, John 49
Maclean, Alison 163
MacNee, Patrick 141
MacOnie, Robin 54
Magpie Productions Ltd 126
Maguire, Martin 142
Main, Stewart 167
Major, Grant 148, 173, 177, 190
Major, Sarah 127, 160
Makepeace, Henry J. 32, 34
Malcolm, James 100
Malcolm, Robyn 165, 166
Malese, Telo 98
Malone, Irene 164, 167
Mana Waka 144
Manchester Productions 110
Mann, Tracy 81
Mansfield Films 119
Mansfield, Katherine 116
Manuel, Mitchell 114, 127, 142
Maori Maid's Love, A 25
Maori War Films Ltd 34
Maoriland Pictures 32
Marachuk, Steve 120
Mareikura, Matiu 79, 99, 154
Marin, Cheech 151
Mark II, 127
Markey Films 46
Markey, Alexander 46
Marquand, Bill Le 97, 137
Marshall, Bryan 120, 187
Martin, Kent 185
Martin, Lew 109, 118, 147, 166
Martin, Richard 127
Mason, Bruce 156
Mason, Patch 43
Mateparae, Denys 139
Matheson, Lara 160
Matheson, Larissa 169, 125, 131, 152
Matte Box Films Ltd 150
Maunder, Denise 62
Maunder, Paul 58, 58, 62, 70
Mauri 138
Maussion, Ivan 152
Mavric, Elizabeth 189
Maxwell, Garth 173
Maxwell, Maggie 72, 76 105, 120
May, Brian 80
Mayersberg, Paul 100
Maynard, George 53
Maynard, John 68, 93, 106, 137, 148, 164, 182
Mayne, Philippa 104
McAllum, Peter 140, 160
McAlpine, Andrew 74, 171
McBride, Chi 191
McCallum, Gordon K. 53
McCarron, Deidre 54
McCarthy, Jack 49, 50

McCauley, Peter 114, 120, 121, 122, 131
McCauley, Sue 105
McClure, Marc 89
McCorkindale, Kiri 128
McCormack, Catherine 182
McCormack, Gary 131, 149, 151
McCoy, Jay 74
McCurdy, Stephen 69, 103, 122, 156
McDermott, Thomas 40, 41
McDonald, Donald 97
McDonald, Garry 102
McDonald, Philip 112
McDowell, Steve 155, 156
McElhinney, Ian 142
McEnroe, Annie 82
McFarland, Grant 164, 173
McFarlane, Hamish 137, 142, 148
McGee, Greg 155
McGlashan, Don 148, 166
McGlone, Carmel 140
McGoohan, Patrick 96 121, 132, 142
McGoram, Wayne 163, 171
McGuire, Pat 90
McIntosh, Judy 101, 105, 114, 120, 124, 128, 142
McKegg, Dorothy 60, 64, 69, 83, 84
McKellar, Ross 142, 156
McKenzie, David 83, 102, 154, 166
McKenzie, Laura 141
McKenzie, Les 55
McKirdy, Dan 127
McLachlan, Craig 165, 166
McLaren, Daniel 81
McLean, Grahame 85, 94, 111, 130, 145
McLean, John 102
McLeod, Rosemary 140
McNab, Murray 189
McNamara, Madeline 189
McNeillage, Dermot 186
McRae, Elizabeth 81, 109, 120, 139
McRae, Katherine 140
McWilliam, John 124
Meet the Feebles 146
Melbourne, Hirini 138
Melies Films 20, 21, 22
Melies, Gaston 20, 21, 22
Melies, Hortense 22
Melle, Gil 120
Mellor, John 131, 165
Melvin, Kenneth 50
Menges, Chris 82
Meredith, Charles 27
Meridian Films 112, 166
Merito, Bill 52
Merrison, Clive 177
Merry Christmas Mr Lawrence 100
Mesmerized 110
Messenger, Peter 53
Mete-Kingi, Lee 149

Meunier, Gilbert 186
Meyer, Stephen 71
Meyer, Werner 188
Michael Forlong Productions 57
Middle Age Spread 69
Miha, Ramai Te 50
Milburn, Oliver 182
Mildenhall, Joanne 83, 111, 123, 169
Miles, Melissa 101, 102
Milligan, Christina 156
Millington, M 34
Mills, Alec 120
Mills, Christopher 112
Mills, Richard 100, 148, 160
Milne, Murray 124, 143, 146 161
Milsome, Doug 99
Minett, Mike 134
Minogue, Dannii 174
Mirage Entertainment Corporation 135, 152
Mirage Films 97, 103, 125, 121, 122, 131
Mirage-Avicom Productions 117
Mirams, Roger 52
Mita, Merata 87, 91, 138, 144
Mitchell, Edmund 20, 21, 22
Mitchell, Roy 142
Mitchell, Witarina 42
Mizrahi, Michael 143
Moa Films Ltd 37
Moana, Guy 171, 175
Molgart, Mathurin 132
Moloney, William 52
Montesse, Lola 32
Monton, Vincent 80
Moodie, Bernard 64, 69, 75
Moody, Elizabeth 81, 161, 177
Moody, Howard 48
Moore, Susanna 89
Moran, Graeme 102, 120
Morgan, Peter 111, 114
Moriarty, Dean 130, 130
Moriarty, Jim 114, 127, 130, 140, 150
Morley, Robert 102
Morrieson, Ronald Hugh 81, 103, 121
Morris, Grant 132, 151
Morris, Judy 93
Morrison, Beth 173
Morrison, Bruce 97, 117, 117, 125
Morrison, Howard 55
Morrison, Temuera 57, 105, 138, 139, 142, 175, 189
Morrissey, Michael 103, 125, 151
Morrow Productions 114
Morse, Helen 109
Morton, Derek 83, 99
Moss, Richard 64, 86 96
Moulder, Helen 79, 109, 123, 166
Mr Wrong 118
Mulheron, Danny 118, 140, 146 158, 166
Mullane, Liz 140, 177

Index

Mune, Ian 57, 60, 64, 73, 76, 98, 103, 117, 122, 123, 142, 156, 171, 175, 192
Murdoch, Daphne 45
Murphy, Geoffrey 61, 76, 87, 113, 118, 138, 139
Murphy, Michael 89, 110
Murphy, Roy 61
Murphy, Val 61, 66
Muru, Selwyn 54
Musaphia, Joseph 55
Mutiny Of The Bounty, The 26
My Lady Of The Cave 30

N

Nambassa Festival 74
Nambassa Trust 74
Napier, Marshall 75, 76, 82, 83, 84, 99, 103, 121, 123, 130, 131, 137, 142
Narbey, Leon 68, 93, 96 105, 135, 149, 164, 167
Narushima, Toichiro 100
Nash, Terre 185
National Film Board of Canada 185
Naughton, Greg 81, 84, 108
Navigator: A Medieval Odyssey, The 10
Neglected Miracle, The 119
Neill, Sam 58, 62, 64, 171, 184
Nemo, Frank 34
Never Say Die 139
New Zealand Cinema Enterprises Ltd 29
New Zealand Film Commission 69, 70, 91, 97, 98, 99, 101, 103, 104, 106 108, 112, 118, 122, 123, 124, 125, 128, 131, 132, 134, 135, 137, 138, 139, 140, 142, 143, 145, 147, 148, 149, 150, 154, 156 159, 161, 163, 164, 165, 166 167, 173, 174, 175, 177, 180, 181, 182, 183, 184
    Short Film Fund 144
New Zealand Film Guild 49
New Zealand National Film Unit 58, 62, 90, 94
New Zealand On Air 156, 189
New Zealand Dominion Productions Ltd 33
Newell, Mike 84
Newey, Murray 101, 139, 159, 183, 192
Newham, Charles 26
Newton, Thandie 182
Nga Kaitiaki o Te Puea Estate/The Te Puea Estate 144
Ngarimu, Kay 52
Ngaromotu-Heka, Diana 188
Ngati 128
Nicholas, Gregor 147, 189
Nicholas, Mark 67, 94, 101, 147
Nicholl, Peter 86 93
Norman, Alan 153
Norton, Bill L. 194
Nuhaka Maori Choir 52

Nutcase 73
Nymen, Michael 171

O

O'Brien, Jillian 121
O'Connor, Simon 111, 123, 177
O'Donnell, Elliot 192
O'Hara, Gerry 120
O'Herne, Pete 134
O'Neill, Sharon 78
O'Neill, Willa 148, 174
O'Connor, Michael 142
O'Connor, Renee 179
O'Gorman, Dean 183
O'Keefe, Michael 95
O'Neal, Tatum 86
O'Shea, John 52, 54, 55, 55, 79, 116, 119, 128, 133, 154
O'Shea, Paul 133
O'Shea, Rory 79, 119, 128, 133, 139, 154,
O'Sullivan, Kevin 99
Oasis Films Ltd 81
Oates, Warren 64
Oberman, Claire 76
Odell, David 95
Oelffen, Petra von 110
Offering, The 186
Off the Edge 63
Okura, Johnny 100
Old Scores 155
Oldmall, Donna 101, 102
Olivera, Angela 32
Olver, Harlewy 105
Omahau, Miro 23
Omahau, Taimai 23
Oman, Wiki 69, 140, 175
On The Friendly Road 49
Once Were Warriors 175
Orinward Ltd 110
Ormond, George 52
Orringham Ltd 105
Oshima, Nagisa 100
Other Halves 105
Outterside, Robin 76
Owen, Rena 175
Owen-Lowe, Paul 81, 97, 102

P

Pacey, Ann 111, 123, 130, 140, 169
Pacific Films 52, 54, 55, 70, 79, 116, 119, 128, 133, 154
Pagonis, Carole 178
Pahu, Jo 98
Pallet on the Floor 121
Palmer, David 57
Palmer, Matt 139, 149

Paltenghi, David 53
Pan Asian Film Distributors Ltd Hong Kong 111
Papps, Stephen 156, 161, 171, 183
Paquin, Anna 171
Paraha, Glynis 149, 171
Paratene, Rawiri 124
Park Avenue Productions 143
Park, Gloria (Chubby) 188
Parker, Dean 103, 155
Parkin, Bill 52
Parkinson, Tom 165, 180
Parry, David 101, 183
Pastrami and Rye 139
Paterson, Tony 102
Patrick, Nick 182
Patten, Tom 37
Patterson, Julie 111
Pattinson, Michael 174
Patu! 91
Paul, Ian 72, 98, 115
Paul, Rim D. 54
Pauli, Gustav 38, 39
Peake, John 48
Pearce, Roy 60, 115
Pearce, Stuart 111
Pearson, Ray 120, 141
Peek, Kevin 82
Peers, Lisa 66
Peirse, Sarah 94, 110, 124, 137, 177
Penalver, Diana 161
Pennington, Lewis 111
Peppard, George 80
Percival, Lacey 35
Perker, Anthony Ray 194
Petaia, Uelese 70, 145
Petherbridge, Louise 79, 131
Phar Lap's Son 47
Phase Three Films 68, 93
Phelps, Peter 131
Phillips, Alex Jnr 186
Phillips, Bruce 117, 131, 165
Phillips, Clinton 150
Phillips, June 32
Phillips, Lloyd 82, 95
Phillips, Tricia 103, 156 173
Phillips-Whitehouse Productions 95
Phipps, Max 95
Piano, Rex 141
Piano, The 171
Picker, Josh 165
Picot, Genevieve, 169
Pictures 79
Piercy, Perry 109, 118, 140, 160, 169
Pigott, Johanna 189
Pilcher, Leo 50
Pilisi, Mark 105, 125
Pillsbury Productions 113
Pillsbury, Sam 58, 81, 113, 131

Index

Pinfold, Dorothee 140
Piper, Emma 96
Pitt, Stewart 45
Platt, Katy 83, 109, 111, 140
Pleasence, Donald 80
Plumb Productions Ltd 178
Poata, Tama 87, 99, 127, 130, 133, 139, 153
Polivka, Steve 194
Pollard, J. J. W. 48
Polonsky, Sonya 186
Pons, Maurice 116
Poore, Richard 99, 102
Portman Productions 188
Potoker, Oscar 46
Potter, Terry 134
Powell, Robert 158
Power, V. 26
Preston*Laing Productions 118, 149, 169
Preston, David 183
Preston, Gaylene 69, 118, 149, 169, 181
Preston, Jan 68, 79, 164, 188
Preston, Ted 37
Prisoners 86
Pritchard, Miranda 97
Prosser, Rod 77
Pugsley, Chris 158
Pullman, Barry 194
Purcell, Noel 53
Purchase, Bruce 105
Purdu, Roland 33
Purkis, Dana 106 165

Q

Queen City Rocker 125
Quetzal Films 186
Quiet Earth, The 113
Quill, Michele 115
Quinn, Anthony 179, 194

R

Rabbit, Tony 98
Race For the Yankee Zephyr 80
Radich, Eva 101, 143
Rae, Iain 140, 149
Ramirez, Adolfo 186
Ramiri Paul, Susan D. 138
Ramsey, Robert 33
Rands, Sylvia 143, 159, 160, 183
Rangi's Catch 57
Rare, Vanessa 149
Rashbrooke, Geoff 153
Rawlings, Kathy 99
Raymond, Sam 49
Read, Melanie 104, 140
Rebels in Retrospect 153

Redford, Jennifer 67
Reece, Murray 60, 83, 180
Reece, Simon 60, 83, 106, 118, 154, 180
Reedy, Tilly 154
Reedy, Turei 140, 166
Rees, Donogh 97, 109, 131, 163
Rees, Spring 111
Regan, Mary 93, 108, 115
Regin, Nadja 54
Regtien, Tina 160, 161, 166 169
Reid, Joan 69, 83, 109, 116, 178, 121, 147, 174, 188
Reid, Sandra 60
Renaissance Pictures 179, 194
Restless 120
Returning, The 150
Rewi's Last Stand 34, 50
Reynolds, Don 58, 104, 108, 113, 115, 123, 124, 135, 155
Reynolds, Harrington 29
Rhodes, Cameron 166 169
Richardson, Bob 117
Richardson, Keith 76, 111, 140, 158, 166
Rickard, Eva 138, 188
Riddiford, Richard 143
Rising, Robert 121
Roberts, John 111
Robertson, Cliff 117
Robinson, Tim 153
Robson, Greer 78, 81, 125, 131
Robson, Lyn 72, 78
Rodgers, Ilona 87
Roe, Allison 104
Roelants, Andy 74
Rogers, Kelly 173
Rogers, Nicholas 114, 127
Romance of Hine-moa, The 38
Romance Of Maoriland, The 43
Romance of Sleepy Hollow, The 32
Romano, Nenad 189
Rongo, Tupatea Kahu 98
Rosas, Guillermo 186
Rose, Mick 169, 178
Rosenman, Leonard 108, 115
Ross, John 141, 164
Ross, Mona 189
Routledge, Alison 105, 113, 122, 150
Rowan, Diana 75, 82
Rowe, Lewis 142, 158, 161, 166
Rowe, Nevan 73, 64
Rowell, Peter 68, 82, 87, 117, 114
Rowell, Tom 54
Rowley, Peter 86, 95, 96, 102, 103, 121, 139, 179
Roy, Ron 63
Royal, Willie 186
Ruby and Rata 149
Ruby, John 134

Rudall and Ramai Hayward Film Productions 56
Ruka, Reg 86, 95, 96 98,
Runaway 54
Rusty 140
Rutherford, Betty 48
Rutter, Peta 89, 164
Rymer, Judy 184

S

Sakamoto, Ryuichi 100
Salter, Jim 189
Samms, Emma 151
Samuel, Fiona 83, 117, 140
Sanderson, Martyn 61, 66, 72, 75, 81, 84, 87, 99, 104, 108, 112, 115, 121, 138, 139, 145, 148, 155, 167, 178, 187
Sardi, Jan 174
Saunders, Rebecca 101, 125
Saussey, Jay 137, 179, 183
Savage, Deborah 187
Savage Islands 95
Scarecrow, The 81
Schaap, Cornelia 71
Schenck, Earl 27
Schmode, Peter 188
Scholes, Peter 167
Scholes, Robin 175, 189
Schurr, Maxine 62
Schwieters, Brett 183, 192
Scott, Daniel 183, 192
Scott, Clyde 54, 64, 73, 75, 76
Scott, George 21, 20, 22
Scott, John 137, 178
Scott, Lloyd 194
Scott, Norelle 101, 147, 164
Scott, Tom 126
Scrimgeour, Rev C.G. 49
Scullion, Michelle 145, 187
Seagrove, Jenny 95
Searell, Marie 56
Second Time Lucky 102
Secrets 174
Seekers, The 53
Segerberg, A. 26
Seidenstein, Ira 86
Selbo, Jule 194
Selkirk, Jamie 72, 85, 94, 98, 111, 130, 134, 146 155, 161, 177, 190
Sellers, Warren 67, 73
Selwyn, Don 57, 64, 70, 76, 96, 103, 110, 112, 138
Senator Film International 187
Send a Gorilla 140
Serbedzija, Rade 189
Serbulo, Mayra 186
Seresin, Michael 64
Sergent, Brian 83, 146, 161, 166

213

Index

Shadbolt, Maurice 133, 158
Shaker Run 117
Shand, Peter 73
Shannon, Paul 161, 166
Shannon, Robert 72, 75
Sharp, David S. 45
Sharp, Peter 56, 96, 149
Shaw, Bryan 141
Shearman, Alan 151
Sheehan, Lucy 143
Shelton, Marlee 194
Shepherd, Geoff 62
Sheridan, David 135, 141
Shields, Gordon 106
Shirley, John 95
Shor, Dan 89, 110
Should I Be Good? 111
Shouler, Kirsten 140, 147
Shrimp on the Barbie, The 151
Siegel, Taggart 186
Sigmund, David 102
Silent One, The 98
Simmons, Brenda 141, 173
Simms, Shane 71
Simpson, Geoffrey 137
Simpson, Joanne 112, 140
Simpson, Megan 165
Sinclair, Harry 161, 164
Sinclair, Kim 159, 165
Sinclair, Stephen 146, 161
Si'ulepa, Nikki 192
Sirder, Daniel 186
Skin Deep 68
Skipworth, Te Whatanui 115, 171, 175, 179
Skolimowski, Jerzy 110
Sledmere, Peter 76, 127
Sleeping Dogs 64
Smart, Dulcie 84, 140
Smash Palace 78
Smit, Robbie 126
Smith, Beaumont 35
Smith, Bill 112, 70
Smith, Craig 134
Smith, Duncan 81, 103, 111, 140, 154, 160, 161
Smith, Ellie 187
Smith, Harry V 47
Smith, Howard 42
Smith, Jonathan 81
Smith, Kevin 130, 167
Smith, Malcolm 58, 70
Smith, Patrick 110, 165
Smith, Pete 105, 113, 163, 171, 175, 188
Smith, Russell 139, 149
Smith, Sam 167, 173
Smith, Shade 73
Smithee, Alan 151
Smuts-Kennedy, Sarah 81, 148, 164, 173
Smyth, Patrick 93, 75, 85, 109, 123, 131, 166

Snell, Geoff 84, 96, 101, 164
Snodgress, Carrie 141
Soldier's Tale, A 152
Solo 66
Solomon, Harata 133, 163
Someone Else's Country 193
Sons for the Return Home 70
Sorbo, Kevin 179, 194, 195
South Pacific All Media Distributors Ltd 94
South Pacific Broadcasting Corporation Ltd 130
South Pacific Merchant Finance Ltd 69
South Pacific Pictures 155, 156
South Seas Films Ltd 47
South Street Films Production 89
Southern Light Pictures 84, 108, 115, 132
Southern, Stella 29
Southgate, William 60, 87, 98
Southland Films Ltd 48
Spence, Bruce 121, 151
Sporleder, Greg 186
Squeeze 72
Stalker, Bill 61
Stalker, Gary 118
Stanley 20, 21
Stanton, David L. 141
Stark, Frank 147
Starlight Hotel 131
Steiger, Rod 178
Stephen-Smith, Fraser 105
Stephens, Jeremy 94, 121
Steven, Geoffrey 59, 68, 93, 93
Stevens, Peter 123, 143, 156
Stewart, Frank 29, 30, 34, 35
Stewart, Penelope 106
Stone, Laurie 102
Stott, David 163, 165
Strata 93
Strawn, Mick 179
Strewe, Chris 74
Stuart, Bathie 35, 42
Sturmer, Richard von 123, 145
Sullivan, James R. 33
Sullivan, Peter 86
Summer, John 165, 179
Summers, Sheila 110, 115
Sumner, Peter 69
Sutorius, Paul 114, 127, 140, 158, 166, 169, 181
Sutton, Arthur 106
Sydney, John Kay 52
Sylvia 115

T

Tait, Peter 83, 99, 139, 143, 167, 173, 188
Taj Mahal 111
Takle, Darien 101, 102, 112, 177
Takle, Emma 112

Tamahori, Lee 175
Tanielu, Amalamo 70
Tarr, George 23, 40
Tarver, Maggie 164, 179
Tate, Wally 29
Taurua, Frank 80, 95, 106
Tawhai, Hera 23
Tawhai, Rua 23
Taylor, David 156
Taylor, Denis 59, 59
Taylor, Noah 174
Taylor, Norma 115
Taylor, Stephen 81, 97, 100, 111
Taylor, Syd 35
Taylor, William Desmond 27
Tayne, Olive 32
Te Kooti Trail, The 40
Teen, Michael 84
Teka, Prince Tui 95, 98
Television New Zealand 127, 148, 156
Telford, David 85, 131, 135, 156
Terry, Nigel 115
Te Rua 154
Test Pictures: Eleven Vignettes From a Relationship 59
Test, The 24
Tetley, Graeme 60, 106, 118, 149, 166, 169
Tetoa, Teina 98
Thomas, Jane 192
Thomas, Jeremy 100
Thompson, Jack 84, 100, 188
Thompson, Ruth 123
Tibble, Michael 73, 128, 177
Tiki Films 29
Tiki, Hei 46
Tilly, Grant 68, 69, 75, 80, 83, 95, 105, 123, 150, 165, 188
Tingarue 38
To Love A Maori 56
Tobeck, Joel 142, 151, 159
Toda, Jusho 100
Todd, Cecil 34
Todd, Chris 143
Toka, Henare 50
Tony Williams Productions Pty Ltd 66
Toon, John 114, 189
Top Shelf Productions 184, 188
Torlen, Rita 186
Total Film 165
Total Film and Television Australia 180
Tourell, Wayne 183
Townsend, Martin 62
Tozer, Stephen 76, 87, 104, 103, 105, 155, 178,
Tracey, Miss 21, 20
Trail, Steven 71
Trainer, Susan 97, 105
Trenholme, Blair 63
Trespasses 96
Trewern, Maurice 106

Index

Trial Run 104
Trilogic Film Productions 72
Trousdale, Alex 83, 85
Trow, Susan 185
Truly, Daniel 194
Tucker Films 183, 186, 192
Tucker Production Co Ltd 101, 159
Tuckett, Graeme 160
Tupu, Lani 70
Turangawaewae Marae Trust, the 144
Turba, Ctibor 93
Turner, Richard 72
Turner, Snow 106
Tutugaro, Marena 189
Tyler-Wright, Stefan 77

U

Uchida, Yuya 100
Umaga, Albert 81, 145
Umbers, Margaret 78, 101, 118, 122, 118, 122
Under The Southern Cross 39, 42
Undercover 160
Unity Pictures Corporation 151
Universal 42
Universal City Studios 194
Universal Pictures 190
Unsworth, Geoffrey 53
Upjohn, William 101
User Friendly 147
Utu 87
Utu Productions Ltd 87

V

Van der Post, Sir Laurens 100
Vanguard Films 77, 153, 193
Vanity, T.R. 48
Vardex Group 143
Vaughan, Martin 97, 180
Venus of the South Seas 33
Vere-Jones, Peter 57, 79, 123, 134, 142, 146, 174, 84, 95
Vernom, Thom 186
Vette, Richard 183
Victorian International Pictures 174
Vigil 106
Vinten, Wayne 140, 160
Vita Film Corporation 25
von Borsody, Suzanne 188
Vujcic, Aleksandra 189

W

Wagon and the Star, The 48
Wahl, Ken 80
Wahren, Tony 84, 85
Wainwright, James 82
Waldron, Claire 187
Walker Films Ltd 124

Walker, Kerry 171
Walker, Mike 114, 127
Walker, Moira 70
Walker, Peter 89
Wallace, Anzac 87, 98, 113, 138
Wallace, Gary 55
Wallace, James 167
Wallace Stone, Dee 190
Wallach, Roberta 130
Walsh, Frances 146, 161, 177, 190
Walters, Craig 111, 119
War Stories: Our Mothers Never Told Us 181
War Years 90
Warbrick, Ani 42
Warbrick, Patiti 42
Ward, Derek 67
Ward, Simon 116
Ward, Vincent 70, 106, 137
Ward-Lealand, Jennifer 123, 164, 167
Waring, Marilyn 185
Warlow, Wayne 155
Warren, Lesley Ann 80
Warren, Peter 154
Warrington, Bill 53
Waru, Sonny 121, 130, 138
Wason, Wendy 71
Watkin, Ian 61, 64, 69, 73, 75, 76, 83, 84, 87, 94, 101, 103, 112, 121, 140, 159, 161
Watkins, Roman 97
Watson, Elizabeth 84
Watson, John 93, 120, 131, 143
Watson, Joy 140, 165, 174
Waugh, Lindsay 96
Wayne, Patrick 141
Weatherley, David 101, 102, 105, 159
Weatherley, Nell 147, 179
Weil, Sam 20, 21
Wells, Peter 167
Wells, Vernon 151
Welsh, Jack 45, 47, 48
Wendt, Albert 70, 145
Wendt, George 139
Werner, Peter 86
Wesney, Roy 123, 137
West, Hazel 30
Weymouth, Belinda 147
Whakatane Films Ltd 40
Whetu, Mark 132
Whitehouse, Davina 64, 66 161,
Whitehouse, Rob 81, 82, 95
Whitten, Frank 120, 124, 141, 143, 150, 151
Whittle, Annie 104
Whole of the Moon, The 192
Who's Counting? Marilyn Waring on sex, lies and global economics 185
Wiari, Apirihana 42
Wiata, Beryl Te 89, 97, 110, 169
Wiata, Inia Te 53
Wiata, Rima Te 180, 140, 165

Wild Horses 99
Wild Man 61
Wildcat 77
Wilkinson, Tom 115
Williams, Anthony 54, 55
Williams, Christian 179
Williams, Kenneth 53
Williams, Mr 50
Williams, Paul 141
Williams, Robert J. 68
Williams, Sam 167, 179
Williams, Tony 66
Willis, Howard 84
Willisson, Simon 150
Willoughby, Kim 125
Wilson, Kevin 68, 79, 99, 114, 123, 148, 158
Wilson, Mike 67
Wilson, Morton 81
Wilson, Roger 102
Winch, Rob 111, 140
WingNut Films 134, 146, 161, 177, 190
Wingrove, John 110
Winslet, Kate 177
Wipani, Marise 103, 183
Wizard, The 76 131
Wood, Arthur 161
Woodham, Teresa 102, 104, 165
Woods, Alma 54, 55, 89, 149
Woolf, Michael 57, 76
Wraight, John 158, 160, 166
Wren, Doug 134
Wright, Arthur 68, 72, 75, 84, 115, 120,
Wright, David 71
Wright, Mark 140, 146 165, 180
Wright, Tandi 109, 166, 169
Wright, W. W. 34
Wyett, Paul 152
Wyndcross Ltd 120

Y

Yallop, David 75
Yandall, Ernest 41
Yandell, Eric 40
Yang, Li 189
Yates, Eric 34
Young, Garth 58
Young, Kenneth 139
Young, Morton 72, 21

Z

Zappa, William 163
Zealandia Photo Play Producing Co 25
Zemke, Ken 103, 117, 145
Zhao, Jing 189
Zilch! 143
Zinsli, Rowena 62
Zweites Deutsche Fernsehen 188